UNDER BOTH FLAGS

CHARGE OF CONFEDERATE CAVALRY AT TREVILIAN STATION, VA

UNDER BOTH FLAGS

A Panorama of the Great Civil War

As represented in Story, Anecdote, Adventure, and
the Romance of Reality

WRITTEN BY

CELEBRITIES OF BOTH SIDES; THE MEN AND WOMEN WHO CREATED THE
GREATEST EPOCH OF OUR NATION'S HISTORY.

AN UNPREJUDICED representation of the issues that
divided our country, as told in the personal recollections
of those who participated in the campaigns, marches,
sufferings, anecdotes, and instances of dauntless
heroism which glorified and ennobled this gigantic
struggle for the supremacy of the Union.

Gorgeously Illustrated

with about 250 superb illustrations from photographs
and drawings accurately picturing the
scenes described

THIS EDITION EDITED BY TIM GROFF

THE LYONS PRESS
Guilford, Connecticut
An imprint of The Globe Pequot Press

ISBN 1–59228–164–8

1 3 5 7 9 10 8 6 4 2

The Library of Congress Cataloging-in-Publication Data is available on file.

A SOLDIER'S OFFERING.

THE laurel wreath of glory
　　That decks the soldier's grave,
Is but the finished story,
　　The record of the brave;
And he who dared the danger,
　　Who battled well and true,
To honor was no stranger,
　　Though garbed in gray or blue.

Go, strip your choicest bowers,
　　Where blossoms sweet abound,
Then scatter free your flowers
　　Upon each moss-grown mound;
Though shaded by the North's tall pine
　　Or South's palmetto tree,
Let sprays that soldiers' graves entwine,
　　A soldier's tribute be.
　　　　　　　　—*George M. Vickers.*

Copyright, C. R. GRAHAM, 1896.

NATIONAL BOOK CONCERN,
352-356 DEARBORN STREET, CHICAGO, ILL.

INTRODUCTION

IN presenting this volume to the public two important characteristics are worthy of special notice: The first is, that every article contained in it was written or the matter furnished by the living actors and witnesses of the events related, and that in no other form can these historical treasures be obtained. The second is, that the truth only, without bitterness or malice, finds place upon its pages; that no word or expression is used that could not with propriety be read by a Northern or a Southern veteran, or to the children of either. Perhaps nothing could better express the sentiment of fairness and fraternity that pervades *Tales of the Civil War as Told by the Veterans,* than the following extracts from the writings of the editor:

"Americans are unlike other people. The manliness which characterizes the American citizen is indigenous to the Land of Liberty; it is confined to no class or condition; it is as widespread as our native golden-rod. The dignity, courage, and magnanimity which are the prominent qualities of American manliness, do not combine in the general character of any other nation. Elsewhere, those qualities are confined to the favored by birth, education, or fortune; with us they are inherent.

"The American is tenacious of his rights, real or imagined, to a degree unknown outside of the United States; he is a sovereign conscious of his sovereignty; therefore, it is always safe to appeal to his manliness. Patriotism is the child of manliness, and we are the most patriotic nation on the earth. Whatever the differences may be that exist in the minds of the people concerning questions of political economy, on the subject of patriotism they are unanimous. This glorious truth may disconcert the plans of demagogues and business politicians; it may deprive them of well-worn texts and inflammatory data, but so sure as the heavens dome Columbia, so sure is this a solid United States.

" Sectional wants and local traditions exert their influences in every commonwealth; the right to think and lawfully express opinion is the essence of liberty; let no man attempt to suppress that right.

"The war of the sixties is over; but the price of its lesson was the blood and treasure it cost. The men of the North and the men of the South each thought differently; but the bravest and most sincere expressed their opinions on the battlefield, and in their glorious record the world recognizes the unparalleled valor of the American soldier. Grant, Lee, Sherman, Jackson were Americans, and it is to our country's glory that their valor is known throughout the world; for of such heroes is our land peopled from sea to sea. How noble, then, the motive that would bind in fraternal bonds the loyal veteran warriors of our land! And such is the sentiment that fills the heart of every true American. How beautiful, if every veteran, whether a Union or a Confederate soldier, would wear a device that would be as pleasing to the citizens of Massachusetts as to those of Mississippi! A tiny badge containing a palmetto and a pine encircled with the simple legend: '*United Veterans, 1861–5*,' would surpass the highest decoration of a king. Imagine the thrill of pleasure that would move the most stolid breast when greeted by the word, 'brother,' and the hearty hand-grasp that would precede the declaration: 'I was with Longstreet,' or, 'I was a Pennsylvania Bucktail.' When the following lines were written the author had been through the South and had satisfied himself that the sentiment of loyalty pervading there was a living truth, as real as the ink which now flows from his pen:

'THE PALMETTO AND THE PINE.

While the months to years are fleeting like a river's ceaseless flow,
And the landmarks old grow dimmer in the distant long ago,
Let us glance once more behind us, where our battle days were seen,
Where our blood, like holly berries, sprinkled thick the grassy green.

There, in rifle pit, on rampart, or upon the open field,
Come the visions of battalions that would rather die than yield—
Come the stately forms of vessels with their crews of sailors brave,
Whose memorial crests of glory are the white caps of the wave.

Once these men were happy, peaceful, till that bloody war, and then—
When it ended they turned homeward from their dead to peace again.
Why they fought, why lost, who triumphed, who was wrong, or who was right,
Matters not ; they were our brothers, and were not afraid to fight.

'Neath the fairest flag that flutters under Heaven's azure dome
Dwell these warriors and their children in sweet Freedom's chosen home.
In his heart each holds a welcome for the soldier at his door,
And he never stops to question which the uniform he wore.

We were soldiers, only soldiers of the nation let us be.
Let us meet and greet as comrades though we fought with Grant or Lee ;
Let us form a noble order with sweet Freedom for our shrine,
And for each enwreathe a token—the Palmetto and the Pine.'

"The sons and daughters of the North and of the South will always honor the gallantry of their American sires. No moral attainder should dim the path of a soldier's child ; and it is to bind together fraternally the millions yet unborn that these truths should be recognized and held aloft now."

In this spirit it is hoped that **Tales of the Civil War as Told by the Veterans** will be accepted and read, never forgetting that the proudest tribute we can pay to the memory of the brave men of both armies is, *they were Americans*.

THE EDITOR.

THE BATTLE OF ATLANTA, GA., JULY 22, 1864.

CONTENTS.

CONTENTS

CONTENTS

CONTENTS

WAR SONGS OF THE NORTH AND THE SOUTH.

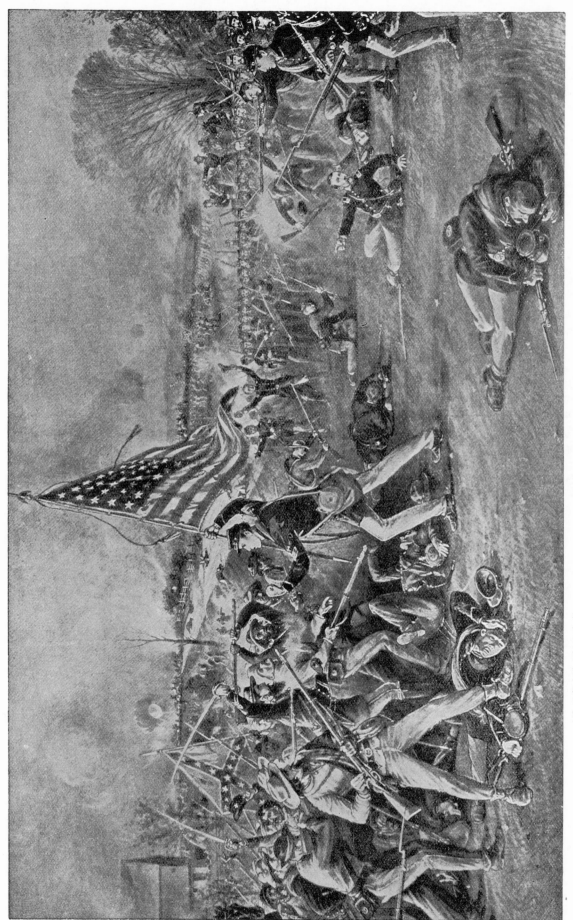

AN HEROIC INCIDENT: COLOR-SERGEANT BENJAMIN CRIPPEN REFUSES TO SURRENDER THE FLAG.

List of Illustrations

LIST OF ILLUSTRATIONS

LIST OF ILLUSTRATIONS

LIST OF ILLUSTRATIONS

LIST OF ILLUSTRATIONS

ON BOARD THE "HARTFORD," BATTLE OF MOBILE BAY.
From the Painting by W. H. Overend.

WITH FARRAGUT ON THE HARTFORD.

I.—FROM MIDSHIPMAN TO COMMANDER.

By Capt. H. D. Smith, U. S. Revenue Marine.

WHEN the change of administration took place on March 4, 1861, the fires of civil war were smouldering, ready to break out at a breath from the leaders. Of all the departments of the government, the navy was the worst off—the least able to respond to the demands made upon it. It could not take care of itself, and was forced to seek assistance from its foster-brother, the revenue-cutter service. To meet the emergency it had neither guns, vessels, nor men. A blockade three thousand five hundred miles in length was ordered, greater in extent than the whole coast of Europe from Cape Trafalgar to Cape North, and a navy had to be created to enforce it. When Mr. Toucey handed the Navy portfolio over to Mr. Welles, it was in anything but a satisfactory condition. Unrest existed everywhere: Southern officers were resigning on every side; bureau officers were under suspicion; and there was a want of confidence in all quarters. The serviceable navy consisted of two sailing frigates, eleven sailing sloops, one screw frigate, five screw sloops of the first class, three side-wheel steamers, eight screw sloops of the second class, and five screw sloops of the third class. But of all these, there were only eight vessels that the government could use immediately, and only four were steamers. At home and abroad the blockade was pronounced an impossibility; but Secretary Welles was equal to the occasion, and he soon had a force of twenty thousand mechanics at work.

The first success of the war was gained by the navy,—the capture of Hatteras,—followed by the possession of Port Royal; and then the department began to consider the practicability of acquiring control of New Orleans and the Mississippi. As early as July, 1861, the plan of establishing a battery at the heart of the passes had been proposed. President Lincoln had become much interested in the important subject of capturing New Orleans, and a conference took place at the residence of General McClellan, who had been lately appointed general-in-chief of the army. The meeting occurred on November 15th, with the President, General McClellan, Secretary Welles, Assistant Secretary Fox, and Commander D. D. Porter present. Ship Island was determined upon as a base of operations and supplies; a co-operating force of the army had been promised. Porter was to have his bomb flotilla, with which he proposed to destroy the forts in forty-eight hours, in which opinion Major Barnard, an engineer officer of the army, fully concurred. The Assistant Secretary, who was an old naval officer, did not think favorably of the bombs, but in deference to military knowledge and the confident assertions of Commander Porter, the mortar fleet was adopted as a portion of the expedition. It now became an interesting question as to who should have the naval leadership. The position must be occupied by a man who would be willing to carry out the views and plans of the department, and sink his own ideas and preferences. It was essential that he should be an officer of known ability and of undoubted loyalty, and one possessing courage, as well as a knack of overcoming obstacles and difficulties. Among the few standing high in the estimation of the department, but who had never been given an important command, was Captain David Glasgow Farragut. Other names, occupying the higher

DAVID GLASGOW FARRAGUT.

numbers on the list, were carefully conned over, with characteristics and merits fully weighed and considered. Undoubted, unswerving loyalty to the country and Constitution was of primary importance. But who to select, and then who to trust, amid the general stampede of secession and resignation that existed at the time, were questions of grave importance to the government. The great body of Southern officers left the service, walking out from under the Stars and Stripes, that had fostered, protected, and paid them for so many years, without a pang of remorse or regret at the time. They were acting under a conviction that their obligations were greater and more binding to their State than to the general government, and chose accordingly. But there were some who remained, whose convictions of duty overruled all love and sentiment of State rights and sovereignty; who cut loose from home, kindred, and friends, to support a principle for which they became exiles, pariahs, and outcasts amongst their best and dearest friends. Prominent among these was Farragut, a Southern man by birth, whose adopted home was Norfolk, Virginia. Nothing could shake his fidelity and reverence for the flag to which he admitted he owed everything. He viewed the doctrine of secession with abhorrence, and disloyalty as a crime for which death alone could atone.

On the eve of the impending conflict, Farragut had arrived from a cruise in the "Brooklyn," had been placed on waiting orders, and was closely watching events from his Norfolk home. When intelligence came that the ordinance of secession had passed the Convention, Farragut realized that Virginia had swung from her moorings, and was no longer a home for him. He would not live under, much less recognize and serve, a flag hostile to that under which he had served for fifty years in every nook and corner of the globe, and for which he had always been ready to yield his life. Two hours after the reception of the news he placed his wife, sister, and their children in a carriage, put his loaded pistols in his pocket, and proceeded to the Baltimore steamer then at the wharf. He reached New York poor in purse, and with means so limited that they would not admit of his remaining in the city. He rented a modest little cottage at Hastings-on-the-Hudson for $150 per annum, where, with plain furniture and one servant, he retired with his family to await events, ready to respond to any call his country might make upon him.

Secretary Welles had met Farragut in Washington fifteen years before, during the Mexican War. John G. Mason was then at the head of the Navy department, and Farragut had submitted a plan for taking the castle of San Juan d'Ulloa. Secretary Mason heard him patiently, but dismissed him and his project as visionary. Welles was present, and the interview made a lasting impression upon the future cabinet official. Farragut's plan was to carry the fortress by boarding; ladders were to be constructed and triced up along the attacking ships' masts; the ships to be towed alongside the walls of the castle by the steamers of the squadron. Secretary Welles once referred to this event after Farragut had made himself famous, and the admiral was greatly pleased at the comment of his superior. He replied that a great many thought him crazy; but he was still satisfied that he could have taken the castle, had he been afforded the opportunity.

Up to 1861 Farragut had never commanded a squadron; and it is doubtful if he would have received their favorable consideration had the opinions of his seniors been asked. His record, in common with others of his grade, was good—nothing more; and whether he possessed to a greater degree the higher qualities which are essential for a leader, and are indispensable for a naval chief, were questions beyond the power of the department to answer. There had always been an intimacy between the families of Porter and Farragut, dating back to the administration of Jefferson, when the father of Farragut had been of great service to the elder Porter, who had reciprocated by placing young Farragut, then a boy of nine years and five months, in the navy as a midshipman. He was taken into the Porter family, and, in gratitude and affection, took the name of David, and was so baptized in the Protestant Episcopal Church at Newport.

Mr. Fox, Assistant Secretary under Mr. Welles, was directed to obtain Commander Porter's opinion of Farragut. Porter had been entrusted with the secret of the proposed expedition against New Orleans, and fully understood the importance of ascertaining the ideas, views, and sentiments of Farragut before intimating in the remotest degree the intentions of the department. Porter was furnished with a written order, covering the purchasing and fitting out of a number of schooners for his proposed mortar fleet, and, with the attendant business as a pretext for interviews, he was to sound Farragut in relation to naval affairs generally. His orders in relation thereto were verbal, it not being deemed advisable to have them in writing. Porter accomplished his delicate mission successfully, reporting favorably to the department, and on the 15th of December Farragut was ordered to report at Washington.

Farragut, still in ignorance of what the department had in view, conversed earnestly and enthusiastically on the subject of subduing the rebellion. He so impressed the Secretary that all further attempts at secrecy and caution were soon abandoned; was shown lists of the vessels, and endorsed the plan of the department as the right one for running past the forts. The mortar boats he did not regard highly, and he placed but little reliance upon that portion of the fleet. But to "obey orders," he said, was his "first duty." The mortar fleet might be of greater benefit than he expected, he explained to the Secretary, and he would willingly adopt it as a part of his command. Farragut was never profuse in promises. He said, however, that he would pass the forts and restore New Orleans to the government, or never return. He might not come back, he said, but the city should be ours. Thus it was that Farragut, a Southerner, was selected as flag-officer, and on the 23d of December was directed to hold himself in readiness to take command of the West Gulf Blockading Squadron and the expedition to New Orleans.

Farragut deserved this recognition from the hands of the government he had served so long and well; and it was a selection that neither the country nor the Navy Department ever had occasion to regret. A few of the prominent features and episodes in the career of America's first and greatest admiral cannot fail to carry with them, to all patriotic readers, a degree of pride and mournful interest in connection with the hero, whose deeds must ever be linked with the history of the Union he was instrumental in preserving.

Farragut was about thirteen years old when he fought his first battle, which, in point of ferocity and stubbornness, was closely on a par with the engagement in Mobile Bay. He was a midshipman on the "Essex," which vessel was attacked by the British frigate "Phœbe" and sloop-of-war "Cherub," in total disregard of the neutrality of the port. Porter, the American commander, was about thirty-two years of age, full of dash and enthusiasm; while Hillyar, the English captain, was a cool, long-headed man

of fifty, who was determined to carry out his orders to "capture the 'Essex' with the least possible risk to his vessel and crew." To give a detailed description of that celebrated action, fit to rank with the "Bon Homme Richard" and "Serapis," would be superfluous in a paper of this kind, and only a few anecdotes relating to Farragut can be mentioned.

"During the action," he said, when speaking of it in after-life, "I was like Paddy in the catharpines—a man on occasions. I performed the duties of captain's aid, quarter-gunner, powder-boy, and, in fact, did everything that was required of me. I shall never forget the horrid impressions made upon me at the sight of the first man I had ever seen killed. He was a boatswain's mate, and was fearfully mutilated. It staggered and sickened me at first; but they soon began to fall around me so fast that it all appeared like a dream, and produced no effect on my nerves. I was standing near the captain, just abaft the mainmast, when a shot came through the waterways, killing four men, and scattering the brains of one over both of us.

"On one occasion it was reported to the captain that a quarter-gunner, named Roach, had deserted his post. The only reply the captain addressed to me was, 'Do your duty, sir.' I seized a pistol and went in search of the fellow, but did not find him. It appeared subsequently that when the ship was reported to be on fire he, with six others, had managed to steal a boat and escape to the shore. Roach had always been considered a leading man in the ship, and once, when the 'Phœbe' seemed about to run into us, in the harbor of Valparaiso, and the boarders were called away, this man stood in an exposed position on the cathead, with sleeves rolled up, and cutlass in hand, ready to board. He was brave with the prospect of success before him, but a coward in adversity.

"It was wonderful to find dying men uttering sentiments worthy of a Washington. In all directions was heard, 'Don't give her up, Logan!' 'Logan' was a sobriquet for Porter. I went on board the 'Phœbe' about eight o'clock in the morning, and was ushered into the steerage. I was so mortified at our capture that I could not refrain from tears. I was aroused by a cry of 'A prize! a prize! Ho, boys! a fine grunter.' I saw at once that an English midshipman had under his arm a pet pig, belonging to our ship, called 'Murphy.' I claimed the animal as my own. 'Ah!' said the captor, 'but you are a prisoner, and your pig also.' 'We always respect private property,' I replied ; and, as I had seized hold of Murphy, I determined not to let go unless compelled by superior force. This was fun for the oldsters, who immediately sang out, ' Go it, my little Yankee ! If you can thrash Shorty, you shall have your pig.' A ring was formed, and at it we went. I soon found that my antagonist's pugilistic education did not come up to mine. In fact, he was no match for me, and was compelled to give up the pig. So I took Master Murphy under my arm, feeling that I had, in some degree, wiped out the disgrace of our defeat."

In that memorable fight, the impressions of which were never lost upon Farragut, he experienced a narrow escape from death. He was standing by the side of an old quartermaster who had the wheel, when he saw a shot coming over the foreyard, in such a direction that he thought it would strike one of them. Farragut told his companion to jump, but he was not quick enough ; for the shot carried away his right leg, and severed the little tails to Farragut's coatee. Lieutenant Wilmer, who had been sent forward to let go the sheet-anchor, was knocked overboard by a shot. His little negro boy servant came on deck, learned of the fate of his master, and deliberately jumped into the sea and was drowned.

Farragut was a somewhat awkward youth of seventeen when, in company with other officers, he was invited to a grand ball at Pisa, given by the Grand Duke of Tuscany. During the dancing his shoe-buckle caught in the flounce of the archduchess's dress. He kicked off the buckle, knelt, and extricated it, with an apology. Soon after he trod fairly and squarely on the grand duke's toe, and made another apology. Disgusted with his want of success, he was looking around for his cocked hat, intending to retire, and avoid further accidents. He discovered a fat old countess was using the hat as a foot-warmer. Farragut drew it away rather unceremoniously, the lady remarking that he " ought not to be offended, but should feel complimented." " Madam," he replied, " it may be looked upon in that light in your country, but not in mine."

When off the Tortugas, Farragut obtained leave of absence to visit his friends in New Orleans. During his absence his father had died. The vessel in which Farragut took passage carried the first load of bricks for building Fort Jackson, one of the defences of New Orleans, which he ran by with his fleet nearly forty years later.

On another occasion Farragut was a passenger on board a merchantman, coming from Gibraltar. He had been ordered home for examination, and was accompanied by two invalided sailors from the squadron. When within a few days' sail of the United States, they fell in with a brig, using sweeps, and it was put down for a pirate. The skipper of the merchantman was so frightened that Farragut, in full uniform, assumed charge, having made up his mind to die fighting rather than be taken and reserved for a worse fate. The two men-of-war's men resolutely ranged themselves alongside their officer, while the merchant sailors huddled irresolutely forward. Such was the difference in training and discipline. The vessel proved to be a Columbian brig-of-war, desiring to have some letters mailed, and so no battle occurred. But for a youth of eighteen to resolve upon a defence almost hopeless, and prepare to meet almost single-handed a vessel supposed to be a pirate, was significant of the officer's nerve and courage. It showed that the stars of an admiral fitted him in every respect, and that he possessed, even then, the spirit that could successfully carry a wooden vessel through plunging rams and formidable iron-clads, and compel the surrender of a craft like the almost invincible " Tennessee."

Farragut was made a lieutenant in 1825, and in 1833 was executive officer of the " Natchez." An officer who sailed with him at this time says : " Never was the crew of a man-of-war better disciplined, or more contented and happy. The moment all hands were called, and Farragut took the trumpet, every man under him was alive and eager for duty. I remember well on one occasion, when he took the ' Natchez ' out of the harbor of Rio, the entrance of which is quite narrow, against a head-wind, by a manœuvre which at that day was termed ' box-hauling.' There were several foreign men-of-war in port, English and French, whose officers and men were watching us closely. Many declared that the manœuvre could not be successfully accomplished ; but it was done splendidly, without a balk or failure, and I shall remember to my dying day the glow of pride and satisfaction which we all felt."

In 1841, Farragut was commissioned commander, and ordered to the " Decatur," on the South American station. She was a fine, weatherly, fast-sailing craft, and, under Farragut's matchless seamanship, beat out of the harbor of Rio against wind and tide. But few instances

are on record where the feat has been successfully accomplished.

In the Mexican War, Farragut had no opportunity to distinguish himself. His plan for the
capture of San Juan d'Ulloa met with little but
ridicule, and he had the misfortune to incur the
ill-will of Commodore Percy. By him he was
ordered to cruise off a reef of rocks, blockading
Tuxpan, where neither credit nor glory was
obtainable. He bore the imposition as patiently
as possible, but finally asked to be relieved from
service under Percy's command, or from command of the ship.

At the breaking out of the Crimean War,
Farragut applied for permission to visit the fleets
of England and France in the Baltic, basing his
request on the fact that he could speak French,
Spanish, and Italian, and had been in the service since he was nine years of age. No action
was taken on the request, but shortly afterward
he was assigned to the important duty of found-
ing a navy-yard on the Pacific coast.

Farragut's linguistic powers were really remarkable, and his reputation in that respect
was well established in the service. On one
occasion an old woman came alongside the
ship in a bumboat, but no one could communicate with her, as she spoke in a strange, guttural
tongue. Some one suggested, "Send for Farragut; he speaks the language of the devil." Accordingly, Farragut came on deck, and having
discovered that she was an Arab, conversed with
her quite freely, to the amazement of those
about him. He had learned the language while
he was at Tunis.

Farragut took a great interest in all athletic
sports. He once won a set of diamond studs in
a foot-race with a brother officer, and even after
his fiftieth year it was no unusual thing for him
to test the skill of his officers with the single
stick. When in command, especially during the
war, he invariably wore or carried his sword on
shore with him, a habit which he had acquired
when serving on the South American coast. In
returning to his ship at night he frequently had
to pass through the worst parts of the seaport
towns, where naval officers were sometimes molested; and, being a good swordsman, he remarked that if he should be attacked he had
more confidence in the sword than any other
weapon. He once remarked, in the cabin of the
old "Hartford," that he really felt more con-
straint as an admiral than when he was a midshipman. Then he had the first lieutenant to
quarrel with; but now he had to face the gov-

ernment, and all his faults were faults that
affected his reputation. He said he made it a
rule never to quarrel with the powers that be; he
did not approve of that in a commanding officer.

When assigned to duty on the Pacific coast,
Farragut took passage with his family for California in the "Star of the West," a vessel which
afterward figured conspicuously in the early
operations of the Civil War. Having decided
upon Mare Island as a site for a navy-yard, and
there being no houses or suitable accommoda-
tions ashore, Farragut and his family moved on
board the old sloop-of-war "Warren," which
had been moored opposite the yard, and turned
over to him by the department. Here, for several months, they kept house and lived comfortably until the houses on shore were in readiness
to receive them. At the expiration of his three
years duty at the navy-yard, so well had he
performed his work, that the department was at
a loss whom to appoint in his place. It had been
the custom for shore duty to be followed by orders for sea; but Farragut was informed that if
he would express a preference to remain it would
be granted. This he would not do, replying
that it was the department's place to give orders
and his to obey. He never asked for official
favors, but awaited orders and obeyed them
without question.

After a residence of four years on the Pacific
coast, he returned East, and was ordered to
command the "Brooklyn," one of the new
sloops-of-war. While in command of this vessel, one of his seamen, confined for drunkenness,
died while in confinement, and Farragut was
roundly abused by the newspapers, and held
personally responsible for the man's death. His
vessel was ordered back from Vera Cruz, and
Farragut was harassed by abuse from pettifog-
ging lawyers. Mr. Charles O'Conor sustained
Farragut, and would accept no fee from him,
saying, "It is a pleasure to defend such a frank
man." Returning to his station, and brooding
over his troubles, Farragut was attacked by
yellow fever, from which he barely recovered.

In 1860, he was detached from the "Brooklyn," and the breaking out of the Civil War
found him at Norfolk. Every day the officers
were in the habit of meeting and discussing the
events of the day. Farragut was termed a
"croaker," and laughed at for his opinions, but
he could see the impending storm gathering.
"God forbid," he once said, "that I should
have to raise my hand against the South, but
my duty must be done."

II.—PREPARING FOR THE FIGHT WITH THE RIVER FORTS.

ON the 20th of January, 1862, Secretary Welles notified Captain Farragut to hold himself in readiness to take command of the "Hartford," and as senior officer to assume control of affairs in the West Gulf Blockading Squadron, to prepare at once for an advance up the Mississippi River, having for its object the capture of New Orleans.

The "Hartford" received her crew the latter part of January, 1862, from the receiving ship "Princeton." They had been carefully picked from over eight hundred men, and probably no vessel afloat at that time under the Stars and Stripes could compare with, much less surpass, the "Hartford's" crew in point of excellence and physique. The frigate's battery consisted of twenty-two nine-inch guns—Dahlgren smooth bores, two twenty-pounder Parrott's rifles, and the tops were protected with boiler iron to shield the men working the howitzers placed there. Farragut believed in wooden ships and plenty of guns.

At the magazine below the city the "Hartford" received her powder, but it was not until the noble frigate anchored off Newcastle that Farragut came on board. It had been rumored on the berth deck that the frigate was to bear aloft the senior officer's flag, and that important work had been cut out for the new commander.

Farragut had never been seen by the crew, and Jack's curiosity on the subject was considerably aroused. He came alongside in a shore boat, alone and unannounced, ascended the starboard gangway ladder with a light, active, springy step and nervous manner; shook hands with the officers, glanced along the spar deck and up aloft; raised his uniformed cap, which was incased in a glazed cover, as he gained the quarter deck, over which floated the Stars and Stripes, and disappeared in his cabin.

Captain Farragut was at this time sixty-three years of age, fifty-two of which had been spent afloat in the service of his country. He was below the average height and slight in figure, weighing about one hundred and thirty pounds, and smooth shaved. The top of his head was quite bald, which fact he tried to conceal by combing side hair across it, or, as the sailors termed it, by "making the after-guard perform

topmen's duty." His manner was dignified but unassuming; his features, while rugged and weather-beaten, were pleasant in expression, but could darken and frown ominously on occasions. He wore the plain uniform of a captain, the frock coat of which was buttoned at the termination of the lapel. It was a peculiarity of Farragut's that he would allow his coat to fly open, and only on special occasions would he button it, as regulations demanded, and then only for a few moments.

Soon after entering his cabin he appeared on deck for a moment and beckoned to a quartermaster (Knowles) who was standing near. "Bring me a small nail, if you please, quartermaster," he said. He held in his hand a framed photograph of his wife, and with his own hand he placed it on a panel of his cabin.

It may appear a strange statement to the general reader that the first impressions of Farragut on the crew were far from favorable. Safe within the boundaries of the berth deck, the men commented upon the appearance of the "old man," as every commanding officers is termed, be he sixteen or sixty, and the general verdict was disappointment in the "cut of his jib." Sailors arrive at their conclusions quickly and are generally correct in their estimates of the officers placed over them; but in this instance, where Farragut was disparaged on all sides as a leader and fighting man, their judgment was wide of the truth. They had yet to learn of the rare qualities lying dormant in Farragut's nature.

It was late in February, 1862, when the "Hartford" anchored off Ship Island, and from the busy hum of active preparation, both afloat and ashore, it was apparent to all that the dismal, barren outlying sand island had been selected as a base of supplies and rendezvous for a large and important expedition. Rumors as to the ultimate destination of the force were many, but the conviction that New Orleans was the objective point at last took possession of the majority of all on board, and the frigate's crew realized that stirring scenes and bloody work awaited them in the near future. The roll of drums, trill of bugles, clatter of artillery, and confused hum of voices, as bodies of men marched and countermarched amid the shifting hills of glistening sand, the white tents, waving banners, glittering uniforms, and horsemen galloping to and fro, with old Fort Massachusetts standing grim and silent overlooking the scene, gave evidence that no time was being lost in preparing the soldiers, under their restless and energetic leader, General Butler, for their part of the programme. On the water the scene was no less spirited and lively; boats, from which fluttered the national colors, dashed in and out amongst the fleet; the word of command echoed over the sparkling waters; guns were being run in and out; the flash of steel, musket, rifle, boarding pike, and cutlass glittered above the hammock nettings, and the notes of preparation went on with little or no cessation.

Farragut, silent and alone, paced the quarter-deck, his head bent slightly forward, plunged in a deep reverie, which no one ventured to interrupt. It was known on board that he was a Southern man, had given up all in his devotion to the flag, and had severed the friendships of a lifetime by remaining true to his convictions. He had relieved Flag Officer McKean of the responsibilities of the station, and Captain Henry H. Bell had reported on board the "Hartford" as fleet captain. Captain Bell's reputation as a fighter had long since been established, and it was current gossip amongst the old tars that he had fought a number of duels with English and French officers, and had always got the best of his antagonists. He certainly was one of the best swordsmen in the United States Navy, and "Jack," who loves dash and plenty of hard knocks, nodded approvingly when the gray-haired fire-eater took up his position on the quarter-deck beside the quiet Farragut. Bell was of commanding presence, tall, erect, and lithe as an Indian, his moustache white and cropped short; steel gray eyes, piercing in their look, imparted a stern expression to his bronzed features. In his intercourse with the enlisted man he was invariably kind and considerate, never refusing a reasonable request emanating from the berth deck. He was the reigning favorite of the ship's company. Farragut's star had not yet risen above the deepening clouds; his opportunity to step into the brilliant path of popularity and glory had not presented itself.

Numbers of vessels attached to the expedition continued to arrive, and on the 7th of March the "Hartford" steamed to the mouth of the Mississippi, where a careful examination by coast survey officers had pronounced in favor of South West Pass as the more desirable channel. The small craft had no difficulty in attaining its object, but with the frigates it meant hard work for both officers and men. All possible means and devices to lighten the huge men-of-war were resorted to. Spars were sent down, magazines emptied, coal bunkers cleared, and even guns removed ere the keels of some of the squadron could pass clear of the mud lumps. Night and day the work went on, the spare articles being deposited at Pilot Town, where the sailors had already planted a flag-staff and hoisted one of the largest ensigns in the fleet. The old salts took upon themselves the privilege and luxury of growling, referring to the good old days that, to their manner of thinking, had vanished forever; but the new recruits were fresh and young, their duties were novel, and they toiled in mud, miasma and sun without a murmur.

The "Brooklyn" and "Hartford" crossed the bar after a number of attempts, the "Mississippi" and "Pensacola" followed, but no amount of coaxing or nautical skill could induce the "Colorado" to trust herself inside amid the muddy waters of the mighty river. This was a great disappointment to Captain Bailey, her commander, and her officers and crew were distributed through the attacking squadron. The number, variety, and rig of the vessels congregated at the bar was a constant source of amusement and study to the sailors. There were lofty transports and diminutive, puffing tugs, large store ships and dingy coal vessels, schooners, barges, mortar boats, trading drafts, square riggers, "fore and afters," in fact the model of every floating craft extant was represented—excepting, possibly, the Ark. Some portions of the vast assemblage of vessels were in motion continually, adding an air of bustle and confusion to the usually deserted and dreary locality. A hospital was established at the wretched settlement built amid the reedy, low and treacherous marshes surrounding Pilot Town; plank walks to the creek landing were laid, guards established, and a strict code of military laws enforced, affecting fisherman, settler, and new comer alike.

One of the first acts of Farragut after crossing the bar was to despatch Bell up the river with the gunboats "Kennebec" and "Wissahickon" on a reconnoissance. The Chief of Staff reported, on his return, that the obstructions seemed formidable. Thirty miles from the Passes were Forts Jackson and St. Philip, situated in a most commanding position at a turn in the river, the former on the west bank, and the latter on the east, which was advantageously situated for raking the lower approach. Fort Jackson was of pentagonal form, with bastions, its river front being one hundred yards from the levee, above which the casemates just appeared. The armament consisted of seventy-five guns, rifled and smooth bore. The water battery of this fort was a powerful work mounting seven heavy guns. The guns of Fort St. Philip were all in barbette, summing up a total of fifty-three pieces of ordnance of various calibre. Each of the forts was garrisoned by about seven hundred men, both of which were under command of Brigadier-General Johnson K. Duncan. In 1815 a single fort at this point had held a British fleet in check for nine days, during which time they threw into it more than a thousand shells.

Just below Fort Jackson the Confederates had obstructed the river with a heavy cable, brought from Pensacola. It was spiked to the under side of a row of cypress logs, which were thirty feet long and five feet in diameter. The logs were but a few feet apart as they were placed in the river, the ends of the cable being made fast to great trees on shore, and the whole was kept from sagging down stream by seven heavy anchors. But the spring freshets piled up a great body of driftwood, before the pressure of which the structure gave way, and the entire mass was swept into the Gulf. The cost to the Confederacy for the boom was $60,000, a costly experiment. It was soon replaced with two lighter chains, supported on a row of eight dismantled hulks anchored abreast across the river. At the end of the cable, on the shore opposite Fort Jackson, a mud battery was planted to drive off parties attempting to sever the barrier. A company of two hundred sharpshooters ranged up and down the banks, to give the forts intelligence of the Federal movements, and pick off men whenever opportunity offered. It may have been these men who conveyed to the Confederate general prompt and accurate information of every movement undertaken on the part of the fleet. At all events, the Confederate camp, by some means, was kept well posted. But they deemed their position impregnable, and laughed at the idea of Farragut's vessels being able to run the gauntlet of the strong fortifications.

On the 6th of April, Farragut, accompanied by Captain Bell, ascended the river in the "Kennebec" for the purpose of closely observing the Confederate position. They came in sight of the forts about noon, and the glasses revealed the parapets crowded with men watching the vessel's movements. Fort Jackson sent as a greeting a hundred-pound rifle shell, which exploded about one hundred yards in advance. Farragut and Bell were in the foretop-mast cross-trees taking notes and observations. A second shot pased over the trucks of the "Kennebec," and she slowly dropped down stream. It was none too soon, for a third shell burst in the river at a point just before occupied by the gunboat. The practice of the Confederate artillerists reflected great credit upon their skill and judgment.

Rafts of logs filled up all available space in the channel way, and the passage between the forts was completely closed. Beyond this, lurking in the deep shadows of the river banks, was a fleet of ironclads and rams, flying the Confederate flag, with guns shotted and manned, ready to greet Farragut and his wooden walls with a tempest of shot and shell, should he succeed in running the fiery gauntlet of forts and water batteries.

To pass the defences, burst through the obstructions, and capture the city, Farragut had six sloops of war, sixteen gunboats, twenty-one schooners each carrying a 13-inch mortar, and five other vessels. The fleet mounted over two hundred guns, and was the largest in number of vessels that, as a whole, had ever sailed under the Stars and Stripes, having for its object a hostile errand.

The 16th of April found all the fleet in position, with mortar schooners ready to open up on the forts. They were moored to the river bank 2,800 yards from Fort Jackson, and 3,860 yards from Fort St. Philip. The Confederates commenced the engagement in a manner peculiarly their own, affording a new and novel experience to the officers and men of the Union fleet. They set afloat a large Mississippi flat-boat piled with fat and resinous wood saturated with tar, rosin, and turpentine. A fresh wind was blowing up the river, which fanned the glowing mass into billows of roaring flames, as it slowly bore down in the direction of the ships. Cables were slipped in a hurry, drums rolled, officers shouted, sailors skipped nimbly about, while the "Mississippi" fired a few shells into the fire raft, without, however, producing any effect beyond casting up clouds of fiery *debris*. The great, roaring, hissing mass whirled through the dodging ships without inflicting damage, and a boat from the "Iroquois" succeeded, with a grappling iron, in towing the unwelcome visitor ashore, where it expended its fury harmlessly. Porter at once organized a boat brigade from the vessels of his mortar fleet, provided with axes, hooks, and tow lines, and they passed in review around the "Harriet Lane," the flagship of Commander Porter. Each officer was questioned by the swarthy-faced chief if he had fire buckets, axes, and all appurtenances as he had prescribed. They were then ordered to pull around the "Mississippi," lying a quarter of a mile ahead. There were not less than one hundred and fifty boats on the river, many of them pulling ten oars, and the trial for supremacy in speed was loudly cheered by the fun-loving sailors of the fleet.

The masts of the schooners had been decked out with green boughs to deceive the enemy and disconcert their fire; but Fort Jackson fired the first shot, to which the gunboat "Owasco" replied. Then for the first time came the deep-toned report of a bomb, and all watched curiously the huge missile, weighing two hundred and eighty-five pounds, as it curved and circled in the direction of the fort, exploding with a dull, heavy concussion. The mortar-men fired slowly, while Porter in person superintended the elevation, length of fuses, etc., until he had arranged all the details to his satisfaction. The forts replied, their balls humming all about the mortar schooners without injuring them materially. The men suffered most from the concussions of the huge engines of war. They stood upon tiptoe and with open mouths to lessen the effect of the stunning concussions. But before the fire ceased, the crews became so accustomed to the sound that they were able to sleep upon the decks of the mortar schooners. It was hard, exhausting work, handling those immense globes of iron; and the men, too tired to go below, would lie along the deck and instantly fall asleep. Quantities of dead fish floated by, killed by the heavy reverberations, while swarms of disturbed bees buzzed angrily through the air as they deserted their haunts in the neighboring swamps. At the commencement of the bombardment, each mortar schooner fired at the rate of one shell every ten minutes, but this was soon increased to a shell every five minutes, averaging two hundred and forty projectiles per hour. One of them broke into the officers' mess room in the fort while they were at dinner, where it lay smoking and sputtering between them and the only exit the place afforded. It was a moment of terrible

suspense, but, fortunately for them, the fuse went out, and the shell was rendered harmless.

During the bombardment, General Butler came over from Ship Island on his little boat. His presence in the fleet always provoked a cheer of welcome, as his advent usually meant news, or mail matter of some kind. He would sit on the poop of the "Hartford," talking over the situation with Farragut, who was getting sadly out of patience with the delay. For six days and nights the mortar schooners had been thundering away, having expended the enormous quantity of 16,800 shells. Porter had calculated upon forty-eight hours as sufficient to reduce the forts to pulp. Farragut granted him time far in excess of that, and still there was no apparent slackening of the enemy's fire. Farragut, in the beginning, had entertained but little faith in the value of the mortars, which were a costly appendage to his fleet, and he would gladly have cut loose from them had he been allowed to do so. As it was, he watched their operations closely. The mortar fleet was divided into three divisions, each taking the duty in turn.

Sunday, April 20th, was Easter Sunday, and just as day dawned, a low, cautious hail was wafted across the water to the keen ears of the officer of the deck. It came, apparently, from a low clump of bushes and rank weeds growing close to the edge of the river. A boat from the "Hartford" was lowered, and brought back a deserter from Fort Jackson, who had made good his escape the night before. He had been an *attaché* of Dan Rice's circus, and had been left behind when the company vacated the city by order of the authorities. He had made his way through the swamps to the fleet, lighted and guided by the fire of the mortars, often floundering in the treacherous, oozy depths of the dreary waste up to his armpits in mire. He was evidently a hard case, if appearances could be taken as a criterion of the man's character. He was at once taken before Farragut, who questioned him closely relative to the condition of affairs in the fort. He represented the garrison as in a desperate and demoralized condition from the effects of the bombs, which had struck in and about the works. One had burst near the magazine door, killing the sentinel and a guard, and it was during the confusion occasioned by that shot that he effected his escape. The ditches had been cut, water was flowing into the works, requiring two steam pumps working continuously to keep the magazines free, while numbers of Union sympathizers were amid the rank and file, who only lacked the opportunity to range themselves under the Stars and Stripes. How much importance Farragut attached to the deserter's information, it was impossible to judge; but never for a moment did the fire from the forts relax.

Captain Bell, with the gunboats "Pinola" and "Itasca," was deputized to ascend the river and cut the cable. The night was dark, while the current ran with more than usual force, and many an anxious eye followed the fleeting outlines of the vessels as they disappeared in the darkness. The mortar schooners had increased their fire, often keeping eight shells at once plunging and whirring on high. Amid the din and gloom the barrier was reached ; a petard, specially prepared to accomplish the work of blowing up the cable, failed at the critical moment. A party from the "Itasca," equipped with cold chisels and hammers, leaped the hulks. At the same instant a rocket shot into the air. The party was discovered, and both forts opened fire ; but under cover of the darkness and smoke, the sailors worked with a will. The chain was severed, the hulks torn from their places, and a breach wide enough to admit of several vessels passing abreast was made. It was a night of anxiety to Farragut, and he did not retire until Bell returned and he was assured of his friend's safety.

The bombardment had been severe, and the mortar boats, or "bummers," as they got to be called, began to run short of everything required—shells, fuses, grape, canister, cartridge bags, and hospital stores. The men had been hard-worked, and were beginning to grumble at their continuous labors, while the sailors of the fleet looked on and jibed them. A council of war was held on the flag-ship. Each commander had his say, and probably the usual diversity of opinion prevailed. Farragut would delay no longer, and it is not all probable that he was influenced by the opinions given at the council. His plans had long since been matured. On the 20th of April, he issued his General Order :

The flag officer, having heard all the opinions expressed by the different commanders, is of the opinion that whatever is to be done will have to be done quickly. * * When, in the opinion of the flag officer, the propitious time has arrived, the signal will be made to weigh and advance to the conflict. * * He will make the signal for close action, No. 8, and abide the result—conquer or be conquered.

Orders to be in readiness for the grand attack on the 24th had been issued from the flag-ship.

It had been Farragut's intention to have the heavier ships take the lead in passing the forts, as they would more readily overcome obstructions in the channel ; but he was overruled by the senior commanders under him. They would not permit the chief to receive the greatest shock of the battle, and it was with great reluctance he adopted the plan of advancing in three divisions, with the "Hartford" in the centre of the line. Captain Bailey led the van in the gunboat "Cayuga" having hoisted his red flag on that vessel.

The English corvette "Rinaldo" had been allowed to ascend the river to the city to look after the interests of English subjects, and about this time returned, every officer, from the commander to midshipman, being deeply impressed with the strength and resources of the Confederate. The commander called on Farragut, who listened courteously to the list of terrors prepared by the Confederates ; while his guest enlarged upon the folly and useless sacrifice of life that would result in an attempt that could only end in defeat and destruction to the Union fleet. The rebel ironclads were magnified into mammoth proportions, while it was argued that even if the forts and ironclads were overpowered, the batteries lining the river to the city were more than sufficient to destroy the invading force. The English officer's advice, no doubt, was sincere and well-meant ; but it had no effect upon Farragut, whose mind was not easily disturbed by an array of difficulties lying in his path.

Every vessel had made such preparations as time and resources would permit to protect the lives of the men and machinery from the fire of the forts. An engineer of the "Richmond" originated the idea of stopping the sheet cables up and down the sides in the line of the engines, which was equivalent to a four-inch plating of iron. The "Brooklyn," "Pensacola," and "Iroquois" followed suit, while others utilized sand bags, coal, hammocks, and clothes bags. Bulwarks were lined with canvas and hammocks, and splinter nettings stretched to catch the flying debris. In some instances, commanders daubed the outside of their vessels with river mud, while others whitewashed their decks so that objects could be seen with greater distinctness. Small anchors hung from yard-arms of the larger vessels, in readiness to drop upon the Confederate gunboats and fire rafts.

The "Hartford's" broad decks had been cleared for action, but no iron cables protected her massive sides. Ports had been lowered, guns shotted and run out, and upon their efficacy Farragut depended; but could he have foreseen what was to come, the stout-hearted old sailor would scarcely have neglected taking additional precautions. In the afternoon, Farragut visited each ship in order to satisfy himself that each commander thoroughly understood his orders for the attack, and that everything was in readiness. The inspection proved satisfactory, and Farragut returned to the flag-ship in excellent spirits. All looked forward to the attack and coming struggle hopefully, but not without anxiety, for it was to be at night, the hour being set for two o'clock A. M.

Rumors ran rife throughout the rank and file of the fleet that an immediate attack had been ordered, and the flag-ship was closely watched by the observant seamen. At midnight the order to stow all hammocks was passed, while the cooks of messes were directed to have coffee and hard-tack ready for serving at one A. M.

The crew of the "Hartford," anxious and silent, gathered in groups between the guns, conversing at intervals in low tones, directing earnest glances up the river in the direction of the enemy's stronghold, and arranging their little affairs in the event of the worst happening. All felt strangely sober and subdued, with the certainty that a hard struggle for supremacy awaited, a struggle that for some would bring peace and sleep—the sleep that knows no waking. Yet the signal for the advance was ardently looked for. The sooner the trial was over with, the better. That was the sentiment prevailing forward. But few slept, and the stillness of death pervaded the vessels; not a glimmer of a light could be seen along the line.

The time crept slowly by, the dark outlines of the ships looming up through the darkness dimly revealed against the gloomy horizon. The night was favorable to the momentous undertaking, the moon would not appear above the distant fringe of trees before three o'clock, when it was hoped it would prove a benefit; the atmosphere was heavy, and a light haze rested on the river, which the faint airs prevailing failed to disperse. The slow, deliberate fire of the bombs, in measured concussions, echoed solemnly through the archway of heaven, and more than one man on the "Hartford's" deck peered curiously aft, wondering when the order to move would come.

The suspense was hard to bear; besides, the men's tempers had not been improved by the loss of their favorite—"Fighting" Captain Bell. He had been ordered to command the third division, which he led in the "Scioto," and the hearty good wishes of the flag-ship's crew accompanied the officer to his new command. The crew of the "Hartford" had but little knowledge of the officers under whom they were to undergo the ordeal of battle. There had been but little time to form opinions or create confidences in the press of hard practical details that had occupied the time and attention of all in the fleet. Lieutenant Thornton, the executive officer, from his constant intercourse with the crew, had become familiar to them; but Farragut, absorbed in study and meditation, appeared more in the light of a passenger occupying the quarter-deck than a leader. Commander Wainwright, the captain of the "Hartford," was also known to the men; but the knowledge that the eve of battle was nigh, insensibly drew officers and crew closer together, as they gazed into the dark void lying between them and the guns of the hostile forts.

Suddenly the mortar fleet, as if furnishing an appropriate prelude to the bloody struggle that was to follow, opened a rapid and furious fire, surpassing all their former efforts. Five, then seven or eight—sometimes as many as twelve—of the tremendous shells could be plainly seen, circling, glowing, hissing, following each other in their fiery paths across the heavens. The noise was deafening; the ships of war trembled under the constant vibration and concussion; the line of woods along the western bank loomed up weird and shapeless in that awful lurid light; men gazed into each other's faces without exchanging a word, listening with a feeling of awe to the crash and roar of Porter's fleet, wondering how much longer they must wait ere their own trusty eleven-inch guns might catch up the death-dealing refrain that was rolling in echoing reverberations over the lowlands of the boasted stronghold. The forts were strangely and ominously silent, scarcely deigning to reply to the fusillade. As it afterwards proved, the enemy had been apprised, through some mysterious and unknown source, of Farragut's intended attack, and were grimly waiting for the Union chief and his vessels to heave in sight, reserving for that event their ammunition and best efforts for the grand assault.

Weitzel, General Butler's engineer, had suggested to Farragut the advisability of running as close as possible to the forts. "The tendency of all men in battle," he said, "is to fire too high, and the gunners of the forts have been for a week firing as high as the guns could be elevated. Besides, they will naturally expect the ships to keep at a distance, and would aim for the middle of the river. The ships, too, will certainly fire over those low forts unless the officers take particular precautions to keep the guns depressed." Fort St. Philip was originally built by the Spaniards, was wholly inclosed by the United States authorities in 1812–15, and since 1841 had undergone extensive repairs and modifications. It was nineteen feet above the level of the river, and all the guns *en barbette*, while Fort Jackson rose to a height of twenty-five feet.

The little steamer "Saxon," General Butler's despatch boat, remained alongside the "Hartford" until a late hour, but the last good-bye was finally uttered, a hearty "God-speed" wished Farragut and his men by the soldiers as they passed over the gangway to the deck of their own craft, which was kept in readiness to move at a moment's warning from the general, who slept on board that eventful night.

Shortly after midnight coffee and hard-tack was given to the flag-ship's crew. There were some growls of discontent from the old hands, who had made up their minds for a stiff allowance of grog; but Farragut detested liquor, and never lost an opportunity to frown down its immoderate use.

The final preparations for action were now made on board the "Hartford." The carpenter's squad produced plugs and planking for shot-holes and fractures, with strings for men to drop over the side and adjust the same; the gunner and his mate inspected the battery for the final touches, testing lock-strings, filling division-tubs with water for use in case of fire, or to drink, and placing buckets of sand in the rear of the guns to be scattered over the deck when rendered slippery by the life-blood of war's victims; the boatswain and his assistants placed extra stoppers on shrouds and backstays, with slings and precenter tackles to secure the lower yards; the surgeon's force adjusted swinging cots at the main hatch for lowering the wounded to the hospital below, where, on a long table, surgical instruments of all kinds gleamed ominously in the bright lamplight. Everything was completed swiftly and quietly, for occupation of any kind was a relief to the men who were chafing under suspense and suppressed excitement.

In the midst of it all a gleam of blood-red light shoots suddenly athwart the turbid waters of the river. Another second reveals a brilliant blaze, that plays upon hull, spars, and rigging of the column of ships, bringing out strongly in the fierce glare the protruding muzzles of the great guns. A dozen signal lights of varied hue throw their brilliant tints upon the river banks, blending with rare effect their vivid colors with the dark, interlaced foliage. It is a fire raft, the last one sent down by the Confederates for the purpose of harassing the Federal fleet, and the swift tide sweeps it onward, a wide zone illuminated by the mass of flaming resinous wood. Over all floats a whirling, writhing pall of dense black smoke, from the midst of which trail flying showers of scintillating sparks and fragments of blazing material. In vast surges and columns of roaring, undulating billows of fire the flames roll on high, casting forth a heat impossible for mortal to withstand. The boat brigade recoils, lying on their oars watching its progress, which they are powerless to dispute. It drifts by the mortar schooners—passes in such close proximity to the "Hartford" that huge blisters are raised on her freshly-painted sides, and the men are compelled to duck their heads behind the hammock nettings as they feel the full influence of its terrific heat. Then, crackling and roaring angrily, it grazes the sides of two gunboats before an eddy tide catches the threatening mass in its resistless grasp and lands the entire fiery structure on the muddy bank of the river.

With the disappearance of the intense light it was some time before the men of the "Hartford" became accustomed to the darkness. The splash of water and a dark, moving object was dimly made out as it crept slowly but surely up against the strong tide, heading toward the barrier which, with replacing and repairing, had cost the Confederacy a grand total of $100,000. Rather a costly war toy, when it is taken into consideration that as an obstruction it had no more effect in retarding the movements of the fleet than a rope of sand. The Confederates made a vital mistake in locating what might have proved a serious obstacle to the fleet. Had it been built just above Fort St. Philip, instead of just below Fort Jackson, the party detailed to cut a passage through would have been compelled to withstand the fire of a hundred heavy guns, in the face of a rapid current, and then retreat under the combined fire of all the batteries for a distance of three miles and upwards. But fate had so ordered it, and what was the Confederate's loss was Farragut's gain.

A closer inspection of the low hull creeping stealthily forward through the gloom revealed, to the watchful gaze of the men of the "Hartford," the gunboat "Itasca" (Lieutenant Caldwell), on her way to the obstructions above, to ascertain at the last moment whether the channel and opening remained intact. She was to display a bright light from her masthead, and hundreds of eyes were striving to catch the first glint of the swaying signal.

The sullen boom of a gun; another and another in rapid succession; the reflection of bonfires burning fitfully along the reedy banks and reflected against the heavens, were sufficient evidences that the Confederates were wide awake, on the *qui vive*, and not to be taken by surprise.

It was, "Silence, fore and aft!" The men breathed in short and excited respirations. With the stroke of two o'clock the shooting, oscillating rays of a white lantern were seen up the river. The passage through the barrier had remained undisturbed. It was the "Itasca's" signal to Farragut. A few moments later the signal to get under way—two ordinary red lanterns—were bent on to the signal halliards in readiness to be run aloft to the "Hartford's" main peak. A newspaper correspondent had asked and obtained permission to run them up to their lofty perch, and the next instant they were sending forth the mute mandate of the great chief to all the commanders of the attacking column.

The click of revolving capstan; the rasping o chains; the subdued rumble and hiss of steam; a low, cautious hum of many voices like the rising tempest afar off followed; and in all directions the fleet was busily obeying the old Roman signal that Farragut had unconsciously adopted. It was half-past three ere all was straightened out and in readiness; the moon had risen above the tree-tops, casting a broad belt of shimmering light over the river; but in the strong gleams of bonfires and blazing rafts its light made but little difference to the Federal chieftain or his men. From the anchorage to a point above the forts, beyond reach of their guns, was five miles; two miles to the forts, one mile under range of their guns, two miles to perfect safety.

The six small steamers attached to the mortar fleet—the "Harriet Lane," "Westfield," "Owasco," "Clifton," "Miama," and Jackson," the last named towing the "Portsmouth"—had been ordered to move up stream nearer to Fort Jackson and engage its water battery while the ships were going by, which they promptly did.

The anchor of the "Hartford" was quickly run up to the cathead and secured; the men required no urging to work expeditiously. The whole fleet was soon under way, steaming steadily into their appointed positions without accident or confusion. Then, with everything secured, ropes laid up, and decks clear, the men of the "Hartford" repaired to their guns.

A light step echoed along the sanded deck, a gleam of lace and buttons betrayed the presence of an officer. It was Farragut, who, night-glass in hand, had moved forward to take up a position in the fore rigging above the sheer pole, striving to peer into the gloom and obscurity ahead. Between the tremendous explosions of the bombs nothing could be heard but the revolutions of the great propeller.

Along the spar and gun deck of the "Hartford" not a whisper was heard as the frigate gathered headway, steaming directly toward the opening ahead. The men were occupied with their own thoughts, and solemn ones at that. Death was nigh; no one could tell what moment might usher him into Eternity, with all its awful uncertainties; and many a brave man shuddered as he gripped his cutlass-guard, longing for the terrible ordeal to be over with.

The fleet advanced in three divisions, one ship close behind the other. Bailey on the eastern bank received the first attention of the Confederate cannoneers. His vessel, the "Cayuga," had barely passed through the opening when both forts discovered him and opened a simultaneous fire. But their marksmanship was poor, their guns had too much elevation, and Bailey suffered comparatively little loss. Not a shot had been fired from the advancing fleet; their guns could not yet be used effectively, and the Confederates, in the beginning, had it all their own way. The smoke settled down over wall and parapet. Not an object on the river could the keen-eyed artillerists discover, and the only mark they had for a guide was the fitful, fleeting flashes of the ship's guns. Captain Bailey and his division steamed three-quarters of a mile under this fire without firing a shot in reply, guided on their way by the gleams from Fort St. Philip's heavy ordnance.

The "Hartford" was about a mile and a half distant from the batteries when she came under fire. The sheltering shores of the river were aglow from the blaze of innumerable fires; while on high the heavens were festooned with glittering trains of fire as the bombs went circling and crashing into the Confederate stronghold. A jet of flame from the parapet of Fort St. Philip, the rush of a solid shot, the rending of timbers, a scream of agony from a poor fellow in the dark shadows of the "Hartford's" deck, and the crimson life-blood mingled unheeded with the coarse, damp sand as the frigate moved steadily on into that vortex of shot and fire.

The right column, under Captain Bailey, was to engage Fort St. Philip; the left, Fort Jackson; and gallantly the ships sustained their part of the conflict. Once abreast of St. Philip, the guns of the "Cayuga" poured in a tempest of grape and canister at short range, and in ten minutes had passed beyond harm. The smoke rolled down densely upon the swift running tide, the "Cayuga" held steadily on her course, emerging suddenly from the choking, sulphurous pall of smoke to find herself surrounded by eleven of the enemy's gunboats. Three of them endeavored to board her simultaneously; but Captain Bailey was closely watching their movements, encouraging the while the men to work their guns rapidly,

but not to throw away a shot. The eleven-inch gun disposed of one of the boats. The projectile tore through her antagonist's timbers at close range, driving her on to the bank of the river, where she was soon wrapped in flames. The Parrott gun on the forecastle drove off another, and before the sailors could manage the remainder, the "Oneida" and "Varuna" had hastened to the rescue of their beleaguered sister ship. The "Oneida" ran at full speed into one of the hostile craft, cutting her nearly in two, leaving her to float down with the tide a helpless wreck. The "Varuna" was ashore on the left bank, with the Confederate vessels "Governor Moore" and "Stonewall Jackson" making a fierce attack upon her. The "Jackson" rammed the "Varuna" twice, inflicting upon that vessel her death wounds, but, ere she sank, her guns had disabled the Confederate, who hauled off, demoralized and on fire. The fire of the "Varuna's" battery was kept up until the water was over the gun trucks, when attention was turned to getting the wounded out of the ship. As the head of Bailey's division reached the first turn in the river above, the "Hartford" was exactly abreast of the forts.

OUR NAVY TO-DAY.

"A ROLLING, ROARING MASS OF CRACKLING FLAMES LEAPED OVER THE BULWARKS."

IT was all but impossible for so many vessels of various degrees of speed to maintain precisely their allotted positions in line, steaming against a four-knot current, exposed to a tremendous cannonade, in addition to fire-rafts, ironclads, and rams, all of which ably seconded the efforts of the soldiers who worked the guns of the forts rapidly and effectively. The greater part of the effective fire proceeded from St. Philip, which had suffered but little from the huge bombs. The "Hartford" and "Brooklyn" kept in position, but the "Richmond" had swerved, lost place, and passed up on the west (or right) bank. The "Iroquois" was forced to proceed independent of fleet tactics and orders, and being very speedy steamed ahead of the vessels of her division. She passed within fifty yards of Fort Jackson without receiving a single shot, and passing beyond the fort was immediately attacked by a ram and the gunboat "McRea," both of which were driven off, and the commander of the latter (Lieutenant Huger) mortally wounded. The

gunners of Fort Jackson had been driven to cover by the rapid fire of the mortar steamers at the batteries. From the light afforded by two immense fire-rafts, objects in the vicinity were revealed as bright as day.

Occasionally from the deck of the "Hartford" glimpses of what was transpiring above and below her could be caught through the drifting banks of smoke. The flagship could only use to advantage her bow guns, with which the enemy's fire was responded to, until, coming into good position, the grand old vessel was sheered slightly, and at the distance of half a mile every gun in the broadside was brought to bear. The storm of grape and canister drove the artillerists from their places, forcing them to seek cover, while the guns were deserted and silent; but the casemate battery was never silenced, and the "Hartford's" compliments were vigorously returned in kind. The entire scene was wrapped in a thick, suffocating canopy of smoke. The ships ahead and the forts had made an already dark night ten times more

15

opaque and dense. The blackness could almost be felt as the "Hartford" passed beyond the radius of the blazing rafts, while the noise was confusing and deafening. The glare from the guns of an entire broadside would illumine briefly the immediate vicinity, then the choking, blinding, sulphurous smoke would settle thickly down, hugging the surface of the river like a filmy gray funeral pall. There was little else to guide the men but the flashes darting from the enemy's guns; and at times, vivid as were the jets of flame, they were obscured. Each individual officer was engaged with his particular duties and could note but little of what was occurring beyond his own division. His ears were filled with the roar of heavy guns, the crash and whir of screaming shells, the shivering, shuddering concussions of falling bombs, the rush of solid shot, crashing of shattered planking and flying splinters, while above all echoed piteously the moans, shrieks, and cries of the wounded.

As the "Hartford" came abreast of Fort Jackson every gun was in motion, each man working as energetically as if the fortunes of the battle depended upon his sole efforts. Not one skulked or wavered, and if a comrade fell his place was at once filled, often without receiving an order from an officer. The flagship was enshrouded in smoke, and on deck it was scarcely possible to recognize a man's face. The guns were trained and fired either at the flashes of artillery or in the direction whence came the heaviest reports. Along the decks the order was passed from division to division to load with grape and canister instead of shot and shell. The sailors knew what that meant—that they were within grappling distance of the foe—and they quickened their movements, though they had been at their guns over an hour, and the ranks were thinned and thinning. From the ramparts of Fort Jackson the vigilant eyes of officers and gunners had discovered and recognized the "Hartford."

An eddying breeze drove asunder the black battle cloud, fiercer and stronger burned and cracked the pine-knot fires, with sheets of flame mounting on high. The sheen of flashing, undulating light lit up the massive proportions of the "Hartford" with the distinctness of day; and from the mizzen, where fluttered Farragut's distinguishing flag, the Confederates recognized and realized that the master spirit of the attacking force was in front of their guns. The deck of the vessel was bright in the fierce blaze, but out over the river was all hideously dark. The fire from the fort visibly increased, but the proximity of the ship to the river's bank caused the gunners to miscalculate the distance, and a large portion of the iron storm passed harmlessly over the heads of the ship's crew. Farragut stood forward, eagerly watching the flashes from the enemy's guns, and occasionally consulting a small compass attached to his watch chain, as the smoke of the battle closed in around him. The wind of a solid shot was felt by the great leader as he stood by the fore rigging, and at the same time his cabin, personal effects, and mess supplies were wrecked by a plunging projectile that performed well its mission of destruction.

A favorable position was reached by the "Hartford" for pouring in a raking fire at close quarters upon Fort Jackson. Farragut was quick to note it, and waved his arm toward the Confederate work. The broadside guns responded without a moment's delay, and at this time fully 200 pieces of ordnance from the fleet and 160 more in the forts were in lively operation. The tracks of the bombs making a semicircle in the air appeared to be coming directly upon the "Hartford," and in reality they were striking at fearfully close quarters. The rending of splintered planks and bulwarks, hiss of steam, and heavy explosions of marine boilers and magazines, the shouts and yells of the combatants, with blazing rafts, burning wrecks of Confederate gunboats and shattered shells of iron rams floating, harmlessly and disabled, with the tide, all contributed to add to a scene terrible in its vividness, that once viewed could never be forgotten.

Each ship was fighting its own battle, each commander intent upon destroying every antagonist and enemy that appeared within range, occasionally directing a broadside at the fortress as opportunity offered.

The "Hartford" forged beyond Fort Jackson, with all her guns in motion, her sides encircled by a wreath of fire proceeding from the deadly muzzles of the battery. Some of the smooth, shining monsters of guns were being run out, others were in process of loading, while some were recoiling with curls of smoke pouring from the hot, discolored muzzles. Each gun's crew strove to outdo its neighbor in the rapidity and effectiveness of its fire; while division officers were careful to prevent wild or useless expenditure of ammunition. The smoke had now increased to such an extent that it was impossible to distinguish an officer from a blue-jacket ten paces distant, and the guns were trained more in accordance with the ear than eye. Every appliance of naval warfare that could be effectively used was brought into play and directed by trained and skillful men toward the subjugation of the foe.

In and out ran the guns; the swinging cots over the main hatch were constantly in use, removing the dead and wounded; fresh layers of sand were distributed fore and aft, water renewed in tubs, while men, with bare breasts and heads, bared arms and faces begrimed with powder, eyes gleaming and teeth clenched, stood by their guns, peering through the splintered ports, intent upon catching sight of what was going on, while around them flew, unheeded, screaming shells, the rush of solid shot, and sharp "ping, ping" of rifle balls.

Colonel Edward Higgens, who had formerly been an officer in the United States Navy, commanded Fort St. Philip, and had the reputation of being a gallant, fearless officer. For forty-eight hours he remained on the ramparts of the position entrusted to his care, unmindful and careless of the bombs falling thickly about him. Amid the bursting, whirling, humming remnants of shell, indifferent to smoke, flying particles of earth and brick, he would sip his coffee, munch a hard-tack, keeping his eyes fastened in the direction of the Federal fleet. He did not believe that any force afloat could succeed in running the gauntlet of the river forts' guns. He was fond of supporting his theory by recounting the facts in connection with the British fleet and their complete discomfiture in 1812, when there was but one poorly planned and uncompleted earthwork. Now there were two forts, planned and constructed by skillful engineers at a cost of a million and a half of dollars, with water batteries and obstructions, an ironclad fleet, and every appliance of modern warfare that human ingenuity and foresight could render available. So confident was the Confederate colonel in his ability to drive back the wooden vessels of Farragut, discomfited, wrecked, disabled, burning failures, that he allowed the leading ship to come abreast of his line of fire before opening with his guns, fearing their deadly execution would deter the majority of the fleet from making the attempt, thereby robbing his doughty artillery men of their coveted prey. When he saw the large, majestic ships and towering spars of Farragut's division steaming steadily on and beyond range of his

boasted guns, he said: "Better go to cover, boys; our cake is all dough! The old Navy has won!"

An ominous glare through the smoke caught the attention of Farragut, and from his position forward he detected an immense fire-raft driving straight down with the tide against the flagship. "Hard-a-port!" was the order from his lips, and from mouth to mouth it was repeated until it reached the ears of trusty old Knowles, a quartermaster, an old-time veteran man-of-war's man. Quick to obey her helm, the vessel's bows fell off, the strong tide acting directly upon them. Taking a broad sheer, the flagship shot across the river, running hard and fast upon a sticky unyielding mud-bank, directly under the guns of Fort St. Philip. The long, tough bowsprit of the old ship was pointed nearly over the parapet, leading the Confederates to believe that it was Farragut's intention to land a force under cover of his powerful battery, and to take the fort by assault. The force stationed in the water battery stampeded at once, leaving their guns silent and deserted—a panic that was fortunate for the "Hartford" and her crew. Never before had the flagship been in such deadly peril or so sorely pressed.

The Confederate tug "Mosher," commanded by a fearless officer, pushed a burning raft alongside, striking the flagship abreast of the fore rigging, and then swinging its entire length aft to the "Hartford's" quarter. A rolling, roaring mass of crackling flames leaped over the bulwarks, swept through the ports, driving the men in disorder from their guns, and lapping with hungry tongues and frightful rapidity the tarred, hempen rigging of the ship. The fierce light streamed with terrible intensity athwart the old ship's deck, revealing Farragut standing abreast of the mainmast, his cap pressed well down over his eyes, the gold lace of his uniform sparkling brightly, as he waved his arms above his head, shouting some order in the ears of Captain Wainwright, whose tall, erect form towered far above his superior.

It was the critical and crowning moment of the battle, and an attempt even to describe the scene seems beyond the power of ordinary ability, to faithfully portray all that was transpiring at that moment. It was an experience of fighting new to every officer in the fleet. Never had they heard of, much less witnessed, such a terrific cannonade. Two hundred and seventy odd guns were thundering with little or no cessation, assisted by twenty mortars; while the swish and whir of splinters, the muffled reports of boilers exploding, the shrieks and screams of scalded and drowning men, burning steamboats, the river ablaze with fire, all combined in filling and rendering complete a horrible, terrible picture of war, desolation, and man's inhumanity to man. "The river," said Farragut, "was too narrow for more than two or three vessels to act to advantage, but all were so anxious that my greatest fear was that we should fire into each other, and Captain Wainwright and myself were holloaing ourselves hoarse at the men not to fire into our ships."

Above all the roar of battle and crackling of flames the voice of Farragut was heard from the quarter-deck, where he had hastened, followed by his aids.

"Go back to your guns, men; don't flinch from that fire; there's a hotter fire than that for those who don't do their duty!"

The firemen were called away, but the men hesitated, gazed into each other's faces, while the guns of Fort Jackson played mercilessly upon the vessel. The "Hartford" appeared wreathed in flames to the very tops; she seemed indeed overwhelmed and doomed. The men had, to a certain extent, lost their heads, when the force and value of discipline asserted itself. The crew depended upon the brains, courage, and leadership of those occupying the quarter-deck to extricate the ship from her peril, and in that trying hour of danger and disaster they did not appeal in vain. Then it was, when Farragut would not leave his burning, grounded vessel, but bent all his energies to save her in the face of almost certain destruction, that the sailors recognized in him the qualities of a great commander, one upon whom they could at all times rely. From that hour he received from the men the not inappropriate sobriquet of "Old Salamander." Through the smoke and obscurity moved a tall form, whose commanding voice was heard far above the existing din and confusion. All recognized at once the presence of Captain Wainwright as he mingled with the men. Trumpet in hand, betraying no excitement or haste, he would quiet the men, start them in the right direction, saying: "Go to your stations, men; it is everybody at fire quarters," and tapping this one and that one on the shoulder, would repeat his words, occasionally calling them by name.

Farragut was by his side, his rugged features lit up grandly by the glare of the conflict, aiding and seconding Captain Wainwright by voice and gesture. Their calm, resolute bearing and the reassuring tones of their voices had its effect instantaneously upon the crew. Lieutenant Thornton was also a power, pointing out, directing, and assisting in getting every man to his post in a quiet, subdued manner, as if an ordinary drill were under way; while the men, reassured by the example of their leaders, worked with a will in combatting the fire. A master's-mate with a section of hose jumped into the mizzen rigging, directing a volume of water with skill and good judgment. The billowy flames succumbed; the thick paint on the vessel's side had contributed to the fierceness of the fire, which was quickly subdued by the firemen.

While the men were giving the finishing strokes to the fire-raft, the marines on the quarter-deck continued to load and fire as sharpshooters, never wavering, swerving from their duty, or turning their faces from the direction of the foe. Brave and reliable as they have ever proved from 1776, they added fresh laurels to their glorious reputation as a corps on that memorable occasion.

Under the shelter of the mizzen-mast, his note-book aglow with the scorching flames, the newspaper correspondent jotted down with a steady hand and clear brain the incidents of the fight as they transpired under his observation.

Captain Wainwright and the chief engineer of the "Hartford" had an interesting interview soon after the fire had been got under control. The men had returned to their guns, which, for a short interval, had been silenced, but the flagship remained hard and fast aground, with the guns of Fort Jackson doing their utmost to destroy the vessel. That relief must come speedily if the flagship was to be saved was apparent to all on board, more especially as the garrison of St. Philip had recovered from their scare, were rallying about the guns and parapet, working like beavers to bring their batteries into effective operation.

The magazines had been closed, all loose powder about the decks destroyed, and every precaution enforced to prevent serious accident. Captain Wainwright, in his concise, business-like way, ordered the chief to reduce the water in his boilers to the lowest possible depth, increase the pressure of steam, at the risk of bursting the boilers—to resort to any means in his department that would facilitate getting the vessel afloat, and that too as rapidly as possible. The engineer required no second bidding, but disappeared below, the effects of the order following with praiseworthy alacrity. The vessel trembled, quivered, strained, beginning to roll and jump in such a manner that it was with great difficulty the men kept their feet.

Out of the blackness and gloom, headed up stream, and seeking for an adversary worthy of her steel, dashed the Confederate ram "Manassas." The broadside of the "Hartford" presented a tempting mark, and she was powerless to escape the blow, which fortunately was a glancing one, striking the flagship on the

him, and from that day to his untimely death he was the reigning favorite on board the scarred and battle-riddled old vessel.

A glimpse was caught of the "Brooklyn" from the "Hartford's" deck, passing Fort Jackson, her broadside guns making it exceedingly lively for the defenders of that post. Out of the smoke and gloom of battle the flagship emerged, well above the forts, affording her men a breathing spell; but the respite was a short one.

Looming up through the darkness was the enemy's fleet. A large steamer filled with men headed for the "Hartford," evidently intending to try a hand at the good old-fashioned game of

"THE SCENE REVEALED BY THE RISING SUN WAS ONE OF DESOLATION AND DESTRUCTION."

counter, shoving her stern in toward the bank, while the bows were twisted in the opposite direction into deep water. The obstinate mud relinquished its treacherous hold upon the "Hartford's" keel, the flagship forged ahead, and sliding into deep water again dashed up stream. The men renewed their efforts to keep up a hot fire from the guns, and amid the enthusiastic cheer, the order was given, "Ahead, full speed!"

There is no doubt but what Captain Wainwright's prompt action, bearing, and coolness saved the "Hartford" from destruction on that occasion. The sailors claimed the honor for

"boarding in the smoke." Captain Broome, of the marines, as gallant and plucky a gentleman as ever handled a sabre, had been watching the dark object keenly. With a steady and practised hand the captain trained a nine-inch broadside gun upon the venturesome craft, and the next instant a shell exploded in the midst of the Confederates. Steamer, men, and all disappeared like chaff before the gale. The "Hartford's" broadside followed, and the splintered wreck drifted silently on into obscurity and darkness.

Engaging the Confederate vessels after the tremendous hammering sustained under the guns of the forts, was but boys' play for the crew of the "Hartford," and short work was made of them. The ram "Manassas" had been particularly active and annoying in her demonstrations, and with the first appearance of dawn, the sharp eyes of Farragut detected the Confederate craft steaming up river in pursuit of the fleet. The "Mississippi" was signaled to take her in hand and run her down. The order was obeyed at once, while all on board the "Hartford" watched the contest with undivided interest. At full speed the "Mississippi" dashed down the river, headed direct for her grim antagonist, but the ram dodged, declining the encounter, running full tilt into the muddy bank, where her crew scrambled on shore, taking refuge under cover of the tall sedge grass of the marsh. A couple of broadsides sealed the fate and career of the ram. Riddled with shot, and flames pouring through the battered casemates, she drifted from the oozy bed upon which she had grounded, drifting with the tide, harmless and deserted, finally to blow up with a heavy report below the forts.

Admiral Porter had made the assertion that the fleet would run past the forts in forty-five minutes, and the time actually consumed from the instant of breaking out the anchors until the forts had been passed was but seventy minutes.

The fighting was over, giving the men an opportunity to look over the scene of battle. Farragut, with Wainwright and a group of officers, occupied the quarter-deck, with marine glasses leveled in the direction of the forts. The scene revealed by the rising sun was one of desolation and destruction. Both banks of the river were lined with burning or sinking vessels that once composed the Confederate fleet. The machinery in some cases was still in motion, the sidewheels revolving helplessly, for the survivors had long since sought safety in flight. Broken spars, shattered planks, streaming cordage, with here and there a body, the uniform torn and discolored with blood, mingled together, floating onward, unheeded and uncared for, while above all the sombre pall of battle hung in deep rifts as if loth to disperse.

The forts, torn and disfigured, but their battle-flags still waving above the shattered ramparts, slowly emerged from the dark mists of the river, with here and there a knot of men discernible along the shell-ploughed parapets. The boasted strength and impregnability of the defences guarding the approaches to the Queen City had been tested by the navy and had failed. Farragut, with his wooden ships and hearts of oak, had scattered the Confederate forces; the sailors had won in the face of tremendous odds, and the United States Navy added another star to its already bright galaxy of victories.

Farragut received the congratulations of his officers with little or no demonstrations of gratified triumph or pleasure. His mind appeared to be preoccupied, his thoughts evidently centred afar off. He did not appear to realize that the work performed had linked his name with imperishable glory on the pages of history. He quickly scanned the reports of killed and wounded, condition of vessels, and then from the flagship fluttered the signal—" PUSH ON TO NEW ORLEANS."

IV.—BEFORE NEW ORLEANS.

THE morning of April 24, 1862, was bright and beautiful. The sun rising in unclouded splendor revealed a scene of tranquillity and peace to the smoke-begrimed sailors on board the flagship. The thunder of guns had ceased; hissing bombs no longer whirled through the air; bursting shell and flying shrapnel had given place to sweet-toned feathered songsters flitting through the dense underbrush, while far to leeward remnants of the sulphurous battle-cloud still lingered low down on the horizon. Over the blackened, shot-battered ramparts of the forts, flying defiantly as ever, appeared the Confederate flags, riddled with holes, smirched and stained from powder and dampness, but still aloft, fluttering from their lofty poles; while the Stars and Stripes, flanked by menacing cannon, bristling steel, and armed, determined men, could be seen both from above and below the Confederate emblems.

But Farragut was impatient of delay; he longed to appear before the Crescent City with his powerful broadsides manned and men at quarters, with the flag he loved once more waving on the majestic expanse of the mighty Mississippi; so David D. Porter, on his flagship, the historic "Harriet Lane",—the brave, impetuous leader of the hammering mortar fleet,— was left to deal with the foe in the rear, while from the "Hartford's" deck a bright lookout ahead was kept for new surprises requiring appropriate responses from broadside guns. Level banks, broad, flowering acres, magnificent sugar plantations, with spacious dwellings and picturesque villas nestling half concealed amid luxuriant, glossy foliage, wide verandas, avenues bordered by stately oaks and magnolias, villages of negro huts, canes shooting up from their drills a foot in height, all nature clothed in a vivid, glorious garb of green, a constant, ever-changing panorama. Such was the appearance of Louisiana, in the vicinity of the river, as the "Hartford" steamed ahead. Over some of the houses waved hastily improvised white flags, but no signs of life or animation were apparent. Doors were closed, blinds drawn, fires in chimneys extinguished; even the flocks of poultry driven to cover and their crowings muffled, as if in fear their notes might be construed as conveying a welcome. Occasionally, from ranks of negroes toiling in the field, a demonstration would be made, as they gazed in astonishment at the massive, grim procession, slowly passing before them, breasting the fierce yellow tide of the great river.

The following incidents regarding the celebrated fight were gathered from the experience of a gentleman, a native of New Orleans, who fought gallantly under the Confederate colors. They are well worthy of a place in connection with unwritten facts and episodes of the river fight. He was one of thirty sharpshooters, volunteers from the St. Mary Cannoneers, to serve in place of a regular marine corps on board the ironclad monster "Louisiana":

"A large number of the forces inside the forts were Northern men, with a sprinkling of foreigners. The armed force that seized the forts early in 1861 was a company of German Yagers, with a liberal representation of Irishmen. In Fort Jackson, there were between 600 and 700 men. Only about one in twenty-five of the shells failed to explode, and the bombs, falling into the ditch close to the walls of the fort, severely shook and weakened its foundation. The discipline was strict, but the placing of young, inexperienced officers, sons of prominent men and wealthy planters, created a great deal of dissatisfaction amongst the men. Suspected men were closely watched, being occasionally subjected to a ducking in the foul, slimy waters of the ditch around the work.

"The chain at first stretched across the river was a powerful and formidable work of defence. It was brought from Pensacola, and was unusually large and heavy. It was kept in place by logs, thirty feet long, only a few feet apart. The chain was kept from sagging by seven enormous anchors, from which small chains ran together to the main chain. The entire structure was swept away by a huge raft formed from floating *débris*, which drifted down the river. It was then replaced by a lighter chain, buoyed by hulks, which remained until cut away by Farragut's marines.

"During the battle, an officer from some back county had charge of the casemate guns which were firing hot shot. He depressed the muzzles, fearing to fire too high, and, being anxious to work his battery well and promptly, ran them out with a jerk, the result being that the balls rolled, hissing and sputtering, into the moat, while the guns thundered with blank cartridges and pressed hay wads. Some officer discovered the oversight, which was at once rectified, and the fire was concentrated upon one particular vessel. This was kept up until the disgusted countryman was told he was throwing away ammunition on one of the *chain hulks*. Between the higher army and navy officers bad blood existed, with no attempt to act in concert and for the best interests of all concerned. The part performed by the 'Louisiana,' an ironclad far stronger than the 'Merrimac,' was a great disappointment."

The "Louisiana" left New Orleans before her steam power, plating, and quarters were in readiness. Even her crew had not been put on board. The day before the passage of the forts, a hundred artisans were at work upon her formidable hull casemates. She was moored on the left bank of the river, about half a mile above Fort St. Philip, from which position she never budged, until her commander, John K. Mitchell, set her adrift, wreathed in flames, to float through the Union fleet, while flags of truce were flying and overtures were in progress for the surrender of the forces. General Duncan, commanding Fort Jackson, had urged Mitchell to drop lower down, to a point bringing him within range of the mortar fleet, but this request is said to have been refused by the naval commander.

From the New Orleans gentleman who served on board the "Louisiana," the following statement was obtained:

"The guns of the ironclad were served by the Crescent Artillery, and at the first discharge were thrown off the trunnions by the recoil, and rendered almost useless. The sharpshooters were stationed in a gallery protected by boiler iron, and three of the detachment met their death there. After the fleet had passed, the detachment was ordered back to Fort Jackson to join the company, who were camped in a

the main fort, an eighteen-pound carronade was trained upon them by those same Regulars and Yagers, and we were warned that if we attempted to thwart these men, who had determined to desert in a body, they would fire upon us from this casemate gun, loaded with canister.

FIGHT AT CHALMETTE.

They then spiked all the other guns, casemate and parapet, and left in a body, taking the levee for New Orleans. The St. Mary Cannoneers was the only company that surrendered with the fort.'' I give this story as I got it.

The "Cayuga," Captain Bailey, kept in advance of the "Hartford" during the passage up the river, encountering none of the batteries which, according to current rumor, lined the river's banks. At eight o'clock in the evening, about fifteen miles below the city, the fleet came to anchor, waiting for daylight to make the final advance. Few slumbered on the flagship that night. Farragut, his hands behind his back, paced the quarter-deck, buried in thought, until long after midnight. The heavens were aglow from the reflections of fierce fires, while dense clouds of smoke rolled upward.

At nine o'clock on the morning of the attack, New Orleans was aroused by hearing from the alarm bell twelve strokes in rapid succession. Like wild fire the news spread that the Federal fleet had passed the forts and was approaching the city. The scenes that ensued must have turned the city into a seething cauldron of violence and excitement. Fifteen thousand bales of cotton were piled on the levee ; a dozen large cotton ships, twenty or more fine river steamboats, dry docks, coal, naval stores, sugar, rice,

bastion of the fort, and from our comrades heard such a story of mutiny and disgrace as made our faces burn with shame. The German Yagers, who had the casemate guns, had acted traitorously, fired blank cartridges, and purposely dropped their projectiles into the morass below. The parapet guns were served by the Louisiana First Regulars, all old United States soldiers, but the St. Mary Cannoneers took no stock in them, convinced that when the emergency came they would be found wanting. There was a well-grounded, deep-rooted conviction pervading the rank and file that the forts had been sold out to Farragut, and that he knew the passage was not a thing impossible when he attempted it. If the guns of Fort Jackson had been served by staunch and true men, not one of the fleet could or would have withstood their scathing fire. The St. Mary boys were never put in charge of a single gun on the main fort. After the fleet passed, and the St. Mary Cannoneers were camped outside molasses,—in fact, stores and materials of all kinds,—were given to the flames.

During the night reports of fire-rafts coming down upon the fleet were numerous, but proved to be groundless. It was a night of alarm and excitement both on river and land; the sailors of the fleet chafing for the first blush of dawn to gild the east as a signal to get under way.

At Chalmette, three miles below the city,—where "Old Hickory" fought his never-to-be-forgotten battle,—batteries on either side were encountered. The "Hartford" and "Brooklyn," followed by the remainder of the fleet, soon silenced their feeble remonstrance, the roar of the Union guns echoing ominously in the ears of the surging mob crowding every available inch of the levee, intent upon viewing the Yankee armada.

Round the bend slowly steam stately frigates and jaunty gunboats, with Stars and Stripes, pennants, and signal flags waving in the early sunlight. Steel bristles from every point, while through open ports protrude the unmistakable, able, eloquent muzzles of Dahlgren and Parrott. In rows and divisions the blue jackets stand mute and motionless, lockstrings in hand, awaiting the word of command, gazing curiously, as opportunity offered, at the city which their prowess had laid at their feet. On the quarterdeck of the "Hartford," standing on the starboard quarter, arrayed in his best uniform as captain, stood Farragut—silent, erect, attentive, with no trace of exultation on his smooth-shaven, round features. The fleet anchored, their broadside presented to the crescent-shaped levee, packed with a screaming, surging mob, who howled themselves hoarse showering abuse on the heads of the victorious sailors.

The scene was one of widespread ruin and desolation. Fires along the shore as far as the eye could reach; the river aglow with blazing steamers and vessels piled with cotton; smoking _débris_, representing millions of dollars, lined the water front, while molasses and sugar had been emptied from cellar and storehouse to be gathered up by whites and blacks.

Farragut's first order was for the seizure of a large ram in process of construction; but ere a boat could be lowered from the "Hartford" the structure, enveloped in flames, floated down the river. Another similar craft was sunk opposite the Custom House, and a number of rams in various stages of construction were given to the flames at Algiers. The amount of property wantonly destroyed must have been represented high up in the millions, for two hundred and fifty thousand (250,000) bales of cotton alone were reduced to ashes.

At noon the "Hartford's" gig was called away, and Captain Bailey, arrayed in his double-breasted uniform coat buttoned to the throat, shook hands with Farragut, and motioned to Lieutenant Perkins, who preceded him over the side into the boat, which was at once headed for the levee. The guns of the "Hartford" were loaded with grape and canister; the men, without beat of drum, silently repaired to quarters, while vigilant lookouts, under direction of the officers, occupied the tops, watching narrowly every movement of the two intrepid officers who sprang on shore, alone and unarmed, facing the desperate mob. Farragut and Bailey were old friends, and the latter had distinguished himself, after passing the forts, by capturing three of the enemy's gunboats and a battery at Chalmette. No braver man than Bailey ever served under the Stars and Stripes, and the fact of his facing a mob with a single comrade by his side, in the streets of a hostile city, indifferent to threats and menaces, as he calmly and resolutely walked on to find New Orleans's mayor, was a wonderful proof of the man's nerve and intrepidity. Farragut loved and honored such men, and he sent this steel-nerved friend to Washington as bearer of despatches containing his account of the capture of New Orleans.

In the so-called "History of the Navy in the Civil War," a chapter is devoted to the disparagement of Farragut in omitting to give Bailey due justice and prominence for his services in running the forts. A mistake was undoubtedly made, an oversight committed in the hurry and rush of exciting events. Bailey failed to receive the thanks of Congress, but the facts in that chapter of history (?) were recounted only so far as served the writer's purpose. Bailey, in common with a number of other officers, was nominated for and received the promotion he merited.

The second party to land from the "Hartford" was a guard of marines under Captain Bell. Two howitzers with ammunition were added to the force. The same mob was there to meet them, but the demeanor of the marines, coupled with their fixed bayonets and clattering field howitzers, had such an air of professional business about it all that the crowd fell back, hushed into silence, as the marines wheeled and proceeded toward the State House. Arriving there the force halted and the howitzers were un-limbered ; Captain Bell ascended to the roof of the building and replaced the Confederate flag with the Stars and Stripes. At the Custom House and Mint the same programme was enacted, the bunting, as it unfolded, being saluted by a succession of cheers from the fleet. The Confederate flags were given to Farragut, who for some time afterward had them in his private cabin.

The "Pensacola," Captain Morris, was an-chored off the Mint, with howitzers in the top trained upon the flag-staff of the building, from which floated the National emblem with no guard to protect it. But the stout-hearted, bluff old Morris had issued orders for those in the top to fire the moment anyone should attempt to haul down the flag.

At noon the crews of all the vessels were as-sembled on deck for prayers,—" to render thanks," as Farragut's order ran, " to Almighty God for His great goodness and mercy in per-mitting us to pass through the events of the last two days with so little loss of life and blood." The services were solemn and impres-sive, a hush and stillness pervading the fleet, unbroken save by the deep tones of the chap-lain's voice.

Suddenly the roar of a gun, followed by whistling, singing missiles, startled everyone in the fleet, and all eyes were directed upon the "Pensacola," from whose maintop curled a dis-solving wreath of blue, fleecy smoke, which lingered around the howitzer's muzzle. Quick as lightning the men's eyes sought the roof of the Mint. The flag-staff was there, but the Stars and Stripes had disappeared.

There was an ominous mutter among the men of the "Pensacola," with black looks and com-pressed lips, but without orders they repaired to their guns, the captains of each eagerly un-coiling the lockstrings, momentarily expecting orders to fire upon the rebellious city. Before the appointed hour for services, a threatened shower had caused the quarter gunners to re-move the primers. It was all that saved New Orleans from a terrible scene of reckoning from the hands of incensed, angry seamen, who then and there would have resented the action of Mumford and his followers. Morris turned livid with rage, muttering passionately as he glared on shore. Had his gums admitted of it, he would have ground his teeth as he chafed neath the audacious act, but, unfortunately, in the haste of dressing for morning services, the gal-

lant old man had left his set in the dressing room of his cabin.

On the 1st of May, General Butler, with troops on the transport "Mississippi," arrived at the city, making fast to the levee, and Farragut gladly turned the city over to that able military governor. A company of the Thirty-first Mas-sachusetts landed first, pressing back the crowd at the point of the bayonet, the column formed under the protection of Farragut's guns, the band of the Fourth Wisconsin played " Yankee Doodle," assisted by a drum corps belonging to the Massachusetts Thirty-first, and, surrounded by his staff, all marching on foot, General But-ler proceeded straight toward the Custom House.

Mumford, the man who had torn down the flag planted by the "Pensacola's" men on the Mint, still walked the streets of New Orleans, proud, defiant, and boasting to his admirers the contempt in which he held both Yankees and their flag. He was a tall, powerful, black-bearded man, about forty-two years of age, with more or less popularity amongst certain classes. He was standing in front of a noted saloon, re-counting, as usual, the flag episode, when a file of soldiers, with a lieutenant at their head, arrested him. For once he had boasted too often, and General Butler determined to make an example of him. He was tried by a military commission, and condemned to be hung on June 7th. The scaffold was erected in front of the Mint, the scene of his exploit, and the gambler met his fate without flinching, in presence of a vast concourse of people.

A French admiral who had volunteered the statement that New Orleans could not, from a scientific standpoint, be taken, was so incensed with Farragut and his great triumph, that he remained his enemy forever after. But Farra-gut's old-fashioned wooden walls, plenty of guns, and rapidly delivered broadsides, followed by Porter's huge bombs, had a most damaging effect upon theory, smashing the staid and vapid lines of scientific warfare all to pieces.

The overbearing, insulting demeanor of offi-cers attached to the British corvette "Rinaldo" (the vessel that bore to the shores of England Messrs. Mason and Slidell after they were sur-rendered by the Government), might have re-sulted in serious international trouble and com-plications. As it was, a great deal of excitement and feeling existed.

The officers and men of the corvette sympa-thized with the Southerners, with whom they were great favorites, and a constant interchange

THE FEDERAL FLEET BEFORE NEW ORLEANS.

of courtesies was maintained. Evenings the Englishmen would join in loud choruses of Confederate songs, and, as they were but a short distance from the "Hartford," Farragut himself noticed the evident intention to arouse the passions of the officers and men in his fleet, and was personally somewhat annoyed over the circumstance. It was Farragut's custom to go on shore in the cool of the evening to visit certain army officers and Dr. Mercer, an old acquaintance. He had many relatives in the city, but they held aloof, not daring to extend a welcome to the officer, whose devotion to his flag was greater than love of his native State. While passing on shore one evening he heard loud cheers for Jefferson Davis from the Englishman's deck, followed by the "Bonnie Blue Flag." Turning to Captain Palmer, who was seated beside him, he said: "We must put a stop to this; and, if it isn't stopped, we shall have to drop down and blow him out of the water." The commanding officer of the "Rinaldo" was informed that the conduct of his men was annoying to Farragut, and orders were at once issued forbidding a repetition of their sympathies.

General Butler had some experience with the same vessel. A crowd of over two thousand people were on the levee one evening listening to the sturdy choruses issuing from the throats of English sailors engaged in singing "Down with the Stars and Stripes," "Bonnie Blue Flag," "Up with the Flag of the Single Star," followed by cheers for Southern rights. Fearing a riot, the crowd was dispersed by an armed force. Afterward an officer of the ship, intoxicated, reeled down the levee singing the "Bonnie Blue Bag." An officer forbade him to continue, but the British officer replied he would "sing what he pleased"; once in his boat he turned, pouring out a torrent of abuse, saying, amongst other absurdities, that "one Englishman can whip ten Yankee curs."

Word was sent to General Butler on the 3d of July that the commander of the "Rinaldo" had promised his Confederate friends that on the dawn of the 4th he would throw to the breeze the flag of the Rebellion. It is authoritatively stated that General Butler registered a solemn vow that, let the consequences be what they might, if the flag was officially displayed from the Englishman's peak, he would open fire from every gun belonging to Nim's battery. The hoisting of the flag, the general considered, would be more than an insult to the Federal government; it would constitute the ship a hostile vessel, and, as such, she was to be fired upon the very instant a Union gun could be brought to bear upon her. What Farragut, Morris, and a dozen other true-hearted leaders in the Federal fleet would have done, had the obnoxious bunting been displayed, is easy to conjecture. Butler would never have had an opportunity to use his guns; but, fortunately perhaps for all parties, Fourth of July came and went, with no cause for affront from the representative of John Bull.

VICE-ADMIRAL KAZNAKOFF AT FARRAGUT'S GRAVE.

(WOODLAWN CEMETERY, SUNDAY, MAY 21, 1893.)

"Sleep in glory in your resting-place, Admiral Farragut. You have served your country well. You have shown us how to fight and what to do. You have added many glorious pages to the annals of your country."—A RUSSIAN TRIBUTE TO FARRAGUT.

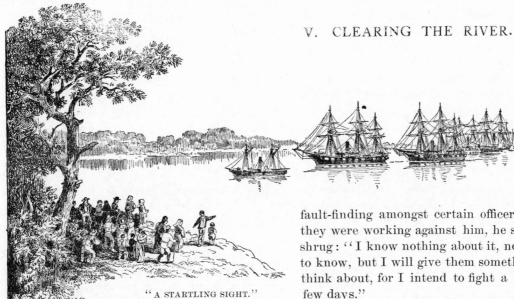

"A STARTLING SIGHT."

ALTHOUGH Farragut had but little to say to the crew, his intercourse being principally confined to his flag captain and one or two principal officers of his fleet, all hands had learned to love the quiet, undemonstrative leader, whose fighting qualities had endeared him to the sympathetic, light-hearted, careless Jack-tar.

Farragut's disposition and temperament was a restless one, chafing under delay, with a leaning toward magnifying the importance of trifling annoyances and reverses.

Co-operating with General Butler, Farragut proceeded up the river, finding the works at Carrollton destroyed and guns spiked. He despatched his vessels on numerous missions, and was soon in possession of Baton Rouge and Natchez, having resolved with the "Hartford" to force his way up the river until he met Foote.

The prospect of keeping sea-going vessels, large, noble frigates, in rivers hundreds of miles from the sea-coast, was anything but pleasant to officers and men, while Farragut, with the privilege of an old and favored salt, growled both loud and deep over the situation.

"I will be kept here," he said, bitterly, "until the vessels break down and the little reputation we have won has evaporated. The government appears to think we can do anything. They expect me to navigate the Mississippi 900 miles in the face of batteries, ironclads, rams, etc."

On another occasion, hearing of jealousies and fault-finding amongst certain officers, and that they were working against him, he said, with a shrug: "I know nothing about it, nor do I care to know, but I will give them something else to think about, for I intend to fight a battle in a few days."

Regarding the fight with the river forts, he said: "Some will find fault with me for not doing them justice in my report of the passage of the forts, but you cannot satisfy all as to the measure of praise, and I have never yet certified to what *I don't know;* as to praising people individually who fought in the dark for gallant conduct, and whom I did not see, that is out of the question. I regret that Bailey did not get the thanks of Congress as recommended by the President. But there is one thing that I cannot be deprived of, and that is the historical fact that we took New Orleans."

Perhaps it is fortunate for the great admiral that he did not live to read some of the so-called Naval Histories of the War, or he might have doubted the fact of his participating at all in the naval affairs of that conflict, and that instead of leading his fleet that he played a minor and subordinate *role.*

After New Orleans had been occupied by the army, Farragut sent seven vessels, under the command of Captain Craven, of the "Brooklyn," up the river. Baton Rouge and Natchez surrendered when summoned; but at Vicksburg, on the 22d of May, Commander S. P. Lee was met with a refusal. On the 18th of June the "Brooklyn" and "Richmond" anchored below Vicksburg, and shortly after Farragut came in person with the "Hartford," accompanied by Commander Porter with the steamers and seventeen schooners of the mortar flotilla. But the flagship had not made the passage without peril to herself and at the risk of becoming a wreck hundreds of miles inland. An accident might prove disastrous, for a vigilant enemy was eternally on the watch to turn every event to his advantage. The appearance of tall, sparred ships, with their long, dark hulls, moving slowly around the bends of the river, must have been a startling sight to many of the inhabitants, who had never seen anything larger afloat than the ordinary river steamer.

It was about noon that the "Hartford" ran hard and fast aground on a mud bank in the middle of the river, and with a falling tide. It was intimated that the pilot had deliberately run the flagship ashore, actuated by sympathies for the Confederacy, but Farragut never entertained the opinion for a moment, although he was both nervous and uneasy over the mishap. The entire fleet worked hard all the afternoon to release the "Hartford," but in vain, and hawser after hawser snapped like pack-thread. The signal quartermaster reported to Farragut that there was a twelve-inch hawser in the hold that had never been used, and it was at once roused upon deck. Two army transports were lashed together, the hawser passed round them, and with a gunboat on either side, all working their machinery together, the "Hartford" finally was hauled clear and again started up stream. It was an all-night job, and at 8.30 A. M., on the morning of the 22d of June, 1862, order was resumed in the naval column. Farragut had been up all night, never leaving the deck even to get a cup of tea. In alluding to the mishap, he said: " It is a sad thing to think of leaving your ship on a mud bank, 500 miles from the natural element of a sailor.''

In connection with the towing of the mortar schooners up the Mississippi, the following anecdote, in the light of the somewhat remarkable controversy that has been made public between Admiral Porter and General Butler, will, perhaps, interest the general reader:

" At the request of a naval officer in high command, Farragut applied to Butler for steamboats to tow the mortar vessels to Vicksburg. Butler replied that he regretted he had none to spare. The officer replied that if Butler would prevent his brother from sending quinine and other contraband stores into the Confederacy, there would be boats enough. This came to the general's ears. He answered. After giving a list of his boats and stating their different employments, he proceeded as follows: ' Now there are two kinds of lying: the first is when a man deliberately states what he knows to be false; the second is when he states what is really false, but what at the time he believes to be true. For instance, when Captain —— reports that the ram " Louisiana" came down upon his gunboats and a desperate fight ensued, he stated what is in point of fact false, for the " Louisiana" was blown up and abandoned, and was drifting with the current, as is proved by the report of the Confederate commander, Duncan; but Captain —— believed it to be true, and acted accordingly, for he retreated to the mouth of the river, leaving the transports to their fate.' "

It was comparatively late on the 25th of June when the " Hartford" anchored below Vicksburg. Farragut viewed the bluffs from his quarter-deck, and wrote: " The work is rough. Their batteries are beyond our reach on the heights. It must be done in the daytime, as the river is difficult to navigate by night. I trust that God will smile upon our efforts. I think more should have been left to my discretion, but I hope for the best."

Vicksburg is 400 miles above New Orleans. The river turns to the northeast five miles before reaching the Vicksburg bluffs, which reach at their greatest elevation 260 feet, sloping gradually to the water. The height of the banks, with the narrowness and peculiar winding of the stream, placed the batteries on the hill-sides above the reach of Farragut's guns, and nature had rendered the position the strongest on the river. At the time of Farragut's first attack, twenty-six guns were in position, some of them commanding a raking fire upon the ships before and after they had passed their front. Half a mile below the town was a water battery about fifty feet above the river, commanded by Captain Todd, a brother-in-law of President Lincoln. It mounted twelve guns, and the sailors of the fleet nicknamed it " The Twelve Apostles." The heaviest gun they called "St. Paul, the great X-pounder," i. e., X-inch rifle.

The distance from end to end of the siege batteries was about three miles, and as the current was running at the rate of three knots, while the speed of the fleet was not over eight, three-quarters of an hour at least was needed for each ship to pass by the front of the works.

The mortars were placed in position and began firing on the 26th of June; but the range was defective, and they moved up closer, opening in earnest on the 28th at four o'clock A. M.

The whole fleet now got under way, and steamed up in the double line of sailing; the

"HARD AND FAST AGROUND ON A MUD BANK."

three largest vessels—"Richmond," "Hart-ford," and "Brooklyn"—on the right forming the starboard column, nearest to the Confederate batteries. As the "Hartford" passed, the steamers of the mortar flotilla moved up on her starboard quarter, engaging underway the water battery, at a distance of 1200 yards, and main-taining this position till the fleet had passed.

The flagship moved slowly and even stopped for a time to wait for the vessels in the rear; seeing which, Captain Palmer, of the "Iro-quois," who had reached the turn, also stopped his ship, and let her drift down close to the "Hartford" to draw a part of the enemy's fire, and to reinforce that of the flag-officer.

Farragut was in his favorite post of observa-tion, the mizzen rigging, when all at once Richard Murphy, the captain of the gun on the poop-deck, wishing to fire at a battery that would require him to train his gun in the direc-tion of Farragut, requested him to move aside, which he did to avoid the concussion. There was not a moment to lose, for scarcely had Farragut shifted his position when the whole mizzen rigging was cut away just above his head. The same shot cut the halyards that hoisted his flag, causing it to drop to half mast without being perceived by the officers or crew. It was

noticed from the decks of the other vessels, however, and led to a rumor that Farragut had been killed.

The "Hartford" fired slowly and deliberately and with fine effect, far surpassing Farragut's expectations in reaching the summit batteries. The broadsides from the ships would drive the Confederate gunners from their position only to return again and reopen as each ship passed. Captain Bell, the friend of Farragut and his fleet captain, was on the quarter-deck beside his chief, and not being able to do much in the management of the fleet, owing to the darkness and smoke, gave his attention to looking after the location of the batteries. Gabaudau, Farra-gut's genial secretary, who acted as aid, was also on the quarter-deck, coolly jotting down all items of importance as they transpired. The "Hartford" received but little injury from the enemy's fire, although she steamed at the lowest rate of speed, and anchored above Vicksburg at six o'clock in the morning.

In writing to the Department, Farragut stated: "The forts can be passed, and we have done it, and can do it again as often as may be required of us. It will not, however, be an easy matter for us to do more than silence the batteries for a time, as long as the enemy has a large force behind the hills to prevent our landing and holding the place.''

And yet but a short time previous, at a conference held by Farragut's captains on the flagship, only one supported him in the proposition to run the batteries that confronted them. In speaking of it to General Thomas Williams, Farragut said: "General, my officers oppose my running by Vicksburg as impracticable. Only one supports me. So I must give it up for the present. In ten days they will be of my opinion, and then the difficulties will be much greater than they are now." He was right. In a few days the officers were nearly all of his opinion, and he did it.

The "Hartford's" stay was short. Receiving the assurance from Flag-Officer Davis that the "Essex" and "Sumter" would take charge of that portion of the river and look after the ram "Arkansas," Farragut returned to New Orleans, arriving on July 28th.

On the 11th of August he received from the Department his commission as rear-admiral, dated July 16th, accompanied with a vote of thanks from Congress, on parchment, to himself and officers for their gallantry in passing the river forts.

On the same day he hoisted at the main his flag, which had been hastily manufactured on board by the old signal quartermaster. It was the first time it had been displayed, and was hailed by the fleet with loud and continuous cheering, to which the "Hartford" responded with an appropriate number of guns. All hands were mustered, and Farragut read to them the act of Congress complimentary of the men's achievements.

Steaming down the river the "Hartford" stopped, off the forts, affording all hands an opportunity to view the strongholds, over which now floated the national colors. Then the old craft resumed her course for the blue, open waters of the Gulf, which were hailed with delight by the seamen after their experience in inland waters, broiling sun, and pestilential vapors.

While at Pensacola, Admiral Farragut was joined by his son Loyall, who remained on board and witnessed the engagement at Port Hudson.

During the rest of the summer and the autumn months, Admiral Farragut's attention was mainly devoted to the seaboard operations of his command. The sickly season, the low state of the river, and the shattered condition generally of the vessels under his command, with the impossibility of obtaining decisive results without the co-operation of the army, compelled Farragut to rest.

FARRAGUT'S FLEET APPROACHING VICKSBURG.

Reports now began to arrive from the commanding officer in the river that the Confederates, with renewed energy, were building batteries above Baton Rouge, and strongly fortifying Port Hudson, about 160 miles above New Orleans. Influenced by the importance of the news which he received daily, Farragut lost no time in returning to the Crescent City, where he arrived November 9th. Demands were at once made upon the admiral for more ships, and out of patience with demands he could not meet, he exclaimed: "Do they think I can make ships here? Everybody is calling for them, which reminds me of the musician's remark: 'It is very easy to say blow! blow! but where the devil is the wind to come from?'"

Farragut was hampered in many ways, and prevented from making an immediate start up the river. There was lack of supplies and munitions of war, but the admiral bore patiently with all the difficulties, feeling assured that sooner or later his day would come.

December came, and with it a change of commanders, Banks having been sent to supersede Butler, who took his departure on the 24th. He spent his last hour with Admiral Farragut on board the "Hartford," for which vessel and her commander General Butler undoubtedly had an affection that was deep and sincere. He had given the admiral a salute when his flag was hoisted, and Farragut, in acknowledging the honor paid him, had promised to return the compliment, with interest, on the first opportunity. The old veteran kept his word, and the heaviest guns of the "Hartford" thundered a ringing farewell to the distinguished soldier as he left the broad deck of the battle-scarred craft.

After much delay, General Banks agreed to support Farragut in a demonstration against Port Hudson, where, as at Vicksburg, the Mississippi makes a sharp turn. The left or eastern bank consists of bluffs fifty feet high, while the fortifications were arranged so that when the lower batteries were silenced other concealed batteries could open with a cross-fire upon vessels attempting to pass. At the time of the passage of the fleet there were mounted in battery nineteen heavy guns, eight of which were rifles, varying from eighty- to fifty-pounders.

In attempting to run the batteries, Farragut was actuated by a firm conviction that by blockading the Red River, by which the Confederacy received vast amounts of supplies, he would be dealing a staggering blow at the waning fortunes of rebellion.

VI.—PASSING THE BATTERIES AT PORT HUDSON.

IT was arranged between Admiral Farragut and General Banks that the former should run by the batteries of Port Hudson, while the latter, with about 12,000 men, attacked from the land side to create a diversion in favor of the fleet.

Farragut, by strenuous exertions, had hastily gathered a few vessels together, consisting of four ships and three gunboats, the ironclad gunboat "Essex" and steamer "Sachem," with the mortar schooners in position a mile ahead, just under Prophet's Island.

At five o'clock on the afternoon of March 14th, Farragut received a despatch from General Banks announcing that his forces were at the crossroads, ready to move upon the land-side defences. Farragut replied that he hoped to pass the batteries by midnight.

The "Mississippi," being a side-wheeler, could not take a gunboat, but one was assigned to each of the other ships, to be lashed on the port side; the fastest gunboat being given to the slowest ship. The following was the order:

HARTFORD . . . . ALBATROSS (gunboat).
RICHMOND . . . . GENESEE (gunboat).
MONONGAHELA . . KINEO (gunboat).
MISSISSIPPI.

By this arrangement, if one of the larger ships became disabled, its gunboat could tow it along and be protected by its bulwarks. All the vessels were trimmed by the head, as was Farragut's custom, so that if they grounded it would be forward first, and they would not be swung around by the current. Every protection to life that the ingenuity of the officers could devise was adopted. The mortar-fleet and its gunboats were to keep up a rapid fire from the time the first gun was heard till the vessels had passed out of range.

It was dusk when the signal (a red lantern) to get under way was displayed cautiously over the stern of the "Hartford." The admiral, nervous and impatient, walked the quarter-deck with one button of his double-breasted frock-coat fastened, his uniform cap pressed well down upon his forehead, while at intervals he played with the strap holding the night-glass that was slung over his right shoulder. Occasionally, he would pause in his walk, exchange a word with Captains Jenkins and Palmer, who, standing in close proximity to their chief, were all attention. Finally, the "Hartford" steamed ahead slowly, and the fleet rapidly dropped into their several positions.

The scene at that moment on the deck of the "Hartford" was one well worthy of the brush and pencil of America's finest artist. Farragut stood on the starboard side of the quarter-deck, gazing intently up the river in the direction of the shore batteries. Captains Jenkins and Palmer were by the fife-rail of the mizzen-mast, conversing in low tones, while a quartermaster was employed in clearing the well-worn signal halyards that dangled from the lofty truck. Along the gun-deck, silence reigned fore and aft ; the men standing by the guns, with breasts and arms bare, their feet grating slightly on the well-sanded deck as they changed their position. Occasionally, a glance was directed aft, where through the gathering shades of night the gleam of gold lace and buttons indicated the presence of their leaders. Not a whisper was heard. The men evidently had no disposition to indulge in banter ; the bluffs, rugged and sterile, prolific only in rifled ordnance and skilled gunners, frowned down upon them, casting shadows of ominous depth and gloom athwart the "Hartford's" hull. An unnatural stillness prevailed both afloat and on shore, that exerted possibly a slighter depressing influence upon the spirits of the sailors, who detested waiting, with opportunities to meditate, when but a cable's length from their adversaries.

On the forecastle was a Sawyer rifle with young Watson in charge, while along the waist, in charge of divisions, stood Hazeltine, Tyson, Read, and Wimple, all officers of experience and tried courage. In low whispers they occasionally admonished the men, or gave some instructions to the captains of the guns, who listened attentively and saluted gravely in response. Captain Broom and Lieutenant Higby, with the steady files of the marines, who were to man the quarter-deck guns, were at their stations, while Ensign Jones, in charge of the wicked Parrott rifle on the poop, stood by on the alert to make the most of his opportunity. Kimberly, the first lieutenant (now rear-admiral), was all life and activity, personally inspecting the details of every department, and satisfying himself that nothing had been neglected or overlooked. Engineer Speights had the post by the bell communicating with the engine-room, for which important position he had been specially selected.

The "Hartford" was slowly forging along, and Farragut, peering into the darkness ahead, scanned anxiously the frowning bluffs along which no sign of life was apparent. His son stood beside him, and as the gallant old ship gradually drew abreast of the lower batteries, the father involuntarily threw his arm around his son's neck, as a rocket darted suddenly on high from the right bank, followed almost instantly by another and another.

A crash from a battery ahead was the response, followed by the swish of solid shot as they sped through the air. It was the opening salute on the part of the enemy, who were not to be caught unawares.

Before the commencement of the engagement, Farragut had been requested by the fleet surgeon, J. M. Foltz, to permit his son to assist him below with the wounded, where he could render important service and where he would be in the best protected part of the ship. He was not in the service, and had nothing to gain, but everything to lose, by exposure on the quarter-deck. But Farragut would not listen to it, and the boy was anxious to be stationed on deck and see the fight, where he acted as aid to his father, assisting in conveying his orders to various portions of the ship.

The dull, heavy clank of the machinery was painfully audible as the flagship passed within range, and the only gun that could respond to the enemy's fire was Watson's Sawyer rifle from the forecastle. Along the shore, at the foot of the bluffs, powerful reflecting lamps, like those used on locomotives, had been placed to show the ships to the enemy as they passed ; and for the same purpose large fires, fed by pitch-pine knots, cast a lurid glare across the turbid waters of the river. The fact that the best water was on the starboard side of the river, led the ships to hug the east shore of the river, passing so close under the Confederate guns that the speech of the gunners and troops could be distinguished. At one time the "Hartford" was in such close proximity to the batteries that a Confederate officer in charge of a number of heavy guns, said he could have killed the officers on the poop-deck with a ship's pistol, and that he trained a gun loaded with grape on the group that caught his eye, but it missed fire, and the "Hartford" passed on, unscathed.

Rapidly the numerous guns on the bluff opened their fire upon the advancing ships, which lost no time in returning the same, as their guns could be brought to bear.

The fire from the fleet and from the batteries on shore soon raised a smoke which rendered it all but impossible to discern objects with any degree of accuracy. Settling down upon the water, in a still, damp atmosphere, it soon hid everything from the eyes of the pilots. As the action became general, and the combined guns of the fleet and shore defences mingled in one great uproar, the crash and confusion fully equaled that experienced in passing the forts below New Orleans. The deep, hollow roar of the mortars anchored below was conspicuous

But the bursting shell and hurtling shot proved too much for the untried nerves of the youngster. He involuntarily ducked his head as shot whistled by, as many a brave and more experienced man had done before him. The keen eyes of the admiral detected the movement, and patting his son affectionately on the shoulder, he said: "Don't duck, my son; there is no use in trying to dodge God Almighty."

There was a brief space of peril for the flagship, but Farragut's good star protected her, and she pulled through in safety. The "Hartford," leading, had the advantage of pushing often ahead of her own smoke; but those who

"THE HARTFORD SEEMED LITERALLY ON FIRE."

above the din of battle, and their fire never flagged or slackened for one moment, eliciting from the admiral more than one warm word of commendation. The thirteen-inch shells, with their burning, hissing fuses, flashed across the dark expanse of heaven like so many meteors. The "Hartford" seemed literally on fire, so rapid and incessant were her broadsides, causing the battle-scarred craft to quiver and tremble as the huge Dahlgrens rang out their death-dealing peal.

Young Loyall stood beside his gallant father during the passage of the batteries, both gazing upon the terrible struggle with intense interest.

followed ran into it, adding to the dangers and difficulties that increased from van to rear. At the bend of the river the current caught the "Hartford" on her port-bow, sweeping her round, with her head toward the batteries and nearly on shore, her stern touching the ground slightly; but by her own efforts and the assistance of the "Albatross" she was backed clear. Then the "Albatross" backing, and the "Hartford" going ahead full speed, she was again pointed head up the river, passing by the last battery without serious injury. Deceived possibly by the ringing reports and flashes of the howitzers in her tops, which were nearly on their level, the Confederates did not depress their guns sufficiently to hit her as often as they did the ships that followed her. One killed and two wounded was the loss sustained, and one marine fell overboard, his cries for help being heard on board the other ships as they passed by, unable to save him.

For an hour and ten minutes the "Hartford" had been under fire, then forging ahead under full steam, with her guns silent to allow the smoke to disperse, with the turmoil and shock of battle echoing astern, all on board realized as the cable rasped and rattled through the hawse-pipe that once more the lucky old "Hartford" had successfully defied the heaviest batteries in possession of the Confederates.

The dense cloud of battle, the gloom of night, and the glaring indistinctness of the fray had given place to a partially clear atmosphere, with only the occasional report of a heavy gun or bursting shell to disturb the usual silence that reigned upon the river. Assured of the safety of his flagship, that she had suffered no vital damage, the admiral glanced about him to note the position and condition of the remainder of his fleet. But not a vestige of one of the boats met the anxious gaze of the chieftain. The sky astern was still aglow from the fiercely burning fires, and reflected there in bold relief were masts and spars that gradually faded from view, while the sullen and irregular boom of heavy guns from the bluffs warned Farragut that his foes were far from being subdued.

Long and anxiously he watched the point around which he evidently expected the remainder of his force to fight their way; but nothing appeared, and in a low tone, as if communing with himself, he muttered : "My God ! what has stopped them ?" No one there could answer the question. All was conjecture, with many speculations as to the cause of the failure of the remainder of the fleet to follow the flagship.

Suddenly a vivid column of light shot on high, and it was reported from the masthead that a large ship could be seen on fire, and that it appeared to be the "Mississippi." It was sad news to Farragut, whose first impulse was to at once drop down the river and renew the contest, and at the same time render such aid to his companions in distress as he could under the circumstances. But a little reflection was sufficient to admonish him that the risk was greater than he had any right to assume. In addition, the firing had almost entirely ceased, which was proof that the remainder of the fleet had, for some reason, retired from the contest.

As he watched the bright flames of the burning ship, Farragut realized that he alone, with his little consort, had accomplished the task of running the gauntlet of Port Hudson's fiery tempest ; that he was effectually cut off from the other vessels of his command, one of which he knew had succumbed to the deadly skill of Confederate gunnery.

In the midst of the excitement and general despondency that existed in the "Hartford," a report ran along the spar-deck that a large steamer was bearing down upon the flagship. The admiral hastily snatched his sword which was lying on the signal-locker (he hardly ever wore it in action), and in person ordered the port-battery to be manned, and boarders to be called away. He evidently intended to take a part himself in teaching the foe a lesson, but the alarm proved a false one. The ruins of an old building on the bank of the river and reflection from burning logs had misled the lookouts, whose nerves had not regained their normal condition.

It was one o'clock in the morning when the "Hartford" had anchored, and the crew of the flagship were too intent upon other matters to pay much attention to the staunch little gunboat that had so bravely shared the perils of the fight with them. The tide caused her to ride rather uneasily alongside, and quietly casting off the lines, the "Albatross" moved up stream to secure a suitable anchorage. But none was found ; the men were tired and exhausted from their efforts, which induced the commander to lose no further time in fruitless search. Dropping down stream, she was soon abreast of the "Hartford," but on the starboard side. Some of the watch on the flagship detected a moving object approaching through the darkness, which loomed up huge and formidable in the obscurity. In an instant the alarm was given, and the cry of "Ram ! ram !" resounded along the deck. It required but a few moments for all hands to muster at the guns, and the entire starboard battery was trained in the gunboat, the captains of the guns waiting for the word to pull the lockstrings. Farragut hailed in person. Lieutenant-Commander Hart replied promptly ; his voice was recognized, and the gunboat was saved from being blown into atoms.

At four o'clock in the morning the "Mississippi" blew up with a dull roar resembling distant thunder, and then Farragut, worn out from excitement and anxiety, consented to leave the quarter-deck for the purpose of obtaining the rest of which he stood so much in need. The ship had been cleansed, decks cleared up, and watch set, and soon the great warship was enveloped in the mists of the river, with silence resting over the scene where but a few short hours before pandemonium had reigned.

The failure of the fleet to run the batteries had not been entirely abortive, although Farra-gut felt deeply disappointed over the result. Two vessels bearing the national colors, backed by rifled and Dahlgren guns, had got above the Confederate stronghold, and Red River was blockaded. The enemy never regained control of the position again ; its death-knell found an echo from the muzzles of the blazing battery of the "Hartford" and her consort as they passed beyond range of the batteries forming Port Hudson's defences.

THE HARTFORD IN NEW YORK HARBOR.

CUT off from all communication with his fleet, left in the heart of the enemy's country with his flagship and one light gunboat, deprived of supplies and even consolation, many men would have lost their heads and brought disaster upon the cause they were serving. The ship's glasses revealed the gleam of arms and accoutrements on either side of the river, while the light air wafted to the ears of the seamen bugle notes from the enemy's troops. Farragut was hemmed in on all sides by a vigilant, energetic foe, who, fertile in expedients and prolific in fortitude and courage, would assuredly make the most of the opportunity afforded them. All this, Farragut from his knowledge of the people and their characteristics, knew and realized; but he never flinched or evaded the great responsibility so unexpectedly thrust upon him.

The morning after the action, the flagship dropped down nearly within range of the upper batteries, to communicate, if possible, by signal with the fleet below, but they could not be seen from her mast-heads, and firing three guns, as a farewell signal, the "Hartford" steamed up the river, anchoring the following morning off the mouth of Red River.

The failure of the fleet to follow Farragut was not through lack of courage on the part of the commanding officers, neither did the guns of the enemy altogether defeat the admiral's plans; but it was rather owing to a combination of circumstances that operated to bring defeat where victory had been wont to perch. Farragut, in writing of the battle, said: "But I have too high an estimation of *each* and *every one* of the officers commanding those vessels to imagine for a single instant that everything in their power was not done to insure success."

The darkness of the night, the stillness of the air, which permitted the smoke to settle undisturbed, the intricacy of the navigation, the rapidity of the current, then running at the rate of five knots, the poor speed of the ships, not over eight knots, all tended to work disaster and disappointment to the ships that followed the "Hartford."

The "Richmond," with the "Genesee" alongside, had reached the last battery, and was about to make the turn, when a shot entered the engine-room, upsetting the starboard safety-valve. The steam was reduced to nine pounds, the gunboat was unable to stem the current with the heavy ship, and Commander Alden was compelled to drop down out of range.

The "Monongahela" and "Kineo" were third in line, and the density of the smoke caused the pilots to miss their way, and the larger ship took the bottom. The "Kineo" received a chance shot that lodged between the stern-post and rudder-post, wedging the rudder and making it useless. Both vessels, after suffering considerable loss and damage, were forced to retreat, with a loss of six killed and twenty-one wounded.

The "Mississippi" had passed the lower batteries and had reached the bend, when she struck, keeling at once three streaks to port. Every effort was made to clear the vessel, but she remained hard and fast, with three batteries that had got the range hulling her at every shot. Captain Smith finally abandoned her, working the starboard battery to the last moment. The ship was then set on fire, the captain and first lieutenant passing down to the "Richmond" in safety. She finally drifted down the river and blew up at 5.30 in the morning, thus meeting the same fate that had befallen her sister ship, the "Missouri," twenty years before, in the harbor of Gibraltar.

With nothing to rely upon but his own resources, Farragut felt that upon unceasing vigilance depended his own safety and that of his flagship. At the mouth of Red River black smoke would occasionally float up above the trees, revealing the presence of a steamer, but it would quickly disappear when the tall spars of the "Hartford" were discovered.

At Grand Gulf a battery opened upon the "Hartford" that annoyed him severely, and entailed a loss of two killed and six wounded. The "Hartford" had passed almost beyond range, when Captain Jenkins remarked to Farragut, "Admiral, this ship goes entirely too slow." Just then a shell exploded in the water under the counter near where they stood, and the admiral answered, dryly: "I should think she did just at this moment."

On the 19th, the "Hartford" came to anchor twelve miles below Vicksburg, and Farragut communicated with Grant's army, learning how affairs stood both afloat and ashore. He was soon in communication with Porter, who had been promoted to an acting rear admiral, and was in command of the naval forces on the upper Mississippi. Reinforced by the ram "Switzerland," Farragut dropped down the river, his vessel well supplied with everything that was needful. At Grand Gulf, the battery opened again; but the guns of the "Hartford" soon silenced the Confederates. Red River was reached in safety. Dropping down to Port Hudson he attempted to communicate with his fleet, but failed. At this juncture Mr. Gabaudau, the admiral's secretary, volunteered to pass Port Hudson in a skiff by night. The boat was covered with twigs, arranged to resemble one of the floating trees so common in the Mississippi.

Equipped with his despatches, a paddle and a revolver, at a quarter past eight in the evening Gabaudau shoved off from the side of the "Hartford." Once grazing the shore, the sentinels were heard commenting on the size of the log, and a boat put out to make an examination. But fortunately for the admiral's secretary, they contented themselves with a glance, returning to their posts. Gabaudau's arrival was signaled from the vessels below at ten o'clock that night.

The "Hartford" was now actively engaged patrolling the river and capturing supplies intended for the Confederate forces, and but little relaxation from duty was afforded the crew. On the evening of May 1st, while the "Hartford" was lying at the mouth of Red River, a steamer was reported coming down that stream. Fifteen guns were soon trained upon her, awaiting only the admiral's command to fire. She proved to be the United States gunboat "Arizona," the first vessel through from Brashear City. When she gave her night signal it was greeted with three cheers from the flagship, for it announced letters from home and a new route to New Orleans.

In the meanwhile Porter's fleet had whipped the Confederates at several important points, including Grand Gulf, and a portion of his fleet having made its appearance, steamed into Red River. Farragut determined to return to New Orleans and look after the affairs of his squadron and the naval operations at the siege of Port Hudson. He felt that with Porter in sight with a well-equipped fleet, his services were no longer needed in that vicinity.

Farragut turned the command of the "Hartford" over to Commodore Palmer on May 6th, and as he left the vessel, the crew manned the rigging, cheering Farragut to the echo as long as he remained in sight. His associations with Palmer were particularly pleasant, and he entertained for that officer a warm friendship. It came about in this way: at the passage of Vicksburg, Palmer commanded the "Iroquois," the leading ship. The flagship stopped her engines for a few minutes to allow the vessels in the rear to close up. Noting the circumstance and thinking possibly that some accident had befallen the admiral, Palmer dropped his vessel down to the "Hartford." Farragut, not understanding the movement, seized a trumpet from the officer of the deck, and, hailing, said: "Captain Palmer, what do you mean by disobeying my orders?" Palmer replied: "I thought, admiral, you had more fire than you could stand, and I came down to draw part of it off." The incident made a deep impression upon Farragut, who never forgot it.

Palmer was something of a character. Under a reserve of manner and dignified bearing which amounted almost to pomposity, Palmer showed a warm and generous nature. He was brave and cool under fire, and always ready to obey his chief's commands.

In point of personal appearance he was as precise and particular as the famous Murat; and before going on deck to face the flashing muzzles of Confederate guns, he would pause to adjust his necktie and button accurately the last clasp on his neatfitting gloves. He died at St. Thomas, West Indies, December 7, 1867, while in command of the South Atlantic squadron.

With the departure of Farragut the officers and crew of the "Hartford" enjoyed a spell of comparative rest and quiet. The old craft remained off Red River, making occasional trips up the river, but little or no fighting was indulged in. Boat and land expeditions were organized, and Captain Palmer had discretionary power to run the Port Hudson batteries; but he deemed it best to remain where he was, and at the end of two months both Vicksburg and Port Hudson surrendered.

The command of the river as far down as New Orleans was given to Porter, while Farragut had instructions to confine himself to coast operations and blockade. Toward the end of July the two admirals met in New Orleans, and, the transfer having been made, Farragut returned to his first love, the "Hartford."

The hearts of all on board the flagship beat high with hope and anticipation when on August 1st, at 6.30 P. M.,

DESTRUCTION OF THE "MISSISSIPPI."

the "Hartford," with all hands at their stations, got under way and steamed down the river. It had been noised about the ship that she was to go north, that the admiral had been directed to take a short leave, for recreation and health, of which he stood much in need.

But few of the original officers who had joined the ship north remained. Many had been promoted, others were tossing on beds of pain in improvised hospitals; some were fighting stoutly in inland waters, and engaged in keeping open the Mississippi wrested from the enemy; while from Galveston to Ship Island, Farragut's veterans were distributed, keeping watch and ward along the coast, all anxious to reflect credit and honor on their illustrious chief. Death, both by battle and disease, had claimed a large percentage of the original picked, stalwart blue-jackets who had joined the frigate at Philadelphia, little dreaming what tremendous scenes they were destined to participate in, in what pages of history they would be instrumental in creating, ere the staunch ship would hoist her long homeward-bound pennant, carrying also the proud flag of a rear admiral.

The "Hartford" was nine days and ten hours in making the passage north, and upon arrival at New York was received with every honor and demonstration of joy possible from the hands of a grateful and appreciative populace.

Upon examination at the navy-yard, Brooklyn, it was ascertained that the "Hartford," during nineteen months of actual warfare, had been struck by shot and shell two hundred and forty times. The "Richmond" and "Brooklyn" arrived at the yard, and the historic ships were objects of great interest to visitors who flocked on board to view them.

The "Hartford" was placed at once in the hands of workmen, who proceeded to give her a thorough overhaul; while Farragut, glad to leave behind him, for a time at least, scenes and associations that were linked with blood, suffering, and carnage, sought the peaceful rest and pleasant society of his family circle at Hastings on the Hudson. He showed his interest in the welfare of the village by donating the first five hundred dollars received as prize money to the erection of an Episcopal church, as a thank-offering for his deliverance from the dangers to which he had been exposed.

Early in January, 1864, in the midst of a violent snow-storm, Farragut hoisted his flag on the "Hartford" which had been placed in complete order and repair by skilled and selected workmen. An old associate, Captain Percival Drayton, commanded the flagship and acted as his fleet captain. Lieutenant Commander J. C. Watson, who had served with Farragut on the Mississippi and to whom he became very much attached, now performed the duties of flag lieutenant.

After a short stay at New Orleans, Farragut visited Ship Island and Pensacola, where large depots of supplies had been stored. He then commenced operations in earnest for the attack on the defences commanding the entrance to Mobile Bay.

Taking the gunboat "Octarora," he made a reconnoissance of the forts, steaming to within three and a half miles of the fortifications. The day was uncommonly fine and the air very clear, enabling the admiral to view the entire situation to his satisfaction. The entrance from the gulf was guarded by two works, Fort Morgan on Mobile Point and Fort Gaines on Dauphin Island. The approach by Mississippi Sound was covered by Fort Powell. The combined guns of the shore defences amounted to eighty odd guns, ranging in calibre from twenty-four pounder howitzers to ten-inch Columbiards and eight-inch Brooke rifles. In the waters of the bay there was a Confederate squadron under Admiral Franklin Buchanan, made up of the ram "Tennessee" and three small side-wheel gunboats, rifled and smooth-bore guns. The "Tennessee" was the strongest ironclad the Confederacy had ever built, and the authorities had made every effort and exhausted their resources in completing the craft. Her plating was six inches thick, backed by yellow pine five and a half inches thick, laid horizontally, and then four inches of oak laid up and down. She was pierced for ten guns but mounted six, consisting of one eight and a half-inch rifle at each end and two six-inch rifles on each broadside. They threw 110-pound and ninety-pound solid shot.

Farragut knew Buchanan, and did not fall into the error of underrating the resources of his antagonist. In point of energy, courage, and determination Buchanan had few equals, while his skill as a sailor was well known to all the old officers of the United States Navy.

In addition to the forts and gunboats, the Confederates had a line of pile obstructions, and then again a triple line of torpedoes *en echelon* extending across the main ship channel to a red buoy, distant 226 yards from the water-battery under Fort Morgan.

To meet the enemy and overcome the obstacles that confronted him Farragut had nothing but wooden ships, having applied in vain to the department for some monitors and ironclads. But the men of the Federal fleet were enthusiastic; their confidence in Farragut, whom they dubbed "Old Salamander," was supreme, and never for a moment did they doubt his ability, in face of forts and piling, rams and torpedoes, that when the hour arrived he would lead them on to victory as he had before. Farragut, on his part, enjoyed a high opinion of the calibre of the "Hartford's" crew. He said: "I have never seen a crew come up like ours. They are ahead of the old set in small arms and fully equal to them at the great guns. They arrived here a mere lot of boys and young men, and have now fattened up, and knock the nine-inch guns about like 24-pounders, to the astonishment of everybody."

Farragut had made repeated applications for light-draught monitors, but months passed without the department taking heed of his requests. His urgent letters calling for the co-operation of

while the "Tennessee" was moved from a position in which she could do no harm to one in which she became the principal menace to the attacking fleet.

Farragut chafed under the enforced delay, and said: "One thing appears to be certain, that I can get none of the ironclads. They want them all for Washington."

Later on he wrote: "I am lying off here, looking at Buchanan and awaiting his coming out. He has a force of four ironclads and three wooden vessels. I have eight or nine wooden vessels. Will try to amuse him if he comes. I am tired of watching Buchanan and Page, and wish from the bottom of my heart that 'Buck' would come out and try his hand upon us. This question has to be settled, iron *versus* wood; and there never was a better chance to settle the question as to the sea-going qualities of ironclad ships. We are to-day ready to try anything that comes along, be it wood or iron, in reasonable quantities."

GABAUDAU RUNNING THE GAUNTLET.

the army in reducing the forts also remained unnoticed; and as he did not like to incur the risk of getting inside with his wooden ships crippled, the forts intact in his rear, and the enemy's ironclads to contend with, he could only wait, compelled in the meanwhile to look on

Toward the end of July the monitors began to arrive. Four were sent to him: the "Tecumseh" and "Manhattan" from the Atlantic coast, and the "Chickasaw" and "Winnebago" from the Mississippi River. The "Manhattan" had been the first to put in an appearance, the "Chickasaw" followed ten days later with the

"Winnebago," but the "Tecumseh" did not arrive, thus preventing Farragut from moving to the attack on the morning of the 4th of August. General Granger had landed his troops on Dauphin Island, and was in plain sight of the fleet, which, however, to the intense mortification of Farragut, was forced to remain idly at anchor. Late in the afternoon of the 4th the "Tecumseh" steamed behind Sand Island and took up her anchorage with the other ironclads.

In forming his plan of attack, Farragut had counted upon a westerly wind to blow the smoke from his guns down upon Fort Morgan, and also upon having a flood tide. As the fleet was to pass within 200 yards from Morgan, little was feared from Fort Gaines, which would be over two miles away; the preparations were therefore made mainly on the starboard side, and port guns were shifted over till all the ports were full. The boats were lowered and towed on the port side. Farragut and Captain Alden, commanding the "Brooklyn," preferred to go in with their topsail yards across, but the balance of the fleet sent down their topmasts.

The "Richmond," while at Pensacola, built a regular barricade of sand-bags, extending from the bow port along the starboard side to the port-quarter, and from the berth- to the spar-deck. Three thousand bags of sand were used, which in places was six feet in thickness.

In the order of battle the wooden ships, as at Port Hudson, were to be lashed in couples, the lighter vessels on the port side. The "Tecum-seh" led the column of ironclads, although Farragut had intended to lead the column, but yielded to the remonstrances of his officers so far as to allow the "Brooklyn" to precede him.

The evening before the action it was raining hard, but toward midnight the heavens cleared, the weather being hot and calm. The preparations were all made, and the vessels lay quietly at their anchors. Later a light air sprang up from the southward and westward, and Farragut, who was not well, sleeping restlessly, sent his steward at three in the morning to ascertain how the wind was. When he learned that it was southwest, he said: "Then we will go in this morning."

The inhabitants of Mobile relied with perfect confidence upon the ability of their combined forces and system of defences to easily win the battle. They entertained no fears so far as the enemy menacing their shores was concerned. Numerous influential citizens and officials came down the river in boats to witness the impregnable ram, "Tennessee," bearing the flag of their pet admiral, swoop down upon and sink the Yankee fleet commanded by Farragut, whom they looked upon as recreant to his trust and a traitor.

The last words that Farragut penned that eventful night were addressed to his wife, and contained the following: "*I am going into Mobile Bay in the morning, if God is my leader, as I hope He is, and in Him I place my trust.*"

VIII.—MOBILE BAY.

CONFEDERATE RAM "TENNESSEE."

AN incident relative to a blockade runner, not found in any naval history, is well worthy of mention here as illustrative of the life and perils encountered by officers and men comprising the Federal navy.

On the night of August 1st, an English blockade runner, favored by circumstances, ran through the fleet, but was pressed so closely by pursuing gunboats that, running too near to the land, her keel took the bottom at a point close under the guns of Morgan. Farragut was much annoyed by the circumstance, and ordered an expedition to be formed, composed of two boats from each ship, amounting to one hundred men, who, under cover of darkness, pulled in for the beach. At three o'clock they returned, reporting that they could not find the wreck. Farragut summoned his aid, Lieutenant Watson:

"Watson, take my barge and a dozen men; go in there and destroy that blockade runner."

Watson required no second bidding; he loved such work. The larger expedition retired chagrined, while the crew of the barge, with white covers on their caps to distinguish them from the enemy, armed with cutlasses and revolvers, pulled at a swinging stroke straight for the entrance to the Confederate works. The fort loomed up through the darkness, stern and forbidding, while a sharp lookout for the hull of the blockader was maintained. She was discovered by a keen-eyed young topman, lying in the deep shadows of an angle of the fort. There was no delay or nonsense about it; no appealing to the men to fight manfully. There was no occasion for that with the men of the "Hartford." The barge was headed direct for her, the men boarding just forward of the starboard paddle-box. The demoralized crew were driven in all directions, many seeking safety in flight ashore, giving the alarm to the garrison. With dextrous hands the sailors strewed combustibles in various parts of the vessel, and placing a large tank of powder in the midst of the machinery, the torch was applied. Fort Morgan had now opened a plunging fire, and as the barge pulled off shore, flames burst from all portions of the doomed craft, revealing a company of soldiers advancing at a double-quick down the broad beach. But the game had slipped through their fingers. The shot from the fort made the water boil and foam around the barge, but none struck her, and as the first red streaks of dawn tinged the east, Watson reported his mission to the admiral as accomplished.

The morning of Friday, August 5th, long before day, the boatswain's shrill pipes summoned "all hands!" and "up all hammocks!" Coffee and hardtack were served to the men, while in the cabin, the admiral, Drayton, and Palmer were partaking of a light and early breakfast. Daylight was breaking, with appearances of rain, which, however, had no effect upon the spirits of the men. The wind was west-southwest, in the most favorable quarter for blowing the smoke of the guns on Fort Morgan, and Farragut expressed his satisfaction at the favorable outlook.

Acting Rear-Admiral Bailey, who led the fleet at the passage of the Mississippi forts and who then commanded the East Gulf squadron, had written to his old chief, "Nothing will please me more than to hoist once more the square red flag, and lead the van of your squadron into Mobile Bay, to the capture of Forts Morgan and Gaines, as well as the city. Put me down for two chances, as the jackass said to the monkey at the lion's ball."

But yellow fever broke out in his squadron, he was stricken down with it himself, and it was not deemed prudent to have the vessels of the two commands brought into contact.

Generals Canby and Granger had visited the "Hartford," and made arrangements that all the troops that could be spared should co-operate with the fleet. There were not enough men to invest both forts, so a body of troops, at Farragut's suggestion, were landed on Dauphin Island, covered by the guns of the "Conemaugh," Lieutenant-Commander De Krafft.

At four o'clock the wooden ships formed in double column, lashed in pairs, in the following order, the first-mentioned of each pair being the starboard vessel:

BROOKLYN, Captain James Olden.
    OCTARORA, Lieutenant-Commander C. H. Greene.

HARTFORD (flagship), Fleet-Captain Percival Drayton.
    METACOMET, Lieutenant-Commander J. E. Jouett.

RICHMOND, Captain Thornton A. Jenkins.
    PORT ROYAL, Lieutenant-Commander Bancroft Gherardi.

LACKAWANNA, Captain J. B. Marchand.
    SEMINOLE, Commander Edward Donaldson.

MONONGAHELA, Commander J. H. Strong.
    KENNEBEC, Lieutenant-Commander W. P. McCann.

OSSIPEE, Commander W. E. LeRoy.
    ITASCA, Lieutenant-Commander George Brown.

ONEIDA, Commander J. R. Madison Mullany.
    GALENA, Lieutenant-Commander C. H. Wells.

The "Brooklyn" was appointed to lead because she had four chase-guns and apparatus for picking up torpedoes. The four monitors, "Tecumseh," Commander T. A. M. Craven; "Manhattan," Commander J. W. A. Nicholson; "Winnebago," Commander Thomas H. Stevens; and "Chickasaw," Lieutenant-Commander G. H. Perkins, formed a line abreast of the four leading ships, and between them and Fort Morgan.

At half-past five Farragut rose from the table, holding in his hand a cup of hot tea, which he was still sipping. He glanced for a moment at Drayton, who, quiet and thoughtful, watched the movements of his superior. "We may as well get under way," he said. Drayton saluted and left the cabin. In one minute answering signals came from the whole fleet, and at six A. M. the ships were all formed in line, moving up the main ship channel, toward the forts, with the Stars and Stripes flying from every mast-head and peak. At half-past six the boom of a gun from the "Tecumseh" announced the opening of the ball, and Fort Morgan promptly responded. The "Tecumseh," with the lion-hearted Craven, had been the last to join the fleet, and was the first to perish on that eventful August morning.

The forts had the advantage, pouring in a raking fire for over half an hour before the ships could get their broadsides to bear, driving the gunners from the barbette and water batteries.

The "Hartford" steamed ahead slowly, coming within short range of the fort before receiving a shot from one of the guns. The order to fire was eagerly awaited, and when it came the old flagship trembled from truck to keelson.

The quarter-deck was occupied by Captain Drayton, with officers of the staff standing conveniently near. At the wheel were three old and reliable seamen, thoroughbreds in every sense of the word, who had been in every engagement known to the vessel, and whose courage and skill were beyond all doubt or question. Their names were McFarland, Wood, and Jassin. Knowles, the signal quartermaster, precise and methodical in his department, walked back-

ward and forward, never for a moment allowing the exciting scenes being enacted about him to divert his attention from his duty.

A great deal has been written relative to the position of Farragut in the Mobile fight, and the incident of being lashed to the rigging has occasioned considerable controversy. Certainly, no question concerning the post occupied by Farragut could arise among those who were on board the flagship and witnessed the engagement.

In the port main-rigging, a few ratlines above the sheer-pole, where he could clearly observe

(FORT MORGAN.)

"THE GAME HAD SLIPPED THROUGH THEIR FINGERS"

all that was transpiring about him, stood Farragut. In the top was stationed Freeman, his pilot, who bravely piloted the flagship and the fleet behind it through shoals and hidden dangers, when to ground might have brought defeat, as assuredly it would death to those exposed to the fort's scathing fire. And yet, but a few years since, this trusty veteran and servant of Farragut sought in vain for a pilot's berth on some government vessel, ultimately meeting death, in his old age, alone, an inmate of a negro's hut— a pauper, with not even the necessaries of life at hand to soothe his last wretched hours on earth.

As the smoke increased, rolling above and a-round the admiral, he mounted the main-rigging higher and higher, until his head was on a level with the buttock band. At that point, Captain

Drayton, fearing some accident might occur, sent Knowles with a piece of new lead line to make the admiral more secure.

The honest old sailor, in speaking of the incident, in 1880, at which time he was quartermaster on the U. S. Steamer "Phlox," stationed at the Naval Academy, expressed himself as follows:

"Pilot Freeman, who was apt to talk too much, I know very well; but that man Baldwin, who yarns it about the admiral and puts him in the *starboard main-rigging*, under the top, he does not know what he is writing about. I was chief quartermaster of the 'Hartford' and the man that lashed the admiral to the rigging, and I ought to know something about it.

"When we got up close to the forts, I heard Mr. Kimberly, the executive officer, tell Mr. Watson, our flag-lieutenant, to have a rope passed around the admiral. I was busy at the time with some signal flags for the monitors, when I was ordered to go up the port main-rigging and put a rope around the admiral. I cut a fathom or two from a new lead line which was lying on the deck, went up the ratlines to where the admiral was standing, with opera-glasses in his hand, just under the buttock shrouds, and made the forward end of the line fast. As I took the after end around the admiral, he passed the remark that the rope was not necessary, but I went on and made the after end secure. I don't think he noticed the rope around him, as we were square abreast of Fort Morgan, and it was pretty hot work; but when the ships got clear of the forts, the admiral had to cast the rope adrift before he could come down."

Regarding the assertion made by Brownell in his poem, "The Bay Fight," where he puts the admiral "high in the mizzen shroud," and for which he has been severely criticised, the incident will be hereafter alluded to.

The painting by Page was presented to the Grand Duke Alexis by the citizens of New York, on the occasion of his visit to this country, the presentation speech being made by General Dix. It at present hangs on the walls of the Czar's winter palace.

A great deal of interesting testimony on the much disputed episode is in possession of the writer, but to introduce it all would add nothing to the interest of the battle. It can be produced, however, if it should ever be wanted.

The scene on the deck of the "Hartford" was now one of bustle and extreme animation. Guns were being worked as rapidly as possible;

every officer and man was busy; powder boys were rushing from point to point; marines, drawn up in double lines, were loading and firing with as much precision as though on the parade ground; while shot shivered and tore the timbers beneath their feet, shells burst above, filling the air with whizzing particles, mingled with splinters torn from sides, bulwarks, and masts, varying from the length of a match to a piece of cord-wood. Men were falling; blood was everywhere, with shrieks, moans, and groans rising above the din, thud, and roar of battle. The fire from the Confederate gunboats now began to tell, while the solid shot from the "Tennessee," weighing one hundred and ten pounds, produced a terrible effect. In the foretop of the "Hartford" was a howitzer, under the management of half a dozen sailors, throwing grape and canister into the water battery in front of the fort, doing good service and assisting largely in driving the gunners from their pieces.

The entire fleet was now engaged, with answering shot and shell from the Confederate gunboats, both parties contending for victory, with the old "Hartford" forging very closely upon the dividing line, marking the decisive point in the battle. A shell burst between the two forward guns, in charge of Lieutenant Tyson, killing and wounding fifteen men. A 120-pound shell, from a Blakely rifle, on the Confederate gunboat "Selma," struck the main-mast, but did not explode; another struck the foremast, while a solid shot, coming through a bow-port, struck a gunner on the neck, shaving his head from the body as quickly as though done with a knife. One poor fellow lost both legs by a round shot; as he fell, he threw up both arms, both of which were carried away by whizzing missiles, which seemed to fill the air.

There was no skulking on that bloody deck, covered with shreds and patches of poor humanity. Men and boys toiled at the guns, shoulder to shoulder; black and white were there, with no thought of social superiority or pre-eminence troubling their brains. No; the smell of blood and the sight of dear friends crushed and mangled about them, filled their hearts with but one desire, stifling all thoughts or sentiments of fear — victory! Triumph over their foes and revenge for the dear blood already spilled— that was what nerved their arms and cleared their eyes, and whenever a telling shot was sent true to its mark, the wild cheers of the "Hartford's" crew would ring out above the roar of the guns. The bodies of the dead were placed in a long row on the port side, so as not to interfere with the working of the guns, while the wounded were sent below until the surgeon's quarters could contain no more. From an elevated position it was easy to trace the course of every shot, both from the guns of the flagship and from the hostile fleet.

At half-past seven the "Tecumseh" was well up with the fort, having the "Tennessee" on the port beam. The monitor's guns had been loaded with steel shot and sixty pounds of powder, which at that time was the heaviest that had been attempted. Craven knew that the eyes of all the fleet were upon him. It was his great opportunity, and his chivalrous nature yearned for a fair trial of strength with the formidable ram and her famous commander. The fire from the fort was scarcely noticed as the monitor steamed toward her adversary, drawing ahead of the "Brooklyn," the other monitors following Craven closely. As they drew near the buoy, Craven, from the pilot-house, saw it so close in line with the beach that he said to his pilot, "It is impossible that the admiral means for this vessel to go inside the buoy; I cannot turn my ship." At the same moment the "Tennessee," which up to that time had lain to the eastward of the buoy, went ahead to the westward of it, and Craven, either fearing she would elude him or unable to restrain his eagerness to commence the combat, gave the order "starboard," heading the "Tecumseh" straight for the ram. She had gone but a few yards, with all hands awaiting the order to fire, when one or more torpedoes exploded under her. She lurched from side to side, careened violently over, and went down, bows first, her screw plainly visible in the air for a moment to all on the "Tennessee," who awaited her onset, less than two hundred yards off, on the other side of the fatal line. The monitor sank beneath the surface, carrying within her iron walls Craven and one hundred and twenty men, helplessly imprisoned. Had the course of the monitor been directed thirty feet more to the eastward, she would have escaped the danger. The pilot leaped from the pilot-house, and half a dozen sailors in the turret managed to jump through the ports. Farragut, from his post in the port main-rigging, hailed Jouett, who was standing on top of the pilot-house of the "Metacomet," to know if he had a boat that he could send to pick up the survivors. Jouett had anticipated the order,

and a boat in charge of Ensign H. C. Neilds, a volunteer officer, was about leaving the port quarter of the gunboat. She pulled round the "Hartford's" stern and broadside, across the bows of the "Brooklyn," toward the wreck, when the pilot, John Collins, and nine of the crew were saved. While on his way, Neilds, who was steering the boat, noticed that the flag was not flying, and, removing it from its cover, unfurled it in the face of friend and foe. The ensign of the forecastle division of the "Hartford," seeing the boat without a flag, and thinking only of torpedoes, was training his rifled gun upon it when he was stopped just in time, as he was about to pull the lockstring. The "Hartford" had passed on when Neilds had picked up the survivors, and, after putting them on board the "Winnebago," he pulled down to the "Oneida," where he served during the rest of the action.

The pilot of the "Tecumseh," John Collins, stated that at the moment of the explosion he was standing with Captain Craven in the iron tower or pilot-house, directly over the turret. Seeing the inevitable fate of the vessel, Craven and the pilot scrambled down into the turret and met at the foot of the iron ladder, leading to the top of the turret through a narrow scuttle, the only exit now left for escape from the doomed vessel. At that point Craven drew back in a characteristic way and said, "After you, pilot." "There was nothing after me," said Mr. Collins. "When I reached the topmost round of the ladder the vessel seemed to drop from under me."

Farragut had witnessed the frightful fate of the "Tecumseh," at the same time the "Brooklyn" stopped causing the admiral a great deal of uneasiness. A moment's hesitation might lose him the battle, and to press on might result in sending fleet, guns and all to the bottom of the bay. Farragut himself, in alluding to the subject afterwards, admitted that the sinking of the "Tecumseh" and the stopping of the "Brooklyn" looked as though all of his plans were to be thwarted, and he was at a loss whether to advance or to retreat. In this extremity his natural impulse was to appeal to heaven for guidance, and he offered up this prayer: "O God, who created and gave me reason, direct me what to do. Shall I go on?" And it seemed as if in answer a voice commanded him to "go on!"

When the "Tecumseh" sank, the "Brooklyn" was about a hundred yards astern of her and a little outside; the "Hartford" between one and two hundred yards from the "Brooklyn," on her port quarter. The admiration of Farragut and his officers was excited, as they passed the "Winnebago," in witnessing Com-

"— THE TORPEDOES ! — GO AHEAD !"

mander Stevens walking from point to point, between the turrets, giving his directions as unconcernedly as though at anchor in some quiet harbor.

Suddenly the "Brooklyn" and her consort stopped, and then began to back, coming down upon the "Hartford." At the same time their bows fell off toward the fort and they soon lay nearly athwart the channel. "What is the matter with the 'Brooklyn'—has she water enough?" demanded Farragut of his pilot. "Plenty and to spare, sir," was the answer. The "Hartford" was forced to sheer, lapping the "Brooklyn" on the port quarter, while the guns were silenced.

"What's the trouble on board the 'Brooklyn'?" came from the flagship.

"Torpedoes ahead!" was the answer.

"D——n the torpedoes!" shouted Farragut. "Four bells, Captain Drayton; go ahead! Jouett, full speed!"

The order to take the lead was received by all on board with loud cheers, which in turn were taken up by the other vessels.

Though the delay had been short, the order to go ahead came none too soon. The "Richmond" had to sheer to avoid collision with the flagship, and all vessels in turn were compelled to stop, their guns partially silenced, while the fire from the enemy's batteries increased, if anything. It was their opportunity.

Clearing the "Brooklyn," the flagship dashed ahead, and had gained nearly a mile lead before the line could be straightened, but she had cleared the torpedo ground, her broadside guns were again in full play, and Farragut, with his blue flag fluttering above his head, pushed on ahead and alone, with the exception of the "Metacomet," lashed alongside, and her gallant, impetuous commander, who was a host in himself.

The following lines well describe this heroic action of the lamented Craven:

"After you, pilot," he grandly said,
And proudly stayed his dauntless tread,
Till up the ladder the pilot crept,
And softly from the turret stepped.
Alas! no after was there for him,
Waiting in turret so close and grim.
Each throb of time with peril fraught,
Weightier growing by doubt distraught,
As the eager flood with gurgling sound,
And rush and roar fast flowed him round.
Fainter and fainter the morning beams
Shimmered through tower in fitful gleams;
Darker and darker grew turret and tower,
Surging and plunging with fateful power;
Faster and faster the torn hulk filled,
A moment more and all was stilled—
For oh! the waters, with pitiless thrall,
Over grand Craven threw their pall,
And shrouded in iron, he sank to rest,
Enshrined indeed, forever blest.
On swept the fleet midst flame and smoke
And thundering roar and cannon stroke,
But the bubbles that rose to the surface brim
Were the last of earth that told of him.
Oh! beauteous bay that saw such bloom
Of valor's flower its deeps illume;
A grace like that by Sidney sealed,
Refulgent ray from Zutphen's field,
Stay not your joys with saddening tear,
As flow your tides about his bier,
But leave to the gulf's aye restless surge
The murmurous chant of ceaseless dirge;
For down the years with freshing glory,
Resplendent glows the lustrous story,
And calling to deeds of likest fame,
Immortal crowns grand Craven's name.

THE LAST OF THE "TECUMSEH."

THE fleet under Farragut carried the heaviest guns afloat. Their total weight of metal was 14,246 pounds, and they threw at a broadside 9,288 pounds. The Tennessee at one discharge could throw 600 pounds, and the remainder of the Confederate craft about 900.

Buchanan fully expected to meet the Tecumseh, whose fifteen-inch guns had been loaded with sixty pounds of powder and cylindrical flat-headed steel bolts that it was supposed would penetrate the armor of the Tennessee.

At that time sixty pounds was the maximum charge for fifteen-inch guns, the largest guns afloat or known to naval warfare. It was afterwards found they could stand one hundred pounds, with a proportionate gain of velocity and battering power.

Before going into action, Admiral Buchanan addressed his officers and men, saying: "Now, men, the enemy is coming, and I want you to do your duty; and you shall not have it to say, when you leave this vessel, that you were not near enough to the enemy, for I will meet them and then you can fight them alongside of their own ships; and if I fall, lay me on one side and go on with the fight, and never mind me, but whip and sink the Yankees or fight until you sink yourselves, but do not surrender."

Buchanan kept his eyes fixed upon the Te-

48

cumseh, whose flat raft of a hull and ominous-looking turret were with every passing second creeping closer to him. Buchanan had passed the order not to fire until the vessels were in contact and the attention of all men riveted upon the monitor, who, with helm put hard-a-starboard, dashed straight at the Tennessee, regardless of the chain of torpedoes of which he had been warned by Farragut. The vessels were not more than a hundred yards apart, when a muffled explosion was heard. A column of water like a fountain shot up from the sea; the monitor lurched heavily, her head settled, her stern went up in the air so that her revolving-screw could be plainly seen, and then she settled beneath the surface in thirty seconds. A cheer rang out from the garrison of Fort Morgan, who imagined that a shot from one of their guns had brought about the catastrophe. A week afterwards, when the divers went down to examine the wreck, they found nearly all the crew at their posts as they sank. The chief engineer, Farron, who had been married in New York only two weeks before and who had received from the flagship's mail his letters while the line was forming, stood with one hand upon the revolving-bar of the turret engine and in the other an open letter from his bride, which his sightless, staring eyes seemed to be reading. He was an invalid, but left his bed at the Pensacola hospital in order to be at his post.

Lieutenant A. D. Wharton, who had command of the forward division of the Tennessee, states that when the Hartford passed the Brooklyn and led the fleet into the bay, she passed square across the ram's bow and not more than 200 yards distant. The seven-inch rifle in the bow of the ram was loaded with a percussion shell, and Wharton congratulated himself that he would have the pleasure of sinking Farragut's flagship under the batteries of Fort Morgan, and that her destruction would defeat the Yankee fleet. He took the lock string from the captain of the gun, taking a long and deliberate aim, giving the commands, "Raise! steady! ready! fire!" He was confident that the shell would tear a hole in the Hartford's side big enough to sink her in a few mintes. It did make a large opening, but it was above the water-line, and the flagship passed majestically on, her sides ablaze with fire from her terrible guns. The keel of the Hartford struck several torpedo cases, and the primers were heard to snap; but the admiral's good star shone over him. They had become so corroded by action

of the salt water that not one of them exploded, and the fleet passed safely through the net-work of danger to which the Tecumseh had fallen a victim.

At half-past eight o'clock the fleet of Farragut's was well into Mobile Bay and past the guns of Fort Morgan. Again had the great admiral proved his ability to run and manœuver his fleet in the face of powerful shore batteries, passing them successfully as he had at New Orleans, Vicksburg, and Port Hudson. Fort Morgan was now out of the fight, but Buchanan with his ram, backed by the gunboats Selma, Gaines, and Morgan, was still lively and full of fight, as the Hartford found to her cost when she took the lead.

The three Confederate gunboats took up positions close on the starboard bow of the Hartford as she crossed the torpedo line, raking her with a galling fire from their rapidly served seven and eight-inch rifled guns. Keeping ahead of the flagship, they used mainly their stern guns at a range not exceeding 1000 yards, and their fire was the perfection of artillery practice. One shot from the Selma killed ten men and wounded five at guns numbers one and two, while that division was strewn with the bodies of the dead and wounded, and fragments of the bodies were hurled on to the deck of her consort, the Metacomet.

Buchanan, through the dense smoke, caught a glimpse of Farragut's blue flag as it floated from its lofty perch. He smiled grimly as he pictured to himself that emblem lowered and humbled, and the ship sinking 'neath the feet of its master. He would give him a taste of the iron ram's quality, which Farragut affected to despise. Everything was in favor of the ram, for the Hartford was still some distance in advance of the column and could look for no assistance from her consorts. The ram dashed at its antagonist, but failed to reach the mark. Shots were exchanged, and the Confederate admiral continued down the bay to meet the advancing Federal fleet. Had the ram kept on, it could hardly have failed to sink the Hartford, for the channel was narrow, with no opportunity for sheering. The ram endeavored in succession to ram the Brooklyn, the Richmond, and the Lackawanna, but owing to the manner in which they were handled, Buchanan was foiled. But what he missed with his iron prow was more than made up for with his heavy broadsides. He rasped alongside the quarter of the Kennebec, putting a shell on her berth deck, killing an officer and four men. He next lodged a couple of shots into the Ossipee, and then swung around under the stern of the Oneida, into which vessel he discharged two broadsides, disabling two guns, carrying away rigging, and robbing Commander Mullany of an arm.

The last few moments the Hartford was under fire of the forts, batteries, and gunboats, was the warmest work the old flagship had ever encountered. Every man on her broad deck appeared to be in motion, and so intent upon his particular line of duty that scarcely a word was spoken. The carefully trained guns seemed imbued with life as they sped in and out of the spacious ports. The hurried run of powder boys and shellmen from the magazines at the stairways and fire-hatches, with supplies for their guns, gave an air of apparent confusion on the deck. The roar of the heavy guns was so great that it was impossible to distinguish the tones of human voices. Occasionally, the peculiar scream of shot passing in close proximity caught the attention of the men, while the bursting of shell and quick snapping crash of flying timber hummed through the air. The cut, frayed rigging swayed wildly to and fro from aloft, and the men, with faces smeared and begrimed with powder, toiled steadily on, peering through the thick pall of battle, watching for the flash and glare of the enemy's guns, and firing in that direction. One gun's crew was entirely swept away, remaining silent until re-manned by men from other portions of the ship. A sailor, fearfully wounded, turned and writhed in the cot used for lowering the wounded to the surgeon's quarters. He fell a distance of thirty feet and his sufferings were at an end. Bulwarks, masts, ropes, guns, and carriages were all more or less smeared with blood and pieces of the human body, over which there was no time to ponder, think, or even grow pale. Captain Drayton and Lieutenant Watson were on the quarter-deck, close observers of all that was passing, and whether fighting or conversing, Watson's face was seldom seen without a pleasant smile, a feature peculiar to him.

Kimberly, the executive officer, speaking-trumpet in hand, walked slowly forward aft the main-deck, seemingly on hand at the very spot where his presence was most required. In caring for the wounded and disposing of the dead, he was tender and careful, looking after all the details as calmly and coolly as though death was miles away, instead of lurking above, below, and all around him.

The Selma, which had been handled with great ability, was still annoying the flagship, causing Jouett to manifest great impatience, finding it almost impossible to curb his ardor. The Metacomet was the fastest vessel in the fleet, and as yet, in all the shifting phases of the great fight, he had been held in restraint, with no opportunity to measure swords with the foe. Three times he had asked the admiral for permission to leave the side of the Hartford and tackle the Selma, but the admiral's answer was, "Wait a little longer." At last the flagship emerged from the channel into the deep water of the bay. Then came the signal: "Gunboats, chase enemy's gunboats;" and with a loud and hearty "Ay, ay, sir!" Jouett seized a hatchet and, in common with his axemen, helped to cut asunder the lashings. Farragut waved his hands to Jouett, whose enthusiasm and courage he much admired, and with three hearty cheers rising from the Metacomet's crew, they steamed at full speed in pursuit of the Selma, who for some time had been having the fun all her own way.

A heavy rain and wind squall had swept in from the gulf, completely obscuring, for a short interval, objects both afloat and on shore. The Morgan, in her anxiety to escape the coming wrath, ran aground, but floated as the squall cleared up, and steamed for protection under the guns of Fort Morgan.

During the mist and uncertainty accompanying the rush of wind and rain, the Federal gunboat was dashing ahead at full speed, while the commander was looking after the effective serving of the forward pivot gun.

"We are shoaling our water, sir," remarked the executive. "I am afraid we shall take the bottom, as we draw twelve feet of water."

"Never mind, sir, never mind. Keep her going," replied Jouett, as he sighted the piece. But the prudent executive quietly ordered a quartermaster to take the lead, and the next instant "Fifteen feet!" was announced. That was all right, and the engine never ceased in its powerful workings. "Fourteen feet!" was the next report. "Thirteen feet!" came sharp and clear from the steady old seaman. The situation was becoming serious! The men glanced quickly at one another, while the officers kept their eyes fastened upon their commander, who turned coolly from the gun, saying, as he walked aft: "Call that man in from the lead. He makes me nervous."

Lieutenant Murphy, commanding the Selma, attempted to escape under cover of the fogs, but

"JOUETT WAS FORGING ACROSS THE BOW OF HIS ANTAGONIST."

his vessel was too slow to escape the Metacomet. At nine o'clock, by which time the sky was clear again, Jouett was forging across the bow of his antagonist, his battery trained upon the gunboat. Their guns rang out; Comstock, the executive officer, and four men fell, to rise no more, and Murphy himself was wounded. Jouett and his boarders were mustering to complete their work at close quarters, when the Selma's flag disappeared in token of submission. In tow of the Metacomet, she was carried back to the Hartford. The gunboat Gaines meanwhile had been chased on shore, under the guns of Fort Morgan, where the torch was applied, the crew seeking shelter inside the fort. The ram, with colors flying and ports closed, had also retired under the shadow of the fort, and the roar of battle died away. Farragut, supposing that the fighting was over for the time being, had anchored about three miles up the bay, signaling his fleet to follow his motions. All hands were at once engaged in clearing the wreck, washing the blood from the decks, and cleansing the ship throughout, while the wounded were made as comfortable as circumstances would permit. The boilers were relieved in part of the great pressure of steam, while the fires were allowed to assume much smaller propor-

tions. Preparations were made as rapidly as possible to give the tired, hungry survivors some breakfast, and stewards and cooks, with fresh uniforms, clean hands and faces, white aprons and jackets in lieu of cutlass, revolver, and cartridge-box, bustled briskly about, with orders flying thick and fast from caterers of messes.

Such of the officers as could be spared from the deck and posts of duty hastened to the wardroom to ascertain how it had fared with friends and messmates who were dead and who had survived. One, Ensign Heginbotham, of the admiral's staff, was mortally wounded. Lieutenant Adams was slightly wounded; all the rest had escaped unhurt. Of the crew, twenty-eight mangled bodies were lying in a ghastly row on the port side of the deck, with twenty-five wounded below. Out of the eighteen officers in the wardroom, strange to state, but one was fatally hurt. Each congratulated the other upon his good fortune, and around the mess-table such a handshaking and exchange of hearty good-will the wardroom had never witnessed before.

Swords, caps, accoutrements of all kinds had been piled hurriedly in one corner of the wardroom, while the grateful aroma of strong, freshly-made coffee pervaded the apartment. In the midst of it all the sharp, piercing tones of Executive Kimberly were heard calling all hands to quarters, and a messenger boy, his young face all aglow with excitement, hurried into the officers' midst with the words, "Gentlemen, the ram is coming!"

Every officer and man repaired to his post, anxious to have the affair decided, for no rest could be expected while the Tennessee remained afloat with the Confederate ensign flying over her.

Farragut and Buchanan were of equal rank in the old navy, Farragut being the senior, having entered the service December 10, 1810, and Buchanan on January 28, 1815. Both received a captain's commission on September 14, 1855. At the outbreak of the Rebellion, Farragut was waiting orders at Norfolk. Buchanan had command of the Washington Navy Yard. He resigned his commission when the Massachusetts troops were attacked in the streets of Baltimore, expecting that Maryland, his native State, would at once secede. Failing in his expectations, he petitioned to recall his resignation, but was refused.

The parapets of the forts were lined with Confederate soldiers, who were beyond range of the guns, and as spectators were greatly interested in the coming contest. Single-handed, the ram, which was believed to be invulnerable, was running straight for the Federal fleet as fast as her powerful double engines could propel her. The monitors, slow and unwieldy, could offer little or no resistance to her approach, and Farragut, who placed his chief dependence upon his stout wooden walls, at once prepared to accept the gauge of battle so bravely thrown at his feet. That the spectators from the forts expected to see the Tennessee whip in detail the Yankee fleet there can be but little doubt, and more than one stout heart on board the Federal vessels beat apprehensively as the distance between the rival admirals lessened.

Farragut stood with his arms folded, his eyes riveted upon the ram, his features bearing a stern expression. With a rapid, nervous movement the great captain unbuttoned his frock-coat, and, turning to his fleet captain, said: "He is after me. Let him come on. Admiral for admiral, flagship for flagship! I'll fight him while I have a gun left or a man to ram home the charge."

Buchanan's previous experience with wooden vessels, when he commanded the Merrimac in Hampton Roads, gave him confidence and strong hopes of winning an easy victory, for the Tennessee was far superior to his former command. But he had antagonists keenly alive to every chance and fluctuation of battle; the vessels, though wooden, were not helplessly anchored, and, above all, there was a ruling master spirit, which, had it been present at Hampton Roads, might have registered a far different result from that won by the astute Confederate admiral.

From the poop of the Hartford Farragut watched the approach of the ram, while from the spanker gaff of the flagship fluttered the signal, "Attack the enemy." Cables were slipped, all anxious to lead in the action, but the Monongahela, with her iron prow, was foremost in the race, and at once rushed at the ram full speed. It had been Farragut's intention, after serving breakfast to the officers and men, to seek the Tennessee in her lair and bring her out to a conclusion, as the advantages of daylight were far in excess of what possibly could have been at night. Buchanan, by his spirited action, had simply anticipated his antagonist's intentions by an hour at most. Under the guns of the fort an opportunity to inspect damages was afforded. A narrow examination revealed a few dents in the armor, and a portion of the smoke-stack carried away. With this slight exhibit, as a result of the heavy fire sustained from the Federal fleet, Buchanan smiled exultantly, and summoning Captain Johnston communicated to him his resolution to once more engage the fleet. "Follow them up, Johnston," he said, "we can't let them off that way." It has been stated that Buchanan was advised not to make his second attack. It was one vessel pitted against three ironclads and fourteen wooden ships. But the iron will and determined courage of the man was proof against all argument. He realized that he was alone, that his squadron had disappeared, that the forts could render him no assistance, but he felt that his vessel was more than a match for a dozen wooden ships; as for the monitors, he knew not their strength, but would not yield until he had squarely tested their merits.

Some fortunate accident might occur—torpedoes possibly rid him of another ironclad—a panic demoralize the Federals through the loss of their vaunted flagship and great leader, who viewed with such scorn the iron plating and swinging shutters of the newly-created iron men-of-war. The battle might yet be won, defeat turned into victory, Mobile saved from disaster and humiliation, and the forts and de-

"HE IS AFTER ME. LET HIM COME ON!"

fences restored to their lost prestige and strength.

Animated with sentiments that caused his cheeks to flush and eyes sparkle, the old warrior answered his advisers: "Let those retire who wish to. I will either be killed or taken prisoner, and now I am in the humor I will have it out at once."

Steadily the Tennessee approached the Federal fleet, which was under way. Not a living being could be seen on board the ram. Every port was closed; the colors waved from a short flag-staff aft; an indescribable air of superiority pervaded the huge vessel, as singly and alone she faced the entire force, as if conscious of her superior strength and resources.

Then ensued one of the most remarkable naval battles the world had ever known, unsurpassed in any age for bravery and fierceness.

MONONGAHELA AND TENNESSEE.

THE Monongahela, with her iron prow and under a full head of steam, was the first vessel of the Federal fleet to try issues with the Confederate champion. But the Tennessee paid no attention to the attack, merely putting her helm to port, which caused the Monongahela to strike her a glancing blow. It crushed the stern and crumbled the iron prow of the wooden ship, who received from the ram two shots that pierced her through and through, while the shot from the nine-inch guns rolled harmlessly off the sloping sides of the ironclad. The Chickasaw sent one of her solid bolts after her, but no harm resulted. The next vessel to meet the ram was the Lackawanna, which succeeded in striking her antagonist at right angles at the after end of the casemate. The concussion was great, but the effect on the ram was scarcely noticeable, while the wooden vessel had her timbers crushed in for a distance of three feet above the water's edge to five feet below. After striking, the two swung head and stern alongside of each other. Two shots from the ram passed through the bow of the unlucky craft whose guns had been pivoted on the opposite side, and but one nine-inch shell was expended on the Tennessee. This struck one of her port shutters, which was distant about twelve feet, destroying it and driving some of the fragments into her casemate. A few of the enemy were seen through the ports, making insulting gestures and using opprobrious language. Both sailors and marines opened upon them with rifles and revolvers; even a spittoon and a holy-stone were thrown by the indignant sailors from the deck of the Lackawanna, before the vessels finally cleared each other. As the smoke drifted to leeward, Buchanan discovered the Hartford coming bows on at full speed. It was the opportunity he had been looking for. There was a clear space between the opposing flagships, and Buchanan felt positive of his ability to send Farragut and his walls of oak, shattered, crushed, beaten, to the bottom of the bay. Up to the commencement of the war they had been warm friends; now each was hoping for the overthrow of the other, and had Buchanan possessed the same degree of dogged determination as his former associate, it is possible both flagships might have terminated their career in the furious onset. Had the ram struck fair, with her power and momentum, she would have forced her way to the foremast of the Hartford, and unable to extricate herself from the shattered frigate would have sunk side by side with her antagonist. But it was ordered otherwise: the Tennessee swerved, struck a glancing blow on the port bow, injuring the frigate but slightly, and the two vessels grated and rasped sullenly by each other.

Buchanan now met with a vexatious turn of fortune which no good seamanship or precaution could have avoided. He could not have wished for a more favorable opportunity to try his powerful guns on his wooden rival, and the order was at once passed to "give it to her!" But one gun after another in rapid succession missed fire, the primers failed to explode except at one gun, which sent a shell through the berth-deck, above the water-line, killing five men and wounding eight—the last hostile shot that ever was fired at the old flagship. The muzzle of the gun was so close that the powder blackened the ship's side. It was the most unfortunate moment of the combat for Buchanan; his would-be victim glided from his side, pouring in a broadside of solid shot as a parting salute, which merely dented the ram's armor and bounded harmlessly into the air.

While the Hartford was about to ram the Tennessee, Farragut sprang into the port mizzen-rigging in order to overlook the manœuver. He was a conspicuous target, in his uniform, for either a rifle or a pistol ball. Lieutenant Watson, his aid, who observed his peril, begged him not to remain in so exposed a position; but he remained that he might better observe the impending collision. Watson picked up a piece of rope off the poop and made a turn around his body, securing the end to the mizzen shrouds. In this position the admiral remained until the two

ships separated; so that Brownell, in his poem of the "Bay Fight," does not err very badly in making use of the line and putting the admiral "high in the mizzen shroud."

Captain Drayton during the ramming was on the top-gallant forecastle, and catching a glimpse of Buchanan's head above the hatch on the casemate, cried: "Infernal traitor, are you afraid of a wooden ship?" and shook his marine glasses in a threatening manner. Lieutenant Watson at the same time fired his revolver at him, which warm reception Buchanan acknowledged by prudently disappearing. So close were the two vessels that Farragut from his position could easily have jumped to the deck of the ram. The ram now dropped astern and was immediately taken in hand by the rest of the fleet, while the Hartford circled around to obtain a favorable position for renewing her fight.

It was a reception Buchanan had not calculated upon receiving. He had hoped for a different state of affairs, with his iron prow carrying panic and destruction through the wooden fleet as at Hampton Roads; and the spectators from the forts began to doubt seriously that the iron ram was so much of a prodigy, after all. At any rate, there was no appearance or prospect of victory appearing on the banner of the ironclad. The flagstaff and its shot-riddled flag had long since disappeared, to be replaced by another lashed to a boat-hook thrust through the grating that covered the casemate. The rattle of the nine-inch shot on the sloping sides of the ram made the stout craft quiver and tremble, while the shocks from the huge wooden vessels ramming him demoralized and disheartened the crew. They were rapidly losing faith in the unwieldy monster, and loudly muttered their dissatisfaction.

Lieutenant Wharton, of the Tennessee, in speaking of the effect of the monitor's fire, thus describes it:

"The Monongahela was hardly clear of us when a hideous-looking monster came creeping up on our port side, whose slowly-revolving turret revealed the cavernous depths of a mammoth gun. 'Stand clear of the port side!' I shouted. A moment after a thunderous report shook us all, while a blast of dense sulphurous smoke covered our port holes, and 440 pounds of iron, impelled by sixty pounds of powder, admitted daylight through our side, where, before it struck, there had been over two feet of solid wood, covered with five inches of solid iron. This was the only fifteen-inch shot that hit us fair, It did not come through; the inside netting caught the splinters, and there were no casualties from it. I was glad to find myself alive after that shot."

As the Hartford turned to renew her attack on the ram, she steamed in front of the Lackawanna, which had already pointed for the Tennessee, and was running down upon her at full speed. Thick clouds of smoke were eddying about, and the Lackawanna, discovering the Hartford too late, reversed her engine, putting her helm hard-a-starboard. The force of the blow was broken, but she struck the flagship two guns forward of the mizzen-rigging, knocking two ports into one, throwing two guns over on deck, carrying away the rail to the mizzen-rigging, and cutting the Hartford down nearly to the water's edge. The collision carried consternation and alarm to the Hartford's men, who imagined that the flagship had received her death-blow, and that from the hands of a friend. "Save the admiral!" was the cry that resounded along the deck, but that official, cool as ever, had sprung into the starboard mizzen-rigging, looked over the side of the ship, and finding there were still a few inches of splintered planking left above the water's edge, instantly ordered the ship ahead again at full speed, after the ram.

The three monitors had now arrived in position, and were paying undivided attention to the Tennessee, which still pluckily continued the fight. The Chickasaw ranged up under the stern of the ram, firing as rapidly as her huge guns would permit, while the Winnebago and Manhattan remained on either quarter. The Hartford proceeded to repair damages inflicted by the Lackawanna, and was soon reported ready. Farragut was anxious to remain in close proximity to the ram, and never, in any of his previous battles, had exhibited so much anxiety.

The Ossipee, Lackawanna, Monongahela, and Hartford were all preparing to run down the ram under full heads of steam, while Buchanan, with closed ports, moved slowly ahead, receiving the thundering blows from the monitor's fifteen-inch guns without once replying to their fire. Feebly and laboriously the bows of the Tennessee were turned toward Fort Morgan, and it was apparent that the champion of the South was sorely beset. Like a knight of old, encased in well-tried armor, surrounded by enemies, with all hope gone and everything lost save honor and reputation, receiving blow after blow upon armor dented and gaping with wounds, yet disdaining to surrender, to such might be likened the

plight Buchanan found himself in. The ram had been shorn of all her glory, naught remaining but her sloping casemates as a target for the guns of the Union fleet. Her smoke-stack had disappeared, flagstaff and ensign had succumbed, steering gear shot away, and several of her port shutters jammed, preventing the working of her guns. Many of her plates had been started by the eleven-inch shot of the Chickasaw, while the smashing of her shield by the Manhattan's bolt added materially to the ram's distress.

The gun-deck was filled by smoke escaping from the stump of the pipe, and the heat was so great that the men, although many of them had stripped to the waist, were in great distress.

Urged on by desperation, Admiral Buchanan had descended to the gun-deck and taken personal charge of the battery. He was a brave man, had always been successful in whatever he had undertaken, and had been held in high estimation by the department previous to the Rebellion. He organized the Naval Academy; co-operated in landing the troops at Vera Cruz, and was one of the leading spirits of the navy at the capture of San Juan d'Ulloa; he was among the first to step foot on the soil of Japan in the expedition of Commodore Perry; and later was honored by the President with the position of commandant of the navy yard at Washington. He had an extensive acquaintance in the service, and should have known the character of the men pitted against him well enough to have considered his task hopeless in conquering such men as Farragut and his rugged lieutenants. Once on the gun-deck, Buchanan sent for a machinist to back out the pivot pin of a jammed stern-post shutter, in order that the gun might be brought into action again, when a shot struck the casemate just outside of where the man was sitting, and the concussion shivered him into atoms as minute as sausage meat; his remains were shoveled into fire-buckets. The same shot started an iron splinter that struck Buchanan and fractured his leg, compelling him to be carried below.

The responsibility of command now devolved upon Captain Johnston, who found that the ram could revolve her screw and use three guns if a foe passed in front of their muzzles, but she could not be steered, and was therefore practically at the mercy of her adversaries. From the pilot-house he listened to the incessant battering kept up on the after end of the shield, which was now so thoroughly shattered that it was a question of a very short time when it must

HARTFORD AND TENNESSEE—"THE TWO VESSELS RASPED SULLENLY BY EACH OTHER."

succumb, exposing the gun-deck to a raking fire. He beheld each Federal ship either cannonading the Tennessee or preparing to ram her. It had been fifteen minutes since she had discharged a gun, while with every moment her armor was growing weaker under the tremendous hammering to which she was being subjected. Filled with regret, Johnston sought the side of Buchanan, communicating to him the true state of affairs.

"Do the best you can, Johnston, and when all is done, surrender," was the reply, as he groaned with pain on his bed of torture.

The Ossipee was within a few yards of the ram when LeRoy saw the white flag fluttering from the Tennessee. He stopped his engines, backing hard to avoid collision. LeRoy and Johnston were old shipmates, and their meeting was marked by warmth and hearty good feeling. Johnston formally surrendered the ram to Commander LeRoy, and his sword and that of Admiral Buchanan were afterwards delivered to Farragut.

The appearance of the white flag was hailed by cheers from all the sailors of the fleet, and many a long breath of satisfaction was indulged in as they viewed the fruits of their valor. The fleet anchored where it had fought, with the Tennessee in their midst, a prize crew on board,

and the Stars and Stripes flying from an improvised flagstaff. Thus terminated the great naval contest, leaving Farragut victor in the most desperate battle he had ever been in—as he expressed it—since the famous fight in the old Essex.

The Hartford was a sorry-looking vessel. She had been struck twenty times by shot and shell, her punishment having been very severe; but in two hours time, all hands working with a will, the marks of the great battle were almost obliterated. The Richmond passed the forts under cover of an impenetrable cloud of smoke, escaping the torrent of shot and shell encountered by the balance of the fleet. When the surgeon's report was handed to the captain, "two men slightly wounded," he was indignant. "What!" he cried, "only two wounded; is that all? How is it there are none killed? They will think at home that this vessel was not in the fight!" An old sailor suggested the propriety of killing two of the after-guard sweepers to swell the report.

Fort Morgan refused to surrender, and steps were at once taken to bring the garrison to terms. Army and navy worked in unison, and a battery of four nine-inch guns were landed from the Hartford to assist the army, Lieutenant Tyson having charge of them. At daylight on the 23d, the bombardment of the fort began from the shore batteries, the monitors and ships

ON BOARD THE TENNESSEE.

"A thunderous report shook us all, while a blast of dense sulphurous smoke covered our port holes, and 440 pounds of iron, impelled by sixty pounds of powder, admitted daylight through our side, where, before it struck, there had been over two feet of solid wood, covered with five inches of solid iron."—Page 55.

inside the Bay of Mobile and those outside, and no hotter shelling was ever maintained for twenty-four hours. It brought the fort speedily to terms, and with the disappearance of the flag from the ramparts, Farragut remained undisputed master of Mobile Bay and its approaches. It was the crowning event of his illustrious career.

The admiral, in alluding to the engagement, expressed himself as follows: "It was the hardest earned victory of my life, and one momentous to the country, over the ram Tennessee. I always said I was the proper man to fight her, because I was one of those who believed I could do it successfully. I was certainly honest in my convictions and determined in my will, but I did not know how formidable the Tennessee was."

The two admirals did not meet. Farragut sent his fleet surgeon, J. C. Palmer, on board to attend to him, and there is no question but that he saved Admiral Buchanan's leg, if not his life. It had been proposed by the Confederate fleet surgeon to resort to amputation, but upon examination Dr. Palmer declined to have the operation performed; and for his skillful management of the case received grateful acknowledgments in after years from Buchanan. The Metacomet conveyed him and other Confederates, under a flag of truce, to Pensacola, where in the hospital every care and attention was bestowed upon the wounded Confederates. Buchanan after the war was president of the Maryland Agricultural College. He died at "The Rest," his splendid residence in Maryland, May, 1874.

In no battle during the war did the sailors exhibit greater courage and determination than in the battle of Mobile Bay, especially when the Tennessee made her attack upon the fleet. Men on the Hartford who were so seriously wounded that they could not stand would crawl back to their guns, anxious to encourage, with their last breath, their comrades whom they could no longer assist. Men with the pallor of death on their faces essayed to cheer when they heard that the Tennessee had struck her flag, and with the knowledge would turn in their hammocks to die contentedly—knowing that to the last they had served their country well. To quote from a celebrated Union admiral:

"It is not always in the excitement of battle that these heroic acts are noticed, and many officers thought enough of their sailors to mention those who had especially distinguished themselves. The medal of honor was as much

as they could expect, but these badges were as much prized as were the decorations which Napoleon served out to his brave soldiers after a victory. It is not the value of the medal, for it is only made of copper; it is the fact that a sailor's services are noticed that makes him the happiest of men, and he treasures the mementos of his services with care and pride."

Admiral Farragut, in relation to the question of attacking Mobile, expressed himself as follows:

"As this is the last of my work, I expect a little respite, unless the Government want the city of Mobile, which I think is bad policy. It would be an elephant, and take a large army to hold it; and besides, all the traitors and rascally speculators would flock to that city and pour into the Confederacy the wealth of New York. If the Government wish it taken, they must send the means to hold it. I must confess I don't like to work in seven and nine feet of water, and there is no more within several miles of Mobile. The enemy has barricaded the channel with forts, piles, and sunken vessels. Now, you know I am in no way diffident about going anywhere in the Hartford; but when I have to leave her and take to a craft drawing six feet of water, I feel badly."

On the 27th of August, Farragut wrote to the Department, stating that his health was failing and that he wanted rest. It had been the intention of the Department to assign him to the command of the Fort Fisher expedition, and orders to that effect were made out on September 5, 1864, but in deference to the admiral's wishes they were revoked and Admiral Porter's name substituted. The action of the Department in giving Rear-Admiral Porter the command instead of Farragut was much commented upon and never fully understood by the country, which had learned to appreciate the noble qualities of Farragut and gave him its unstinted confidence. Secretary Welles has stated that "the great admiral always regretted—though on his account I did not—that he had reported his physical sufferings and low state of health before any orders were received or even issued."

After a short visit to Pensacola and New Orleans the Hartford sailed for New York, where her crew were discharged at the Brooklyn Navy Yard, December 24, 1864. Of the 380 men that formed her crew when she sailed from Philadelphia three years before, but forty remained. During that period Farragut had fought eleven battles. Some of the ship's company had deserted, many had succumbed to the malarial diseases common to the Mississippi River, and the balance were killed or wounded in battle. Of the officers but three remained—Admiral Farragut, Lieutenant Watson, and Lieutenant Tyson.

At the Brooklyn Navy Yard, Farragut bade a final adieu to his well-beloved and battle-scarred ship that with him had shared his perils, his triumphs, and final success. Her staunch timbers bore him from Southern seas to the snow-clad North, where a grateful nation bestowed upon him another laurel, a fresh honor worthily won, a commission as vice-admiral, bearing date December 23, 1864. It was a Christmas gift that the old sailor might well view with pride and satisfaction. As senior rear-admiral, Farragut hoisted a plain square blue flag at New Orleans, on the main masthead of the Hartford. Afterwards the flag was shifted to the mizzen; thence, on his promotion to vice-admiral, it waved from the fore; and on his elevation to full admiral, July 25, 1866, it floated again high up on the main.

A SORROW OF '62.

LEONORA BECK.

INTO the moonlight he rode swift away,
  Bearing her kiss on his smiling red lips;
Fragrantly dying, upon his breast lay
  A rose, fastened there by her sweet finger-tips.
Booted and spurred and wearing the gray,
  Boldly he galloped, and gaily he sang:
"I love you, my love; we will love on for aye!"
  Tender the words were and clear the notes rang

    *   *   *   *   *

In at her casement the moonbeams still streamed,
  Dancing with fairy feet through the rose-vine,
While the bright maiden, reposing there, dreamed
  Of her brave lover just crossing the line.
Well that she heard not the hiss of the lead
  Piercing a path through the rose on his breast,
Nor saw the gray coat, now bedabbled with red,
  Nor caught his last sigh, as he murmured "Celeste!"

Fort Morgan.   Manhattan.   Tecumseh.   Brooklyn.   Octorara.   Hartford.   Metacomet.   Richmond.   Fort Royal.   Lackawanna.   Monongahela.
                                                                                                                          Seminole.   Kennebec.

FARRAGUT'S FLEET PASSING FORT MORGAN.

61

WITH BUCHANAN ON THE TENNESSEE.

D. B. Conrad, M. D., late Fleet Surgeon, U. S. Navy and C. S. Navy.

THIRTY years ago this month (August, 1894) a memorable action was fought in Mobile Bay, between iron-clads of different type, design, and armament; one with a shield and rifled guns, the other with turrets and Dahlgrens (smooth-bores). Many men are now living in New Orleans and Mobile who participated in or saw this conflict; there are many sons and daughters of the men living who have heard of it at the fireside. There are many others who have never heard of the fight, fought so near their homes. For these, too, I write.

The Bay of Mobile was of infinite use and importance to the Confederates, who guarded and held it by two forts, Morgan and Gaines, at its entrance. By holding it they held safe the city of Mobile from attack by water; it could only be captured by a combined army and navy attack, so it was a safe depot for blockade-runners, easy to go out of and enter, and if it was such to the Confederates, how much greater was it to the Federals? For they were compelled to keep their large blockade fleet outside, exposed to all the storms of the gulf. They could only be victualed and watered by going away, one at a time, to Pensacola, their only port; their sick had to be transported to the same place, and the wear and tear both to vessels and crews was fearful, as a constant, vigilant, and never-ceasing watch, both by officers and men, had to be kept up, day and night, year in and year out. The officers were in three watches, the men in two, guarding themselves against night attacks by torpedo-boats or assault by the Confederate gunboats, and seeing that no vessel came out and that none went in. All this had to be endured, or the bay captured and held by the fleet. This was finally determined on by Farragut, and he only awaited the arrival of iron-clads to make sure his end. Finding this plan determined on, the Confederates bestirred themselves. At the hamlet of Selma, on the river above, they built one iron-clad, on the plan of the Merrimac, their resources being exhausted to do even this. Slowly the wooden structure approached completion, then more slowly was it ironed all over above the water-line, then towed down to Mobile, where it was equipped with eight-inch rifle-guns.

Then, when officers and men, provisions and water had been taken on board, all ready for action, she started down the bay, nearly thirty miles, to go outside in rough water and attack the enemy's wooden fleet before the ironclads arrived; when, on arriving at the bar of sand caused by Dog Run emptying into the bay, it was found that the bar had shoaled to such an extent that the iron-clad, now christened the Tennessee, drew three feet more water than there was under her. The only expedient that offered itself, which was safe and speedy, was to build of huge square timbers two enormous air-tight tanks, each as high as a two-story house. They were to be towed alongside of the ram and sunk to the water's edge by opening the valves, then all lashed together securely, making one vessel, as it were, of them; the water was pumped out of these tanks, and the air entering, they, by their buoyancy, lifted the huge ship clear of the bottom, then steam tugs towed her over the bar. This was done in May, 1864; it should have been so many months before, for these so-called "camels" were finished in March. But on their arrival off Mobile they were burned by Federal emissaries, who were paid well for their daring deed.

Right here we may interrupt our story to say that the secret service fund was well spent by Admiral Farragut, for we were delayed several months in building two more "camels," and by that time his ironclads were built and on their way to him. I must mention the desertion of five men the day after the destruction of the camels; they had been working on our ironclad, and furnished him with all details of her construction, all her weak points, of the character of her engines, the calibre of her armament, of all of which information he availed himself when the eventful day of action came. In addition to this, they were to be received into the Federal service if they destroyed these camels. These large bribes were offered for the reason that the fleet lying outside of Fort Morgan were solely wooden ships, and could not cope with nor resist the attack of our ironclad, and the Federal ironclads had not yet arrived. Finally, one June day we were towed over the bar down the bay; then, casting loose, we steamed out to attack the Federal fleet. Reach-

ing the passage between the two forts, we encountered rough water and found that, owing to
want of buoyancy, we were in great danger of
being water-logged and sunk by the amount of
water that swept inboard. The ram lay deep
in the water, solid and motionless as a cast-iron
platform or raft, and every sea tumbling over
her came inboard in such masses that the fires
in the engine-room were nearly put out and the
empty vessel itself filled with salt water. So,
discomfited, we put back under the fort, in
smooth water, and all thought of attacking the
fleet outside was dismissed. Then the defects,
which this short cruise of ten hours had developed, were looked into. Our engines had been
taken from an old river boat; they were weak
and old, and could only force us through the
water about two miles an hour. They could
not be strengthened by any method. The
rudder-chains, by which the ship was steered,
were found to be exposed to the enemy's shot,
being in their whole length outside the iron
deck; they were covered over by a slight coat-
ing of iron rail. The capacity of the ram inboard to accommodate her crew was fearfully
deficient; all officers and men, when the weather
admitted, slept outside on top of the iron shield
and decks, but in rainy times it was awful to
endure such close quarters at night; but we
bore it June and July, under the sloping sides
of the shield, in shape like the roof of a square
house, about twelve feet in height and forty-
eight in length. On July 26th, Admiral Buchanan and staff came aboard; for, from his information, a fierce fight was imminent, when,
on the 1st of August, 1864, we saw a decided
increase in the Federal fleet, which was then
listlessly at anchor outside of Fort Morgan, in
the Gulf of Mexico.

This reinforcement consisted of ten wooden
frigates, all stripped to a "girt line" and clean
for action, their topmasts sent down on deck
and devoid of everything that seemed like extra
rigging; they appeared like prize-fighters ready
for the "ring." Then we knew that trouble
was ahead, and wondered to ourselves why they
did not enter the bay. On the 3d of August we
noticed another addition to the already formidable fleet—four strange-looking, long, black-
monsters, the new ironclads; and they were
what the Federals had been so anxiously waiting for. At the distance of four miles their
lengthy, dark lines could only be distinguished
from the sea, on which they sat motionless,
by the continuous volume of thick smoke

issuing from their low smoke-stacks, which appeared to come out of the ocean itself. These
curious-looking craft made their advent on the
evening of the 4th of August, and then we knew
that the "gage of battle" was offered.

———

We had been very uncomfortable for many
weeks in our berths on board the Tennessee, in
consequence of the prevailing heavy rains wetting the decks, and the terribly moist, hot
atmosphere, which was like that oppressiveness
which precedes a tornado. It was, therefore,
impossible to sleep inside; besides, from the
want of properly cooked food and the continuous
wetting of the decks at night, the officers and
men were rendered desperate. We knew that
the impending action would soon be determined
one way or the other, and everyone looked forward to it with a positive feeling of relief.

I had been sleeping on the deck of the admiral's cabin for two or three nights, when at
daybreak on the 5th of August the old quartermaster came down the ladder, rousing us up
with his gruff voice, saying: "Admiral, the
officer of the deck bids me report that the
enemy's fleet is under way!" Jumping up,
still half asleep, we came on deck, and sure
enough, there was the enemy heading for the
"passage" past the fort. The grand old admiral of sixty years, with his countenance rigid
and stern, showing a determination for battle in
every line, then gave his only order: "Get
under way, Captain Johnson; head for the leading vessel of the enemy, and fight each one as
they pass!"

The fort and fleet by this time had opened
fire, and the Tennessee replied, standing close
in and meeting each foremost vessel as it came
up. We could see two long lines of men-of-war;
the innermost was composed of the four monitors, and the outer of the ten wooden frigates,
all engaging the fort and fleet. Just at the
moment we expected the monitors to open fire
upon us, there was a halt in the progress of the
enemy's fleet. We observed that one of the
monitors was apparently at a stand-still; "laid
to" for a moment, seemed to reel, then slowly
disappeared in the gulf. Immediately immense
bubbles of steam, as large as cauldrons, rose to
the surface of the water, and only eight human
beings could be seen in the turmoil. Boats were
sent to their rescue, both from the fort and fleet,
and they were saved. Thus the monitor Tecumseh, at the commencement of the fight, struck by
a torpedo, went to her fate at the bottom of the

gulf, where she still lies. Sunk with her was her chivalric commander, T. A. M. Craven. The pilot, an engineer, and two seamen were the only survivors picked up by the Federal boats, and they were on duty in the turret. The pilot, with whom I sometime afterwards conversed at Pensacola on the subject, told me that when the vessel careened so that water began to run into the mouth of the turret, he and Captain Craven were on the ladder together, the captain on the top step, with the way open for his easy and honorable escape. The pilot said: "Go ahead, captain!" "No, sir!" replied Captain Craven. "After you, pilot; I leave my ship last!" Upon this the pilot sprung up, and the gallant Craven went down, sucked under in the vortex, thus sacrificing himself through a chivalric sense of duty.

There was dead silence on board the Tennessee; the men peered through the port-holes at the awful catastrophe and spoke to each other only in whispers, for they all knew that the same fate was probably awaiting us, for we were then directly over the "torpedo bed," and shut up tightly as we were in our "iron capsule," in another moment it might prove our coffin.

At this juncture the enemy's leading vessel "backed water" and steered to one side, which arrested the progress of the whole squadron. But at this supreme moment the second vessel, Admiral Farragut's flagship, the Hartford, forged ahead, and Farragut, showing the nerve and determination of the officer and the man, gave the order: "—— the torpedoes! Go ahead!" and away he went, crashing through their bed to victory and renown. Some of the officers told me afterwards that they could hear the torpedoes snapping under the bottoms of their ships, and that they expected every moment to be blown into high air.

The slightest delay at that time on the part of Farragut, subjected as he was to the terrible fire of the fort and fleet, would have been disaster, defeat, and the probable loss of his entire squadron, but he proved to be the man for the emergency.

We in the Tennessee, advancing very slowly, at the rate of about two miles an hour, met the leading vessels of the enemy as they passed and fought them face to face, but their fire was so destructive, continuous, and severe that after we emerged from it, there was nothing left standing as large as your little finger. Everything had been shot away—smoke-stacks, boats, davits, staunchions, and, in fact, "fore and aft,"

our deck had been swept absolutely clean. A few of our men were slightly wounded, and when the last vessel had passed us and been fought in turn, we had been in action more than an hour and a half; and then the enemy's fleet, somewhat disabled, of course, kept on up the bay and anchored about four miles away. So ended the first part of the fight. Farragut had already won half the battle; he had passed the fort and fleet and had ten wooden vessels and three monitors left in good fighting trim.

———

Neither the officers nor men of either fleet had as yet been to breakfast, and the order was given: "Go to breakfast!" For us on the Tennessee to eat below was simply impossible, on account of the heat and humidity. The heat below was terrific; intense thirst universally prevailed. The men rushed to the "scuttle butts" or water-tanks, and drank greedily. Soon "hard-tack" and coffee were furnished, the men all eating standing, creeping out of the ports of the shield to get a little fresh air, the officers going to the upper deck. Admiral Buchanan, grim, silent, and rigid with prospective fighting, was "stumping" up and down the deck, lame from a wound received in his first engagement in the Merrimac, and in about fifteen minutes we observed that, instead of heading for the safe "lee" of the fort, our iron prow was pointed for the enemy's fleet. Suppressed exclamations were beginning to be heard from the officers and crew. "The old admiral has not had his fight out yet; he is heading for that big fleet; he will get his 'fill' of it up there."

Slowly and gradually this fact became apparent to us, and I, being on his staff and in close association with him, ventured to ask him: "Are you going into that fleet, admiral?" "I am, sir!" was his reply. Without intending to be heard by him, I said to an officer standing near me: "Well, we'll never come out of there whole!" But Buchanan had heard my remark, and, turning round, said sharply: "That's my lookout, sir!" And now began the second part of the fight.

I may as well explain here why he did this much-criticised and desperate deed of daring. He told me his reasons long afterward, as follows: He had only six hours coal on board, and he intended to expend that in fighting. He did not mean to be trapped like a rat in a hole and made surrender without a struggle. Then he meant to go to the "lee" of the fort and assist

General Page in the defence of the place. This calculation was unluckily prevented by the shooting away of the rudder chains of the Tennessee in this second engagement.

As we approached the enemy's fleet, one after another of Farragut's ten wooden frigates swept out in a wide circle, and by the time we reached the point where the monitors were, a huge leading frigate was coming at us at the rate of ten miles an hour. A column of white foam, formed of the "dead water," piled in front of its bows many feet high. Heavy cannonading from the monitors was going on at this time, when this leading wooden vessel came rapidly bearing down on us, bent on the destruction of the formidable ram, which we on board the Tennessee fully realized as the supreme moment of the test of our strength. We had escaped from the "torpedo bed" safe and "on top," and were now to take our chances of being "run under" by the heavy wooden frigates that were fast nearing us. Each vessel had her own bows heavily ironed for the purpose of cutting down and sinking the Tennessee, as such were the orders of Admiral Farragut.

Captain Johnson, in the pilot-house, now gave the word to officers and men: "Steady yourselves when she strikes; stand by and be ready!" Not a word was heard on the deck under its shelving roof, where the officers and men, standing by their guns, appeared, silent and rigid, awaiting their fate. Captain Johnson shouted out: "We are all right; they can never run us under now!" As he spoke, the leading vessel had struck against our "overhang" with tremendous impact; had shivered its iron prow in the clash, but only succeeded in whirling the Tennessee around as if she were swung on a pivot.

I was sitting on the "combing of the hatch," having nothing to do as yet, a close observer as each vessel in turn struck us. At the moment of impact they slid alongside of us, and our "black wales" came in contact. At a distance of ten feet they poured their broadside of twenty eleven-inch guns into us. This continued for more than an hour, and as each vessel "rammed" the Tennessee and slid alongside they followed, discharging their broadsides fast and furious, so that the noise was one continuous, deafening roar. You could only hear voices when close to the speaker, and the reverberation was so great that bleeding at the nose was not infrequent.

Soon the wounded began to pour down to me.

Stripped to their waist, the white skins of the men exhibited curious dark blue elevations and hard spots. Cutting down to these, I found that unburnt cubes of cannon powder that had poured into the port had perforated the flesh and made these great blue ridges under the skin. Their sufferings were very severe, for it was as if they had been shot with red-hot bullets, but no serious effects followed.

———

Now all the wooden vessels, disabled and their prows broken off, anchored in succession over a mile away. Then Admiral Farragut signaled to the monitors: "Destroy the ram!" Soon these three grim monsters, at thirty yards distance, took their position on each quarter of the Tennessee as she lay nearly motionless, her rudder having been shot away with grape in the fight. We knew that we were hopelessly disabled and that victory was impossible, as all we could do was to move around very slowly in a circle, and the only chance left to us to crawl under the shelter of Fort Morgan.

For an hour and a half the monitors pounded us with solid shot fired with a charge of sixty pounds of powder from their eleven-inch guns, determined to crush in the "shield" of the Tennessee, as thirty pounds of powder was the "regulation amount." In the midst of this continuous pounding the port-shutter of one of our guns was jammed by a shot, so that it would neither open nor shut, making it impossible to work the piece. The admiral then sent for some of the firemen from below to drive the bolt out. Four men came up, and two of them holding the bolt back, the others struck it with sledge-hammers. While they were thus working, suddenly there was a dull sounding impact, and at the same instant the men whose backs were against the shield were riven into pieces. I saw their limbs and chests, severed and mangled, scattered about the deck, their hearts lying near their bodies. All of the gun's crew and the admiral were covered from head to foot with blood, flesh, and viscera. I thought at first the admiral was mortally wounded. The fragments and members of the dead men were shoveled up, put in buckets and hammocks, and stuck below.

Engineer J. C. O'Connell, one of the wounded, had a pistol ball through his shoulder. "How in the world did you manage to get this?" I asked him. He replied: "Why, I was off watch and had nothing to do, so while the Hartford was lying alongside of us a Yankee cursed me through the port-hole and I jabbed him with my bayonet in the body, and his comrade shot me with his revolver." Cutting the ball out I proposed to give him morphine, as he was suffering terribly, but he said: "None of that for me, doctor; when we go down I want to be up and take my chances of getting out of some port-hole." Another man was wounded in the ear when fighting in the same manner as the engineer, but he always declared he got even by the use of his bayonet. I merely mention these facts to show how close the fighting was, when men could kill or wound each other through the port-holes of each vessel.

While attending the engineer, Aide Carter came down the ladder in great haste and said: "Doctor, the admiral is wounded." "Well, bring him below," I replied. "I can't do it," he answered; "haven't time. I'm carrying orders for Captain Johnson." So up I went, asked some officer whom I saw: "Where is the admiral?" "Don't know," he replied. "We are all at work loading and firing; got too much to do to think of anything else!" Then I looked for the gallant commander myself, and lying curled up under the sharp angle of the roof discovered the old white-haired man. He was grim, silent and betrayed no evidence of his great pain. I went up to him and asked: "Admiral, are you badly hurt?" "Don't know," he replied, but I saw one of his legs crushed up under his body, and, as I could get no help, raised him up with great caution, and clasping his arms around my neck carried him on my back down the ladder to the "cockpit," his broken leg slapping against me as we moved slowly along. After applying a temporary bandage he sat up on the deck and received reports from Captain Johnson regarding the progress of the fight. Captain Johnson soon came down in person, and the admiral greeted him with: "Well, Johnson, they have got me again. You'll have to look out for her now; it is your fight." "All right," answered the captain, "I'll do the best I know how."

In the course of half an hour Captain Johnson again made his appearance below and reported to the admiral that all the frigates had "hauled off," but that three monitors had taken position on our quarters. He added that we could not bring a gun to bear and that the enemy's solid shot were gradually smashing in the "shield," and not having been able to fire for thirty minutes the men were fast becoming demoralized from sheer inactivity, and that

from the smashing of the "shield" they were seeking shelter, which showed their condition mentally. "Well, Johnson," said the admiral at this precarious juncture, "fight to the last; then, to save these brave men, when there is no longer hope, surrender."

In twenty minutes more the firing ceased, Captain Johnson having bravely gone up alone on the exposed roof with a handkerchief on a "boarding-pike," and the surrender was effected. Then we immediately carried all our wounded up on the roof into the fresh air, which they so much needed.

————

From that elevated place, I witnessed the rush of the petty officers and men of the monitors which were nearest to us, to board the captured ship, to procure relics and newspaper renown. Two creatures dressed in the blue shirts, begrimed and black with powder, rushed up to the wounded admiral and demanded his sword. His aide refused peremptorily, whereupon one of them stooped as if to take it, upon which Aide Forrest warned him not to touch it, as it would only be given to Admiral Farragut or his authorized representatives. Still the man attempted to seize it, whereupon Forrest knocked him off the "shield" to the deck below. At this critical moment, when a fight was imminent, I saw a boat nearing, flying a captain's pennant, and running down as it came alongside, I recognized an old shipmate, Captain Le Roy. Hurriedly explaining to him our position, he mounted the "shield," and assuming command, he arrested the obnoxious man and sent him under guard to his boat.

The sword was then given to Captain Giraud by Admiral Buchanan, to be carried to Admiral Farragut. Our flag, smoke-stained and torn, had been seized by the other man and hastily concealed in his shirt bosom. He was brought before Captain Le Roy, and amidst the laughter and jeers of his companions, was compelled to draw it forth from its hiding-place, and it was sent on board the flagship.

Captain Le Roy, who was an old friend of us both, immediately had private supplies brought and did everything in his power to aid his former shipmate, the wounded admiral. He brought a kind message from Admiral Farragut, in which the latter expressed regret to hear of Admiral Buchanan's wound, and offered to do anything in his power, wishing to know what he desired. This was accepted by Admiral Buchanan in the same kind spirit in which it was given, and as one of his staff-officers, I was sent on board the Hartford with the reply that, appreciating the kind message, he had only to ask that his fleet-surgeon and his aides might be allowed to accompany him wherever he might be sent, until his recovery from his wound. Boarding the Hartford by Captain Le Roy's steam launch, and ascending by the "man-rope," I mounted the hammock netting, as the whole starboard side, amidship, and the gangway had been carried away, as I was afterwards told, by one of their own frigates having collided with the Hartford, after "ramming" the Tennessee. From the hammock netting the scene was one of carnage and devastation. The spar-deck was covered and littered with broken gun-carriages, shattered boats, disabled guns, and a long line of grim corpses, dressed in blue, lying side by side. The officer accompanying me told me that those men, two whole guns' crews, were all killed by splinters, and pointing with his hand to a piece of "weather-boarding," ten feet long and four inches wide, I received my first vivid idea of what a splinter was, or what was meant by a splinter.

Descending, we threaded our way, and ascending the poop, where all the officers were standing, I was taken up and introduced to Admiral Farragut, whom I found a very quiet, unassuming man, and not in the least flurried by his great victory. In the kindest manner, he inquired regarding the severity of the admiral's wound, and then gave the necessary orders to carry out Admiral Buchanan's request.

We then thought that the admiral's leg would have to be amputated that evening or the next morning. In speaking to the admiral about his chances of recovery and the proposed amputation, he replied: "I have nothing to do with it. It is your leg now. Do your best." It was this spirit of firmness and equanimity which not only saved Admiral Buchanan's life, but ultimately saved his leg also. He was carried on board of Captain James Jouett's ship, the Metacomet, which was temporarily converted into a hospital. We remained on board that night and were cared for in a very kind way by Captain Jouett, to whom Admiral Buchanan always expressed himself as deeply indebted.

———

The next morning, at my suggestion, a flag of truce was sent to General Page, commanding Fort Morgan, representing our condition, sending the names of our dead, wounded, and the great number of Federal dead and wounded on board, and asking, in the name of humanity, to be allowed to pass the fort and convey them to the large naval hospital at Pensacola, where they all could receive the same treatment. To this request General Page promptly responded, and we passed out, and in eight hours were all safely housed in the ample hospital, where we were treated by old naval friends in the warmest and kindest manner. Medical Director Turner was in charge, and we remained there until December, when Admiral Buchanan, being able to hobble around on crutches, was conveyed to Fort Warren, with his aides, and I was sent back to Mobile in Captain Jouett's ship, under flag of truce.

Daily with the admiral in the hospital at Pensacola for four months, he explained his whole plan of action to me of that second fight in Mobile Bay, as follows: "I did not expect to do the passing vessels any serious injury; the guns of Fort Morgan were thought capable of doing that. I expected that the monitors would then and there surround me and pound the shield in, but when all the Federal vessels had passed up and anchored four miles away, then I saw that a long siege was intended by the army and navy, which, with its numerous transports at anchor under Pelican Island, were debarking nearly 10,000 infantry. Having the example before me of the blowing up of the Merrimac in the James River by our own officers, without a fight, and their being caught in such a trap, I determined, by an unexpected dash into the fleet, to attack and do it all the damage in my power; to expend all my ammunition and what little coal I had on board (only six hours' steaming), and then, having done all I could with what resources I had, to retire under the guns of the fort, and being without motive power, there to lie and assist in repulsing the attacks and assaults on the fort."

The unexpectedness of the second attack is well illustrated by Admiral Farragut's remark at the time. After having anchored, all hands were piped to breakfast, when the officer on duty on the deck of the Hartford, seeing the ram slowly heading up the bay for the Federal fleet, reported the fact to Admiral Farragut while he was taking breakfast. "What! is that so?" he inquired. "Just like Buchanan's audacity! Signal to all frigates to immediately get under way and run the ram under, and to the monitors to attack at once."

The greatest injury done to the Tennessee was by the Chickasaw, commanded by Captain G. H.

Perkins. Our pilot, in pointing it out to Captain Johnson, said : " That —— ironclad is hanging to us like a dog, and has smashed our shield already. Fight him ! Sink him, if you can !" The Chickasaw really captured the Tennessee.

Admiral Buchanan was in form and physique one in a thousand. Upright in his carriage, he walked like a game-cock, though halting in his gait in later years, in consequence of having received a minié ball in his right thigh, while commanding the Merrimac in the first ironclad fight in the world. It was while he stood on the deck after sinking the Congress, that he was shot by some Federal infantry on the shore, and from 1864 to his death, in 1871, he was very lame in both legs, the left particularly, which was terribly shattered in the fight when on the Tennessee. He always complained of his " bad luck " in his two great actions ; in the first he was struck down at the moment of victory, and in the last at the moment of defeat. At sixty-two years, he was a strikingly handsome old man ; clean shaven and ruddy of complexion, with a very healthy hue, for he was always remarkably temperate in all his habits. He had a high forehead, fringed with snow-white hair ; thin, close lips ; steel blue eyes ; and projecting conspicuously was that remarkable feature which impressed everyone—his strongly-marked aquiline nose, high, thin, and perfect in outline. When full of fight, he had a peculiar way of drawing down the corners of his mouth until the thin line between his lips formed a perfect arch around his chin.

The Confederate torpedoes, planted at the entrance to Mobile Bay, were the first, and were very primitive in their construction—merely a large beer keg, filled with powder and anchored by chains to a big, flat piece of iron, called a " mushroom." Projecting from the swinging top, some four feet under water, were tubes of glass, filled with sulphuric acid, which, being broken, fell into sugar or starch, causing rapid chemical combustion, and finally a mass of fire, thus exploding the powder. They had been planted so long that many leaked, only one out of ten remaining intact, and this fact explains why so many were run over by the Federal fleet without exploding.

During the four months that we were guarding the entrance to Mobile Bay, we were not by any means safe from the danger of our own contrivances. One hot July morning, we officers were up on the flat deck of the ram, enjoying the sea-breeze, when a floating black object was observed, bobbing up and down. We supposed at first that it was a sort of devil-fish, with its young, as we had killed one, with its " calf," only a few weeks previously ; but the motion was too slow, evidently. A telescope soon revealed the fact that it was a torpedo drifting in with the flood tide. Here was literally the " devil to pay." We could not send a boat-crew after it to tow it out of the way. We could not touch it ; we could not guide it. There were no means in our power to divert it from its course. Finally, at the suggestion of Capt. David Rainy, of the marines, he brought up his whole guard, with loaded muskets, who at once commenced to shoot at the floating keg and sunk it, and not a moment too soon ; for it only disappeared under the water about twenty feet from the ram.

As this sketch is confined exclusively to operations inside the " shield " of the ram Tennessee, I have not thought it germane to detail anything in relation to the other three gunboats of the Confederate fleet, which, being wooden vessels, were sunk or captured early in the first action.

It may be interesting to state the cause of the wound received by Admiral Buchanan. It was by a fragment of iron, either a piece of solid shot or part of the plating of the ram, which fractured the large bone of the leg, comminuting it, and the splintered ends protruding through the muscles and skin.

The admiral's aides were Lieutenants Carter and Forrest ; they tenderly nursed him during the entire four months of his confinement in the hospital at Pensacola, accompanied him to Fort Warren, cared for him while there, and brought him back to Richmond after his exchange. The former is now a prominent citizen of North Carolina ; the latter, until ten years ago, lived in Virginia, since which time I have lost sight of him.

GETTYSBURG.

GEN. MAHONE AT GETTYSBURG.

A FEW sentences will cover what I have to say respecting the great battle of Gettysburg.

At that time I commanded two brigades of Anderson's division, Hill's corps. The morning of the first day's fight, General Lee moved out from Cashtown with Longstreet's and Hill's corps, the latter leading. Ewell was at Carlyle. Early in the forenoon of that day the two leading divisions of Hill's corps came upon and engaged the Federals northwest of Gettysburg, and drove them southward beyond the town.

GEN. MAHONE.

Meanwhile Anderson's division, of 8000 muskets, rested on the side of the road leading from Cashtown to Gettysburg, in full hearing of the battle ahead. Why it especially was not *put in*, I do not know, but suppose it was because General Lee as yet did not know of the whereabouts of the Federal army. He had not heard from General Stewart.

Anderson's division was moved up to the field, over which the day's fighting had taken place, about sundown of that day, and as soon as I had bivouacked my brigade, as was my habit, I rode over much of the field where the battle had taken place and possessed myself, as far as practicable, with a knowledge of the ground. My impression then formed was that "Cemetery Hill" was absolutely essential to the further

success of General Lee's army on that field, and I so expressed myself to Captain Robert H. Fitzhugh, of General Hood's staff. The second day we took the position of Hill's corps in the centre, on Seminary Ridge.

When the order of battle for the third day came to my knowledge, I rode over to General Anderson, my division commander, and begged him to go with me to the crest of Seminary Ridge and take a look at the field over which it was ordered the assault should be made. I said to him what was plain to my mind—that no troops ever formed a line of battle that could cross the plain of fire to which the attacking force would be subjected, and live to enter the enemy's works on "Cemetery Hill" in any organized force; that I could not believe General Lee would insist on such an assault after he had seen the ground. General Anderson declined to go with me or to see General Lee, saying, in substance, that we had nothing to do but to obey the order. The result of the heroic attack was as I had predicted.

Lately a pleasant opportunity was afforded me, in company with distinguished personages, to go over the whole field at Gettysburg, and the wonder to me is that General Lee should ever have made the fight the third day. He had some supreme reason for it, we must presume, but I could see then, as the more clearly I see now, that Gettysburg should never have been fought. If General Lee could not have moved his army to his right and compelled General

RAILROAD CUT—SCENE OF THE CAPTURE OF THE MISSISSIPPI REGIMENTS, JULY 1, 1863.

EASTERN EDGE OF SEMINARY RIDGE; LOOKING TOWARD CEMETERY HILL AND THE ROUND TOPS. POSITION OF PICKETT'S DIVISION BEFORE THE CHARGE, JULY 3, 1863.

Meade to give him battle on his own chosen ground, it were better that he should have fallen back and fought on some field where all the advantages of position were not against him.

The order for me to go in after Pickett's assault had failed was countermanded.

WILLIAM MAHONE.

THE FIRST DAY'S FIGHT.

I OBSERVED a notice of the death of General James A. Hall the other day, and that recalls to my mind an incident which occurred at the battle of Gettysburg. General Hall was commanding a Maine battery, and I was serving on the staff of General Abner Doubleday, who commanded the 1st corps. General John F. Reynolds commanded the left wing of the army.

COL. M. L. JONES.

As we approached Gettysburg, but yet were a couple of miles distant, General Doubleday ordered Major E. P. Halstead and me to ride forward to the front and communicate with General Reynolds, and find out from him what disposition was to be made of the troops as they arrived.

Shortly after leaving General Doubleday, and while we were passing over a hill, we noticed that the cavalry was skirmishing, and saw that the small batteries were engaged.

Major Halstead and I pressed forward at top speed, and, passing the head column, entered the Lutheran Cemetery, where we found General Reynolds, as usual, at the very front. As we approached, we met Lieutenant-Colonel Sanderson, of General Reynolds' staff, who directed me to return and bring up, as quickly as possible, the first battery I could find.

I immediately rode back to the approaching column of infantry and along its line, until I came up with the 2d Maine Battery, commanded by General Hall.

I communicated my order to him, and with wonderful celerity he soon had his battery reversed to the front position, indicated by Colonel Sanderson, and to which I directed him. This incident is important, from the fact that this was the first battery placed in position and opened fire in this memorable battle. I take some personal pride in having thus brought up the first battery to open fire, thereby virtually opening the engagement.

General Hall was a brave and efficient officer, and stood high in the estimation of his comrades and fellow-officers.

When I returned, General Reynolds had gone to the front. I never saw him again. He was probably one of the finest officers in the Army of the Potomac, if not in the whole United States. His wise selection of the position on the first day—and which was afterward maintained so stubbornly by General Doubleday—was the principal thing in preserving to the Army of the Potomac their almost impregnable position which they occupied on the second and third days, and against which the hosts of Lee were hurled in vain.

I remember hearing Hon. Oliver P. Morton deliver an oration at the unveiling of a monument on Cemetery Hill, several years ago, in which he dismissed the fight on the first day somewhat thus: "The first day was of varying success." I felt like interrupting him to say that it was more like the sacrifice at Thermopylæ, with this exception—that we accomplished our object, which was to keep the advancing Confederates, who far outnumbered our men, at bay, in order that the advance of the Army of the Potomac might occupy Cemetery Hill and the flanking eminences, which later insured the Federal victory at Gettysburg; and while the efforts of the first day seemed to fail and we fell back, the result was a grand success.

From ten o'clock in the morning to eight in the evening the 1st corps contended, inch by inch, the space intervening between Willoughby Run and the Cemetery. The dead, who lay in windrows, as it were, at our feet, testified to the courage and determination with which our brave boys held their ground; and while the events of the third day and their momentous results overshadowed the earlier movements, the struggle

HOUSE TO WHICH GEN. REYNOLDS' BODY WAS CARRIED, JULY 1, 1863.

of the first day should ever be memorable and shed lustre upon the men engaged.

MEREDITH L. JONES.

AN INCIDENT AT CEMETERY HILL.

I ENLISTED in 1861, in the 73d Pennsylvania Volunteers. My father was killed at Missionary Ridge, November 25, 1863, and I was severely wounded in the same engagement. I saw four years' of service, and did all I could to defeat the "Johnnies"; but since 1865 I have considered that the brave Americans against whom I fought are my friends and brothers. God bless the blue and the gray! United as they are to-day, they can defy the whole world.

I remember well the evening of July 2, 1863, when the "Tigers" charged up Cemetery Hill into the very teeth of our best batteries. Our brigade, charging through the cemetery, met a sight of awful sublimity—our artillerymen de-

"HIGH-WATER-MARK," JULY 3, 1863—MONUMENTS OF THE 106TH AND 72D PENN'A VOLUNTEERS.

fending their guns with rammers and stones, and the "Tigers" struggling like their fierce namesakes for possession. It was a grand, though gory, example of the heroism of the American soldier.

After the fight we picked up the wounded. I remember one poor fellow clad in gray, who was shot in the head. We carried him to the pump back of the cemetery gate. He was moaning piteously and rubbing his hand over the gaping wound from which his brains were oozing. How we pitied the poor wounded man—ten minutes ago a foe, now a helpless comrade needing our care! One of our boys, with tears in his eyes, put his gum blanket under the sufferer's head, and said, in a choked voice, "There, my poor fellow, that will make you rest easier;" and other comrades moistened the feverish lips with water from the pump.

If this government had become involved in a war with European powers in 1865, over the Mexican question, I know that the soldiers of Sherman and Johnston would have been found side by side, fighting with equal valor for their common country. I know that when I read in a recent publication of the dream of the Confederate who "awoke screaming the rebel yell" while charging a French battery, I involuntarily answered that "rebel yell" with a good old Union cheer. ANDREW DIEMBACH.

JOHN MOSELY.

WHEN the war commenced, among the numberless mere boys who left their plays and schools to fight for what their hearts told them was right, was one young lad from Alabama. He was John Mosely. "Bravely he fought, and well," until the fatal battle of Gettysburg, where he was mortally shot. The surgeon told him that he could not recover; so, asking for paper and pencil, he wrote this manly and eloquent letter to his mother, in Alabama:

DEAR MOTHER :—I am here, a prisoner of war and mortally wounded. I can live but a few hours, at farthest. I was shot fifty yards from the enemy's line. They have been exceedingly kind to me. I have no doubt as to the final result of this battle, and I hope I may live long enough to hear the final shout of victory before I die. I am very weak. Do not mourn my loss. I had hoped to have been spared, but a righteous God has ordered it otherwise, and I feel prepared to trust my case in His hands. Farewell to you all! Pray that God may receive my soul.

Your unfortunate son, JOHN.

GENERAL VIEW OF THE GETTYSBURG BATTLE-FIELD FROM SUMMIT OF LITTLE ROUND TOP, LOOKING WEST.
SEMINARY RIDGE IN THE DISTANCE.

LINCOLN'S DEDICATION SPEECH.

IT was my privilege to be present at the dedication of the Soldiers' National Cemetery at Gettysburg, on the afternoon of November 19, 1863, and to hear the now world-famous address of Abraham Lincoln on that occasion. I can bear witness to the fact that this address, pronounced by Edward Everett to be unequaled in the annals of oratory, fell upon unappreciative ears, was entirely unnoticed, and wholly disappointing to a majority of the hearers. This may have been owing in part to the careless and undemonstrative delivery of the orator, but the fact is that he had concluded his address and resumed his seat before most of the audience realized that he had begun to speak.

MONUMENT OF 29TH PENNA. VOLS.

It was my good fortune as a newspaper correspondent to occupy a place directly beside Mr. Lincoln when he delivered this brief oration, and on the other side of the speaker was Hon. W. H. Seward. Other members of the Cabinet had seats on the stand, and I also noticed Governors Curtin, Seymour, Tod, Morton, and Bradford, Hon. Edward Everett, and Colonel John W. Forney.

At the conclusion of Mr. Everett's scholarly oration, Mr. Lincoln faced the vast audience. He looked haggard and pale, and wore rather a shabby overcoat, from an inside pocket of which he drew a small roll of manuscript. He read his address in a sort of drawling monotone, the audience remaining perfectly silent. The few pages were soon finished; Mr. Lincoln doubled up the manuscript, thrust it back into his overcoat pocket, and sat down. Not a word, not a cheer, not a shout. The people looked at one another, seeming to say, "Is that all?"

The full text of Mr. Lincoln's address was as follows:

Fourscore and seven years ago our fathers brought forth on this continent a new nation, conceived in liberty, and dedicated to the proposition that all men are created equal.

Now we are engaged in a great civil war, testing whether that nation, or any nation so conceived and so dedicated, can longer endure. We are met on a great battle-field of that war. We have come to dedicate a portion of that field as a final resting-place for those who here gave their lives that that nation might live. It is altogether fitting and proper that we should do this.

But, in a larger sense, we cannot dedicate, we cannot consecrate, we cannot hallow this ground. The brave men, living and dead, who struggled here, have consecrated it, far above our poor power to add or detract. The world will little note nor long remember what we say here, but it can never forget what they did here. It is for us the living, rather, to be dedicated here to the unfinished work which they who fought here have thus far so nobly advanced. It is rather for us to be here dedicated to the great task remaining before us—that from these honored dead we take increased devotion to that cause for which they gave the last full measure of devotion—that we here highly resolve that these dead shall not have died in vain—that this nation, under God, shall have a new birth of freedom, and that government of the people, by the people, for the people, shall not perish from the earth.

REYNOLDS' MONUMENT.

I am well aware that accounts have differed as to the manner of this address and its reception by the audience. I was an eye-witness and hearer, and my position was immediately beside the speaker, therefore the foregoing account may be relied upon.

W. H. CUNNINGTON.

THE GRANDEUR OF THE BATTLE.

OUR camp near Fayettesville, Pennsylvania, was struck on July 1, 1863, for the march to Gettysburg. General Mahone's brigade of Anderson's division, Hill's corps, reached a point near Gettysburg early in the afternoon, and bivouacked in an oak woods for the night.

The morning of the 2d of July, we were or-dered forward, and formed in line of battle on the western boundary of a small grove of large oaks, to support McIntosh's artillery, which was unlimbered on the east of this grove, along a stone wall, which

WM. H. STEWART. guarded the open field between the contending armies of Lee and Meade, where we remained during the eventful 3d of July. The morning was consumed in placing the different columns in position ; those were long hours of breathless anxiety, for the very stillness seemed to foretell of the iron storm, which began at one o'clock P. M., fringing the crests of those frowning hills with the lurid glare of 200 guns, whose terrible thunder resounded like some hidden volcano, bursting from the very centre of the earth, and scattering the smoking fragments from its bowels over the trembling hills. The terrific cannonade made the air hideous with the shrieks of the shot and shell, which ploughed

THE SUMMIT OF LITTLE ROUND TOP.
POSITION OF 95TH PENN'A, AND 140TH NEW YORK.

the earth in bloody furrows. Now and then, on either side, a well-trained gun would drop a shell on a magazine, which would send a blazing spout high up towards the sky, and there around lay dead and wounded gunners, weltering in blood. Occasionally, a solid shot would scream through the infantry column, making a death-wail pierce the roar of a hundred guns, all majestic, grand, sublime, awful! For two hours the mighty duel raged, and as the dial marked the hour of three, two columns of infantry rose in line of battle under the thunder-bolts of war, and, at the word of command, pressed fearlessly forward toward the triple-armed hills of their foes. The fire of our artillery slackened, not very long, then we were ordered to forward into the great open field of

CORNER OF THE "PEACH ORCHARD."

EAST CEMETERY HILL, SHOWING POSITION OF RICKETT'S BATTERY AND THE CHARGE OF THE
"LOUISIANA TIGERS," JULY 2, 1863.

death, but there the halt and retreat were ordered, for the magnificent charge of Pickett's
4,500 was over, and the remnant, 400 unofficered
soldiers, were retreating.   From the time men
first met men in deadly strife, no more
unflinching courage was ever displayed by
the veteran troops of the most martial people,
than Gettysburg witnessed in the determined
valor of Pickett's Virginians.   Then and there
they made an imperishable name, which will
sound down the centuries, thrill unborn heroes,
and inspire all generations to emulate their
valor.

The battle closed with night, and then came a
trying ordeal for our regiment.   We were deployed and advanced about one-half mile, as
pickets for the resting army.   All that night
and the following fourth day of July and night,
we were hotly engaged.   The flashes of musketry
gleamed through the darkness thick and fast.
The minié ball's shrill shriek appeared more
fearful and deadly by darkness than by light,
and the prayers of the dying, and the groans of
the wounded, made existence on that bloody
field, during that gloomy night, too terrible for
pen to portray.   The army of Northern Virginia remained in line on the 4th of July, and
commenced to withdraw after nightfall of that
day, but the whole did not get in motion until

after sunrise of the 5th of July, and late in the
forenoon our pickets took up the line of retreat.

The greatest battle of the intersectional war
was over, and as we stand thirty years away,
we look upon it as an event in American history
of which the defeated can feel as proud as the
successful side.   The animosities of the soldiers
who fought there are dead with the intervening
years, and they are now truest friends wherever
they meet.   As the blending of the white and
red roses was the glory of great England, so the
intermingling of the blue and the gray embraces
the splendor of American martial fame.

The magnetic leadership of Robert E. Lee,
and the unfettered courage of Ulysses S. Grant,
are co-ordinate jewels of this mighty union of
States, and all Confederate and Union soldiers,
without a single cross to mar or tinge, love, re-
vere, and cherish the memory of George Washington, the Father of our Country.   What a
glorious trinity of heroes to magnify, glorify,
and perpetually solidify this magnificent union
of States!   Thank heaven the blue and the
gray have joined hands before this fourth day of
July, 1893, upon our Saviour's great command-
ment, in friendship, citizenship, and brotherhood ; enemies no more forever, but all rejoicing
in that grandest appellation, American citizen.

W. H. STEWART.

WOUNDED AND CAPTURED.

WHEN the battle of Gettysburg was fought, I was a boy of nineteen, fresh from the University of Virginia, full of vigor, enthusiasm, robust in health, and radiant with hope. I marched from Fredericksburg to Gettysburg without a suggestion of weariness. The trip had rather the air of an excursion, than the dismal seriousness of "grim-visaged war." I was with Ewell's corps during the three days of Gettysburg, and belonged to Daniels's brigade, Rodes's division, of that corps. During the first two days I escaped without any greater calamity than being once or twice covered with dirt ploughed up by shot and shell. It was on the third day that my disaster occurred. My brigade had been detached from its division, and sent about five o'clock, on the morning of July 3d, to reinforce General Edward Johnson, in an attack upon the Federal position upon Culp's Hill, the extreme right of Meade's army. About ten o'clock on the morning of that fateful day, I was shot down, a ball having passed through the flank of my right knee, just grazing the bone. In a moment everything was transformed into darkness. I retained consciousness enough to sit down under a large tree, and was soon picked up and carried off to an improvised hospital, some distance in rear of our line of battle. Once or twice shell fell almost at my feet. By a merciful Providence they did not explode, but buried themselves harmlessly in the earth. My wound was dressed, and I was removed to our principal hospital beyond the range of the Federal fire. The surgeons, Federal and Confederate, pronounced my escape from amputation most remarkable. I lay for three months prostrate in Frederick, Maryland, and in Baltimore, to which points I was removed by the Federal authorities, into whose hands I fell after the retreat of General Lee's army across the Potomac River. I was captured with our ambulance train on the night of July 4th, in the mountain passes between Monterey, Pennsylvania, and Hagerstown, Maryland. My experience was most thrilling and memorable. In its desperate attempt to escape, our train drove through the contending lines of cavalry—the one striving to capture, the other to protect. I was utterly helpless and disabled, and the ghastly recollections of that gloomy, stormy night, when I was driven through the lines of battle—unable to raise my hand, and in momentary peril of my life—can never be dimmed or effaced. Since the close of the Civil War I have repeatedly visited Gettysburg, surveyed the ground, and endeavored to fix localities accurately. I was able to identify the precise spot, I think, at which I was wounded on Culp's Hill; the blacksmith shop, which was my first hospital, and, of course, the creek, over which I was carried in the arms of a

PROF. H. E. SHEPHERD.

MONUMENT OF 5TH NEW HAMPSHIRE VOLUNTEERS.

U. S. SOLDIERS' MONUMENT, GETTYSBURG, CEMETERY HILL.

stalwart Confederate soldier, who bore me off as if I had been a mere child.

My reminiscences of Gettysburg might be expanded indefinitely, as they have all the freshness and tenacity that characterize a youthful memory. I can recall the struggle on the railroad track, July 1st—the "Tapeworm"—when the blue and gray lines almost melted into each other, and the unsurpassed brilliancy of the pyrotechnic display on the evening of

POSITION OF GEARY'S BRIGADE AND MONUMENT OF 28TH PENN'A VOLS.

July 2d, as the opposing batteries illumined with their radiance the spires of the quiet town, which seemed to nestle between the confronting lines. It was on this day that one of my company was struck fairly in the head by a shell, and, with no sign or word, lay motionless in death. On the day before, a young officer was shot directly in the throat while advancing on Seminary Hill, and with the simple utterance, "God have mercy!" he fell asleep.

Thirty years have passed, and I have seen, like Ulysses, many phases of life and many changeful experiences; but the memory of Gettysburg is as clear, vigorous, and undimmed as it was on that July morning in 1863, when I heard the faint, hardly perceptible sound of distant cannon and rushed on with my command to engage in the most celebrated struggle of the American Civil War.   HENRY E. SHEPHERD.

A SURVIVOR OF PICKETT'S DIVISION.

TAKING the feelings of Company K, 9th Virginia regiment, as evidence, I will venture to say that no troops ever made a charge with more confidence than Pickett's division did at Gettysburg.

The impression seemed to be that General Lee had selected the division for this special duty,

JAMES H. WALKER.

believing that they could carry Cemetery Heights by assault, and they, having sublime faith in his opinion, started in the charge, satisfied that they would accomplish what he ordered.

The division never was in better shape, and they were in the highest spirits, being elated with the success of our army in the fights of the two previous days; and, besides, they thought they would be enabled to transfer the war to the Northern territory, and eventually end it by causing the burden to fall upon the homes of our foes.

The men did not seem to dread this battle as many others they had been in. It was rumored that this division had been selected because they were Virginians, and that they were expected to be successful where others had failed. It is not probable that this was so, but it created a feeling of determination not often shown by men about to enter a desperate battle.

State pride and the great admiration for General Lee was no doubt the great incentive, but, whatever the cause, it is a fact that no troops ever displayed their flag in front of the enemy with more confidence.

That soldiers could be halted and dressed under such fire is remarkable, and must prove that they were under no dread of failure. When this was done, at least a fourth of the division had fallen, but they did not seem to be aware of it. They still kept their eyes to the front and on the enemy, marching forward with the gait and air of soldiers on parade.

The flag of the 9th Virginia went down repeatedly, the last time when about fifty yards from the Stone Wall, when it was picked up and carried forward by a member of Company K.

Probably no large body of troops ever lost in any fight as many men as Pickett's division did in this battle. It was particularly fatal to officers, as out of four generals three were killed and wounded, and seventeen field officers were disabled out of eighteen.

Now, the country should look upon this charge as showing the valor of the American soldier, and that, if necessary, this drama could be enacted against a foreign foe.

The time may yet come when Virginia can show to the American people its devotion to our great and united country.   JAMES H. WALKER.

FROM POTOMAC TO SUSQUEHANNA.

I N May, 1863, the cavalry brigade of General A. G. Jenkins was transferred from the Greenbriar region of Western Virginia to the Shenandoah Valley, and formed the advance of General Ewell's corps in the Pennsylvania campaign.

I was, at that time, a private in Company C, Seventeenth Virginia cavalry regiment. After

JAS. H. HODAM.

the return of our brigade to Hagerstown from the raid on Chambersburg, our regiment, commanded by Colonel Wm. H. French, reported to General Early at Shepherdstown, and acted under his orders and with his division from the Potomac to the Susquehanna and back to the bloody contest at Gettysburg.

Our route was by the way of Waynesboro, Greenville, Gettysburg, and York, to Wrightsville, some seventy-five miles from Philadelphia, if I remember correctly.

ENTRANCE TO NATIONAL CEMETERY, GETTYSBURG.

Our duty was such as generally falls to cavalry—mostly foraging for quartermaster stores, scouting, and picket duty. All saloons and liquor shops were closely guarded, and the law of total abstinence was enforced in a way so complete that a modern prohibitionist might have been proud of it. While on picket near Waynesboro early one morning, four or five people were seen running to a farm-house near by. It was too dark to fully distinguish them, but from their actions we supposed it was a party of Federals interested in our movements. Five of us were sent to the house to look after

them. We dismounted in the yard of a substantial farm building, and found no one about but three or four women, who seemed perplexed and frightened at our early visit. We were informed that the men had fled east with their most valuable property, and at first they denied that any one was concealed on the premises ; but learning that we intended no personal harm, and that our purpose was to search the house, they reluctantly told how, a few minutes previously, five persons, worn out with fatigue and hunger, had sought refuge with them and were now concealed in the upper part of the house.

With revolvers in hand, we cautiously ascended two flights of stairs to the dark garret, expecting every moment to encounter an armed foe. As we reached the floor, an Irish comrade put his foot into a crock of apple-butter sitting near the stairway ; the noise and vigorous oath occasioned thereby were echoed by a wail of fear and distress from the darkest corner of the room, where, in a kneeling posture, instead of armed Yankees, we beheld four men and a woman, who proved, as our Irishman remarked, to be nobody but "dirthy nagurs, black as the ace of sphades." On informing them that we were looking for armed men instead of such defenceless creatures, their fear was turned to joy and thanks. They were free negroes from Maryland, and had been told that if caught by the "rebels," they would be killed or taken South as slaves. They had been fleeing from the supposed wrath to come for three days without food or rest. Assuring them of safety from molestation by our people, we left them devouring with ravenous haste the food we divided with them. The women were much surprised when we returned down stairs without killing or making prisoners of the miserable fugitives. They gave us an excellent breakfast, and we departed, leaving the impression with them that the Southern soldiers were not all barbarians.

General Early tarried long enough at Greenville to destroy the iron works in which it was understood the great Pennsylvania commoner, Thaddeus Stevens, had an interest. About that time, we were anxious to give Mr. Stevens a free ride to Richmond to offset his losses at Greenville.

The country through which we passed toward Gettysburg seemed to abound chiefly in Dutch women who could not speak English, sweet cherries, and apple-butter. As we marched along, the women and children would stand at the front gate with large loaves of bread and a crock of apple-butter, and effectually prevent an entrance of the premises by the gray invaders.

As I said before, the women could not talk much with us, but they knew how to provide " cut and smear," as the boys called it, in abundance.

CULP'S HILL, OVERLOOKING GETTYSBURG FROM POSITION HELD BY 7TH INDIANA REGIMENT AND KNAPP'S BATTERY.

The cherry crop was immense through this part of the State, and the great trees often overhung the highway laden with ripened fruit. The infantry would break off great branches and devour the cherries as they marched along. Regiments thus equipped reminded me of the scene in Macbeth, where " Birnam's wood do come to Dunsinane."

Near Gettysburg, we captured the camp and equipage of a force of Pennsylvania militia, and after an exciting chase of several miles our regiment succeeded in picking up over 300 of the " band-box boys," as we called them. But few shots were fired by either side, but the yelling on our side would have done credit to a band of Comanche Indians. The main body of the flee- ing enemy kept together in the highway, but many, as they became exhausted, sought refuge in the fields, orchards, and farm buildings by the way, and many laughable incidents occurred as we gathered them in. Six were found hid among the branches of a large apple-tree. One portly lieutenant, in attempting to crawl under a corn- crib, had stuck fast by the head and shoulders, leaving the rest of his person exposed. Com- rades Charlie Hyson and Morgan Feather had hard work to drag him out by the heels. But the most fun came when we dragged from a family bake-oven a regimental officer, who, in his gold-laced uniform, was covered with soot and ashes. He was a sight to behold.

While returning from escorting a lot of prisoners to the rear, I met a large party of prisoners hurrying by, while a short distance behind them a little drummer boy was trying to keep up. He was bareheaded, wet, and muddy, but still retained his drum.

" Hello, my little Yank, where are you going?" I said.

" Oh, I am a prisoner, and am going to Richmond," he replied.

" Look here," I said, " you are too little to be a prisoner; so pitch the drum into that fence-corner, throw off your coat, get behind those bushes, and go home as fast as you can."

SPANGLER'S SPRING—POSITION OF LOCKWOOD'S MARYLAND BRIGADE.

"Mister, don't you want me for a prisoner?"

"No."

"Can I go where I please?"

"Yes."

"Then you bet I am going home to mother!"

Saying this as he threw his drum one way and his coat another, he disappeared behind a fence and some bushes, and I sincerely hope he reached home and mother.

At Gettysburg, Company C, commanded by Captain Waldo, reported to General John B. Gordon, and we acted in the advance of the Georgians, and "Extra Billy" Smith's Virginia brigade on York and Wrightsville. After a longing look at the blue-coated sentinels on the Columbian shore of the Susquehanna, we rejoined General Early and our regiment. I shall not attempt a general description of the battle of Gettysburg. Thirty years have obliterated from my mind much of the topographical surroundings of the place, and many of the scenes and incidents dimly present themselves as dreams of the long ago, rather than of actual experience.

Toward noon on that memorable first of July, the 17th Virginia cavalry reached the vicinity of Gettysburg, from the direction of York, closely followed by the division of General Early.

Heavy firing of artillery and musketry had been heard for some time in the direction of the town, and we realized that hot work was before us. Our regiment was halted near a strip of woods that intervened between us and the battle-field, while the infantry brigades and artillery hurried to the front and disappeared in the timber.

Infantry of those days generally held the cavalry service in light esteem, and as we sat on our horses by the roadside, we were the subjects of many good-natured remarks and much badinage from those gallant fellows who, with quick step, were marching into the jaws of death. As Gordon's and Smith's brigades passed, a hearty cheer was given as we recognized our comrades in the march to the Susquehanna.

During the time the infantry was passing to the front, the noise of the battle was increasing on our right, and in a short time shells from the enemy were screaming over our heads, tearing through the tree-tops, and plowing up the ground in our vicinity. For nearly two hours we remained here under fire, waiting for orders, and all old soldiers will acquiesce in the fact that our position was not a desirable one. Much rather would we have preferred a call to the front, where we could have returned the fire and participated in the excitement of battle. The firing in our front was terrible. No such sound of musketry ever greeted my ears before—and scarcely ever afterward, except at the battle of Five Forks. Soon the "rebel yell" could be distinguished in the mighty roar, and conveyed to us the gratifying intelligence that our boys were getting the best of the fight, and a signal officer of a station near by soon verified the fact that the enemy was retreating from every position. Then the welcome order came for us to quickly advance to the front.

"By fours, march!" was the sharp command of Major Smith, and we spurred our horses along the road for Gettysburg. Through the timber, across a small stream, and the battle-field was before us in all its horrors and excitement. In our front were open fields and orchards, and, a little further on, the town. Many pieces of artillery occupied the high ground to our right, but their thunder was silenced now, while the heaps of dead and dying around them told how the boys in blue had bravely stood by their guns. A little beyond, to judge from the windrows of dead, a Union regiment had been blotted out. Along the road the blue and gray veterans lay thickly. On a large pile of fence-rails by the roadside, several of the Federal and Confederate soldiers grimly faced each other in death, with their muskets interlocked. Dashing forward, we came up with our infantry, driving Howard's corps through the town. Confusion seemed to reign in the Federal ranks, and thousands were made prisoners in a short time. The enemy opened a heavy fire on us from their batteries on the hills to the south of town. Our lines were re-formed, skirmishers advanced beyond the town to the south and east, while our regiment engaged in gathering up the prisoners. It was now about four o'clock, and the enemy's fire ceased for a short time, and but little of their line was visible to us. My captain sent me forward to our skirmish line to locate the battery that so fiercely shelled us. While returning, the enemy began a brisk fire from several guns; a shell exploded just in front of me, and just over a woman as she ran across the street. She disappeared in a cellar, unhurt. Then came a blinding flash in my face, and the next thing I realized was being carried to the sidewalk by three or four infantrymen. My horse had been killed by a piece of shell, but I escaped with a few bruises and a general shaking-up. I was ready for duty the next day. Our regiment guarded the prisoners the following days of the battle. During those days I had many sociable talks with our prisoners, many of whom belonged to the 11th corps, which had suffered so severely a short time before at the hands of Stonewall Jackson. I still cherish as a valuable memento a canteen I traded for with a Pennsylvania Bucktail.

JAS. H. HODAM.

THE NEW YORK MONUMENT.

THIS is the thirtieth anniversary of the battle of Gettysburg, and on the first three days of July this year 10,000 battle-scarred and weather-beaten defenders of the Stars and Stripes will tread the grounds in peace and safety that they trod 'mid falling shot and bursting shell thirty years ago.

The occasion that brings them together is the unveiling of a monument commemorative of the deeds of those men who died for their country. It is to give to the world evidences of their love for their comrades, and honor in their deeds. A generous State has made it possible that her people should thus honor her fallen heroes.

New York, the Empire State, will give to the world assurances that her sons' deeds are not forgotten, and that republics are not ungrateful where the endeavor is for right. From one of the historic hills of Gettysburg a handsome monument has risen ninety-two feet in the air. It is the result of many years' labor by General Daniel E. Sickles. The monument cost $62,000; but the amount of thought and work which it cost its promoters can hardly be estimated.

NEW YORK STATE MONUMENT, GETTYSBURG—DEDICATED JULY 3, 1893.

Peculiar circumstances were connected with this monument. Ninety-eight organizations from New York took part in that memorable battle, and almost as many organizations wished to honor their members. In 1887, a bill passed the New York Legislature creating a New York State Board of Gettysburg Commissioners. General Daniel E. Sickles was made Chairman, and his colleagues were men whose names are a guarantee of earnest work. They were Major-Generals Henry W. Slocum, Joseph B. Carr, and Josiah Porter, and Major Charles A. Richardson. A month after the Governor signed the bill, work was begun, and the Committee determined to place the monument in the front rank of Gettysburg memorials.

GENERAL SICKLES.

The new monument is seventy-six feet high, with a heroic statue in bronze of a girl sixteen feet nine inches in height, holding a wreath of laurel in her hand outstretched over New York's unknown dead. The figure is a superb execution, and adds a grand appearance to the monument. The base is twenty-seven feet in height and built of Hallowell granite, with a polished shaft.

On the plinth is a bronze trophy, with a New York State eagle over the State's escutcheon, and on the base, in bold relief, stand out the words "New York." Along the upper line of the base are the badges of the First, Second, Third, Fifth, Sixth, Eleventh, Twelfth, Cavalry, Engineer and Signal Corps, and the artillery which took part in the fight.

Around the base of the shaft in *alto relievo* is a bronze circular divided in four panels. The first represents General Sickles immediately after he has been shot; he is removed from his horse and leaning on the shoulder of General Joseph B. Carr. Besides General Carr, in this group are also General S. K. Zook, who was killed on the second day, the day General Sickles was wounded; General S. H. Weed, a native New Yorker, who was killed on the third day; General C. K. Graham, one of the Third Corps commanders; General R. B. Ayres, General J. H. Hobart Ward, and General Henry E. Tremaine, member of General Sickles' staff, and the first one to reach him after he was shot.

On the obverse is a representation of General Henry W. Slocum, of Brooklyn, N. Y., surrounded by a group of general officers. General Slocum was commander of the right wing of the Union Army. On his right is General Geo. S.

Greene, whose magnificent generalship preserved the Union Army on the first night. General Greene is the oldest living graduate of West Point. Besides General Greene, there are represented General James S. Wadsworth, who was killed at the battle of the Wilderness, in May, 1864; General David A. Russell, who was killed at the battle of Winchester, October 19, 1864; Brigadier-General Henry J. Hunt, Chief of Artillery on General Meade's staff; General Alfred Pleasanton, Chief of Cavalry of the Army of the Potomac; General Henry A. Barnum, General Joseph J. Bartlett, and General Alexander Shaler.

The right panel represents General John F. Reynolds' death. Over him are leaning General Abner Doubleday and Major-General John C. Robinson, who lost a leg at Spottsylvania, while around them are grouped General Francis C. Barlow, General A. Von Steinwehr, and Colonel Thomas C. Devin. General Reynolds' sister says that the likeness on the panel is the best she has ever seen of her brother.

Around General Hancock, whose wounding the left panel represents, are grouped General Kilpatrick, General Warren, Chief of Engineers on General Meade's staff, General Butterfield, who was Chief of General Meade's staff, and

LEFT PANEL—WOUNDING OF GENERAL HANCOCK—NEW YORK MONUMENT, GETTYSBURG.

General Alexander S. Webb, who commanded the famous Philadelphia brigade which received the full force of General Pickett's charge on July 3d.

As all can see from the illustrations which accompany this article and this brief description, this monument will be one of the handsomest at Gettysburg. New York State has spent $260,000 on this single field in commemorating the deeds of those of her sons who fell there, and this last monument is an eloquent and fitting period to the eulogium of which it is a part.

Too much honor cannot be paid by a State to her brave dead, who fell fighting her cause, and the example which it sets to the younger generation is in the highest degree stimulating, exhilarating, and inspiring. By such actions heroes are made. They see the honor paid to patriotism, and strive to emulate those who merited it by true worth, and proved their loyalty by shedding their blood.

Many a State had troops at Gettysburg, but none did more than those that came from New York. Many a State has erected marble shafts to the memory of its dead at Gettysburg, but none more choice and lovely than that which will be unveiled there to 10,000 survivors of that battle on July 3d, by the New York State Commission. This monument is worthy of the blameless and heroic lives of those "dead but sceptered sovereigns who still rule our spirits from their urns."

"Yes," answered the surgeon. "What can I do for you?"

The sufferer caught him nervously by the arm and in a manner eloquent with emotion, said: "What do you think, doctor? I am wounded and dying in defence of my country, and these people are trying to force me to take the oath of allegiance to theirs."

The crowd scattered, and the doctor bowed his head in honor of the gallant fellow on whose brow the damp shadow of death had already gathered.

OBVERSE PANEL—GEN. SLOCUM AND HIS OFFICERS—NEW YORK MONUMENT, GETTYSBURG.

RANDOM TALES BY CONFEDERATES.

A PHYSICIAN of the Army of Northern Virginia was in the 2d corps hospital at Gettysburg on the third day of the fight. A crowd of idle spectators were around, and he was pushing his way through when his footsteps were arrested by hearing a feeble voice call out to him, "Doctor, doctor!" The surgeon halted and found that the cry proceeded from a wounded Confederate from one of the North Carolina regiments. The wounded man said:

"You are a Confederate surgeon, are you not?"

In the first battle near Gettysburg, the Northern soldiers showed a determination we had never before seen in them. General Hill said that he saw a Federal soldier plant his regimental colors in a railway cut, and that there they made an excellent stand. The men, after planting their colors, fought with a determination and obstinacy that was almost invincible. When, at last, they were compelled to retire, the color-bearer was the last to retreat, and General Hill says that he was honestly sorry when he saw the brave fellow meet his doom, for he retreated with his face toward the foe and shook his fist at every backward step.

In the second day's fight, General Lee, to my own knowledge, sat most of the time on the stump of a tree. He was quite alone, and I especially noticed that he received and sent only one message during the entire day.

It was on the third day. Pickett's division had just come up. It was to bear the brunt of the

GENERAL SLOCUM.

engagement; it was weak in point of numbers, comprising only about 5,000 men. After the battle was opened, I joined General Longstreet. I was surprised at the number of wounded. However, I had not seen enough to give me any idea of the amount of mischief that had been done. When I got near General Longstreet, I saw one of his regiments coming toward us in good order. I thought I was just in time for a good engagement, so said to General Longstreet, "I wouldn't have missed this for anything."

The general was seated on the top of a fence, and looked perfectly calm. "The devil you wouldn't!" he replied, grimly. "We have attacked the enemy, and have been repulsed."

Looking around, I saw our men slowly and sulkily returning toward us, under a heavy fire. Some of them were straggling, and General Pettigrew came up and said:

"General, I can't get my men up again."

"Very well, then, general," answered Longstreet, curtly, "just let them alone; the enemy is going to advance, and will spare you the trouble."

I think about the best thing I saw on that bloody field was General Lee's action toward General Wilcox. The latter wore a straw hat and short jacket; he came up and explained, almost crying, the condition of his brigade. "Well, never mind, general," said General Lee, shaking him heartily by the hand; "all this is my fault; it is I who have lost the fight, and you must help me out of it in the best way you can."

After our rout at Gettysburg, General Lee was engaged in riding about encouraging and trying to rally the broken troops. His face did not give the slightest evidence of annoyance or disappointment, and almost to every soldier he met he said something encouraging. As he

passed me I heard him say: "This will all come right in the end, but you all must rally, and we will talk it over afterward. We want every good man now."

General Lee said to an English officer, who was a correspondent, standing near: "This has been a sad day to us, colonel, a sad day; but we cannot always expect to gain victories."

It was then that an incident occurred which made me almost idolize him afterward. General Lee was always loved by his officers, and more so by his men, but none of us, I believe, ever knew the full depth of kindness of his heart. A mounted officer, who was riding past us, began beating his horse because it shied at the bursting of a shell.

"Don't whip him, captain, don't whip him," said General Lee, "I've got just such a foolish horse myself."

I think that one of the saddest incidents of the war which I witnessed was after the battle of Gettysburg. Off on the outskirts, seated on the ground, with his back to a tree, was a soldier, dead. His eyes were riveted on some object held tightly clasped in his hands. As we drew nearer we saw that it was an ambrotype of two small children. Man though I was, hardened through those long years to carnage and bloodshed, the sight of that man who looked on his children for the last time in this world, who, away off in a secluded spot had rested

RIGHT PANEL—DEATH OF GENERAL REYNOLDS—
NEW YORK MONUMENT, GETTYSBURG.

himself against a tree, that he might feast his eyes on his little loves, brought tears to my eyes which I could not restrain had I wanted. There were six of us in the crowd, and we all found great lumps gathering in our throats, and mist coming before our eyes which almost blinded us. We stood looking at him for some time. I was thinking of the wife and baby I had left at home, and wondering how soon, in the mercy of God, she would be left a widow, and my baby boy fatherless. We looked at each other and instinctively seemed to understand our thoughts. Not a word was spoken, but we dug a grave and laid the poor fellow to rest with his children's picture clasped over his heart. Over his grave, on the tree against which he was sitting I inscribed the words:

"Somebody's Father,
July 3, 1863."

I heard a story related about Major-General Howard, of Maine, which I believe to be true, from what I have seen of him. It is said that after the battle of Gettysburg, one of our (Southern) soldiers lay in a house near the battle-field, dying. The major-general rode up and, dismounting, entered the house. He knelt down beside the man and, after talking to him sometime, took out a little black book and read: "Let not your heart be troubled. Ye believe in God, believe also in me. In my Father's house are many mansions."

He then offered up a prayer to God for the dying soldier, and, leaning over him, kissed him and said: "Captain, we will meet in heaven."

FIRST PANEL—WOUNDING OF GENERAL SICKLES—NEW YORK MONUMENT, GETTYSBURG.

WHAT MIGHT HAVE BEEN.

GETTYSBURG has acquired a sentimental importance, that distinguishes it in the Northern States above all other battles of the Civil War. There the "backbone" of the Confederacy is said to have been broken, and no doubt the issue contributed largely to the final result of the war.

Among Southerners, also, at least among Virginians, the fight is regarded as exceptional in the rare valor displayed in the assaults upon Meade's line. And no ex-Confederate could listen, except with a full heart, to the panegyric heaped upon Pickett's men at the cyclorama of "Gettysburg," recently exhibited in New York, by the old soldier of the Grand Army of the Republic, who was charged with the duty of explaining to the public the scenes set forth on the canvas.

The interest of the military critic hangs mainly upon speculations as to what might have happened in different dispensations. The battle was an accident, and its main details were accidents, lost opportunities, and frustrated plans. Its mention is inseparably associated with a volume of ifs and exclamation points, and it will be well if the many mistakes of many of the leaders on both sides become enveloped in the veil of romance that is gradually settling upon the hills of Gettysburg.

Had Stuart informed Lee of the movements of the Federal troops, the week that was frittered away supinely about Carlisle and Cham'ersburg might have been spent in picking up in detail the widely scattered corps of Meade. Had Ewell run over Doubleday when they met in front of the town, instead of allowing himself to be occupied by an inferior force a whole afternoon and night; had he even pushed Doubleday back a few minutes longer—beyond Culp's Hill—had Longstreet been prompt on the morning of the second day; had Sykes delayed the occupation of Round Top a little longer, etc., etc., a wholly different turn would have been given to the affair.

But when on the morning of the third day he was confronted with the fish-hook line planted upon Culp's Hill, Cemetery Ridge, and Round Top, he was forced to break through its centre (the only vulnerable point) or withdraw from Meade's front at great peril to his army. In this alternative he was justified in trusting to his old soldiers, for the infantry with which he had just crossed the Potomac have never been surpassed by any body of troops in history. And even in front of Cemetery Ridge we are tempted to speculate upon what might have happened had Pickett been better supported, or had Lee's ammunition held out.

Not less interesting is the consideration of the possibilities had Meade followed Pickett back to his lines, or assaulted Lee in force the next day, or pressed him while he was retiring beyond the mountains, or attacked him while he lay for a week about Williamsport, impeded by the swollen Potomac.

The most interesting figure in the fight is that of Lee. He generously assumed the burden of the failure, and it is not certain that some of his officers have not sought to shift to him the responsibility for their own shortcomings. But whatever may be his merit or demerit, he is brought out into massive relief by the poise and equanimity which lifted him above the vicissitudes of fortune, and preserved to him the command of his individual resources as fully in defeat as in victory. He received and parried the crushing blow that Pickett suffered with unequaled intrepidity, and withdrew from Pennsylvania as calmly as the tide recedes upon an ocean in repose.

Gettysburg as a fact has passed into history, and as the stones rise upon its field to testify the glory that the various commands gleaned in its harvest of death, its hills are clothed with a halo brighter than that of Yorktown or Bunker Hill. During the next generation the traditions of the North and the South will have united in one stream, and Gettysburg will have become a shrine to which the whole people will devoutly turn. Upon its field was brought to naught the most momentous campaign of the Civil War; it was the turning-point of a war that could not have logically had any other result than that which actually befell. And this distinction will make of it the Mecca of liberty.

WM. J. HARDY.

MARCHING INTO PENNSYLVANIA.

A BRAVE OLD SOUTHERN WOMAN.

J. O. SMITH.

THE summer of '64, with Sherman's army, was a continuous succession of battles and skirmishes. From Rocky Face Ridge and Mill Creek Gap, Johnston's army of the Confederacy had been forced back by successive stages of battle, assault and flanking detour, until the early days of June found the Confederate army at Marietta, with its strongly defensive chain of surrounding hills, the key to which was the impregnable heights of Kenesaw Mountain, at which a determined stand was made to stay the onward and victorious progress of the Union army. Its wooded and rugged slopes presented an insurmountable barrier to the Union forces, while its towering summit afforded to the Confederate commander unobstructed oversight of every movement within in the lines of Sherman's army. From the 4th of June to July 2d, Johnston succeeded in baffling every effort of Sherman to overrun or force him from his position, and only when the old tactics of flanking, by extending the Union right and overlapping, and endangering his sources of supply and retreat, was Johnston forced back once more toward Atlanta.

The army supply depot was at Big Shanty, a very primitive town on the Georgia Central Railroad, the then nearest point to "the front" to which the railroad had been repaired after its destruction by the Confederates, in the wake of their retreating army. Here gathered the trains from every part of Sherman's army for supplies, and the motley gathering of quartermasters, commissaries, ordnance officers, clerks, wagon masters, teamsters, contrabands, and the much-abused, but indispensable, army mule, made a small army in itself. "First come, first served," was the rule, and as the facilities were not equal to the demand, it frequently occurred that a wait of two or three days was required before your "estimate" was reached in the list and your supplies obtained.

Being detailed as receiving clerk of the commissary department of the First Division, Twentieth Army Corps, it became my duty to visit this place, and it also occurred that I once had some three days waiting time on my hands. Having filed my "estimate," I wandered about to watch the interesting activity that the continual coming and going of supply trains; the push and hurry of those who had obtained, and the scramble to get into place of those who were yet to get, their supplies; the shouting of the wagon masters, interlarded with plenteous and frequently unique profanity; the coming and going of the railroad trains, with their loads of supplies and their burdens of suffering humanity, as the wounded were placed in these same cars to make their long journey to the rear, afforded a scene that only the supply depot of an advancing, fighting army can present.

"SHE STOOD UNDAUNTED AT THE OPEN DOORWAY."

With the freedom that pervades such a community, I unhesitatingly entered the invitingly open door of one of the houses, and found myself in an exquisitely neat little home, the presiding genius, a motherly-looking old lady, who evidently must have been a very handsome woman in her early life, and which beauty still lingered about her personality.

I soon learned that her husband was with the army of Northern Virginia; that her only son had given up his life for the Confederacy at Aldie, Virginia, in the fierce cavalry fight at that point, in the summer of '63; that her loyalty to "the cause" was unquestionable and unswerving, even to the point, if need be, that her "dear old man" should be laid, too, a sacrifice on the altar of his country. She firmly and ardently believed the cause at stake was the enslavement of the Southern "poor white" element and the freedom and social advancement of the "niggers." No argument could swerve her from this belief, and her detestation of the Yankee and anything from the North was strong and pronounced. She had no education, or as she termed it, "schoolin'," and expressed a full contempt for any such "useless book larnin'." She used the vernacular peculiar to the class she represented, that even the slave element characterized as "de low down white trash!"

Though her conversation was surcharged with disloyalty to the Union cause, her evident honesty and fearless announcement of and defence of fealty to the cause of the South, was to me interesting, and at times very amusing. I, therefore, led her on while I discussed a cup of hot coffee and a corn "pone" that she had provided me with, as her feelings of aggression toward the Yankee were not personal and did not include coffee. This last was the one and only good thing she would "allow" the Yankee had brought her, as parched rye as a substitute for Java or Mocha had lost its illusory effects, and

she welcomed this Yankee innovation on Southern soil with hospitable acclaim.

I finally led her up to talk of the battle of a few days previous, when Johnston had been forced back to the position he then held. Her description of the fight, and her criticism of the several generals, was so refreshingly original in both manner of expression and characterization of persons, that I enjoyed it most heartily. She persisted in designating the several generals of the armies as Mr., ignoring their military titles entirely. It was Mr. Johnston and Mr. Sherman, notwithstanding an effort on my part to assist her by prompting "General" on each use of the prefix, Mister, in the earlier stages of her story.

"You'uns," she declared, "don't fight fair. Mr. Johnston and we'uns' men want to fight like men; to stand right up to it, fair like. But Mr. Sherman is 'fraid to force we'uns; he keeps dodgin' around the flinks. Then there's your Mr. Kilpatrick, with his critter company, keeps fighting endways, and tearin' around we'uns' flinks, and comin' in the back way. Why don't you'uns fight like men, and not keep dodgin' about as like you were scart to fight?"

"SHE PICKED UP THIS FULL-GROWN MAN."

The indignant air with which she uttered this challenge to the valor of "we'uns," was as warlike and suggestive of pride in her cause and its brave defenders as might have graced the presence of one of those old-time and oft-quoted Spartan mothers.

She described the Confederate lines of battle, that had fought so bravely, yet faultlessly; so stubbornly, and yet steadily and irresistibly had they been forced back by the overpowering strength of the Union army. These she called "long strings of fight," that had passed over her little garden and pasture lot.

From the fierce enthusiasm with which she described how the Confederates had clung to every tree, fence, or other point of defence, until forced back by the steady import of numbers and discipline, was suggestive of the thought that only the instrument and opportunity was required to have made an Amazonian warrior of this kindly old soul. She had stood undaunted at the open doorway, with bullets whistling all about and around her, as was fully testified to by the scores of bullet marks on the door-posts, and adjacent parts of the woodwork, and "with a heroism worthy of a better cause," with her arms rolled in her ample apron, stern-visaged and defiant, had braved the Yankee onset; had seen the heroic struggle of her defenders, as they fell dead and wounded all about her little home.

Her sympathetic nature finally overcame all other feelings, and reckless of flying bullets and charging battle lines, she rushed out to the nearest of the wounded Confederates, and with the superhuman strength, born of the moment and by the needs of the occasion, that dear old soul, who would seem physically incapable of carrying a five-year-old child, picked up this full-grown man, and carried him within the shelter of her little home. But her heroic work did not halt at this; by the time the Union line had passed to and beyond her, she had no less than three wounded sufferers, in butternut uniforms, within the shelter of her improvised hospital, and was attending them with all the means and skill at her command. The Union surgeons had their wounded brought to the house, and assumed charge, but the old heroine would not surrender the care of "her boys;" she attended them until, with all others, under direction of the surgeons. they were removed to the general

hospital. It was not entirely from her lips I gathered the story of this act of true heroism, but from one of the Federal officers who had been an admiring witness of this scene. I secured from her a reluctant and more detailed account of it. She seemed to have come to a realization that she had done something out of the ordinary, when spoken to by others, that at the moment had not occurred to her, and she shrank from the fame that she had so nobly and so bravely achieved.

Unlettered and uncouth in her language as she was, she was a true woman, and more cannot well be said. There was an innate nobleness in her that would assert itself. With a religious belief in the righteousness of the cause of the South, she was willing to do and dare, to suffer and struggle on; to "walk through the valley of the shadow of death;" give up her first-born and only boy, and even part with the lover of her youth, the companion and comrade of her later life, if so God willed, that the cause might prevail.

Despite this stern and unflinching loyalty to the Confederacy, she had a motherly and sympathetic heart, that I congratulated myself I succeeded in reaching, for at her earnest invitation, almost command, I made my home with her during my stay, and no son could have received more hospitable treatment than did this Yankee boy at the hands of Mother Allen. And when I parted from her, with a heartfelt, earnest, in substance, "God bless you, my boy; may you get safely through it all," I thought I detected a suspicious moisture in her kindly old eyes, that warranted the belief that she did not detest all the Yankee boys.

THE BATTLE OF STONE RIVER.

AS SEEN BY ONE WHO WAS THERE.

Rev. R. B. Stewart.

THE battle of Stone River, if not the greatest, was one of the greater battles of the war, and that not because of the numbers engaged, the character of the fighting, or the victory won, though in all these it was hardly second to any; but because of its place in the history of the war, the encouragement it gave to the people of the North, and the confidence and experience it gave to an army hitherto untried in battle.

The Army of the Cumberland, or the 14th Army Corps, was the immediate successor of the Army of the Ohio. It was simply the reorganization of the old army with a large number of new regiments distributed to its several brigades. Since the battle of Shiloh the older regiments had seen very little fighting, but a great deal of marching. The newer ones had seen very little of either. At this time the Army of the Potomac, after a summer's fruitless campaign, was stuck fast in the Virginia mud; the Army of the West was pounding away at the Mississippi forts; the Army of the Ohio, after a five months' pleasant promenade through the rich valleys and over the rugged mountains of Kentucky and Tennessee, found itself facing its partner between Nashville and Murfreesboro. Only one incident occurred to mar the pleasure of our trip to Louisville; that was the battle of Perrysville. This battle was a mistake, that might have resulted seriously. It was brought on by the imprudent and somewhat impulsive nature of one of our division commanders. By his generalship Buell succeeded in putting a stop to the battle before it had gone too far, and Bragg quietly and willingly withdrew to a safer distance. Both generals apologized and parted good friends. The victory of Stone River, although poor, was to us a rift in the clouds, a streak of sunshine promising a brighter day. It gave hope to the anxious watchers at home and confidence in itself to the Army of the Cumberland.

The closing year of 1862 found us in camp near the lunatic asylum, a few miles south of Nashville. We were in comfortable winter-quarters, and, seemingly, for all winter. By drilling, camp duty, picket duty, foraging, and an occasional reconnoissance, we were kept in exercise and from forgetting that we were in front of the enemy.

It was here that the reorganization of the army was completed and the change in commanders made. However good a military man General Buell may have been—and on horseback he was a model—on parade he was every inch a commander. He never won the love, and entirely lost the confidence, of the army he commanded. There was silent rejoicing everywhere when Rosecrans took his place. Other changes followed that were not so popular and that suggested serious work ahead.

Until now we had been using the Sibley tent, a tent large and comfortable enough for camp purposes, but hard to manage and heavy to transport, and when our wagons got behind, as they often did for days together, we had to do the best we could, with only the heavens above us for shelter.

One day there was issued to each one about two yards square of heavy cotton, with buttons and button-holes along three sides and small loops of cord along the other. We were seriously informed that henceforth these were to be our burden by day and our shelter by night, and they might answer for flags of truce in a time of need. Of course the big tents were to follow us, as usual, and be used in regular camp, so that we were not nearly so mad as we felt like being, but somewhat disgusted and a great deal in doubt. However, being helpless, we turned our disgust into fun and frolic, gave our doubts to the winds, and, taking up our little squares, we folded them away for whatever emergency they might happen to suit.

It was the morning after Christmas, 1862, when orders came to strike tents, fold them up, and turn them over to the quartermaster (and that was the last we ever saw of our "Sibleys"), draw three days' rations, and be ready to march at a moment's notice. We obeyed, of course, but not without grumbling, and the notice came before we were ready. We gathered up our traps, said good-bye to our quarters, and were soon in our place on the road. We were hardly fairly started before it began to rain, and to rain only as it can rain in that Southern country. Soon the earth was all mud beneath us, the heavens all dark above us, while sounds that were not thunder gave us a hint of business before us. We tramped on and on, encountering nothing worse than the enemy's pickets, who retreated slowly over the hills.

In the evening we halted near Nolinsville. The rain had ceased to pour, but fog was settling heavily and night was near at hand. We were wet and tired and hungry. There was an abundance of good cedar rails near by, and soon roaring, fragrant fires gave us what cheer they could. Hot coffee, crackers and pork soon helped to modify the situation, so that things were not nearly so bad as they seemed. When we began preparations for the night our minds went out to our squares of muslin. If ever they might be useful, now was the time. We unfolded them carefully, spread them out gently, and studied their anatomy. Evidently they were constructed with reference to each other; they seemed to be social in their nature, and must somehow go together. The buttons and the buttonholes suggested at least a pair to begin with. We went to work and buttoned two pieces together, then stretched them over a ridge-pole made of a cedar rail, and, with pegs through the loops, made them fast to the ground. We now had a shelter about four feet high, long enough and wide enough for two persons. The idea thus far developed seemed to strike us favorably, and we wondered if they would shed the rain.

We paired off, selected our ground, pitched our united squares, and in a little while the evening gloom was all lighted up by the snowy whiteness of our shelter tents. Spreading our blankets and putting our knapsacks under our heads, with jest and joke, we took possession of our strange, new quarters. When all seemed to be settling down into the quiet of the night,

some sleepless fellow stuck his head out and began to bark. Soon another followed, then another. The idea was swiftly contagious, and in a few minutes the whole camp sounded like a vast dog convention, where all kinds of dogs were barking for a prize.

The shape of the tent, the way of getting into it, and all the surroundings gave to some one the idea of a dog kennel and he felt constrained to bark. The tents were henceforth christened "dog tents," which in a little while degenerated into "purp tents," and by this name they were ever after known. It rained during the night, and, as we were dry in the morning, the last question was answered to our entire satisfaction. But so far the tent was only a roof. We were not long, however, in discovering that by three or four persons going together, or by one person managing to get possession of three or four squares, a very close and comfortable shelter could be erected in a very few minutes, and, when in camp, with the help of a few rails or logs or boards, we could have quarters fit for the General himself — better in every way than the old wall or Sibley tents. And then,

MAJOR-GENERAL W. S. ROSECRANS.

though our baggage train was cut down to its lowest limits, we were always pretty sure of a house over our heads. The man who invented the "dog tent" ought to have a monument.

The next day we reached Triune, the enemy contesting every inch of the way and sometimes making our further progress doubtful. Finding the little village almost deserted, we took possession of such live-stock and provisions as we could conveniently carry along, and the next day being the Sabbath, we rested from all our labors and feasted upon the spoils.

Early on Monday we took up our burdens, and leaving the good road to go its own way to the right, we struck across lots. Through cedar forests and dismal swamps we plodded patiently along, stimulated by the occasional booming of cannon far off to our left and front. We knew that the other divisions of the army were somewhere on the road and forcing their way along, but we did not know where they were. But as to that, we did not know where we were ourselves.

Night found us joining them on Stewart's Creek, a few miles north of Murfreesboro. It now became evident that unless Bragg should keep going on and traveling faster than we, there was going to be trouble pretty soon. Rosecrans was not on the war-path just for the fun there was in it.

We all felt exceedingly homesick that night as we lay under the clouds and in the mud. But we still had some hope that the situation was not so serious as it seemed to be; that Mr. Bragg would think better of it and get out of our way before it would be forever too late. We had been on friendly terms so long and had so often managed to avoid each other that our hopes, however vain, were not without foundation. Thinking a great many thoughts about home and the morrow, we dropped off at last into a restless sleep.

Morning dawned cloudy and cold. We ate our breakfast in silence, rolled up our blankets, and patiently waited for orders. Rumors and reports of what had taken place the day before were plenty, but none of them were very encouraging except to those who were longing for a fight, and that class was not conspicuous. We lay under arms all day and made but little change in our position. At irregular intervals, somewhere in front of us, cannon kept thundering away, not as in battle, but as though searching for a foe. All day long regiments of other divisions kept marching past us and on to the front, disappearing in the woods and dark thickets of cedar.

In the evening came our turn to move, and we marched to the right, through woods and across fields, until we came to the Franklin Pike. Here we formed the extreme right of the line of battle, a part of our division curling around like a dog's tail until some of us fronted to the rear. Behind us was a large field of corn-stalks, the ground sloping gently back for a mile or more to the creek. On the right were open fields as far as the eye could see. On the left, a cedar thicket with large limestone rocks covering the ground. In front were heavy woods, dark with cedar underbrush and full of we knew not what. But we had some reason for thinking that there was nothing there worse than the silent gloom. Night came on clear, cold, and frosty, almost too cold for sleep, and we were allowed no fires. We made our beds among the rocks and under the cedar branches. Though everything was quiet and our sleep undisturbed, we were glad when morning came.

The morning of December 31, 1862, came on with a cloudless sky and a ringing, frosty air. With the first streak of dawn we were all up and lively, with fires kindled, coffee boiling, and meat frying on the coals. The night had passed without any alarm, and the early light revealed no signs of an approaching storm. The pickets were all at their posts, thinking only of the coming relief. The battery horses were away to watering. General Willich, who commanded our brigade, alone seemed uneasy and was out inspecting the picket line.

Just as I had taken my meat and coffee from the fire, and was sitting down on a cold rock to eat my breakfast, a few shots rang through the woods in front. We had hardly time to be alarmed before others followed, and we heard bullets singing uncomfortably near and saw the pickets rushing in, followed by a line of gray, yelling and shooting like demons. There was no need nor time for any order to " fall in." We just tumbled over each other to get in. Dropping our pots and pans, leaving our haversacks and blankets, we snatched up our cartridge-boxes and rushed for our guns, only to find ourselves in ranks with our backs to the foe. Before we could change front to rear they were upon us, not a skirmish-line, but a line of battle; not one line, but two or three, it seemed to us. The woods were just full of them. They swarmed, they overflowed, they were a regular flood. We stood to deliver our fire and say good-morning, then took to our heels and ran. But not all of us. Some fell right there; many lingered too long with their breakfast dishes, but most of us ran. Our way was through the corn-field. The stalks were yet thickly standing. The ground was frozen and rough. I could hear the bullets striking the stalks. I could hear them strike a comrade as he ran; then there would be a groan, a stagger, and a fall. I could hear the wild yelling behind and the roar of the guns that were now getting into action. I saw, by a backward glance, a gray mass covering all the ground where our camp had so lately been. I saw the fields on the right filling up with regiments and columns and armies of gray. I felt like running.

I felt as though I would like to be all legs, with no other purpose in life but to run.

At the lower side of the field was a high rail-fence. No fence ever stood so much in my way. I could not get to it for the crowd that was ahead of me. We all wanted to get over it first. But many never got over it at all. None of us sat on the top rail to rest. Some tumbled off and ran no further. There was an old house a little way ahead. I reached it safely, and sheltered behind its big chimney, reloaded and fired, and loaded again. I do not know that I hurt anybody. I am not sure that I shot at anybody in particular, but it was a good thing to do. It made me feel better. My fingers were so cold that I could hardly handle the cartridges; but they very soon warmed up to the work. A team of battery-horses came dashing along without riders, and passing between two gate-posts; one of them struck a post and was killed. By this time we were so scattered and mingled that hardly two of a company were together, and there did not seem to be anyone to give us a word of command. It was a plain case of "everyone for himself, and the devil take the hindmost."

The pursuit had now somewhat slackened and the noise behind us was not so furious, but we continued our retreat until we crossed the small creek about one mile from where we started. Here we seemed to be at a distance safe enough to stop and breathe, and gather ourselves together. The flag was still with us, and one or two of our regimental officers made it a rallying point. In a few minutes a large fragment of the regiment had clustered around, not nearly so badly whipped as they thought, but hardly knowing what to do. The panic was over, the scare was out of us, and we were ready to retreat in an orderly manner, if further retreat was necessary. We had not lost all hope, but we had lost our breakfast, and now began to realize the emptiness of our stomachs. But it was, no doubt, the loss of our breakfasts that saved our stomachs, for the enemy, finding it all prepared, tarried long enough to gather it up. That short delay gave us time to get beyond their reach.

Having taken our breath and refreshed ourselves from the clear waters of the creek, we consulted together and studied the situation. The battle was raging on our left and front with increasing fury, and we could see the lines of gray swinging around our right. It was dangerous to go further back, for we saw signs of rebel cavalry in that direction. We did not dare to tarry longer where we were. The only thing to do was the thing we did. Deliberately moving off to the left and front, and to the rear of the still unbroken centre, we gathered up fragments of our own and other regiments, until we had quite a respectable company. The right wing having been thus broken, the centre was left to bear the whole force of the attack, which was now being made upon both its flank and front with an energy increased by present success and confidence in future victory.

But the centre was not so easily put to rout. Having had some time to prepare for the shock, it was ready to meet it, the positions of the regiments being changed only so far as necessary to resist the flank approaches of the enemy.

In the meantime, Rosecrans had hurried his left division to the right, and uniting them to the centre, formed a new line of battle almost at right angles with the old. This line was strongly posted, and formed a rallying place for the demoralized regiments from the right. Here we all halted, and together gave the first real check to the exulting foe. All the afternoon the battle raged among the cedars, shifting from one point to another, until night drew her curtains between the combatants and ordered a truce until morning.

It was a long, cold night that followed, and a busy one to both the armies. Lines were reformed, weak places strengthened, and breastworks of logs and stones hastily thrown up. What was left of our brigade was sent back to the right and rear to guard against cavalry, and give warning of any danger from the north. We had nothing to eat. Our blankets were giving comfort to the enemy, and we were allowed no fires. All night long we could hear the sounds of preparation for the coming day, and we felt gloomy and doubtful and miserable enough. We had time to think over the events of the day, to count up the missing, and wonder what was their fate; to think of our homes, so many of them soon to be clouded with sorrow. There was no chance for sleep and no occasion for motion, so we just sat and waited, and watched the old year out and the new one in.

When morning came it brought us a little comfort in the softer atmosphere and pleasant sunshine, but no breakfast. All remained quiet on the lines of battle. The morning passed and gave place to noon, and still we waited for the opening gun. The afternoon had almost passed when a furious uproar began near the centre of our line, and we were hurried to the rear of

A FIERCE DASH AT STONE RIVER.

Shells shrieked over us, and bursting, scattered their fragments through our ranks. But it was "close up," "guide right," and still forward until Stone River was reached, and we paused for a moment on its bank. A part of the line passed over and the Southern ranks were broken. They fell back and doubled upon their centre, which, already strained to its utmost, gave way, and the battle ended just where it was intended that it should begin.

At night we rested where our work ended, but to most of us there was no rest. There was comfort in the thought that our defeat had turned to victory; that we who had fared so badly under the first stroke of the enemy were permitted to lay the last stroke on his back. All night long the rain poured down as though it would wash away every stain of blood. All night long we listened to the cries of the wounded where they lay upon the field. All night long the ambulances were busy gathering in the sheaves of this fearful harvest. All night long we waited and watched and wondered if the battle were really over.

The morning came, dark and damp and gloomy enough, but revealed no enemy. The pickets gave no alarm. The scouts reported Bragg in full retreat and many miles away. We quietly took possession of Murfreesboro and turned her churches and public buildings into hospitals and store-houses. The wounded were gathered in, the dead buried, the losses counted up, the news sent back to the anxious North, and the battle of Stone River became history.

where the battle was in progress. It continued only a short time. The enemy having made the assault was repulsed so decidedly that nothing more was heard from him that evening. A little food had by this time been secured and some blankets hunted up. The night was not nearly so cold, and we began to take a more hopeful view of the situation. The morning came too soon.

The third day of the battle passed with only skirmishing enough to let us know that we were not deserted. It was late in the afternoon when an attack was ordered on the left, in which the broken regiments of the first day's battle were to take a prominent part. We heard the orders with no particular pleasure, though we were anxious enough to redeem our reputation. We had a very general idea of the work before us and believed we were going to win. The order was given and we started forward. Down through the open fields we rushed, keeping in as good order as possible. Cannon thundered before us, to the right of us, and behind us.

WIGGINS OF OUR STAFF.

General Horatio C. King.

I DOUBT if any one knew Wiggins of our staff as well as I did. He was a strange mixture of frankness and reserve, and just when you thought you had his entire confidence, he would shut himself up like a clam.

I had been spending a couple of weeks in idleness, at Sheridan's headquarters, near the old battle-field of Cedar Creek, waiting for an assignment to Merritt's staff, where I could exchange my single-breasted captain's coat for a major's uniform, with two rows of buttons down the front. I had been over to see Merritt and the boys, at the stone house, about a half mile from Sheridan's. Some of them I had known in the Army of the Potomac, and Merritt especially, who had picked up a star by his brilliant conduct at Brandy Station, in one of the brightest cavalry fights of the war, that brought out the mettle of our troops, and made Custer a brigadier-general, also.

HORATIO C. KING.

There was Dana, our assistant adjutant-general, who was in over thirty general engagements without a scratch, and lost an eye a few years after the war, in chopping a stick of wood (such is fate) ; and Bean, Drew, Baker, Halberstadt, and Gordon (an inexhaustible humorist), and others equally brave and jolly, whose names have for the moment gone out of my memory. All these had more or less of a history, but all said: "You must see Wiggins. He's home just now ; got a scratch at Cedar Creek ; shot through the fleshy part of the thigh—and was very much disgusted, he said, because no one could tell, from the character of the wound, whether he was advancing or retreating—the ball sort o' ploughed through the flesh, fore and aft, and Wiggins himself wouldn't have been sure whether he was hit from the front or rear, if he hadn't known he was going to the front, under a permit and order from Merritt." You see, it happened in this way:

Every one knows, who has read anything about that great battle, that Jubal Early was awake very early, and got in some fine work before any of our soldiers were fairly out of bed. I have heard it stated since the war, that General Gordon was largely responsible for this surprise, but as Jubal Early was his senior, he, of course, got the credit of it.

Four o'clock is not very early when one sits up all night, but it does seem a trifle premature for waking up a whole army. But this is what Early did, and under cover of a thick fog, the advance walked right over the left of the line, occupied by the eighth corps, under General Crook. Wiggins said that Wright made a mistake here, in not having a cavalry vidette in advance of his infantry picket, but somehow or other, all the cavalry had been sent over to the other flank, where they were not particularly needed. In fact, after the terrible rout at Winchester, I doubt if any one had serious thoughts of another battle in that vicinity. Sheridan, in his official report, says that the surprise was due probably to not closing in Powell, or that the cavalry divisions of Merritt and Custer were sent away over to the right, where there was no turnpike, and but little danger of attack.

The enemy came upon our pickets with such suddenness that they had no opportunity to give the alarm, and the lively Confederates were actually prodding our bunks with their bayonets, before the eighth corps men could get their clothes on. Molineux, with a brigade of the Nineteenth corps, happened to be up for a reconnoissance, and did manly work in checking the advance. But the unceremonious treatment of the Confederates was very demoralizing, and the line was forced back a couple of miles, leaving some twenty-four guns in the enemy's hands. I suppose they needed them very much at that time, for it was common report in Richmond that Sheridan had been making rather free with the Confederate batteries in the valley, and that on the last battery of Armstrong's, kindly introduced through the blockade by our English friends across the water, some wag had written the address, "General Jubal E. Early, commanding Army of the Shenandoah, near Winchester, Virginia, care of General Philip H. Sheridan." I saw this battery, but not the address, and therefore do not vouch for its truth, but then there was a good deal of fun on both sides, notwithstanding the serious business in which we were engaged.

I was told Wiggins actually saw the address, but he never admitted it, though he was in at the capture of the battery and got the scratch, of which I am going to tell you later.

Our line got a lively walloping, and didn't get its wind fairly until it had reached a point between Middletown and Newtown. Sheridan was in Washington, and Wright was in command. Wiggins used to say that if Sheridan hadn't gone to Washington there wouldn't have been any surprise, because the Confederates wouldn't have wasted any time to surprise Sheridan, who always slept with one eye open; but then you can't almost always tell. The Confederates never had any trouble to find out all about our movements, and Early himself says he knew Sheridan was in Washington when he planned the attack.

Well, Sheridan came up in the nick of time. Our stragglers were rushing back toward Winchester in great numbers, carrying exaggerated accounts of our reverses. One straggler can make more noise and tell more lies than a whole company of brave men—so Wiggins used to say in one of his moments of frankness, and I guess, if he were alive to-day, he would find these same laggards in the front rank of pension claimants, howling vigorously for the "old flag and an appropriation."

The story about Sheridan and the black horse was every bit true. Read's poetry has the usual license, but the horse was there, and the rider too; and when there was any fighting to be done, they moved together with lively rapidity. When Sheridan arrived, Wright had his lines re-formed, and the impression prevailed that a fresh advance was not contemplated. I remember making this statement once at an Army meeting, and I came near having to fight a duel with every member of the 6th corps, with that prince of good fellows, Colonel Andy Smith, at the head. So I do not repeat it, but simply say that Wiggins said so. However, Sheridan took in the situation, rode along the lines, received a royal ovation, and gave the command, "Forward!"—and here is where Wiggins got his scratch, as he called it. The first cavalry division was holding the pike—and it was the only decent road in the valley—and that battery of new Armstrongs opened on the boys in the meanest kind of way—and in a way, Wiggins said, not to be tolerated. So he asked Merritt if he couldn't take a regiment and make a flank movement and silence that fire. Merritt said he might, and in about five minutes Wiggins was behind that battery, hacking away at the gunners and acting like a madman. The

gunners found it was no use, and took to the rear (those who didn't throw up their hands), and Wiggins was so wild that he jumped astraddle of a gun and fairly hugged it with delight. If he had been on his feet and in less exposed position, he couldn't have got that ball through the fleshy part of his thigh, as I have told you, and he wouldn't have had to explain that when he was struck he actually had his back to the enemy; though I never could see how he could have had it any other way so long as the guns he captured were faced toward us—and Wiggins, of course, wouldn't have faced any other way than toward the muzzle.

Well, you all know the result. The reverse of the morning was turned into a victory in the afternoon. The good things in our camps were too much for the Confederates, who hadn't been living on Delmonico fare or dressing in Raymond's best suits for some time. Sheridan got all his guns back, including that Armstrong battery, sent, as I have intimated, to his care, and one of the guns had a liberal splashing from Wiggins' thigh, all because he didn't know the difference between gunback and horseback, and that the meanest place for a cavalryman is astride of a gun in a heated engagement.

Well, as I was saying, everybody said to me, "You ought to know Wiggins; he's a brick. You'll like him, if you can only get to understand him." I began to think I was not going to get to know him, it took so long to make out my assignment to Merritt. But Colonel Harry Page finally succeeded in cutting the red tape, and I reported for duty, and, as luck would have it, was quartered in Wiggins' tent, which I had all to myself for a few days. These I spent in tidying up the place and burying a few horses that were lying around after the fight. One morning, I was sitting outside (for this was early in October, and still very pleasant), when a strapping red-headed six-footer came limping up the walk. Wiggins, by the way, was in the signal corps, and his red head was a good substitute for a torch in night-signaling. He came right up to me and stuck out his hand, and gave me a hearty grip which fairly made my knuckles crack. He said he was not feeling very strong (for which I felt grateful), but hoped to be all right in a few days. I asked him what he did with the gun he captured, and he said he had turned it over to the government to make up into medals—some of the same, I suppose, which by a gentle fiction still enter into the composition of Grand Army badges.

Wiggins and I soon grew intimate. I had the picture of a lovely girl that I had left behind me in Brooklyn, and when I wanted to arouse Wiggins I used to take it out and show it to him. He would gaze at it long and earnestly, and several times I observed he was on the point of saying something, but stopped short, and, so to speak, swallowed his words. I tried hard to draw him out, but he always turned me off by telling a story, which, by the way, he did very well. I recall one which struck me as amusing, and I have since heard Major Brodhead, of happy memory, get it off at Grand Army encampments with great unction. The story goes that a patriotic private was doing picket duty on the Rappahannock that terribly cold winter when Burnside lay along Falmouth keeping watch of Lee on the Fredericksburg side. It was one of those mean winters, when it would freeze for three days and thaw the balance of the week, and it was colder when it was thawing than when there was an honest freeze. The night was bitter cold, and as the picket walked his beat, he dropped into soliloquy. When a soldier hadn't anybody else to talk to, he found comfort in talking to himself, and this particular soldier ran on in this style:

"Yes, I love my country, but just look at those shoes; nice protection they are for such a night as this. But (straightening himself up and grasping his musket more firmly) I love my country; but look at this shoddy overcoat and these pants. Fine lay-out this for a grateful government. But I love my country; but if I ever get out of this scrape, I'll be d—d if I ever love another country."

Sheridan found we were too far from our base of supplies (we had to cart everything from Martinsburg), and so we moved back to Winchester, and in a little while had the railroad in running order to that point. In one of his confidential moments Wiggins let fall the fact that he had left his heart at home in the keeping of a sweet girl, who, by the way, was not in the best of health. Every once in awhile when the mail came and brought him a letter, I would find him very low-spirited. I knew, without his telling me, that she was growing worse, and one day a black-bordered envelope foretold the news that the worst had happened, and that she had been taken home. If he was moody before, he was desperate now, and chafed under the restraint and monotony of winter quarters.

But I must skip over the dull winter months until the early opening of the spring campaign,

the raid down through Virginia (I thought we would go entirely *through* the State, the mud was so deep), which brought us out on the Pamunkey, and finally to Hancock Station, near City Point.

Wiggins had attracted my attention by his recklessness during the raid. He always wanted to go where there was any special danger, and begged to lead every scouting party on the march.

We were lying together one night in the tent, and he said to me: "King, if anything happens to me, I want you to take charge of a little package which you will find in my breast-pocket. It will make some things clear to you."

I was tempted again to draw him out, and I said, "Wiggins, why don't you tell me exactly what you want and what troubles you?"

"My dear fellow," he said, "nothing troubles me, except living. My heart was buried long ago." And then he told me the story of how he had loved a sweet girl; how he had left her to enter the army, and how she had sickened and died. It had preyed upon his mind until he was desperate, and the one thing he desired was to meet her.

We started out on the raid which culminated in the battle of Five Forks. Wiggins was in the fore-front all the time, but seemingly bore a charmed life. I saw him lead a regiment into action, and he was devoid of fear. The death he courted didn't come, while many a poor fellow who wanted to come out safely, received his quietus.

In all the three days' fighting Wiggins was constantly exposed, and yet he told me that he never saw anything so slow. He said if Warren had got the 5th corps into action sooner there might have been a better chance for Sheridan to shove the 1st cavalry division to the front, and then he might have seen some livelier fighting. I think I never saw a man so foolish. It did look to me as if he thought dying was the most delightful occupation of life.

But if this was his idea, luck failed him, and he came into headquarters at Jettersville thoroughly disgusted, and declared that the whole thing was a farce, and that Lee ought to have been bagged in that Five Forks engagement. He was brimful of fight and disappointment.

There was a short halt at Jettersville, and breastworks were thrown up. Lee's plan to make a stand there was abandoned, because Merritt was reaching out on his left and keeping the Confederates in motion. It was a lively stern chase, and we kept banging away at the retreating forces whenever we could see a soldier or a wagon. How the teamsters did quail before the shot and shell, and I guess they wished that they had been in the rank and file with muskets in their hands. It was safer than being teamsters.

It was just after the halt at Jettersville that I saw Wiggins again. He had had a little trouble with Meade's headquarter train, which got in the way of the advance of the cavalry, and were disposed to be uncivil. The infantry were in the habit of taking more equipage for the general and staff than the cavalry thought of carting around for a whole division. I knew Wiggins was angry and dispirited and the prey to foolish fancies. He told me that after he had gotten through with the captain of Meade's headquarter guard, the 3d infantry, who had charge of the palatial outfit, he pushed on to catch up with Devin. The night was exquisitely beautiful. Not a cloud obscured the sky, and the stars shone brilliantly. The scene was so beautiful, he stopped at the first stream to water his horse, and, leaning on the saddle, took in the beauty of the outlook.

Gazing up into the sky, he declared to me that he saw as distinctly as if he had held her in his arms the dear girl he had lost. He insisted that it was no figment of the imagination, and that if ever man did see the spirit of one who had gone before, then he saw his beloved one.

I think this made him more desperate than ever, and his one idea seemed to be that she had made this disclosure to him to entice him to her. He told me this, and nothing could dissuade him from this notion, and after this he was more reckless than ever and foolishly courted danger.

The chase grew very hot, until Lee made up his mind to give the boys a rest, by ordering Ewell to hold his corps as a rear guard at Sailor's Creek. The position was a desperate one. Sailor's Creek was a little Virginia stream, across which any one could wade at that season without getting seriously wet. But on both sides there were commanding hills. The Confederates placed their men at the base of the hill on their side, and our forces took position on the opposite side with our batteries on the left

and commanding an enfilading fire of the enemy, who had formed line of battle following the line of the creek. I remember a natural rifle-pit at the base of the hill, formed by the rush of the rains down the main road. It was filled with Confederates, and from it they poured a deadly fire upon our lines. I saw Wiggins turn to Devin and ask him if he couldn't take a regiment and clear out that party. Devin hesitated for a moment, but finally said: "All right, Wiggins, go ahead, but don't let them get away from you." Wiggins rushed off like mad, and in almost less time than I can tell it the rifle-pit was silent and the fight was over. Ewell and almost all his entire corps fell into our hands as prisoners of war, and among them my old friend Henry Kyd Douglass, with whom I had had many pleasant college associations before the war. Wiggins did not return, but that did not worry us much, because he was so erratic; but the next morning when he did not report, Devin asked me to take a detail from the 5th cavalry and look him up. We crossed over the creek, and the sight I then saw I have never forgotten. That raking fire had done its deadly work. The ground was so thick with corpses the horses would not move. You can't make a horse tread on a live or a dead body if he can help it, and the dead were so thick there was no chance to jump them. So we had to get down, move the bodies aside, and make our examination on foot. On the right of the road was that natural rifle-pit I have spoken about, and it was filled with Confederate soldiers. I had noticed this from a little distance, and as I came nearer I saw a soldier kneeling, with his eyes open, and his hands clasped above his head, as if in prayer. The form set my heart beating wildly; I approached it, and, as I live, it was Wiggins! His face bore a triumphant smile, as if dying in the hour of victory. Close to his heart was the package he had asked me to take charge of. It was only a daguerreotype of a very sweet woman, and in the case were these words: " I lived for her and my country. I shall rejoice to die for my country that I may be with her." Wiggins was a strange fellow, and I guess I was the only one of our staff who even approximately understood him.

VICKSBURG.

IN FRONT OF VICKSBURG, 1863.

A WAR ARTIST AT VICKSBURG.

"KINDNESS used up the 42d Georgia—finished ravages of campaign and siege," said Colonel L. P. Thomas, as captain and ranking officer marched the 42d Georgia out of the Vicksburg fortifications, July 4, 1863. "I ought to tell you, Davis," continued Colonel Thomas, heartily, "how that thoughtful consideration, evidenced by Grant's men from first to last, and from each to all, was appreciated. Looking for nothing of the sort when we marched out of Vicksburg that morning, downhearted and bitter, ragged and hungry, bitterly cross, we found Grant's men well fed—yes, when we did find them. You know they were withdrawn from the front until we had stacked arms and hung our equipments on the stacks, and rested our colors upon the guns with which we had defended those flags so well. Then, guided, we marched to camping-grounds, plainly the best to to be found near by. Then every opportunity was given us to tidy up, enjoy better food, better everything, have a rest, and get acquainted with you all.

"Yes, Grant's men were well fed. It was, however, a surprise to see their clothes about in the same plight as our own. Good hats were scarce. We had shot up each other's headwear, and burrowing and living like gophers used up

clothing. When you rode up and spoke to us that morning, we knew that you were a respectable somebody, although appearances were against you, my dear boy," said Colonel Thomas, treating himself to a laugh at the meeting in the intricate maze of sap, parallel, and rifle-pit, to successfully emerge from which there was need of a guide.

Perhaps I should explain that this conversation was in part a chat between Colonel L. P. Thomas, late of the gallant 42d Georgia—but the then sheriff of Douglass County, in which is Atlanta— and myself, then busy working out the preliminaries of what General Joseph E. Johnston named the best battle picture he ever saw. It was the great battle cyclorama of the terrific encounter known to every veteran of the Western army, whether he wore the blue or the gray, as the battle of the 22d of July.

For a quiet afternoon, the colonel had joined me in escaping an aggregation of friends, who were over-ready "to come along" on our reconnoissance. An old army talk was our theme while trudging through Edgewood, a thrifty suburb of Atlanta, to a point where nearly a quarter of a century in the past we had met in a desperate fight. It was the precise locality of this point which we were now to determine, aided by the worn and defaced field note-books in my pocket. The memorandum sketches are to-day the only existing data by which to establish locations; that is, so far as I know of. Our point is directly in the now thrifty village of Edgewood, among its villas and lawns, and beneath the grand old oaks whose branches show how riven and torn they were by shot and shell, a storm of iron not easily forgotten by the brave men who experienced it. I cleared up for the sheriff in our Vicksburg chat, points—until then his knowledge was mainly gained by inference—telling him of Grant's simple instructions, to "remember that our guests to-morrow were soldiers, and that the meeting was an unarmed one; from circumstances, our guests would need to be fed and lodged, the best in our power, and that the incident of stacking arms should take place without the presence of more than a picket guard, and later the men of both armies might meet unarmed and thus fraternize like the pickets' truce, which no one knew of an instance in which consideration for one another was not fully acted out."

I told Sheriff Thomas of how officers of McPherson's and Logan's staffs vied with each other in the darkness of the night of July 3d, searching for grounds fitted for camping because of shade, water, drainage, and lay; and how, finally, before dawn of the 4th, camp grounds had been found for double the number of guests expected, and how the commissary and quartermaster trains had been loaded and pushed up from the Yazoo River, to points convenient for distribution along the front, and how, on the morning of the 4th, General Grant had waited patiently, by the head of the sap, near the white house, until word was brought that Pemberton's men had stacked arms and were ready for direction as to movement. Then General Grant rode in through the saps, taking the route which has since become the highroad, between Vicksburg and Jackson—another instance of army road building on campaign grounds.

The illustrations of this article are elaborated upon the exact lines of the pencil memoranda made on that eventful morning, which is now thirty years back, in the nineteenth century. These illustrations are not intended for highly finished drawings, it being concluded that, as war notes, every effort should be made to simplify the facts.

Vicksburg veterans yet with us, will find little difficulty in tracing out the zigzag course by which they once made safe progress from the ravines, thickly dotted with little earth-roofed dugouts, in the hillsides, down past head-logged saps, with twisted grapevine gabions and fascines of cane, to finally creep into the ditch of a principal fortification known to us as Fort Hill. The ex-Confederate insists that this work was either unnamed or bore a different designation, and I have regretted not asking Colonels Montgomery, Saunders, and Lockett, of General Pemberton's staff, when I met them that morning of July 4th, on the parapet of this fortification, to designate it for me; but they were so anxious to know what West Pointer directed the serving of the "cohorns," that, after a moment's thought, I took them hastily to the point where Tressalian's wooden mortars, the supposed cohorns, had been fired until they burst, always handled by some calculating private, who exploded the two-ounce charge that tossed the twelve-pound shell the few feet to its mission, live ashes from the soldier's pipe being used to explode loose powder priming to the "cohorn's" charge.

I won't attempt a description of their amazement. One of the gentlemen remarked, "Hell!" and the rest said, *sotto voce*, "They made it one!"

In the general view, the Vicksburg oak is seen to the left, near by an orchard group of trees. Beneath the spreading branches of this oak, Grant and Pemberton met, under the truce preceding capitulation.

The two generals alone then walked slowly a hundred or more feet to the front, where, seated on the sloping earthwork's side, they arranged a basis for preliminaries, while the then veteran, General A. J. Smith, and General McPherson, standing on the works, still farther to the right, chatted with General Bowen and Colonel Montgomery, of General Pemberton's staff.

Of the group remaining beneath the tree, the only ones alive to-day are the veteran editor, Charles A. Dana, and the author of this article.

The larger illustration is sketched from a line point of view, but several hundred feet west of the location from which the first sketch was made. The point was just in advance of Coonskin's tower, a novel structure of timber, built under the direction of Captain Foster, an Indiana officer, whose odd headgear gained him his cognomen.

Since the ditches of the Confederate fortifications were, in many instances, held by Grant's men, Pemberton's men, to complete the terms of surrender, marched out of their own works into those of General Grant's.

This is mentioned to explain why the arms were stacked in what appears to be singular locations.

Beneath the salient of the chief fortification will be seen a dark spot in the upright side of the ditch. This was the entrance through which more than a ton of powder was carried a hundred feet or more, along a narrow gallery, beneath the works.

The explosion of this powder drove out a huge mass of earth, leaving a crater, to be instantly seized, under the protecting veil of dust, and for a few days the Stars and Stripes stood marking the extreme advance, as shown in the sketch. The battle-flag then waved where, in the illustration, the flag of truce is located.

We had chatted back and forth at this point, perhaps to arrange for a social event, such as a vocal serenade by the Lombard brothers. "If you fellows will only quit your blame shootin'," or, as in another instance, a protest came expostulating that our thoughtless use of soap in washing clothes "in every doggoned crick that runs from you un's camp into we un's works," was a serious matter, and it pleases me to-day to say that this plaint was promptly heeded, and some runs, among the several winding toward the Mississippi through each corps, were guarded, that they might flow, with the same purity we wot of, to the appreciating men who were beleaguered. Even mules and horses were not watered in these little streams.

There were courtesies by and between soldiers which were not made prominent to officers. The boys did it in their own ways, and I am satisfied that lives were purposely spared by brave men, who were ready to fight and die in the cause each believed to be fully the right, but to use an army phrase, "There was nothing mean about them."

The face of nature changes rapidly under the luxuriant foliage growth of a semi-tropic climate. The war was only a year or two in the past, when I made a careful inspection of the "old" Vicksburg ground.

Rain, cultivation, and nature had generally effaced earthworks and smoothed the shot-torn earth; jagged crests no longer marked shell explosions, which on this 4th of July, 1863, showed everywhere.

Cottonwood trees, twenty to thirty feet high, were growing in rank luxuriance on earthwork,

magazine, and tent site. Exactly where Logan's tent had formerly been pitched a cottage stood, and noting this structure to be without a cellar, at my suggestion the owner of the cottage came with me, bringing an axe and brush-hook, and he presently had a cellar not sufficiently distant from his home to be inconvenient. I had uncovered for him the heavy outer door of wood,

HEAD OF M'PHERSON'S SAPS.

and later worked open a second door, to show him quite a spacious apartment, ceiled, sided, and floored with heavy two-inch plank, taken originally from the flooring stuff of our pontoon train. The boards were still in fair condition, and a few bags of powder were yet there—cartridges once for the nine-inch guns, formerly in battery near by, and the powder being too coarse-grained for use in small arms, it was suggested to celebrate with it. I gained favor as a cellar-finder, when on other days I repeated this action, and became known as an individual who was better posted about springs—good ones, too, that had been washed out and lost—than "a'ry" chap who had come along yet.

Odd meetings in the vicinity of revisited battle-fields have resulted in acquaintances and friendships, and there is yet to be an instance where a veteran ex-Confederate was not a kindly self-constituted host to me, and a willing companion over ground where once a conflict raged in which we were on distinctly opposite sides.

Plainly there is yet the same feeling that led Grant's men to treat the soldiers who capitulated at Vicksburg as guests, not prisoners, and thus, to use my friend Colonel Thomas' expression, "work a scatteration among his Georgia boys," which in present and future will surely event in a concentration which can be best comprehended by a veteran.

THEO. R. DAVIS.

GENERAL PEMBERTON'S HEADQUARTERS, VICKSBURG.

COURTESY OF GRANT, THE CONQUEROR.

AMONG the gallant defenders of Vicksburg, was Brigadier-General Thomas P. Dockery, of Arkansas. On the day following the surrender, Mrs. Dockery, accompanied by a neighboring planter, made her way to the Federal lines, in the rear of Vicksburg, in the hope of receiving tidings of her husband, who had so long been penned up in that beleaguered city. During all that tedious siege, Mrs. Dockery had been waiting, with the planter's family, a few miles from the town, listening to the ceaseless roar of cannon, and hoping against hope for the safety of her husband. When Vicksburg fell, she persuaded the planter to secure an old, dilapidated buggy, which had escaped the general destruction, and, with the aid of a mule, picked up along the highway, and harness improvised from pieces of old straps, ropes, and strings, the lady and her host set out for Grant's headquarters.

All was confusion and bustle, but the boys in blue were all in excellent humor, and after a dusty drive, the mule was halted close to General Grant's shady retreat, about three miles in the rear of the city. Here the guard declined to let the party pass, declaring that "the old man" was too busy to see them. Mrs. Dockery, with tears in her eyes, begged the soldier to go to Grant and tell him that a lady in deep distress wished to see him "just one little minute." Thus entreated, the sentry strode to the tent of the general, and instantly returned with an invitation for the lady to come at once, accompanied by her escort.

Mrs. Dockery and the planter left their ancient equipage with the guards, and started for the general's tent, with fear and trembling.

They were now to face the grim warrior who had rendered vain the formidable defences of Vicksburg. To their infinite relief and surprise, Grant met them cordially; and having courteously given them seats, ordered his attendants to provide cool water for his jaded guests, also insisting that Mrs. Dockery occupy the "easy chair" vacated by himself.

As soon as the lady could command her over-wrought nerves, she stated her errand to the Union commander, and requested the favor of a pass, so that she might proceed to Vicksburg, and learn the fate of her husband. Grant replied, "Madam, General Grant has issued an order that there shall be no passing to and from Vicksburg, and he cannot set the example of violating his own orders."

Mrs. Dockery tearfully said, "Then what shall I do?"

General Grant smiled pleasantly, and replied, "Oh, don't distress yourself, madam. I will take it upon myself to get news from your husband. He must be a gallant fellow to have won such a devoted wife."

"But when can I know, general? Don't you see this suspense is killing me?"

"You shall know at once," said Grant, "and you shall be my guest until my orderly can ride to General Pemberton's headquarters and return with the news."

A moment later, a courier was galloping toward the city, with a note from Grant to Pemberton, requesting information regarding General Dockery, and advices of the lady's whereabouts.

Meantime, dinner was served, and Mrs. Dockery and her friend dined with the great Northern captain and his retinue of officers, not one of whom spoke a word to wound the feelings of the anxious guests. The general himself was exceedingly agreeable, and, eschewing war topics, talked of the South and its products with all the vim and interest of a Southern country gentleman.

In due time the orderly returned, with a note from Pemberton, stating that General Dockery was in excellent health, and would visit his wife as soon as General Grant would permit him to do so. Handing the note to the now happy wife, Grant remarked, "You shall see him in a day or two; just as soon as we can fix things a little. I shall not forget your name, and, of course, shall have to remember him."

Upon his visitors' departure, Grant expressed his appreciation of their call, and wrote on a scrap of paper a pass, permitting General and Mrs. Dockery to return to their home, signed his name, and politely bade them adieu.

* * * * *

The editor is indebted to Miss Octavia Dockery, daughter of the general, for the subjoined anecdote of "Grant's dog," which story, coming from a valiant officer, under Pemberton, shows how completely the chivalrous Grant won the hearts of the soldiers he conquered. In this connection, Miss Dockery writes:

The world loves a great name, and listens with interest to even the remotest incidents connected with greatness. This manuscript should find welcome among your readers, since it tells an incident in the most eventful part of the great general's life. It was given me by the writer, a brave Confederate soldier, who has fought his last battle on earth, and I take pleasure in sending it for publication, as I know the author himself would have done.

The little dog belonged to my mother, and became well known throughout Arkansas. My earliest recollections are of "Truce" and her family, all as snowy as herself, fresh from the bath, toddling in on the rich old-fashioned velvet carpet, in the spacious parlors of "Lamartine," to receive the guests, who always asked to see "Grant's dog."

The following is a story of "Truce":

We so often hear of the terse and seemingly abrupt manner of speaking peculiar to the late General Grant, that it is the impression of many that he was not a man given to saying pretty or complimentary things; but a little incident witnessed by the writer, who was among the defeated at Vicksburg, proves the great general's ability to say a graceful thing at the proper moment.

It was one morning, a few days after General Pemberton's surrender, and the Confederate troops were marching out of the fated city. The officers' wives and families were in conveyances. The victorious Grant stood watching the retiring Confederate army, the habitual cigar in his mouth. A white spitz dog lay curled at his feet. This dog was a pet of the boys at Federal headquarters, and a great favorite of the general himself.

As the carriage occupied by Mrs. General Thomas P. Dockery drew near, General Grant caught up the little snow-white dog and handed it in to that lady, saying, gallantly: "Let this be a flag of truce between us, madam, and if my

PRESENT ASPECT OF SPOT WHERE GRANT AND PEMBERTON MET; WITH MONUMENT.

men continue to possess the courage you have shown during the siege, I would not say, 'I may conquer,' but 'I have conquered,' the South."

The dog was ever afterward called "Truce," and soon became as much the pride of the boys in gray as it had been the joy of those who wore the blue.

* * * * *

We were in bivouac one night, after a long march, and the soldiers lay stretched on the hard ground, sleeping soundly. I was aroused by something tugging at my sleeve and a distressed whine. Yes, it was "Truce," and, not a little annoyed, I drove the dog from me. Nothing daunted by my scolding, she made a successful effort to awaken the soldier next to me. Just then a bullet whizzed over our heads and the report of a musket fell on the still air; another and another, one ball grazing the tree where my head had been resting. By this time we were all awake and ready for the fray, and were not surprised to find that we were the targets of sharpshooters on the Federal side. The keen perception of danger natural to the dog had saved many lives.

"Truce" was looked upon as a "mascot" after that by the soldiers of General Dockery's command. Confederate veterans served as pallbearers when this heroic little war dog was laid to rest, and its silky, snowy little body reposed in a white satin-lined casket. YAZOO.

LANDING OF THE FEDERAL FORCES AT INDIAN BEND, LA., APRIL, 1863.

"IMPREGNABLE VICKSBURG."

WITH the axiom, "All's for the best," it might seem proper that on days of national jubilee we should regard our tribulations as blessings which blazed the way to the land of promise. Still, an old Confederate of the right mettle, and with an average amount of human nature, has no satisfaction in dwelling upon a day of defeat and surrender. It is more pleasant for us to think of Manassas, Chickamauga, and the brilliant campaign of Jackson in the valley, than it is for us to talk of the disaster at Vicksburg, for the fall of Vicksburg sundered the Confederacy and sealed its fate. Further contest was war against the inevitable.

Vicksburg was regarded as the Gibraltar of the South. Farragut had thundered vainly against its lofty bluffs and steep red hills. Sherman's legions met irretrievable disaster in seeking approach by way of the Yazoo swamps. Grant spent men and money without stint in the futile effort to turn the city by changing the channel of the Mississippi River. The South considered the fortress impregnable. President Davis, even, seemed blind to the possibility that the stronghold could be captured.

When Grant's transports passed the batteries of the city and crossed his army over to Port Gibson, the Federal forces might have been in extreme peril had the Confederate detachments been concentrated and effectively handled. But the Confederate troops, instead of being united, were left to be beaten in detail. Bowen was disposed of near Port Gibson; Joe Johnston waited at Jackson until Sherman came out and drove him across Pearl River, and Pemberton's unsupported army was overwhelmed at the Big Black, and the shattered remnants then cooped up in Vicksburg.

While generalship on the Confederate side was not manifest in any part of the campaign, the Confederate soldiers made their usual record of valor and endurance. The attenuated line of defence could not be broken by a circle of fire from land and water, by subterranean explosions or by charge after charge of columns of infantry. The garrison yielded only to starvation.

Surrender on the Fourth of July, of course, enhanced the glory of conquest, and it naturally intensified the pain of surrender. But Grant spared his prisoners unnecessary humiliation, showing then the spirit of magnanimity which subsequently reflected so much lustre on him at Appomattox.

To the credit of the victors, they were courteous, humane, and considerate to the non-combatants. And the soldiers? Why, the blue and the gray fraternized then as they do now, and as they always will do so long as any of them are left to talk over the hardships and gallant deeds of the "boys" of either army.

AN EX-CONFEDERATE.

FRATERNITY AT VICKSBURG.

THE sentiment which permeates Tales of the War was founded on battle-field, when both sides were contending for what each thought right.

At Vicksburg, General Tom Taylor was commandant of the post, and I was provost marshal. About a week before the surrender one of our companies captured about forty Illinois soldiers, three of whom were officers, one being the captain. As he was sick, I asked and obtained permission from General Pemberton to keep the officers in the court-house,  JOHN F. BLACK. instead of in jail. The captain dined with me every day during his stay. Just prior to the surrender of Vicksburg the officers, under partial parole, were sent back to their company, because of the over-crowded condition of our prisons.

As the officers were leaving us, the captain turned and, seizing my hand, shook it warmly, at the same time remarking that my horse was very thin.

I told him that it was because we had no oats, and it was compelled to subsist only on what grass it could pick.

The day after our surrender I was surprised to see a wagon stop before our headquarters and unload a bale of hay, two or more sacks of oats, and a lot of fine canned goods for my own table. It was from the Union captain, whose name I cannot recall. I consider that one instance of the pleasant personal feeling existing between our two armies.

After the surrender of Vicksburg, General McPherson (whom I consider one of the most perfect officers and gentlemen I ever met) had General Taylor's position, commandant of the post. He took possession of the headquarters, and I spent many a pleasant day and evening with him.

One afternoon, while we were sitting talking together, two squads of soldiers, of about ten or twelve each, passed us. One was Union, the other Confederate.

General McPherson said: "Look here, captain, if you had come into Vicksburg, without knowing which army had been victorious, and seen those two squads pass, which would you have selected as the victorious?"

I asked him to excuse me, as I hardly cared to answer the question.

"Come," said he, "be frank; answer as you think."

"Well, then, general," I replied, "the Union soldiers are very well dressed but seem very slouchy. Their coats are all open and they don't appear like soldiers, while the Confederates, not as well dressed, have their coats well buttoned, their side-arms (which they were allowed to keep by the terms of surrender) well cleaned and in order; therefore I must give the palm to the Confederates."

"Perfectly correct; same opinion struck me as those men passed. Your army has been defeated, but no one would know it from the appearance of soldiers or officers," was his laconic answer.   JOHN F. BLACK.

SIGHTS AND SCENES OF SIEGE AND SURRENDER.

IN the action at Vicksburg, on December 29, 1862, only two divisions, Morgan's and Steele's, were actively engaged.

We could see the movements of the Confederates and Vicksburg was plainly seen. Some of us were restless; we wanted to rush on, but knew that it was impossible to take the city, and galled under our forced inactivity.

That night it rained incessantly. The next morning there was no change for us, but the enemy's artillery assumed a threatening position. It was evident they intended to storm our position. Our men withdrew, so as to clean their guns, which had rusted from the night's exposure. On Wednesday both sides, in the presence of the other, began to make preparations for offence and defence, throwing up new works, digging new pits, etc.

On Tuesday afternoon the cries of our wounded could be heard all over the field, and an impromptu relief was sent to them. As this, however, was irregular and unauthorized, the flag of truce was fired upon. The dying of Blair's and Thayer's command had to lie there and await the tedious process of official communication.

On Wednesday morning, everything being quiet, a flag of truce was run up, in order to obtain time to attend our sick. This being regular, an interval of four hours was granted to bury our dead. As they always did, the pickets and sharpshooters took advantage of this to talk to each other. The conversation was opened by one of our pickets, who asked:

"How far is it to Vicksburg?"

"So far that you'll never git thar," answered the "Confed."

"How many men have you got?" asked another of our men.

"Enough to clean you out," answered the same "Reb." Another of the gray boys thought he would give us something to think about, and said:

"Banks has been whipped out at Port Hudson, Memphis has been retaken, and you blasted Yanks won't get Vicksburg till Hades freezes over."

In a short time the field was cleared, and everything was quiet on the lines. Shortly after the fight recommenced.

Sitting around the camp-fire one night, one of my comrades was telling about different sights he had seen in Vicksburg in 1863.

VICKSBURG FROM THE RIVER.

There was a church, very small, situated on the top of a hill. Floor, pews, and altar were all gone. Even the string-pieces that had supported the floor were gone. Some negroes sat in the corners, cooking. A marble font lay broken on the ground, while the bowl was used for ordinary ablutions and washing dishes.

"How did this happen?" asked my friend.

"You see, sah, as how de secesh dey done gone and hab camp in yere and bu'nt de pews and pulpit, and we, sah, only bu'nt de flo.'"

In the cemetery, graves were opened and bodies exposed. One grave had the embalmed body of a celebrated duelist, who had been killed in Arkansas, opposite Memphis. Fresh young faces looked up through glass covers, with smiles on their faces, as if pleasant dreams were passing through their minds. The fences had been burned, and all was desolation. Desecration sat there—the mournful reminder of a curse too deep for words to express.

———

However, the most melancholy sight that I ever witnessed was the surrender of Vicksburg. Brave men had been conquered and humbled, and no matter what the cause for which they fought, the sight of their humility was a sorrowful spectacle. They were brave men, and many a hard-fought battle will bear witness to the fact that better soldiers never followed abler leaders in a "Lost Cause."

They marched out of their intrenchments in regiments on the grassy declivity, stacked their arms, hung their colors in the centre, laid off their knapsacks, belts, cartridge-boxes, etc., and marched down the Jackson road to the city. I watched the whole proceeding, and as I watched my eyes grew dim with unshed tears, as I saw the cheeks of bronzed and brave Confederates wet as they looked upon the colors which they were leaving. The men went through the scene with downcast look, never uttering a word. The officers spoke the necessary words of command in a low tone, much like what we hear at funerals. Generals McPherson, Logan, and Forney watched them as they left.

It would be impossible for me to describe their clothing, and more impossible to conjecture how men clothed as they were could fight as they did. The troops were from Texas, Alabama, Mississippi, Louisiana, Georgia, and Missouri. Their flags were new to me, being a plain red field with a white cross in the centre.

After the troops had left, the officers, Federal and Confederate, mounted their horses and swept on to the city, at the outskirts of which was situated a stone house, built in real old Southern fashion, and almost hid in an exuberance of foliage. This was General Forney's headquarters. Here we met General Pemberton. Shortly after General Grant came in, and after talking about five minutes with General Pemberton, completed the terms of capitulation.

Generals McPherson and Logan then went toward the camp to bring in the latter's regiment, and a party started for the city, about a mile distant, to raise "Old Glory" over the court-house, while the officers left behind were chatting as pleasantly as if a short time before they had not been trying to kill each other. At 11.30, on July 4, 1863, Lieutenant-Colonel William E. Strong flung out the Star-spangled Banner to the winds.

In my heart to-day there is no hard feeling to the South because of the war. Both fought for what we thought the right—and we won. In my heart of hearts I have two favorite colors, and those are "blue and gray."

A "G. A. R."

A MIDNIGHT RAMBLE IN THE DITCHES.

I REMEMBER it as if it were yesterday. The pale moon rose calmly, and shone as tranquilly on this troubled section as if we were obeying the command of Him who said, "Love one another." Together a comrade and I climbed a parapet and viewed the siege. The beauty of the scene was enhanced by the rays of the moon, and the mellow light nullified, as far as possible, the grim aspect of war.

Vicksburg was in front of us, beyond the enemy's works. But we could not see it, for it was hidden from our view. The spires of the court-house and of one or two churches alone were discernible through the dim light. The mortars were playing that night, and the sight was *horribly* grand. These words seem to be opposed to each other, but they express my idea more nearly than any others could. I stood awhile entranced. The awful beauty of the scene had a peculiar enchantment for me, which held me to the spot. There the dark court-house tower stood, where the Confederates, in the early part of the siege, had a watch, but our guns made it too dangerous for them. It was lightless; the guards had fled.

I stood contemplating the scene in silence, thinking of how little actual quarrel I had with the men I was now ready to kill, or they me, thinking of the wife I had left home while I went to fight for a cause I was certain was right, and the other side as positive was wrong. Suddenly, off in the direction of Young's Point, beyond the city, the sky became illumined, and a huge, meteor-like object rose in the air, with a long tail almost trailing the ground. Quickly it rose, and then shot over our heads towards the city, where it exploded with a shock that shook the earth for miles around. Near us McPherson's guns were belching forth death-dealing missiles into the ranks of gray, while further to the right Sherman's eight-inch monsters were playing havoc in the enemy's lines. Again a ball shot past us, and we knew by the peculiar sound which followed it that there was but one gun on either side that could have sent it forth — the celebrated Confederate "Whistling Dick." Just then my comrade touched me on the arm and said, "Come on, Bill, let's see how they are getting on with the mine."

Together we walked about one hundred yards to the right of where we were, and entered a deep trench, which we followed down under the winding hills until we reached the opening of a huge cave. A puff of damp air fanned our cheeks, and the close atmosphere made it seem impossible to stay there any length of time.

Away off in the distance we saw the dim flicker of numberless torches, and heard the dull thud of numerous picks as they dug out the tough soil of Mississippi, and gradually drew nearer to a point where we could blow up the enemy's intrenchments. Our men worked night and day.

Finally we came out into the moonlight again, into a wide, deep trench, filled with soldiers. A heavy parapet of cotton bales and earth was flung up towards the enemy. We mounted this parapet. The men lying on the ground behind us were *our* men. The soldiers in gray, only a few feet farther away, were our foes— Wall's famous Texas legion.

We jumped down and entered the other mine. It led towards the enemy's works. Here, as before, the close air; men wheeling barrows of earth and others swinging picks, greeted us. Again we emerged into the fresh air, and this time retraced our steps, for the moon was waning and my garrison opened at midnight.

As we returned, shot and shell shrieked past us. Men wounded were carried off the field, while others, too severely hurt to be moved,

were attended where they had fallen. I reached my tent. It was eleven o'clock. I caught a short nap, and then my company was ordered out. My thoughts of sentiment were gone. I was then again the grim soldier fighting for his country.   A FEDERAL SOLDIER.

A VICKSBURG MENU.

HOTEL DE VICKSBURG.

BILL OF FARE FOR JULY, 1863.

SOUP.
Mule Pie.

BOILED.
Mule Bacon, with Poke Greens.   Mule Ham, canvassed.

ROAST.
Mule Sirloin.   Mule Rump, stuffed with Rice and Vegetables.
Peas and Rice.

ENTREES.
Mule-Head, stuffed, a la mode.   Mule Beef, jerked, a la Mexicana.
Mule Ears, fricasseed, a la gretch.
Mule Side, stewed, new style, hair on.   Mule Liver, hashed.

SIDE DISHES.
Mule Salad.   Mule Hoof, soused.   Mule Brains, a la omelette.
Mule Kidneys, stuffed with Peas.
Mule Tripe, fried in Pea Meal Batter. Mule Tongue, cold, a la bray.

JELLIES.
Mule Foot.

PASTRY.
Pea Meal Pudding, Blackberry Sauce.
Cotton-wood Berry Pie.   China Berry Tarts.

DESSERT.
White-Oak Acorns.   Beech Nuts   Blackberry-Leaf Tea.
Genuine Confederate Coffee.

LIQUORS.
Mississippi Water, vintage of 1498, superior, $3.
Limestone Water, late importation, very fine, $2.75.
Spring Water, Vicksburg brand.

MEALS AT ALL HOURS.

Gentlemen to wait upon themselves. Any inattention on the part of servants should be promptly reported at the office.

JEFF. DAVIS & CO., Proprietors.

CARD.—The proprietors of the justly celebrated Hotel de Vicksburg, having enlarged and refitted the same, are now prepared to accommodate all who favor them with a call. Parties arriving by the river, or by Grant's inland route, will find Grape, Canister & Co.'s carriages at the landing, or any depot on the line of intrenchments. Buck, Ball & Co. take charge of all baggage. No effort will be spared to make the visit of all as interesting as possible.

A HEROINE OF THE SIEGE.

HERE is a letter written from the "City of the Hills" by an officer of high character and undoubted veracity:

I must tell you of a feat performed by a young girl, as told me by one who saw it, on the day of the hardest fight. Her brother belonged to one of the batteries, and hearing that he was wounded, she started alone and on foot for the battle-field, and, against the remonstrance of all who saw her, walked along the line of intrenchments and across an open field, swept by a murderous fire of musketry, grape, and canister, as if she had been going to church to show her new bonnet, to the point where his battery was. You can imagine that the men whom she passed did not fight the worse for the sight.

ANTIETAM-SHARPSBURG, 1862.

Colonel A. H. Nickerson.

THE "BURNSIDE BRIDGE" TO-DAY.

GENERAL McCLELLAN professed to find in the result at Antietam occasion to thank God for a great victory, and General Lee, with apparently the same reverence, and just as much sincerity, thought that the people of the Confederacy had similar reason to return thanks to the same God for having vouchsafed to them a great victory at Antietam, or, as he called it, Sharpsburg. Both of these great generals were men of unimpeachable veracity and unquestioned sincerity, and yet it was hardly possible for both to be victors on that occasion.

Without attempting to cast doubts over either of these paradoxical claims, let us glance at some of the incidents upon which each must base his plea. On the threshold of our inquiry, however, we are met with the stubborn fact that both the contending armies virtually camped on the field of battle, so that neither can lay exclusive claim to this usually unanswerable argument in favor of the right to wear the victor's wreath. McClellan says his army slept that night conquerors on a field won by their valor, and Lee says that his army remained there till the night of the day following the battle.

Antietam was a sort of an accident, or necessary sequence to the capture of Harper's Ferry. In fact, the invasion of Maryland was unexpectedly precipitated by the extraordinary victory

COLONEL A. H. NICKERSON.

to the deliverer. The Confederacy was certainly disappointed by Maryland's failure to respond.

If Antietam was not decided at Harper's Ferry the Confederate success at the latter place at least saved the army under Lee from certain destruction.

As so frequently happened upon other notable occasions, on the success or failure of the flanking column, under the indomitable Stonewall Jackson, depended the wisdom or folly of Lee's stand at Sharpsburg. What would have become of Lee, and that portion of his army that was on the north bank of the Potomac, had Jackson failed to capture Harper's Ferry? The chances would surely have been greatly in favor of their defeat and destruction. Then why, we may further ask, did Lee take such a fearful risk? Stonewall Jackson himself could hardly have asked for a higher compliment than that paid him by what the Confederate Commander-in-Chief did on that occasion.

Why did Wellington await Napoleon's attack at Waterloo when he knew that if Blücher did not come he must be defeated? Simply because he had the same confidence in the old Prussian Field Marshal that Lee had in Jackson. Wellington knew that about the only thing that would prevent old Marshal "Vorwarts" from being at Waterloo, as he had promised, was death.

Lee had a similar faith in Stonewall Jackson, and neither he nor Wellington were disap-

at the Second Bull Run; though Lee gave as one of the principal reasons for it a desire to give the citizens of Maryland an opportunity, as he expressed it, of recovering their liberties. The lack of enthusiasm with which they availed themselves of the opportunity thus afforded them of freeing Maryland from "the despots' heel" must have been somewhat disheartening

ANTIETAM BATTLE FIELD FROM OLD DUNKER CHURCH.

PART OF THE BATTLE FIELD.

pointed. But there was a striking difference between the task performed by Blücher and that accomplished by Jackson. The Prussian Field Marshal had only to steal away and leave Grouchy to fight the air, as it were, while Jackson not only defeated the forces he was sent to neutralize, but he captured the whole of them, officers and men, horses and artillery, quartermaster, commissary, and ordnance stores; as Mr. Mantelini would say, "the demnition total," bag and baggage.

And what a difference between the movements of this greatest of Confederates and those of McClellan, as he loitered*up through Maryland. Jackson could hardly wait to parole the prisoners captured at Harper's Ferry, but, delegating that duty to Hill, off he posted to Antietam, where Lee was anxiously counting the minutes in anticipation of his coming. Wellington did not examine his watch more anxiously, nor sigh more earnestly for night or Blücher, than did Lee long to see Stonewall Jackson's lank veterans wading across the Poto-

mac. Had McClellan possessed some of Jackson's "ginger," he would hardly have waited for Lee to be thus reinforced, but hurrying up his tardy regiments, he would have hurled all the troops he had in hand at Lee's weak battalions that were being concentrated at Sharpsburg. Of this matter Lee himself makes the remarkable statement that McClellan's advance was so slow at the time the Confederates left Fredericktown as to justify him in the belief that his army could capture Harper's Ferry, and concentrate afterwards, before they would be called upon to meet the Union army. Surely, confidence in an antagonist's supineness could go no further. Little

OLD DUNKER CHURCH, ANTIETAM.

* Having been a soldier of the Army of the Potomac on the march from Bull Run to Antietam, I cannot agree with Col. Nickerson.— ED.

ANTIETAM CREEK, LOOKING UP FROM "BURNSIDE'S BRIDGE."

diately making the same movement that he did with Hooker's corps twenty-four hours later. Had he done so the battle that was fought—or commenced—on the morning of the 17th would have been fought and won on the 16th. Jackson's advance guard could hardly have often on the ground before it would have been all over with Lee's comparatively small force; and that, too, must also have suffered a similar fate, if vigorously attacked.

wonder that many of McClellan's most faithful adherents were beginning to believe that before he could be persuaded to attack the enemy an aide-de-camp would ride out at the front, take off his chapeau, and politely ask:

"Gentlemen, are *you* ready?"

When McClellan arrived in front of Lee's position at Sharpsburg, on the afternoon of September 15, he found two of his own divisions in position, Richardson's and Sykes's. The heads of the remainder of his columns were close at hand, and coming on as fast as they were allowed to come. He was warranted in imme-

All the information that McClellan had, including Lee's field order of operations, which had accidentally fallen into his hands, went to show that a large part of the Confederate army was either at Harper's Ferry or, at the worst, barely on its way to Sharpsburg. In fact, many of the Confederate troops did not arrive from Harper's Ferry until late in the afternoon of the 16th, and Hill's troops did not come till in the afternoon of the 17th.

It was the opportunity of McClellan's life. The proverbial tide in his affairs was at its

BURNSIDE'S BATTLE GROUND.

NATIONAL CEMETERY, ANTIETAM—GRANITE STATUE, "AT REST."

flood. After the brief interval embracing the second battle of Bull Run and Chantilly, the Army of the Potomac had welcomed him back as the Commander-in-Chief with an enthusiasm that was little less than idolatry. Under him, with this great confidence in his abilities, that army was capable of performing its grandest achievements. No commander of that great army ever had such a devoted following as those men gave to McClellan. They fought many battles after he left them—fought them with heroic devotion and sublime courage; but to no commander did they again give the warm affection which characterized that lavished upon McClellan.

While he thus dallied on the banks of the Antietam, those precious moments, like the sands of the hour-glass, ran swiftly out, until they had lengthened into golden hours; and yet

Irresolutely he waited on the banks of the river,

while the grand opportunity

Flowed on and flowed past him forever.

On the other hand, it is but justice to McClellan to say that, at that time, no Stonewall Jackson had then been developed in the Union army to lead his flanking columns. Probably Hooker, at this date, approached more nearly than any other Union officer the example of this ideal soldier, and yet the defects in Hooker's character were as pronounced as were the virtues of his great Confederate contemporary.

Burnside, who commanded on the Union left flank, was, so McClellan says, ordered again and again to assault and carry the bridge in his front and the heights beyond, but it was not until many hours after it should have been done that the bridge was finally carried; and after the bridge had been taken by the Union troops, two hours delay before the assault upon the heights beyond gave time for the last of the Confederates from Harper's Ferry, consisting of Hill's corps, to come up and render that assault nugatory.

Does anybody doubt what would have happened had Stonewall Jackson stood in the place of Burnside? No one ever heard of Jackson's getting more than one order to do the same thing. Unfortunately for the Union cause, these dilatory officers always appeared to be in the most important positions.

When, a little later, Burnside succeeded McClellan in the command of the Army of the Potomac, it was said in the public prints that at last "Masterly Inactivity" had been superseded. They might have added, with equal truth if not propriety, that he had been succeeded by "Gigantic Stupidity." *De mortuis nil nisi bonum* will not do when we are discussing matters of history, otherwise we should be obliged to say nothing but good of Caligula or Benedict Arnold.

Probably the most stupendous and bloody blunder ever committed during our civil war

AFTER THE BATTLE.

Copy of the celebrated painting by Captain James Hope. From a sketch made at "Bloody Lane" on the evening of September 17, 1862.

Copyrighted. Engraved by special permission.

was at the first battle of Fredericksburg—the only battle, fortunately, fought by the Army of the Potomac under Burnside's command. He has been much commended for his magnanimity in assuming the whole responsibility for that awful slaughter—those thousands of heroic lives that were, absolutely and without excuse, sacrificed in front of the Confederate position on Marye's Heights on that melancholy December day. Of course he was responsible; many officers protested against the movement, and at least one subordinate was temporarily in arrest because he asserted that it was murder to put men into such a trap as that. Burnside's acknowledgment that he alone was responsible

that "Most of us think that this battle is only half fought and half won. There is still time to finish it, but McClellan will do no more. What I want you to do is to see Hooker, find whether he can mount his horse, and if he can ask him whether he will take command of this army and drive Lee into the Potomac or force him to surrender."

This was represented to be after Hooker had been wounded. As the correspondent *näively* says: "It was, perhaps, the most astounding request ever made by a soldier to a civilian."

Leaving to one side the utter absurdity of this proposition, there is no doubt that a good deal of what is put in the officer's mouth was true.

BLUFF NEAR SHARPSBURG, WHERE PHILADELPHIA CORN EXCHANGE REGIMENT SUFFERED SEVERELY.

only emphasized a fact, patent to every one, that, in addition to being a general without ability, he was stupid and stubborn. Such was the man who commanded the Union troops in one of the most important places on that bloody battle-field—Antietam-Sharpsburg.

Had the Burnside bridge been carried only two hours before it was, even McClellan's dilatory tactics might not have saved the Confederate army an overwhelming defeat.

A distinguished journalist, in a recent paper*, tells an extraordinary story about his experiences on the field of Antietam. Condensed, it is that an officer serving on McClellan's staff told him, during a lull in the battle on the 17th,

---

* Smalley, Harper's Magazine for August, 1894.

But he must either have been a madman, lunatic, or an idiot, to suppose such a scheme practicable, or even possible. A staff officer who would make such a proposition upon a field of battle could have no possible excuse to offer when, standing in front of a platoon of soldiers, he would be asked if he had anything to say why sentence of death should not be executed upon him. While agreeing with much which this writer says on the subject of the battle, and making due allowances for such errors as stating that Hooker's fight on the evening of the 16th was simply a skirmish between two companies of cavalry and the Confederate outposts, and that the great battle of the 17th was fought on Thursday, we must be permitted to take that

LOOKING DOWN BLOODY LANE, AUGUST, 1894.

part of the story about the "staff officer" *cum grano salis.*

The conspicuous points on the field of Waterloo were Hogomount, La Haye Sainte, and the sunken road of Ohaine. The latter, however, is somewhat hidden in the mists of the past, and its existence even largely dependent upon the tradition due to Victor Hugo's reference to it.

The two similarly conspicuous points on the field of Antietam are the "Sunken Road" and the bridge now known as the "Burnside Bridge." The former was a sort of a blind road or lane, sometimes called "Bloody Lane." The Confederate troops occupied this roadway, and used the low but steep banks through which it was cut as a sort of a breastwork, piling rails up on them to make them higher. Many times during the progress of the battle these men would have been glad to be safely out of it, and sometimes they were so cut off as to be willing to surrender. But it was impossible to get out. Occasionally a man, more hardy than wise, would make the attempt, and the moment he appeared crawling up the bank or over the fence that stood between the roadway

NEWSPAPERS FOR THE ARMY.

and a cornfield back of it, he would be literally riddled with bullets. Several men got partly over the fence, and there hung across the rails, their bodies being actually made into sieves. Once, apparently by "unanimous consent," they concluded to try and surrender, and so hung out on the points of their bayonets any sort of a cloth available, that had once been white, as flags of truce; and before the Union troops could get down to where they were a reinforcement came up in the cornfield back of them and commenced firing over their heads. At once down came the tokens of surrender, and out went the whizzing, deadly bullets again. Finally, however, in a charge of the Union troops that swept up to, over, and beyond the roadway, all the occupants that were still living were captured. After the battle was over no spot on that field presented a more horrible appearance than the "Sunken Road" and its immediate vicinity. The roadway was bankful of dead men, and the slopes that approached it were covered with windrows of the harvest of death.

The bridge, now known as the Burnside Bridge, was probably the next most important position. Before they got to it, while crossing, and as they *debouched* from it, the Union troops were all the time exposed to a point-blank fire from the Confederates posted on the Sharpsburg side, in a sort of a natural *tête de pont*, reversed. That is to say, it defended the opposite end from that which a regular *tête de pont* would.

A few years later the writer was sitting by a meagre fire in the wilds of Oregon, trying to keep from freezing to death, and not daring to lie down to sleep for fear of never waking up again. He was engaged in a winter campaign against the Snake and Piute Indians, with General George Crook, who commanded one of the brigades of Union troops engaged at the Burnside Bridge, in the battle of Antietam. Crook then said that many lives were uselessly sacrificed at this point, because the plainest military precautions were not observed in making that crossing. In fact, that he went himself and superintended the posting of two pieces of artillery in such a position that they nearly compelled the occupants of the defensive position to vacate, and so materially reduced their fire that the passage of the bridge, after many failures, was rendered practicable. All the assaults made previous to the posting of that section of artillery had been unsuccessful, and were attended with fearful loss of life. It had up to that time been a Burnside battle of Fredericksburg on a smaller scale. An officer who was capable of such a *contretêmps* should never have

had the opportunity of doing the same thing again, only on a grander scale, as, barely three months later, Burnside did at Fredericksburg.

On the march through Maryland the Army of the Potomac was joined by a good many newly-organized regiments. They were, in the majority of cases, the rawest of the levies, and were therefore sandwiched between the veteran regiments. Each four-regiment brigade thus became a six-regiment organization. Numerically, of course, they were a great reinforcement, but, in another sense, that they were an element of weakness no one acquainted with the facts can deny. It was not an agreeable sensation for even a veteran organization to feel that its next-door neighbor, on its right or left, might take it into its composite head to vanish and leave an open space on that flank, for the enemy to swoop in upon them. And this was not greatly to their discredit; in fact, it could hardly be expected to be different, inasmuch as most of them had never heard a hostile shot, and some of them had not yet had time to learn the difference between "about face" and "forward, march." Their "baptism of fire" was not to be a mere sprinkle, but an immersion, a cold plunge, or perhaps we should say, the hottest kind of a shower. How they would stand it depended a good deal upon circumstances. If, when they met the first shock of battle, received their first volley, while they stood on their feet,

VIEW FROM NATIONAL CEMETERY TOWARD M'CLELLAN'S HEADQUARTERS.

and they remained standing, kept their formation, and faced to the front, they were likely to continue to stand fast, and become heroes. If, however, they had lain down, either on their own account or by order taken shelter, or begun to look back when the first gust of the storm came, they were gone. It would be hard to get them to stand up again or to come out from their place of safety; and if, on their feet, they had indulged in a longing look to the rear, the whizzing bullets were quite likely to decide the matter; and when they once started to run away, a battery of Gatling guns would hardly have had any effect in stopping them. They seemed to lose all control of themselves, and neither shame, threats, nor actual violence would serve to check or rally them.

How far this may have influenced McClellan in his decision not to risk a renewal of the battle, either on Wednesday or on Thursday morning, no one will ever know. A man who was a prospective candidate for President could hardly be expected to mention such an unpleasant truth. All through the war, men who represented a large popular vote, whether of Teutonic, Celtic, or native birth, had to be told that they were heroes, though in every fight they ran like sheep. However, at Antietam many of these undisciplined organizations did perform deeds of valor worthy of Cæsar's Tenth Legion.

A Pennsylvania regiment, when it first joined, had excited the commiseration of the veteran organizations of the brigade to which it was assigned, because its colonel kept them standing in line so long when halted at the end of each day's march, throwing out markers, and compelling each restless soldier and impatient officer to "toe the mark" until the alignment was perfect enough to suit him. Other troops gathered in the fuel and such camp perquisites as were in sight; still he would not break his ranks and allow his men to go until each company front was an absolutely straight line.

On the day of the battle, when the brigade to which this regiment belonged moved into line of battle and opened fire on the enemy, the position that fell to this regiment was a conspicuous one on the side of a gentle slope that fell off toward the Sunken Road. Here the colonel's line was formed, just as rigidly correct as it had been at the close of each day's march. And there, too, those men stood and stayed. The brave colonel was killed; officers and men were falling like autumn leaves, all along the line, and yet "dressed on the centre," where their colors were flying, just as they had been taught to do at the close of each day's march, and this, too, comprising about all the "drill" they had ever had, they continued to load and fire as regularly as if at target practice,—a striking evidence of the effect of even a little discipline, and an example of heroism worthy of the best and bravest.

Antietam-Sharpsburg may then, perhaps, properly be called a drawn battle. There was no great display of strategy or grand tactics on the part of either of the Generals-in-Chief, and as they have long since passed beyond the reach of praise or censure, there let them rest. The "honors are easy," and can be awarded to no one general on either side. "Joe" Hooker was, undoubtedly, on this occasion at his best; and, as McClellan wrote him after the battle, had he not been placed *hors de combat* the result on the Union right might have been different.

The veteran Mansfield died too early in the battle to show more than the splendid example of an heroic death. Of the other Union Corps Commanders there is not much to be said. Lee's great lieutenants—Jackson, Longstreet, and Hill (A. P.)—comprised the same grand trio it ever remained until it was forever broken by the death of Jackson at Chancellorsville.

There were, however, generals of division and brigade who here gave indications of the grand achievements of which they were capable. Hancock, Sedgwick, Meade, Howard, and Sykes, of the Union army, and Hill (D. H.), Ewell, Gordon, and Hood, of the Confederates, here began to illume the military horizon with the splendid promise of an early fruition.

The heroic deeds of regimental and company officers would fill many volumes; while, towering far above them all, stands the magnificent figure of the American citizen-soldier, his well-worn uniform of faded Union blue and dingy Confederate gray splashed with the crimson tide of that mighty conflict that, nearly a third of a century ago, rolled along the Antietam, his sincerity unquestioned, his courage unchallenged, his name and fame immutable, immaculate, and immortal.

GENERAL ROBERT E. LEE AND HIS SON AT ANTIETAM.

119

BURNING OF THE GUNBOAT UNDERWRITER.

D. B. CONRAD, M. D., LATE FLEET SURGEON, C. S. N.

IN January, 1864, the Confederate naval officers on duty in Richmond, Wilmington, and Charleston were aroused by a telegram from the Confederate Navy Department, ordering them to detail three boats' crews of picked men and officers, fully armed, equipped, and rationed for six days, who were to start at once by rail for Weldon, North Carolina, reporting on arrival to Commander J. Taylor Wood, from whom they would get further instructions.

So perfectly secret and well-guarded was our destination, that not until we had all arrived at Kingston, North Carolina, by various railroads, did we have the slightest idea of where we were going or what was the object of the "naval raid." We suspected, however, from the name of its commander, that it would be "nervous work," as he had a reputation for boarding, capturing, and burning the enemy's gunboats on many previous occasions.

Embarking one boat after another on the waters of the Neuse, we found that there were ten of them in all, each manned by ten men and two officers, every one of whom was vigorous, fully alive, and keen for the prospective work. Now we felt satisfied that it was going to be hand-to-hand fighting; some Federal gunboat was to be boarded and captured by us, or we were to be destroyed by it.

Sunday afternoon, February 1, 1864, about two o'clock, we were all quietly floating down the narrow Neuse, and the whole sunny Sabbath evening was thus passed, until at sunset we landed on a small island. After eating our supper all hands were assembled to receive instructions. Commander Wood, in distinct and

PREPARING TO REPEL BOARDERS.

terse terms, gave explicit orders to each boat's crew and its officers, stating that the object of the expedition was to board that night some one of the enemy's gunboats then supposed to be lying off the city of New Berne, then nearly sixty miles distant by water from where we were. He said that she was to be captured without fail. Five boats were to board her on either side simultaneously, and then, when in our possession, we were to get up steam and cruise after other gunboats. It was a grand scheme, and was received by the older men with looks of admiration and with rapture by the young midshipmen, all of whom would have broken out into loud cheers but for the fact that we had been enjoined to observe the strictest silence.

In concluding his talk, Commander Wood solemnly said: "We must now all pray," and thereupon offered up the most touching appeal to the Almighty that it has ever been my fortune to hear. I can remember it now, after the long interval that has elapsed since then. It was the last ever heard by many a poor fellow, and deeply felt by every one.

Then, embarking again, we now had the black night before us, our pilot reporting two very dangerous points where the Federals had out pickets of both cavalry and infantry. We were charged to pass these places in absolute silence, our arms not to be used until we were fired upon, and then, in that emergency, we were to get out of the way with all possible speed, and pull down stream in order to surprise and capture one of the gunboats before the enemy's pickets could carry the news of our raid to them.

In one long line, in consequence of the narrowness of the stream, did we pull noiselessly down, but no interrupting pickets were discovered, and at about half-past three o'clock we found ourselves on the broad estuary of New Berne Bay. Then, closing up in double column, we pulled for the lights of the city, even up to and around the wharves themselves, looking, but in vain, for our prey. Not a gunboat could be seen—none were there. As the day broke we hastened for shelter to a small island up the stream about three miles away, where we landed, dragged our boats into the high grass, and established numerous pickets at once. Those of us who were not on duty, tired and weary, threw ourselves on the damp ground to sleep during the long hours that must necessarily intervene before we could proceed on our mission.

Shortly after sunrise we heard firing by infantry ; it was quite sharp for an hour, and then it died away. It turned out to be, as we afterwards learned, a futile attack by our forces, under General Pickett, on the works around New Berne. We were obliged to eat cold food all that day, as no fires were permissible under any circumstances, so all we could do was to keep a sharp lookout for the enemy, sleep as much as possible, and wish for the night to come.

About sundown one gunboat, which proved to be the United States Steamer Underwriter, appeared on the distant rim of the bay. She came up, anchored off the city some five miles from where we were lying, and we felt that she was our game. We began at once to calculate the number of her guns and quality of her armament, regarding her as our prize for certain.

As darkness came upon us, to our great surprise and joy a large launch, commanded by Lieutenant George W. Gift, landed under the lee of the island. He had, by some curious circumstance, been left behind, but, with his customary vigor and daring, had impressed a pilot, and, taking all the chances, came down the Neuse boldly in daylight to join us in the prospective fight. This was a grand acquisition to our force, as he brought with him fifteen men and one howitzer.

We were now called together again, the orders to each boat's crew repeated, another prayer was offered up, and then, it being about nine o'clock, we started in double column directly for the lights of the gunboat, one of which was distinctly showing at each masthead. Pulling slowly and silently for four hours, we neared her, and as her outlines became distinct, to our great surprise we were hailed, "man-of-war fashion, "Boat ahoy !" We were discovered, and, as we found out later, were expected.

This was a trying moment, but Commander Wood was equal to the emergency. Jumping up, he shouted, "Give way hard ! Board at once !" The men's backs bent and straightened at the oars, and the Federal blue-jackets at the same moment opened upon us with small-arms. The long, black sides of the gunboat, with men's heads and shoulders above them, could be distinctly seen by the line of red fire, and we realized immediately that the only place of safety for us was on. board of the gunboat, for the fire was very destructive. Standing up in the boat with Commander Wood, and swaying to and fro by the rapid motion, were our marines, firing from the bows, while the rest of us, with only pistol in belt and hands ready to grasp her black sides, were all anxious for the climb. Our coxswain, a burly, gamy Virginian, who by gesture and loud words was encouraging the crew, steering by the tiller between knees, his hands occupied in holding his pistols, suddenly fell forward on us dead, a ball having struck him fairly in the forehead. The rudder now having no guide, the boat swerved aside, and instead of our bows striking at the gangway we struck the wheel-house, so that the next boat, commanded by Lieutenant Loyall, had the deadly honor of being first on board. Leading his crew, as became his rank, duty, and desire, Loyall jumped and pulled into the gangway, now a blazing sheet of flame, and, being near-sighted (having lost his glasses), stumbled and fell prone upon the deck of the gunboat, the four men who were following close upon his heels falling on top of him stone dead, killed by the enemy's bullets, each one of the unfortunate fellows having from four to six of them in his body. Rising, Lieutenant Loyall shook off his load of dead men, and by this time our crew had climbed up on the wheel-house, Commander Wood's long legs giving him an advantage over the rest of us. I was the closest to him, but had nothing to do as yet except to anxiously observe the progress of the hand-to-hand fighting below me. I could hear Wood's stentorian voice giving orders and encouraging the men, and then, in less than five minutes, could distinguish a strange synchronous roar, the meaning of which I did not understand at first ; but it soon became plain. "She's ours ! she's ours !"

everybody crying at the top of their voices, in order to stop the shooting, as only our own men were on their feet.

Jumping down onto the deck I slipped in the blood and fell on my back and hands. Rising immediately I caught hold of an officer standing near me, who, with an oath, collared me, and I threw up his revolver just in time to make myself known. It was Lieutenant Wilkinson, who, the moment he recognized me, exclaimed: " I'm looking for you doctor; come here !" Following him a short distance in the darkness I examined a youth who was sitting in the lap of another, and in feeling his head I felt my hand slip down between his ears, and to my horror discovered that his head had been cleft in two by a boarding-sword in the hands of some giant of the forecastle. It was Passed Midshipman Palmer Saunders, of Norfolk. Directing his body and those of all the other killed to be laid out aft on the quarter-deck, I went down below looking for the wounded in the ward-room, where the lights were burning, and found half a dozen with slight shots from revolvers. By the time I had finished my examination a half-hour had elapsed, when, again ascending to the deck, I heard the officers of the various crews reporting to Commander Wood; for immediately after the capture of the vessel, according to orders, the engineers and firemen had been sent down to the engine-room to get up steam, and Lieutenant Loyall, an executive officer, with a number of seamen, had attempted to raise the anchor, cast loose the cable which secured the ship to the wharf just under the guns of Fort Stephenson, while the marines, in charge of their proper officers, were stationed at the gangways and guarding the prisoners. The lieutenants, midshipmen, and others manned the guns, of which there were six eleven-inch, as it was our intention to convert her at once into a Confederate man-of-war, and under the captured flag to go out to sea, to take and destroy as many of the vessels of the enemy as possible.

But all our well-laid plans were abortive; the engineers reported the fires out, and that it would be futile to attempt to get up steam under an hour; and Lieutenant Loyall, too, after very hard work, reported it useless to spend any more time in trying to unshackle the chains—as the ship had been moored to a buoy—unless he could have hours in which to perform the work. Just at this moment, too, to bring things to a climax, the fort, under which we found that we were moored, bow and stem, opened fire upon us with grape and solid shot. Some of those who had escaped had reported the state of affairs on board, and this was the result.

In about fifteen minutes a solid shot or two had disabled the walking-beam, and it then became evident to all that we were in a trap, to escape from which depended on hard work and strategy. How to extricate ourselves in safety from the thus far successful expedition was the question, but events proved that our commander was equal to the emergency.

Very calmly and clearly he directed me to remove all dead and wounded to the boats, which the several crews were now hauling to the lee side of the vessel, where they would be protected from the shots from the fort. The order was soon carried out by willing hands; they were distributed as equally as possible, each boat in charge of its own proper officer, and subjected, under that heavy fire, to that rigid discipline characteristic of the navy, manned by their regular crews; and as they lay in double lines hugging the protected lee of the ship as closely as possible, it was a splendid picture of the discipline a body of trained men can show under circumstances of great danger.

After an extended search through the ship's decks, above and below, we found that we had removed all the dead and wounded; and then, when the search was reported ended, Commander Wood, still on deck giving his orders, although the fire from the fort was very deadly and searching, called up four lieutenants to him, to whom he gave instructions as follows: Two of them were to go below in the forward part of the ship, and the other two below in the after part, where, from their respective stations, they were to fire the vessel and not to leave her until her decks were all ablaze. At that juncture they were to return to their boats and report.

The remainder of us were lying on our oars while orders for firing the ship were being carried out, and soon we saw great columns of red flame shoot upward out of the forward-hatch and wardroom; whereupon the four officers rejoined their boats. Immediately, by the glare of the burning ship, we could see the outlines of the fort, with its depressed guns, and the heads and shoulders of the men manning them; as the blaze grew larger and fiercer their eyes were so dazzled and blinded that every one of our twelve boats pulled away out into the broad estuary, safe and untouched; then we all realized fully our adroit and successful escape.

Some years after the affair I met one of the Federal officers who were in the fort, and he told me that they were not only completely blinded by the flame, which prevented them from seeing us, but were also stampeded by the knowledge of the fact that there were several tons of powder in the magazine of the vessel, which, when it exploded, would probably blow the fort to pieces; so, naturally, they did not remain very long after they were aware that the ship had been fired. This all occurred as we had expected. We in our boats, at a safe distance of more than half a mile, saw the Under-

were, and that, as a natural consequence, they would be treated well.

Continuing to pull for the remainder of the night, we sought and found, by the aid of our pilot, a safe and narrow creek, up which we ascended, and at sunrise hauled our boats upon a beach. There we carefully lifted out our wounded men, placed them under the shade of trees on the grass, and made them as comfortable as possible under the circumstances. Then, as soon as we had partaken of our breakfast, of which we were in so much need, we laid out the dead, after carefully washing and dressing

ATTACK UPON THE UNDERWRITER.

writer blow up, and distinctly heard the report of the explosion, while those at the fort, a short distance from the ship, had, luckily for them, sought a safe refuge.

Fortunately, there were no casualties at this stage of the expedition. I boarded boat after boat, in my capacity of surgeon, attending to the requirements of those who demanded immediate aid, and I witnessed many amusing scenes, for among the prisoners were some old men-of-warsmen, former shipmates of mine in the Federal navy years before, and of the other officers also. Their minds were greatly relieved when I made known to them who their captors

them. All hands were called, a long pit was dug in the sand, funeral services were held, the men buried, and each grave marked. We remained there all that day, recuperating our exhausted muscles, and when night came again we embarked on our return trip. All through that night and the four succeeding ones we cautiously pulled up the rapid Neuse, doing most of our work in the darkness, until, when near Kingston, we could with impunity pull in daylight.

Arriving at Kingston the boats were dragged up the hill to the long train of gondola cars which had been waiting for us, and then was presented an exhibition of sailors' ingenuity. The boats were placed upright on an even keel, lengthwise on the flat cars, and so securely lashed by ropes that the officers, men, and even the wounded, seated in them as if on the water, comfortably and safely made the long journey of a day and two nights to Petersburg. Arriving there the boats were unshipped into the Appomattox River, and the entire party floated down it to City Point, where it debouches into the James. It was contemplated, when City Point was reached, to make a dash at any one Federal gunboat should there be the slightest prospect of success; but learning from our scouts, on our arrival after dark, that the gunboats and transports at anchor there equaled the number of our own, at least, we had to abandon our ideas of trying to make a capture, and were compelled to hug the opposite bank very closely, where the river is nearly four miles wide, and in that manner slip up the James, pulling hard against the current. By the next evening we arrived, without any further adventure, at Drury's Bluff, where we disembarked. Our boats were shown as mementoes of the searching fire we had been subjected to, for they all were perforated by many Minié-balls, the white wooden plugs inserted into the holes averaging fourteen to each boat engaged; they were all shot into them, from "stem to stern," lengthwise.

Among the many incidents that occurred on the trip there were two which left a lasting impression on my mind, and to this day they are as vivid as if they had happened yesterday. As we were stepping into the boats at the island that night, the lights of the gunboat plainly visible from the spot on which we stood, a bloody, serious action inevitable, several of the midshipmen, youth-like, were gayly chatting about what they intended to do, joyous and confident, and choosing each other for mates to fight together "shoulder to shoulder," when one of them, who stood near me in the darkness, made the remark, as a conclusion, as we were taking our places, "I wonder, boys, how many of us will be up in those stars by to-morrow morning?" This rather jarred on the ears of us older ones, and looking around to see who it was that had spoken, recognized the bright and handsome Palmer Saunders. Poor fellow! he was the only one who took his flight, though many of the others were severely wounded.

On our route down to Kingston by rail we were obliged to make frequent stops for wood and water. At every station the young midshipmen swarmed into the depots and houses, full of their fun and deviltry, making friends of the many pretty girls gathered there at once, who asked all manner of questions as to this strange sight of boats on cars filled with men in a uniform new to them. The young gentlemen explained very glibly what they were going to do, —"To board, capture, and destroy as many of the enemy's gunboats as possible." "Well, when you return," replied the girls, "be sure that you bring us some relics—flags, etc!" "Yes, yes! We'll do it," answered the boys. "But what will you give us in exchange?" "Why, only thanks, of course!" "That won't do;— give us a kiss for each flag, will you?" With blushes and much confusion, the girls consented, and in a few moments we were off and on our journey again. On the return trip the young men, never for an instant forgetting the bargain they had made, manufactured several miniature flags. We old ones purposely stopped at all the stations we had made coming down, in order to see the fun. The young ladies were called out at each place, and after the dead were lamented, the wounded in the cars cared for, then the midshipmen brought their flags, recalled the promises made to them, and demanded their redemption. Immediately there commenced a lively outburst of laughter, denials, a skirmish, followed by a slight resistance, and the whole bevy were kissed *seriatim* by the midshipmen, and but for the whistle of the train, warning them away, they would have continued indefinitely.

CARRYING DESPATCHES TO FARRAGUT.

By "Yvan."

UNITED STATES WARSHIP RICHMOND.

ON July 9, 1863, the gunboats Princess Royal, Winona, Kineo, and New London were at anchor off Donaldsonville, Louisiana. It became necessary to communicate with Admiral Farragut, at New Orleans. Captain M. B. Woolsey, senior officer present, selected the New London, Lieutenant-Commander (now Captain retired) George H. Perkins, to convey the despatches to the admiral. A better man could not possibly have been chosen, but a better ship could have easily been detailed. The machinery of both the Kineo and Winona was below the water line, and they were regularly constructed gunboats, while the New London was a purchased merchantman, with all her machinery exposed. Perhaps it was Perkins's reputation for gallantry and dash that caused him to be assigned the task. So he started off. Almost the whole distance between Donaldsonville and New Orleans (eighty-five miles) the river was lined with batteries, masked and otherwise, in possession of the Confederates.

On the morning of the 10th, we heard that the New London had been disabled and driven ashore, and was then under the fire of the enemy. Captain Woolsey, in his report, makes the following statement:

On the morning of July 10th, I received a message that the U. S. S. New London, which had been sent down the river during the night, with important despatches for Ad-

miral Farragut, was aground near College Point, some twelve miles below; that she was disabled and under the enemy's fire, and her officers and crew behind the levee. Before going down to the assistance of the New London, I landed —— ——, with orders to go down behind the levee to the New London, get the despatches from Lieutenant-Commander Perkins, fasten a bit of lead around them, and, if possible, to proceed down to New Orleans with them; to seize horses as he wanted them, and to dash through the enemy's pickets and suspicious places with all speed; but if surrounded by the enemy, to pitch the despatches into the river.

I will now, in his own words, give the description of the trip by the young officer who was selected—or rather, who volunteered—for this perilous service:

I was pulled ashore from the ship and landed. I was dressed like a tramp, and had no arms but a revolver. I fully recognized the nature of the service I was to perform and also the danger attendant on it, which was no less than that of being hung as a spy should I be captured.

I reached the New London and found a sad state of affairs. She had been driven ashore, and a lot of the men scalded and wounded. A shot had (as might have been expected) gone through her steam-chest and at once disabled her. I had no time to lose, so I got the despatches from Lieutenant-Commander Perkins and started off at a great pace. I had a very good horse, but had ridden him so hard I found

I should soon have to give him up and get another. Four or five miles from the New London the horse broke down entirely, and I was obliged to abandon him and proceed on foot until I could "confiscate" another horse. I soon found I was in great danger of being "confiscated" myself.

GUNBOATS AND MORTARS ON THE MISSISSIPPI.

I just got into the woods in time, as half a dozen guerillas came along the road, evidently going to inspect the condition of the New London and her crew. I was now obliged to go along very carefully. In the next four hours I made about three miles. I concluded to hail the first negro I saw and see if I couldn't be secreted until I deemed it safe to go on. I also wanted to get some sleep, as I intended traveling all night. At last I found a negro who could give me a place to sleep for a while, and a little something to eat. I told him to wake me at midnight, as I must again be off towards New Orleans. I got all the information I could from

him, but saw no prospect of getting a horse. I got up at midnight and went on my way. It was a pitch-dark night, and I moved as rapidly as the circumstances would permit. I heard footsteps and voices once or twice, but found no difficulty in concealing myself.

I suppose I had made about ten miles when daylight began to appear. I met another negro, who gave me shelter and thought he could arrange so I might get a horse. I had certainly not been in the hut more than a few minutes when we heard the approach of horsemen. The negro told me to lie down on the bed, and "de ole woman" would "kiver" me. She did, sure enough. She weighed about 200 pounds, and threw herself on top of me. This had hardly been done when the soldiers entered the hut. They had heard of me on the road, and were determined to capture me. The negro told them there was nobody in the cabin but "de ole woman;" that she had the rheumatism so bad she couldn't move, etc., etc. I was hoping they would leave soon. It was only a question as to whether I should be smothered or captured.

At last, to my great joy, they disappeared, and I was released from a very uncomfortable position. I was obliged to remain *perdu* most of the day. The negro promised he would have a horse for me before sundown, and, sure enough, he did. I had no saddle—only a halter. However, I was so glad to get the necessity I cheerfully dispensed with the luxuries, and started off after dark, down the road, on a dead run. I

UNITED STATES STEAMER OSSIPPEE.

concluded it was my only chance. I judge I had made about ten miles when I thought I heard horses in pursuit, and at once jumped from my horse, gave him a smart cut with a switch, and sent him running down the road. I then concealed myself and waited to see what was to come. I knew if horsemen were after me they must soon overtake me, as my horse was pretty well tired out.

Soon I heard the horsemen close at hand. There were five of them, and at the gait they were going I thought they would get up with my horse in about twenty minutes. He, of course, being relieved from my weight, would go much faster. I followed along after them as fast as I could go, intending, as soon as they caught my horse, or I heard them returning, to quietly drop overboard and float down stream until I could, with safety, go ashore.

It turned out just as I had expected, only the horse must have given them a longer chase. I concealed myself behind the levee and awaited their return. I hoped I would not be obliged to take to the water, as that would deprive me of the use of my revolver, my only weapon of offence. It was a long time before they returned. They had evidently been searching for me farther down the road and had given up the task as hopeless. They never for a moment thought I was concealed so far from the place they had overtaken the horse.

My progress now was, of necessity, very slow, as I had to exercise the utmost care and caution. New Orleans seemed a terrible distance away.

I doubt if I made more than a mile an hour for the next half dozen of hours. I was in a very ticklish position. I kept on my way as best I could, running where I thought I had a clear field, and hiding, resting, and walking alternately. I made up my mind that if I got through this adventure safely it would be the last of the sort I would undertake. (I made two or three others, just such trips, subsequently.) Proceeding as described above for the next three days, without anything startling taking place, I arrived safely in New Orleans the most completely "played-out" fellow you ever saw. I delivered my despatches to Admiral Farragut, and was very highly complimented by that glorious and gallant officer.

Captain M. B. Woolsey, U. S. N., says: "The cheerfulness with which —— —— volunteered to perform this hazardous duty, and the energetic and successful manner in which he performed it, would certainly have been noticed by the government had my report, in which the circumstances were stated, been received. The distance performed by —— —— was eighty-five miles, and through the enemy's country."

Admiral D. G. Farragut wrote on the subject as follows: "I distinctly remember that this officer was very active and energetic in conveying despatches on the Mississippi River in 1863, and I therefore cheerfully endorse his conduct during that period (as set forth by his commanding officer), and consider him well entitled to government recognition."

MEMORIAL DAY.

GEORGE M. VICKERS.

LIKE stars that sink into the west,
  So one by one we seek our rest ;
The column's brave and steady tread
With banners streaming overhead,
Will still keep step, as in the past,
Until the rear guard comes at last.
Ah, yes, like stars we take our flight,
And whisper, one by one, " Good night ;"
Yet in the light of God's bright day,
Triumphant, each again will say,
' Hail, comrade, here has life begun,
The battle's fought, the victory's won ! "

COLONEL CHARLES MARSHALL'S EULOGY OF GENERAL GRANT.

ONE of the finest examples of patriotic American oratory was the address delivered by Colonel Charles Marshall at the tomb of our great soldier-statesman on May 30, 1892. This address has never been published in permanent form, and the veterans North and South have thus been deprived of the privilege of preserving for their own delight and for the inspiration of their children one of the most brilliantly patriotic orations our literature affords.

Colonel Marshall was the military and confidential secretary of General Robert E. Lee, and is the grand-nephew of the great Chief Justice John Marshall, of the United States Supreme Court. He is now a resident of Baltimore, and is recognized as the leader of the bar in that city.

This oration was delivered in the presence of a vast assemblage, made up in part of veteran organizations, among which was the Confederate Veteran Camp of New York. The full text is as follows :

COLONEL CHARLES MARSHALL.

I know nothing in history that resembles the close of the war between the States. No more bitter and obstinate conflict was ever waged between different nations or different parts of the same nation. Millions of men had been in arms against each other; myriads had perished on each side, and countless treasure had been expended. Yet in a moment the mighty struggle ended and peace was proclaimed throughout the land. So suddenly did the great army of combatants disappear that

"It seemed as if their mother earth
Had swallowed up her warlike birth."

No such peace as our peace ever followed immediately upon such a war as our war. The exhausted South was completely at the mercy of the victorious North, and yet the sound of the last gun had scarcely died away when not only peace, but peace and good-will were re-established, and the victors and the vanquished took up the work of repairing the damages of war and advancing the common welfare of the whole country, as if the old relations, social, commercial, and political, between the people of the two sections had never been disturbed.

Not only was the union of the States restored, but, what was far more important, the union of the people was re-established, to be broken, please God, no more forever. To my mind this is the most striking event connected with the war and it is one which generations yet unborn shall rise up and bless. When we remember the legacy of hate and revenge that successful war has usually left between the victor and the vanquished, a hate that in some cases has outlived centuries,

"The unconquerable will
And study of revenge, immortal hate,

and when we remember that such a state of feeling between the people of the North and South would have been absolutely inconsistent with a complete and lasting union of the kind that all patriotic men desired, we can better appreciate the magnitude of the services of those to whom we are indebted for such a happy ending of a bloody war.

It is not easy to express the thoughts that the scene before me inspires in my mind and in the mind of every man who understands the full meaning of this occasion.

Men who once were arrayed against each other in deadly strife are now met together to do honor to the memory of one who led one part of this audience to a complete and absolute victory over the other, yet in the hearts of the victors there is no feeling of triumph, and in the hearts of the vanquished there is no bitterness, no humiliation. Both look back across the tempestuous sea of blood and tears that separate the old from the new order of things, and both rejoice that the voyage is ended and they have safely arrived in a haven of lasting security and peace.

I am here to-day, with some of my late companions-in-arms, and with the belief that I express the feelings of every Confederate soldier, to bear witness that the American people are indebted for this great blessing, for all the good that followed it, and for the exemption from the countless evils that were averted by it, to the illustrious man whose grave we strew with flowers of gratitude and affectionate veneration more than to any other, and to none is the duty of recognition of his great services more grateful than to the soldiers of the Confederacy.

I think that this great service of General Grant has not been as fully understood and appreciated as it deserves. To me it seems the most illustrious of all his illustrious deeds, and entitles him to a high place in the history among the benefactors of his country and of mankind. Great as were his achievements in war, I think his crowning glory was that of a peacemaker, and that to him belongs the blessing promised to the peacemaker.

Before I bring to your attention the facts that I think warrant what I have just said of General Grant, I will tell you part of a conversation between General Grant and General Lee, as related by the latter, the day after the surrender at Appomattox.

You all remember that when General Grant first opened the correspondence with General Lee which led to the meeting at Appomattox, General Lee proposed to give a wider scope to the subject to be treated of between him and General Grant and to discuss with the latter the terms of a general pacification.

General Grant declined to consider anything except the surrender of General Lee's army, assigning as a reason for his refusal his want of authority to deal with political matters or any other than those pertaining to his position as the commander of the army. The day after the meeting at McLean's house, at which the terms of surrender were agreed upon, another interview took place between General Grant and General Lee upon the invitation of General Grant, and when General Lee returned from that meeting he repeated, in the presence of several of his staff, the substance of the conversation, one part of which I am now about to state, and I think you will see in it, as I did and as we all did, the feeling that controlled all the actions of General Grant at that most critical period.

The conversation turned on the subject of a general peace, as to which General Grant had already declared the want of power to treat, but in speaking of the means by which a general pacification might be effected General Grant said to General Lee, with great emphasis and strong feeling : '' General Lee, I want this war to end without the shedding of another drop of American blood.'' Not ''Northern'' blood, not ''Southern'' blood, but ''American'' blood, for in his eyes all the men around him and all those who might be then confronting each other on other fields over the wide area of war were ''Americans.''

These words made a great impression upon all who heard them, as they did upon General Lee, who told us, with no little emotion, that he took occasion to express to General Grant his appreciation of the noble and generous sentiments uttered by him, and assured him that he would render all the assistance in his power to bring about the restoration of peace and good-will without shedding another drop of ''American'' blood. This ''American'' blood, sacred in the eyes of both these great American soldiers, flows in the veins of all of us, and let it be sacred in our eyes, also, henceforth and forever, ready to be poured without stint as a libation upon the altar of our common country, never to be shed again in fratricidal war.

It is in the light of this noble thought of General Grant that I have always considered the course pursued by him at the moment of his supreme triumph at Appomattox, and, seen in that light, nothing could be grander, nobler, more magnanimous, nor more patriotic, than his conduct on that occasion.

Let us go back for a moment and look at the state of affairs on the morning of the 9th of April, 1865.

The bleeding and half-starved remnant of that great army, which for four years had baffled all the efforts of the Federal Government to reach the Confederate capital, and had twice borne the flag of the Confederacy beyond the Potomac, confronted, with undaunted resolution, but without hope save the hope of an honorable death on the battle-field, the overwhelming forces under General Grant.

At the head of that remnant of a great army was a great soldier, whose name was a name of fear, whose name is recorded in a high place on the roll of great soldiers of history. That remnant of the great Army of Northern Virginia, with its great commander at its head, after the long siege of Richmond and Petersburg, had been forced to retreat, and on the 9th of April, 1865, was brought to bay at Appomattox, surrounded by the host of its great enemy. There was no reasonable doubt that the destruction of that army would seal the fate of the Confederacy, and put an end to further organized resistance to the Federal arms, and there was no reasonable doubt that if that remnant were driven to desperation by the exaction of terms of surrender against which its honor and its valor would revolt, that resistance would have been made, and General Grant and his army might have been left in the possession of a solitude that they might have called peace, but which would have been the peace of Poland, the peace of Ireland. Under such circumstances, had General Grant been governed by the mere selfish desire of the rewards of military success, had he been content to gather the fruits that grow nearest the earth on the tree of victory—the fruits that Napoleon and all selfish conquerors of his time have gathered, the fruits that our Washington put away from him—what a triumph lay before him !

What Roman triumph would have approached the triumph of General Grant had he led the remnant of the Army of Northern Virginia, with its great commander in chains, up Pennsylvania avenue, thenceforth to be known as the ''Way of Triumph.'' But so simple, so patriotic, was the mind of General Grant that the thought of self seems never to have affected his conduct. He was no more tempted at Appomattox to forego the true interests of his country for his own advantage than Washington was tempted when the time came for him to lay down his commission at Annapolis. I doubt if the self-abnegation of Washington at Annapolis was greater than that of Grant at Appomattox, and it is the glory of America that her institutions breed men who are equal to the greatest strain that can be put upon their courage and their patriotism.

On that eventful morning of April 9th, 1865, General Grant was called upon to decide the most momentous question that any American soldier or statesman has ever been required to decide.

The great question was : How shall the war end ? What shall be the relations between the victors and the vanquished ? Upon the decision of that question depended, as I believe, the future of American institutions.

If the extreme rights of military success had been insisted upon, and had the vanquished been required to pass under the yoke of defeat and bitter humiliation, the war would have ended as a successful war of conquest—the Southern States would have been conquered States, and the Southern people would have been a conquered people, in whose hearts would have been sown all the enmity and ill-will of the conquered to the conquerors, to be transmitted from sire to son.

With such an ending of the war there would have been United States without an united people. The power of the Union would then have reposed upon the strength of Grant's battalions and the thunder of Grant's artillery. Its bonds would have stood upon the security of its military power, and not upon the honor, and good faith, and good-will of its people. The Federal Government would have been compelled to adopt a coercive policy toward the disaffected people of the South, which would soon have established between the Government and States the relations now existing between England and Ireland, and some Northern Gladstone would now be demanding for the Southern people the natural rights that the English Gladstone is claiming for the Irish against their haughty conquerors.

Does any man desire to exchange the present relations between the people of the Northern and Southern States for the relations of conqueror and conquered? Does any man wish to have a union of the States without a union of the people? Now, General Grant was called upon to decide this great question on the morning of April 9, 1865.

The Southern military power was exhausted. He was in a position to exact the supreme rights of a conqueror and the unconditional submission of his adversary unless that adversary should elect to risk all on the event of a desperate battle, in which much "American" blood would certainly be shed.

And I will say here that the question was gravely considered in Confederate councils, whether we should not accept the extreme risk and cut our way through the hosts of General Grant or perish in the attempt.

This plan had many advocates, but General Lee was not one of them, as will be seen by his farewell order to his army.

Under such circumstances General Lee and General Grant met to discuss the terms of the surrender of General Lee's army, and at the request of General Lee General Grant wrote the terms of surrender he proposed to offer to the Confederate general. They were liberal and honorable alike to the victor and the vanquished, and General Lee at once accepted them. Any one who reads General Grant's proposal cannot fail to see how careful he is to avoid unnecessary humiliation to his adversary. As far as it was possible, General Grant took away the sting of defeat from the Confederate army. He triumphed, but he triumphed without exultation, and with a noble respect to his enemy.

There was never a nobler knight than the Grant of Appomattox—no knight more magnanimous or more generous. No statesman ever decided a vital question more wisely, more in the interest of his country and of all mankind than General Grant decided the great question presented to him when he and General Lee met that morning of April 9, 1865, to consider the terms of the surrender of the Army of Northern Virginia.

The words of his magnanimous proposal to his enemy were carried by the Confederate soldiers to the farthest borders of the South. They reached ears and hearts that had never quailed at the sound of war. They disarmed and reconciled those who knew not fear, and the noble words of General Grant's offer of peace brought peace without humiliation, peace with honor.

The decision of General Grant imposed upon the Southern people the solution of a great problem, and I invoke for them while engaged in its solution the good-will and tolerance of General Grant, while I demand of them and promise in their names the good faith and fidelity of General Lee to all his promises made in their name.

At the entrance of the great harbor of our commercial metropolis stands the representation of "Liberty Enlightening the World." In her hand the figure holds the torch toward which the artist desired to draw the eyes of all nations, the hope of the oppressed and helpless of mankind.

Here upon this sacred spot, my brethren, raise a noble and grand temple, the hope and assurance of the defenders of our national faith, and upon this altar inscribe for the teaching of the coming generations of Americans the illustrious name, "Grant of Appomattox—Grant the magnanimous."

GENERAL U. S. GRANT.

GEORGE M. VICKERS.

[Read by Frances E. Peirce at the Annual Reunion of the Independent Literary Society, August 8, 1885.]

GO search the annals of the human race,
Go hear the legends that the heathen tell,
And learn that hist'ry, sacred or profane,
Records no hero like the mighty Grant.
Columbia proudly claims him as her own
And rears her monuments with love and pride;
But millions scattered o'er the face of earth,
And millions yet unborn, will share that claim:
Who serves mankind is deemed the friend of man,
And nations nationalize him in their hearts.
Since that first famous Battle of the Kings,
Of which we read in holy writ, no sword
E'er leaped from scabbard in a juster war
Than that which made our country free indeed,
Which, until then, was only free in name.
The bond of unity that Washington
To us bequeathed, Grant's loyal arm maintained;
Emancipation of the dusky race
By Lincoln's heaven-inspired pen, by Grant's
Unsullied sword was made complete!

How well
He proved the potency of equal rights,
And how he dignified Democracy
The monarchs of the world have told, thrice told,
In homage, hospitality and love.
No land is free where dwells a slave: to-day
In all our land there dwells no slave, and we
Are free, forever free!

"Let us have peace."
Clasp hands across the ashes of the dead.
No, no; Grant is not dead, he cannot die;
The body is the worn-out coat of mail,
That with his sword and shield the warrior casts
Aside when life's campaign is o'er, and home,
Eternal home, is reached.

He is not dead
Whose power still exists; and Grant will live
A life of immortality while yet
Our starry banner floats for liberty,
Which, thanks to God, will be forevermore.

PERSONAL RECOLLECTIONS OF "STONEWALL" JACKSON.

MAJOR JOHN G. GITTINGS.

JOHN G. GITTINGS.

Late Adjutant 31st Virginia Infantry and Major Confederate Cavalry.

MAJOR Thomas Jonathan Jackson was a professor at the Virginia Military Institute, at Lexington, Virginia, when the writer, a cadet, first met him in the year 1852.

A relative of Jackson and coming from his native town, the writer bore a letter of introduction to him, which letter, however, was not presented, for this young recruit, a boy of sixteen, had met with such a warm reception from the older cadets on his arrival, and was, withal, so depressed by the rigid discipline of the school, that he feared to face this professor, whom he looked upon even then as a hero, one who had received the "baptism of fire" in Mexico, and was "the only officer promoted twice in one day"—as he had been informed by the village chronicler, who thus dilated on the achievements of Jackson in the war against the Mexicans.

One evening the sergeant of the guard came with the order that I should report to the quarters of Major Jackson without delay. On receiving this order, my first thought was that I had violated some one of the innumerable military rules and was about to be called to an account therefor; so it was with some trepidation that I went to the major's quarters.

However, he met me with a smile and greeting that somewhat relieved my anxiety, but it did not put me entirely at ease, as I still felt some awe in the presence of this military officer in full uniform, whom I had been told was a stern and rigid disciplinarian. The major took my cap, placed it carefully on the table, then made me take the best chair in the room, after which he took a seat himself and, with apparently a labored effort, tried to make things pleasant. Though entertaining, he appeared ill at ease, and this, I noticed afterward, was characteristic of him when conversing in the presence of strangers.

This was my first interview with "Stonewall" Jackson. He was then about twenty-eight years of age, six feet tall, with gray-blue eyes, a well-chiseled Roman nose, and a very fair and ruddy countenance. He wore side whiskers, and one noting his very fair complexion and reserved manner might have mistaken him for an Englishman, but here the resemblance ceased, for in thought and expression this quiet, unaffected man was all American. As I sat in his presence and observed his diffidence, this thought passed through my mind: Can this modest man be the one who fought so bravely in Mexico and who stood by his cannon after all his men had been killed or driven away?

It was not until my second year at the Military Academy that I came to recite in the classes taught by Major Jackson; but in the meanwhile I was under his instruction at artillery practice, which consisted principally, as far as the "plebes" were concerned, in drawing the pieces and caissons. This was for the first year only; the second year the new cadets were promoted to the position of cannoneers.

At the artillery practice we soon learned that Major Jackson was a very strict and exacting officer. He expected every man to do his duty —and every horse, too. One day on the parade ground a fellow "plebe" managed, in some way, to draw out a linchpin from a wheel of the limber at which I was pulling, and, as a consequence, in trotting down an incline at a fast pace, the wheel flew off with considerable force,

"STONEWALL" JACKSON AS A CADET.

and, as the fates would have it, rolled directly toward "Old Jack," who was looking in an opposite direction. He turned his head in time to see its approach, and although it passed within a few inches of his person, he did not budge from his tracks. A cadet remarked: "He would not have moved if it had been a cannon-ball going right through him!" But we soon observed that his gaze was fixed intently on our battery in a way that made us feel very uncomfortable, and in a brief space we were placed under arrest—officers, cannoneers, horses, and all; and as a result this breach of discipline was settled in a way that did not invite any repetition of the offence.

Professor Jackson was an able instructor of artillery tactics, but in the regular collegiate course he did not appear to have any special genius for teaching; yet he was always a conscientious, laborious instructor.

It was the custom at the Military School to fire salutes of artillery on the Fourth of July and Washington's birthday. In honor of such occasions Major Jackson would always don his best uniform and wear his finest sword, a very handsome one, which the cadets said had been presented to him by the ladies of New Orleans at the close of the Mexican War.

In the gray dawn of the morning he would come marching on the parade-ground, with his fine sabre tucked well up under his left arm. He had the long stride peculiar to the dismounted cavalryman, and on such occasions his manner would be brisk, if not cheery, for he took special pride in these celebrations and was very punctilious in all their observances.

Major Jackson married a daughter of Doctor Junkin, president of Washington College, during the second year of my stay at Lexington. He then took up his residence in the town.

Before his removal from the barracks, however, an incident occurred which will go to show the estimate in which he was held, even by the most intractable characters. A number of cadets who were about to be dismissed, through incompetency in their studies or for excess of demerit-marks, while on a Christmas frolic made a raid on the professors' rooms in the barracks and literally despoiled them. Major Jackson's room alone was left intact. It is difficult to determine why these young vandals should have respected his quarters when they seemed to respect nothing

HOUSE WHERE "STONEWALL" JACKSON WAS BORN.—CLARKSBURG, W. VA.

BULL RUN—GENERAL JACKSON'S POSITION, NORTH OF WARRENTON PIKE.

else. Some suggested that, as cadets, they respected his military fame won in the battles of Mexico. It is a notable fact that even at that time the cadets had an abiding faith in Jackson as a military man, and perhaps very few of them were ever afterwards much surprised at his great achievements in war.

He was one of the most scrupulously truthful men that ever lived, and even carried his exactitude of expression and performance to extremes in small matters.

On one occasion he borrowed the key of a library of one of the literary societies, and promised the secretary to return it within an hour. However, becoming absorbed in his book, he put the key into his pocket and did not think of it again until he had reached his boarding-place in the town, nearly a mile away. Then, although a hard storm had sprung up in the meantime, he turned about and marched all the way back through the rain to deliver the key as he had promised, though he knew the library would not be used, and the key would not be needed on that day.

In conversation, if he ever happened to make an ironical remark, even if it were so plainly ironical that none could misapprehend it, yet would he invariably qualify his expression by saying: "Not meaning exactly what I say." This peculiarity of speech became almost a by-word with the cadets, and subjected him to much

embarrassment, but such was his regard for truth that he would not depart from it, even in jest, without immediately correcting his statement.

He belonged to a literary society in Lexington which embraced in its membership many men of learning and ability. It was the custom of the society to hold a series of public lectures during the winter season. This was one of the few entertainments the cadets were permitted to attend, and when Major Jackson's turn came to lecture there was considerable interest evinced by them in anticipating the subject of his lecture and the manner in which he would acquit himself.

When he appeared on the lecture-platform he was embarrassed, it is true, and his lecture lacked in oratorical effect; yet it was said at the time to have been one of the best of the whole course, and was very entertaining. The subject of his discourse was "Acoustics," and he discussed very effectively all that was then known about the properties of sound. He said it was "an undeveloped science," and that no doubt in the near future progress would be made in it, and discoveries, especially in the "transmission of sound." This prediction has since been verified in the perfecting of the telephone.

It must be admitted that Major Jackson was regarded by the cadets and others as an eccentric man. His health had been impaired by his

"STONEWALL" JACKSON—1862.

service in Mexico, and he always seemed to be more or less sensitive and ill at ease in his intercourse with strangers.

Speaking from a social standpoint, no man ever had a more delicate regard for the feelings of others than he, and nothing would embarrass him more than any *contretemps* that might occur to cause pain or distress of mind to others. Hence he was truly a polite man, and while his manner was often constrained, and even awkward, yet he would usually make a favorable impression, through his evident desire to please.

However, before he became famous in war he was generally underrated by his casual acquaintances, for in such society he was a taciturn man, and would listen in silence, while others discoursed at length upon subjects in which he was himself well versed. He would thus create a false impression of his own acquirements, which were very considerable outside of collegiate learning, and embraced a wide knowledge of men and things.

About the second year of my stay at the Virginia Military Institute, Major Jackson was suffering from weak eyes, and he would not read by artificial light. So, when near one of the examinations, our class had prevailed on him to give us a review of a difficult study, he was compelled to hear us after dark, the only time he had to spare for the purpose. We used to meet in the "section room," in the dark. Professor Jackson sat in front of us on his platform and, with closed eyes, questioned us over many pages of a complicated study. This work

required a strong effort of memory and concentration of thought, and no doubt it was just such exercise that fitted him for his duties in the field—in holding in his mental grasp the countless details that perplex the mind of a commander of armies.

It was one of the marked characteristics of Major Jackson that he always inspired confidence in those who knew him intimately. The cadets believed in him as a religious man, although he would sit placidly and sleep through a greater part of the long and tedious sermons of the Presbyterian divine, in whose church he was an elder! They knew that he slept because of physical weakness, and that insincerity was not a part of his nature.

Governor Letcher, who had been familiar with him for a number of years, appointed him to a colonelcy at the beginning of the war, and he never had a doubt of Jackson's capacity to fill any rank in the army, however great.

Major Jackson had the great misfortune to lose his wife the second year of his marriage. The Rev. Dr. White, an aged minister of the Presbyterian church, officiated at the funeral, to which the cadets marched as a guard of honor. After the services were over at the grave, and the attendants had all left the grounds except the cadets, who were forming their ranks at a distance, it was noticed that Jackson was standing alone, with uncovered head, by the open grave, as one distraught. The venerable minister, who was a lame man, was compelled to hobble all the way back from the gate, and lead him away, as he would heed none other.

It is not the purpose of this narrative to record General Jackson's military achievements, but to recount briefly a few personal incidents of which the writer was an eye-witness and from which he formed impressions of this grand historic character.

Soon after the outbreak of war, the writer was ordered to Harper's Ferry to see General Jackson on military business, and appeared at his office about daybreak on a morning in May. This was his regular office hour for receiving the reports of his subordinate officers; and after hearing the reports of the officer of the day, officer of the guard, scouts, and others, he would despatch business in a very prompt and energetic way. He knew exactly what ought to be done, and how it should be done. There was no wavering in opinion, no doubts or misgivings; his orders were clear and decisive. It occurred to me at the time that Jackson was much more in his element here as an army officer than when in the professor's chair at Lexington. It seemed that the sights and sounds of war had aroused his energies; his manner had become brusque and imperative; his face was bronzed from exposure; his beard was now of no formal style, but was worn unshorn.

As the war progressed and his fame grew apace, whenever he would appear riding along the lines of infantry, on his chestnut-sorrel horse, clad in his old, faded uniform, the loud cheers of his soldiers would follow him for miles along the dusty roads. He was a good rider, but not a very graceful one, except on the occasions mentioned, when the soldiers were cheering

They paid little heed to any other officer or soldier of the passing column. The old man "only wanted to see Jackson once before he died," and the young ladies were "just crazy to see him!"

Soon thereafter, a post-quartermaster rode by; his bright uniform presented a striking contrast to the dust-begrimed regimentals of the officers of the column; and the young ladies were sure this fine-looking soldier must be the great "Stonewall," the hero of their imaginations. Finally, when General Jackson did appear on the scene, it was difficult to make these ladies believe that the travel-stained horseman, with his faded cap drawn low over his sunburned, bearded

HOUSE IN WHICH GENERAL JACKSON DIED—GUINEA STATION, VIRGINIA.

him; then he would straighten himself in the saddle, and ride erect, with uncovered head and at a rapid pace, as if to escape this ovation of his troops.

On one occasion during the Valley campaign, as our troops debouched from a narrow crossroad into the turnpike, we saw a carriage drawn up by the wayside, in which were seated an elderly gentleman and three young ladies. As we rode by the old gentleman halted us and inquired anxiously for General Jackson. It at first occurred to us that he had news of importance to communicate to the general, but the young ladies soon made it apparent that their only object in being there was to look upon this now famous officer, whom they had never seen.

face, was the famous "Stonewall" whose name had wrought so great a spell in that valley.

On the day of Malvern Hill I saw "Stonewall" Jackson in the thick of the fight and under circumstances that moved the very depths of his nature. The sun was sinking toward the western sky when our wearied troops emerged from the pine woods, which were being torn and riven by shot and shell. We stood there obscured from our formidable adversary only by the black cloud of sulphurous smoke that overhung the bloody field like a pall shrouding the windrows of the slain. McClellan's grand army, 90,000 strong, confronted us on those heights, which bristled with 300 field-pieces and great siege-guns, reinforced by the monster cannon of the

"STONEWALL" JACKSON AT MALVERN HILL.

river boats. All these guns, banked in tiers, extending the distance of a mile, now belched forth in streams of flame and iron hail, that mowed down ranks and regiments, and forest trees far in their rear. The incessant din and concussion of the bursting bombs seemed to rend the firmament and shake the solid earth.

As we moved forward into action we marched within a few paces of "Stonewall," who at that time was giving orders to a battery which was being actually destroyed by the concentrated fire of McClellan's artillery. He sat erect on his horse, in this hurricane of canister and grape; his face was aflame with passion, his eyes flashed, his under jaw protruded, and his voice rang out sharp and clear. Before he was entirely obscured from our view, the soldiers would turn, at brief intervals, to look back on him, as if for the last time. And indeed it was the last time for many of us.

Toward the close of his career, whenever "Stonewall" Jackson appeared to citizens who had known him only by reputation, he was always regarded by them with great interest. Many had clothed him in imagination with almost supernatural powers; others believed him

to be a chosen leader, especially favored of heaven on account of his religious character and pure life.

But his soldiers knew that his success lay in his eternal vigilance, his untiring energy, his personal supervision, and perfect knowledge of the topography of the field of his operations, and the exercise of those qualities that bring success to other generals. Yet he possessed qualities that were peculiar to him as natural gifts; he had a resolute mind and never halted between two opinions; and he had the intuitions and instincts of the born soldier, quickly to take advantage of any mistakes his adversary might make. Above all, he had a realizing sense of the inestimable value of time, in its connection with the operations of war. He was always on time. It was a tradition with his soldiers that when, at Richmond, Lee heard the sound of Jackson's guns away off on McClellan's right, he took out his watch and calmly remarked: "Jackson is on time."

General Lee knew all that this remark implied—the arduous toil and sleepless energy—yet he expressed no surprise; he expected nothing less of Jackson.

Shortly after sunrise on the morning after the battle of Fredericksburg, as I was walking along the ridge above Hamilton's Crossing and about thirty yards from one of the batteries, I passed within a few feet of General Jackson, who had taken up his position alone on this vantage-ground for the purpose of reconnoitering. But he was not doing very much of it just at that time, for he was seated on the ground, leaning against a hickory sapling, and fast asleep. He held his bridle-rein in one hand and his field-glass in the other, and did not awaken as I walked along the path within touching distance of him, but seemed to be sleeping as calmly as I had seen him sleep years before in the church at Lexington.

which they had had no leisure to do the day before while the battle was raging.

Several days after this time I met General Jackson riding across the battle-field, about two miles below Fredericksburg. He was riding alone and very slowly, with his head hanging down, as if in profound thought. He halted for a few minutes and spoke in a kindly, friendly way, but made no allusion to the battle, the sad, melancholy evidences of which were all around us.

A few weeks before his death I visited his headquarters for the last time. He at that time occupied for his office an outbuilding of an old manor-house at Moss Neck, on the Rappahannock, which had been used in happier times as a sporting lodge. On the walls of this room

CHANCELLORSVILLE—STONE MARKING THE SPOT WHERE GENERAL JACKSON FELL.

However, his slumbers were destined to be of short duration, for a battery of heavy guns on the Stafford Heights soon opened with a volley, directed against the battery near the spot where Jackson was quietly sleeping. The fire of these guns continued only for a short time, but while it lasted the din was terrific, not to speak of the destruction wrought by the hurtling missiles, for the very first gun that opened this morning salute sent a shell right into the muzzle of the cannon nearest to the general, broke it from its trunnions, killed two horses, and hurled the piece back into the barbette, which the gunners were trenching out at the time, an operation

still hung pictures of race horses, game cocks, and the trophies of the chase. One was impressed, on entering here, with the ludicrous incongruity of these pictures to the grim surroundings and to the taste of the grave, religious soldier who occupied these quarters. After a pleasant conversation of half an hour, I took my leave, as it proved, forever, of General Jackson, who had now won a world-wide fame, and was still the same modest, diffident man I had met for the first time at Lexington, eleven years before.

When Jackson died, many of his intimate friends believed that his death portended the downfall of his cause, and never had much hope

ROOM IN WHICH GENERAL JACKSON DIED.

The Duke of Wellington once expressed the opinion that the presence of Napoleon on a field of battle was worth all of 20,000 men. It would be difficult to compute how many men the presence of Jackson on a battle-field was worth. There was but one "Stonewall" Jackson. His presence in any battle where the victory wavered in the balance, his soldiers thought, was worth all the difference between victory and defeat.

"Brave men lived before Agamemnon," and there were brave and able officers living after Jackson, but his constant success had wrought such faith in his old soldiers, and they were so dazzled by the popular applause and enthusiasm which his presence everywhere inspired, that they truly believed there was none to come after him that could fill his place.

been here, things would have been different!" of its success from that fatal day; but his soldiers grieved his loss as no others could grieve for him. Afterward, on every battle-field where the tide of war made against them, they would exclaim in their extremity: "Oh, if Jackson had

TWO BROTHERS.

Paul Laurence Dunbar.

HERE stands the house as it used to stand,
Ere the curse of strife came on the land ;
It stands as it stood that fateful day,
When the two brave brothers marched away.
But the rooms are cheerless, bare, and still,
And a lone bird sings on the window-sill.

*　　*　　*　　*　　*　　*　　*

They were two brave boys and a mother's pride,
She had watched them growing, side by side,
And she prayed for both as mothers pray,
For the one in blue and the one in gray.
For they could not think alike, and so
They parted, grieving ; each to go
And add his little tithe of might
To help uphold what he deemed right.
Each did the right as right he knew,
What more could saints or angels do ?

*　　*　　*　　*　　*　　*　　*

And one came back, and one was left
Where fleet Death wove his crimson weft.
But both were brave ; since this is true,
What matters it about the hue
Of coats they wore into the fray ?
Brave hearts beat 'neath both blue and gray.

OUR GENTLE ENEMY.

MARIA LOUISE EVE.

HE slew our kinsmen in the field ;
　　He fought our brothers, hand to hand ;
And stern and sad, amid the fray,
　　And terrible, he gave command.

But when the work of death was done,
　　He knelt beside our wounded men
And soothed their anguish till they smiled
　　And blessed him for an angel then.

The livelong night his vigil kept,
　　Beside the dying and the dead ;
And never woman's hand was half
　　So gentle as his touch, they said.

He sits among us at our board ;
　　He kneels beside us at our prayers.
You would not think, to see him thus,
　　How stern a look he sometimes wears.

But on the morrow beat the drum,
　　And buckling on his sword once more,
His brow grew sad, his gentle eye
　　Its look of pain and pity wore.

Again I saw him, when the shouts
　　Of victory had died away,
Where, in the solemn evening light,
　　Amid the gathering shades he lay.

Upon his brow a ghastly wound,
　　But on his lips a smile of peace,
As if his gentle soul were glad
　　That now its cruel work might cease

And never gentler spirit, sure,
　　Was sent on such a stern behest
As this, our foe who fought so well,
　　As this, our gentle, sad-eyed guest.

Thus, looking on his beauteous clay, his simple epitaph I said,
　　And felt that we had lost a friend, our gentle enemy was dead.

WITH EWING AT TUNNEL HILL.

GEORGE W. McBRIDE.

SHERMAN, leading three divisions of the 15th Corps and one of the 17th, reported to General Grant November 21, 1863.

He had with him the 1st division of the 15th Corps, General P. Joseph Osterhaus, commanding ; the 2d, General Morgan L. Smith ; the 4th, General Hugh Ewing ; and the 2d division of the 17th Corps, commanded by General John E. Smith. Osterhaus was on the march from Bridgeport, but was so far back that he did not arrive in time to participate with Sherman, but joined the forces of Hooker and fought with Geary on Lookout Mountain. Sherman had been hurried so fast that he was compelled to leave his 3d division behind, and take in its place the division of John E. Smith, of the 17th Corps. On the march from Vicksburg, Sherman had overcome obstacles that would have stopped others, but with that push that marked him one of the greatest military leaders of modern times, he was at last in touch with his chief and in line with the Army of the Cumberland—rain, mud, high water, and everything that could possibly retard his progress was with him and about him—out of it all he came to the assist-

ance of his comrades with as rugged a lot of men as there was to be found in all the Union army. Morgan L. Smith crossed his division over the Brown's ferry bridge on the 21st. Ewing arrived soon after, to find the bridge broken by the enemy's sending down against it rafts and flood wood, which kept the column in waiting that day and the night following.

General Giles A. Smith's brigade, of the 17th Corps, was sent under cover of the hills to North Chickamauga, with orders to man the boats intended for the pontoons, and at midnight to drop down with the current to a point above the mouth of the Chickamauga, then land two of his regiments and capture the enemy's pickets posted along the river, then to pass hastily down the river below the mouth of the Chickamauga and land the balance of his command and send the boats across the river for a fresh load. This movement was executed with complete success, as the enemy was taken by surprise and captured.

Morgan L. Smith's division was then hastily ferried over. John E. Smith followed, and by daylight of the 24th, two divisions of 8,000 men

139

were on the east side of the Tennessee, and intrenched.

General William F. Smith, with his engineers, commenced the construction of pontoon bridges

MAJOR-GENERAL JOHN M. CORSE, U. S. A.

across the Tennessee and the Chickamauga. The steamer Dunbar arrived in the forenoon and ferried the balance of Ewing's division across the river. At one o'clock on the afternoon of the 24th the command moved out in three columns *en echelon*, the left, General Morgan L. Smith, the column of direction. The day was like those that immediately preceded it, wet and misty, with low hanging clouds that shut out the view of the enemy on Lookout. Sherman pushed ahead and occupied a range of hills. Skirmishers were thrown out and crept up the ridges, with a strong support following. At 3.30 in the afternoon he was in position.

A brigade from each division was thrown forward to the top of the hill, where they encountered the veterans of Cleburne's celebrated command. Smith's Texans opened fire on the Federals, and Giles A. Smith was wounded, and his brigade passed into the command of Colonel Tupper, of the 116th Illinois. Sherman's position was over the tunnel, where the East Tennessee and Georgia Railroad passes through Missionary Ridge. The rivers and the ridge here form three sides of a square.

The valley between was, as a rule, level and cleared. In the Federal front and about 1200 yards north and about 600 yards west of the tunnel was a high detached ridge, commanding

every point within cannon range. This ridge was the disputed point. Between the two armies was a deep valley, commanded by the guns of both. To reach either, this valley must be crossed, and that, too, in the face of the concentrated fire of the entire line and the artillery. Orders were given to Ewing to fortify the ground he held, which was done that afternoon and night. One brigade was held in reserve on the hills; one of Morgan L. Smith's closed the gap to Chickamauga Creek; two of John E. Smith's brigades were thrown back to the base of the ridge and held in reserve; Ewing's right was extended down the ridge to the plain, thus crossing the ridge in a general line facing southwest; General O. O. Howard, commanding the 11th Corps, sent three of his regiments to Ewing, and they were placed in prolongation of that officer's line to his right, thus connecting Sherman with the army at Chattanooga. Night came, but the work went on.

Sherman was ordered to attack the enemy at dawn. He was told that Thomas would attack in force early in the day. The enemy occupied the range of hills with his infantry and artillery, and was strongly intrenched. General Corse, with his brigade, was ordered to attack from the right-centre, and to use such portion of his command as he could operate along the narrow ridge. Lightburn sent to Corse the 30th Ohio Infantry. Morgan L. Smith was to move along the east base of the mountain with two brigades of John E. Smith's division. The forces selected for the attack were the brigades of Corse and Loomis, of Ewing's division, together with the 30th Ohio and the two regiments of Buschback's brigade, of the 11th Corps, and only such portions of this force as the formation of the ground would permit.

Bragg concentrated a mighty army to meet these veterans from Vicksburg and the Potomac. Cleburne's dashing division, with the brigades of Liddell, now commanded by Govan, and the brigades of J. A. Smith, Polk, and Lowery, with the batteries of Calvert, Dodge, Semple, and Swett, were in position, well protected by fieldworks and slashing. Lookout Mountain sent the brigades of Generals J. C. Brown and Alfred Cummings; Breckenridge sent Lewis's brigade; Walker sent Maney; and Buckner sent Reynolds's brigade. Smith faced Corse; Lowery was posted south of the tunnel, and Govan on the high spur overlooking the whole field. During the night Smith was changed from the advanced position and given another, to the rear of the one held by him the evening before. Withdrawing Smith, Cleburne left the works erected by this brigade standing, and between the two contending lines.

Roger Q. Mills, of Texas, commanded a regiment in Smith's brigade, and occupied a line that ran close under the crest of Tunnel Hill. Swett, with four Napoleon guns, held the top of the ridge and commanded the ground that Corse and Loomis charged over. Douglas's battery was posted in the line of Govan, and was so situated as to enfilade a line approaching the front of Smith's position, while Calvert's guns were intrenched on the hill above the tunnel. Three regiments of Brown's brigade were formed between the tunnel and Smith.

The sun was just gilding the tops of old Cumberland with its golden splendor on the morning of the 25th, when the same bugler, with the same bugle that sent the Six Hundred forward at Balaklava, sounded the advance of Corse's brigade. This bugler was Jimmy Burk, of the 15th Michigan Infantry. As the bugle-call ceased, the line advanced, the 40th Illinois, with Companies A, F, and B of the 103d Illinois as skirmishers, supported by the remainder of the brigade and the 30th Ohio. At its head was that peerless soldier, John M. Corse. Down the hill, across the valley, and up the opposite ridge goes this splendid line. Up the hill goes the gallant Corse, down the hill drives the enemy's fire that wraps the blue line about like a vestment. The movement of the brigade is the signal for the opening of the artillery on both sides, and the crash and roar of the guns is thrown from rock to rock, multiplying the sounds of the conflict. The crests of the ridges are ablaze with the flame of cannon, the gorges are volcanoes in eruption, and their lava is lead. From out this seething furnace slowly arises the smoke from the combatants; and as it ascends it joins with the mists from the mountain, and the two unite to form a mystic bridge that spans the ridges and covers, like a canopy, the contending forces.

Have you ever stood and watched the coming of a cyclone, with its broad sweep, its shifting clouds, its matchless grandeur, and the power of the elements, as it comes to you in the splendor of the lightning's flash and the roll of the thunder? Would you see the cyclone intensified, and would you also know the meaning that morning to the followers of Corse? If so, just stop a moment in this valley that separates the blue and the gray and look about you. The hills are a blaze of fire, the heavens are shut out of view; looking upward, you see streams of flame burning through the curtain of smoke as the cannons throw their double charges of canister into the ranks of the forces that oppose them. On every side the musketry crackles like the falling of rain on a roof; the mists are constantly giving up the bleeding and wounded, who seek a sheltered spot to gasp the name of "home" and "mother," and then fall asleep forever. You would not call that blue line back if you could, for it would have lifted you into the zone of the heroic and made you a member of the column that attacked the thunder and lightning, that crouches on yonder ridge—an attack that set in foment the powers of the mount, as did the pleadings of the divine god-

MAJOR-GENERAL "PAT" CLEBURNE, C. S. A.

dess on Olympus of old. But on this mountain are gathered the thunderbolts forged by the hand of modern warfare, and in the grasp of the trained cannoneers of the South the bolts of Zeus are thrown in sheets of fire, while the roar of battle shakes the heavens and the earth.

Into this storm goes the intrepid Corse and his command. Across the mystic bridge pass hand in hand the dead of both armies, as they journey together into the presence of the sweetest and gentlest force of the human race, their Comforter and Redeemer.

Without a waver the splendid line of blue advances, and pushes its way into the fiery blast that covers the hill from base to summit. Smith's Texans, Brown's Tennesseeans, Cummings's

Georgians, Swett's Napoleons, and Calvert's Battery open a murderous, direct fire upon this heroic line; while Douglas's cannons enfilade and sweep it with a storm of shot and shell. Lowery's infantry get a long-range fire upon its flank. Corse well knows that the Army of the Cumberland is watching and waiting for him. This, with the thought that the ridge can be cleared of its defenders, nerves this intrepid soldier to the attack, and into the human cyclone he carries his followers to its very centre, the flaming crest of the ridge. With a shout his regiments drive

GENERAL MORGAN L. SMITH, U. S. A.

Mills and his men in confusion; he occupies the ridge within eighty yards of Cleburne's main line, halting here to reform his men, which he does by placing the 40th Illinois and one wing of the 103d on the skirmish line, with the balance of the brigade as support. The halt is short, for the ground is hot with shell and the deadly musket ball. At the word the brigade moves forward, with orders to storm the ridge at the tunnel. As true as the sweep of a sword-blade moves the line as it cuts its way to the front, up to within fifty paces of the Confederate line, when Smith's Texans arise and charge them, while batteries and infantry pour into the Federal ranks a continuous stream of lead. Corse falls wounded, and the command of the brigade passes to Colonel C. C. Walcott, of the 46th Ohio, who is pressed back to the works built by Smith's men the day before; but the fight goes on. The Confederate General Smith, Colonel Mills, and Lieutenants Shannon and Ashton of Swett's battery, are all wounded in this charge, and the battery is commanded by

Corporal Williams. The gunners are shot down and a detail of infantrymen is made to man the guns. The roar of the conflict carries word to the Army of the Cumberland that the fight is on, and that it is to the death.

Word is sent to Loomis of Corse's advance, and he is ordered forward. His brigade consists of the 26th and 90th Illinois, the 12th and 100th Indiana, and has with him the 27th and the 73d Pennsylvania Infantry, of Buschback's brigade.

At 10.30 A. M., Loomis, with the Pennsylvania troops in reserve, moves out into the open country and faces the fire of the circular line of the Confederates. His movements are in plain sight of the enemy on the ridge above him. Hardee at once masses the commands of Cummings, Maney, and Lewis on his front; Cleburne moves a part of Govan's brigade to the crest of the ridge over the Tunnel; Swett's battery is changed to the ground occupied by Douglas, and Key takes Swett's place; Warfield, with his famous regiment of Arkansans, is hastily moved to the westerly of the works and outside of the intrenchments on the crest of the ridge. Loomis sweeps across the open ground, receiving the concentrated fire of Key's artillery and the infantry, that tear through his ranks from both front and flank, but without a waver or a halt these veterans from other fields close up, and with a halloo to the grim spectre that stalks amongst them, they drive straight for the base of the hill. As they reach its shelter, a Federal cheer rolls up the ridge, followed by the line of blue. As Walcott falls back, Loomis halts and shelters himself as best he can. He reforms his line and awaits orders.

At 12.30 P. M. Loomis is again ordered forward, and to charge the works in his front. With a cheer that rings along the ridge like a pæan, his line, or so much of it as can be used, rushes forward and captures and holds the works. Taft's Pennsylvanians drive Cummings from Glass's house and over the hill, the 27th occupying the ground within a few feet of the enemy, where they lie down and open fire on their foes. Loomis joins with the 27th, and sends Cummings, Brown, and Govan into their works. The Federal fire is converged into a space not more than forty yards in width, and the space is swept by the leaden storm clear of all living things. Key and Swett are silenced, while the infantry cower behind their works, unable to face the awful Federal fire. Cummings details the 36th and 56th Georgia to drive the Federals back. These Georgians are fresh from Lookout and are full of fight. They sweep to the attack and are repulsed, losing each its regimental commander. Warfield is still holding his position, but his dash is gone and the cry for help is sounded; even this splendid regiment yields to the fire that is poured upon it. Walcott is holding his ground against the rushes of Granbury (now commanding Smith's brigade) and Lowery, and is punishing these commands most frightfully. Callender on the ridge behind Walcott, Wood with Lightburn, and Dillon's batteries are planting their shot where they will do the enemy the most harm.

Hours go by and the struggle continues. Matthias's brigade, of John E. Smith's division, is ordered to the support of Loomis, and the heroes of Champion's Hill move out across the open ground and come up on the flank of Loomis, and the "Old Ironsides" are at it again. Colonel Raum, with his brigade, is also ordered to the support of his comrades. These brigades are forced to the westerly face of the ridge because of the narrow crest, there being no room for their deploying in line with Walcott. They are caught in flank by a force sent against them by Hardee's reserves from the hollow, which are sheltered by the ridge and the underbrush so completely that the Federals do not see them until they are in part surrounded by an overwhelming force and are driven back. As they go, Granbury and Cummings follow them up in a charge. As soon as the gray line opens out before Walcott, it is swept with a murderous fire that sends the gray legions back to their works. The Federal fire is so continuous and the effect so disastrous to Cleburne that he is compelled to either fall back or drive the Union men down the hill. He therefore masses the brigades of Cummings and Maney, together with the regiments of Warfield, Mills, and the 9th Texas, and sends them down against Taft and his Pennsylvanians. Just here the fight becomes a hand-to-hand struggle. The Pennsylvanians stand to the front and riddle the Confederate ranks with a fire that kills. At the same time they face as deadly a return. The 73d springs forward; with clubbed muskets and fixed bayonets they fall upon Cummings, and, amid the smoke and confusion, the two lines close in deadly grapple for the mastery. The stubborn and continuous resistance of the Federals permits their enemy to close in on their flanks, and the Union colors and a portion of the regiment falls into the hands of the Confederates, and the balance fall back. The house of Mr. Glass is burning, and sends up a cloud of smoke. The fire is no more red than the fire of the combatants, nor is it as red as the blood that crimsoned that awful field.

The failure to drive Cleburne off the ridge was not the fault of the Federals alone, but due rather to the fact that Pat. Cleburne defended, —and that meant much—and to the further fact that the Union forces had no room to stand upon. It was the old myth over again—no ground for their feet to touch to make them mortal.

Corse carried into the fight 920 effectives, and stood, a wall of adamant, against the surging of the Confederate hosts. Loomis, with about the same number, stood in his might and glorified the name of the American soldier. The 90th Illinois had its colonel (O'Meara) killed, Lieutenant-Colonel Stewart wounded, and 160 men and officers, out of 370 that went into action, were stricken with the bloody rain. Man never saw such heroism. The

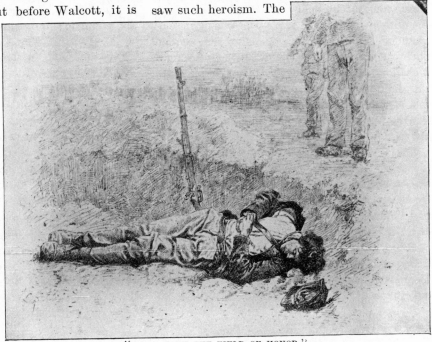

"DEAD UPON THE FIELD OF HONOR."

90th rushed upon Warfield's men and clubbed them with the butts of their muskets. The 100th Indiana, the "Persimmons," drove straight at the 50th Tennessee and tore them to pieces. Generals Corse, Giles A. Smith, and Colonels Matthias and Raum all wounded; Colonels O'Meara, Putnam, and Torrance and Lieutenant-Colonel Taft lay dead upon that field of honor.

The Smiths were out in force that day, but they left their mark on their enemy and on the page of their country's history. Let no man doubt their worth. Each of them, whether wearing the blue or gray, acquitted himself with distinguished honor.

Had Corse remained on the field, the result might have been different, for he possessed the faculty and rare ability to carry a body of men further into a conflict than any other brigade commander of the army of the Mississippi; he routed the forces of Cleburne and sent them in confusion back onto their reserves, and stayed not until he fell, sharply wounded, at the very threshold of his foe. The only time his followers wavered at all was when he was being carried from the field. Sherman knew this brigade; he saw it stand at the bridge crossing Owl Creek at Shiloh and beat back the legions of Beauregard until its dead carpeted the field and made it famous with their matchless heroism. It had been tried and found true, the struggle was desperate, and it was equal to the requirements. Sherman waited for the attack of Thomas that came not, so he held the huge mass of his enemies in his front. He made the fight continuous. The splendid regiments sent against Cleburne carried the gauge of battle and flung it with defiance into the faces of their foes. Worn out and bleeding from ghastly wounds, Ewing in the afternoon established his line where Smith's Texans were the day before, and intrenched for the night.

The Federal dead, with white, upturned faces, lay along the ridges. The wounded shivered in the cutting blasts of the mountain air and prayed for the coming of their friends and the morning; and Chattanooga became famous, touched by the hand of immortality.

Bragg's army, flushed with the triumph at Chickamauga, was master of the valley of the Tennessee, and was confident of the ultimate overthrow of Thomas and his half-starved fol-lowers. He had thoroughly fortified a position which engineers pronounce the strongest, naturally, on the American continent; to this he brought an army trained in the art of war, commanded by educated soldiers from the best military school in the world.

Man and Nature were acting hand in hand in Bragg's defence. The Tennessee and Chickamauga, with their broad and deep currents, hemmed the field in on one side, while the mighty walls of Lookout Mountain and Missionary Ridge stood barriers in the way of escape towards the south. His men lay along the ridges, intrenched, and with the most approved artillery posted so as to sweep all approaches. From Lookout's summit he could see every move his enemy made, and he knew as accurately the strength and disposition of his forces as Grant himself. With perfect assurance of success, Bragg awaited with complacency the coming of his foe.

Sherman's headlong rush at Cleburne sent Bragg's army side-stepping to the right; it closed in mass to confront Sherman, and thereby lost the battle. The bearing of the Confederates in this fight was of the dashing, reckless kind that won for them the admiration of their opponents. No other soldiers but Americans would have stood before those toughened veterans, led to the attack by Corse and Loomis and Morgan L. Smith. Cleburne was a fighter; he maintained his reputation on the bloody steeps of Tunnel Hill.

There is something weird and wonderful about the whole action of the 23d, 24th, and 25th days of November, 1863. Who gave the orders to storm the ridge in Granger's front? has been asked, and not yet satisfactorily answered. It was the same unexplained something that swept the columns of Hooker into the splendors of the cloud-capped Lookout, the soldiers of Corse and Loomis into the fiery hell of Tunnel Hill, and the battalions of Wood and Sheridan up the sides of Missionary Ridge and into deathless story.

The Federal soldiers seemed to catch an inspiration from the towering grandeur of the mountain and the mighty sweep of the river; and, rising into their sublimity, they made those bleak November days immortal, and the valley and the mountain monuments more enduring than chiseled marble or polished brass.

Oft on the field has this sight been seen,
Where the wounded have "drank from the same canteen."

WE DRANK FROM THE SAME CANTEEN.

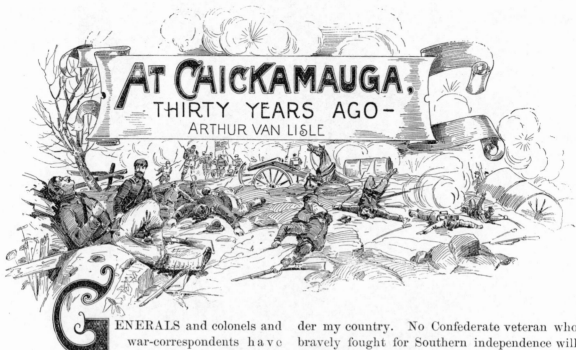

AT CHICKAMAUGA,
THIRTY YEARS AGO—
ARTHUR VAN LISLE

ENERALS and colonels and war-correspondents h a v e been heard, and the historian has begun to write, but the private soldier who fought the battles has had but little to say:

> " His not to reason why,
> His but to do and die."

Well, I did my duty as an humble private, although I did not die, nor lose my reason; and since I survive and still retain my faculties, I now propose to tell my story, and relate, with such poor powers as I possess, the observations and experiences of one who carried a musket and who loyally and conscientiously obeyed the orders of his superior officers.

I was in the Union army four years,—from 1861 to 1865,—only one of the two million who made up that magnificent army, and therefore a very insignificant factor of the whole. My experiences were those common to my comrades. I went into the service of my country to do my duty and to take all the consequences. I have no apologies to make for the part I bore; indeed, I am proud of the fact that I was a Union soldier, and of the little service I was able to render my country. No Confederate veteran who bravely fought for Southern independence will deny me or begrudge me the honor which I so proudly shall share in common with the grand army that saved the nation from disruption. With me it was a war for principle, as it was with the great mass of Southern soldiers. Men do not voluntarily surrender their personal liberties and their right to reason; they do not submit themselves to the rigid discipline of the army; leave home and loved ones and the comforts of life to suffer the *ennui* of camp and the fatigue of the march; to endure the horrors of battle, the agony of wounds, and die,—unless animated by some exalted motive. At least, no intelligent, free-born American would do this unless he felt that his country was in peril or his honor at stake.

I was but a boy in those troublous times; but such even then was my course of reasoning, and it made me feel great respect for the Confederate, who, I believed, was inspired by the same spirit of patriotism that animated me. Surely these brave men (my enemies) were human beings,—aye, more: they were Americans,—and held life as dear as I did myself, but honor more dear than life. I did not, and could not, fight these men in malice. I deprecated their action; but did they not equally deprecate mine? There was, however, an "irrepressible conflict" which only the sword and the arbitrament of arms could settle. I engaged in that settlement, and many a time during my four years of service, when the heavens were dark and rations short, did I feel (and this feeling was not peculiar to myself, but quietly shared by many a comrade too brave and proud to make open confession) that our cause, if not lost, was at least not assured. But such feelings, although depressing for the time, would only nerve me for more determined effort.

ARTHUR VAN LISLE.
1863.

As it was with me, so it was with my comrades, and so it must have been with our enemies; for they, too, had their seasons of success and defeat before the final and decisive blow was struck at Appomattox.

All this is merely introductory to my story. When I began to write, it was to express my gratitude to an unknown Confederate to whom I have ever felt that I owed my life, and to recite the circumstances under which the episode occurred. I had been shot. True, a Confederate soldier shot me; that was his duty as a soldier, just as it was my duty to shoot the Confederate—and to shoot to kill. War is barbarous even among the most civilized nations; it was not my duty to go out of my way to save the life of a wounded Confederate, neither could I expect a Confederate, in the heat and fury of battle, to stop and sympathize with me, writhing in pain and wallowing in blood. But that a Confederate soldier did so, and that to him I owe the fact that I am living to-day to tell the story, impels me—now that the opportunity is afforded through the medium of this patriotic magazine—to express to him my unbounded love and gratitude, and through him to all those lofty souls, on either side, who, while they bravely fought, were yet brave enough to sympathize with suffering and relieve distress wherever it was in their power to do so. There were thousands of cases like mine which will never find record in the annals of the war; but the angel of mercy, looking down from above, has recorded them in a book of gold treasured in the celestial library, to be opened in the presence of those whose names are inscribed in that glorious volume of Christ-like deeds when the roll of honored Federals and Confederates is called in heaven.

———

It was at the battle of Chickamauga. For several days previous to the final onslaught there had been marching and countermarching, back and forth, up the mountains and down into the valleys, like the king's men who "marched up the hill, and then marched down again." There was considerable skirmishing, too; for every day we encountered the enemy, who seemed to be omnipresent, and determined to annoy us if not to check our progress. The fact that the Confederates were cautious, as if timid, and that they uniformly retired after a few shots, was not nearly as cheering as one might suppose. There was too much method in this apparently desultory programme. We had seen too much fighting, and knew too well the character and qualities of our adversary, to feel any particular elation over their systematic withdrawals. They were only feeling us, to discover our strength and position, while their army was choosing its ground, luring us on while its formidable lines were moving into battle array. Such was our conjecture, and it was probably correct. The privates had theories of their own, as well as the generals, and they grasped the true condition of affairs as readily.

On Friday, September 18, 1863, there was a foretaste of what was to follow. The enemy had ceased to dash and retreat, and made a resolute offensive movement. Off to our left, in the direction of Ringgold, there was heavy firing. We were ordered in that direction, and hastened to the scene. As we approached we encountered riderless horses dashing wildly toward us; then came ambulances burdened with mangled forms, groaning in the agony of gaping wounds. As we drew nearer we saw the Union lines stubbornly falling back, while an aide, with fire in his eyes, mounted on a frothing steed, rushed toward us with orders to double-quick into line and forward.

This order was executed with a will, and with a shout we dashed to the front. Suddenly halting, we fired a deadly volley into the advancing "graybacks," under which their lines reeled and staggered, withdrawing from the field as soon as they had recovered from the unexpected blow. This settled the affair for that day, so far as our part of the line was concerned; still we anticipated that another day would be required to rout the hostile host and send them scampering over the Georgia mountains. A true soldier never thinks of defeat before the battle: he only realizes it after the battle has been fought and lost. So we never dreamed but that the "Johnnies" were doomed when once we fairly engaged them.

But the next day, Saturday, September 19, 1863, proved to us that our cousins "Johnnie" were equally hopeful and confident, and more determined than we, their Yankee cousins, had ever found them before. We learned, too, the solid basis of their hope: they had been reinforced by a corps of the best troops in the world, —a portion of General Lee's army, from Virginia. This we learned to our sorrow, and at frightful cost, but too late to make amends.

The question occurring to me now is, Could the Chickamauga campaign have been conducted with more skill and with better results, had we known in advance that Longstreet, with his magnificent divisions, had come to the relief of Bragg? To have retreated and abandoned the field, in consequence of this knowledge, would have been demoralizing and disastrous, if not disgraceful. We had the year before, in 1862, advanced on Chattanooga, under Buell, only to abandon the project of its capture and follow Bragg back into Kentucky, in order to save Louisville and Cincinnati from falling into his hands,—a masterpiece of strategy on the part of the Confederate commander, worthy of the highest military genius. It saved Chattanooga to the South for the time being, and prolonged the war at least another year. No; to repeat such tactics was out of the question. We were in front of the enemy, and this time he must not again pass us to menace our borders. If General Rosecrans knew that General Bragg had been reinforced (and he probably did, though not to what extent until after the battle), he felt that his only safety consisted in giving battle— by aggressive demonstrations, or at least by vigorous resistance—to the combined Confederate armies of the East and West. I write as a private soldier, who only knows what transpires under his immediate observation; but I then felt, and have always felt, that General Rosecrans, considering all the circumstances, did the best and wisest thing that any commander could have done. That we wrenched Chattanooga from the hands of the enemy, and held it, is to his everlasting credit. This was the objective point of the Chickamauga campaign, as I then believed and as I still believe. If there was any other object in view, I have never yet heard what it was. Chattanooga, at all events, was taken, and

never again passed out of our possession. It was the centre of the Southern railroad system, and the key to the interior situation. But I must cease these reflections, and confine myself to the narrative.

Our work on Friday, the 18th, had not been very serious in its results to us, and we congratulated ourselves on having put a sudden quietus upon the enemy, who had evidently assaulted our lines with a view of breaking through and getting into our rear, and thus demoralizing our forces; or, confident of his strength, it might have been with a purpose to precipitate a general engagement. Whatever the motive, it had miscarried. That night we threw out a heavy skirmish line; then ate

ARTHUR VAN LISLE.   1893.

our hardtack, drank our black coffee, and lay down to rest. We were very much worn with the heavy marching for several days, and the double-quick affair of that afternoon, so we slept quite soundly during the night, every man with his rifle at his side, which, in a half-conscious, mechanical way, he would transfer to the other side as he rolled over in his sleep.

There was no sounding of the reveille the next morning, that memorable Saturday, September 19th, but every man was astir at the first dawning, still weary, stiff in every joint, bones aching, muscles sore. A pint of strong black coffee, however, relaxes the system, and soon we feel somewhat refreshed. An occasional shot is heard here and there, on the right or the left; but no one regards that, although we are expecting every moment either to be attacked or to make the attack ourselves. We are formed into line and rest at ease, but ready.

The Confederates, too, are stirring; they take the initiative; they advance upon us as coolly as if on dress-parade or manœuvring to show us the precision of their drill. We are eager, anxious witnesses of this grand, warlike spectacle; we view it intently, and cannot restrain our admiration for their unbroken, advancing lines; yet we know too well what their approach portends. Involuntarily we seize our rifles and examine them critically to see that all is in order; we place our hands upon the cartridge-boxes to assure ourselves that they are unfastened and well filled; we thrust thumb and forefinger into our cap-pouches to ascertain their condition, for no less depends upon these items than upon our courage; but all the while our eyes are intently fixed upon the advancing foe. On they come, like a long-extended, great gray billow surging toward our position, destined to overwhelm us; nearer and nearer. We are cautioned to maintain our position, ready, but not to fire until ordered. Men nerve themselves for the final onslaught; their breathing is quick and heavy; the suspense is awful. Was ever tongue or pen that can describe the sensations of the soldier awaiting such an attack? There we stand, realizing what is before us and what must follow. We feel that the eyes of the nation are upon us—the eyes of all the nations; we think of our loved ones far away in our Northern homes; we know that it means death or wounds to some of us; we look upon the old flag which we have borne in triumph through Kentucky and Tennessee, and we make up our minds that after all it is not such a terrible thing to die, and that die we will rather than yield—that to die in defence of our flag, representing the freest and best government on earth, is a glorious privilege and an exalted duty.

Such were the thoughts that rushed through my mind, inspired my courage, and reconciled me to my fate, whatever it might be. Were my comrades who stood shoulder to shoulder with me on that eventful morning any less concerned, thoughtful, and resolute? No! They were reared on the adjoining farms, in the same neighborhood; they attended the same country school and the same village church near by; our early education was the same, and we naturally thought the same thoughts, and experienced the same sensations; we enlisted in the same squad with a full realization of duty to be performed and dangers to be encountered. Once again we stood as we had at Shiloh, and Perryville, and Stone River. We recalled the awful scenes there enacted, and thought of the comrades, the playmates of our boyhood days, who fell upon those bloody fields. They had surrendered their lives for their country, and they met their death like patriots. Was it now ours to die like them? If so, we were ready!

On they come, that long gray line, so long that the flanks extend beyond our vision; steady is their step and perfect their alignment, save here and there as they meet an obstruction in the way of a farm-house or a fence. There is heard to the right and left some irregular firing, and occasional cannon shot, and then for a moment a crash and rumbling like the thunders

rolling from cloud to cloud. In our immediate front, however, all is quiet. It is that dread silence which precedes the approaching storm. On it comes, and now a general shout breaks forth. It is the "rebel yell,"—HEY—YEH—YEH! HEY—YEH—YEH! They have started on the double-quick toward us. The scene is one of supreme awe—well calculated to strike terror to the soul of the most hardened and stoical.

But we are not to be terrorized by this sublime exhibition of intrepidity on the part of our assailants. We have witnessed similar demonstrations before and have withstood them. We only clutch our rifles more firmly, and brace ourselves to receive the shock. That we do not flinch or fire no doubt surprises the charging host. Suddenly they halt. They are probably eighty rods distant, and are about to give us their first volley.

We are nervously awaiting their nearer approach, that our first fire may do the more effective execution; but the moment they halt, and before they have time to adjust themselves in position, or bring their guns from a right-shoulder-shift, we are given the command, *Ready! Aim! Fire!*

A sheet of flame issues from our ranks; a cloud of smoke fills the air and obscures our vision. We reload and await results as we watch the vapor rising from the ground. We see a flash as of sheet-lightning; we hear the report; we see our comrades falling, some never to rise again, some mortally wounded, weltering in blood, others crippled and writhing in agony. Now "forward" is the order, and we advance on the enemy, leaving our stricken comrades behind us where they have fallen. The battle is on in earnest. We do not see the enemy's lines, for they are hidden by the intervening cloud of smoke; but we know where they are, and we keep up an incessant fire as we steadily, but cautiously, move on. The enemy, too, maintains his fire, pouring into our ranks a regular shower of lead. All is turmoil and confusion. Artillery in our rear is firing over our heads into the enemy beyond. A battery pushes up to our line shotted with grape and canister, which it pours into the enemy before us. But our ranks are growing thin, our losses are frightful. It is becoming evident that the "Johnnies" are too many for us. We are without doubt doing terrible execution among them; but we certainly cannot long endure their murderous fire, which is sweeping along our lines and mowing down our men like grass. Our condition is desperate, our position untenable. We are forced to retire; only temporarily, we hope, for surely reinforcements will come to our aid.

I fall. I try to rise, but cannot. What's the matter?

My thigh is torn, the bone is shattered, although I did not feel the shot that struck me.

Here I lie among the dead and wounded. Our men have fallen back. Over our prostrate forms the bullets are hissing and shells shrieking.

In the endeavor to ease my cramped position my wounded limb becomes twisted, and oh! the agony of pain which I now feel for the first time.

What horror surrounds me!

Here I am, helpless and bleeding, my flesh lacerated, my thigh-bone broken; the dead so ghastly, the dying and the wounded all about me; my regiment falling back, the enemy advancing.

What will become of me?

Oh, my country! is it possible that my fate is but a portent of yours?

To the wounded soldier, deserted on the field, the day is ever lost. How can he feel otherwise? To him it is a day of disaster, of irretrievable ruin; for he can judge only from what he sees and feels; he feels his own utter helplessness, and sees nothing but death and defeat. And yet he hopes that all is not lost; that the enemy may yet be repulsed. But it is a doubtful hope, for on comes that terrible line of gray, in all its fury, pressing back the boys in blue.

Now they halt, but still they fire.

The rattle of rifles and the roar of artillery are simply awful. No sounds ever heard can bear comparison to this deafening, deadly, rattling, crashing, roaring, thundering noise, which fills the heavens and shakes the earth.

Now the enemy falls back.

Our boys are coming. Thank God, I shall be rescued!

But, oh, how long I wait! How much longer must I wait? Can I—can I survive this terrible ordeal?

I am growing weak, oh! so weak; my tongue is dry, my lips are parched. I cannot move my body, but with an effort I turn my head to see if my comrades are really coming. Oh, how I long for their presence; for I am so thirsty, and they will give me drink, and carry me to a place of safety in the rear. But, better than all this, the battle is not lost, for the troops in gray are still falling back, and our own boys are still

advancing. I see the flag, our beautiful flag; never were its colors more resplendent than now, as it whips the Southern air and moves on to the front. My eyes are riveted to that glorious old banner. I had followed its folds for many a weary mile; but I cannot follow it now, though never more adored. Will it ever reach the spot where I have fallen? Will it recover its lost ground, and save the boys who fell where it first advanced? Will it ever reach me? Oh, the suspense, the sickening, killing

"I WATCH THE FLAG."

suspense! The anguish of mind drowns the agony of pain.

But how vain the attempt to describe such a scene and such sensations. A Hugo would shrink from such a task. It is not in power of mortal man to do it. The soldier may witness the scene, and feel the horror of the situation, but he can never tell the story of either; and it is well that he cannot, for all who would hear his words would feel their hearts grow sick, and their blood chill in their veins.

I watch the flag, for I can see it, although occasionally obscured by the smoke of battle, but I cannot see our boys nor the opposing line; but surely our boys are coming, and their foes retreating,—hope borne above despair.

The whizzing, sizzing balls fly over my head, and over the slain, that surround me on all sides; the earth trembles with the thunders of the cannon; the tumult of sounds and the turmoil and confusion of battle continue fiercer and fiercer.

What a scene to contemplate! And here am I in the midst of it, to see it, to feel it, helpless, and without help, feverish from pain and loss of blood, but still borne up by the hope that my comrades will come to my relief.

The battle still rages—rages furiously, and the horrors which environ me are being enacted all over that bloody field for miles around; for not only in front of me and behind me, but to the right of me and to the left of me, and above me, is heard the crash of musketry and the belching of artillery, the earth trembling under the reverberations and enveloped in one dense cloud of smoke.

How long, oh, how long must this continue?

For me it is all that dreadful day and all that dreadful night.

What thoughts crowd upon the feverish brain in the midst of such a scene! Can there be a merciful God, and He see His children suffer like this? But have not we, His children, departed from His divine law of love and bid Him defiance? It is not His punishment,—it is self-imposed and self-inflicted. God would not that any of His children should suffer.

Now there ensues a temporary lull in this pandemonium.

Is the battle over? And who are the victors?

God grant that this holocaust of fire and blood and death has come to an end.

But these are only fleeting thoughts, inspired by the momentary lull in the battle,—hopes born of the heart's desire, only to be chilled and doomed to die.

The end is not yet. The enemy open fire with even greater fury than before, and again take the offensive. They are coming from among the pines (to which they had retired) like a horde of ferocious, unreasoning, starving beasts, bent upon their prey. Our boys cannot withstand their withering fire and desperate onslaught, and are compelled to fall back to escape complete annihilation. Backward and forward surge the contending lines, and now, oh, my God! the enemy comes with a wild rush and that ominous, terrifying "rebel yell." They are passing over me, stumbling over our dead and wounded, falling among us, passing on. We are left behind, and the moans and groans of Union and Confederate wounded mingle in the smoke-stifling air, while many a poor fellow's agony is ended by stray shots which strike in our midst.

Can I survive this awful anguish? Must I die here, to be laid in an unknown grave by the hands of the enemy? How long must I endure this torture of mind and body. Hope is gone,—all is lost. The day is waning,—what a terrible day it has been! Night approaches,—what horrors will it bring forth! Surely if my comrades cannot help me I must die, and I must die here,

with no friend to soothe my last moments or tell the story of my death to the loved ones at home? I am growing weaker and weaker from the loss of blood, which is now drying upon my body and stiffening my clothing; fever is in my veins, and I am perishing from thirst. Oh for a drink! *Water*, WATER, WATER!

Again the firing slackens, but it does not cease.

Have my comrades, my regiment, my brigade, been driven from the field? And what of our army? Oh, the uncertainty, the terrible despair of the situation!

While I thus bemoan my condition there comes a sudden crash of artillery; the fight is renewed, and here comes back the line of gray with its thinned and thinning ranks, trampling upon the dead and the wounded as they retire, for they keep their faces to the front. They are falling thick and fast, some of them upon our dead, and some upon their own. Back they go, sullenly, defiantly; they do not think of death, but of victory.

It was during this repulse, the crisis in the day's battle, that a Confederate soldier, standing over me, bravely fighting, seeing my bloody side and parched lips, stooped down, and, throwing the strap of his canteen over his head, put the nozzle to my mouth, saying, as he did so,—

"Drink, Yank; I reckon you're powerful dry."

I drank, and never did Ganymede serve the gods with nectar more delicious or refreshing.

Meanwhile the shower of shot and shell and hissing balls from our front was frightful, and the brave Confederates were forced still farther back, and my benefactor with them, while I still held his old cedar canteen to my lips, draining its contents. Too kind, too humane, too noble to take it from me, my Confederate friend rose to join his retreating comrades, when I offered to return it, feebly raising the canteen above my head with outstretched arm.

"Jest you keep it," I heard him shout back as he retired, loading his gun.

I never saw that noble, tender-hearted Confederate soldier again; but he has been to me a good Samaritan, an angel of mercy, all my days. I had always entertained an exalted opinion of the courage and fortitude of the Confederate soldier; but from that eventful day to this serene moment he has seemed to me the soul of honor, brave and generous, true to his cause, however mistaken, and true to (and never mistaken in) the higher instincts of humanity. Thus one man may exalt the good name of an entire

"JUST YOU KEEP IT!"

people or a whole army by his moral heroism and his own exalted character.

My story is already too long. Were I to dwell upon what followed that night and the the next day, it would be only to repeat the sad-dening sights I had witnessed and the sufferings experienced all that day.

Three decades have passed over our heads since that memorable battle, and yet to-day I survive, a living and a willing witness of Confederate kindness. The water from that old cedar canteen refreshed and revived me so that I survived that awful night, and early next morning I was rescued by my comrades and taken to Chattanooga, where my wound was dressed. I lay for many weary weeks a great sufferer; but finally, though slowly, I regained strength, and my wound healed.

I recovered, and although a cripple for life, never while I live shall I cease to feel the deepest love and most profound gratitude for that humane action of an unknown Confederate soldier.

God grant him joy of heart if living yet;
    Blest be his memory if he be dead;
Yet living or dead I cannot forget,
    But ever pour blessings upon his head.

THE LAST SALUTE.

GEORGE M. VICKERS.

YES, the ranks are growing smaller
    With the coming of each May,
And the beards and locks once raven
    Now are mingled thick with gray;
Soon the hands that strew the flowers
    Will be folded still and cold,
And our story of devotion
    Will forever have been told.

Years and years have passed by, comrades,
    Though it seems but yesterday
Since the Blue-garbed Northern legions
    Marched to meet the Southern Gray—
But a day since Massachusetts
    Bade her soldier boys good-bye—
But a day since Alabama
    Heard her brave sons' farewell cry.

Those are days we all remember,
    In our hearts we hold them yet;
And the kiss we got at parting,
    Who can ever that forget?
And it may have been a mother,
    A fond father, or a wife,
Or a maid whose love was dearer
    To the soldier's heart than life.

Then the silent midnight marches,
    And the fierce-fought battle's roar,
And the sailor's lonely watches,
    Gone, please God, forevermore:
Though these ne'er can be forgotten
    While the dew our graves shall wet,
Yet the color of our jackets
    Let each gallant heart forget;

For the ranks are growing smaller,
    And though decked in blue or gray,
Soon both armies will be sleeping
    In their shelter-tents of clay.
But the loud reverberation
    Of the last salute shall be
Oft re-echoed through the ages
    As the tocsin of the free!

For we both but did our duty,
    In the Great Jehovah's plan,
And the world has learned a lesson
    That all men may read who can;
And when gathered for the muster
    On the last and dreadful day,
May that God extend His mercy
    Sweet, alike to Blue and Gray.

CUTTING OUT THE "UNDERWRITER."

A BRILLIANT EXPLOIT IN A SOUTHERN HARBOR.

CAPTAIN H. D. SMITH.

THE planning of the capture of the United States Steamer "Underwriter" came from a number of naval officers meeting in the vicinity of New Berne. They were unemployed, applications for duty afloat remained unheeded and unnoticed by the authorities at Richmond, and they determined to rub the rust from their ardent temperaments by meeting the Federal blue-jackets with such means as they could command.

It was a dashing and daring undertaking, well worthy to be classed among the brilliant deeds of American seamen, side by side with the lamented chivalrous Decatur and the bold, lion-hearted Cushing. For the fact remains, that, though fighting under different flags, with opinions and principles variant, the blood and birthright of the combatants remained the same—all were American sailors.

The " Underwriter " was a side-wheel steamer of about 341 tons, and was purchased by the government for use in the naval service in the early part of 1861. She cost $18,500, and when ready for service made a very respectable cruiser. She carried four broadside guns, with the usual quantity of small arms, and rendered good service in the sounds of North Carolina, to which locality she was ordered from the Brooklyn Navy Yard. She participated in the capture of Roanoke Island, Elizabeth City, Edenton, and New Berne, under the able leadership of Commander S. C. Rowan, and was captured February 2, 1864, in a night attack, after a desperate resistance.

The story of the capture was related to the writer by a participant, whom he met by chance at a hotel in Weldon, N. C.

The old sleepy town of New Berne is situated on a point of land bordered on the one side by the muddy waters of the Neuse, and on the other by the sluggish Trent. It fell into the hands of the Federals soon after the reduction of Roanoke Island, and had been used as a base of supplies and military operations, having been strengthened by extensive field fortifications, extending over twenty miles of surrounding country. A naval rendezvous was also formed at the juncture of the two rivers; two or more gunboats were continually at the station or cruising on the rivers.

For some time the Confederates had entertained the idea of cutting out one of the gunboats, which would form a welcome addition to their skeleton fleet. There were a number of Southern naval officers drifting about on shore, with nothing to do, and temperaments peculiarly fitted for an expedition of the kind proposed. A meeting of the officers was held in a spur of pine woods some miles distant from the town, and it was resolved that one of the number should proceed to New Berne in disguise, reconnoitre, and gather all the information possible for the benefit of the attacking party. This was successfully accomplished by a young fellow who played the rôle of an up-country farmer, in which guise he visited the " Underwriter " at the wharf, ascertaining her force, number of guns, mode of keeping watch at night, and all particulars relative to discipline and routine duties.

The rendezvous for the bold spirits had been selected on a clear knoll bordering on the Neuse River some forty miles above the town. Men had been recruited, boats secured, while for rations and supplies the surrounding country afforded ample means of support. Commander Wood, of the Confederate navy, had been chosen as the leader, his reputation as a cool-headed fighter and man of judgment being well established. Lieutenant B. P. Loyall was selected as second in command, and the arrangements for an immediate attack were rapidly perfected. There were Lieutenants Hoge, Kerr, Porcher, Gardner, Roby, Wilkinson, and Gift, with Engineer Gill, Midshipman Saunders, and others whose names have faded from memory with the lapse of time. The force was organized upon the same principles as that of the famous whale-boat navy of the Revolution, and a few days were spent in the sylvan retreat getting the men into shape. All had been under fire, had listened to the whistling of balls and bursting of shells in many a hot engagement; but fighting afloat was a new experience to many of the men, who, however, looked forward to the cutting-out expedition with enthusiasm, and were full of confidence as regarded the result.

In the meantime Commander Wood had communicated with General Pickett, who agreed to make a demonstration along the Federal lines, and divert their attention from the water front. The general had with him two brigades only,— Clingham's and Hoke's,—while General Barton had been sent up the Trent to fall simultaneously upon the town with those in front. In addition to this, Colonel Dearing, with a small force of infantry, a battalion of cavalry, and two pieces of artillery, had been sent across the Neuse to threaten Fort Anderson and prevent reinforcements from Little Washington.

Pleased with the hearty and cordial co-operation of the land forces, Wood returned to his party, reporting his success.

On the morning of Sunday, January 31, 1864, the little frail fleet of boats and canoes was launched on the placid surface of the Neuse, and were pulling down to the appointed place of meeting, about twenty-five miles above New Berne. One by one they struggled in and were hauled up on the shelving beach, where cheery camp-fires had been lit and numerous camp kettles placed in position. All was in readiness, save the presence of Commander Wood, who had been detained looking after some matters of supplies. About two o'clock he rounded the point, his men pulling with long, sweeping strokes, and soon he was surrounded by his comrades, anxious to hear the latest news.

He was a fine-appearing man, with a commanding presence, every inch a sailor, and an accomplished officer, and had stood high in the estimation of his superiors when serving under the old flag. He was dressed in a simple suit of gray, tight-fitting, with brass buttons, a slouch hat, and insignia of rank embroidered in gold upon his standing collar. His old navy sword hung by his side, while the long cumbersome naval Colt, ready for instant use, was suspended in front. His hair and eyes were dark, complexion swarthy, with a muscular frame, possessing, in fact, a physique far above the average allotted to man.

The men were clad in homespun, with no attempt at a uniformity in apparel. The arms had been carefully looked to, ammunition distributed, the final directions given to each officer, and at three o'clock the party embarked. The boats were formed in two divisions, Wood leading, while Loyall headed the other.

Night soon enveloped the scene in impenetrable shadows, rendering progress both uncertain and extremely slow; gradually the heavens became obscured, heavy clouds gathered, followed rapidly by a mist and drizzling rain, but fortunately the worst part of the trip was over. The open country above New Berne had been gained, the river widened, the shores grew low and marshy, and soon the lights of the town loomed up as the boats rounded a sharp bend. It was four o'clock when a point in front of the quaint old place was reached ; the fog was so thick it was impossible to distinguish objects fifteen feet distant : but a search for the Federal boat was at once made, with every man on the *qui vive* for the order to board.

Suddenly the deep, muffled boom of a piece of artillery was heard, followed by the rattle of musketry. Pickett had opened fire on the outposts, and the long roll of the drums, mingled with hoarse shouts and galloping of horses, testified that the Federal forces had taken the alarm. No time was to be lost so far as the boat expedition was concerned, every moment was fraught with life or death, but pull as they would no gunboat could they discover.

For an hour the resolute band cruised from point to point, trying in vain to make out the glimmer of a light or battle lantern. Daylight was close at hand, detection could end in nothing but disaster, and with curses both loud and deep the cutting-out party, foiled and disappointed, their ardor dampened and hopes blunted, were forced to pull at a lively rate up stream and seek cover. So far as they were concerned their mission had been a dismal failure. There were no gunboats in the Neuse.

Dull, leaden streaks of light along the eastern horizon admonished the leader of the folly of remaining longer in the river before the town. Skirting the left bank of the river closely, the expedition silently withdrew, while the boom of cannon and rolling fire of musketry from the land forces effectually occupied the attention of those in the town. Not a man among them dreamed of such a thing as an attack from the water.

A landing was effected, and as the sun rose the men stretched themselves upon the grass, and soon the party were sleeping soundly, with not a solitary sentinel or picket thrown out to keep watch. All that day the battle around New Berne raged, but the roar of cannon and the sharp reports of bursting shells disturbed not the slumbers of the tired men.

It was shortly after 10 o'clock at night when the boats were again afloat. The fog had rolled up, the stars were out, and, although it was cloudy, objects could be distinguished with tolerable distinctness.

Keeping well within the shadows of the overhanging bank, the boats made good time, passing within a short distance of the tumble-down wharves of the town. Suddenly the clang of a bell, struck seven times, rang out sharp and clear, and then, but a short distance ahead, loomed up the outlines of a long, substantial-appearing gunboat. She was moored head and stern close to the shore, with her broadside guns commanding the principal street of the town, while in close proximity were three powerful batteries, fully manned, and ready for action. The hour, as proclaimed by the bell, was half-past eleven, and Wood, standing erect, waved his sword aloft, pointing expressively toward the silent gunboat. The boats glided forward in beautiful order, leaving the friendly cover of shadows and banks.

"Boats, ahoy!" hailed a gruff voice; "Boats, ahoy! Lay on your oars, or I'll give you a shot!" "Give way!" shouted Commander Wood. "Give way, my lads; give way as you never did before!" echoed Lieutenant Loyall; and as the men bent to their work the whirr of a huge rattle resounded upon the still night air. It was the summons on board the gunboat for rallying the men at quarters. The seamen, half dazed by sleep, and taken by surprise, scarcely realized their danger before the boats were upon them.

The boats crowded together, all making for the forward part of the steamer, with the exception of Wood, who maintained a position amidships. The glare of a dozen lanterns triced up on board now illuminated the scene, revealing a crowd of sailors, jostling each other, evidently panic-stricken, while the word of command from officers, casting loose guns, and rattle of accoutrements were distinctly heard amid the confusion of sounds arising from her decks.

The first blow was struck by the Federals, who poured into the faces of the attacking party a volley of rifle-balls. The larger portion flew wide of the mark, passing over the heads of the Confederates, and ere a second could be delivered the boats were rasping alongside. The great guns of the vessel were thus rendered useless; the men, led by Wood and his officers, clambered over the rail, cutting, shooting, thrusting with pikes and bayonets at the dense ranks of sailors, who had now gathered in force and were pouring in a hot fire from their small-arms.

The flashes came full in the faces of the Confederates, lighting them up with a deathly pallor, while the sulphurous smell of burning powder pervaded the air. Gradually the sailors were forced back, the weapons wrenched from their hands by the sturdy homespun followers of the Confederacy, being used with terrible effect upon their late owners. The officers endeavored in vain to stem the current of disaster sweeping along the gory deck of their floating citadel. They did all that brave men could do to repair their lost prestige. An effort was made to drag a howitzer into position, that its stream of leaden balls might carry a whirlwind of death through the ranks of the Southerners; but the keen eye of Wood detected the movement, and he at once charged upon the knot of seamen gathered about the piece. His sinewy, nervous arm swung aloft his irresistible sabre; one, two, men went down before it, the deep blue of their uniforms tinged with a crimson flow of life-blood. Two marines, with charged bayonets, rushed upon the tall form of the Confederate leader, while the "rebel yell" rang out defiantly as a dozen brave fellows rushed to their chieftain's rescue. The woodwork of the gunboat had caught fire, the light, ornamental material quickly augmenting the flames, but there was no time then to pay attention to the devouring element. The ruddy blaze revealed a hideous sight,—the white deck streaming with blood, while homely, homespun-clad figures lay motionless side by side with the popular and patriotic uniformed seamen of the United States Navy. A stalwart marine had fallen beside a companion-way which he had guarded faithfully to the last.

Driven into close and contracted gangways, hemmed in and confronted on all sides by the fierce, unkempt Confederates, the sailors of the "Underwriter" lost heart, and, throwing down their arms, called for quarter.

Wood, from the hurricane deck, ordered all the fighting to cease. The "Underwriter" was won, the cutting-out party had been successful; and the hands of the cabin clock pointed to the hour of midnight.

Poor Gill, the engineer, was lying in the starboard gangway, shot in four places, and Midshipman Saunders, cut down in the hand-to-hand encounter, was breathing his last a few paces distant, his face upturned to heaven, unable to respond to his grief-stricken friend who bent over him. Loyall, wounded from a jagged splinter, leaned weary and exhausted against one of the after-guns, and the mortality among the men had been great.

The rattle of small-arms and shouts of the combatants had not passed unnoticed. The soldiers in the batteries had been summoned, and, regardless alike of friend and foe, sent a shell with deadly precision into the hull of the "Underwriter." Another burst amid the machinery, while a third exploded on the main deck, throwing up a cloud of splinters, and shaking the vessel from trucks to keelson. It required not the work of the Federal batteries to wrest from the hands of Wood and his gallant followers the hard-earned fruit of their victory. The unchecked flames had gained such headway that to save the steamer would have been impossible. In addition, fires had been hauled by the orders of the Federal commander, and no water was in the boilers.

The wounded, together with the prisoners, were placed in the boats, and Lieutenant Hoge and his men, who had trained the guns of the captured vessel upon the nearest battery, were ordered to retreat at once. But for considerations of the wounded and helpless, Wood, with his bull-dog tenacity, would have returned the fire, despite the burning _débris_ around him.

The boats were manned, the oars soon sent them whirling up the river, their course partially lighted by the flames of the doomed vessel. Neither clothing, stores, paymaster's chest, or booty of any description rewarded the needy Confederates. They had had their fill of fighting, also, especially afloat, and Commander Wood, with his brother officers, organized no more expeditions of a semi-naval character in the neighborhood of New Berne.

The "Underwriter" was burned to the water's edge, together with the bodies of those who had fallen on her decks. But the result of the attack was not entirely barren of results.

Pickett had met the Federals in force at Bachelor's Creek, killed and wounded about one hundred in all, captured thirteen officers, two hundred and eighty prisoners, fourteen negroes, two rifled pieces and caissons, three hundred stand of arms, four ambulances, three wagons, forty-five horses, a quantity of clothing, camp and garrison equipage, and two flags.

THE GENERAL LOST HIS WHISKEY.
H. J. HEALY.

EVERY one has heard of General Robert O. Tyler, the gallant officer from Connecticut, who on several occasions was rewarded by promotion for his bravery. It is with him that this anecdote has to deal.

Like many other good soldiers, General Tyler was a good judge of whiskey, and could drink his portion without at all incapacitating himself for military duty. Consequently it was not surprising that he should have a certain amount of liquor as a part of his tent equipment. One day he received a ten-gallon keg of whiskey, which was safely stored away in one corner of his tent, and which gave promise of many soothing potations and any amount of entertainment. But all these hopes were soon dashed to the ground. That night General Tyler had for a guard a big, raw-boned Irishman, named Kirwin, who, in the drinking line, could give the General points, and even go him one better. Kirwin was particularly instructed to report any trouble without the camp, for General Mosby was prowling around at that time and was making it particularly warm for the Unionists. The General retired; but Kirwin had either seen the keg when it was being brought in, or later, and in his anxiety for its welfare, forgot all about Mosby. Assuring himself that the General was asleep, he called a council of his bosom companions and told them the status of things. It was unanimously decided to steal the keg, and Kirwin hauled it out from the end of the tent and rolled it down into a near-by ravine, where his thirsty companions were in waiting, like young eaglets in the absence of the mother-bird. They made shorter work of the liquor than I can of the story, and all got patriotically drunk.

In the morning, when General Tyler looked for an "eye-opener," he was surprised to find the keg missing. Ascertaining the name of his guard the night before, he sent for Kirwin. The latter was still drunk when he entered the tent, but cleared himself, after denying all knowledge of the whereabouts of the keg, by saying, "General, Mosby must have stolen it." General Tyler smiled and dismissed him.

A few days after, when the men were on dress-parade, Kirwin had a place in the front rank, but was now sober. As General Tyler marched down the line, in review, Kirwin endeavored to avoid the keen, searching eye, but to no purpose, for the General stopped directly in front of him, and said, with a smile, "Hello, Mosby, what are you doing here?" He passed on, while Kirwin remained severely quiet.

THE BEGINNING OF SHERMAN'S ADVANCE.

BATTLE OF RESACA.

ROBERT SHACKLETON, JR.

"NOW, Alice, he's seen the coat; so bring out the sash, and he'll have seen your grandfather's whole uniform."

The daughter blushed furiously as she turned to look for the sash. The father smothered a gurgling laugh. "Not the whole——!" he exclaimed, and suddenly checked himself. The mother looked sedately prim.

It was on the little-visited battlefield of Resaca, some two miles northward from the village; and when we by chance called at the little farm-house, we had no thought of there meeting a man whose father was a colonel in the Mexican war, and who still preserved the old-fashioned buff-blue coat of the colonel's uniform.

The interesting little town of Resaca is one of the quietest and sleepiest imaginable. Were it not that the railroad trains run through it, it is difficult to imagine what could give it any life. An old-looking well, walled in with brick, the wall extending several feet above the level of the ground, is in the centre of the little common, and over it is built a wooden roof supported on wooden posts. It is a public well and is much used by by the citizens, including even such as have wells of their own, for this public well furnishes particularly good water.

Alighting from the train, we approached a large frame building which stands at one side of the common. An elderly man was leaning against one side of the porch.

"Is this the hotel?" we asked.

"No," he replied, with slow deliberation, and as if accurately weighing the exact meaning of his words. "No. It's not good enough to call a hotel; but I reckon you can get something to eat here."

We were amused to find that he was the proprietor, and we were glad to find, too, that, although he was perhaps right in the first part of his description of his own place, we could really get something to eat there.

There are but a few buildings in the town which stood there at the time of the war. The principal of these is the Hill homestead, a low unattractive structure of frame, standing prominently on a low rise of ground not far from the common. This building was used as headquarters by the commanding officer of whichever

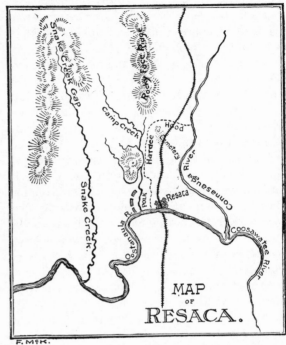

RESACA AND VICINITY.

force happened to be in possession in the course of the war. It suffered a little, but not much, from the fighting that took place here, and Mrs. Hill showed us the spot, still marked by a great scar, where a cannon-ball went through the house.

General Sherman, with his army in front of the impregnable Rocky Face Ridge, very early became convinced of the necessity of flanking Johnston out of his position; and so, while his forces were tentatively attacking the Confederates at different points, he was sending McPherson to the southward, with over 30,000 men. McPherson was to push his way through Snake Creek Gap, a wild and narrow valley, some five or six miles in length, to the westward of Rocky Face Ridge.

Sherman dared scarcely hope that this effort to get through to Johnston's rear could be successful, without at least serious opposition and heavy fighting; but the attempt was one that was well worthy of trial. Should McPherson get through, his orders were to advance against the railroad at Resaca and do his utmost there.

The march was successful to an unlooked-for degree. In passing through the narrow gap there was scarcely any opposition; there was but a handful of Confederate troops in the defile; and McPherson, without having encountered any difficulties, was advancing right upon Resaca, which, some miles south of Dalton, and upon the railroad, it was vitally important for Johnston to hold. The plan of Sherman was simple and comprehensive, and threatened, thus early in the campaign, the complete defeat of Johnston and the scattering and rout of his army. For with the Federals in firm possession of the railroad above Dalton, north of his army, and at Resaca, to the south, and holding Snake Creek Gap open as a line of communication, Johnston would indeed be helpless. Should he dash himself in force upon McPherson, that able officer could be trusted to keep him in check until ample reinforcements should arrive, for additional troops were rapidly hurrying forward. He could not go to the north; he could not go to the west; his only course would have been to remain at Dalton until starved into surrender, or else retreat eastward over difficult roads and through a rough and hilly country. Sherman, with his superiority of force, would undoubtedly crush him after gaining such a superiority of position as well.

Such was Sherman's hope, and it was well founded. He felt, too, that he must do something decisive in order to keep his agreement with Grant, who was depending upon his so actively occupying the attention of Johnston that it would be impossible for the Confederate commander to send any aid to Lee. Grant, for his part, had just fought the terrific battles of the Wilderness, and there was great danger that Johnston, if allowed to think himself safe, would send part of his force to Virginia.

Browning, in a poem on Napoleon at Ratisbon, has called attention to a chance to which even the greatest of generals are always liable:

> "Just as, perchance, he mused, 'My plans
> That soar, to earth may fall,
> Let once my army-leader Lannes
> Waver at yonder wall.'"

A chance such as the poet imagined with reference to Lannes and Napoleon served to effectually spoil Sherman's comprehensive plan for Johnston's utter destruction. McPherson, able and trustworthy though he was, wavered at Resaca. The Confederate position there was defended by but two brigades. Sherman thought that there was only one, but in reality there were two. McPherson, however, with the tremendous possibilities that depended upon his

action, should have advanced upon them and seized the post. There would have been a hot struggle. There would have been loss of life. But the chances were that the campaign would be so promptly terminated that in the end an immense saving of life would result.

McPherson advanced toward Resaca, after emerging from the narrow gap. He cautiously reconnoitered. Then, instead of attacking, he decided that it was impracticable to go any farther. He halted, and prepared to wait until reinforcements should arrive.

Sherman was bitterly disappointed, and had it been some less trusted officer who had thus failed to perform all that was expected of him, he would have been sharply rebuked, and perhaps even relieved of command. But he had a strong personal friendship for McPherson, and highly trusted and honored him, and therefore only told him, when they met, that he had "missed a great opportunity." In his "Memoirs" he remarks that such an opportunity as was presented at Resaca occurs only once in a lifetime. Even as it was, he had good reason to feel cheerful. He had made a safe flank movement with quite a portion of his force, and was in position to fight Johnston on what, compared with Rocky Face Ridge, was favorable ground indeed.

Learning that Sherman was, without any doubt, preparing to make a massed attack upon Resaca, Johnston first forwarded reinforcements to that point, and then, on May 12, 1864, evacuated Dalton and concentrated his entire force there. On the 13th, General Howard entered Dalton, and then followed the Confederates southward.

Resaca stands on the Oostenaula River, and the Western and Atlantic Railroad crosses the river at this point. Westward of Resaca some three-quarters of a mile, and parallel with the railroad, is a creek. This creek, shown on maps as Camp Creek, is not known by that name in this neighborhood. As, however, scarcely any two citizens agree upon the same name for it, we may as well call it Camp Creek as anything else.

The Confederate line began where the creek empties into the Oostenaula; thence it continued northward some two miles; then it curved eastward toward the Connasauga. The Connasauga, flowing in a generally southerly direction, is east of the town, and, flowing into the Oostenaula (or, to be more exact, uniting with the Coosawattee to form the Oostenaula), leaves

Resaca in an angle, with large rivers in every direction from it except toward Camp Creek and where the railroad comes down from Dalton. In case of disaster, retreat from such a position might become hazardous in the extreme, and it is not at all likely that Johnston expected to make a lengthy stand there, for he was too prudent a general to needlessly expose his men to danger.

The Confederate line did not extend to the western bank of the creek, except at its mouth. At that point, however, was a hill which commanded the railroad bridge, and therefore it was strongly fortified, and General Polk was placed in command there. Hardee was in charge in the centre, and his command extended to about where the Confederate line swung eastward. From Hardee's position to the Connasauga River was held by Hood. Moving on an interior line, Johnston could promptly get his entire army to Resaca and into position there, and Sherman, realizing this, did not hurry his own forces forward to the attack until he had practically all of them in hand.

On the 14th, however, vigorous fighting commenced, and for some time the struggle was very fierce near the angle where Hood's and Hardee's commands met. Schofield's men, the Army of the Ohio, charged bravely across the creek. The Confederates, however, defended their position with desperate valor; and although the Union forces made some little gain, it was at the expense of a serious loss in men. Later in the day the divisions of the Twentieth Army Corps being sent to that portion of the field, the Confederates were forced to yield considerable ground to their opponents.

Meanwhile, on the left of the Confederate position, brisk fighting was going on, and the Federals succeeded in gaining a foothold on the eastern side of the creek, and late in the afternoon General Logan ordered an assault upon the hill occupied by Polk's forces on the western side. It was desperately defended, for its possession by the Federals would render the entire position at Resaca most dangerous; but the troops charged upon it with irresistible valor, seized it, and then, although shot and shell fell thick among them, hastily made preparations to hold it against any effort to retake it.

In the course of the evening the effort was made, but the Federals repulsed it, and, thus holding the hill, made the Confederate position most precarious. Johnston fully realized this, and, exerting his splendid faculty of getting his

men out of desperate straits, that night had a pontoon bridge constructed across the river about a mile above the railroad bridge. Of course, if Johnston, after all, could not be compelled to retreat, the matter of bridges was of no importance except from a precautionary standpoint. Both armies fully realized this, and there was hot fighting on the 15th. Sherman's endeavor was to break the Confederate line at its northwestern angle and then force Hood into the Connasauga and Hardee and Polk into the Oostenaula. Johnston clearly saw this danger, and therefore, in this quarter, made furious onslaughts upon the Federal forces.

In the midst of the fighting the Confederates were compelled, at one portion of the line, to leave a four-gun battery in possession of the Federals. In turn, the captors themselves were driven back, and then so fierce was the storm of bullets that swept over the ground from both sides, that neither army was able to draw off the guns. When night came, however, a detachment of the Fifth Ohio rushed forward, seized the guns, and took them within the Union lines. This achievement is the more noteworthy from the fact that, so the Confederates claim, these guns were the only field trophies captured by the Federals from the opening of the campaign till the time that both armies reached the Chattahoochee.

Sherman was planning another flanking movement farther to the south, and, in fact, had already sent a force in that direction. Johnston saw that it would be fatal to longer remain at Resaca. Even as it was, he was in a position from which few generals could have escaped with safety. In the night of the 15th he withdrew beyond the Oostenaula, burning the railroad bridge as he retreated, and on the following morning Sherman entered the town.

The terrible scenes about a battlefield were forcibly brought to mind, at the time of our visit to Resaca, by the narrative of a woman who lived there as a little girl.

"How long ago *was* the war?" said she, musingly. "Let me see. Wal, Johnny, he's thirty year old now, I reckon, an' he war a baby then —must hev' been nigh about thirty year ago."

Thus she located the time, and she further explained that she was then some ten or twelve years old herself. Her home was made into a field hospital, and she, being but a child, was allowed to go about as she pleased. She remembers that the wounded officers were carried into the house, and that the privates were laid upon the ground outside. She counted one hundred and thirty lying there at one time.

Surgeons were there, too. Where they came from she did not know, but they were there, and she shudders as she remembers how freely and rapidly they cut and hacked, and how, apparently, without the slightest concern.

"It was like killing cattle," she says, and she adds that "it affects her more now, to think of it, than it did then to see it." She was little, and did not well appreciate what was done, and then, too, both the surgeons and soldiers themselves took it coolly, and as a matter of course. Eight men died there, and were buried by the fence. They were merely rolled in blankets, and laid closely side by side. Since the war the bodies have been taken up and carried to one of the national cemeteries.

A man, a resident of the battlefield, who returned to his home there immediately after the close of the war, he having been in the Southern army until then, tells of how he found in the "bresh" (Georgian for "brush") the bodies of soldiers, who, wounded, had crept under thick piles out of sight, and there died. On his farm, too, was a trench some seventy yards long, in which Union soldiers had been buried closely side by side. But the trench was shallow,—there had been heavy rains,—and for a distance of seventy yards a row of shoes was actually protruding above the ground. The bodies were all disinterred afterward, and transferred either to the national cemetery at Chattanooga or to that at Marietta.

It was raining when we were at Resaca, and the snow which we had met at battlefields farther north had disappeared. Heavy rain alternated with damp drizzle, and it was anything but a pleasant task to go about the fields of miry clay. It was well on in the afternoon when we arrived there, and we at once went to the farther side of Camp Creek, and first examined the position from the Federal standpoint. After going about among the hills and woods for some time we prepared to recross, and wished to do so without going back to the bridge.

"I don't know whether you can cross on the log, though," said a resident, doubtfully; and we did not know, either, when we came to it. It was a heavy log, but it had cracked and sunk in the middle, and at the break there was a tangle of drift, and the water, being high, ran over the broken part. The log obligingly held together, but it certainly surprised us by doing

so. Even then, too, we found that the creek was but a branch of the main stream, and in a little while we had the larger creek to cross, on a narrower and longer log. Everywhere the creeks and runs were high and swift. Everywhere the ground was boggy and soft.

Next morning we set ourselves to thoroughly go over the Confederate line, and, of course, began where the railroad bridge crosses the Oostenaula. The broad and deep river, with its current swirling and swift, went hurrying onward. Black rocks here and there jut out into the water, and fringes of trees line each bank. The river being in flood, there were many of the trees with the water well up their trunks. Right by the bridge, in the war time, stood the magazine. It was constructed within a little knoll, and upon this knoll, the magazine space having been filled in, a house now stands. The owner complained to us that the ground, even now, has a tendency still to settle. Close by the magazine is a strongly fortified hill, while across the road from it is a hill which, from the shape of the heaps of earth upon it, was evidently the location of a strong battery.

The entire position is a series of detached hills and swells, of varying heights, and lines of earthworks may still be followed, zigzagging everywhere, along the crests and across the lower intervening spaces. Now and then, in the trenches, the head logs may be seen, still in place, just as they were put there when the trenches were made.

Amid thick woods, at a lonely spot, some two miles from the village, is a Confederate cemetery, occupying some two acres of ground. We have seldom seen a more pitiful sight. The place was once well cared for; but the fence is

BATTLE OF RESACA.

now greatly dilapidated and broken, and every-thing shows the utmost neglect. Numbers of the wooden head-boards have been broken down and scattered about the ground, and fires, burning the brush and leaves throughout the woods, have from time to time crept within the cemetery enclosure, and burned and black-ened and scorched. No efforts are made to keep the cemetery in order or to repair damages to it.

Quite a number of graves were marked with neat tablets of iron, and these, of course, are still standing, except such as have been deliber-ately knocked over (and some have been), and such as have fallen through the flooding and washing away of the graves, for a little brook runs right through the cemetery, and, as it fre-quently floods, much of the ground is marshy and wet. The explanation of the choice of such a location is that it was selected in a very dry season by some one unfamiliar with the neigh-borhood.

In the centre of the cemetery, upon a little mound of earth, stands a plain stone cross, with a pathetically simple inscription:

"TO THE UNKNOWN DEAD."

The entire effect of that lonely cemetery in the woods is unspeakably desolate and sad. It is at least ten years, the villagers say, since there were Decoration Day exercises at the cemetery. Since then the graves had been decorated by but a tangled growth of bushes and vines, and by layers of fallen leaves.

A good-looking, bright-eyed girl, living in the village, told us that until within a few years past the cemetery was a favorite resort of couples who were "courting"; only she pronounced the word, Georgia fashion, without either the "r" or the final "g." But the young men, she added, have left the village, and the girls are consequently alone there, and so the cemetery is no longer used for "co'tin'."

THE BATTLE OF ATLANTA.

J. S. BOSWORTH, Co. K, 15th IOWA.

IN May, 1864, the Union armies began active operations. Grant, with the Army of the Potomac, commenced operating against the Confederate capital, while the other armies, under the different commanders, were supposed to co-operate to such an extent that it would be impossible for the Confederates to reinforce the Army of Northern Virginia, at that time defending Richmond.

This article has only to do with the struggle for Atlanta, and the battle known as "the battle of Atlanta," fought July 22, 1864.

Sherman commenced his forward movement, as agreed upon by himself and the general of the army, who went together from Nashville to Cincinnati, in March, 1864. On this journey Grant and Sherman talked over the plan of the coming campaign, arranged details and all other matters pertaining to the campaign, which broke the back-bone of secession, no matter how seriously it might have been strained in the battles of Gettysburg and Vicksburg.

Consequently, the first part of the month of May, 1864, saw all the armies of the Union in motion,—the one under Meade, with Grant personally present, and that of Sherman and Banks, each operating upon lines of their own, all subject to such orders as the general-in-chief might give.

A furious contest began with Sherman's advance, every hill being fortified and defended. The battles of Resaca, Dallas, Peach-Tree Creek, and others too numerous to mention, followed. But, on the 20th of July, Hood, who had succeeded General Joe Johnston in command of the Confederate army opposed to Sherman, made a sortie, which was handsomely repulsed by the 20th and 4th corps, commanded by Generals Hooker and Howard. The 14th corps also had considerable to do with this battle, known as Peach-Tree Creek.

On the evening of July 20th, the 17th corps, to which the writer belonged, passed through Decatur, skirmishing every foot of the way with a very persistent enemy. General Walter Q. Gresham, the present Secretary of State, was commander of the 4th division of the 17th corps. He, as usual, was with the skirmish line, and while directing the advance was wounded in the leg so severely that he never again took the field. The writer was a witness of his being carried to the rear on a stretcher, and remembers to this day the look of agony upon his handsome face as he was carried past our regiment.

When he was made Postmaster-General by President Arthur, I accosted him at the Arlington Hotel, saying that I saw his leg shot off. General Gresham responded by stating that I was mistaken, as he still used his old leg, but that he had a hard task to convince the surgeons that his leg was all right; and said he, "My boy, they knew more about it than I did, for, if the thing had been cut off, I would not have suffered half so much as I do now."

On the 21st of July, the Iowa brigade, to which I belonged, and, in fact, the whole 17th corps, made a charge on the enemy's works. We went clear up to the line of breastworks, were ordered to lie down, and await results on the right and left of us. This was the biggest mistake, perhaps, of the war, for we could have gone into their works, and doubled them up to the left and right of us, and allowed the other parts of our line a lodgment, which they failed to make.

The consequence was, that we had to fall back through a cornfield, from an enemy who, a few moments before, had been so cowed that not one of them dared show his face above the works; but now that we were on the retreat, showed boldly above the breastworks, and fired into our unresisting rear, killing and wounding almost half of the men in line.

That night, July 21st, we were moved to the extreme left of the army, and commenced and completed a small line of breastworks. The 17th corps was placed in a *refused* position, in military parlance,—that is, instead of facing toward Atlanta, our backs were to the city.

We felt perfectly secure in our new position, as the woods and underbrush were so thick one could not see a man 100 yards away. Rations were issued an hour previous to the battle, and everybody was seeking the repose necessary to a very hot July day in a Southern clime.

Suddenly, at twelve M., two or three shots were heard in our front. They were reports that any soldier knew came from the guns of an enemy pointing toward us; clear, distinct, and something to be dreaded.

Blackberries were ripe and in profusion, and I had a can of them on the fire, boiling. The order came, " Fall in !"

I grabbed my can of seething fruit and my gun, got into the works, and foolishly tried to eat the blackberries. As a matter of fact, my mouth was severely scalded by the operation.

In less than two minutes the skirmishers of my regiment came rushing back through the *abatis*, Lieutenant Muir in command, hatless and out of breath.

Big, brawny, and brave Belknap, colonel of the regiment, jumps onto the works and orders Muir to take his men back into the woods and protect our front. Muir tried to do his duty; but hardly had Belknap's order passed his lips, until Givan's brigade, of Arkansas, was upon us.

Then began a struggle seldom witnessed in the " late unpleasantness." General Oliver O. Howard, who, a few days later, became the commander of the Army of the Tennessee, said, in an article in the " Atlantic Monthly," that, although he had been with the Army of the Potomac during the severest part of its fighting up until Gettysburg, he had never seen anything to equal the ferocity of the enemy or the gallant defence of the 4th division of the 17th corps on that occasion.

The Crocker Iowa brigade (3d), of the 4th division, 17th corps, held the extreme left of the line, and my regiment (15th Iowa) was the left of the brigade. The Confederates overlapped us, and got into our rear. Here was the first time we ever used the breastworks, although we had been working upon them since the battle of Shiloh.

We drove the enemy back handsomely from our front, but had hardly done so until we found they were taking us in the rear. We jumped the works and repulsed our new enemy, and had hardly done so until the ones in our front made a new attack. The order was to retreat by a side step to the right, which was executed by the men jumping first from one side of the works to the other and driving back the charging Confederates.

This was a fight in which there was no rear, and where the cowards and " bums " had not the slightest chance.

General McPherson, commander of the Army of the Tennessee, was killed within 100 yards of the writer's regiment, and one of the soldiers of Company D, 15th Iowa, George Reynolds, was presented with a gold medal for his heroism in succoring the general in his last moments and recovering the dead body.*

We continued to fight and side-step to the right until we got into the works of Leggitt's (3d) division, and then helped to repulse several charges made upon Gold Hill, the key to our position.

I will never forget the appearance upon this field of General Giles A. Smith and his Adjutant-General, Colonel C. Cadle, Jr. They came down through the brush and stopped with Colonel Belknap, asking how the battle was going.

Smith had succeeded General Gresham, and had been sent from the 15th corps, much to our discontent, as we thought we had men in our own ranks who ought to command us. Smith and Cadle rode down through a very tempest of fire, stopped, and commenced talking to Colonel Belknap.

" General," said Belknap, " get off your horse, for they are shooting grape and canister up through here by the bucketful every minute, from cannon captured from us."

The faces of these brave men were as white as the paper upon which this is written, but they remained on their horses and talked about the battle as unconcernedly as I now write about it. It was an exhibition of nerve and coolness that I have never seen equalled.

During this fight, General Belknap, then Colonel of the 15th Iowa, won his commission as brigadier-general by personal bravery. He was in every exposed position and urging his men to stand fast. The 45th Alabama (Confederate) charged upon Belknap's regiment. If any of them got away, we did not know it at that time. Lampley, colonel of the 45th, came clear up to our lines, and was hauled over the works by General Belknap by the " scruff of the neck and seat of the breeches." This is a fact, which can be proved by any man of the Crocker Iowa brigade present on that occasion, and by the fact that our " Old Uncle Billy Sherman " made him a brigadier-general a few days later for " conspicuous gallantry," although there were several officers in the brigade who ranked him, one of whom was so incensed that he immediately resigned.

Upon the death of General McPherson, General John A. Logan took command of the Army

---

* When the Army of the Tennessee met in Washington to unveil the statue to General McPherson, it was conceded on every hand that I and one other were the last persons to see General McPherson alive. This after a cross-questioning by all the prominent officers of the Army of the Tennessee.

FALL OF GENERAL, JAMES B. McPHERSON, NEAR ATLANTA.

FROM THE ETOWAH RIVER TO ATLANTA.

Robert Shackleton, Jr.

KENESAW MOUNTAIN FROM THE SOUTHEAST.

HIS story was told me by a Union veteran whom I met, some two years since, at a little town on the Ohio River, and he said that it was an actual conversation between pickets, in the course of the Atlanta campaign, and that he himself heard it:

"Who's your gen'ral now?"

"Sherman. Who's yours?"

"Ourn's Sherman, too."

"What! You don't mean that you've got a general named Sherman?"

"Nope. But whenever you'uns gits marchin' orders we'uns allus goes too!"

And, indeed, he might well say this, because for mile after mile, after evacuating Resaca, Johnston steadily retreated toward the southward, managing to just keep out of the way of Sherman's flanks and centre.

Lincoln once said of the Army of the Potomac: "If McClellan does not want to use the army I would like to *borrow* it," but he never had occasion to make such a remark about the army of Sherman, for its commander kept it very busily engaged from the opening to the

close of the campaign. It was a constant succession of battles and marches and skirmishes. It may be mentioned, too, that there was a great deal of burning and destroying as well. The mayor of one of the towns that Sherman visited in war time was afterwards asked if he had injured it very much.

"Injured! Why, he took it with him!"

The town had been burned, and as the army marched off the wind blew the smoke and ashes in their direction.

After passing Resaca, the Oostanaula River flows in a southwesterly direction, and at Lay's Ferry, some few miles below Resaca, there was a sharp engagement on May 14, 1864, between a Confederate force posted there and the troops sent by Sherman to advance toward Johnston's flank and rear. The Federals, however, succeeded in making a crossing. On the following day a strong effort was made to force them back, and the Confederates charged upon them with desperation. The effort, however, was a failure, and, Federal reinforcements arriving, the position of the Confederates became hopeless, and Johnston retreated farther South.

The country south of Resaca is exceedingly beautiful. There are broad and fertile fields. There are pleasant homes. There are fine views of the mountains in the distance. It is one of the most attractive farming regions that I have

165

ever seen. The land is sufficiently diversified by rolls and swells to be beyond the charge of tameness, while it is not rough enough to interfere with the farming. There is a large quantity of corn grown in this section; a great deal of cotton, and some wheat. Now and then, dilapidated little cabins may be seen, with poverty-stricken occupants, but the general aspect of the country is prosperous, and there are many comfortable homes. Some of the houses are really fine.

Johnston intended to offer battle at Adairsville, fifteen miles southward from Resaca, but deciding, after careful consideration, that the valley was too broad to give him the advantage of position that he desired, he went on farther to the southward. From Adairsville the railroad continues southward eleven miles to Kingston, on the Etowah River. Then, instead of crossing at that point, it bends easterly and southeasterly, until it reaches Cartersville, ten miles farther on, and at that town the river is crossed.

Sherman thought that if Johnston intended to cross at Cartersville he would take his men right across the country by the most direct route, instead of following on by the right-angle line made by the railroad. When, therefore, from all indications and from reports of country people, he concluded that Johnston was moving with his main force toward Kingston, he thought that the Confederate leader was surely intending to cross the river at that point.

Johnston, however, was endeavoring to mislead Sherman, and succeeded in doing so. Sherman thought that his main army was marching by way of Kingston and only a smaller force across country toward the southeast; while, as a matter of fact, it was just the other way. Even those marching toward Kingston were not to cross the river there, but were to hurry on toward the east and join the rest of the army.

Sherman, believing as he did, pushed on the bulk of his own forces toward Kingston, and sent only a weaker force toward the southeast. It was Johnston's intention to engage this weaker left wing with his whole army and crush it before help could arrive. He had chosen a position of splendid strength at Cassville, a town located a short distance from the railroad, some seven miles northwest of Cartersville, and felt confident of success. Sherman was deceived; but even when he learned this, he did not consider his own position as at all dangerous. He had already given his corps

commanders orders to hazard the bringing on of a battle, without regard to the question of reinforcements, if they could do so before Johnston should cross the Etowah. He was confident that if a weak wing should go into action he would be able to send it sufficient help in time to prevent disaster.

The battle, however, most unexpectedly did not take place. Johnston found that both Hood and Polk were in a critical and half-hearted mood, and that he could not rely upon them to do their best in the anticipated engagement. With bitter disappointment, therefore,—for he believed that in the position that he had selected he would certainly win,—he was compelled to relinquish the plan and to retreat over the Etowah River at Cartersville.

Sherman's advance guard pursued the retreating forces to the crossing-place. There the Confederates burned the railroad bridge, and the Federals made no effort to pursue farther. At Kingston, however (now an unattractive town of fair size, in the midst of an attractive region), Sherman secured two bridges, so as to be ready to cross at any time, and there halted. He did not wish to cross the Etowah at Cartersville, because to do so at that point would have brought him into the dangerously rugged country in the vicinity of Allatoona Pass. He was, therefore, planning another, and more delicate and elabo-

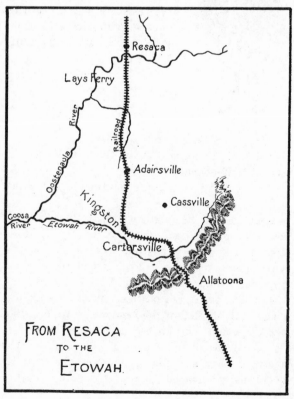

FROM RESACA
TO THE
ETOWAH.

rate, flank movement, and wished to thoroughly rest and recuperate his troops and accumulate a great quantity of supplies before cutting loose from the railroad and entering upon the new advance. On the 22d of May he issued his orders for the contemplated movement, and his army, crossing the Etowah at Kingston, was once more in motion.

I have a war relic from this region which to me is quite interesting. I met at a little cabin, at quite a distance from the railroad, a man who showed me a buckle with the letters "U. S." upon it.

"Was it you'uns or we'uns that used this?" he asked.

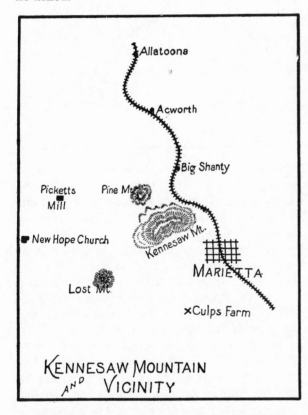

KENNESAW MOUNTAIN
AND VICINITY

Thinking that I must have misunderstood his question, I asked him to repeat it, and found that he really did not know whether it was a buckle of the Unions or the Confederates. I explained, and he was highly gratified.

"I've been a-keepin' it, for I thought as how some time I would meet some of you'uns as could tell me."

His curiosity satisfied, he had no further use for the buckle, and it is now in my own collection, a memento of something more than the war.

After crossing the Etowah, Sherman advanced in a southerly direction until his forces were west and southwest of the Confederates, who were

strongly posted in the unfavorable country that Sherman was making the flank movement to avoid. He threatened Johnston's rear; and, to meet this danger, the Confederate commander also moved toward the westward and massed his troops in a position of great defensive strength at New Hope Church, about fourteen miles west of the town of Marietta. Heavy fighting ensued, and Sherman found that he could not hope to reach the railroad to the southward of the opposing army. To meet his advance, however, the Confederates had been compelled to leave unoccupied some of the rugged country in which it had been their desire to fight him, and he thought that now he might be able to seize the railroad a little south of the formidable Allatoona Pass.

The fighting was fierce and destructive, and a curious incident was the bursting of a shell between Johnston and Hood, while those two generals were standing but a few yards apart. Neither, however, was injured.

Moving steadily, day by day, to the eastward, extending his left wing more and more in that direction to seize the railroad,—such was the plan which Sherman set himself to carry out, while the firing of pickets, and the volleys from rifle-pits, and the booming of cannon filled the air with a constant and dismal roar. On the afternoon of May 27th, there was a general battle at Pickett's Mill, and the troops under Howard made an attack which was remarkable for the superb gallantry of both the officers and the men who engaged in it. Gallantry, however, was of no avail, for the Federals fatally misunderstood the character of the defences and the number of Confederates who were at that point, and Howard admitted that his loss was 1,500 men. The Confederates also lost heavily, but not so severely as their opponents. Then the Confederates, believing that by the movement to the eastward the Federals must have seriously weakened their right wing, attacked that part of the army with great determination, only, however, to be driven off with heavy loss.

On June 1st a portion of the Union army occupied Allatoona Pass, and within a few days afterward—days of constant fighting and manœuvring—Johnston retreated from his position about New Hope Church and Pickett's Mill, and took up a new position about Kenesaw Mountain.

The losses up to June 1st had been very heavy on both sides, each army having lost, since the opening of the campaign, at least 9,000 men, and probably even more.

Sherman, facing Johnston before Kenesaw, had no thought that any serious opposition would be offered there. He believed that within a very few days he would pass the mountain and occupy the town of Marietta beyond it.

Kenesaw Mountain is but an isolated height. Lost Mountain, another point held by Johnston in his new position, is of a similar character. From the summits of these mountains, looking down upon the surrounding lower country, the appearance is as if all were but level plain, while in reality that plain-like country is cut up by low hills and tangled ravines, by ridges and watercourses and valleys. While Sherman, surprised by the unassailability of the Confederate position, was slowly working toward Kenesaw, Grant had fought the awful battle of Cold Harbor, and had begun the siege of Petersburg. The famous " Alabama," too, in this same month of June, had had its last fight and had been beaten and sunk.

To Sherman's soldiers the month was a time of constant struggle, and even when it was more than half over the position of Johnston seemed as unassailable as ever. Efforts were made to reach Marietta, south of Kenesaw, by flanking with the right wing, and then advancing upon the town from the west, and on June 26th, the extreme right, under Schofield, was directed to make a strong demonstration in that direction.

From the summit of Kenesaw the movements of the Federals could well be seen, and the advance of Schofield caused Johnston much uneasiness. But he realized that if a serious movement should be made in that direction he would be unable to check it, and that therefore it would be worse than useless for him to weaken his forces at the mountain by detaching a large body to oppose Schofield. Should the Federals, however, dare to attack him in his chosen position about Kenesaw he would, so he firmly believed, win a victory. But would Sherman dare to make such an attack?—Johnston scarcely dared think of it as a possibility.

Kenesaw Mountain is about two miles north from the town of Marietta. It is in reality two separate heights, connected by a considerably lower ridge, and the two heights are called the Big and the Little Kenesaw. The Big Kenesaw is somewhat the higher of the two; and the view from the summit, about 700 feet above the surrounding country, is splendidly imposing.

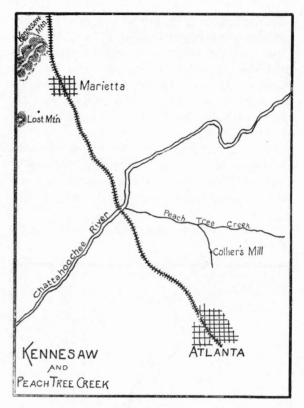

KENNESAW AND PEACH TREE CREEK

The mountain rises abruptly, and there are no ranges of heights within a distance of many miles to shut in the view in any direction, and so the eye glances over a widespread stretch of country.

Near by is Marietta. In the distance Atlanta may be plainly seen. Lost Mountain rises impressively, while farther off the majestic mass of Stone Mountain looms grandly up. Allatoona Signal Mountain shows its wooded summit near by the ridge of Allatoona Pass.

In some directions the plain is hemmed in by lines of hills. In others it stretches off illimitably, and the eye fails at length to farther follow it. So sharply does the mountain rise that one upon its top may look right down upon the farm-houses and farms round about, and can see and watch every detail. Standing there we could well understand how the Confederates could so well follow every movement of their opponents; for from that point of observation they could not only watch the marches of divisions and brigades and regiments, but they could even tell whenever a courier galloped to some officer with a message, or when that officer mounted or dismounted or changed his position in the slightest degree. All the motions of the Federal army for miles around were revealed to them.

The summit of Big Kenesaw is quite rocky, and the ridge between the two heights is even

THE BATTLE OF KENESAW MOUNTAIN.

more so. Many of the stones are huge and massive, and were alone sufficient to form a cover for the men. On the top of the highest portion there still remain earthworks, while lower down are long lines of extremely strong fortifications, constructed of earth and stone. In many places the huge rocks are themselves made use of by being included in the lines.

On Little Kenesaw there are even more sheer surfaces of rock and more huge rock formations than on the other portions. The northern slope is scattered thickly with stones of all sizes; and we noticed one broad stretch of rock, sloping at an angle of fifty-five degrees, slippery with spring water which runs down over it, and with only patches of half-loose moss to offer a precarious foothold. The mountain is bare of trees in many places, while in others there is but a stunted and straggling growth.

About nine o'clock in the morning of the 27th of June the Union columns went forward with heroic bravery to the attack, and the splendor of their assault was freely admitted even by their enemies. But the appalling fire that was opened upon them, no fortitude, no bravery could withstand, and at every point the attack completely failed. But even to retreat was, in many places,

as dangerous as to advance, for the men would have to pass over open stretches that were completely commanded by Confederate guns. In desperation, then, some of the commands hastily constructed shelters and ditches where they were, and in them they crouched, being the only places of possible safety. This was the measure of what some have considered partial success, and which has been described as "holding their lines within a few yards of the Confederate trenches, and there covering themselves with defences." The Federal attack was magnificent, but no flesh and blood could survive the shower of lead and iron that swept down that rocky slope.

In the course of the battle there occurred a pathetic incident, showing that "blood is thicker than water." At one place on the mountain the dry leaves and brush began to burn, and the creeping flames encircled many a poor fellow lying helpless and in agony on the ground. The Confederates at that portion of the line were ordered to cease firing; and then one of their officers called to the Federals and offered to suspend hostilities long enough to allow the removal of the disabled. While the Union soldiers bore their comrades to the rear, the Confederates looked on with sympathetic pleasure, and then the fighting was again renewed.

"The bullets were scattered over the ground like dust,"—such was the forcible description given me by one whose home was at the mountain's base.

And the battle was, after all, unnecessary. Even while it was in progress the Union right was engaged in the very flanking movement that Johnston was unable to oppose, and immediately after the battle Sherman set himself to carry the movement to completion. The consequence was that on the night of July 2d Johnston evacuated Kenesaw Mountain and fell back toward the Chattahoochee. His lines along the river were of splendid strength; and for some days there was much of manœuvring and skirmishing, until Johnston, seeing that he could no longer safely keep his army on the northern bank, drew it off to the southern side, again displaying, in this delicate operation, his remarkable faculty for conducting a safe retreat.

Sherman cautiously followed with his own army, laying pontoon bridges, and also beginning at once to prepare for the rebuilding of the railroad bridge that the Confederates in their retreat had destroyed. Johnston took up a new position south of Peach Tree Creek, a stream which, entering the Chattahoochee near the railroad bridge, forms an east and west line about five miles north of Atlanta.

Sherman determined to outflank his adversary, and, by moving easterly and then to the southward, compel him to retreat. Johnston, meanwhile, determined to attack the Federal right wing as soon as it should become isolated by the flank march of the rest of the army.

On the 17th of July, Johnston was unexpectedly ordered to turn the command over to General Hood. This news was received with gloom and discontent by the Confederates, and with corresponding joy by the Federals, for both armies believed that Hood was by no means Johnston's equal.

On the 20th came a heavy assault on the Federals along the line of Peach Tree Creek. It was made with desperate courage, and Hood's men rushed again and again to the attack; but the Union veterans stood firm, and with terrible volleys of musketry, and with shrapnel and canister and grape mowed down the charging ranks. Sorely cut to pieces, the Confederates drew slowly off, after a loss, as nearly as can be

"A PATHETIC INCIDENT, SHOWING THAT 'BLOOD IS THICKER THAN WATER.'"

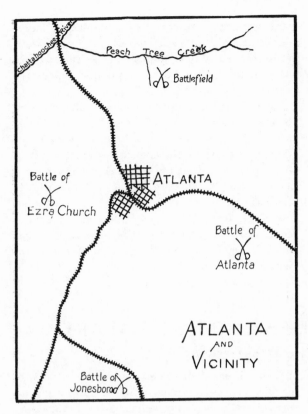

ATLANTA
AND
VICINITY

ascertained, of about 5,000 men. The Federal loss was less than 2,000.

Although so near Atlanta, much of the battle-field is covered with a tangle of woods or with poorly cultivated farm land. It is a roughly wild country; and one, as he crosses the creeks and clambers up the banks of the ravines, can appreciate the difficulties which both armies experienced in fighting over such broken land.

Collier's Mill, where there was greater loss of life than at any other single point, has disappeared, but there still remains a section of stone retaining wall to mark the spot where it stood.

Though disheartened by defeat, the Confederates were still ready to fight for the possession of the city that was the immediate object of Sherman's campaign.

On July 22d, occurred the battle of Atlanta. McPherson, with the left wing of the army, had advanced to a point east and a little south of the city, and upon his command fell the Confederate attack. Taken between two lines, that portion of the Federal army was to be captured or destroyed. The assault was vehement and unexpected, and for a time could not be checked. McPherson himself, galloping to the location of the firing, came unexpectedly upon a body of the enemy, and was shot and killed. There was desperate hand-to-hand fighting in the trenches, and at times the assaulted troops

could scarcely tell whether to face to the front or rear, for the enemy were all about them. The Confederates, however, with a loss of perhaps some 10,000 men, were defeated. The loss of the Federals was probably about 3,500.

The fighting was plainly heard in the city. The thundering of the cannon, the rattling discharges of musketry, and even the shouts and cheers of the men, came to the ears of the women who tremblingly waited at home. Even after this, the Confederates still firmly held the city. Deciding upon a complete change of plan, Sherman advanced his right flank, and, withdrawing his left, placed a large portion of his troops westward of the city. There, at Ezra Church, on the 28th of July, the Confederates made another tremendous assault, but were again beaten off.

Still unsuccessful in getting into Atlanta, Sherman now came to an entirely new resolution, which was, to leave a strong body of his troops, well intrenched, at the crossing of the Chattahoochee, and with all the remainder, the great bulk of his army, cut loose from communications, and plant himself well to the southward of the city. From his new position, he would be able to effectually cut off Hood's railroad communication, and compel him to evacuate the town.

On August 25th, the movement began. Hood realized that he was in peril, and moved his own army toward that of Sherman, and on the 1st of September, at Jonesboro, fifteen miles south of the city, there was another hard struggle.

The campaign was now really at an end, and a most arduous campaign it had been. The record of the 118th Ohio may give some idea of the trying times that the soldiers experienced. For 121 consecutive days that regiment was within hearing of hostile firing every day but one. For sixty consecutive days they were more or less actually under fire. For one particular week there was probably not even the space of five minutes during which they were out of hearing of the shot and shell.

Soon after midnight of the 1st of September, there was heard the noise of heavy explosions in the direction of Atlanta, and Sherman anxiously wondered what could be the explanation.

A lady who lived in Atlanta at that time told me of the scenes of that dismal afternoon and night of September 1st. The Confederate garrison marched out, calling "good-byes" in as cheerful tones as possible to the helpless women, who, weeping and sad, were left behind.

And then, after midnight, when the women and children had lain down to seek for a little rest and slumber, all were awakened by terrific and continued explosions. This lady's home was but about half a mile from the magazines, and she tells of how the bullets rained down upon her house like hail, and how awfully grand were the thunders and the flashing lights of the tremendous explosions. Unable, in the haste of his retreat, to save the magazines, Hood had blown them up rather than let them fall into the hands of the enemy.

Slocum advanced and took possession of the city, and sent a message to Sherman telling him of what had occurred. The news was received by officers and men of the army with profound gratification, and by many with almost extravagant joy. Even the stately and usually undemonstrative Thomas snapped his fingers and whistled and almost danced, while the soldiers laughed and cheered, and could not sufficiently express their delight.

Regarding the total losses from Chattanooga to Atlanta, there is much doubt, as each army was desirous of making its own losses seem light, and those of the enemy heavy. It would seem, however, that the Federal loss must have been at least 30,000 men, while Federal authorities claim that the Confederate loss must also have been in the neighborhood of that amount. Some, however, claim that the united losses of the two armies amounted to very much more than 60,000, and it is unfortunate that there is no way of deciding the question.

SCOUTING IN THE SHENANDOAH VALLEY.

Thad. J. Walker (a confederate scout.)

THE life of a scout in the lines of the enemy is a dangerous and very exciting one, especially with the cavalry. And in the valley along the winding banks of the Shenandoah were enacted many scenes of dash and daring which will make the warm blood course quicker in the veins of many an old veteran trooper who participated in them, and who yet survives their memories. Although nearly thirty long years have passed away, it seems but yesterday that we can recall the bugle's charge at Brandy Station, Aldie, Winchester, Fisher's Hill, Kearnstown, Cedar Creek, and all along the pike from Harper's Ferry to Staunton, across the Massennutten Range, through the Luray Valley, over the North Mountains to the Moorfield Valley, where, along the fertile banks of the south branch of the Potomac, many fat beeves were gathered to feed the Army of Northern Virginia; recall many desperate encounters with Sheridan and his men, with such leaders as Stuart, Fitz Lee, Rosser, Imboden, Mosby, Harry Gilmor, the two Whites, McNeil, and others. " Little Phil" had his hands full when he had occasion to cross our path.

The lower counties of Clarke, Jefferson, Loudoun, Farquier, Fairfax, and the lower Shenandoth and along the banks of the Occoquan and Opequan, was called " Mosby's Confederacy," and invaders, even the redoubtable Phil himself, had to feel and fight his way, harassed and disputed at every step. But I am frank to admit that on all occasions when we received any intimation of the advance of Sheridan into our territory we felt pretty well convinced that there would be hard and sharp work ahead for us. But it is interesting to note that we did not always run away from him, as is proved by the fact that a large number of our men, of Mosby's, Gilmor's, and McNeil's commands, were fully equipped with Sheridan's horses, saddles, Spencers, etc., and good ones they were, too; for it is well known that General Sheridan's troopers were better equipped for service than any other cavalry in the field. To possess one of his outfits was our greatest ambition, and I will relate a very " close call " a portion of our command had on one occasion while trying to gratify it:

In the spring of '63, as well as I can remember, Captain Nick Burke, of Harry Gilmor's command, left Mount Jackson, where we were encamped, with twenty men, dismounted, for scout duty, and intending, if possible, to capture horses from Sheridan, whose command at that time was in camp at and around Martinsburg. Our plan was to proceed cautiously by night, keeping under cover by day, so as not to be observed by any one in sympathy with the enemy who would betray us, or by Jessie Scouts, a well-known and dangerous enemy to Union and Confederate scouts alike, who were always on the alert to waylay, murder, and rob any who came in their way. This treacherous class of pirates, generally comprised of deserters from the armies of both North and South, too cowardly to face the music on either side, can well be remembered by the old veterans, both blue and gray, who served in the lower Shenandoah during the last year of the struggle.

One incident in connection with those men, described in Major Harry Gilmor's book entitled "Four Years in the Saddle," will be read with interest:

We were in the saddle, leisurely proceeding on one of our expeditions, when from the thick foliage that lined the roadside came a faint curl of smoke and the sharp report of a rifle, fired at our leader with murderous intent, striking him with earnest aim in his left breast over his heart, when, by one of those singular instances of fate, his life was saved by a pack of playing-cards in his breast-pocket. Momentarily staggered, he instantly recovered, and retribution came swift and sure to his almost hidden foe. With accurate aim from one of a pair of short, single-barreled Derringers, which he always carried and with which he was very expert, he fired, and, although partly a chance shot, a hurried search a few moments later revealed his enemy breathing his last, clutching at the herbage around him in his death-struggles. A short time after this, seven of those murderous wretches were captured and hung in retaliation for crimes committed by them.

But I am digressing.

Finally arriving at our destination, a place suited to our purpose, we went into ambush at a spot called "Ash Hollow," between Winchester and Berryville, to lie in wait for any straggling bands of cavalry who passed us, and who were not too large for us to attack. Having the advantage of sudden surprise, we almost invariably met with success, without resorting to bloodshed. A dense growth of ivy bushes lined each side of the road and completely obscured us from sight. We were only a few feet away from the edge of the hard, white pike, winding along, looking from the bushes like a line of silver gleaming in the moonlight. We grasped our carbines and revolvers, and silently awaited the approach of the enemy.

Many large bands passed us, mounted on splendid chargers, making us more eager to secure some of them at any cost, but as yet they were too strong for us, and we were taking no chances. We could not afford to do so, as our defeat meant the wiping out of our little band. On they passed, leaving us once more to silence and gloom, unbroken save by the plaintive song of the night-birds and the chirping of crickets. Finally our ears again caught the sound of horsemen in the distance, approaching from the direction of Winchester. They came leisurely on until we could readily distinguish their number, which appeared about thirty well-mounted men. Silently whispering, "Now, boys, get ready," our leader gave the command to glide slowly and cautiously to the edge of the road, ready to spring out upon the unsuspecting foe. On they came, some singing, some laughing, and when seemingly they were not more than twenty yards away from us, suddenly there came a suppressed whisper from our leader and a warning signal to lie still. Away in the distance could be heard the sound and clash of approaching squadrons. A few seconds more and our fate would have been sealed, as the party we were about to attack proved to be merely the advance guard of a large body of cavalry returning from an expedition up the valley as far as New Market.

You can well imagine our feelings and chagrin when obliged to lie there, afraid to move a muscle, watching those handsome chargers as they passed us. It was a trying and exciting moment for us, and it seemed as if they would never get past. We could fully realize the true meaning of the sentiment that "distance lends enchantment to the view," and we were exceedingly anxious to get safely away from "Ash Hollow," which eventually we did, sadder and wiser men, with all the fight knocked out of us for the time being. We succeeded in reaching camp safely, as foot-sore foot cavalry, to wait for a more congenial and convenient season.

MEADE AT GETTYSBURG.

RANDOM RECOLLECTIONS OF THE GREAT CONTEST.

L. W. WALLAZZ.

DURING a recent visit to Petersburg, the writer called up the fact that two very important advantages were gained by the Union forces on Independence Day—Vicksburg and Gettysburg. In the latter case a Philadelphian, Major-General George Gordon Meade, was the victor, while at Vicksburg Major-General Pemberton, an accomplished native of the Quaker City, was vanquished.

In the course of the conversation, the query came up as to the sentimental phase of these two great events. They had a most profound effect upon the people of both sections, but in the North they seemed to say, "These victories show you the augury of the end—the triumph of the Union cause." This was accentuated by the fact that, previously, the advantages were largely and numerically to be credited to the Confederates. Was there any design in bringing on these affairs? I have been told that General U. S. Grant wearied the patience of his subordinates with his delays at Vicksburg, but abundantly requited them for their forbearance by his triumph on the Fourth of July, and probably doubled the effect of the victory in the army and among the people by having victory consummated on the natal day of national independence.

My Confederate friend said he was in Richmond at the time that General Lee's campaign was under consideration, and that it was understood that the Confederates were to advance to Harrisburg as a feint, and suddenly concentrate in Maryland, move on the capital, and take possession of it on the Fourth of July. As soon as this was accomplished, President Davis was to have proclaimed his terms of an equitable settlement of the difficulty. My friend is still of the opinion that there was this sentimental element of design all through the scheme, and he believes that the result was only another verification of the adage that man proposes, but God disposes.

This leads me to the field that virtually settled the war between the States. Not long ago, the surviving great actors of that portentous struggle went on the site of the carnage and fought the battle over again in their minds.

As is usually the case, General Meade was severely criticised for not following the Confederates after the battle. "Had General Grant been in command," said the venerable General Longstreet to the one-armed Howard, "he would have crushed us." Possibly he would have done so, but General Trumbull has recently observed very shrewdly that on an occasion not entirely unlike—Shiloh—General Grant did not follow up Beauregard, after Johnson's death, and crush the victor of Manassas.

Technically, the writer was at the battle of Gettysburg; that is, he was within the sound of the guns. Having been for a long time a war correspondent, he became familiar with the factors that controlled the battle. Take a glance at the situation. Word came that Lee was advancing northward to take the offensive. It was plain his object was a demonstration against the capital of the country. It was still the policy of the government to plug up all the holes, so as to keep the Confederates from running through the North as General Sherman scurried through Georgia. So, while the old Army of the Potomac was being mustered in Maryland in a hurry, an army of defence was quickly organized on the Susquehanna, under the command of Generals Darius N. Couch and Napoleon B. Dana.

General Meade was only nominally in command, because he was not like Grant—supreme. Meade was a great captain, an excellent organizer, a careful, able leader, but he was modest, unassertive, and, above all, obedient to his superiors. He had many commanders, and among them was the irascible and arbitrary Secretary of War. Meade really did not know exactly what was going on at the front, for he was astonished when the brave but rash General Reynolds precipitated the fighting beyond the famous battle-field.

Instantly, however, he acted, and with a result that proved his wisdom. He put in the van the Chevalier Bayard of his army, "Hancock, the Superb." That dashing officer, who was one of the few who was ever first in the fight but never foolhardy, selected the vantage ground and held it, and so disposed of his troops that when General Meade came up he could only approve of everything that had been done. For a few moments he glanced over the field, and from that time forward he seemed to have perfect control of affairs. He was remarkably cool and self-possessed, and ever appeared to be confident that this time the Army of the Potomac was not to be whipped, even by the steel-muscled veterans of the South, who were confident of success, because of their many triumphs.

The battle ended after three days of bloodshed and the Confederates withdrew—repulsed but not conquered; beaten but not dismayed; broken by the murderous fusillade of the grandest park of field artillery ever arrayed, but they still were unconquered. They were yet full of fight. The law of war said they should have been followed and destroyed. "Had you come on us then, flushed with your success, there would have been resistance, of course, but finally it would have been a foot-race for the fastnesses," said a distinguished Confederate officer. Most of General Meade's men had been in the fight—so had all the Confederates. Here they were even, but the latter were hungry, footsore, and on the retreat, having failed in their object after long, terrible marches and desperate fighting for three days. A few miles north, there was an army of fresh Union troops, forty thousand strong, with enough re-enlisted veterans to steady the lines. They were within sound of the guns of Gettysburg and ought to have been in the battle, or at any rate in the pursuit of the flying Confederates. It is a matter of record that Generals Dana and Couch had no orders to move forward, but had they assumed the offensive they would have been warranted by the results. They did not move, although they must have known the situation of affairs. The writer

had been caught by some Confederates moving south from Hagerstown, and so learned that Lee's army was in full retreat. He telegraphed this news and all the other intelligence he could gather to the New York *Herald*, for which paper he was correspondent, and it confirmed the news of the Union victory, then unknown to him, to such an extent that it was given first place in the paper and recorded in those lively days as a "scoop."

As was observed before, General Meade was ruled from Washington. He had done all he was ordered to do: he had saved the capital. He had done more: he had beaten a hitherto victorious veteran enemy; he had repelled the invasion. He concluded to "let well enough alone." Had he done more he might have been superseded. He had not gained the supremacy of Grant. He could not tell President Lincoln that Secretary Stanton must mind his own business and not interfere with grand tactics or operations in the field. These were potent reasons for General Meade's actions. He was too good a soldier to exceed his instructions; too patriotic to risk too much at that critical moment; too perfect a gentleman to assume anything more than the performance of duty, and hence he modestly excused his determination not to follow hard on the retreating Confederates by reciting the exhausted condition of his brave veterans of the Army of the Potomac, who had climaxed that army's marvellous record of endurance, bravery, and devotion, physically and mentally, by winning a grand triumph, without prestige, and after having been experimented with by a dozen commanders, for some of whom they were forced into a lack of respect and confidence if not a feeling of actual contempt.

FREEDOM'S BANNER.

D. J. DONAHOE.

While the stars in the blue remain,
　And the rosy shafts of morn
With their peaceful light shall cleave the night
　For the day that is newly born,—
　　For the hope of the day that is born,—
　　So long shall Freedom reign !
And the red, white and blue, as her banner true,
　Shall float over land and main.

And the waves of the surging sea,
　And the winds that sweep the sky
Shall sing of her birth to the listening earth,
　While her colors are streaming high,—
　　While her banner is waving on high,—
　　No traitor shall there be !
For Freedom's hand shall guard our land,
　And her flag shall rule the sea.

A ROMANTIC EXPERIENCE.

J. M. WADDILL.

THE flood-tide of battle was at its height in the Wilderness, May 5, '64. The roar of musketry ebbed and flowed all along the line, and hundreds lay gasping under the tangled undergrowth which extended for miles on either side of what was known as the Plank Road, near which my company, lying or kneeling, the better to see the enemy through the dense thicket, as well as for protection, were firing as rapidly as their unfavorable positions would allow.

Our captain had fallen early, shot through the head, and First Lieutenant Rowe was soon thereafter borne away by the litter-bearers, desperately wounded. There was little for me to do, every man of the company doing his duty, as I passed along the line, crouching from the rain of bullets, and speaking words of cheer here and there, few, if any of which, were heard in the din and roar of the conflict. Pausing for a moment, the shrubbery was parted, and little Johnny Julian, courier for the colonel, came through the bushes, shielding his face with both hands, as if from the light, and yelled in my ear: "The colonel's orders are that you take your company at once to the rear, and report to Colonel White on the Plank Road."

Within a few seconds we were double quicking down the road, stooping as we went, the better to escape the shower of balls which whistled through the brush on every side.

Soon we came upon the Third Corps Ordnance train standing in the road in a double row, horses harnessed and drivers mounted, ready to move instantly.

Half a mile further on we met Colonel White. "Lieutenant, take your company a quarter-mile further on, with Cooke's wagon train, with guns loaded, ready to repel cavalry," he ordered, and off he galloped toward the front.

Obeying his orders, we reached our position, and threw ourselves by the roadside to rest. A little later I heard from the thicket near by what seemed a groan of some one in pain. A second time the sound reached my ears, and I determined to learn the cause.

Thirty or forty steps from the road, in a perfect tangle of brush and vines, I espied a blue uniform on the ground. Approaching nearer, I discovered a Federal soldier lying face down-wards, apparently dead. Pulling aside the brush, I knelt and turned the body over as gently as I could, to ascertain if life was extinct. With a groan and a shudder his eyes opened, while his lips moved as if to speak, but no sound came from them. Raising his head slightly, I placed my canteen to his lips, and in a few moments he seemed much revived. "What regiment?" I asked.

In a weak voice he replied, "Fifth New York Cavalry," which was confirmed by the brass letters on his forage cap lying near.

Hardened as I was by scenes of blood and suffering, my sympathies were deeply aroused as I looked in the face of the young soldier, for he seemed not more than twenty years of age—a mere boy, though taking a man's place under man's most trying circumstances; a fair, frank, blue-eyed boy, dying, perhaps, far from home or friends.

"How are you hurt?" I asked.

Pointing to his hip, a slight rent and a blood spot or two told the story.

Placed in as easy a posture as possible, and his thirst again satisfied, he gave a brief account of himself, his name, where from, etc., after which I left him for a short time to rejoin my company.

Finding everything quiet, I called one of the men, and together we returned to the wounded youth. With our pocket knives we cut away the brush and tangle for some twenty feet around him, and carefully swept up the leaves and rubbish, as fire was raging in the woods not far away. We then built a slight shelter of green branches above his head for protection from the sun, filled his canteen from the creek near by, and divided our rations of bacon and bread with him.

He seemed very grateful; offered his watch in return for our services, which I placed in his pocket again, and, bidding him good-bye, promising to see him again, went back to my company.

The expected cavalry raid proved a false alarm, and within an hour or two the several companies along the road, mine among others, were hurried back to the battle line, and I saw no more of my Fifth Cavalry man, and thought no more of the circumstance.

Grant attacked early next morning, and we were being steadily pressed back, when Longstreet, with his twelve thousand heroes, moved up at the double quick, with Lee at their head; the tide was turned and the day saved.

Then began the movement by the flank, with great blood spots marking the line of march, on the 10th and again on the 12th of May, on the 3d and 23d of June, and on to Petersburg, which I never reached, for, together with some hundreds of others, I was captured at Hanover, and hustled off to meditate at Elmira over the uncertainties of a soldier's life.

My circumstances and surroundings at Elmira were not of a joyful nature. Discipline was strict, and the days were remarkably alike. My daily life is quite accurately described in the daily entry made by Jack in his diary of "Innocents" fame, as follows: "Got up, washed, went to bed." The monotony was slightly varied by the daily appearance of visitors to the prison, ladies and gentlemen of the city, a limited number of whom were at that time admitted to gaze at the prisoners and to ask questions. Most of us were quite willing to be noticed and interrogated thus, as there were not wanting among the visitors kindly hearts whose promptings occasionally blessed us with small gifts, which, in our forlorn state, were received with a degree of gratitude far out of proportion to their intrinsic value.

Thus it came to pass one day that a lady, accompanied by a very pretty girl, passed near me, and incidentally inquired from what State I came. Being civilly answered, the elder of the two asked if I needed anything for my personal comfort. Inasmuch as my entire earthly possessions consisted of a tattered Confederate uniform, a pocket knife, and a blanket, I was prepared to enumerate a long list of needs; but as the girl was very pretty, my pride very extravagant, and my common sense *nil*, I replied that I needed nothing. My name and regiment was asked for, and they passed on,

with a pleasantly worded wish for my speedy return to my friends.

Several days passed, and the couple again appeared, and again approached me with a kindly recognition. We had quite a little chat

"HOW ARE YOU HURT?"

this time, the young lady asking a number of questions about army and prison life, and again they bade me adieu, the younger of the two placing in my hand, as she turned away, a small copy of the New Testament. Opening it to see whose name I should find, I was surprised to see on the fly-leaf, written in a delicate feminine hand: "Would you place yourself in the hands of a friend, and assume the attendant risks? If so, tie a bit of white cord to the bottom button of your coat, when we come next week. Confide in no one else, and destroy this." Instantly I tore out the leaf and chewed it into pulp. There was no sleep for my eyes that night. What did this mean? Who and what were these people who thus interested themselves in me? And why? Was it a trap? No; surely these two women couldn't entertain such a thought toward a poor devil of a prisoner. These, and a thousand such thoughts, occupied my mind all the night through, and, when reveille sounded, I had decided to trust them fully. The next few days were full of anxiety and suspense, but my purpose of confiding in them never wavered.

Within a week they came again. I deemed it prudent not to approach them too soon, but stood aloof, waiting for them to dispose of some trifles. When I presented myself, with my bit of white cord conspicuously displayed according to orders, my angel put into my hands a religious tract, and, with a most indifferent, unconcerned look, passed on. I held the tract carelessly for some moments, and placed it in my breast pocket. How beautiful she looked, and, though I was wild with anxiety to see what my tract contained, I could but linger to watch her.

It was no easy matter to find seclusion in that crowded enclosure, but waiting my opportunity, at length I found myself alone, and tremblingly opened the tract. On a blank page, pinned inside, was written: "Two weeks from this date, a woman, with a red-bordered handkerchief in her belt, will give you a thin linen coat and vest. Carry them to your quarters, conceal them, and return immediately. An old man, with gold eyeglasses, will give you pants, shoes, and collar. Do likewise with these and return. We will give you a hat, in the lining of which will be found a permit, signed by the Commandant, allowing Mr. William J. Pool, of Syracuse, to visit the prisoners. As soon as possible, without exciting attention, put on your new suit and walk quietly to the exit, surrendering your permit to the guard. When outside, walk slowly, straight away from the prison for two hundred paces, when a young man will meet you. Trust yourself to him, and confide in no one else. Should anything transpire endangering you or us, cut the two bottom buttons from your coat."

Having thoroughly memorized my instructions, they were likewise chewed up, and I began to have visions of freedom, conspicuous among them being the picture of the fairy who was taking this hazard on my account.

The days went by as do the months now. I grew nervous and anxious, fearful ever that some one would read my thoughts. Not only were my fears for myself. What if I brought my fair benefactresses to grief? Truly were the two intervening weeks filled with a variety of conflicting emotions, and I more than once wished I had never given the signal of assent to the offer of freedom.

At length, after a sleepless night, the eventful day came. All through the morning I battled with my excitement, but gained only a partial victory. The usual knots of visitors began to arrive, but not my benefactresses. Watching the throng, I at length espied the woman with the red-bordered handkerchief. I noted that she carried several goodly-sized packages of what appeared to be food, which she distributed indiscriminately. As I approached, she gave me a thin, hard-pressed bundle, which I placed in my pocket, and, shortly going to my quarters, hid it under a small wooden box which served the purpose of a seat, and immediately returned to the crowd of visitors.

I waited only a short time for my old man. There he was, giving out tracts and Testaments, with a package or two in his pockets. As I drew near him, he placed one of the packages in my hands, with a benediction, and, having lingered a short time, this was placed under the box with its companion.

A tedious half-hour passed before I saw my two angels. Coming near, the young lady said to me: "Here's a Yankee hat from a Yankee girl. Will a rebel accept it?" "No, Miss," I replied, "but a Southern gentleman will," and, suiting the action to the word, I placed it on my head, as she unconcernedly went her way, handing a pair of half hose to one, a handkerchief to another, until I lost sight of her.

A little later I was in my quarters, trembling all over. Should I try the risky experiment now, or later? "Now or never," I thought, in desperation, and began to don my new attire. While thus engaged, one of my messmates came in hurriedly, but left as quickly, not observing me.

Dressed as a citizen, I paused a moment to collect myself, and stepped forth for freedom.

As I walked across the grounds, my heart beat so loudly that I feared others would hear it. On I walked, mingling with the visitors, no one seeming to notice me. As I neared the gate, Walter White, one of my fellow-prisoners, recognized me. He was in the act of speaking when I drew my knife from my pocket, and, speaking loud enough for the guard to hear me, said: "Here, reb, take this to cut your beef with," adding in a whisper, "For God's sake, say nothing."

He understood instantly; was most profuse in his thanks for the knife, and we parted. Passing slowly through the exit, I surrendered my permit, and was free.

It was with the utmost difficulty that I kept from running; however, I restrained myself, and, following my instructions, found a young man waiting for me, who, without a word, took my arm, and together we sauntered away from the locality as if we had been friends for life. Some distance from the prison we hastened our steps, when, for the first time, my companion spoke:

"My name is Avery Chauncey, and I am taking you to my father's residence. You will remain in hiding with us for some time, until the noise made over your escape subsides. The two ladies you first met are my mother and sister; the lady with the fancy handkerchief is my aunt, who lives with us, and the old gentleman with the tracts is my father, so you perceive it has required the whole family to pull you out of that hole. We will have to furnish you with rather cramped quarters for awhile, being no more than a cuddy fitted up by my father and myself, just under the roof, within the last fortnight; and our hospitality cannot equal what we would like, for you must not be seen by the servants."

I replied that this was not the time for a suitable expression of my gratitude, and that I would obey orders implicitly. Shortly after, we entered a fair-sized frame dwelling, and I was immediately taken up two flights of steps and hurried into a little six-by-eight box of a place, just under the rafters, the door of which was not more than two and a half feet square, against which a table was placed, the woolen cover of which hung down nearly to the floor, completely hiding the entrance to my "den."

"Make the best of it," he said. "It's a pretty tough place, but I guess it's better than the prison. I must show myself now, for our house may soon be under suspicion. A couple of taps on your door will be my signal," and off he went.

I found my den very cosy—a trifle warm and a bit dark, being lighted and ventilated only by the removal of two shingles from the roof, which could be replaced in case of rain.

The furniture was suited to the size of the room, with several books with which to beguile the period of my confinement; but that which probably gave me the greatest pleasure was a neat suit of dark clothing and a change of linen, which, by the by, I had not known for some

months. A lunch was spread on a tray, which I lost no time in devouring.

I cannot recall in my whole life a feeling of more thorough contentment than that experienced by me as I threw myself on the low bedstead to think over the events of the day. Nature, however, prevailed over mind, and I soon fell asleep.

How long afterwards I know not, I was awakened by two raps on the door, to which I replied in like manner, and soon some one scrambled into the room.

"I'll put up your ventilation shingles, so as not to cause the neighbors to think the roof is on fire when I strike a light," said Avery, in the darkness, proceeding to light the lamp.

"Here's some supper and a few cigars, and, if you don't object, I'll sit by and see you enjoy them, after which we'll have a chat."

I bade him do the talking while I ate, and afterwards I would do my share with him. He informed me that there was no talk of an escape (and, indeed, it appeared later that my departure was never noted by the prison officials, or that they kept the matter quiet), that every member of the family wished to see me, but that I should not venture out for several days, as the town was always full of detectives and no one was safe from suspicion, and that though he had been a Union soldier his people were as likely to be suspected as others.

Some hours were spent in conversation, when he bade me "good-night," and again I resigned myself to slumber, and knew nothing until next morning.

Thus for four or five days I was kept a close prisoner, young Chauncey being most attentive during the time, no one else being admitted except Chauncey, *pere*, who visited me several times. The old gentleman was kindness itself, assuring me that he would gladly do all in his power until such a time as I wished to return South. One evening Avery crawled through the door into my den, saying: "The ladies are expecting you in the parlor this evening, and we think there will be no risk, though you must hold yourself in readiness to retreat, should there be a ring at the door."

I was rejoiced at this, for my confinement was growing irksome, and I longed for a time when I could see my fair deliverer, and thank her and the others for their great kindness.

Having arranged my toilet, we descended to the parlor. The entire family were assembled: Mrs. Chauncey, Miss Sarah Chauncey, the aunt.

and Miss Esther, my angel, to each of whom I was duly introduced. The evening passed in delightful conversation, and at a late hour I ascended to "the den," accompanied by Avery, who sat with me until after midnight, which

"I HAVE DECIDED TO MAKE AN IDIOT OF MYSELF."

time I would much rather have spent in the parlor with Esther, but the fates decided otherwise.

Each evening thereafter I spent in the parlor, generally with the family, occasionally with Esther, whom I simply worshiped the more I saw of her. But recently, I little thought that any hated Yankee could ever so influence me; so it was, nevertheless, and I began to realize that life must be worthless to me without her.

I had as yet said nothing of my sentiments to her, though I suspected that she was not totally ignorant on that subject. A young man's affections are hard to conceal from the object of his love, but I failed to discover that she cared more for me than a hearty sympathy for a prisoner of war, in an enemy's country.

I determined to make known my feelings, and not many evenings passed before the opportunity came. If she was indifferent, there was nothing for me to do but leave, and get across the lines, South, as soon as possible.

The family were gone out, leaving us alone in the parlor. Summoning all my courage, I said to her :

"I have decided to make an idiot of myself, Miss Esther."

"Surely you are not thinking of leaving us yet," she replied, looking steadily in my face.

"That would be wisdom, in comparison with my purpose," I answered, in steady, deliberate tones.

I think she began to divine my intentions, for her gaze fell upon the carpet at her feet, and a blush tinged her cheek as she replied :

"I cannot imagine your meaning."

I was sorely tempted to take her in my arms and tell her the old, old story, but prudence and reason prevailed, and I sat quietly, framing my next sentence.

"A poverty-stricken prisoner, with little to recommend me, a stranger and a beggar, indebted to the charity of hitherto unknown friends for the very clothing I wear, yet I cannot longer forbear declaring that from the first I have been madly in love with you. I know my words are those of a simpleton, but the worst you can do is to speak your contempt for my passion. I cannot help taking that hazard."

Great tears filled the blue eyes, and in a moment she was folded in my arms.

It were a task I am unequal to, that of recording the tender, loving words which fell from our lips during the blessed moments which followed. By her gentle but firm command I resumed my seat, and became again partially rational.

"So it was you who selected me from among the hundreds as the object of your most disloyal intentions," I exclaimed.

"Yes; we looked carefully over the entire collection," she answered, with a happy smile, "and I decided that you should be the favored one."

Again I would have taken her to my heart, but order prevailed, and I was not allowed to do so.

" And why, pray, was I selected?" I inquired, angling for a compliment.

" We never told you the story, did we?"

" No."

" Well, last spring, brother Avery was badly wounded down in Virginia. A rebel—I mean a Confederate—officer was very good to him, giving him food and water, and protecting him from a fire which would soon have burned him to death. When he was able to move we brought him home, and he often said that when he recovered he would return the kindness to some Southerner. He has never regained his strength sufficiently to return to the army, so he decided to pay his debt by releasing one of the prisoners, all of us promising to help him. The selection of the victim was left to me, and I thought you —you looked—nice, and I felt more sorry for you than any of the others, and——"

Again I tried to do the clasping act, but she ran out to attend a ring at the door, not trusting a servant for that purpose, and when she returned the whole family followed.

I tried to look very unconcerned, and joined in the general conversation for some minutes, when, turning to Avery, I asked:

" Were you ever in Virginia?"

" Yes, and I carry very undesirable proof of the fact in my hip now."

" Got it at the Wilderness, I guess?"

" Yes; sister told you, I suppose."

" Fifth New York Cavalry, I imagine?"

"Yes."

" Lay in the bushes and came near being burned?"

"Yes."

" Fellow came along and fixed you up in some sort of way?"

" Yes."

" Brought you some water and left a mouthful of rations, and took your watch for pay?"

" No," he blurted out; "I gave it to him, and he refused it."

" Would you know the fellow again if you met him?"

Gazing at me for a moment, he sprang forward, throwing his arms about me, saying:

"YOU ARE THE VERY MAN, OLD FELLOW!"

"Well! well! well! you are the very man, old fellow! Since the first time I saw you I had a notion I had seen you somewhere. What a fool I was not to have known you!"

There were tears and a general handshaking all around. The two old ladies hugged me again and again, and I thought at one time that Esther would do likewise, but she thought better of it, and only whispered in my ear: "Why didn't you tell me before?"

A proposition was submitted by Avery to kill the fatted calf, but the old gentleman insisted on adjourning to the dining-room and making a night of it, which was done in the most thorough manner.

Next morning old Mr. Chauncey and Avery came up, bringing my breakfast, and as they crawled through the doorway, Avery said:

"Esther is just outside, and wants to come in if you will let her."

I glanced around the room; it was awful, but I replied: "Certainly, I shall be only too happy."

The door was opened, and I dragged her through as gently as I could.

After she had eyed the little room over, admired it, and said "how cute" everything looked, etc., she said to her father, with eyes on the floor:

"Mr. B—— told me a still more wonderful story last night, father."

"What was that, my daughter?"

Hesitatingly, she continued:

"He said that he loved me, and—wanted me to marry him—but I didn't think you would let me."

"Let you! Why, my boy, you couldn't please me better. Yes, yes, I say, certainly you shall marry her. I can take care of you both, and you shall live right here with me."

There was another handshaking, varied by a kiss from Esther.

Ah, those were happy days, indeed! The servants were dismissed, and my "den" was bidden a final adieu, and the run of the house given me.

The wedding didn't take place, however, for I could not consent to leaving Lee's army to do battle without me any longer. So one night, armed with a railroad ticket to Baltimore, a little purse of gold, and a photograph of the dearest girl in the world, I took my departure for the South, if I should happily succeed in getting through the lines.

Providence (or the photograph, as Esther said later) protected me from shot and shell from Petersburg to Appomattox, and I returned home, but not to stay.

When something of quiet was restored, I once more took my way to Elmira, but with emotions very different from those which filled my breast on my first visit.

The wedding was a quiet one, the family not being quite ready *then* for my story to be known.

This was twenty-seven years ago, and my Esther, gray and more sedate now than then, is yet the dearest woman on earth to me.

Another Esther, her mother's image, was the pet of the household for some twenty years, until we gave her to the son of a neighbor, and her baby Esther, a toddler of three summers, spends half her time with us in the old homestead, not far from the capital of the old Palmetto State. Avery has paid us a visit once every year from his home in Albany, and the dear old people are long since in their graves, near the scenes of their honored and useful lives.

A WAR TIMES BALL IN DIXIE.

A TRUE STORY.

By a Participant.

IT must not be supposed that in those dire, dreadful, and dreary times we had nothing but horrors and havoc; nothing but lamentation, wailing, and woe; nothing for the "boys in gray" to do but fight, whilst the lassies stayed at home only to sew and pray.

It would be all wrong to suppose that even in a city before which the great ironclads did sentinel duty, whilst monster cannon, with devoted energy, sent shot and shell, with an occasional sprinkling of grape, into our midst, and oftentimes over our heads, by night as well as by day, there were no times of hope, happiness, and hilarity; of merry-making, love-making, and match-making; of music, dancing, and balls.

In the effulgence of silvery beauty still shone the moon over our beleaguered city. The soft salt zephyrs sped their way over turret and top-sail, and there was no "blockade" to the perennial bloom of our rich tropical flowers with their ravishing odor upon the midnight air. If there were brave boys in Dixie, they were gay ones, too; and maidens ever ready for fun, frolic, and mirth.

We had learned, by the spring of '64, to gauge the distance of the shot and shell thrown by the fleet into the "City by the Sea." It was noticed that beyond a certain street no missile had fallen. In consequence of this, the lower part of the city was deserted, beautiful houses became tottering, dismantled walls, broad piazzas hung like the gardens of Babylon, and in the busy thoroughfares, once echoing with the tread of prancing steeds, the grass grew, long and damp, with no sound save that of the whizzing bomb. Life existed only in the suburbs. Here every house assumed rubber-like dimensions, and—a seeming paradox—without peace there was hearty good-will.

On the broad bank of the Cooper River, stood an ancient residence, whose Ionic columns gave support to wide and beautiful piazzas, and commanding from the summit of its picturesque cupola a full view of old ocean, with the besieged fortresses and the flotilla beyond.

The sunlight played between the folds of a graceful flag—not the "Stars and Bars," nor yet the "Stars and Stripes"; but, high up-lifted from the dome of this mansion and given to the breeze, floated the Cross of St. George, making the headquarters of the British consul, also the abiding-place *pro tem.* of himself and family, whose guest chambers were always full. Out of the reach of the guns and their fiery work, the house became the centre of attraction for the soldier beaux of the times. The spacious parlors held gay gatherings, albeit the tell-tale mirrors betrayed the incongruous dress of the fair ones and the paucity of their wardrobes by reason of the wear of time and the vigilance of the blockaders outside our harbor.

It was under these circumstances that whispered rumors reached us of the social event of the times, and soon we were overjoyed and yet dismayed by an invitation to attend a ball to be given by the commandant at the arsenal, all the way "cross town." There were two things to be considered, confronted, and overcome,—two things quite startling to us young maidens of the mansion, and most nearly concerned,—viz., how to get there and what to wear.

The edict had gone forth that we could not avail ourselves of "outside escort"; "proper chaperonage" would be necessary for the decorum of such an event. The distance was too great to be walked, and conveyances must be had for the "discreet" ones, as well as for ourselves. The depleted stables stared at us gloomily, as all "able-bodied" animals had long ago been conscripted and sent to the field, and we retired to our rooms to breathe treason, denunciation, and rebellion; but, nothing daunted, to find a way to go, and, with certain reservations, a way also to get back.

A venerable quadruped, whose hoary age rendered him exempt from military duty, but which was sufficiently imbued with life for his latter day avocation of hauling wood, was led from the stable and subjected to a process of massage and grooming, administered by a small boy, whose sympathy had been enlisted by the stimulating aid of a teacup of molasses. Then followed a fortuitous discovery of an old set of harness, which, with a splicing of twine, was made to "do." Remembering an old, battered, and wrecked "carry-all," long ago consigned to disuse, we repaired to the darkened and musty quarters of the carriage house, and, by united strength and working with a will, brought out into the light the ancient vehicle. By the aid of mop and brush, with greasing of lard applied by our own hands, safe from observation under cover of luxuriant foliage, we effected a metamorphose which quite recompensed us for our labor. The conduct of our gayly caparisoned steed, during a trial trip around the carriage house, gave us every assurance that there would be no runaway accident. Our pride was assuaged by the knowledge that, since we would leave under cover of darkness, no one at the ball need know the state nor the speed which marked our journey. All we had to do was to go slowly, "sit lightly," thus running no risk of a breakdown.

Next in turn loomed up the dress question. As the fortunate owner of a "blockade runner" (all articles coming in this way were so termed), my friend's pale-green muslin paled further before the greener jealousy of my heart, until I was appeased by the discovery of some scraps of lilac silk, out of which a hasty jacket was constructed. This, worn with a skirt of pink and white muslin,—strongly suggestive of the striped lines of mint candy,—made the wearer thereof sincerely hope that the analogy would not be further carried out, and that she would in no way be found to "stick."

But the greatest trial awaited us in the contemplation of our well-worn, well-rubbed, and sickly-looking *boots*. No slippers ever slipped the blockade, and we wore only home-made brogans of the times. Blacking—we had none. As necessity is the mother of invention, so an improvised polish of soot and molasses, diluted with water, gave to our faded footgear a most gratifying "shine." All things being ready, it only remained to go to the ball.

Driving slowly along, in diligent search of secluded by-ways, "sitting lightly," holding our breath by way of a precaution the value of which was not clear to our minds, but indulged in by a sort of concord of agreement that it might lessen our weights—thus we went "cross town." But there was no subduing the steady creak of the wheels, the alternate grating drag of the one, whilst its mate seemed to have become too short, and inclined to spin; then the swaying, leaning, and lurching of the top-cover awakened great fear of a turn-over at any moment. We began to ask each other, nervously, would the ball be over before our arrival, or would we get there at all?

But we did get there, and, alighting at a distance safe from obtrusive eyes, wended our way up the graveled walk between stalking sentinels with glistening bayonets, around murderous cannon, and pyramidal piles of shot. Met by gallant swains, the vicissitudes along the way were forgotten, our stiffened limbs caught inspiration from the full strains of the band, and, without formality, we fell into the mazes of the waltz under the sheen of the silvery moon, and upon the greensward under our willing feet.

Our late arrival gave us an opportunity for a survey of the ball, now at its height, with the accompaniment of gliding steps to a strange medley of sounds. Far above the exhilarating and joyous strains of the military band, and at short intervals of studied precision, came the ominous whirring and whizzing of bombs in mid-air, quickly followed by the reverberating roar of explosion—harmless agents doing work only among abandoned homes and forsaken streets.

The brilliant uniforms, in gray and gold, with crimson sashes and dangling swords, stood in beautiful contrast to the quaint, unique, and old-fashioned but picturesque costumes of these war-time belles. Antique relics of heavy silks and velvets had been rescued from the depths of trunks, and donned by demioselles who danced *vis-a-vis* with maidens looking lovely in the latest *calico* "blockade runner," costing far more in dollars than any ancient dame's heirloom! Resuscitated tarlatans and checkered "homespun" lent additional brilliancy to this kaleidoscopic scene. Then supper, of strawberries, cream, and sorghum sugar. The "grand promenade" gave an interval for that delightful saunter under moonlit skies amid the perfume of sweet flowers and the rhythm of soft music. And how we plotted, planned, and intrigued—my companion and I! How we agreed that it was too unsafe to venture to return the way we had come, and, going back to the ball-room, plead in plaintive tones to be allowed to accept "outside escor,t" for, as "a merciful man is merciful unto his beast," we would thereby lighten the load, and, with a fleeter steed, we would get home ahead of our chaperons, and be "waiting!" How we promised not to "lose the way," and many more promises of a conciliatory nature! I distinctly remember that after devious detours and serpentine wanderings, conveniently losing the way, and finding it again, we arrived to find *them* waiting for us.

What matters it all? Those were war times, and "all's fair in love and war."

HIS SON'S FRIEND IN BLUE.

Mrs. C. P. F.

THE boom of cannon and heavy artillery at intervals and the constant crack of sharp-shooters' rifles had been heard since daybreak. From the house in the valley the battle on the hill was plainly visible. Now and then shells hissed through the air, just grazing the tops of the grand old oaks, and fell with loud explosions in the grove beyond. From time to time, children playing in the old-fashioned yard, frightened by the whistling bullets or by some deserter dashing by with clanking sword and panting horse, scampered into the house.

The house (built in the irregular style of architecture so common in the South "'fo' de wah"), with the surrounding plantation, was the property of General ———, a wealthy Southern gentleman. While loving his sunny birthland devotedly, he still clung to the old flag under which he had served during the Mexican War, believing that "in union there is strength." Thus it was a trial hard to bear that both of his oldest sons were soldiers in the Southern Army, and almost as bitter was the knowledge that wife and children were sympathizers with the same cause, though this, through deference to the husband and father, was rarely even hinted at.

The day was as warm and balmy as if a June, rather than a March, sun was smiling—a day musical with the voices of many birds, some wanderers just returned, while others were old friends who had remained faithful through the short winter months. The trees were peopled with the ubiquitous tree-frogs, with their unending challenge and answer; and early spring flowers nodded coquettishly in the gentle air, as if daring the zephyr just gone by to kiss them again; a day filled with the airs and graces spring knows so well how to assume, when all the world is flattering himself or herself, as the case may be, that winter is a thing of the past, and that summer, with her beguiling way, is almost within reach. It seemed a sacrilege that anything so gracious as that day should be marred by so ungracious a thing as war.

In the battle on the hill one of General ———'s sons was fighting, and father and mother, knowing so well his daring spirit, that

scorned any place but the thickest of the battle, were fearful that any hour might bring the tidings of his death.

The day is closing with a great display of brilliant coloring, alternately brightening and fading. The birds are twittering in the low cedar hedge separating the yard and orchard, fluttering from place to place in search of a suitable night's lodgement; the frogs in the hollow over the way are furnishing a deep basso to the shrill falsetto of their cousins, the tree-frogs; while the swish and hum in the air reminds one that the bugs are out for an airing on their new wings. The dying sounds of the battle chime strangely with these peaceful sights and sounds; and General ———, walking hastily back and forth on the walk over which the maple boughs meet fraternally, turns for the first time a deaf ear to Nature's wooing. His youngest child toddles after him, striving in vain to keep pace with her father's impatient steps.

At the gate opening on the highway his wife stood watching, her heart aching with the suspense of waiting for news of her brave boy. The twilight lingered, as if anxious still further to lend her light; and the children, who had been playing "hide-and-seek," for which game the fine box-trees offered such splendid inducements, were now gathered in a silent group around their mother.

Just as the moon came up from behind a distant hill, smiling serenely, as if sure of her welcome, there fell on the ear distantly, but distinctly, the beat of horses' feet. After some moments of breathless waiting, a squad of soldiers came slowly around the bend, the greater part of them mounted, while a number were walking, and bearing on their shoulders what, at that distance, seemed a litter. The moon shone on buckles and swords, making them flash brightly, and each soldier's form stood out clearly as they advanced in perfect order. As they neared the gate the mother's heart chilled almost to death as she saw the gray uniforms; but before her mind actually conceived the thought that they were bringing her son,—wounded, perhaps dead, —a handsome soldier rode from the rear, and springing lightly to the ground, caught her to him, exclaiming: "Little mother!" Then, as the soldiers came to a halt a few feet back, he stepped to the side of the litter, drawing his mother with him, and said, cheerily : " Captain, I am going to put you into the hands of the best nurse in the State, and I will lay any wager you like that she will pull you through." And then he repeated the formal introduction, bowing with courtly grace, and placing his mother's hand in that of the wounded man, whom he introduced as Captain ————, of the Union Army.

Mrs. ————'s heart filled with pity for the " boy in blue " as she saw the agony of suffering on his face, and she spoke a kindly welcome, her sweet voice and gentle touch soothing him inexpressibly. His gray eyes, half full of tears, searched her face longingly as he thanked her in a voice broken by pain. General ———— now came up, and grasping his son's hand, with a fervent " God bless you !" turned and courteously welcomed the stranger ; then, seeing the blue uniform, said delightedly : " Why, my boy, you are wearing my colors !" The poor boy— for boy he was though an officer—said : " I am glad to know that you are my friend ; but," he added quickly, " no one could be kinder than these noble men in gray, especially the young officer, who, I think, is your son "—this last inquiringly.

" Yes," answered General ————, with a shade of disappointment in his voice that he could not conceal. " Yes, my son and a noble boy and brave soldier."

Mrs. ———— had been watching the wounded soldier with concern, and now perceiving his growing weakness, drew her son's notice to the fact, and he at once directed the bearers to carry him to the house, himself following with father and mother, his arm thrown fondly around the latter. The children, usually so noisy in their welcome of their favorite brother, now forebore any demonstration, only pressing close to him, their childish hearts awed by the solemnity of their elders.

As the bearers stepped into the great piazza with their burden, a great sigh rustled through the trees and lost itself in the grove beyond.

They laid him in " young master's " room, and the bearers retiring, the family commenced their efforts at relief. It was evident that relief could be but temporary, for death even then stood waiting. When all had been done that was possible, and the sufferer seemed sleeping, the son explained, in a low voice, the circumstances of their finding him, and that he was a Southern man whose loyalty for country was greater than love for his native State.

The sounds peculiar to night on a plantation smite familiarly the dying man's ear as he stirs from his sleep. In memory he is again in his childhood's home ; he is listening to his " ole mammy " as she tells again the oft-told story of " Bre'r rabbit an' de tah baby," nodding his head vehemently now and then as his childish heart kept pace with " Bre'r rabbit's " indignation as he found his weapons of defence, one after the other, stuck tight to that most wonderful of all babies, " de tah baby." Once more he is bird-nesting, or fishing with bent pin ; again his heart thrills with the awesomeness of a hunt with the " old uncles " through the moonlit woods for " old man coon." He has grown to a young man, and feels again the rush of feeling when he hears that the Stars and Stripes have been fired upon, and clasping his mother to him bids her farewell, to enlist his fortunes with the Union.

As the night wanes, and the sounds hush, he goes back yet again to the loved home. The beautiful woman by him, with the exquisite pity in her eyes, seems to him his mother, and, so thinking in his longing, he takes her hand, and holding it, repeats from beginning to end the pathetic prayer of childhood, " Now I lay me down to sleep." As he enunciates the last word, death lays his seal on his lips, and the boy in blue sleeps his last sleep !

ROMANCE OF THE GREAT LOCOMOTIVE RAID.

Hon. D. Thew Wright.

THE 2d Regiment Ohio Volunteers was organized in Southern Ohio. Leonard A. Harris, a man afterward in public life, was its colonel. He will be well remembered as mayor of the Queen City.

"His bones are dust ; his good sword rust."

Captain James Warnock, also a Cincinnatian, was a captain in this regiment, though he entered the service as a lieutenant. Through Captain Warnock, it was my good fortune to become acquainted with some of that regiment, one of whom was afterwards engaged in one of the most daring and desperate adventures of the war. He was an East Tennesseean by birth, although he had spent most of his life in the western portion of that State. He was a mere private in the ranks when I knew him, but he was a man of considerable education, a machinist by occupation, and a man of great decision and force of character. He came from Memphis to the North simply for the purpose of enlisting in the Union army. We will call him Jacobs, for the purposes of identification only, for that was not his name, and he perished upon a Southern scaffold. It is probable that to-day his own family do not know of his fate.

The 2d Ohio Volunteers was in the division of General Ormsby MacKnight Mitchel, who was certainly one of the most remarkable men and one of the most brilliant generals of his day. This division was lying at Shelbyville, Tenn., from which place Mitchel moved and captured Huntsville, Ala., to the entire surprise and discomfiture of the rebels. It was early in 1862, just before the battle of Shiloh, about which, to the present day, people are being continually convulsed, as to whether Sherman was or was not surprised. While engaged in the Huntsville campaign, Mitchel, who was restless and active in his disposition of untiring energy, and never satisfied unless occupied in overcoming the impossible, conceived an enterprise, brilliant in its nature, bold in its execution, and in the light of what was then and is now known, entirely feasible.

It was well understood at that time that East Tenneesee was thoroughly loyal. Brownlow was alive, and the flag waved in the hearts if not in the homes of the people. Mitchel's plan was to get into East Tennessee with his division ; there uniting with General Morgan, who was at Cumberland Gap, a considerable army would be collected. With this as a nucleus, the loyal people of that region would rally to the standard to the extent of sixty or eighty thousand men. Supplied with arms and munitions of war by the general government, they would be able to defy the whole Southern Confederacy, and Chattanooga would have been ours two years before it was taken by Rosecrans. But to ensure the safety of such an expedition, it was necessary to break and disable the Western and Atlantic Railroad, the line of communication between Chattanooga and Atlanta ; for, at that early period of the war, troops were collecting in all parts of the Gulf States, and pouring from Atlanta north to reinforce Beauregard and Sidney Johnson at Shiloh.

To accomplish the end in view, Mitchel organized the great railroad raid, as it has been called. Twenty-four volunteers were called for from the army under his command. They were only told they were to go on a secret and dangerous expedition into the enemy's country ; that every man risked his life, with the chances largely against him. This kind of desperate adventure exactly suited the Northern soldier, and pretty much all of Mitchel's army wanted to go. Colonel Harris selected four men from the 2d Ohio, Captain Warnock having named Jacobs from his company as one of the most reliable, as well as one of the fittest men, where pluck, nerve, and skill were required. The only orders the men received were to don citizens' clothing, and repair to a certain spot in the woods that evening, a few miles from Shelbyville.

The night was dark. A rising storm was growling through the distant mountains, and occasional flashes of lightning lit the gloom, as twenty-three men met at the appointed rendezvous. One had failed to come. There in the sombre surroundings of the forest, the leader of the party imparted his instructions to his men. They were to break up, and singly, or in squads of not more than two or three, make their way through the mountain passes and an unknown and hostile country to Chattanooga, one hundred and three miles away.

All immediately set forth upon the long march, from which eight of that devoted band never returned. They made their way as best they could. They slept in the open fields; sometimes a friendly shelter would be given them, upon the representation that they were on their way to join the Southern army. Their lives were in daily peril, as they encountered parties of armed Confederates who were hunting up stragglers and deserters from their ranks.

As they approached the town of Chattanooga, they began to hear the news of distant Shiloh. In that sanguinary engagement, according to the floating rumors, all the Yankees in the United States had been killed, millions of cannon captured by the Confederates, and five hundred Union gunboats sunk in the turbid waters of the Tennessee. This was quite exciting and "highly important, if true," but the boys were not as yet completely discouraged.

Reaching Chattanooga, the party united, and took a train on the Western and Atlantic Road for Marietta, a small town twenty miles north of Atlanta.

When the expedition started, the date had been assigned for the execution of the enterprise, but unfortunately the leader had changed that date and made it one day later. This was fatal, and disaster was the result. The morning after their arrival at Marietta, twenty out of the twenty-three men took the train for the North. The plan was to capture this train; rush for Chattanooga; burn every bridge they passed; tear up the track; cut telegraph wires; do all the damage they could; switch off at Chattanooga for Huntsville and there report to Mitchel, who was then to start for East Tennessee like a cyclone double-shotted with dynamite.

How clear to us all are the errors of yesterday! How easily might they have been avoided had we only known! But the mistakes of to-morrow are forever a sealed book. Had the party started as was first intended, one day sooner, the entire road from Marietta to Chattanooga was clear, and they could have made the run in three hours, without a single obstacle in the way.

It was a peculiarity of our Western armies that its ranks were filled with all sorts of artisans and mechanics of every description. When Mitchel wanted to build a bridge he called for volunteers, and forth from the lines stepped carpenters, blacksmiths, stonemasons, water-rats, and every imaginable character useful in the construction of such a work. So, in this party about to steal a train, were locomotive engineers, firemen, conductors, brakemen, and for this particular occasion all were thieves.

There was, however, no Pullman car porter, but this modern railway appendage was scarcely needed.

Eight miles from Marietta the train stopped for breakfast at Big Shanty. Among other pleasant surroundings, here was a Confederate camp of 10,000 men, and, besides, a guard had been placed to watch the train. The leader of the expedition contemplated the situation and made up his mind it was "now or never."

The engineer, conductor, and officers of the train were at breakfast. The locomotive, baggage cars, and two box cars were quickly uncoupled from the passenger coaches; the selected man sprang to the throttle; a fireman was at his side in an instant; the rest tumbled on board; a jerk at the lever, and they were off for the land of liberty and the North Star.

As they pulled out from the station and the flying wheels began to spin over the iron way, in the first moments of exultation they congratulated themselves on their now assured success, but there were factors in the problem they had not consulted. At the first alarm the conductor and engineer rushed from their breakfast and saw they were left. Without a moment's hesitation they put forth up the track on foot, at the top of their speed, after the train now rapidly vanishing in the distance, a performance that was greeted by the crowd with shouts of laughter. But they kept going, and, strange as it may appear, they caught up with the runaways. After a run of about three miles they came to some trackmen with a hand-car. Pressing the gang into the service, they sped on till they came to a place where our people had torn up the track and cut the wires. Off the hand-car went, head over heels, into the ditch, but it was a case where nobody was to blame, for nobody was hurt. They righted the car and on they went, muscle against steam.

At the Etowah River, twenty miles from Marietta, on a side track, stood an engine fired up and ready for action. The leader of the Union expedition, Andrews, thought he would stop and disable it. So easily it might have been done! The removal of a single small pin would have made the iron monster as helpless as an inshore whale at low tide. But so certain was he now of success that he thought the precaution unnecessary. This mistake was fatal, for without that engine they would never have been caught. On came the remorseless hand-car with the vindictive conductor, who had a head for the business he was in. He yanked this locomotive onto the main track in less time than it takes to mention Mr. Robinson's name, "gave her all that was in her," and it was now steam against steam, iron horse against iron horse. This conductor's name was Fuller. He was in a towering rage at the Yankee trick played upon him, and, entirely reckless of consequences, he made his empty engine dance and bounce over the rails like a cork in a gale of wind.

Further on, at a place called Cass Station, Andrews stopped and leisurely proceeded to take wood and water, entirely ignorant that the avenger was after him, though yet a long way off.

Up to this time he had been running on blind chance. He had no time-card and no schedule of trains, and knew nothing of what he was to meet on the road. He was sweetly unconscious of the fact that at any curve or tunnel he might dash into some train, head on, or crash into one that he had overtaken, and with all this oblivion of his danger, he had been tearing over the face of the earth at the rate of sixty miles an hour.

We have heard of the faith that can remove mountains, but the faith that can run a train under such circumstances beats the old style out of sight.

At Cass Station Andrews procured a time-card from the station agent, under the plausible statement that he was running a special train loaded with powder for Beauregard's army, and that his orders were to run regardless of anything and everything in existence. On examining his time-card, Andrews found that he had secured it none too soon, as at the next station he was to meet a freight train. This was about as near a collision as he cared to approach. They reached Kingston, the station in question, where they took a side track to let the freight train pass. As they were felicitating themselves that the way would now be clear, to their horror they discovered that this train carried a red flag, indicating that another train was following. So they had to wait and wait, while each minute was worth a life. But even yet their pursuers had not come in sight, and they were not aware how hotly they were being followed.

Andrews thought he had so obstructed the road that he could not be overtaken. At various places he had torn up the rails, loaded them into his box cars, and carried them off. But Fuller was not to be beaten at that game. When he came to a break, he took up the rails

behind him, laid them in front, and on he went—madder than ever.

There is sometimes in the composition of the human race a sublimity of impudence that is beyond all admiration. This impudence Andrews possessed to a degree rarely seen among men. At one station where he stopped, he knew that Calhoun was nine miles distant, and at this point he would meet the down passenger train. He had the coolness to, and *did*, telegraph that train to sidetrack for him and let him pass, telling the powder story; and this train, although entitled to the road, actually obeyed his orders. He ran that nine miles in seven minutes and a half, and went past the Calhoun station so that the people standing there said they could hear or see nothing but a buzz.

At the Oostenaula bridge they stopped to take up a rail. While busily at work they heard the scream of a whistle behind them. This was the first they knew that the foe was so close. When Fuller had reached Kingston, he found the Rome train lying there. He abandoned his first locomotive and took the engine, which was a first-class passenger machine.

At the Oostenaula the quarter stretch was reached, and the final race for life began. Andrews barely got his men aboard when the chase hove in sight. The engineer put his engine at it. In a minute the wheels were striking fire, so rapid were their revolutions. The roadbed itself was in poor shape, rough and uneven, and the engine rocked backward and forward, and the men in the box cars rattled about like peas in a gourd. But like the tireless wolf that scents his prey, the Rome engine, like the gray mare, was the better horse of the two. As they turned a curve, Andrews cut off one of his box cars, hoping to derail his pursuers, but Fuller was riding on the cowcatcher of his Rome engine, expecting exactly some such trick, and he was not caught napping. He simply stopped, coupled the box car to the front of his engine, and away he went to the next sidetrack, where he switched off his box car and went on unencumbered.

It was not long before Andrews, at the end of a long stretch, saw the smoke of his coming fate. His engine had run nearly one hundred miles. They were out of wood, water, and oil; the terrific speed had melted all the metal from the journals, and the brave horse that had carried them so gallantly and so far was quivering in every fibre of his iron frame. They cut a hole in the rear end of the box car, in which they had loaded the rails they had taken up. As the road was a crooked one, when the pursuer was too close, at the first sharp curve they would shove out an iron rail and let it fall upon the track. They hove overboard a lot of cross-ties in the vain attempt to disable Fuller's engine, but in every instance Fuller's quick eye saw the danger and averted it.

They were within fifteen miles of Chattanooga, when they tried to fire the Chickamauga bridge, but they were too late. The Rome engine was within four hundred yards, and Andrews gave the order for each man to look out for himself. They jumped from the cars and scattered into the woods. All were subsequently captured, and the story of the sufferings they endured is something too pitiful to relate. Eight were hung as spies, and Jacobs among the number. Jacobs had run the engine from Big Shanty to her last gasp at Chickamauga bridge. Fuller, during the chase, swore a terrible oath that he would see the man who run that engine hung, and he did.

Although this story has for many years had more or less of public notoriety, its chief interest to me was that I had heard many of its particulars from Colonel Harris and Captain Warnock long before I ever saw them in print. This, and one other fact, in the nature of a coincidence. Captain Warnock told me that the night before starting on the raid, Jacobs left with him some papers, to be opened in case he did not return. After being assured of the soldier's death, Warnock opened these papers. They contained a few personal ornaments, such as jewelry and the like, and a letter to be sent to a certain young lady (naming her) in Memphis, Tenn. Warnock had sent to Memphis and made every effort, after the war, to discover the person named, but without success; and he was satisfied she must be dead.

Nearly twenty-five years after the war had closed — ten years after Captain Warnock's death — it so happened that my interests and pleasure had called me to spend my summer in Western North Carolina. I met there some very pleasant people, but scarcely any who had not in some way suffered from the events of the war. I made the acquaintance of a gentleman there, of large wealth, residing upon one of the most beautiful plantations of that beautiful country. His wife was a lady past middle age, and upon first meeting her I was struck with her appearance. In youth she must have been a very beautiful woman. Now she was of commanding, stately presence, but there seemed

to be a tinge of sadness in the expression of her face that at once awakened my curiosity and interest. She was a lady of cultivation and keenness of intellect. I very well remember the first evening passed at her house. There had been an assumption abroad in the land that I was an adept at cards. There was a challenge for whist by two of the crack hands of the neighborhood, and there was to be a star performance. With the lady as partner, at a certain stage of the game one of our adversaries asked, referring to the points, "How do we stand?" I replied, "We are seven." Quick as a flash she capped the line—

"And two of us at Conway dwell,
And two are gone to sea."

I was so completely taken off my feet I gasped at her with the astonishment of an idiot, trumped my partner's ace, and lost the odd.

I inquired about her of the friends with whom I happened to be staying, and they told me she had a history with a romance, although she herself never spoke of her early life.

She had come from Memphis. Before the war "There was a youth, etc., etc." She was an ardent Confederate. He was for the old flag and went North to join the Union army. They parted in anger, in silence and in tears. She never heard of him again. After the war was over, her bitterness of soul remained. She hated the North; she hated the Yankees. In particular, she hated the "Lincoln hirelings." But somehow, there was one Lincoln hireling she did wish would come back. He did not come. She waited — five years — ten years. Meanwhile, a gentleman, many years her senior, but blest with all those material aids that tend to make life pleasant, wooed her, and she was very poor. Her family had been stripped by the war and driven from their home. With entire frankness she told him her story, and said, "If he does not come in five years." The five years elapsed, and like a sensible woman as she was, she married this gentleman, who gave her every comfort and happiness that a true heart, backed by no end of a bank account, could give.

The last time I was ever at her home, I was turning over the pages of an old family Bible. Between the leaves I came across a photograph. It was faded and worn. I gazed at it in amazement. I knew that face. I turned it over, and on the back of it a name was written. I knew that name. I closed the book and went away. I did not think it was for me to awaken a sorrow that so long had slumbered, but the lady in question was Jacobs' sweetheart.

"PRIVATE" BILL GARRETT'S DISGRACE.

J. M. WADDILL.

IT was in December, '62. Citizens of historic old Fredericksburg were fleeing from Burnside's threat of burning the city. Extra trains carried the well-to-do to places of safety. The muddy roads were crowded with vehicles of every description, while pedestrians thronged the roads and fields, all flying from the coming storm.

Many were burdened with such lighter household goods as could be carried, seeking no particular place, bent only on escape from the old city.

A melancholy spectacle it was—feeble old men and women, mothers with groups of little children clinging to their skirts, wearily making their way out of harm's reach. Little knots of desolate, homeless ones paused by the roadside, with wet feet and bedraggled garments, knowing not which way to turn their steps.

Very soon outhouses, barns, and stables were taken possession of by these houseless ones, while temporary huts were hastily constructed for shelter from the storm, but there was much suffering.

It was just before the great battle, and our regiment, the ——th North Carolina Infantry, was in camp, near the now famous Marye's Heights.

Bill Garrett and I were messmates and chums. Bill was known as one of the best, warmest-hearted fellows in the world, rough of exterior, but a jewel at heart; quiet, sensitive, brave, and the soul of honor.

One morning, to the surprise of every man in the regiment, Bill was marched forth under arrest and put in the guard tent.

Upon inquiry, I learned that he had been caught the night before stealing from the commissary's store tent. The evidence was undoubted, and Bill submitted to the punishment without a murmur—marching back and forth before the guard tent all day, with a big placard suspended from his neck bearing the word "THIEF" in great black letters.

That night, when Bill came to our mess fire, I felt so disgusted with him that I scarcely spoke; for while thieving in the army was not exactly the same as in civil life, I could not but feel a contempt for him, the synonym of all that was noble and proud in the regiment.

"What on earth could have caused you to descend so low, Bill?" I asked, as we drew our only blanket over our heads that night.

"Well," said he, with a yawn, which showed far too much indifference, "I felt that I was just bound to have a whole side of bacon once more."

"I wouldn't have believed it of you, Bill," I replied, with no little contempt in my tones, "and," I continued, "you must bunk with some one else hereafter."

"We'll see about that to-morrow," he answered. "I'm too sleepy now to talk much," and in a minute he was sound asleep and snoring.

The next day, a good many of the boys turned the cold shoulder to Bill, but he seemed so hardened and brazen that I felt no delicacy in again referring to his disgrace.

"What were you going to do with your plunder, Garrett?" I asked, when we were alone.

"Don't you think our mess-table could stand such an addition and not suffer?" he replied, with so little of shame in his manner that I felt a far greater contempt for him than ever.

"Our mess doesn't wish any help by such means," I answered, and turned on my heel to leave him.

"Hold on a minute," he said, and I half turned to hear what he had to say.

"The boys are pretty hard on me, don't you think so?"

"No harder than they should be," I answered, coldly, but a bit of compassion overcame me for the moment, and I continued:

"How is it, Bill, that you, whom every one regarded as the soul of honor, should so far forget yourself as to descend to the level of the lowest scum of the regiment?"

The great burly fellow looked full in my face and burst into a loud horse laugh.

I instantly left him without another word, but he called to me to come back. Taking no notice of him, he again called me in a more earnest manner, which prompted me to pause and wait for him to draw near.

"I think I'll make a clean breast of the whole matter, if you won't give me away," he said, in a more serious manner.

191

"My respect for your people at home must prevent my adding to your disgrace," I answered.

"Then meet me at sunset, on the telegraph road, near the Tennessee Brigade, and I'll tell you the whole story," and we separated.

I went that evening to the place he appointed and found him already there.

"Come along," he said, leading the way down the road some distance, neither of us speaking a word. Turning into a narrow path which led into the forest, he glanced over his shoulder and beckoned me to follow.

Having passed through the wood, we entered a small clearing, near the centre of which stood a solitary tumble-down log cabin, toward which he led the way. As the door was reached he gave a double knock, and looked into my face laughing.

The door was lifted away, for its hinges had long since disappeared, and we entered. I shall never forget the sight which greeted my vision. A poor, meanly-clad, middle-aged woman, surrounded by five little children, received us. There was nothing attractive about the woman save the look of gratitude with which she gazed on Bill.

"Well, and how are we getting on now?" he asked, patting one of the tow-headed boys with his big brawny hand, at the same time placing on a rude shelf a package which I had noticed under his arm as we came.

The tears sprang into the woman's eyes as she turned away, unable to speak, during which time I took a hurried inventory of the contents of the cabin. A camp kettle, frying pan, a piece of pork, a bag of something, a pile of hay in a corner, and a short piece of board supported by two goodly-sized stones, comprised the entire furniture.

"Oh, cheer up, mother; we'll soon be all right; to-morrow we're going to thrash Burnside, and you and the little chicks can go back home," said Bill, in a cheery tone, as he kicked the fire and laid on another huge log.

"God will reward you, Mr. Garrett," said the poor woman, through her tears, and again her voice left her.

"That's all right, mother," spoke Bill, and grasping the kettle he started out, saying to me as he disappeared: "There's a pile of wood about a hundred yards back of the cabin." I understood the hint, and by the time I returned with my load, Bill was back from the spring with the kettle full.

"I'll try and come again to-morrow evening, mother; keep a stout heart; good-bye, little chick," and he strode out into the starlight. But Bill failed to keep his promise, for the next evening he lay on the hillside just back of the stone fence on Mayre's Heights, shot through the shoulder.

As we reached the wood, on our way to camp, I said to him: "I feel like falling down before you, Bill, and kissing the dust from your feet; and *this* was what you stole for, and *this* is where you went alone, and *this* was what you marched all day long for in front of the guard tent, with that awful placard, and I was one of the first to turn my back on you. Can you forgive me, old fellow?"

"Come along, you great idiot," he said, good-naturedly. "Didn't I know you couldn't understand?"

"Tell me all about it, old chap. May I touch you?" I said, passing my arm through his, as we entered the telegraph road.

"There isn't much to tell," the noble fellow answered. "I found that poor creature with her five little brats in that old shanty, with not a thing but what they wore on their backs; that was about sunset. I found the pile of wood where I sent you, and that night I stole a part of Company 'B's' rations, which I carried to her. About day I made a raid on the commissary department, and got that bag of meal, and as I passed Archer's Tennesseeans, I hooked the camp kettle and frying pan which you saw. The next night, one of Major Hayes' men caught me just as I had taken a big side of bacon from under the tent. Next day I trotted before the guard tent, you know, but that night, after you were asleep, I hooked a piece of meat from Walker's commissary, which will run them several days. This is about all there is about it, but you must keep quiet, for I'll catch it again if Cooke hears of it."

I never saw the woman again, for when three days later I went to look after them, the cabin was empty.

———

In the winter of '63-'64, while we were in winter quarters on the Rapidan, Bill and I were sitting in our "shuck" one day, when a big, rawboned cavalryman looked in the door and asked, "Is this Private Bill Garrett's house?"

"Said to be mine in part," answered Bill. "What can I do for you?"

"I learned sometime since," replied the cavalryman, in a brusque tone, "that you acted toward my wife in such a manner as must demand my attention, and which I do not propose to forget, sir.''

"My dear friend," said Bill, in his usual lazy tone, "you are on the wrong track; I haven't spoken to a woman in six months."

"That may or may not be so, but it won't do for me, sir," he answered. "But I happen to know that you were guilty of conduct toward my wife which, to say the least of it, was very unusual, and I've come for a settlement."

"Yes, sir," continued the cavalryman, entering the door, "I have learned that while my wife and little ones were houseless and freezing and starving, on the hill behind Fredericksburg, you sheltered and fed them; and I've come from up on Robinson River to say to you,"

and he offered his great big hand, "that I can't live without thanking you and asking God's blessing on you; and I want to say, more, that while you and I live, if you ever want a friend to stand by you to the last drop, if need be, Jim Blake, of the —rd Virginia Cavalry, is just the man to come at your call, whether you are a hundred or a thousand miles away,"and he wrung Bill's hand until he cried out with the pain.

Bill lived under a cloud for a while after his punishment, but the truth finally leaked out, and he was again the popular private Bill Garrett of former days. He now lies up in the "land of the sky" in his native Western Carolina, as much honored as a citizen as he was beloved as a soldier.

DEATH OF GENERAL PHIL KEARNEY.

COLONEL W. L. GOLDSMITH.

THE death of no Federal general caused so much genuine and sincere sorrow as the untimely taking off of the gallant one-armed Phil Kearney, who was killed September 1, 1862, at Chantilly, Va. He was a Mexican veteran, who had left an arm in the land of the Montezumas, and we had several Mexican war veterans in our regiment (14th Georgia). Our brigadier-general, E. L. Thomas; our division commander, A. P. Hill; our corps commander, Stonewall Jackson, and our army commander, R. E. Lee, were all veterans of the Mexican war, and loved General Kearney very much. Early in the war we heard more about him than any other Federal general, and the army of Northern Virginia had great love and respect for him. His death occurred in this way, and I, perhaps, was largely responsible for it:

The battle of Chantilly was fought late in the afternoon, amid a severe storm of wind and rain. It was a gloomy, dark, depressing afternoon, and night was fast approaching. Our brigade had not fired a gun, but was on the extreme left of our forces and behind a worm rail fence, grown up thick with saplings and bushes—an excellent place for ambushing. The fighting was all to our right. I had charge of the skirmish line, some two hundred yards in advance of our line of battle, and in a cornfield which gently sloped up toward the direction of the Federals. Fortunately, I saw a line of blue majestically moving toward us, several hundred yards away, and I remember distinctly the powerful impression it made on my mind at the time. As it came forward, slowly and grandly, amidst the thickening gloom of that dreary September evening, it reminded me of an inrolling blue wave of the great ocean coming toward us. They had no skirmish line, and I withdrew ours back to the main line, and as far as I could I tried to get the men to hold their fire until the enemy came close up. I could not find General Thomas, and therefore failed to carry out my idea, and having a good many new recruits in our brigade at that time, our discipline was nothing like it was in 1863 and 1864, or we would have annihilated the Federal line. As it was, some of our men commenced firing before the enemy came close enough, which spoiled the whole game. The Federals were checked and driven back so easily that we knew something was the matter, and attributed their timidity to the demoralizing influence of defeat at Second Manassas only a few days before; but on re-establishing our skirmish line, we discovered that the gallant General Phil Kearney had been killed, and this was the cause of the Federals' weak attempt. The grief of our entire army was marked and sincere over this sad news, and General Lee sent his body through the lines next day, to the great satisfaction and approval of us all. General Kearney was killed by the 49th Georgia Regiment, beloved and mourned by both blue and gray.

"HARDTACK AND TOBACKER."

MATTHEW H. PETERS.

THE armies were camped on opposite hills,
　The river flowed on in the valley between,
The sound of the bugle and fife sent their thrills
　Through the veins of the vet'rans who viewed the scene.

A picket line guarded each river bank,
　And at night all along those lines we could hear
(On one side the Johnny, on t'other the Yank,)
　The challenging picket, "Halt! Who goes there?"

The answer came back at the rifle's click,
　Which in the dead silence rang down the line,
"Grand Rounds;" the picket responding quick,
　"Advance, Grand Rounds, and give the countersign."

All the night through, from the beat of tattoo
　'Til the reveille sounded at dawn of day,
Could be heard the voice of the picket who
　Would challenge each object that came his way.

Those were nights of suspense, for neither knew
　What the other side intended to do,
Though both sides felt that a fight must ensue
　In the valley that lay between the two.

But when the sun in his lustre arose,
　And the pickets could look upon each other,
They exchanged their greetings like friends, not foes,
　And spoke as a man should speak to a brother.

"Howdy, this morning," says the Yankee lad.
　"Oh, bully; come closer, I'm no bushwhacker,"
Was Johnny's response, who, advancing, would add,
　"Got any coffee to swap for tobacker?"

"No, Johnny, I'm sorry that I have not,
　And but very little pork or cracker;
But I will trade with you what I have got—
　Hardtack and hog for a bit of tobacker."

"All right, Mister Yank, we'll call it a go;
　You lay down your gun and I will leave mine,
We'll meet half way in the river below,
　And we'll swap tobacker for hardtack and swine."

They meet in the midst of the stream as agreed,
　(No matter how swiftly the river runs),
Exchanging their greetings and rations, then speed
　Back to their stations and take up their guns.

"Say, Johnny," the blue-coat calls over the river,
　"Who are you, and where do you live when at home?
I'd much like to know, for if you should ever
　Fall into our hands I might help you some."

"Much obliged to you, Yank, that's kind of you;
　My name in full is Coligni De Vina;
I belong to Wade Hampton's Legion true,
　My home's at Sumter in South Carolina.

"I glory in Huguenot blood and name,
　To the Palmetto flag I point with pride,
With the Sumters and Marions I share the fame
　Of the fields on which my ancestors died.

"Now, since I've given my name and address,
　Please give me yours, for it may be that I
Might do you a favor sometime in distress;
　It looks very much like a fight were nigh."

"Thanks to you, Johnny, it's right that we should
　Do what we can to help a suff'ring one;
For even in war we can do some good,
　And feel better for it when the war is done.

"So I'll cheerfully tell you who I am,
　For I'm proud of my name and place of birth;
I hail from the land of the cod and clam,
　The spot to be born in of all the earth.

"Though I'm but a private, I'm proud of my name,
　John Alden Standish, of Mayflower note;
From old Massachusetts my birthright came,
　And I live in Salem, where Hawthorne wrote."

"Well said, brave Yankee, you may well feel pride
　In your native State and the name you bear;
Your grandsires and mine battled side by side
　In days of old, and their glory we share.

"Then let us pledge in the name of our sires,
　Who valiantly fought under Washington,
To still be friends—'tis their spirit which fires
　And stirs the heart of each patriot son.

"Let the issue of battle be what it may,
　We'll bide the result when the war shall cease:
We'll honor the blue, you'll honor the gray—
　Honor shall bind us forever in peace.

"We have learned to respect each other the more
　Since in battle we met as Greek met Greek;
We have tested each other in peace and war,
　And each of the other's valor shall speak.

"But here comes the sergeant with the relief,
　So farewell, Yank, may good luck attend you;
If we meet on the field and you come to grief,
　I hope to be there to help and befriend you."

"Good-bye, God bless you," from a heart elate,
　The answer went back from blue to the gray,
"Your generous words I reciprocate,
　Yet I hope we may both survive the fray,

"And after the war is done, 'twould be sweet,"
　Says the Bay State lad, "and my greatest joy
In the bonds of honorable peace, to meet
　Coligni De Vina, the Palmetto boy,

They meet, heart and hand, to tell the story
  Of generous deeds and valor revealed
On deadly fields where the Nation's glory
  In the mingled blood of her sons was sealed.

And thus may they meet—may their campfires burn
  Bright with memories of duty well done
To the last tattoo, when their children in turn
  Shall raise the proud banner of "Many in One."

OF CARDS.

W. C. ELAM.

"I do not know what it will be," she said, doubtfully. "Another Bible or Testament would seem too much of a good thing."

"Give me these cards," he said.

"Oh, no!" she protested, glancing at him as if alarmed.

"Now, Mary," he urged, turning quite red and speaking very low, "I know what you think; but give me these cards, and I promise you that they shall never be defiled by gambling, and that no other cards shall smirch my hands. I only shall use these, playing *solitaire* in memory of our parting and in hope of our meeting."

She gathered up the cards and placed them in their leather case.

"Be a good boy, Harry," she said, with tears in her eyes and words, as she handed him the case.

He kissed the case, and put it tenderly in his left breast-pocket. And then very quietly, but very fondly, he kissed her. She couldn't help it; and, for that matter, neither could he. The next day Mary Conway waved her moist handkerchief to Harry Norridge as he marched away, and he responded with his cap.

Big Bethel was Harry's baptism of fire. Since leaving home he had taken one "wild tear," and then subsided into a very orderly fellow, much given to solitude and *solitaire*. He was thus occupied when the long roll called him to the fight. It was a tumult and a convulsion; a series of fearful and quick succeeding scenes, only dimly perceived and not at all understood; a hail-storm of musketry, with all the thunder of artillery; breathless rushes and awful pauses; shouts, huzzas, groans, flame, smoke, wounds, and death! The boys stood it well.

"Norridge is down!" cried John Conway, who was near him.

"Take him to the rear, you and Barker," ordered Captain Stokes.

They raised Harry's body and hurried off with it. The ranks closed up. The fight went on.

parting. Both equally sought to make the separation appear pleasant, yet it was obvious enough that each felt most painfully all the possible vicissitudes that might intervene before their next meeting. They had been telling each other's fortunes, more ruefully than gaily, with a pack of playing-cards that now lay on the table, while they sat silent, both filled with thoughts and feelings which neither could wholly dissimulate, nor either would openly reveal.

"I will write as often as I can," said he hesitatingly, "to—to—my sister Sarah."

"And I," she said, "will write every day to brother John, and he will write to me."

"So we shall hear from each other," he suggested, with a faint smile and something of a blush, "even if—if we—don't write to each other."

"Yes," rejoined she; "and that will be better," she added, although as one asserts that self-denial is meritorious.

"You will give me a keepsake," he whispered, for Miss Eliza Conway, an elder sister of the girl, was visible in the adjoining room, where she was thrumming snatches of old songs on the piano.

That was the paramount business, requiring the strictest attention, and allowing little thought of anything else. Still, somebody had observed a bullet-hole in the left breast of Norridge's coat as his body was borne away, and this fact passed from one to another. A brief career! Who next?

Conway and Barker came back pretty soon, and with them came Harry Norridge. The impact of the ball had knocked him down and rendered him for awhile breathless and unconscious; but his carriage to the rear had resuscitated him, and he was little the worse for the hit. The case of cards in his breast-pocket had stayed the ball, and he was again all right. He participated in the glory of victory, and all the more exultingly that Mary's keepsake had saved him.

It was, of course, known all over camp soon after the fight that a pack of cards had prevented Harry from being killed. The chaplain seemed to take it very ill. Surely death should have been all the more inevitable because of the cards. At any rate, it was unorthodox, and disreputable, if not iniquitous, to owe life to such means, instead of to a regulation Testament. Still, the incident plainly showed that to carry playing-cards was "to court death," "to fly in the face of Providence," and the chaplain exhorted accordingly.

"Burn the accursed things," he urged Norridge. "You have had a solemn warning!"

"I don't see it in that light," replied Harry, "and as the cards preserved me, I'll preserve them."

Yet it was to be regretted that some of the more reckless lads instituted a test of the comparative bullet-proof capacity, at a hundred yards, of packs of cards and Testaments.

When John Conway and Harry Norridge left home, it was expected of the former to look after the latter, as Harry was not as tame as could be wished, while John, twenty-five years old, was reputed to have no vices and no ill-habits,—being a sober-sided fellow, with little to say, who was as regular in his ways as a chronometer. But, without giving an analysis of the processes which brought about the results, it is enough to say that John and Harry had not been six months in the field when it was noted that they were exchanging their conduct, if not their characters. War had settled Harry and unsettled John, in so much that the now steady and exemplary Harry was kept busy in looking after John, who had taken to drinking and gambling with the same zeal he had shown in business. And so it happened, in early June, 1862, when Harry had been sent from camp on some temporary detail, John Conway and three of his sporting friends badly wanted a pack of cards, their own, perhaps, having been "played out." At all events, no available pack being elsewhere readily obtained, Conway went to Norridge's knapsack and borrowed the pack he knew his friend sometimes kept there.

At that period the regiment was supporting certain artillery, doing entrenched picket-duty along certain portions of the Chickahominy River and its swamps, facing similar pickets on the Federal side. "Artillery duels" had been frequent enough, but on this particular morning all was quiet, and John Conway and his friends were soon seated on a blanket spread under an umbrageous oak. John knew very well how highly Harry valued the cards, and that they had once saved Harry's life; but whether he knew who gave them to Harry cannot be said. However, Conway was in no mood for nice scruples, and he soon dealt the cards around, scarred as they were.

"Spades are trumps," he said.

But hardly had he spoken (and before a card was played) when a screaming shell came rushing over and fell upon the blanket amidst the card-players, bursting as it fell. The four men seemed torn to pieces; but only three of them were killed outright, John Conway still surviving, though badly wounded in no less than six different places.

"Gather up Norridge's cards for him," he was able to murmur; and then he became unconscious. That evening he was sent to hospital in Richmond.

Whatever may have been Harry Norridge's feelings when he returned to camp and learned for what "base uses" his cards had been taken, he was glad enough to recover them, though with additional fractures and now powder-burnt and blood-stained.

Obtaining leave to go to John that night, Harry found his friend in a desperate condition, and he telegraphed home to the Conways. Before he could repeat his visit to the hospital, the Seven Days' Fights around Richmond began, and Harry was in the thick of much of that great struggle, carrying his case of cards tenderly next his heart.

It was Mary Conway who came to Richmond to assist in nursing John at the hospital, and he was out of danger when the wounded from Malvern Hill were brought in. The matron of John's ward took Mary aside to tell her about one of these wounded.

"The young fellow," said she, "had his right leg badly shattered, and it was amputated here at the knee last night. The double shock has been too much for him, and he is dead, or dying. He had a dirty pack of old playing-cards, in a shabby leather case, when he was brought in, and these he would never allow out of his grasp while he was able to hold them. At last, this morning, as he seemed near his end, and as cards looked out of place on a death-bed, I took the case to my room."

Mary, pale and trembling, sank into a chair.

"The reason I tell you this," continued the matron, glancing at Mary, and then looking away, "is that I thought you might know the young man, or know of him; for, on examining the old card-case, I found on the inside of the flap the name of 'Mary Conway,' which is your name, I think."

"Let me see the case," gasped Mary.

The matron took it from her pocket. Mary needed only one look at it to recognize it, notwithstanding the rubs it had received.

"Take me to him at once!" she cried.

Yes, there lay Harry Norridge, dead, or in a stupor that looked like death.

"Oh, Harry, Harry, Harry!" exclaimed Mary, falling on her knees at the head of his cot.

He opened his eyes feebly. She repeated his name with tender anguish. He looked at her indifferently. But, as he looked and listened, he smiled.

"Doctor, you will not let him die!" she implored, turning to the surgeon with clasped hands.

"You have already raised him from the dead!" said the surgeon.

And so it proved. Mary's voice and presence had saved him. The cards, unable to save him this time themselves, had brought her to the rescue. As Harry looked at her and grew strong, he saw that the war experiences of a little more than a year had developed the pretty girl into a beautiful and lovely woman:

> "When pain and anguish wring the brow,
> A ministering angel."

John Conway resumed his place in the ranks, and came out of the war a famous colonel. Harry was disqualified for arms; but, in losing his leg, he had won wife and home—a happy home, where that battered pack of old playing-cards is a sacred monument.

A STORY OF THE SHENANDOAH VALLEY IN 1862.

THE FIRST PROVOST-MARSHAL OF HARRISONBURG, VA.

C. W. Boyce, late of 28th N. Y. Volunteers.

"When hearts whose truth was proven, like thine, are laid in earth,
There should a wreath be woven, to tell the world their worth."

EVERY survivor of the little army known as "General Banks' Division" will always remember the many charming beauties of the Shenandoah Valley, as it appeared in the spring of 1862. To this division was given the favored privilege of being the first Union troops to march into Winchester and up the valley as far as Harrisonburg. General Patterson's army, the previous year, had only reached Martinsburg and vicinity, in their vain attempt to hold General Johnston's forces and prevent their union with General Beauregard's army on the eventful field of Manassas.

The valley varies from ten to twenty miles in width, the wooded heights of the Blue Ridge Mountains rising on either side, the landscape constantly changing from green meadows and fields of grain to wooded and undulating lands, watered by many rapid-flowing streams. The scene which presented itself to our army then never appeared so lovely again during the war. The harsh order that later applied the torch and laid waste this valley has often been questioned, and it is very doubtful if the national cause was advanced by this severe measure. We saw this "Garden of Virginia" in all its natural beauty before it had been marred by the destroyer's hand. On every side large fields of wheat were waving in their beautiful green; many cattle were grazing on the hillsides; the fruit trees were just opening their lovely bloom, while the houses, buildings, and well-filled barns showed no evidences of the devastation that soon visited this entire section. It was a scene combining mountain, valley, river, and woodland, scarcely excelled in this country.

General Banks' army consisted of two divisions, commanded by Generals Williams and Shields. We had almost daily skirmishes with the enemy, consisting of General Stonewall Jackson's forces, Colonel Ashby's cavalry acting as their rear-guard. On April 17th the advance continued from Woodstock, through Edenburg and Mount Jackson, to New Market, the enemy burning bridges and in every way trying to impede the progress of our troops. At Mount Jackson a scene of destruction presented itself. Here was the terminus of the Manassas Railroad; and the engine house, railroad engines, passenger and freight cars were found in ruins, burned by the Confederates in their retreat, to prevent their falling into our hands.

CAPTAIN E. A. BOWEN—1862.

The advance was continued, and on April 25th the division, led by the old First Brigade, consisting of the 10th Maine, 5th Connecticut, 46th Pennsylvania, and 28th New York regiments, entered Harrisonburg, with colors waving and bands playing national airs.

Captain Bowen, of the 28th N. Y., having been ordered to act as provost-marshal on our arrival in Harrisonburg, had obtained permission to march his company—who were to act as provost guard—in advance of the brigade. We followed the cavalry, which led the division, and thus had the honor of being the first Federal infantry organization to enter Harrisonburg, thus enabling us to have guards posted at the street crossings to prevent straggling from the regiments, as they marched through the town.

Let us, for a moment, make the reader acquainted with our captain as he undertakes the arduous duties of a provost-marshal.

Captain Erwin A. Bowen was a model soldier and could never be other than a perfect gentleman: a man of fine physique, tall and erect, with black hair, quick, flashing eyes, and a commanding voice that inspired his men with the same enthusiasm that controlled himself. Quick, sharp, and sometimes stern when in the active command of his company, in the quiet of his tent life he was charming. He was one of our best disciplinarians and as a drill-master had no equal in the regiment. When off duty, no one could be kinder or more approachable. He organized the company that became Company D, of the 28th Regiment, at Medina, New York, at the first sound of war, and no better organization ever left the State than this became under his able leadership and constant drill. It was composed of some of the best young men of the county. He had commanded a company of the 66th Regiment State Militia for years and was well qualified for the position of captain, being thoroughly posted in military affairs.

The members of his company had loved him as a friend and soon learned to admire him as a brilliant soldier. We were proud of our captain, and he always spoke of his company in words of highest praise. His subsequent career as lieutenant-colonel in command of the 151st New York Volunteers was one of great credit and honor. He carried to that organization, as he had ever exhibited in ours, the splendid qualifications of a brave and gallant officer, and led his regiment into battle with the same unflinching courage he had displayed as commander of his company in the 28th New York.

His modesty and his uniformly courteous manner endeared him to all who knew him. His most intimate associates can recall no word or expression of his that could not have been used in the presence of a lady. No man ever had a truer friend than Captain Bowen, and I do not think he had an enemy in the regiment. At his death, which occurred at Medina, New York, in 1889, Western New York lost a highly respected and leading citizen—one of Nature's noblemen. Such was the man who was to be the executive officer of the army, as provost-marshal, on this first occupation of Harrisonburg by the Union forces.

As the division came up, the cavalry moved out, driving the enemy four miles beyond. The several regiments went into camp near by, and Captain Bowen established his headquarters in the county clerk's office, on the Court House Square, our company being assigned to the Court House and adjacent buildings. General Williams and General Hatch, who commanded the cavalry, located their headquarters on the square, the former in the beautiful Bank of Rockingham, one of the finest buildings in the town.

Captain Bowen addressed himself at once to the difficult task of the provost-marshal's office with energy and spirit and a conscientious purpose to do his duty without fear or favor. The citizens were assured they would not be molested, but protected in all their rights; guards were placed in every part of the town, and the streets and alleys cleaned; the post-office was opened, printing-presses started, and every saloon closed. It is said by citizens still living, who were there in 1862, that the good order preserved was fully equal to that maintained in times of peace. The testimony is very general that "Your men were the most gentlemanly that ever occupied the town." Not a drunken soldier was to be seen on the streets, and we had emphatically a temperance place. On the two Sundays we occupied the town, the churches were opened as usual, many soldiers uniting with the citizens in divine worship.

Harrisonburg was the county seat of Rockingham County and the finest town we had seen in the valley. It contained—besides the Court House, situated in the centre of the public square, which was a beautiful park—several stores, two or three hotels, half a dozen churches, two printing offices, and many fine residences. While not so large, this town was far superior in appearance to Winchester. A very interesting feature on the square was the mammoth spring, situated at one side and covered with a dome-shaped roof, supported by eight pillars. Stone steps descended to the water; a large stream, clear as crystal, was running from this spring, and it was constantly surrounded by thirsty soldiers. Many estimated that the discharge of water was nearly a thousand barrels an hour.

At first the citizens were very much alarmed. They had the natural prejudices against the Yankee soldiers and had become so frightened that many had deserted their homes, while others, if they saw our entry into the place at all, must have done so from behind drawn curtains or closed blinds, as few persons were to be seen. They had little respect for our army, which had come into their midst declaring martial law and taking forcible possession of their town, and had naturally feared our visit would be one of pillage. When they saw the protection given them in life and property, the many special acts of kindness shown them by the provost-marshal, and the orderly conduct of the soldiers, they learned that the invading army were actuated by no feelings of hatred or animosity against them as peaceful citizens, but were fighting to save the Union from disruption. They daily became more friendly and soon made the captain's acquaintance. Many had business with him, and all, whether officially or socially, found him uniformly courteous and obliging. He would not allow them to be interfered with in the transaction of their usual business, and any wrongs perpetrated on them were promptly redressed.

Besides these general acts for the protection of their interests, others could be recalled that endeared him to the citizens in an especial manner. A few such will suffice. A citizen had

been arrested for some slight cause and started down the valley as a prisoner. It was brought to the captain's notice that his wife was very ill and her life in great danger from the excitement of his arrest. Captain Bowen, by unusual effort, procured his release and return to the bedside of his wife, to her great relief and gratitude.

A Confederate officer, Captain E. A. Shands, had been killed outside our lines, in the eastern portion of the county. He had been a resident of Harrisonburg, and his wife, hearing of his death, visited the provost-marshal's office to procure, if possible, permission to go and bring in her husband's body for burial in the village cemetery. This, in the exciting times of war, was an unusual request, and it was with great difficulty that the general in command could be persuaded to allow Captain Bowen to grant the permit. The correspondence between the two officers is said to have been very warm, the general at first returning the paper unsigned, with this question : "Why —— —— do you ask for such an order?" It was returned again by Captain Bowen, with the following endorsement: "I did not enter the service to fight dead men, women, or children." This time the order came back approved, and the widow was allowed to

COURT HOUSE AND PUBLIC SQUARE, HARRISONBURG, VA.

COLONEL E. A. BOWEN—1880.

go on her sad errand, provided by the captain with an escort and ambulance for the return of the body. Thus he showed his humane spirit and kindliness, and each day the respect and gratitude of the citizens for him increased.

In the midst of these pleasant surroundings, the time passed all too quickly, and just as we had become accustomed to our new duties as provost-guard, came the sudden order to march, and, to the great surprise of all, we started down the valley instead of in the advance!

Our purpose, however, is to follow the history of the army only so far as it concerns our story. General Banks' division soon became a part of the "Army of Virginia," commanded by General John Pope, and we left the Shenandoah Valley for the vicinity of Culpepper. To the unusual and severe orders of this general, whose "headquarters were in the saddle," we must here refer, as they have much to do with our article.

This Western officer had just been transferred, and had introduced himself to the Army of the Potomac by the bombastic address which is so well known—that we must "discard all ideas of lines of retreat, etc."; that under *his* superior leadership "we should see only the backs of the enemy, as his policy would be one of attack, and not defence." He had evidently not learned the ancient maxim of soldiers, "not to despise your enemy." The sneering tone of this address was considered a reflection on this army's previous history and strategy, and brought upon this general the dislike, if not the contempt, of the soldiers. Many orders especially offensive to the Confederate authorities followed; citizens were to be held responsible for any damage to railroads, etc., in their vicinity; those not taking the oath of allegiance were to be sent South, and if again found within our lines, to be treated as spies, and shot; and many others of a like character. Such orders were considered infamous by the Confederate authorities, and in retaliation similar ones were issued by them against any officers captured from General Pope's army, who were to be held as felons, and not to receive the usual treatment accorded to prisoners of war.

About the time these orders were published, our division marched out from Culpepper, and was soon engaged in the battle of Cedar Mountain.

General Banks claimed he fought this battle under positive orders from General Pope to "attack the enemy immediately, and be reinforced from Culpepper." That he was not so reinforced, and that his division suffered defeat, was no fault of the troops composing his command. Abundant reinforcements were near, and yet we were allowed to be greatly outnumbered by General Jackson's forces. At this battle, Captain Bowen was taken prisoner, with many others of our regiment and brigade, after having bravely borne their part in the unequal contest, in which nearly every line officer of our regiment was either killed, wounded, or taken prisoner.

General Halleck, general-in-chief of the army, in his address to General Pope, on this battle, said: "Your troops have covered themselves with glory, and Cedar Mountain will be known in history as one of the great battle-fields of the war;" and General Williams, the division commander, in his report of the battle, claims that "a combat more persistent or heroic can scarcely be found in the history of the war."

Captain Bowen and other soldiers captured at Cedar Mountain were taken to Richmond and incarcerated in Libby Prison. Soon after arriving there, an order was issued from the Confederate War Department that all officers from General Pope's army, in accordance with the orders previously referred to, should be allowed no intercourse with other prisoners, but be treated as common felons. The captain and the other officers were at once taken to rooms more secure in the prison, had additional guards placed over them, and also informed that they were not entitled to the benefit of cartel, for parole and exchange as prisoners of war, but were to be held as hostages, and in the event of any citizen being executed by virtue of the orders of General Pope, would be shot—man for man. This, they learned, was in retaliation for the severe measures proposed by this officer. The prisoners had yet to learn that General Pope, who was the cause of their present unfortunate condition, had been relieved of the command of the army, and been succeeded by General McClellan.

Their condition and feelings can be imagined, daily fearing that the order for their execution would be issued. In the midst of this anxiety, the guard one day called for Captain Bowen, of the 28th New York. Surely, this is the first victim, is the thought of all. The captain was brought before Captain Wirtz, then in charge of Libby Prison, who handed him the following paper:

H'DQ'RS DEPARTMENT HENRICO,
    RICHMOND, VA., Sept. 11. 1862.
CAPTAIN ERWIN A. BOWEN,
        C. S. Military Prison.
Sir:—I am instructed by the general commanding this department, to inform you that, in consideration of your kind treatment of our citizens while acting as provost-marshal at Harrisonburg, the Secretary of War has directed that you be treated as a prisoner of war, to be exchanged at an early day.
        Respectfully,
            W. S. WINDER, A. A. G.

With feelings of gratitude and joy at his release, he tried to find to whom he was indebted for this unusual order. This General W. S. Winder, who had signed his release, was the father of General Chas. S. Winder, of the Confederate army, killed at Cedar Mountain, while bravely trying to repel the charge made by our brigade. General Winder would give no information beyond the fact of the order, and the captain could learn nothing more. It was so unpopular to show sympathy for General Pope's officers, that General Winder was not at liberty to disclose any names. Not until long afterwards did he find that this kindness was the result of the action of the citizens of Harrisonburg, but we give the facts here as they have been verified since by some of the participants.

His friends there saw, among a list of prisoners received at Richmond, the name of their former provost-marshal, Captain Bowen, and learned that he, as one of General Pope's officers, had been subjected to the retaliatory orders of the Confederate authorities. They had called a meeting, circulated a petition in his behalf—which was signed by many citizens—had appointed a committee to visit Richmond, and, if possible, secure his release on parole and his early exchange. They visited Jefferson Davis, and their mission was successful in securing the above order for the captain's release. Among the citizens who were instrumental in this action, were Mr. Allen C. Bryan, a prominent member of the bar of Harrisonburg, Mr. E. J. Sullivan, postmaster there in later years, L. W. Gambill,

MAMMOTH SPRING, HARRISONBURG, VA.

county clerk, A. S. Gray, Andrew Lewis, Sam'l Shacklett, Isaac Hardesty, D. M. Switzer, A. C. Rohr, and others.

Captain Bowen was granted the freedom of Richmond on his parole, which he improved by visiting many places of interest, and in a few days he was exchanged. Then came the question of leaving his comrades behind. In correspondence with the writer on the subject years afterward, he said: "Feelings of duty and honor suggested remaining and taking my chances with my brother officers, but they urged me to go. 'No good can be accomplished by remaining in prison; going to Washington may benefit all.'" Before leaving the prison, he arranged a cipher by which he could inform them of the result of his efforts at Washington in their behalf. The prisoners, in the cipher, were to represent Captain Wilkins' *horse;* if they were to be exchanged soon, the captain would write, " The horse had been turned out to *pasture;*" if not, " The horse had been *stabled.*" He was soon on his way to Washington, where he immediately made known the sufferings of his companions in Richmond to President Lincoln, the Secretary of War, and Adjutant-General Thomas. In his interview with Secretary Stanton, he asked what word he could send his companions as to their speedy release. The Secretary turned upon him fiercely, with the response, " Would you *presume,* sir, to send such information through the mails?" Upon being informed of the cipher agreed on, he said, " Oh, very well! You may say to your comrades that they are soon to be exchanged!" The cipher letter was at once forwarded to Libby Prison. The guards there must have wondered what had possessed the "Yanks," as they made the grim old walls ring with their shouts of joy at the glorious news. Their expectations were very soon realized, and within a few weeks all were released and exchanged.

The modesty of the captain, and his generous nature in not taking all the praise to himself but sharing it with the members of his company who assisted in maintaining order at Harrisonburg, is shown in the following extract from the letter above referred to, written by him in 1884: "Thus, you see, the soldierly, manly course and conduct of the members of old Company D, at Harrisonburg, not only benefited me as their captain, but improved the condition and hastened the release of those outside our company and regiment."

Ten years since, when the survivors of the 28th New York made their memorable trip to Virginia, to renew their acquaintance with the field, a stop was made for several hours at Harrisonburg, that the citizens might show in a public manner their appreciation of Captain Bowen. The town was gaily decorated with flags and bunting, a public reception was given and lunch prepared on the Court House Square. Mayor Bryan, son of Allen C. Bryan, who had been instrumental in securing the captain's release from Libby Prison, made a speech of hearty welcome to all and personal eulogy of the captain. Captain Bowen responded, with much feeling, and the ovation which followed showed that he still held a warm place in the hearts of his Southern friends. Every member of the regiment present was gratified to see the honors thus shown him, and no one who ever knew Captain Bowen, either as soldier or as citizen, will say this feeble tribute to his memory is in any manner overdrawn.

Halleck's words in memory of his friend Drake can be said so truly of Captain Bowen, that we use them in closing as we did in opening:

> " Green be the turf above thee,
> Friend of my better days;
> None knew thee but to love thee,
> None named thee but to praise."

A SONG OF BLUE AND GRAY.

Ervana Bowen Bissell.

A SONG of a pretty maiden's eyes—
　Sauciest eyes of blue—
Blue as the distant sapphire skies
　When stars are shining through.

A song of two eyes of deepest gray—
　Gray as the early morn
Which lies so still in the arms of Day,
　Before the light is born.

A gentle, blue-eyed, Northern lass,
　Tender, loyal, and true;
A wild rose springing from out the grass,
　Sparkling with morning dew.

A Southern lad with as brave a heart
　As man's breast ever bore,
But cruelly pierced by Cupid's dart.
　Could woman ask for more?

Again a meeting of "blue" and "gray;"
　No flash of sword or gun;
The blue-eyed lass is a bride to-day!
　This "war" the *gray* has won.

PETERSBURG—THE BATTLE OF THE CRATER.

A. M. DAVIES, Co. C, 34TH VIRGINIA.

"BY the left flank, forward!" was the unending command of General Grant from the bloody angle at the Wilderness to the closing days of March, 1865, when the calamity culminated on the Petersburg right, and the heroic Cockade City, the Saragossa of the South, fell after a twelve months siege (almost).

Vigorously assaulted, it had been valiantly defended, and elaborate in the highest degree were the defences, for the best engineering skill in the two armies had been employed alike in its protection and reduction. Day in and night out warfare was waged by all the means of modern invention against its death-dealing battlements, from the fearful mortar to the unerring repeating rifle.

Impregnable and invincible in front to every attack, the fall only came from the breaking through of the extreme right flank, under the crushing preponderance of overwhelming numbers. Then, and only then, when longer resistance was hopeless, did its grim-visaged defenders sullenly retire from the trenches they had held so long and at such deadly cost, every inch of which had been crimson with their blood and memorable by their devotion. The defiance of these formidable earthworks in the past seemed to impress respect upon the enemy even when their power of successful resistance was broken, and the long beleaguered troops occupying them moved back and out without menace or molestation.

Beauregard and Lee had exhausted their store of engineering skill upon the Petersburg front, and nothing was left undone in perfecting its impregnability. Earthworks, complete and massive, single, dual, triple, reinforced by curtains, traverses, bomb-proofs, covered ways in flank and rear; *abatis* and *chevaux-de-frise* in front; the angles and salients bristling with field and siege batteries, and amply supported by veteran infantry, constituted this position one of imposing strength—too strong for any ordinary attack, as every attempt to storm it had proved in blood and death, and so resort had to be had to the extraordinary method—*mining*.

The lines of the confronting forces at the crater front were about 170 yards apart, and so accurate were the sharp-shooters that a hat raised on a ramrod ever so slightly above the crest of the parapet was sure to be soon perforated with balls; indeed, ceaseless vigilance was the only guarantee against injury at any point along these lines, and incredible as it may seem, it is nevertheless true that soldiers facing to the front, and with the earthworks between the enemy and themselves, were frequently struck in the back by the bullets just grazing the edge of the parapet in passing over with downward inclination, striking some hard substance behind and glancing diagonally forward. Hence there was not always discredit in being wounded in the back while serving in these trenches.

On one occasion, General Lee, while making an observation, stepped to a somewhat exposed position to secure a better view, and thus stood for a moment at personal risk, when General Gracie, who was in the party, quietly stepped before General Lee, without obscuring his view, and remained thus covering the body of his superior until the field-glass was lowered and the danger over—a simple, quiet act, but showing cool bravery and self-sacrificing spirit.

Sleep under trying circumstances was the feature within these entrenchments; though noise, danger, and death were around during the bombardment, the soldiers quietly reposed when mortar shells and cannon-balls were crushing into the embankments that stood between them and the enemy. Nature's demands could not be resisted, and sleep was one of these, although terror was abroad in the breastworks.

Danger became such an hourly occurrence, that its presence made it jocular with the soldiers. When a broadside would issue from a Federal battery, and the heavy missiles come hurtling toward our works, the cry, "*more bread*," would go up from the near-by soldiers, which meant that as soon as night or a flag of truce allowed, the fragments of metal would be exchanged for fresh bread with the junk dealer and baker from Petersburg; and these loaves were indeed a relief from the monotony of hard-tack and coarse corn-meal, called "grits," and often sour.

Read before the Confederate Veteran Camp, New York, and republished through courtesy of Colonel Edward Owen, Treasurer of the Camp.

By the intuition of soldiers it was known by the useless random firing along the picket lines when the " fresh " troops came on duty, as contradistinguished from the veterans, who were as quiet as possible and abstained from conduct that had no result but annoyance to both sides, for the spiteful spirit of the one would bring about similar reply from the other.

Toward the close of 1864, while the fortunes of the Confederacy were waning, these picket guards for the most advanced posts (those nearest the enemy) had to be carefully selected from men of known devotion. This was a guard against desertion, which was prevalent at that period, but the most of it could be more properly termed " absence without leave," the soldiers going off sometimes singly, sometimes in squads, to see their people at home, who likely had lately given disheartening news of suffering. It was this tale of suffering and home destitution that unmanned the Southern soldier and urged him to hurl his musket to the ground when duty called upon him to press it more closely to his shoulder.

Fresh meat was a delicacy along the lines, and while horse-flesh was not on the ration list, yet when an officer's horse was shot down between the breastworks, the soldiers of the South, under cover of the darkness of night, crept over their works and cut fragments of this flesh, bringing the same into camp and hugely enjoying it ; so much so that a sick soldier in the hospital, hearing of the occurrence the next day, sent a message to his messmate to go out the next night and get him a piece, and to cut it from the " breast " and broil it. (These are the words of the poor fellow's semi-delirium.)

For some time prior to the crater explosion, there were rumors along the lines that mining was going on somewhere, but no one knew where. Countershafts were sunk at various points along the front as a guard against this subterraneous danger, two of which shafts were in front of the very salient exploded, but missed the mine. The lines where the explosion occurred were about 170 yards apart, Bushrod Johnson's command occupying the Confederate and Burnside's corps the Federal position. The natural formation suggested a mine to the officer commanding a Pennsylvania regiment, which was from the mining region of that State and which was posted at the spot where the ground sloped downward from the inner side of the Federal works, thus creating a depression that shielded the work of mining from the Confederate view ; and by the aid of green leaves and branches, the fresh dirt as taken from the gallery or channel of the mine was covered to divert attention therefrom. When this mining undertaking was proposed by this Pennsylvania colonel, General Meade and his chief engineer discouraged it, but Burnside warmly advocated it, and under his urgency it was adopted. General Grant did not take any interest on either side and left it to be determined by the others. The difficulty of the undertaking under the imperfect facilities, and the constant care necessary to prevent detection, were deterring, but this Pennsylvania regiment bravely set to work on the 25th of June to dig the mine, and it was completed on the 30th of July following. The plan was good, the execution bad, hence the crater was a boomerang of the first order. The purpose was to break the Confederate line ; to pass troops forward through the break to Blandford Hill Cemetery, about 1,000 yards in rear of the explosion point, thus commanding Petersburg and being in flank and rear of the Confederate front ; to compel Lee's forces to abandon the extension fortifications thus rendered untenable, and fall back, thus uncovering Richmond on this side and giving up the three railways centering at Petersburg and furnishing army supplies. A dangerous, well-devised plan, and only prevented of execution by the dilatoriness of Burnside's forces in not pushing forward to Blandford Heights and fortifying the same, instead of hovering in the crater chasm until certain destruction came upon them.

A good idea of this mine is to consider a tunnel in which a man could about stand erect, 170 yards long, with a lateral branch to both right and left. The termination of the main stem was under the salient of the Confederate works known as Pegram's, and held by the battery of this name, with Elliott's South Carolina brigade as support.

These branches to the right and left were filled with magazines arranged in pairs, side by side, containing 8,000 pounds of powder, the same connected throughout by a fuse and to be simultaneously ignited thereby.

When this underground gallery reached a point below the Confederate works, the noise above, from spiking down a gun platform, advised the miners that the proper point had been reached, and from this point they completed the mine by running out wings to right and left, conforming the same, as near as they could, to the overhead course of the menaced angle. The hour for the explosion was well chosen—just before day, when sleep is deepest and when the drowsiness of the watch is most pronounced—but there was delay from a defective fuse, and not until two brave men of this same Pennsylvania regiment, Lieutenant Doughty and Sergeant Rees, took their lives in their hands, and coolly entering the mine, repaired the half-consumed fuse so as to fire the train at the next effort, which was at five o'clock on the morning of Saturday, July 30, 1864.

A deep, dull, rumbling sound, like a half-suppressed earthquake, with a heavy cloud of dust rising from the spot of explosion, in which was mingled timbers, muskets, and men, gave sudden notice to the Confederates near this fatal spot that a peril of no ordinary moment was upon them. For some moments the hush of consternation was upon the Southern troops near the crater, and the faces of veterans, who had braved death unflinchingly upon a score of battle-fields, blanched with horror in anticipation of a fate against which nothing could shield. The redoubt blown up was occupied by about 150 men of the 18th and 22d South Carolina and a section of Pegram's battery of artillery; and pitiful, indeed, was the situation of those poor fellows who had escaped sudden death only to find themselves half buried amid the boulders of the explosion and powerless to extricate themselves, bruised, scorched, bleeding, and mangled as they were. Swift upon the sound of the explosion came the rush of heavy bodies of Union troops toward the chasm made by it; and they crowded into the irregular ravine, which was about 150 feet long, thirty feet deep, and fifty feet wide; also spreading out until nearly half a mile of the Confederate breastworks was held by them. To the credit of the Union soldiers be it said that they lent kindly aid in helping the poor, crushed, and mangled Confederates out of their perilous places, and this while a hot fire was opening upon them from both artillery and infantry. From five to eight A. M. the Federals thus crowded the crater chasm and the abandoned half-mile of earthworks, from which the troops had fled under the terror of the awful upheaval or had been pressed back by the force of numbers, until our supporting traverses and batteries checked their further encroachment.

About eight o'clock a division of negro troops, some 5,000 strong, charged over from Burnside's line and swept beyond the crater front, a distance of several hundred yards, toward Blandford Cemetery, which they appeared bent on taking; but this force became entangled in the complex works and were so harassed by a furious fire upon them from both flanks and front as to force them back upon the crater line. A second attempt was made to seize the hill in their front and thus gain command of Petersburg by the possession of said (Blandford) hill; but the golden opportunity to do this had passed, for the onset was met by a fierce charge from Mahone's and Bushrod Johnson's forces, and the Federals were driven back to the shelter of the crater, in which they took refuge, or crowded that spot in dense masses, which were thus exposed to a destructive fire of infantry and artillery. The effect of this fire upon the dense masses of troops huddled in the crater ravine was deadly in the extreme, and, to aggravate the distress of the Federals, a July sun was pouring down its fiercest rays from a cloudless sky, while no water was to be had, save what was brought at the peril of life from the Union lines in the rear.

For the first time the Army of Northern Virginia met colored troops in considerable body, and this sight had its effect in intensifying the bravery of the Confederates, while the valor of these negroes was beyond question. There were rumors that these colored troops were plentifully supplied with whiskey to stimulate their courage in the first charge, and that their battle-cry was "Remember Fort Pillow," and that no quarter was asked or given; but such reports are sensational rather than truthful, for bravery without brutality was the characteristic of both sides in this fiercely-contested battle.

It may be said, however, that when the white and colored Union troops were crowded closely together in the chasm made by the explosion, under a severe fire and momentarily expecting to be charged by the Confederate forces, then forming for that purpose, there was chafing and irritation between them, for the whites thought the presence of the negroes under arms would so incense the Southern soldiers as to cause desperation and butchery. This supposition was groundless as to the butchery feature, but the presence of the negro, under arms, did naturally inspire and nerve the Southern soldiers beyond any influence that could have been applied, but beyond this there was no effect.

When the reserve troops were called upon to retake the crater position, which was then held by Federal lines, five deep, with eleven battle-flags floating along the front, there was grave fear that it was too late, and it was well-nigh so, for Mahone's brigade met the colored charge, bayonet to bayonet, and forced the negroes back toward the crater; the order from Mahone being to reserve fire until the edge of the earthwork near the Federals was reached, and then to pour it in with muzzles almost touching, and then to complete the deadly work with the bayonet. This was done to the letter, Captain Girardey leading the charge and Wright's Georgia brigade co-operating on the left. Wright was repulsed in two gallant charges, but the Mahone brigade swept all before it, and by one o'clock the final assault was made, in conjunction with some of Bushrod Johnson's command, which led to the recapture of the whole Federal force and position at the crater, and closed one of the bloodiest battles of the war—a battle in which the Union loss was 5,000 and the Confederate 1,500.

The troops participating in this conflict were: Elliott's (South Carolina), Wright's (Georgia), Mahone's (Virginia), Lander's (Alabama) brigades, with portions of Johnson's and Hoke's divisions and the batteries of Wright, Haskell, Lampkin, Gibbs, Langhorne, and Preston. Burnside's corps, with portions of the 5th and 2d in supporting range, were upon the Union side.

Where such stubborn fighting was general on both sides, the instances of individual valor were equally marked. Notice has already been taken of the cool bravery of the Pennsylvania officers in entering the mine and relighting the half-consumed fuse; but this was only one of the many brave deeds of this eventful day. There was Lieutenant Pennell, of Burnside's colored division, killed with the battle-flag in his hand, and the flag taken by a private of the 41st Virginia; Chamberlayne, leaving a sick bed, and fighting the guns, which the cowardly cannoniers abandoned early in the day; also Preston, of the Wise brigade, manning with his artillery-trained infantry similarly deserted guns, and falling dead (apparently) while working the same at short deadly range upon the crater's occupants.

To the ladies of Petersburg the honor of a devotion beyond words is due; they were ministering angels to many a sick and wounded soldier, and in all the long, bloody siege, with its daily death harvest, there was never flinching or faltering in these brave daughters. Their tender care and consideration to the war-worn soldiers led not one, but many of them, to do and dare unto the death in defence of the gallant little city that had its strongest bulwark in its devoted daughters.

A quiet, blessed Sabbath followed the dreadful drama of the crater, and the flag of truce on Monday witnessed the burial of the brave dead on the Union side—and the tragic tale passed into history.

THE PROUD FLAG OF FREEDOM.

GEORGE M. VICKERS.

THE proud flag of freedom, unsullied, behold
　How cluster about it the glories of years,
As skyward and westward, 'mid purple and gold,
　In the land of the sunset, its home, it appears.
America's token of faith never broken,
　Sweet signal that flutters o'er mountain and sea;
That mutely repeats what our fathers have spoken,
　That tells the oppressed they may come and be free!

O proud flag of freedom, how swells with delight
　The breast of the wand'rer who meets thee afar;
What home-visions come with the gladdening sight,
　And how fond dwells his eye on each stripe and each star!

Thus be it forever, while oceans may sever,
　Or fate hold in exile, a man from our shore!
Tho' fairer the clime, an American never
　Forgets his own colors, but loves them the more.

Thou proud flag of freedom, so lovely in peace,
　So awfully grand in the dread crash of war,
Float on in thy beauty till nations shall cease,
　While there's room in the blue for another bright star:
From tyrants defending, still onward, ascending,
　The hope of mankind and the envy of none:
E Pluribus Unum, our motto transcending,
　Till earth's constellations are blended in one!

CAPTAIN W. N. GREENE, OF THE ONE HUNDRED AND SECOND NEW YORK REGIMENT, CAPTURING THE BATTLE FLAG OF THE TWELFTH GEORGIA REGIMENT AT CHANCELLORSVILLE.

DARING EXPLOIT AT DONALDSONVILLE.

By "YVAN."

AFTER leaving the Rappahannock, I was ordered to the United States steamer Princess Royal, fitting out at Philadelphia. She was a captured blockade runner and had been transformed into a man-of-war. She had a very heavy armament. It consisted of six nine-inch guns, two sixty-pounder Parrott rifles, and four twenty-pound howitzers. We were ordered to the West Gulf squadron, commanded by Admiral David G. Farragut. We had rather a pleasant passage to New Orleans. Shortly after our arrival there, we were ordered down to the mouth of the Rio Grande, to look after some vessels said to be loading with cotton from Texas. We arrived there and found a large vessel, named the Sir William Peel. Most of us felt sure she was in American waters, but our captain was a very conservative man, and would not act without being sure she was in our waters. So her position was laid down, and Lieutenant (now Lieutenant-Commander, retired) C. E. McKay and myself were landed at Boca del Rio Grande, with orders to go to Matamoras, Mexico, and have the question decided as to the position of the Sir William Peel. The enemy from the Texas shore watched all our movements closely and carefully. We were given a little house to sleep in for the night, by the Alcalde. We were informed by some Mexicans that the last Yankee officers who slept in that house were captured by the Texans, taken across the river, and shot. This was pleasant news to go to sleep on—quite an opiate, indeed. We concluded to stand watch and watch during the night, and to start bright and early next morning for Matamoras. We were disturbed but once during the night. We thought a party had come over from Texas, but were driven back by the Mexican sentries. We started next morning in a coach drawn by four wild mustangs. A Mexican held each one by the head until the order was given to let go, when they all jumped quickly aside, and the mustangs bounded off on a wild run. We had relays about every eight miles, where the same performance took place. At last we arrived safely in Matamoras, having been followed on the Texas bank the entire distance by the enemy. We found that the Sir William Peel was in *our* waters, but the night we left she quietly slipped her cable and dropped over into Mexican waters.

Thus we lost a nice sum of prize money, which prompt action would have given us.

After blockading the river for a while, we were ordered to return to New Orleans. Upon reaching that place, we were sent up the Mississippi, with orders to attack any batteries we might find and silence them, and finally take our station off Donaldsonville, at the mouth of Bayou la Fourche, for the protection of a small fort we had there, called Fort Butler. The garrison consisted of 125 sick and convalescent soldiers, and were subject to constant attacks by small parties of the enemy. These attacks were supposed to be only preliminary to a grand attack as soon as the enemy could muster the force. We had a very lively fight just before we reached Donaldsonville. The enemy had embrasures cut in the levee at College Point, and they certainly gave us a very warm reception. Their shot entered one side of us and went out of the other. The vessel's sides were constructed of one-fourth-inch iron, and this was all the protection we had. We fought them for about two hours, when we succeeded in silencing them. On our arrival at Donaldsonville, we were informed that the enemy was massing troops, and the commandant of Fort Butler, Major Bullard, informed our captain that he was daily expecting an attack. I spent most of my time on shore. I had a speedy little black horse, and used to get as near the enemy's pickets as possible, for the purpose of getting information. In this I was greatly assisted by a gallant young officer, Acting Ensign (now Lieutenant-Commander, retired) F. A. Miller. He was then a mere boy, but utterly fearless. He too was mounted.

About this time the enemy sent in a flag of truce and demanded the surrender of the fort and town. This demand was, as a matter of course, refused. We were then given three days in which to remove the women and children from the town. I went ashore without giving anybody information as to what I proposed doing. When ashore I disguised myself as a refugee from New Orleans and a prisoner aboard the gunboat. I watched my chance and ran through our own pickets. They promptly fired on me, and I narrowly escaped being shot. The enemy's pickets received me with open arms. I told my story, and was then asked as to the number of men, guns, etc., in the fort and on board the gunboat. I was perfectly aware that the enemy knew the exact number as well as I did, so told them the plain truth in the matter. This, naturally, gave them full confidence in me. I remained with them all day and part of the next night. I began to fancy they were losing confidence in me. I had already found out when and how they were to attack us, and thought it a good time to get back, if possible, with a whole skin. I lay down to sleep at "taps," and as soon as everything was quiet I edged away from the place slowly and carefully. I had a presentiment that if I remained till morning, I would be found out. I got safely away and rapidly increased my pace in the direction of Plaquemine. Shortly after daybreak, when, I should judge, about three miles from the river, I saw a small party of the enemy approaching from up the river. I made my way as quickly as possible toward the river. I saw now that discovery was inevitable, or at least I thought so. Suddenly the party struck inland, and I felt safe for the moment, but nevertheless ran like a deer for the river. I suppose I was within about a mile of it when I heard the enemy in pursuit. I reached the levee some good distance in advance of them, and my heart was made glad by the sight of a gunboat. I made frantic signals, threw off my boots and most of my clothing and plunged into the water. I never saw a boat manned and shoved off so quickly. But as quick as they were, the enemy had reached the levee and blazed away at me. The gunboat promptly fired into them and dispersed them. I was quickly taken into the boat and pulled aboard. The gunboat proved to be the Winona, Lieutenant-Commander (now Rear-Admiral) Weaver. I was completely exhausted and had to be assisted in getting aboard. The surgeon of the ship, Dr. Arthur Mathewson, gave me a good, stiff dose of brandy which greatly revived me. He took excellent care of me and soon made me as good as new. I told my story, and the Winona took me down to Donaldsonville and set me aboard of the Princess Royal.

Captain Woolsey reprimanded me severely for taking so great a risk and then complimented me highly on my performances. I told them the whole story, how and when the enemy would attack, etc. I was not, it appears, missed from the camp, and the party I met in my escape was composed of guerillas from up the river; otherwise the plans of attack would probably have been entirely changed.

The next night at twelve o'clock, just as I had predicted, the enemy made the attack, and a fierce one it was. Our guns were loaded with grape and canister, and we played havoc with the enemy. We kept under weigh all the time, and not only kept firing into the attacking party, but also over the fort into the reserves. The Winona came down and joined in the fight. It was fierce and bloody, and lasted a little more than four hours. The fort had a wooden stockade, three inches thick, pierced for musket firing. Our men would put their guns through and fire, and the enemy would fire back *through the same holes*. A party, headed by a young Texan lieutenant, approached the stockade with axes and endeavored to cut their way through. Our grape and canister riddled them, and the next day we found eighteen bodies in one heap and the stockade partly cut. Others of the enemy waded down into the Mississippi River and seized the broken bricks with which the fort was surrounded, and threw them into the fort. We captured all the men who entered the river. It was the hardest fight up to that time I had ever been engaged in. Our loss was comparatively trifling, while that of the enemy was very great. Our ship was full of prisoners, some of whom recognized me, and their language to me was unparliamentary.

I received great credit for my exploit. Captain Woolsey, in his official report, stated that for the information which led to the overwhelming defeat of the enemy, "I am indebted to ——, who was out for three days on his own horse and on foot, reconnoitering *in* and about the enemy's camp." I received a letter from the gallant old Rear-Admiral Andrew A. Harwood, in which he said: "I perfectly remember your capture of Captain Charles Lawson, of the 55th Virginia Cavalry, while attached to the Potomac Flotilla, then forming part of my command. Your gallant conduct on that occasion has been eclipsed by your exploit at Donaldsonville. It deserves a place, however, on the list of your gratuitous, patriotic services."

This was the only position we held between Port Hudson and New Orleans, and it was of the greatest importance that we should keep it. I knew we could not hold out against the force about to attack us, unless fighting under some great advantage, and that is the reason I took the risks I did.

GENERAL GORDON AT APPOMATTOX.

Edwin D. Newton, M. D., late surgeon A. N. V.

AFTER the death of General "Stonewall" Jackson, General John B. Gordon may be said to have been the "right hand" of General Lee, owing to his thorough knowledge of strategy, his habits of watchfulness of the movements of the enemy, and the irresistible dash with which he led his daring veterans upon the field of battle.

General Gordon is a born soldier, a true son of Mars. He is as modest as he is brave, and, of course, in his recent lectures did not tell of his own many deeds of valor, as they were witnessed or known to the veterans of Lee's army. I was at Appomattox and beg leave to mention a few incidents connected with the gallant Gordon:

By order of Surgeon LaFayette Guild, medical director of the Army of Northern Virginia, we had improvised a small field hospital for the wounded, from our last "skirmish" on the morning of the surrender. On the day following, whilst taking a little rest from our labors and in conversation with my brother medical officers, we were most agreeably surprised by a salutation from General Gordon, as he rode up to our camp fire. General Gordon and I were college boys together, at the University of Georgia, he a Senior, and I a Freshman. He addressed me in his old, familiar manner: "Ned, get your horse and ride with me, I am now on my way to make a last address to my soldiers of the Second Corps and the right wing of the army."

In a few moments we were facing the soldiers who loved him so well and were ever proud to follow him in battle. Still in his saddle and surrounded by his staff, all of whom were mounted, General Gordon advanced a pace to the front, and with all the winning grace of a true soldier, removed his hat and addressed his veterans. I can only give the ideas in a crude form, for the address, with the lapse of years, is now but a memory of this sad and eventful occasion:

My countrymen and fellow-soldiers: Already has our great commander, General Robert E. Lee, spoken an affectionate farewell to the Army of Northern Virginia. No pen or words can add to his touching and patriotic address. I beg however, as your late corps commander, the privilege of a few words in this sad hour of parting. Let me assure you that my heart goes out to each and every one of this gallant corps in this dark hour of disaster.

Do not doubt, my fellow-soldiers, that the future historian will give to you the full measure of your martial glory. Yon battle-flags, now furled, tell of your heroic achievements. Thousands of your comrades, on almost every plain in historic old Virginia, sleep the sleep of death, yet the death of glory. But few survive the fierce conflict of civil war, and only a remnant is before me to-day, to tell the story of the battles and privations of the 2d army corps—the old corps of Stonewall Jackson. This corps and this Army of Northern Virginia will be remembered as long as the names of Stonewall Jackson and Robert E. Lee will be treasured by a grateful people. Overwhelmed by superior numbers and almost inexhaustible resources, together with the untiring energy and dauntless courage which has ever marked the military movements of the great leader of the Federal army, General Ulysses S. Grant, the Army of Northern Virginia, an army of heroes, decimated by battle, disease, and privation, through four years of almost continuous warfare, will now disband, never, perhaps, to meet again.

With our last parting let me impress upon you one or two thoughts, which I trust will go with you to your homes and firesides. Remember that in God's providence we have surrendered not to a foreign foe, but to our own countrymen. In the exhibition of your fortitude in the face of disaster, ever be as great and as good as citizens as you have been great and heroic as soldiers. Ever be the model citizen, as you have been the model soldier. Obey the civil law, no matter how odious the same may be temporarily. Discharge every duty as a citizen to your respective States and to the general Government. Sustain the poor, help the feeble, and succor the unfortunate in your midst, and by so doing you will command not only the admiration and respect of the world, but win the friendship and confidence of those who are now your political enemies. Fellow-soldiers, with my love and my benediction resting upon each and every one within the sound of my voice, I now bid you farewell. May God, in His infinite mercy and kindness, protect and bless you and yours, now and forever.

No words can truly express the touching eloquence and tender pathos of the speaker or paint the scene of that sad parting. It was like a last good-bye from brother to brother. With moistened eyes the veterans grasp the hand of their gallant leader. They retire, form in groups, and speak in subdued tones. Comrade and comrade shake hands and part. Slowly they return to their bivouacs in the open field, where stand the stacked arms, in mute eloquence, the bayonets clasping each other as if in the last embrace of death. The battle-flags, rent with shot and shell, are now furled forever. The 2d army corps of the Army of Northern Virginia is no more, except as it shall ever live in history and in story, in poesy and in song.

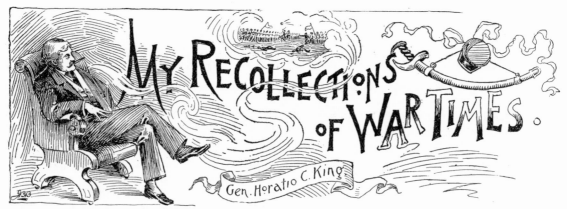

My Recollections of War Times.

Gen. Horatio C. King.

CHAPTER I.

Just now, in connection with the recent dedication of the New York monument, where our State generously aided seven thousand survivors of that battle to be present, much is being written of the brief address of Lincoln at the dedication of the soldiers' monument in the cemetery there. I was at Dickinson College, at the commencement exercises, in June last, and Colonel McClure delivered a most interesting address before the literary societies. He referred eloquently to the great commoner, Lincoln, and cited particularly that dedication speech, which now ranks among the great classics. The gifted Everett was orator of the day, and delivered a masterly oration, every sentence beautifully rounded, and the whole the perfection of Addisonian English. But that address has been wellnigh forgotten, and, as Colonel McClure said, if any should ask who made the great speech at Gettysburg, the reply would be "Lincoln."

And yet, at the time of its delivery, it made little impression upon its hearers. Those who heard it have told me that Mr. Lincoln seemed weary. He read from manuscript, in a low tone, and when it was completed, the crowd waited in expectation for more. They were evidently disappointed.

Several years ago I met the venerable and always to be venerated war governor of Pennsylvania, Andrew G. Curtin, at Chamberlain's, in Washington. My honored father, Horatio King, was also present. As we sat at table, Governor Curtin referred to this incident, and stated, as near as I can recall, how the address was prepared. President Lincoln, with Curtin and other distinguished men, came upon a special train from Hanover Junction. Mr. Lincoln had no speech prepared at that time. It was either on the cars or at the Eagle Hotel, in Gettysburg, that Mr. Lincoln drew from his pocket some letters from which he removed the envelopes, and, cutting them open, wrote on them, with pencil,

that gem of English. Rapidly dashing it off, he handed the slips to Governor Curtin with the request that he would have a fair copy made. This was speedily done. The governor returned the copy to the President, and then, to use the somewhat emphatic language of Governor Curtin, "Instead of keeping the slips, which would be of priceless interest and value now, I, like a blasted fool, tore them up and threw them away." I may have forgotten some of the minor minutiæ of the governor's recital, but the account is true in all substantial details.

* * * * *

At the outbreak of the war and for two years previous (being a resident of Washington) I was a private in the National Rifles, the crack company of the city, and one of the best drilled organizations I have ever known. Schafer was its captain, and his superior as a drill officer could not be found. But, unfortunately, his sympathies were with the South, and, as the inauguration approached, the War Department felt nervous about him, and relieved him of the command. The individual members of the company were about equally divided in their views, but it is to the credit of the pro-Southern men, that, while sworn to support the Constitution, they refused to commit any overt act against the Union in their capacity as militia. About half the company, who were known to be sound Union men, were detailed to act as sharpshooters along the line of the inaugural procession, and my station was on Wall's Opera House, on Pennsylvania avenue, between Ninth and Tenth streets, where, with forty rounds of cartridges in my pouch, I spent the time from the advance to the return of the procession—about six hours—with beating heart, awaiting the attack which the authorities feared, but which happily was not made. That it would have been made but for the extraordinary precautions taken by Mr. Buchanan and his Cabinet,

I have no doubt. The light batteries of Regulars in the line had a very wholesome influence upon the noisy secession element which infested the capital.

*   *   *   *   *

After my graduation, in 1858, I studied law with Mr. Stanton, who was then Assistant Attorney-General, having had charge, on behalf of the government, of the land claims set up by the Mexican residents of California. Mr. Stanton was of heavy build, and possessed undoubted courage. He had been a prominent lawyer in Pittsburg, and was a warm friend of Judge Jeremiah S. Black, the United States Attorney-General, who had selected him for this work. San Francisco was overrun with land thieves, who were claiming title to the most valuable sites on the basis of alleged conveyances by worthless Mexican priests. Stanton went out to investigate the frauds, and so exasperated these rascals that he was in constant danger of assassination. For months he did not lie down to rest without a faithful guard at his door. I recall one of these cases and its argument by Judge Black before the United States Supreme Court while Taney was Chief Justice. The dignity of the Supreme Court is not surpassed by any judicial body in the world, and it takes a high degree of effrontery to perpetrate a joke in its presence. The claim was for the land on which the Mission Dolores stood, and was worth millions. The claimants alleged titles through a pauper priest, who started on foot from somewhere in Oregon and landed in San Francisco, where he averred he had purchased the Mission property, and sold it for twenty horses. Black, with irrepressible humor, traced the course of the claimant, who had never had a dollar in the world, and when the court was quite ready to explode with laughter, he seized the occasion and exclaimed, " And this fellow claims that he received twenty horses as consideration for the transfer. What proof is there of this? What evidence is there that the priest became possessed of this sudden wealth? This learned court knows that if you put a beggar on horseback, he will ride to the—your Honors know the adage; but put him on twenty, and where will he ride to?" The court was convulsed with laughter, and, to shorten the story, the title to the lands embraced in that Mission was not disturbed by this alleged equestrian and acrobat.

*   *   *   *   *

I had been with Stanton scarcely a month when the Sickles trial began. The defence tried hard to secure Attorney-General Black, but he declined to take any work outside of his official duties, and referred Sickles to Stanton. No trial in Washington had ever excited so much interest up to that time; and none since, except the trial of the conspirators who assassinated Lincoln, and of the half-crazy Guiteau, who murdered Garfield. The court-room was packed daily during the month consumed in the trial, and a more brilliant array of counsel I have rarely seen in a criminal case. Stanton sat some distance from the table set apart for counsel and alongside the enclosure (prison pen) in which Sickles was kept. Ould was District Attorney, and James G. Carlisle acted as counsel for the prosecution at least part of the time. Stanton had the aid of James T. Brady and John Graham, the eminent criminal lawyers of New York, and of Daniel Ratcliffe, of the District bar, and, I think, of one or two others whose names I do not now recall. There was one scene which is forever impressed upon my memory. Ould had been greatly annoyed by the objections of Graham, the keen thrusts of Brady, and the aggressive attacks of Stanton, whose savage manner, backed up by a stentorian voice, carried everything before him. Finally, Ould lost patience, and, addressing the court, said, in substance, " If your Honor pleases, it seems to me that in this tragedy there has been assigned to the representatives of the defence their several acting parts: to my Websterian and learned opponent (bowing to Brady) the part of high tragedian; to the great objector (turning to Graham) the part of low comedian; to my learned friend and associate from this district (bowing to Mr. Ratcliffe) the part of walking gentleman, and to lesser lights the lighter characters; but to the distinguished counsellor who sits next to the prisoner's box (turning savagely toward Stanton) has been assigned the part of the bully and the bruiser."

Quick as thought, Stanton sprang to his feet and poured the vials of his wrath upon Ould. So rapid and violent was his utterance that the reporters laid down their pencils in despair, and no verbatim report or even an approximately correct transcript of any kind was ever made of his remarks. They combined the rush of an avalanche with the impetuosity of a cyclone.

I remained with Stanton until after he was taken into Buchanan's Cabinet as Attorney-General along with my father as Postmaster-General, and found him always genial, helpful, and kind. The change which came over him a year later, when he was made Secretary of War by Mr. Lincoln, was a complete surprise to me and always inexplicable. He became the very incarnation of bearishness, and offended and estranged his best friends. The strain upon him was terrific, no doubt; but even this was insufficient to account for his almost unceasing incivilities. With a single exception, however, he always maintained toward me his old-time pleasant demeanor, and that exception happened in this way.

*   *   *   *   *

I was in Washington, at the suggestion of Governor Morgan, of New York, who promised to give me an appointment as adjutant of a battalion of light artillery, then being organized by a recent professor in Union College, and a foreign officer of some experience in Germany. I called on Mr. Stanton, who referred me to Assistant Adjutant-General Townsend, by whom I was informed that no appointment of adjutant could be allowed under the act of Congress, except to a full regiment. Greatly disappointed, I turned my steps toward General Casey's headquarters, near the Long Bridge, where I had some New York friends. As luck would have it, I found General Casey much in need of a staff officer, and, taking a letter from him, I applied to Mr. Stanton, and in less than an hour was sworn into the service and assigned to duty on the general's staff. This was just after the Peninsular campaign, and while Pope was floundering about in Virginia, trying to reach Richmond by the always impracticable route, via Fredericksburg. The desertions had been very numerous at this time, and especially of men who had been furloughed on sick-leave. A few days after I entered upon my duties, a refined lady from Germantown, a friend of General Casey's, came on to take her wounded son home for treatment. The young man had been paying-teller in a bank, was educated and refined, and in a spirit of true patriotism had enlisted as a private. His wound was by a Minié ball, which had passed through the calves of both legs, and, while not dangerous, was exceedingly slow in healing. Mr. Stanton had issued a very stringent order against furloughs, and he alone could modify it. In her extremity, the lady called on General Casey, and I was detailed to accompany her and aid in pleading her cause. We entered the War Department at the usual reception hours, and, taking our place on the long line of visitors, finally reached Mr. Stanton, who, black-bearded and frowning, greeted us rather stiffly. The lady stated her case, and received in reply an apparently inexorable "No!" I attempted to explain that she was a lady; her son was a gentleman, and that he would honorably keep a promise to report for duty as soon as his condition would permit. He turned abruptly upon me, and said, brusquely, "I do not wish to hear anything further. I will not grant it."

The poor mother burst into tears, and we left the room. Completing some work that I had in hand, I returned to our headquarters in about an hour, and there was advised of a verbal order from Mr. Stanton directing me to report at once to him. I was new to the business then, and green, and my heart was in my mouth. Visions of court-martial or summary dismissal rose up before me. When I entered the War office and asked for Mr. Stanton, I own to feeling some degree of nervous apprehension. Mr. Stanton at once sent for me, and I was ushered into his private room. Extending his hand to me, he asked, "Horatio, what is the name of the lady you brought here to-day?" I gave the name. "Where is she?" I replied she intended to return home on the 4 P. M. train, and it was then 3.30. Taking a sheet of paper, he wrote an order to the surgeon in charge of the hospital, I think in Judiciary Square, to grant a furlough to the wounded lad; he to report for duty as soon as sufficiently recovered.

"Do you think you can catch her?" said Mr. Stanton.

"I'll try," I replied, my spirits rising with the occasion.

"Well, take this and hurry! But, stop a moment, Horatio. I gave you an appointment in the army to attend to army matters, and I want you to do it, and not to come here bothering me about side affairs." With this remark he shook hands and dismissed me with a pleasant smile. I galloped with all speed to the depot; found the lady; made her radiant with happiness by the message, with which she hastened to the hospital; and from that day to this I have not seen or heard of her. I took the advice given me by Stanton, and did not bother him again until I applied to be assigned to duty with Sheridan in the Shenandoah Valley, a request he promptly granted.

CHAPTER II.

THE rapidity of the pursuit of the Army of Northern Virginia, after the battle of Five Forks, distanced the trains and left our army with scant supplies. I had been sent back to hurry up the cavalry wagons, and reached Sailor's Creek just after the brief but desperate engagement at that point. Many of the wagons being empty, we loaded the wounded upon them (all the ambulances being in use) and sent them with their ghastly loads to Burke's Station, where the principal hospital had been established. Pushing on to Farmville, we halted long enough for a hasty dinner of ham and eggs at the hotel, for which we honestly paid a dollar each (and not in Confederate scrip either), and then hurried on, not even stopping at night, except a sufficient time to mass and feed. It was in this hotel that General Lee had slept only two or three days before.

The next day we had reached a point from four to five miles from Appomattox, when we received an intimation that the end was near and to park a great part of the train, the rest going to the front with a full supply of rations, which were subsequently issued to the half-starved Confederates. We had hardly settled ourselves for the much-needed rest when the rain came down in torrents. The provisions for shelter were not palatial. One wall tent fly for six officers was the maximum, and the end men were partly submerged by the water which overflowed the insufficient ditching on both sides of this scanty protection. But I doubt if a happier or more contented company ever lay down to rest. A big camp-fire blazed with genial warmth, and was kept fed by the orderlies, and little sleep came to our eyelids that night. We knew the war was practically over, and our hearts were full of the thoughts of home to which our lips gave full utterance.

Across the road from our camp was an humble cabin of hewn logs, so common in Virginia, the cracks filled in with mud. It was tenanted by a colored man and his family, and the old aunty (she was everybody's aunty) exhausted her resources in supplying corn pones at fifty cents a "dodger." It must have been about the middle of the day, when we saw far down the road a brilliant cavalcade, and it was not long before we recognized the headquarters flag of the cavalry corps, floating gayly in the rear of "Little Phil." Those who knew the great cavalry leader late in life could hardly realize how Sheridan obtained his sobriquet, but during the war he weighed scarcely more than a hundred and thirty pounds, and on foot he seemed almost diminutive; but on horseback he appeared much taller, his body being somewhat out of proportion to the length of his legs. The advance had the appearance very much of a Mardi-gras festival, for "Little Phil" had ordered all the captured flags and their captors to ride at the head of the column, which was a festive rainbow of multitudinous ensigns. The effect was kaleidoscopic. The line of interested spectators who flanked the road took the review with feelings which no one can describe. They were those not of exultation at the downfall of our foes, but of gratitude that the fratricidal war was over, and that those who had struggled so valiantly, in what we felt to be a mistaken cause, were once more to be our friends and unite with us in rebuilding the waste places in a restored Union. Sheridan, the central figure, was all smiles, and we gave him and the "boys" rousing cheers as they rode by. We were speedily hooked up, and, following in their wake, went into camp at Nottoway Court House.

From the time we left City Point, on the 29th of March, no opportunity had been given us for a change of clothing, the extra baggage being with the wagons in the rear. The Appomattox furnished the first chance for an all-round wash, and the scene rivaled Coney Island in the height of the season. Discipline was greatly relaxed, pickets were dispensed with, and the command was given over to rest and jollification. From this dream of peace we were rudely awakened by the assassination of Lincoln. The meagre news first received intensified the mystery, and the Confederate government was supposed to be responsible. Picket lines were reestablished, and the most watchful vigilance was renewed. Happily the excitement, held in restraint by the perfect discipline of the army, was speedily abated by the arrival of correct intelligence, but the genuine sorrow which affected all hearts it was difficult to dispel. Sadly we resumed our march homeward, and came to a halt at Petersburg to recuperate and repair damages.

Our headquarters (the First Cavalry Division, under General Thomas C. Devin) was in a house near the outskirts of the city, which had been recently occupied by the brilliant Confederate General A. P. Hill, who, at the evacuation of Petersburg, while attempting to make a junction with General Heath, was killed by our stragglers. Hill was one of the best soldiers of the Confederacy, and at Fredericksburg and Chancellorsville showed that high degree of soldierly ability which secured for him promotion to a lieutenant-generalcy. We took one-half only of the spacious residence, the other half being left in control of the owner, a handsome widow, who declined any association with her Yankee visitors. As we had the parlor and the piano, we managed to pass our time pleasantly, though the presence of ladies would have served to temper our somewhat boisterous revelries.

While there I saw General Roger A. Pryor, whom I had known in Washington as a fire-eating editor and Congressman, and the hero of many duels. He was about entering the provost marshal's office to take the oath of allegiance, being one of the first to accept the situation and take a hand in the restoration. His removal to New York, his successful career at the bar, and his recent appointment and subsequent election as Judge of the Court of Common Pleas, are well known to the reading public.

Our stay in Petersburg was a continued round of festivities, marred only by the delay of Johnston in making up his mind that the cause was lost through the surrender of Lee, and in letting us go home to our friends and families. To our great regret, the hope of a speedy return was dashed by an order to pack up our traps and move with all convenient despatch to the

support of Sherman, who was still holding Johnston at bay down in North Carolina. The day was beautiful when "boots and saddles" was sounded and we moved off at an easy gait down the Boydton plank road, our objective point being Danville. The halt for the first night was made at Dinwiddie Court House, around which, only a month before, we had had some heavy encounters with our active brethren. The headquarters was in the residence of a tax collector, or, more properly, a tithe-gatherer, for much of the taxes was paid in produce, which had greater value at that time as a circulating medium than Confederate currency. There we found several young ladies, including a pretty "school marm" from New England, who had been there during the entire war, holding Union sentiments, and at the same time retaining the affection of her Southern sisters. The tithe-gatherer was a genial gentleman, with that genuine hospitality which everywhere characterizes the South, and he did not consider it a violation of his duty to grant us access to his cellar, which was full of barrels of apple-jack, and, under the circumstances, contraband of war. It is but fair to say that we destroyed only so much as we could conveniently stow away under our vests and carry off in good-sized flasks, which each member of the staff next morning plunged into his capacious bootleg. This experience was very agreeable, and we felt like echoing the sentiments of the Irishman who spent days basking in the sun on the grassy slopes of Suffolk and accosted his commanding officer with the remark, "Gineral, if this is war, let us never have pace!"

After passing Ream's Station, which still bore evidence of the bloody conflicts had there, we turned southward, passing through a country which, superficially, exhibited little of the results of the devastating war, which had well-nigh impoverished the inhabitants of that section. At length, our progress was impeded by the narrow, but deep and swift-running Meherrin River. For some reason, the pontoon train had been left behind, and as the only convenient bridge had been burned, we had to erect a structure of logs, and level the steep approaches, which delayed us several hours. But our engineers were equal to any emergency, and labor that would have occupied several days under ordinary circumstances was condensed into a few hours. As the Army of Northern Virginia had been paroled and started homeward, never to take up arms again, our advance was more like that of an exploring expedition than angry war. All marauding was forbidden, and for supplies necessarily taken receipts were given. Our next obstacle was the Dan River, a narrow but unfordable stream. In anticipation of our arrival, Sheridan had sent scouts up and down the river to collect and concentrate, at the point selected for crossing, all the bateaux used at the numerous ferries. They were frail structures, capable of holding one ordinary farm wagon and horses, and seemed wholly unsuited for the passage of heavy

and the constant hammering by the wheels several times parted the chains, and caused one mishap somewhat ludicrous in its character. An adventurous and ease-loving commissary had picked up, *en route*, a dilapidated buggy, which looked as if it might have come out of the Ark. Driving along, in the rear of a heavily-loaded team, he aroused the envy and jeers of his less fortunate companions. But pride must have its fall. The weight of the team was too much for the flimsy structure, which broke apart. Two boats filled with water

"FISHED OUT, MORE DEAD THAN ALIVE FROM FRIGHT."

teams and the heavier artillery. But Yankee pluck was not to be deterred by trifles of this character. The extra chains from the wagons were called into requisition, the bateaux were placed end to end, and held as firmly as possible by the chains, secured by railroad spikes, or staples, or whatever came handy. The boats were shallow, and inclined at the ends to the height of about two feet. The men and horses crossed over with little difficulty, but with the wagons and artillery it was more serious business, for while the horses or mules were in one boat the wagon or gun would be in another,

and sank, leaving the whole layout, including horse, buggy, and driver, floundering in the muddy river. The horse and driver were, however, fished out, more dead than alive from fright, and this unmilitary rig no longer encumbered the procession. Nine thousand men and horses, with a battery and lengthy train, crossed without further mishap, a feat that could not have been successfully accomplished in the face of even very slight opposition. We had scarcely had time to mass the force, before word was received from General Wright, who was at Danville with the Sixth Corps, that

Johnston had surrendered, and the great conflict was over.

Our return, by easy stages, was even more of a picnic, though the strictest orders, involving even directions to shoot marauders caught in the act, continued in force.

I recall an incident of our first day's halt, at a stately mansion owned by a Mr. Marshall. Here I was ordered to take out an expedition with a company of cavalry, to secure forage. We came upon a well-to-do farm house, whose inmates, all women and children (for the male members had not yet returned from the army), were in a state of the wildest excitement. Hastening with a small detail to the house, I soon discovered the cause to be the presence of one of those worthless vagabonds who infest every army. He had gone through all the apartments, threatening the women with death, while he loaded himself down with jewelry and anything of value which struck his fancy. In view of the orders, I would have been justified in killing him on the spot, but it is not an easy thing to shoot a man in cold blood, so I contented myself with stripping him of his uniform, restoring the valuables to the grateful owners, and sending the rascal under guard to the provost-marshal, who dealt out summary though not capital punishment. I have forgotten the names of the ladies thus happily relieved, but I shall not forget their expressions of gratitude, which were overwhelming.

After a short sojourn at Petersburg, we began the overland march to Washington, passing through Richmond *en route*. For some reason never explained, General Crook, who was in command, made forced marches, the first day from Richmond covering about forty miles. A terrific storm came on at night, making the roads almost impassable, and the train was stretched out for a distance of at least twenty miles. The wagons were heavily loaded with forage and commissary supplies, and it was simply impossible to keep up with the procession; so I gave orders to lighten the teams, and thousands of pounds of corn and oats were left along the road to be speedily appropriated by the residents. Thus, almost my last official act in the war was one of benefaction to the impoverished inhabitants of the great State which had borne the brunt of the fight. And it was not without its beneficial side to myself, as it enabled my "affidavit man" to square my forage accounts with the quartermaster's department, which had become somewhat mixed by the exactions of a lengthy and wasteful campaign.

A few weeks later, and the grand review in Washington, compared with which all subsequent pageants have seemed trivial and commonplace, closed the most stupendous and momentous struggle in modern history.

A MESSAGE FROM THE SKIES.

CHARLES KINGLY SHETTERLY.

IN golden twilight, one sad day,
  A soldier of the gallant gray
Is kneeling o'er a mound of dew
Where sleeps a boy who wore the blue.
From his sweet eyes love's hallowed tears
Are falling for those bloody years,
When face to face each, dauntless, stood,
Contending for the masterhood.

"I was a 'rebel' in the fight,
  Because I thought it just and right;
The South I lov'd; her flag was mine,
Her fields and hills and skies divine;
I lov'd her as no other could;
Was not her cause born in my blood?
Against a storm of shot and shell
I fought for country, loved so well.

"But he who in the blue was dressed
  Was champion of a race oppressed;
He died that freedom's cause should stand
Supreme, in this—fair Freedom's land!
Now o'er his mound sweet flowers I strew,
I ask forgiveness of the blue.
I love the flag; I clasp the hand
Of every patriot in our land."

From mansions in the far above
There comes a voice in tenderest love,
A voice that sweetly seems to say:
"God bless the boy who wore the gray!"
In answer to th' angelic voice,
As if to make the world rejoice,
Up through the ether these words flew:
"God bless the boy who wore the blue!"

CAVALRY *versus* INFANTRY.

Col. W. L. Goldsmith.

WHEN a boy, before the Civil War, I was a great student of war history, and learned to have exalted ideas as to cavalry charges. The splendid charges of the French cavalry, led by the dashing Marat and Kellerman, and the crushing attacks of the Prussian cavalry, led by the iron-hearted Blucher, caused my young heart to thrill and throb with intense excitement. It took the sturdy English infantry, in squares, to resist the terrible charges of Napoleon's splendid cavalry at Waterloo.

With such dread of cavalry charges I entered the "late unpleasantness." This idea was dispelled at Cedar Mountain, August 9, 1862,—Stonewall Jackson against General Pope. I was at that time captain of Company K, 14th Georgia regiment, Thomas's brigade, A. P. Hill's division. Our brigade was in reserve, and soon after the battle opened there was much confusion on our extreme right, held, I believe, by Talliafero's brigade. We were ordered to support Talliafero, and double-quicked to that part of the field, under heavy artillery fire. As we went in, Talliafero's men poured through our ranks. A few volleys and a vigorous charge soon restored the line and sent the Federals back to their original position. My company was in and across the Culpepper road, and the Federal "black-horse" cavalry, no doubt on account of Talliafero's confusion, charged down the Culpepper road, but not in it. I saw the cavalry when several hundred yards off, and ordered my men to stop firing, but to load and wait for orders to fire, stating that the enemy's cavalry was charging us.

On they came, in splendid style, to within fifty or sixty yards, when I shouted to the command to fire, and horses and riders went down in a conglomerated tangle. The cavalry hastily turned and went back, some of them having come within twenty yards of our line.

I would like to know how many of those brave soldiers fell at that discharge; but Stonewall Jackson rode up a short time thereafter and led us in person against the enemy's infantry, in the woods some two hundred yards in our front.

We were very proud to have "Stonewall" to lead our regiment, and we easily cleared the field in our front.

After that, we never had the least dread of a cavalry charge, but rather thought it was a "picnic" to fight cavalry, and this led our brigade into serious trouble in 1864. While at Hanover Junction, General Fitz Lee requested General A. P. Hill to give him a brigade of infantry to drive some Federal cavalry back across the North Anna River at Jericho Ford. General Grant had placed some batteries on the heights across the river, and, under their protection, some infantry crossed to our side. When we reached the place and formed a line of battle, the Federal artillery opened upon us, and we were highly elated because told that there was nothing but cavalry in our front. So we moved forward with great glee and contempt for the cavalry, little dreaming that we were to meet a force of Federal infantry.

We ascended a gentle slope, and when within about fifty yards of the top of the ridge a line of bluecoat infantry arose as one man and poured a dreadful volley into our unsuspecting and confident ranks, which completely shattered our brigade, and we could not rally our men, but heard on all sides, "Cavalry be d——d!"

The deception practised upon us, that we were to fight cavalry, caused this "recoil and scatteration"; for just a few days before this, at Spottsylvania Court House, when trying to recover the breastworks taken by the gallant Hancock from the Confederate General Johnston, our brigade came unawares right up to a Federal line of infantry in a thick pine thicket, and received a volley within thirty yards, but did not hesitate or show much disorder, but charged over all resistance.

I always found it best to tell the men exactly what was required of them—never to deceive them. If hard and desperate work was to be done, I told them so, plainly and truthfully, and could depend upon them; but when deceived and they found it out, they would recoil in disgust, and seemingly because of the deception practised.

SHILOH, AFTER THIRTY-TWO YEARS.

George W. McBride.

IT was more than an ordinary group of men that assembled on the battlefield of Shiloh, on the thirty-second anniversary of that famous struggle, April 6 and 7, 1894. Of the Union generals there was John A. McClernand and Lew. Wallace, commanding divisions; and there was also the hero of the Hornet's Nest, General Wm. T. Shaw, of Iowa; also General McGinnis, of Indiana; Captains Waterhouse, McCallister, Rumsey, and Brown, of the artillery, and subordinate officers to the writer unknown. The gray was represented by the dashing Chalmers, one of the two living generals of that side—the others have joined the army of the dead. With Chalmers was Major Bynum, of the 2d Mississippi, who helped to make famous the railroad cut that first day at Gettysburg. There was also Captain Gracy, of Cobb's battery; Major Robert McMechan, of the 4th Alabama Cavalry; Captain Erwin, of the 1st Confederate Cavalry, and others, whose names the writer did not learn. There were many of the rank and file of both sides, with their families; there, too, were the young man and his " girl," busy with the old, old story.

At the Landing, and on the bluff overlooking the river, is situated the Government Cemetery, where lie more than 4000 Union soldiers, the representatives of every command of the Federal army that participated in the fight. The graves were marked with small flags, while overhead swung in its splendor, and in the bright sunshine of the South, the Stars and Stripes of the Republic. A full band from Monticello, Illinois, played national airs. The Southern soldiers were a little careful at first, and looked upon the " Yankees " with suspicion; but as the purpose of the coming together unfolded and the objects were better understood, the restraint passed away and " Johnny " became interested; the coldness melted into a warm, friendly greeting that opened both hands and hearts.

There were various styles of conveyances furnished by the people living in that vicinity, for the accommodation of those desiring to ride over the field. It is a custom of that country to ride a horse or mule-back, and the custom was carried out, for a great many people came from far and near to meet us, and the woods about the Landing were alive with horses and mules, presenting the appearance of a cavalry camp of the old army.

The writer disembarked from the boat at the same spot that he did thirty-two years ago the night before. Then the Landing was blocked with the munitions of war; now it was a sea of bright faces that came to greet us at the same

GRAVE OF THE DRUMMER BOY OF SHILOH, NATIONAL CEMETERY, PITTSBURG LANDING, TENN.

MAJOR-GENERAL LEW. WALLACE, U. S. A.
(From a war-time photograph.)

of river-boats was moored, is now the silence of the river and its banks. The road or cut in the river bank, by which we passed from the boat to the crest, has changed and is wider and made more easy of ascent. The old log-house, used then as a post-office, and the small summer-house are both gone; the ground is cultivated and is fenced; several houses have been built since, and the general appearance of the foreground has greatly changed since 1862.

It is the opinion of the writer that there will come to any one who visits the field for the first time since the war, a feeling of disappointment, and with it a tinge of regret, that he does not find the field as he has pictured it for these busy years since then. All the roads that then led to the

"PAT" CLEBURNE, MAJOR-GENERAL, C. S. A.

Landing. Out in the river, where the gunboats Lexington and Tyler lay that Sunday night and threw their great shells into the ranks of the Confederates, are now seen, passing and repassing, the skiffs and row-boats of the people coming to see the "Yankees"; and where the fleet

various camps are closed up, and the regular Corinth road is the one that you will take in your journey to the front; in this you will meet with disappointments, for you will find the field has grown up to a thick underbrush of black gum and oak, so that it is impossible to pass through in places. You will miss the openings that enabled you to see the coming of the Confederate hosts on the Sunday night, or the rally of their forces on the morning of Monday, as the reformed and reinforced Federals gave them the iron glove.

The writer, believing that he could locate at least two positions, started out alone to find them; but after a thorough search, he was compelled to cry quit and seek some one that knew more of the field than he did. The road is the one thing that will remind you of the

SPRING, NEAR THE SHILOH CHURCH, WHERE HUNDREDS OF WOUNDED GATHERED FOR WATER.

OFFICERS OF THE SHILOH BATTLEFIELD ASSOCIATION AT THE OLD CHERRY MANSION.
(General Grant's headquarters were in this house, and it was in this old mansion that General C. F. Smith and W. H. L. Wallace passed away.)

past; the hills are not so high as they seemed in the long ago.

I passed on out over the ground where the last stand was made on that Sunday night. There is to be seen the remains of the earthworks thrown up by Colonel Webster, for the placing of his heavy guns; further on you come to the forks of the road where the Corinth and Hamburg roads separate; here the country is more like you expected to see it. The trees are larger and there are new clearings, and the appearances are different. The line of Hurlburt's camp is traced more by the ridges and the "lay of the land" than by any marks that survive the years. Taking the Hamburg road, you pass just to the south of the Hornet's Nest, and skirt the south edge of the Bloody Pool and the Peach Orchard. Passing on, you cross the line of battle formed by Hurlburt, Prentiss, and McArthur, in the rear, and to the left of Prentiss's camps, and come to the place of Prentiss's first line formed in the morning; here the field is natural. Peabody's brigade and the command of Colonel Miller can be traced with ease. Retracing your steps to the Peach Orchard, and turning around Bloody Pond, or Pool, you pass by a path to the northward of the Orchard, and enter upon an old road; to your right, as you move to the northward, is a cedar tree growing in a small field—which the 3d Iowa defended for awhile that afternoon— which is pointed out to you as the spot where

General Albert Sidney Johnson died. Still further on, you enter a woody slope, down which runs an old road, overgrown with grass and with the branches of the oaks interlocking overhead, and you are on the ground known as the Hornet's Nest.

Moving further on to the northward, you come to the Corinth road, and turning to the westward

MAJOR-GENERAL ALBERT SIDNEY JOHNSON, C. S. A.

you approach the camps of McClernand and Sherman, and reach the Shiloh Church. As you journey out, on this later April day, you see groups of men and women in and about the church and down toward the springs; here you will find that the hand of time has been laid more sparingly than at other places on the field. The old log church has disappeared, and a new frame structure has taken its place, in about the same spot. About twenty rods to the rear of this church is another one of the same denomination —Methodist—which is known as the Northern church, while Shiloh Church proper is a Southern church, and the two are not united. The parade

and 14th Iowa Infantry on the Federal centre in the action. He points out the position of the 14th, 12th, 8th, 7th, and 2d Iowa Infantry; also the 31st and 44th Indiana Infantry. There are with him members of the 4th, 5th, 52d, and 154th Tennessee Infantry. General J. R. Chalmers, of the Confederates, is also there, and they tell of the charge and counter-charge in a plain, simple, straightforward way, but with a power that thrills the listener as with an electric shock.

Moving up and down that sunken road the past arises before us again, and we see the splendid division of Hindman charging through the close thicket, and the blue line crouching upon their knees with shotted guns awaiting the coming of their foe, and, as the sunken road is reached, the word is given, and a sheet of flame bursts out from the line that waits, and the gray line reels and falls back. Hindman seeks to rally his men, but the fire is more than mortal can stand, and the line is swept back in spite of its heroic leader. Cheatham leads his Tennesseeans to the charge and selects the open field for his line of advance. These veterans close up and rush to the assault; they, too, meet a storm of leaden hail and are repulsed.

THE "HORNET'S NEST" AND SUNKEN ROAD.

ground is called Ray's farm and is used for growing cotton.

Such, in brief, is a description of the ground over which the contending forces fought and surged on that other day in April. You are in the grove known as the Hornet's Nest; it is still, and the Southern song-birds are calling to each other in the thick underbrush where so many brave men died. The writer entered into its silent shadows as a member of a group of Federals and Confederates who had contended for the mastery on that awful field. One of the principal figures of that group was General Wm. T. Shaw, of Iowa, who commanded the 12th

Gibson leads his Louisianians to the attack, and they, too, go back to re-form; four times they move to the assault and four times they recoil from the fire that they face, and are finally drawn off, broken and bleeding, from the fight. Bushrod Johnson and the knightly Maney lead their forces to face the line of Federal fire and are sent reeling to the rear.

The quiet recital of that white-haired old man who defended the Nest was eloquent in its simplicity and power, as he repeated the story of the eight hours of constant fighting on his part. The position of the Federals was just to the rear of the sunken road and in a thicket and on a backward slope, giving to the line the protection of the ridge in their front; at the same time they were protected from an enfilading fire by a ridge on their flanks. This was a natural defence that made their position impregnable to

GENERAL J. R. CHALMERS, C. S. A.

a direct assault. In this hollow the intrepid Shaw held his forces and bid defiance to the combined powers of his foes as long as they faced him. Prentiss and Hurlburt were on his left, and the balance of Wallace's division joined him on his right. You will see that this line presented an unbroken front to the enemy, and as long as the attack was in the Federal front it was unsuccessful.

Standing on that historic spot in the pleasant April day, listening to the story as told, how that other April day comes to mind, with the names of men that have fallen out of human speech, and the sight of faces that have become beautiful in memory. The blue and the gray are both touched by the unseen presence, and in the quieting influences of our better impulses the touch of nature makes us one again, and there, over our dead that were flung along that sunken road as offerings on the bloody altar of a distracted country, intuitively grasp the friendly hand, and in the sacredness of their memory, that is stronger than the hate of the past, we pledge our lives and future to the Republic and its flag.

While the Confederates were being driven back in bloody repulse in the front, and while Ruggles was massing forty pieces of artillery to open on the ground so stubbornly held by the Federals, Chalmers was reaching out beyond the Federal left, and in a hand-to-hand fight drove Stuart, and the left is turned. Hurlburt and Stuart are driven back. Chalmers closes in on Prentiss's left, while the concentrated fire of Ruggles's guns makes the road to the rear of the nest impassable, and the regiments sent to the relief of the heroic Prentiss and Shaw recoil before their savage fire. Anderson and Cheatham are slowly but surely closing in on the Federal right. W. H. L. Wallace hastens to meet this new danger and is shot down. Maney and Russell push to the front, the line of iron is broken, and the men seek safety in flight. Shaw

LOOKING DOWN THE TENNESSEE FROM PITTSBURG LANDING.

NATIONAL CEMETERY, PITTSBURG LANDING.

runs into the arms of Chalmers's men and is taken prisoner, with his fighting 12th and 14th Iowa. Prentiss seeks to elude his captors and moves to his right rear, but is taken, with the remnant of the 12th Michigan, 16th Wisconsin,

MAJOR-GENERAL JOHN A. M'CLERNAND, U. S. V.

18th, 21st and 25th Missouri, and others of his command.

Chalmers gathers up his own and Jackson's brigade and moves on to the front. Cheatham,

Johnson, and Maney join with Cleburne, and the triumphant legions push on over the rough and rocky country. Chalmers deploys his Mississippians and sends them against the bluff held by Colonel Webster with his great guns. Here he finds the united forces presenting an unbroken front, against which his and Pond's columns dash themselves to pieces.

Let no man think that the combined army of Beauregard could have dislodged the Federal army from its last stand. It was then occupying the only connected line it formed that day, and it was in a position where it could not have been flanked; the enemy would have found another "hornet's nest" all along the line and the fight would have gone against them whether Buell came or stayed.

Such, in brief, is the story of the part taken by the left of the army on that first day.

The divisions of W. H. L. Wallace, McClernand, and Sherman occupied the field on the Federal right in the order named, as you pass to the front from the Landing, and each bordering on or close to Owl Creek. Sherman's line was well to the front, facing in a westerly direction, with McDowell's brigade on his right, and its right covering Owl Creek; Buckland's brigade to McDowell's left, and joining Shiloh Church; Hildebrand on the left of the church. Waterhouse's battery was posted to the left and in front of the church, and to the rear of Hildebrand. Taylor's battery was in position to the left of the church. McClernand was to the rear, and his right rested on Owl Creek; his right was thrown back and was farther from Sherman's line than was his left. It was nearly a mile from the left of Hildebrand to the right of Prentiss's camp. Peabody's brigade, of Prentiss's division, was thrown out to the front in the early morning, and there developed the enemy. The gap between him and Sherman was sufficient to admit an entire brigade of the enemy to pass through, which they did, and attacked some of McClernand's and Wallace's men, sent to the support of Sherman. There is a dispute as to whether the fight opened on Prentiss's or Sherman's front, but whichever is correct, this is a fact, that Prentiss fought the main part of Hardee's command that morning. Hardee formed the first line of the Confederate order of battle, with Hindman's division in the centre, and Gladden on his right. Hildebrand's brigade was destroyed in the first onslaught, and Buckland soon fell back, leaving the gap the larger, through which the enemy poured in furious haste and crushed the flanks of the Union force. This strange spectacle is seen: two distinct conflicts going on at the same time, the one in the front of Prentiss and Sherman, and the other in the rear of these commands, against McClernand and Wallace. The Confederates took order of battle in two lines, with a reserve, Hardee commanding the front line, composed of Cleburne's, Wood's, Hindman's, and Gladden's commands, in the order named, from their left to right. Hindman's right struck Peabody in front of Prentiss's camp, and the fight opened in earnest at about the same time Wood and the right of Cleburne encountered Hildebrand and Buckland, while Wood's right and Hindman's left passed through the gap between Prentiss and Sherman, and swept Waterhouse and Taylor out of the road; Gladden fell upon the right of Colonel Miller, of Prentiss's left, and the fight became desperate. Chalmers was called up from the line of support and thrown on the extreme left of Prentiss, whom he outflanked. The 15th Michigan Infantry arrived on the line at the time of Chalmers's advance. The Michiganders were without ammunition, and stood and watched the Mississippians shoot. The useless regiment was ordered to the rear, leaving the flank of the 18th Wisconsin exposed. Chalmers threw the 10th Mississippi on to the flank of the line and drove them. A. P. Stewart's brigade was ordered to the support of

GENERAL W. J. HARDEE, C. S. A.

the Confederate right, and joining Chalmers. Prentiss was beaten back. The order of battle on the part of the Confederates was to turn the Federal left and crush it if possible. The first line wheeled to their left and fell upon Sherman's and McClernand's left flanks and sent them to the rear. Polk and the reserves were sent to the Confederate right, and the wheeling of Hardee sent him to the left, when the two wings became in a measure separated and the battle became two. Cleburne at first became entangled in the morass in Sherman's front, and only a portion of his force became engaged in the morning. Trabue's Kentucky brigade was sent to the support of the Confederate left, and, joining with Cleburne, they made a common cause against Sherman and McClernand, which was in time increased by the commands of Ruggles and Pond. Thus slowly were the overmatched Federals fought back toward the Landing. In the course of the afternoon, Sherman took position in front of a bridge crossing Owl Creek, and stationed the brigade of McDowell as its guard. This was the road by which Lew. Wallace was expected, and the fighting here was between McDowell on the Federal side, and Pond, Cleburne, and Trabue on the other. It was to the death, and stands as the high-water mark on the Federal right on that day of slaughter. The time came when the whole Federal line formed for the last fight with Sherman, McClernand, and the remnant of Wallace,

Prentiss, and Hurlburt, in the order named, from right to left. This line was assaulted by the Confederates in the evening after the fall of Wallace.

It was the good fortune of the writer to make the tour of this field in the company of General Chalmers and others of the gray, and many of the disputed points of the battle were gone over in detail, and the foregoing is in brief the result of the conference.

This reunion brought the blue and the gray together, forming an incorporated company, for the purpose of making the battlefield a national park, wherein each shall have equal and exact privileges to mark their positions on the field, to erect monuments to their fallen, and to join in the memorial services over their dead. It is the commencement of the end. It is the offering of those who fought, of a fraternal brotherhood to the future. It is the burial of the hates and animosities of the past. It is the pledge of national unity for the future. It means much, for the dead that sleep so well beside the Tennessee are the outer guard that watch the coming of the republic's greatness, and in their name, and by the sacredness of their memory, there shall go out into every home, North or South, a power that will strike to the earth any man or set of men who seek to set aside the decree of the God of battle, written by the hand of war, on that and other fields of the Rebellion.

SCENE AT THE GRAND REUNION AT SHILOH, APRIL 6 AND 7, 1894.

A MESSAGE FROM OUR COUNTRY'S DEAD.

Thad. J. Walker.

THIS willing tribute let me gladly lay,
  In memory of our heroes slain
On battlefields where blue and gray
  Met in war's relentless train.

Beneath Virginia's soil they rest,
  In phalanx orderly arrayed ;
Like soldiers still, they, breast to breast,
  Lie marshaled in death's last parade.

Upon each scarred historic plain
  The flowers—"God's smiles"—have come to bloom
Once more ; nor do they come in vain,
  But help to lift the old-time gloom

That once o'erhung the hearts of those
  Who looked upon these mounds so still,
And thought of the great strife's cruel throes,
  As it surged at the monster's will.

Have these martyred forms no voice to speak ?
  Yes, if we'll but bend to hear ;
Then take these whispers to some lofty peak,
  And herald them both far and clear.

"There is peace, yes, peace with the dead," they say.
  "Shall the living prolong the strife ?

And the heroes who wore neither blue nor gray
  Imperil the Nation's life ?

"Was the battle not bravely fought and won ?
  And our blood, was it shed in vain,
That the heroes born since the war was done
  Should fight it all over again ?

"If battle they must for the Nation's good,
  There are causes many and just,
Which call not for the patriot's blood,
  Nor the soldier's deadly thrust ;

"But which loudly call for courage stern
  To war 'gainst *wrong* in myriad forms,
Where a noble zeal may brightly burn
  In conflict with its sullen swarms.

"For higher than all war's proudest gales
  The pæans of peaceful victories rise.
Go, win them, patriot ! And change the wails
  Of your country's woe to joyful cries."

So seem they to speak to my spirit to-day,
  These shades of our honored dead.
Oh, may their sons this message obey,
  And pathways of *true glory* tread !

A DAY WITH MOSBY'S MEN.

Colfax Schuyler.

THE bold Shenandoah shook the icy wrinkles from its morning face and rolled smoothly away before me into the gorgeous forest of crimson and gold, below Front Royal.

Julia, my favorite mare, neighed impatiently in front of my tent, just as the bright sunrise of early autumn was gilding the hills. The morning was cold and brilliant, and the first crisp

CAPTAIN COLFAX SCHUYLER.

frost had just sufficiently stiffened the sod to make a brisk gallop agreeable to both rider and horse.

A thousand army wagons were already rolling away from Sheridan's headquarters, down the famous Valley Pike, to bring food and raiment to a hungry and shivering army. I sprang into the saddle, and Julia, in excellent spirits, evidently thought she could throw dust in the eyes of Mosby or any other enemy who might dare follow her track. It was nine miles to the place where the wagon train was parked, and before I

arrived there the last wagon had passed out of sight and the picket gate of the army had been closed for an hour behind it. Giving Julia the rein, I dashed on at a sweeping gallop until I came within sight of the train, a mile ahead, winding its way through the little village of Newtown, nine miles south of Winchester.

"Mosby be hanged!" I said to myself, as I slackened speed and passed leisurely through the town, noticing the pretty women who, for some reason, appeared in unusual force at the doors and windows. One or two of them waved their handkerchiefs in a significant manner which, however, I failed to understand, and I rode heedlessly forward. Who would suppose that a handkerchief in the hands of a pretty woman could be a sign of danger? Evidently no one but a cynic or an old bachelor, and as I was neither, I failed to interpret the well-meant warning.

I had nearly passed the town, when I overtook a small party, apparently of the rear-guard of the train, who were lighting their pipes and buying cakes and apples at a small grocery on the right of the pike, and who were in charge of a soldier whose uniform betokened a non-commissioned officer.

"Good morning, sergeant," I said, in answer to his salute. "You had better close up at once. The train is getting well ahead, and this is the favorite beat of Mosby."

"All right, sir," he replied, with a smile of peculiar intelligence; and nodding to his men, they mounted at once and closed in behind me, while to my surprise I noticed three more of the party, whom I had not before seen, in front of me.

An instinct of danger at once possessed me. I saw nothing to justify it, but I felt a presence of evil which I could not shake off. The men were in Union blue and wore in their caps the well-known Greek cross which distinguished the gallant Sixth Corps. They were young, intelligent, cleanly, and good-looking soldiers,

Captain Colfax Schuyler was born in Bordentown, New Jersey, in 1835. He was educated at Peddie Institute, Hightstown, New Jersey, and at the age of eighteen years entered the Military College at Bordentown. At the outbreak of the Civil War, Mr. Schuyler enlisted under the first call for volunteers in the 9th New Jersey Regiment, but that regiment having already been fully recruited, he was not permitted to join, but enlisted again on May 3, 1861, in the 1st New Jersey Cavalry, being commissioned second lieutenant. Mr. Schuyler served with this regiment throughout the war, being promoted to a first lieutenancy at Malvern Hill, and a captaincy on November 29, 1863. The 1st New Jersey was one of the first regiments of volunteer cavalry to enter the Confederate service, and was one of the last to leave it. According to official report, the Adjutant-General of this regiment was engaged in no less than ninety-seven actions, including many of the most noted battles of the war. The flag of the regiment was carried through ninety-two of them.

armed with revolvers and Spencer repeating carbines.

We galloped on merrily, and just as I was ready to laugh at my own fears, Wash, my colored servant, who had been riding behind me and had heard some remark made by the soldiers, brushed up to my side and whispered, through teeth chattering with fear, "Massa, secesh, sure!" At these words I turned to look back, and saw six carbines leveled at me at twenty paces distance, and the sergeant came riding toward me, with his revolver drawn, and the sharp command, "Halt! Surrender!"

I remembered the military maxim that "a mounted man should never surrender until his horse is disabled," and hesitated an instant, considering what to do, and quite in doubt whether I was myself or some other fellow whom I had read of as captured and hung by guerillas; but at the repetition of the sharp command, "Surrender!" with the addition of some impolite words and the somewhat disagreeable presence of the revolver immediately in my face, I concluded I was undoubtedly the other fellow, and I surrendered accordingly.

My sword and revolver were taken at once by the "sergeant," who proved to be Lieutenant C. F. Whiting, of Clark County, Virginia, and who remarked, laughing, as he took them, "We closed up, captain, as you directed, and as this is a favorite feat of Mosby's, I hope our drill was satisfactory."

"All right, sergeant," I replied. "Every dog has his day, and yours happens to come now. Possibly my turn may come to-morrow."

They were a jolly, good-natured set of fellows, who evidently thought they had done a big thing; and as I scanned them more closely, the only distinction in appearance between them and our soldiers, which I could discover, was the Greek cross on their caps was *embroidered* in yellow worsted.

I was offered no further indignity or insult and was allowed to ride my own horse for the time out. I was quietly informed on the way that Mosby had threatened to hang the first officer he could catch, in retaliation for the hanging of some of his men as guerillas at Front Royal, and that I would undoubtedly be the unfortunate. With this consoling information I was ushered into the presence of the redoubtable John S. Mosby, then lieutenant-colonel, C. S. A.

He scarcely noticed me as I approached, but fixed his gaze on the noble horse I rode as evidently the more valuable of the two. As I dismounted he said to his servant: "Jack, take that horse," and I knew the time had come when I must part with my beautiful Julia, whom I had ridden nearly three years on many a bloody field and who loved me with an almost human love. Twice during the last three miles as I came to a space of open country had I resolved to dash away and trust to her nimble feet to distance the deadly rifles, and twice the sweet faces of home had appeared to urge me back to propriety.

The lieutenant ventured to protest against Mosby's appropriating the mare to himself, but he was silenced and ordered to content himself with his choice of the other two horses he had captured, which he did by taking both of them. While this colloquy was passing, Mosby was quietly examining my papers, and looking up with a peculiar gleam of satisfaction on his face he said: "Oh, Captain Schuyler, of the Jersey cavalry? Good morning, captain; glad to see you." Mosby then assumed a grim smile and told Lieutenant Whiting to search me. My watch, chain, several rings, buttons, some coins, a Masonic pin, etc., and three hundred dollars, letters and pictures, and a small Bible were taken. Then a board of officers was assembled to appraise their value, also that of my clothing, and to determine the ownership of each of the articles.

When all this was concluded, immediate preparations were made for the long road to Richmond and Libby or Castle Thunder. A guard of fifteen men, in command of Lieutenant Whiting, acted as our escort, and we were accompanied by Colonel Mosby. We started directly across the country, regardless of roads, in an easterly direction toward the Blue Ridge. We were now in company of nine more of our own men who had been taken at different times, making eleven prisoners in all, besides my indignant "contraband," whom it was thought prudent to send to the rear for safe keeping. I used every effort to gain the acquaintance and confidence of my companions, and, by assuming a jolly and reckless manner, I succeeded in drawing them out and satisfying myself that some of them could be depended on in any emergency. I had determined to escape if even half an opportunity should present itself, and the boys were quick to understand my purpose and intimated their readiness to risk their lives in the attempt.

Two of them in particular—Frank McCauley, of Virginia (commonly known as "Mac"), and

"THIS WONDERFUL PANORAMA OF FOREST AND RIVER, MOUNTAIN AND PLAIN."

one Joseph Brown, of Blaser's scouts—afterward proved themselves heroes of the truest metal. We bivouacked for the night in an old school-house. Our party of eleven was assigned to one side of the lower floor of the house, where we lay down side by side with our heads to the wall and our feet nearly touching those of the guards, and thus we dropped off to sleep until the morning broke dull and rainy.

The march began at an early hour and our route ran directly up the Blue Ridge. We had emerged from the forest and ascended about one-third the height of the mountain when the full valley became visible, spread out like a map before us, showing plainly the lines of our army, its routes of supply, its foraging parties, and my own camp at Front Royal. We now struck a wood path running parallel with the ridge of the mountain, along which we traveled for hours, with this wonderful panorama of forest and river, mountain and plain, before us in all the gorgeous beauty of the early autumn.

"This is a favorite promenade of mine," said Mosby. "I love to see your people sending out their almost daily raids after me. There comes one of them now, almost toward us. If you

please we will step behind this point and see them pass. It may be the last sight you will have of your old friends for some time."

The coolness of this speech enraged me, and yet I could not help admiring the quiet and un-ostentatious audacity which seemed to be the prominent characteristic of its author. I could hardly restrain an impulse to rush upon him and

"Try this quarrel hilt to hilt,"

but the important fact that I had not even a hilt, while he wore two revolvers, restrained me. Looking in the direction he pointed, I saw a squadron of my own regiment coming directly toward us, on a road running under the foot of the mountain, and apparently on some foraging expedition down the valley. They passed within half a mile of us under the mountain, and Mosby stood with folded arms on a rock above them—the very picture of stoical pride and defiance.

We were hurried on through the gap and down the eastern slope of the mountain, and, turning southward, in a few hours we passed Chester Gap, finding it occupied by Mosby's men in force, and we were only able to approach it after exchanging the proper signals.

After passing Chester Gap we descended into the valley and moved toward Sperryville, on the line to Richmond, the last gate of hope seeming to close behind us as we left the mountains. We were now far within the Confederate lines, and our guard was reduced to Lieutenant Whiting and three men, well mounted and doubly armed, and our party of eleven prisoners had seven horses to distribute among us as we pleased, so that four of us were constantly dismounted. There was also a pack-horse carrying our forage rations and some blankets. To the saddle of this horse were strapped two Spencer carbines, muzzle downward, with their accoutrement complete, including two well-filled cartridge-boxes. I called Mac's attention to this fact as soon as the guard was reduced, and he needed no second hint to comprehend its significance. He soon after dismounted, and when it came his turn again to mount he secured, apparently by accident, the poorest and most broken-down horse in the party, with which he appeared to find it very difficult to keep up, and which he actually succeeded in some way to lame. He then dropped back to the lieutenant, and modestly asked to exchange the lame horse for the pack-horse. Being frank

in his address, his request was at once granted, without a suspicion of its object or a thought of the fatal carbines on the pack-saddle. I used some little skill in diverting the attention of the lieutenant while the pack was readjusted, and as the rain had now begun to fall freely, no one of the guard was particularly alert. I was presently gratified with the sight of Mac riding ahead on the pack-horse, with the two carbines still strapped to the saddle, but loosened and well concealed by his heavy poncho, which he spread as protection from the rain.

The carbines were seven-shooters, and loaded from the breech by simply drawing out from the hollow stock a spiral spring and dropping in the cartridges, one after the other, and then inserting the spring again behind them, which coils as it is pressed home, and, by its elasticity, forces the cartridges forward, one at a time, into the barrel at the successive movements of the lock.

I could see the movement of Mac's arm by the shape into which it threw the poncho; and, while guiding his horse with his left hand, looking the other way and chatting with the boys, I saw him carefully draw the spring from the carbines with his right and hook them into the

"THE BULLET WENT CRASHING THROUGH HIS BRAIN."

upper button-hole of his coat, to support them while he dropped in the cartridges, one after another, trotting his horse at the time to conceal the noise of their click, and finally forcing down the spring and .glancing around at me with a look of the fiercest triumph and heroism I ever beheld.

I nodded approval, and, fearing he would precipitate matters, yet knowing that any instant might lead to discovery and be too late. I rode carelessly across the road to Brown, who was on foot, and dismounting, asked him to tighten my girth. During this time I told him as quietly as possible the position of affairs, and asked him to get up gradually by the side of Mac, and, at a signal from me, to seize one of the guns and do his duty as a soldier if he valued his liberty. Though a plucky fellow, Brown was of quite a different quality from Mac. He was terribly frightened and trembled like a leaf, yet went immediately to his post.

I scanned the country closely for chances of escape if we should succeed in gaining our liberty. I knew that to fail or be recaptured would be instant death, and the responsibility of risking the lives of the whole party, as well as my own, was oppressing me bitterly. I also had an instinctive horror of the shedding of blood, as it were, with my own hands.

We were on the immediate flank of Early's army. His cavalry was all around us. The country was thickly inhabited. It was almost night; we had passed a Confederate picket but a mile back and knew not how near another of their camps might be. The three guards were riding in front of us and on our left flank, our party of prisoners was in the centre, and I was by the side of Lieutenant Whiting, who acted as rear-guard, when we entered a small copse of willow, which for a moment covered the road.

The time was propitious. Mac looked around impatiently. I wove the fatal signal, "Now's the time, boys!" into a story of our charge at Winchester, which I was telling to distract attention, and at the moment of its utterance, I threw myself upon the lieutenant, grasping him around the arms and dragging him from his horse in the hope of securing his revolver, capturing him, and compelling him to pilot us outside of the Confederate lines.

At the word, Mac raised one of the loaded carbines, and in less time than it takes to write it, shot two of the guards in front of him, killing them instantly, and then turning in his saddle and seeing me struggling in the road with the lieutenant, the chances of obtaining the revolver apparently against me, he raised the carbine, and as I strained my now desperate antagonist to my breast, with his livid face over my left shoulder, Mac shot him directly between the eyes as he could have done if firing at a target at ten paces distance. The bullet went crashing through his skull, the hot blood leaped from his mouth and nostrils into my face, his hold on me relaxed, and his ghastly corpse fell from my arms, leaving an impression of horror and soul-sickness which can never be effaced.

I turned around, in alarm at our now desperate situation, and saw Mac quietly smiling at me, with the remark:

"Golly, cap, I could have killed five or six more of them just as well as not!"

Brown had not accomplished so much. He had seized the second carbine at the word, and fired at the third guard on our flank, but his aim was shaky, and he had only wounded his man in the side and allowed him to escape to the front, where he was now seen, half a mile away, at full speed, and firing his pistols to alarm the country.

Our position was now perilous in the extreme. Not a man of us knew the country except its most general outlines.

The hostile camps could not be far away, the whole country would be alarmed in an hour, and I doubted not that even before sundown bloodhounds would be on our track. Half of our party had already scattered at the first alarm, and, "every man for himself," were scouring the country in every direction.

But five remained, including the faithful Wash, who immediately showed his qualities by searching the bodies of the slain and recovering from them, among other things, my gold watch from the person of Lieutenant Whiting, and over $1100 in greenbacks.

We instantly mounted the best horses and, well armed with carbines and revolvers, struck for the mountain on our right; but knowing that would be the first place we would be sought for, we soon changed our direction to the south and rode for hours directly into the enemy's country as fast as we could ride. Before darkness intervened, we were fully thirty miles from the place of our escape; then, turning sharp up the mountain, we pushed our exhausted horses as far as they could climb, when we abandoned them and toiled onward on foot all night, to the very summit of the Blue Ridge, whence we could see the camp-fire of the enemy and view their entire lines and position, just as daylight was breaking over the valley.

We broke down twigs from several trees in line to determine the points of compass and the direction of the hostile forces and pickets after it should be light, and then crawled into a thicket to rest our exhausted frames and await the return of friendly darkness in which to continue our flight.

The long days and nights and the terrible pangs of hunger and thirst which we suffered on this mountain pertain to the more common experience of a soldier's life, and I need not describe them here. After days of untold suffering, I shall never forget my joy on seeing the glorious old Stars and Stripes and standing once more beneath its protecting folds.

LAST MEETING PLACE OF THE CONFEDERATE CABINET.

WALTER L. MILLER, ESQ.

THE BURT MANSION, ABBEVILLE, S. C.

I BELIEVE it is an open question where the last meeting of the Confederate Cabinet was held. I have seen the statement that it met for the last time at Washington, Georgia. It is universally believed by my fellow-townsmen of Abbeville, South Carolina, that the Confederate Cabinet held its last meeting there. Abbeville lies just across the Savannah River from Washington.

Much historic interest attaches to Abbeville and Abbeville County. Here John C. Calhoun was born and reared, and here he had a law-office and practised his profession. Before the Civil War, it was one of the most prosperous of all

our counties. Its people were above the average in point of intelligence. A great many of the distinguished men of the State were reared here. George McDuffie, Governor Noble, Hon. David Wardlau, Hon. Armistead Burt, Drs. John T. Pressly and Robert C. Grier, and Dr. Waddell, of Willington-school fame; and I could easily add to these a long list of distinguished names. Abbeville County had much to do also with shaping the policy of the State upon public questions. It had unbounded faith in Mr. Calhoun, and accepted his utterances as those of an oracle. In their views, our people were Southern to the core, and above all did they believe in South

Carolina and State sovereignty. The village of Abbeville numbered a little less than 2000 inhabitants, and was noted far and near for its culture, wealth, and refinement. It contained a large number of elegant private residences, and many of these were surrounded by flower-gardens, which, with their spacious grounds,

WALTER L. MILLER, ESQ.

beautiful shrubbery, and lovely flowers, charmed the eye and delighted the taste. The people of the town were noted for their hospitality, refinement, and good manners.

But the four years of warfare made a wonderful change. The stores were closed; business was at a standstill; many of the bravest of Abbeville's sons had fallen upon the field of battle; gloom and despondency could be read in every eye and upon every countenance, while the great Civil War was rapidly drawing to a close. It was evidently only a question of time—and of short time—when the struggle would end.

Mr. Davis and his Cabinet were hurriedly making their way South. One lovely morning, in the spring of 1865, they entered Abbeville. Coming up Washington Street, they rode to the public square and turned the corner at the Marshall House, which was the principal hotel of the town. Here about thirty men were standing. One of them, raising his hat, waved it in the air, and offered three cheers for Mr. Davis, who gracefully acknowledged the honor by lifting his hat in return. This was probably the last time that cheers were ever called for in

honor of the Confederate chief. Mr. Davis and a portion of his Cabinet were entertained at the residence of Hon. Armistead Burt. The other members of the Cabinet stopped at Colonel T. C. Perrin's, who resided just across the street. Both of these residences were splendid mansions, with large, beautiful flower-gardens surrounding them. The members of the Cabinet who accompanied Mr. Davis were John C. Breckinridge, Secretary of War; Judah P. Benjamin, Secretary of State; S. R. Mallory, Secretary of Navy; and John H. Reagan, Postmaster-General.

A daughter of Colonel Perrin, who was at that time a young girl, says:

We were expecting Federals at the time, and at first we thought Mr. Davis and his men belonged to the Federal army; but as soon as we saw Mr. Mallory, we knew from his uniform that they were Confederates. Messrs. Breckinridge and Benjamin were well dressed, but Messrs. Mallory and Reagan looked as if they had been meeting with the hardships of war. Messrs. Breckinridge, Mallory, and Reagan seemed to realize that a great calamity had befallen us; but Mr. Benjamin was more jovial and did not seem depressed. The last named spent a good while out in the garden, admiring the flowers. A Cabinet meeting was held in the afternoon, at Mr. Burt's, and that night discharges were issued to about 8000 soldiers, Mr. Benjamin and his secretary giving these discharges in my father's library.

After the last soldier left, father went into the library, where Mr. Benjamin was burning the official papers. The latter pointed to the seal, which was lying on the table, and said he did not know what to do with it, as he could not burn it and yet he was unwilling for the Federals to get it. Father suggested that he throw it into the Savannah, which he had to cross, and he said he would do so. Mr. Benjamin gave father a handsome inkstand and he gave mother a small box of loaf-sugar and also about five pounds of tea in a little tin box. Mr. Benjamin and Mr. Reagan left their trunks at our house. Mr. Benjamin afterward had his trunk shipped to England, and Mr. Reagan came for his in person, a few months later.

Hon. William H. Parker, a prominent member of the Abbeville bar and at one time president of the South Carolina Bar Association, was at home at the time of this occurrence, and saw Mr. Davis and his party as they entered Abbeville. He says:

That night a council of war was held, at which it was resolved that further resistance was useless, and before morning, at about two o'clock, Mr. Davis and a portion of his escort left for Georgia, crossing the Savannah River at Fort Charlotte Plantation, below Vienna, on a pontoon bridge; and here it is reported that the Secretary of State threw into the river the great seal of the Confederacy. The day after they left Abbeville, a portion of the cavalry escort returned through the town, with a white flag displayed at their head, looking for Union troops to whom to surrender. It was thought at the time that the Federals were near at hand, but they never came to Abbeville. The soldiers threw away a great many of their arms and accoutrements the morning they left Abbeville.

Hon. J. S. Cothran, formerly a circuit judge and for several years a member of Congress from this district, says:

I got home from Appomattox the last of April. A few days afterwards Mr. Davis and his Cabinet reached Abbeville, on their way, as it was then said and believed, to the trans-Mississippi Department. While Mr. Davis and his Cabinet were in Abbeville, a body of cavalry, that had been moving to cut off the presidential party, was a few miles away, moving upon the town. A hasty council of war was summoned and the officers were called upon to say whether successful resistance could be made. The council consisted of President Davis, the Secretary of War, Mr. Benjamin, General Bragg, General Breckinridge, and Brigadier-Generals Vaughan and Basil Duke. The youngest officer, according to military custom, was first called upon to speak, and in the inverse order to that mentioned above they proceeded, in the language of the inspired Elihu, to show forth their opinion. So far as they expressed their opinion, it was unanimous that further resistance was useless. When all had so spoken, I heard Mr. Burt, at whose house the council was held, say that Mr. Davis fell back in his chair, threw his pocket-handkerchief over his face, in perfect silence save a single groan of unutterable anguish, when his kind friend and host took him gently by the arm and led him to his bedroom, hard by. *El ultimo suspiro del Moro.* Hurried preparation was then made for their departure, and, before daylight of the next morning, the party wended their way westward. The last idea of any further resistance was abandoned at the conference just alluded to.

Hon. Armistead Burt, referred to above as Mr. Davis's host while at Abbeville, was a distinguished lawyer, and practised his profession in Abbeville and the adjoining counties for about sixty years. He died in 1883. He was a member of Congress for ten years, beginning in 1843, and at one time Speaker *pro tempore* of of the House of Representatives. At the beginning of the war he was appointed and served as a Commissioner from South Carolina to the State of Mississippi, to induce that commonwealth to cast her lot with the Confederacy. Hon. Ellis G. Graydon, for several years a law-partner of Mr. Burt, says that the latter often told him that the last meeting of the Cabinet was held at his house. Mr. Graydon also says that Mr. Burt was a personal friend of Mr. Davis, and carried on a correspondence with him. Some time after the war our old court-house was burnt, and a new one has since been built on the same spot. The Marshall House, referred to above, and the Perrin residence have also been burnt; but the Burt mansion, now historic, still remains. Strangers who visit Abbeville invariably have pointed out to them Secession Hall, where the first secession meeting took place, and the Burt house, where the last meeting of the Confederate Cabinet was held.

I think the facts stated above warrant the belief that prevails, as I have already said, in this community, that the last meeting of the Confederate Cabinet was held in Abbeville. The statements here given coincide with the account

SPOT WHERE FIRST SECESSION MEETING WAS HELD, ABBEVILLE, S. C.

given by Mr. Davis himself in his book, entitled " The Rise and Fall of the Confederate Government." From it we learn that Secretaries Benjamin and Breckinridge and General Vaughan, who had been accompanying him, were not with him when he reached Washington, Georgia. The quotation is as follows :

The Secretary of State, Mr. Benjamin, being unaccustomed to traveling on horseback, parted from me at the house where we stopped to breakfast, to take another mode of conveyance and a different route from that which I was pursuing, with intent to rejoin me in the trans-Mississippi Department. He had breakfasted at a farm-house near the Savannah River. * * * * * * *
At Washington, the Secretary of the Navy, Mr. Mallory, left me temporarily to attend to the needs of his family. The Secretary of War, Mr. Breckinridge, had remained with the cavalry at the crossing of the Savannah River, and I gave him authority to draw from the silver coin, under the protection of the troops, enough to make to them a partial payment.

So we find that the account which Mr. Davis gives coincides in every particular with the events we have already mentioned as having occurred at Abbeville.

CONFEDERATE RAM RAID OFF CHARLESTON, S. C.

XANTHUS SMITH.

N view of the vast amount of ingenuity and money which has been applied since the close of the Civil War to the planning and construction of armored ships, and the great losses that have resulted to both life and property by their peaceful collisions, it is strange to look back and see how little was really accomplished during that war by either the Federals or the Confederates with their ironclad vessels, in comparison with the amount expended upon them.

The first day's exploit of the Merrimac was the one success of ironclad construction, as far as the Confederates were concerned. Whether she paid for herself in the destruction of the Cumberland and the Congress, and why she was finally blown up without taking any risk in further conflict with the Monitor and the fleet of wooden vessels at Fortress Monroe, are simply matters for discussion ; but certain it is that the Monitor, in her one encounter with the Merrimac, earned very many times over all that was expended in her construction and equipment.

The career of the Merrimac was typical of that of all of the Confederate ironclads—one grand dash or sally, which in three or four instances only, resulted in inflicting any considerable amount of damage upon the enemy, and even in these cases not attaining the slightest advantage for the Confederate government.

In the operations on the lower Mississippi little was accomplished, in comparison with what might have been supposed would be, by the rams brought into action there, though it is true that the most formidable were not sufficiently completed to be considered serviceable. The Albemarle, Palmetto State, Chicora, and Atlanta, though in an ample state of completion each, were brought but once regularly into action.

The Atlanta, in encountering at the outset the Weehawken, of course met much more than her match in invulnerability and weight of metal, and necessarily succumbed at once. But why more was not accomplished with the Charleston and New Berne, ironclads, seems strange, considering the success of the first dashes made by them.

Of the raid made by the Palmetto State and Chicora upon the blockading fleet off Charleston we would give some little account, for the engagement, though brief, was a gallant one on the part of the captains of the blockaders.

The most favorable time possible was seized upon by the Confederates, namely, the only occasion upon which all of the regular men-of-war, except one, were away from their station, and during the prevalence of a thick, hazy atmosphere.

About four o'clock on the morning of the 31st of January, 1863, the dash was made. The first vessel encountered was the Mercedita, Commander Stelwagen. She was a light iron ship, presenting much freeboard, and, like all vessels of her kind, offering no security to her engines or boilers, and with a light spar-deck battery, incapable of making defence against a low-lying adversary at close quarters. She had been

"A DESPERATE ENCOUNTER FOLLOWED, THE KEYSTONE STATE RAMMING THE IRONCLAD AGAIN AND AGAIN."

called from her station some two hours before by an alarm in connection with a supposed blockade-runner, had returned and come to anchor, and those of her officers and crew not actually on watch had turned in. Suddenly the Palmetto State made her appearance upon her starboard quarter. When first seen from the Mercedita the enemy was but a few yards distant. The officer of the watch hailed and received an unintelligible reply. There was neither time nor chance for defence, for even had there been time the guns of the Mercedita could not have been sufficiently depressed to do injury to the ironclad, which immediately crashed her ram into the frail craft, at the same instant firing her bow-gun, charged with a shell, which, passing through to the opposite side of the ship, exploded in the gunner's room, blowing the side out of it and instantly killing the gunner, who was just turning out in answer to the summons to quarters. Other shots followed in rapid succession, one of which played sad havoc by cutting away steam-pipes, thereby scalding the engineers and firemen, and causing such a rush of steam that, together with the in-pouring of water from the effects of the ramming, the impression was that the ship was sinking, and all on board were thrown into con-

fusion. And what crew would not have been thrown out of discipline, taken thus abruptly, in a vessel in no wise suited to cope with an ironclad?

There was no alternative but to surrender at demand. A boat was hurriedly sent to the victor, when parole was given the vanquished. There was no time for better disposition to be made of the prize, for the firing had roused the other vessels near at hand on blockade, and more work was to be done, and quickly done.

The next vessel encountered was the Keystone State, commanded by the gallant Le Roy. Le Roy was quick and bold. He was not the man to pause to consider the odds against him. But the light having now somewhat increased and the haze lifted, he took in the situation at once, and dashed with his frail wooden ship headlong at the enemy, receiving shell after shell as he approached. A desperate encounter followed, the Keystone State ramming the ironclad again and again, hoping to run her down. Shots were rapidly exchanged. Around about each other the vessels flew, but the high wooden sides and in every way exposed engines and boilers of the Keystone State were as mere paper against the shells of the enemy, which, exploding one after another within her, soon set her on fire.

A halt was now necessary on the part of the brave Union commander. He found it necessary to haul off and extinguish the fire. This done, the attack was renewed, the smaller ram, the Chicora, also taking part. But the second encounter was brief, for a shell coming in almost fore and aft, pierced the steam-chest of the Keystone State, a disastrous scalding followed, and the water pouring out of the port boiler the ship heeled to starboard and the engines stopped.

By this time the steamers Augusta and Quaker City, also high, light, elegant vessels like the Keystone State, being attracted by the firing, had approached sufficiently close to exchange shots; and now comes the strange part of the story, for the Confederates, instead of holding

some delicacy about coming in close contact with her, but she was, after all, but a wooden ship, unprotected in any way with iron, and there were two ironclads to cope with her, and considering the complete devastation which they were making with the improvised men-of-war, it seems very strange, as a writer says, if "they did not remain outside of the bar during the day at least," that they did not venture an hour or two more of a conflict in which they were having it all their own way. Indeed, in such haste were they to get back to Charleston, that they did not tarry to make any disposition of their prize, the Keystone State; and why well-constructed ironclads, covered with four inches of iron plating and armed with two eighty-pound Brooke rifles,

MERCEDITA AFTER THE FIGHT.

their ground, made a grand sort of circuit, and put back to a position safe and snug, under the guns of Forts Sumter and Moultrie, being followed, as far as prudence permitted, by the United States sloop-of-war Housatonic, whose captain, William Rogers Taylor, was stationed with his vessel on the extreme northeasternmost point of the line of blockaders, and who, hearing the firing and seeing black smoke, had slipped his anchor and hurried to the scene of action, only arriving in time, however, to give chase to the ironclads and exchange shots with them at long range.

True it is that the Housatonic was a regular man-of-war, and the Confederates may have felt

besides shell guns, should have been in such a hurry to make off from frail wooden structures, made solely for carrying freight and passengers, seems really unaccountable, and especially in view of the testimony of those of the Keystone State, that the shots fired by her, which struck, even at comparatively close quarters, did no apparent injury, and the Confederate flag-officer, Ingraham's, statement in his official report of the affair, that they were not struck by a projectile during the raid.

This ironclad episode certainly did not in any way redound to the credit of the Confederates. They made a dash under the most favorable conditions, disabled two vessels, and just as their work had really only fairly begun, took fright and put back under cover, never to make their appearance again outside Charleston bar.

It would perhaps be unkind to refer at this late date to the farcical manifesto issued by General Beauregard and Flag-Officer Ingraham, on that same day, declaring "the blockade by the United States of the said city of Charleston, South Carolina, to be raised by a superior force of the Confederate States, from and after this 31st day of January, A. D. 1863." The fact is that all the blockading squadron save two remained in their places and held in their possession one of the most valuable prizes of the war, the Princess Royal, which had just been captured.

One or two little circumstances are curious, in connection with what transpired on board the Keystone State during the engagement. One of the first shots to penetrate the vessel passed through forward, under the spar-deck, precisely on a line with the hammocks of four marines who had not yet turned out. It cut the heads off three of them and the feet off the fourth. The latter had just come off duty and had turned in wrong way about. Another shell entered just on a level with the berth deck, cut it clean through and through, until it arrived amidships, exploding there and tearing a hole several feet in diameter; and another, about spent, coming over the starboard quarter, grazed over the head of the cabin boy, who dropped the captain's coffee and rushed down the cabin hatch, exclaiming, "I am killed!" It then entered the armory, taking an entire row of muskets, which were ranged along one side, from end to end, turning them into about a cart-load of scrap iron and splinters. Of all the shells that entered the vessel, only one did not explode, and that was the one which entered the steam drum, and by so doing it played greater havoc than if it had exploded before entering the boilers. We give an accompanying sketch of it. It was fifteen inches long, seven inches in diameter, and weighed 102 pounds.

LEADERS OF THE CIVIL WAR.
JAMES B. MC PHERSON—CLEMENT A. EVANS.

JAMES BIRDSEYE McPHERSON, one of the most efficient general officers of the Federal army during the Civil War, was born in Sandusky County, Ohio, November 14, 1828. He entered the West Point Military Academy in 1849, and graduated with high honors and at the head of his class, June 30, 1853; received the rank of brevet second lieutenant of engineers and assistant instructor of practical engineering at the academy. This position he maintained until 1854, when he was appointed assistant engineer on the defences of New York harbor. After devoting three years to this important work, Lieutenant McPherson was transferred, in 1857, to Fort Delaware, where he was placed in charge of the construction of that fortification, and subsequently he superintended the erection of the works on Alcaltras Island, in San Francisco Bay. Early in 1861, he was transferred to Boston and placed in charge of the harbor fortifications there.

About this time he was made captain, and in November, 1861, became aide-de-camp to General H. W. Halleck, in the Department of the West, with the rank of lieutenant-colonel. From this time on, his promotion was rapid and his skill in practical engineering was of profound value to the Federal armies of the West, especially during the expeditions against Forts Henry and Donelson, during which period Colonel McPherson was chief engineer of the Army of the Tennessee.

In May, 1862, he was commissioned brigadier-general of volunteers, and the following month became superintendent of the military roads in western Tennessee. In September, 1862, General McPherson was on the staff of General Grant, whom he accompanied throughout the Vicksburg campaign, and he commanded the 17th Army Corps from December 18, 1862, until promoted to the command of the Army of the Tennessee, early in 1864. He was placed in charge of Vicksburg after its capitulation, and, as an acknowledgment of his valuable services in that campaign, was given the rank of brigadier-general of the regular army, this rank dating from August 1, 1863.

During Sherman's march to the sea, McPherson was one of his chief lieutenants, commanding, as we have seen, one of the three grand divisions of the former's forces, the Army of the Tennessee, composed of the 15th, 16th, and 17th corps. It was at the battle of Atlanta that this gallant soldier met his fate. During a lull in the engagement, and while the lines of the contending armies were being somewhat shifted, General McPherson, almost unattended, and with the lack of precaution as to personal safety that ever distinguished him, attempted to ride through a piece of woods to ascertain the position and disposition of a portion of the 17th corps. In a few moments after he had disappeared in the woods his horse came galloping back, riderless and wounded, while the brave McPherson lay dead under the trees—killed by a volley from the Confederate skirmish line, which had been rapidly advanced under cover of the forest.

MAJOR-GENERAL JAMES B. MC PHERSON.

McPherson's death was a great blow to Sherman, and was deeply regretted not only by the men under his command, but also by the rank and file of the opposing army, who knew and admired his sterling soldierly qualities. By direction of General Sherman, the body of the fallen officer was taken to his old home in Clyde, Ohio, where it now reposes.

In personal appearance, General McPherson was a striking figure. More than six feet in height, and well proportioned; straight as an arrow, and soldierly in bearing; honest, frank, and winning in manner; bold and resolute in action—these were characteristics of the Ohio boy who commanded the Army of the Tennessee, and closed a brilliant military career before he had reached the age of thirty-six years.

CLEMENT A. EVANS was one of the fighting generals of the Confederate army. He is a native of Georgia and received his first military training through the militia companies of which he was a member in early life. In 1861 he enlisted in the 31st Georgia regiment, and shortly became its major. Later he rose to the rank of colonel, and at the close of the conflict was in command of one of General Gordon's divisions, with the rank of brigadier-general. He was wounded several times, and earned an enviable reputation for dash and courage.

General Evans's life has been less eventful but not less distinguished since than before the war. Abandoning law and politics, in which a brilliant future awaited him, he carried into effect a purpose which he had cherished for some time, to enter the Methodist ministry at the close of the war. He was received into the Georgia conference and served three years on a country circuit. Since that time he has served the principal churches of Augusta, Rome, Athens, and Atlanta.

At the present time, General Evans is Commander-in-Chief of the Georgia division of the United Confederate Veterans, with headquarters at Atlanta, Georgia. His division is a part of an organization that covers the entire Southern States, composed of soldiers, sailors, and other Confederates. The objects of this association are purely benevolent and non-political, and it is designed to promote good-fellowship among old soldiers everywhere. General Evans is engaging his

BRIGADIER-GENERAL CLEMENT A. EVANS.

division in the work of collecting and preserving the history of his State during the Civil War, and is carefully protecting it from being entangled in politics. The relations between the Confederate associations in Georgia and the "boys in blue" are particularly pleasant. It is a significant fact that a man possessing broad national views should have been selected as the head of the United Confederate Veterans in the great State of Georgia. Under his wise and temperate leadership the last vestiges of bitterness are sure to pass away, while the fraternal spirit which should, and in a large measure does, fill the hearts of all the survivors of the Civil War, North and South, will be deepened and intensified as the years roll by.

General Evans rarely alludes to his military career, and always in terms of self-depreciation. Like thousands of other thoughtful, earnest men he cast his fortunes with his State in 1861, believing that in so doing he was fulfilling his duty and acting the part of a true patriot. That he had the courage of his convictions his record on half a hundred battle-fields fully proves; and that he honestly accepted the legitimate results of the war, and at its close became not alone a Georgian but a loyal citizen of the great republic, has been amply shown by his life and deeds thereafter. Nearly twenty years ago, in the presence of a large audience in Augusta, he spoke these words, which reflect the real feeling of the general and his followers: "But the Confederacy has expired. We have buried it. We do not intend to exhume its remains. We were utterly defeated, but we have dismissed all our resentments. Sadly we furled the cross of stars which we followed through many storms of shot and shell; but with the true hand of Southern honor we take the staff that holds the flag of stars and stripes."

General Evans enjoys the thorough respect and esteem of his fellows. The portrait accompanying was engraved from a recent photograph.

A BURNING SHAME.

DIXIE WOLCOTT.

THAT there wasn't a saucier rebel
    In all the sunny South,
'Twas easy to tell by the mischievous eyes
    And the smile of her roguish mouth.

But how she hated the Yankees,
    She couldn't bear the *name*;
"How dared they come and whip us;
    It was a burning shame!"

One of those self-same Yankees
    Came to her Dixie one day,
And ere the week was over
    She'd stolen his heart away.

But how should she treat her captive?
    He couldn't be shot, you know,
Because the war was ended
    Two dozen years ago.

So in order to keep him prisoner
    The rest of his life instead
She reckoned she'd have to marry him, tho'
    "'Twas a burning shame," she said.

IN MEMORY OF THE KEARSARGE.

J. W. MORTON, JR.

THE KEARSARGE ON RONCADOR REEF.

NOW that the Kearsarge has gone to pieces on Roncador Reef, more than half the people of this nation feel a sensation as of the loss of an old and dear friend. Nations are sentimental to some degree, and have their pets, as do individuals. The loss of one of our expensive new white cruisers would hardly have been felt so keenly as is the destruction of the homely old corvette, whose chief value consisted of a certain halo that hung around the name. It was, in fact, the name and the memory that our people cherished; for the Kearsarge of late years was quite a different craft from the Kearsarge of 1864, and her days of practical value were nearly numbered.

When the Kearsarge was launched at the Portsmouth, New Hampshire, navy yard, on September 11, 1861, she was described as a third-rate screw sloop of 1031 tons, built of white oak; length, 201 feet 4 inches; breadth, 33 feet 10 inches; maximum speed, 14 knots; ordinary sea speed, 8 to 11 knots. She was completed in January, 1862, at a total cost of $272,515. The

Oneida, Wachusett, and Tuscarora belonged to the same class. The Kearsarge of 1864 carried seven guns, of which two were of eleven-inch calibre and very formidable as ordnance was in those days. At the time of her wreck the corvette mounted four nine-inch smooth bores, two eight-inch muzzle-loading rifles, and one sixty-pounder breech-loading rifle in her main battery; one three-inch howitzer and one Gatling in her secondary battery. The eleven-inch guns which won renown in 1864 were long ago removed; and the whole vessel had been rebuilt and somewhat remodeled, remaining, however, a warship of the ancient pattern, of little use in these days of steel.

The chief event in the history of the Kearsarge was her historic duel with the Alabama, off Cherbourg, France, in 1864. There are two reasons why this combat has remained a subject of continual interest and a source of national pride. In the first place, it is the only naval duel, in which an American warship was one of the principals, that has occurred since the gallant days of 1812-1815. The operations of fleets and squadrons never possess the romantic interest that has always attached to a battle to the death between two ships of fairly equal strength. Secondly, while the Alabama fought under the Confederate flag, and her officers were Americans, she was built, armed, and equipped by England; most of her seamen and nearly all her gunners were British, and the fight was, in reality, a combat between American and British sailors, in which America, as usual, came out ahead. In view of these facts, the whole Nation may, and should, join in honoring the memory of the gallant old corvette and the invincible American sailors who brought the British privateer to grief.

The Kearsarge went into commission in January, 1862, and was at once despatched under command of Captain Charles W. Pickering, on a search for the privateer Sumter. This vessel was found in the port of Algeciras, across the bay from Gibraltar. Captain Pickering anchored outside the port and lay in wait for his victim, but the commander of the Sumter wisely remained quietly in the neutral port. So matters stood until September 29, 1862, when word came that the Alabama was cruising off the Azores and playing havoc with American vessels. Captain Pickering put off in search of the Alabama, but when he reached the Azores the Alabama had sailed for parts unknown; so he returned to the Sumter. Not long thereafter the latter was sold by the Confederate authorities as she lay in port, so the blockade was raised.

It was not until nearly two years later that the Kearsarge again caught up with the Alabama. She was then commanded by Captain John A. Winslow, and found the Alabama under command of Captain Raphael Semmes, in the port of Cherbourg, France, where the privateer had come for the purpose of refitting and repairing. Winslow anchored off Cherbourg early in June, and awaited the appearance of his adversary.

Up to this time the Alabama had succeeded in avoiding a collision with armed vessels, excepting when she fought and sank the Hatteras, but she had destroyed merchantmen and merchandise worth some $15,000,000, and her name was a household word everywhere. In point of size and armament there was little difference between her and the Kearsarge. The latter was of 1031 tons and the Alabama 1150 tons; the privateer carried eight guns, while the corvette had seven; but two of the latter were of larger calibre than any on board the Alabama. In point of speed they were well matched, but the Kearsarge had a crew of some 165 men, while the Alabama had only 150. It must be remembered, however, that while the combat occurred in neutral waters, the surroundings were all favorable to the Alabama, while Captain Winslow and his men were not only cut off from all hope of assistance, but were in the midst and practically in the waters of nations whose sympathies were wholly with his enemy. This deed of Winslow and his brave American tars, in point of heroic bravery, ranks with the best achievements of Perry, Decatur, and John Paul Jones.

On the other hand, Captain Semmes showed true American grit. Doubtless he hoped to win the victory, but he must have known that the chances were not at all in his favor. As Americans we must all be glad that he did not show the white feather in the presence of the British, who, be it always remembered, loved the Confederacy simply and only because it touched their purse-strings and promised revenge for Yorktown, Lake Erie, and New Orleans. This truthful view of the matter will hardly escape our Southern brethren of to-day, though it may not have been quite apparent thirty years ago.

On the 14th of June, 1864, Captain Semmes requested Captain Winslow, through the American consul at Cherbourg, to remain near at hand for a few days, until he could complete his arrangements for coming out and fighting him. This bold defiance required no reply, for Winslow had already sent a silent challenge when he dropped anchor outside the harbor. The next four days were spent by Captain Semmes in active preparation for the conflict, and about ten o'clock on Sunday morning, June 19, 1864, the Alabama steamed out of the harbor, attended by the French warship Couronne, the latter remaining with the privateer until she reached the limits of French waters and entered the high seas. At a respectful distance followed the English steam yacht Deerhound, having on board her owner, Mr. Lancaster, and some other English friends of Captain Semmes.

Winslow immediately put out to sea, being determined that no question should arise as to the neutrality of the fighting place, and probably to draw his adversary as far as possible from friendly shores. Reaching a point about seven miles from shore, the Kearsarge came suddenly about, her decks cleared for action and her guns pivoted to starboard, and bore down upon the Alabama. Coming within about a mile, the

END OF THE DUEL BETWEEN THE KEARSARGE AND THE ALABAMA

OFF CHERBOURG, FRANCE, JUNE 19, 1864

latter opened fire, which was not returned by Winslow, who steered his vessel directly down upon the enemy, and received three broadsides in silence and with little if any damage. When within 1000 yards Winslow opened with his starboard battery, and planted a solid shot in the Alabama's frame. Then the battle raged furiously for an hour. The British gunners on the privateer served their pieces rapidly, but with poor judgment and poorer aim; the sturdy Americans fired with deliberation and deadly precision. The vessels circled round and round each other, Winslow vainly attempting to secure a position where he could rake his adversary fore and aft with the terrible bolts from his eleven-inch guns. This effort, with Semmes' counter-effort to avoid it, explains the rotary course of both ships, and aided by the powerful current, the combatants gradually drew nearer the shore, until they came within five miles of the French coast.

About noon, Captain Semmes, finding that the rudder of his ship was becoming unmanageable and that the vessel was rapidly filling, set all sail and headed for the coast, hoping to reach neutral waters and protection. The Kearsarge, still in good form and not much damaged, frustrated this design by running across the bows of the Alabama, where she could rake the doomed craft with her heavy guns. At this point the Alabama struck her colors, and ran up a white flag in token of surrender.

Two guns were fired by the Alabama after Winslow had ceased firing in obedience to the signal of surrender, and Winslow reopened hostilities during the few moments that elapsed before the officer, despatched by Captain Semmes for the purpose, reached the Kearsarge and formally surrendered the privateer. This unfortunate circumstance may be readily understood and partially excused when we consider the condition in which the Alabama was at that time, and the inevitable confusion on board the sinking ship. It is certain that Captain Semmes did not "give up the ship" until her fate was unquestionably sealed, and that Captain Winslow proposed to take no chances of the battered wreck escaping into neutral waters.

At twenty minutes past twelve, while the Kearsarge was still several hundred yards from her adversary, the Alabama, with a great plunge by the stern, her bow rising high above the water, went down in forty fathoms. Her crew clung to boxes, spars, and other floating wreckage, drifting helplessly on the sea. Two of the boats of the Kearsarge, which remained uninjured, were set to pick up the drowning men, and the Deerhound coming within hail, Captain Winslow requested her master to aid him in the work of rescue. The Deerhound picked up Captain Semmes and several of his officers and seamen, and made off for the English coast. Captain Winslow was loath to recognize this exhibition of British treachery, and was too busy with his humane work to give chase until the Deerhound was well out of reach. With the assistance of two French pilot boats the survivors were picked up, and about three o'clock the Kearsarge started for Cherbourg, with seventy prisoners on board.

The success of the Kearsarge was undoubtedly due to the intelligence and bravery of her officers and crew. Her guns were well served, while much of the Alabama's fire was wasted. Of the 370 shots fired by the Alabama, only twenty-eight hit the Kearsarge and only fourteen "hulled" her. As we have already remarked, the gunners on the Kearsarge were Americans, and those on the Alabama were chiefly, if not entirely, British. Much stress has been laid upon the fact that portions of the Kearsarge's sides were protected with armor. The truth is that her coal-bunkers which, from their position, normally afforded a partial protection to her engines and boilers when full, were at this time empty, and the "armament" consisted simply of sheet cables stopped from her upper works and covered with inch boards, affording no better protection than would the coal-bunkers had they been filled, which they were not. The Alabama's bunkers were full. I may add that only three shots from the Alabama struck the "armor"; two were small missiles that could not have done much harm, and the third passed through and out on the other side. It was not this improvised chain-armor that gave Winslow a victory; and it may be questioned whether he would not have been compelled to make an even harder struggle for his prize had the rank and file of both contesting forces been composed of men of true American nerve and valor, such as those who piled the fields of Gettysburg and Chickamauga with heaps of mingled blue and gray.

The news of this splendid victory filled the North with enthusiasm, and gave the name of "Kearsarge" a place of high honor and reverence. The effect in the South was naturally different at the time; but now that it is all over, and it has been made plain that the triumph of the Kearsarge was an important link in the chain of events that have given the Southland a permanent place in this glorious Republic, it is safe to say that all our friends of the gray now join in the proud memory of an American victory over the hireling sailors of an alien nation which then professed great regard for them and felt none.

The career of the Kearsarge since 1864 has been uneventful, as is always that of a man-of-war in time of peace. She was partially rebuilt and rearmed; has served on the various foreign and domestic stations; has seen her effectiveness dwindle and disappear before the prestige of ships of iron and steel; and was recently employed in the rather commonplace duty of blowing up "derelicts." At the time of her disaster she was flagship of the North Atlantic Squadron, and carried the pennant of Rear-Admiral Stanton, who was on board.

The Kearsarge sailed from Port au Prince, Hayti, on January 30, 1894, for Bluefields, to look after American interests during the invasion by the troops of Honduras. She was under command of Commander O. F. Heyerman, and, in addition to the officers, carried a crew of 200 sailors and marines. Roncador Reef, on which the corvette struck, is well known to navigators of that sea as a dangerous and treacherous spot. It is about sixteen miles in length, curved backward at each end, and is of coral formation. At one end it rises above the sea, forming a small island, or "cay," covered with sand and some vegetable growth. The reef underneath the water is covered with sandy shoals. It has wrecked many a good ship, the prevailing winds and currents rendering it extremely dangerous. The "cay" has no human habitations, save one or two huts which are sometimes occupied by turtle-fishers. It is about 800 yards in length and not more than 300 yards wide. Water of an inferior quality may be obtained by digging shallow wells in the sand.

At six o'clock, on the evening of Friday, February 2d, the Kearsarge was dashing ahead under full sail, on her way to Bluefields. A few minutes later the lookout cried, "Breakers ahead!"—a cry that always carries terror with it. By an unfortunate error, not fully explained, the corvette had run close upon the dreaded Roncador Reef, and all the efforts of officers and crew could not save her. The weather was clear, but the wind was high and the sea was running fiercely. Far and near the white caps chased

each other across the watery waste like maddened, foam-flecked steeds; but now the practised eye of the officer on the bridge sees only too plainly the mighty breakers tumbling over the hidden reef. No time to turn, no time to think, until the doomed craft crashes upon the coral rocks and pitches over to port. In vain the heavy guns are torn from their carriages and flung into the boiling waters. The ship will not right herself, and her keel clings to the bottom with deadly tenacity. "Cut away the masts!" and the men swing their axes amidst the spray of the angry waves, now dashing over the fated corvette and threatening to carry them off their feet every instant.

With a crash, the mass of masts, spars, and canvas went by the board, and as the Kearsarge partially raised and righted, a giant wave swept her further on and up the shelving rock, where she pounded and beat until the banked fires under the boilers were scattered in all directions, adding the dangers of conflagration to the perils of the sea. Willing hands soon mastered the flames and kept them from the magazine, and then ensued a night of dreary waiting. At daylight the boats were lowered, and the short but perilous trip to the "cay" was accomplished by all the crew save one. Provisions, hastily thrown overboard, were washed ashore, where a camp was established, with rations for a month.

Lieutenant Frederick R. Brainard volunteered to make an effort to reach the mainland, and taking with him a selected crew, in one of the ship's boats, he set out for the nearest land. He reached New Providence, ninety miles distant, on the morning of the 5th, and proceeding thence by schooner, reached Colon, 230 miles south, on the 7th of February. The story of the relief of the castaways by the steamer City of Para is well known to all.

Visitors to the National Encampment of the Grand Army of the Republic, at Washington, in September, 1892, will remember that one of the great attractions on that occasion was a model of the Kearsarge, which was erected on the "White Lot." It will ever be a source of regret that this famous old vessel was not put out of commission and into a place of safety before she met her fate in the Caribbean Sea. A gallant craft of such historic memory deserved better treatment and a less cruel fate.

Stonewall Jackson's Grave

BY ERNEST N. BAGG

"Let us pass over the river and rest under the
shade of the trees."

This is the hallowed place!
A hero's dust lies 'neath this grassy mound!
" Under the shade " of these wide-arching trees
His armor " rests " secure from war's alarms.
His soldier soul hath passed " the river " o'er!
Upon its earthly shore still stand and mourn
The yet unvanquished army of his friends.
In blue as well as gray these legions are—
One " burning bush " within the solemn scene,
Kindled to vestal flame by Autumn's hand,
Reveals a small " stone wall " of spotless white,
Unsullied, pure as was his character.

Down the long village street
Sleeps Lee the valiant, and his truest friend.
Perhaps (I love to think) their spirits blest
Now and again to this fair scene return,
Hold sweet communion in this sacred grove,
This green-arched, peaceful " hall of Chancellors,"
And bless the day that saw the dawn of Peace,—
The new-born brotherhood of blue and gray,—
The glad hand-clasping of the reconciled.

But deftly chiseled, stately marble tomb
Is not more eloquent than this plain stone
With naught thereon but " Stonewall " Jackson's name,
Telling of deadly combat nobly waged;
Of field of battle honorably lost;
Of mastery of self; of courage strong;
Of words of truth; of martyrdom at last,
In the mistaken cause he served so well;
Of knightly deeds, immeasurably great;
Of stainless life, unutterably grand!

NOTE.—In the picturesque village of Lexington, Virginia, close by the street, in the common cemetery, is the grave
of "Stonewall" Jackson, marked only by small white marble tablets, bearing no inscription but the general's eloquent
name. The burial place of General Lee is but a short distance away, in the Lee Memorial Chapel, beneath Valentine's
magnificent recumbent statue. It was a beautiful and noteworthy incident when, in 1886, and again in 1888, blue-clad
veterans of the war, belonging to a Northern Grand Army Post, visited these two graves and expressed, in almost the
same words, some of the sentiments recorded above.

Dorchester, Mass.

FROM VICKSBURG TO NEW ORLEANS, THROUGH THE ENEMY'S COUNTRY.

By Yvan.

DURING the siege of Vicksburg, it became of vital importance to communicate with Admiral Farragut, at New Orleans, as speedily as possible. It was much easier to talk of this feat than to accomplish it. The whole intervening country was held by the enemy, except one or two places like Donaldsonville, Louisiana. Still, the commanding general concluded to try it. I was a young lieutenant of cavalry and had made several trips into the enemy's country, and had also more than once carried despatches safely. I was sent for and asked if I would undertake the task. The forlorn hope of the project, and the extremely slim chance of getting through with all the dangers incident to the trip, were duly placed before me. Nevertheless, I cheerfully accepted the mission. In these trips I never carried any documents when I could avoid it. I had none on this occasion.

After receiving my full instructions, I made my plans to start off that very night, as there was no moon. There was an old suit of "butternut" furnished me, and the only weapon I took with me was a large, keen-bladed bowie-knife. Firearms would be of no possible use to me, as I intended to swim the river that night, and expected to have to take to it frequently during the long journey before me.

I slipped into the water about ten o'clock that evening, and noiselessly made for the opposite shore. Swimming was my forte, and I was really an expert. There was scarcely any light, the current was not very strong, and no difficulty was experienced in reaching the other bank. But here it was necessary to exercise great care in landing. I landed very quietly, not even having the privilege of a dog—that of shaking myself. There was no evidence of life about. I may remark, *en passant*, that I landed some distance below Vicksburg, as I had gone down easily with the current. I crawled along behind the levee, slowly and carefully, making no noise whatever, and listening attentively for the slightest sound.

After traveling in this manner for an hour or two, I distinctly heard voices and footsteps. I crouched down, and made myself as small as possible. The persons, whoever they were,

passed by without seeing me. It seemed a little dangerous about there, so I again quietly slipped into the river, and swam and floated about half an hour or more, when I again landed. I was exceedingly anxious to strike some place where I could conceal myself before daybreak.

The banks all along the Mississippi River were infested with guerillas, and they were very dangerous fellows to meet. There was no use attempting to "spin a yarn" to these fellows. They were altogether too sharp and too familiar with the country. One's only chance was to keep out of their way.

About four hours must have elapsed since leaving. I had made about eight or nine miles, and was very tired. Daylight was due about four o'clock, and I concluded to make a few more miles on land before that time, as I must find a hiding-place before dawn. After going along stealthily for nearly three miles further, I found a clump of trees that seemed a fair hiding-place. (The personal pronoun "I" figures very prominently in this narrative, but there seems to be no possible way of avoiding it.) I crawled into the woods, and found it more dense than it at first appeared. I dropped asleep almost immediately after lying down. When I awoke, it was bright daylight, and I found myself in a very nice secluded little place. My great hope now lay in seeing some of the scout's invaluable and ever-faithful friends, the negroes. I was very hungry, and hoped to get something to eat, as well as information, from them.

I heard some one approaching, and soon a little negro girl came in sight. She was so small I feared I might alarm her, and concluded to await further developments. Shortly after, a colored woman came along, calling after the child. I called softly to her, and then showed myself. She was at first a little frightened, but soon took in the situation. She said she would find her "ole man," and send him to me with something to eat.

A few minutes after, her "ole man" came along, bringing me a piece of corn-bread and a small piece of bacon. He informed me that I was about fourteen miles below Vicksburg, and that there were lots of guerillas around. I asked him if he couldn't take me back a little in the country, so that I might avoid the guerillas. He said he could, but was a little afraid, but he was finally persuaded. He took observations and found the coast clear, so we crossed the road, and went back a piece into the country. He said he knew a cabin where he could hide me till sundown, when he would bring me some food and direct me how to go.

This was too slow work. I felt at this rate the war would be over before I reached New Orleans. I hoped to meet a gunboat about Donaldsonville that might be going down the river, and get aboard. I asked him if he could not tell me of some place near by where I could get another negro to guide me. He told me of a place about seven miles further on, and gave me his friend's name, telling me how to find him. He said he was a first-rate guide, and afraid of nothing. I gave him a little money, and concluded to take my chances.

I went along very quietly and carefully, avoiding the roads as much as possible. I had been traveling for about an hour, when I suddenly spied a guerilla, on horseback, making straight for me, and a minute after a bullet whistled by my ear, and on he came, and was on me almost before I knew it. He attempted to ride me down, but I quickly stepped aside, and plunged my knife into the breast of the horse. The poor beast fell to the ground, and the rider under him. Before he could recover himself, I was on him, and almost severed his head from his body. I took his rifle and pistol, and got back farther into the country as quickly as possible.

It now behooved me to get as far away as I could from my deceased friend. I went as rapidly as prudence would allow, only stopping to wash off the blood. In about an hour I discovered the place to which the negro had directed me, and after a good many futile attempts, succeeded in arresting the attention of an old darky. He at once came to me. After telling him my story and the danger I was in, he said he would find my guide at once and send him to me. I told him I was awfully hungry, and to send me something to eat.

In about fifteen minutes, along came another negro, who was the man I was after. He brought me a piece of pork and corn-bread. He said it would be better for me to hide right there until after sundown, as the country would be roused if anybody found the body.

I insisted on going ahead, and he said all right, he would do the best he could; and his "best" proved to be very good. I asked him

if, in case we were attacked, he would be afraid to fight. He said no, indeed; that they would kill him anyhow for showing a Yankee the way, so he might just as well fight for his life. I then gave him the pistol and some ammunition, cautioning him not to use it unless ordered by me to do so. He agreed to take me down to the vicinity of St. Joseph, which is about thirty-five miles from Vicksburg, and about thirteen miles from our present position. We were obliged to be very careful, and made slow progress. My great desire was to put as much space as possible between the defunct guerilla and myself.

We had several alarms on our way down, but reached our destination about nightfall, very tired and very hungry. My guide now left me, saying he would find his friend and return in about an hour, and would bring me some more rations. When they returned, they found me fast asleep. I had been away from Vicksburg about twenty hours, and had made about thirty-five miles.

After eating my corn-bread and pork, I told the new guide that the other guide and I would take a nap, and to wake us up in about three hours, when we would resume our journey. The old guide was afraid to return, so I concluded to keep them both.

At the time appointed, we were awakened, and again started off. We heard heavy firing on the river, and I wanted to go down, thinking we might reach a gunboat, but the new guide, Sam, strongly protested, saying we would surely be "cotched" if we did. We made about fifteen miles during the night, when, on reaching what we considered a safe place, we lay down for a little snooze, Sam keeping watch as before. After a short nap, we again proceeded on our way. It was agreed that Sam should go ahead, and on the least appearance of danger he was to begin whistling. When the whistling should cease and be renewed, we were to go on. He did all the foraging. We made about forty-five miles in the next twenty-four hours. We were now in the neighborhood of Bayou Sara, on the opposite side of the river. We had made just about the distance I expected and hoped to do. Sam found an acquaintance here, who gave us food and a place where we could take a sleep.

We went on as before, each taking his turn watching while the others slept, for the next two days, when we reached Plaquemine. Here we got an old negro to take us down the river at night, to Donaldsonville, which we reached safely in less than five days from the time I left Vicksburg.

I was cordially received by Major Bullard, commanding Fort Butler, at the mouth of Bayou La Fourche. The gunboat "Princess Royal," Captain Woolsey, was lying off the fort, but as General Greene's forces were in the neighborhood, and might at any moment attack the fort, he did not feel justified in leaving.

After a good rest, I started for New Orleans alone. I gave the negroes ten dollars each, and Major Bullard told them they were free. They promptly enlisted in his command.

I traveled steadily for nearly twenty-four hours, without stopping, when I lay down in a secluded place, thoroughly exhausted, and immediately fell fast asleep. I don't know how long I had been asleep when I found myself seized, and looking up, I saw four men around me. I felt "tired." I tried to pass myself off as a refugee from Donaldsonville, but it was no use. They took me to their camp, near the levee, and their commanding officer at once ordered me to be hung as a spy. A rope was found and put about my neck. They didn't bind me; as the officer said, "Just haul him up, and fill him full of holes." The order had scarcely been given, when a fierce bombardment of the levee began. There were embrasures cut in the levee, in which guns were mounted. My captors all instantly made for their guns, and I quite as rapidly removed the rope from my neck and ran for my life down the road. I met men hurrying to the scene, and told them all for heaven's sake to make haste, as the Yankees were upon us. I did not stop running until I fell prone on the ground. As soon as I could get up, I crawled into the woods and concealed myself. I found afterward that the United States Steamer "New London," Lieutenant-Commander (now Captain) George H. Perkins, (who was always looking for a fight, and was generally found wherever there was one,) had, fortunately for me, steamed up the river, and it was his guns that had diverted attention and saved my life. I continued my course, as soon as I was able, down the levee. On arriving at a little bend in the river, to my inexpressible joy I saw another gunboat coming up. I jumped with glee, and made the most frantic signs to them. At first I think they were disposed to fire on me, but they finally concluded to send me a boat. I lost no time in getting in, and was pulled aboard.

The vessel proved to be the United States Steamer "Kineo." I believe the captain's name was Waters. I remember distinctly that the executive officer was Lieutenant (now Captain) Fred Rodgers. I told my story, and was treated like a prince. They turned around and steamed down to New Orleans. On arriving there, I was taken aboard the flagship, and ushered into the presence of the grandest naval hero the world ever saw, Admiral David Glasgow Farragut. I delivered my message, and the gallant admiral thanked me heartily.

I have already been too prolix. Suffice it to say, that on my return to my regiment, I was made a major.

The foregoing narrative is strictly true, the name and command of the brave officer being disguised, out of deference to his wishes.

OUR BLUE AND OUR GRAY.

Mary Baird Finch.

BROWN are the branches out there in the meadow,
    Moaning and sighing as mortals in pain,
Pleading for summer bird, blossom and shadow,
    Stirred with a mem'ry of leaves in the rain ;
Waked with the blue mist blown from the mountains,
    Sweet with a promise of dews by and by ;
Soothing our sleep with the tinkle of fountains
    And song of the mocking-bird under the sky.

Airs from the Southland, whose cypress and willow
    Touch the last tints of the gray and the blue,
Thrilling the maple, whose musical billow
    Sings " hail and farewell," then bourgeons anew
A message of hope, not a burden of sadness,
    Tho' each has long cherished its blue and its gray,
While bare branches wave in carols of gladness,
    And sweep the dull mist of our winter away.

In harbors of hate we were wont to remember
    We bury the canker of wearisome years ;
Northland nor Southland keep not that December
    That darkened the spirit once drowned in its tears,—
Tears for the true friend, the father, and lover,
    Sad woe for the nation a-reaping its rue,—
Soon shall the house of the wild rose discover
    The soul of the South wind 'mong lilies of blue.

A harp in her hands from pine trees that murmur,
    A tear in her trumpet-blooms, poured on the sleep
Of the blue and the gray from manhood's brief summer
    Mnemosyne guardeth on valley and steep ;
Yet bare boughs are sweet with the dreams of that singer,
    The angel of peace, with her preludes of song,—
A sheaf from our harvest we hasten to bring her
    To banish hyenas of hatred and wrong.

AN ARRESTED BULLET.

H. M. HOKE.

AS Albert Garthman's intimate friend, I feel it my duty to make known, as simply as possible, the extraordinary circumstances which preceded and attended his early death. I have been deterred—inexcusably perhaps—from hitherto writing this account by the fact that, while the sensation of the supernatural is enjoyed when excited by a mere tale, the practical modern scouts any actual obtrusion of the inexplicable into the tangible and analyzable, and regards the sincere relator of such interference with amused pity. But, having lately been informed that, in certain quarters, the mystery of my friend's death has been explained on the theory of suicide, I have determined truthfully to narrate the incidents as they came under my wondering observation.

For several years prior to the late war Garthman and I, as law students, and new members of the bar, had been close friends. Upon the call to arms we enlisted in the same company, and, without accident, engaged in many of the fearful conflicts of 1861 and 1862. Upon the night after the beginning of the struggle at Gettysburg, the first of the "extraordinary circumstances" I have mentioned, warningly and vividly outlined itself against the perils and horrors of war. We were at work upon the fortifications on Cemetery Hill, when Garthman, who had complained of fatigue after our day of danger and repulse, became ill, and I, as his usual tent-mate, was detailed to attend him to the rear.

At some distance from the confusion I placed him upon the ground as comfortably as possible, and hurried away to find a physician. Failing in this, I returned to do all in my power for him. I found him sitting up, staring wildly about, trembling violently, and moving his hand before his eyes, as if to brush away some hideous sight.

"I have had a dreadful vision," he replied at length to my repeated inquiries.

"Haven't you been delirious in your fever?" I strove to reassure him.

"No. My eyes were open, and my fever is almost gone. Feel if it isn't."

I placed my hand upon his forehead, and replied,—

"Yes, it has subsided. You must have been dreaming, then."

"If it was a dream, it was the plainest one I ever had. The apparition was as clear before my eyes as you are now. I was lying here, wondering how long you would be gone, when suddenly I saw that I was in a wild, rugged place, where huge rocks were crowded together, and piled up in a wonderful mass.

"Crouching behind two of the rocks was a Confederate sharpshooter in the act of reloading his rifle. He took a bullet from his box, and laid it upon a little natural shelf in the rock before him, and I heard him say, as distinctly as I heard you speak just now, 'I'll try this one now.' I seemed to be standing directly behind him, but with these words he turned his head, and I saw the strangest face I have ever seen or heard of. His eyes gleamed fiercely from deep hollows, and the scar of a sabre-cut on his right cheek glowed through the powder-stains like the crescent through smoke. His face wore a look that I cannot describe and the stains did not dim. The look was not cruel or murderous, but it seemed to warn me that I was about to see something miraculous. Ramming the bullet home, he set the rifle in the small space between the beveled tops of the rocks, and took long and careful aim.

"As he aimed, my eyes strangely followed his line of sight, and I saw that the rifle was pointing at a soldier standing upon the summit of Little Round Top. His figure seemed distant, but suddenly, like a flash, my sight became telescopic, and I saw that it was *myself* at whom the rifle was aimed. In great wonder I watched the sharpshooter pull the trigger, and I saw the bullet dart from the muzzle of the rifle. My magical sight followed it in its course, which was straight for my heart. With a whirl of emotions at the prospect of seeing myself shot down, I followed the bullet, when, instantly, abruptly, as quickly as if it had struck a solid substance, the ball was stopped in its flight, and I saw it hanging perfectly still in the air. 'Success, success,' muttered the sharpshooter. 'Years and months after this it will lodge in that Yankee's heart.'

"A remarkable feature of the situation was that I knew I was lying here upon the grass, yet, at the same time, I seemed to be standing in that rocky place behind the sharpshooter. In this double sensation my amazement and fear at the stoppage of the bullet belonged to the consciousness of lying here on the ground, but there was no wonder connected with the sensation of standing behind the Confederate. I thought I stepped forward to question him, but before I could speak the vision faded, together with the sensation of standing, and the full, undivided sense of lying upon the ground returned. I have had vivid dreams, Leighton, but never anything like this. What does it mean ?"

"Mean ?" I echoed, thrilled by the recital, but striving to make light of it. "It means that you are flighty, that's all."

"No, it doesn't," he gravely disagreed. "I was no more flighty than I am now. It means that during this battle I shall be sent to Little Round Top with orders, and while I am there I shall be shot through the heart by a Confederate sharpshooter. I'm not superstitious, as you well know, but this vision was too plain to be scoffed at. You and I have often heard of men who had presentiments of their death. Their warnings came vaguely, but mine has come sharply and clearly to the sight. I'm going to prepare myself for death."

I tried to argue the apparition away, and finally to ridicule it, but to no purpose. He persisted in writing messages to his home folks, and giving me directions as to the disposal of his body, in accordance with such grim wishes as we all cherish in health, concerning our most solemn hour.

History has recorded how the evening of July 2, 1863, brought a lull in the furious struggle, and how the night of the third hid in its shadows the horrors which make up the cost of a great victory. I stood at our tent-door that evening, awaiting Garthman. My apprehensions fell heavier with the shadows. Again and again Garthman's vision set itself up as an explanation of his long delay, and each time I fought it down with greater difficulty. At last I discerned a figure approaching in the gloom ; it grew more distinct, and I sprang forward with a glad cry, and caught Garthman's hand.

"The battle is won !" I exclaimed, triumphantly ; then, my rebounding mind naturally taking the direction of my fear, "and where is your apparition ?"

"I haven't been shot as I expected," he replied, solemnly checking my elation ; "but I believe in the warning of the vision as firmly as I did. I gave it the wrong interpretation, that is all. I expected to be killed, but——." He stopped, looked steadily at me, and continued : "See here, Leighton, I suppose you'll think my brain has gone wrong, but I believe as firmly as I stand here that this morning a sharpshooter over in Devil's Den, which is a place exactly like the one I saw in the vision, shot a bullet at me, and that it was arrested in the air and will pause there for 'years and months,' as he said, when it will start on its way again and strike my heart, wherever I may be."

"Nonsense, Garthman !" I exclaimed. "This is superstition."

"It may seem so now, but listen : This morning I was sent with an important message to the commander of a battery on Little Round Top. As I stood waiting a few moments until I could get to him, I looked about me and was startled at the scene, which was precisely as it appeared in the vision. After this fact struck me, I had not time to feel any great fear or to move from the spot, before my heart gave a sudden bound, such as I have never felt before, with a keen pain darting through it. The sensation was so weakening that I fully believed I was shot and that I was experiencing the tumult of thought in the few seconds between a mortal wound and death. But I remained upon my feet, and gradually the sensation left me, my heart resumed its regular beat, and I felt as well as before. Nothing you can say, Leighton, will convince me that at that moment a sharpshooter did not fire a bullet at me from Devil's Den, and that somewhere up in the air it has been arrested until the same mysterious power that stopped it shall start it again on its deadly flight. I believe this, nonsensical or extraordinary as it may seem, and if my death occurs suddenly and unaccountably, you will understand."

* * * * * * *

From Appomattox, Garthman and I returned home and resumed our interrupted practice. Amid its activities the apparition of Cemetery Hill dimmed in Garthman's mind ; but there were times when it warningly brightened and he talked morbidly of a bullet fatefully paused over Gettysburg's silent field. At these periods I tried, as before, to enliven him, but arguments, ridicule, expostulations, and entreaties to set his manhood against such superstition were alike ineffective ; he clung despondently to the belief that he was rapidly approaching the end of his miraculous respite.

Striving further to lift this incubus, I persuaded Garthman to go with me into the fashionable society of the city. At a reception one winter night he was introduced to Miss Marie Drumford, daughter of Alexander Drumford, one of the eminent lawyers of the State. She was a girl of rare beauty, superior accomplishments, and of a gentle, loyal, and lovable character. When Garthman came to me, with eyes sparkling more brightly than for many a day, and frankly confessed that he was falling in love, I congratulated him and inwardly rejoiced. During the previous month or two he had been relaxing his hold upon life, and I believed there was no power like that of a good, beautiful woman to recapture his interest and exorcise the unmanning vision.

With satisfaction, therefore, I watched his love strengthen, and, with all the encouragement and help in my power, I sought to increase its beneficial influence upon him. From the night he met her until his death, only once did the fear—unnatural as I then thought and called it—seem to depress him. That one occasion was on an evening when I walked with him to the Drumford house, and he told me that he wished to ask Marie to be his wife, but that he still regarded himself as a doomed man; that he had done wrong in trying to win her love, and would do worse to take her as a wife when he might be suddenly and strangely stricken by her side.

"Why *will* you cling to your belief in that bullet?" I asked, with some impatience. "You have everything to make you happy, instead of weakly yielding to this foolishness. You can become celebrated as a lawyer if you will not allow this vision to sap your energies. Besides this, you have now won Marie's love, and it is your duty to assert your manhood and be the worthy husband you should and could be. Exercise your will-power, Garthman, and throw off this silly belief. Depend upon it, if that sharpshooter in Devil's Den did aim at you, he missed you, and you are as safe from the bullet as I am."

"No, I am not," he gloomily dissented. "And even if I were, the apparition was so vivid that it has irreparably unnerved me. It isn't right for me to ask Marie to be my wife when I will become a miserable, apprehensive man, always afraid of this impending stroke of a bullet. Even if it never comes, the expectation will make me too melancholy a husband for such a happy woman."

I saw the force of this view. His condition was, indeed, a serious one. Believe that a bullet would ever strike in the way he feared, I could not; neither could I shut my eyes to the fact that the vision had changed my friend from an active, alert, keen-minded man to a despondent, irresolute one. But, relying upon the cheering, uplifting companionship of a loving wife, I urged him to follow his wishes.

Next morning he came to me, almost happy, and told me he had been accepted and that he meant to fight and conquer the consuming influence of the vision. I heartily promised him my help, and, indeed, under my encouragement, and in the active preparation for and happy expectations of his marriage, which had been appointed for an early day, he became more like my old, light-hearted friend than he had been since the war.

Three evenings before his marriage day I walked with him to the Drumford home to help with the final details. It was a soft spring night, the sky cloudless and the full moon serene in the east,—a time when, with the expanding leaves and opening flowers, love of life springs anew within the heart. Garthman was unusually hopeful. Five years and ten months had safely passed since the vision of the bullet had appeared to him; and now, his love whispering that life was precious, he was inclined to join my skepticism and to attribute the apparition to fever. I was so happy in my belief in his final release that I could not help congratulating him enthusiastically upon the fact, and on the union he was soon to make. Marie met us in the hall, and the happiness upon her face completed, as I thought, his restoration.

In the elegant parlor we sat, merrily arranging the final details of the approaching ceremony. As I looked from him, gay and hopeful, to her eyes, sparkling, and her face glowing with admiration and increasing love, I thought, "If any power can break the influence of that unfortunate vision, it is the affection in those looks." But, almost instantaneously with the thrill of this thought, Garthman uttered a sudden exclamation of fear, put his hands before his eyes, and began trembling violently. We hastened to him, and I, surmising the trouble, said a few assuring words, while Miss Drumford implored him to tell her what had alarmed him.

"The—the vision!" he gasped, looking at me in terror.

"Nonsense!" I said. "Don't give way to it."

"It is not nonsense," he repeated, trembling. "It is all over! I——"

His voice failed and he sank weakly into his chair, overcome.

"What does this mean, Mr. Leighton?" faltered Miss Drumford, turning to me.

"Albert has been working too hard. Close application and the excitement have been too great a strain upon him. I will send for a physician."

"A physician can do me no good," Garthman feebly objected. "You think it is simple nervousness. It is not; it is an impending tragedy. Before a doctor can come I shall be gone. Please call your father, Marie, and I will explain."

She was too bewildered to comply, and I left them, seeing her, as I walked through the door, bending entreatingly over him and wringing her hands in perplexity and distress. I dispatched a servant for the nearest physician and brought Mr. Drumford from his upstairs library.

"Mr. Drumford," Garthman said, as we entered the parlor, "Mr. Leighton will tell you what has happened. Tell it all from the beginning, Frank."

I saw that he was rapidly sinking to complete prostration, and that an explanation was necessary. I shrank from the task, fearing that the lawyer would break his daughter's engagement with a man mentally afflicted, as was poor Garthman. I hesitated, but Miss Drumford turned to me, and implored me to speak. She clung apprehensively to her father, while I,

standing close to Garthman, related the story of the apparition, of the peculiar sensation at my friend's heart upon Little Round Top, and of his subsequent anxiety.

"But this is only a form of nervousness," observed Mr. Drumford, when I had finished. "A physician can cure——"

"No, sir, I am doomed," interrupted Garthman. "Only this evening I thought as you do, but while we were talking here, Marie, sitting in front of me, suddenly disappeared from my sight, and in her place I saw the same sharpshooter, with the same blackened face and scar, with the same look in his eyes, kneeling by the rocks, aiming his rifle at me. Then I knew—but see, see, there is the vision again!"

He partly arose from the chair in horror, and we followed the direction of his pointing finger. And near the door, in the full glare of the gas, we all saw the figure of a "gray" sharpshooter in the act of firing. His great eyes gleamed fiercely from his blackened face, and a crescent-shaped scar glowed through the powder-stains. Marie sprang forward to go to Garthman, but her father stayed her, and then, rigid as the figure of a statue, we gazed with horrified eyes upon the portentous vision.

Slowly it faded, and instantly upon the dying of its last shadowy outline the silence of the room was cut by a sharp, unnerving hiss, as of a bullet. I sprang forward in time to catch my poor friend as he fell to the floor and expired.

THE OLD CANTEEN.

O F all the faithful friends we had
On weary march, when gay or sad;
Of all the comforts ever nigh
When throats were parched, when lips were dry,
Oh, comrades, none there was, I ween,
More welcome than the old canteen.

When powder grimed our faces black,
'Mid cannon's roar and rifle's crack;
When charging brave the foe to meet,
When falling back from grim defeat;
One thing we had on which to lean,
Our bosom friend, the old canteen.

How oft the wounded's lips have pressed
The old tin spout whose water blest;
How oft when on the battle-field
The soldier's eyes in death were sealed,
A smile upon his face was seen—
Asleep, beside his old canteen.

Ah, comrades, if there is one thing
Which memories from the past can bring,
One symbol that in time's swift flow
Binds hearts to friends of long ago,
'Tis this—enwreathed with laurels green—
The soldier's friend, the old canteen.

GEORGE M. VICKERS.

THE BATTLE OF PORT ROYAL.

ROBERT CHISOLM.

NO more sublime spectacle, connected with the late war, has ever been witnessed than that presented in the attack made by the United States navy, under Commodore Dupont, on Port Royal, South Carolina, in 1861.

Bay Point, on the east, and Hilton Head, on the west, guarded the entrance to the spacious harbor. A great, ma-

ROBERT CHISOLM.

jestic basin of water, deep enough to float the largest ships, and four miles in width, flowed in between these two points from the Atlantic. On each point a powerful earthwork battery, carrying the heaviest ordnance then made, had been erected by the Confederates. The fort on Bay Point, named after General Beauregard, was immediately in charge of Captain—afterward Brigadier-General—Stephen Elliott, who commanded his volunteer company, the Beaufort Artillery, a company composed mostly of young men, and all men of means, education, and refinement.

On Hilton Head, a Charleston company, composed of Germans under Captain Wagener, had charge of Fort Walker. Both commands were well drilled and, in the case of the Beaufort Artillery, first-rate shots. The Confederates on Bay Point were under the command of Colonel Quay Dunnovant, a distinguished veteran of the Mexican War—the same gentleman who had fought, some years before, the celebrated duel with his friend Legare. His command consisted of the artillery company named, a regiment of about 1,000 men, besides a cavalry company commanded by the subsequent attorney-general of South Carolina, then Lieutenant Leroy F. Youmans, to-day the most accomplished and finished orator in his State.

Admiral Dupont, then a commodore, had arrived with his entire fleet, consisting of thirteen men-of-war and about fifty transports of troops, with which to establish a base for future land operations in South Carolina. The "Wabash," a double-decker, mounting sixty-two guns, was

his flagship. This enormous fleet of near seventy ships arrived on Monday before the battle, and were, during the afternoon, anchored over the bar, about four miles from land. The masts and smokestacks in the distance looked like a forest in the ocean, and the heart would swell with emotion as its purpose was fully understood. With us on land, it was a mere matter of dismounting twenty barbette guns, to do which about 500 guns were to enter the contest against us.

There is much circumstance around a naval conflict, and it is the only battle which ever looks like a picture. The old-time ships loomed so high out of water, black, as a rule, with square white port-holes; in movement they are slow and grand. Nothing is done in a hurry, and the battle must be fought in accordance with navy rules, learned when a boy in the Naval Academy, or it is not a correct fight. Our garrison were in high spirits over the prospect of a fight. Many a silent, private tear told what the result had to be, but there was none the less determination to do all and more than duty in the approaching struggle, and if now and again an unheard prayer was made that Providence would scatter the enemy by a storm, it was only what the world's best soldiers have ever done.

The gallant commodore must have appreciated the inequality of the struggle also, for he brought his ships close enough to the forts during the engagement to let the garrison sink them if they could.

Commodore Tatnall, of the Confederate navy, was also there, with his "Mosquito" fleet of five boats. These were inland river steamers and tugboats, carrying one gun each, the recoil from which was almost enough to upset the small craft. Captain John M. Moffit, the distinguished commander of the "Florida," was second in command, and, during a short visit made by Tatnall to the battery, Moffit signaled his fleet and brought on a small-sized movement which came near destroying the entire Confederate navy in those waters, the result of which was he was placed under arrest as soon as the commodore could get aboard. His young son, Midshipman Eugene, asked permission to go ashore and fight in the fort, which Tatnall allowed him.

On Tuesday morning, three of the enemy's ships came in to reconnoitre and feel the strength of the batteries. Exchanging some 300 shots with each other, they retired to their anchorage about nine A. M. The rest of the time passed without incident until Wednesday night, when the soft sounds of music over the water and the crossing of lights in the fleet showed us plainly that the attack was to be made in the morning.

The morning of that November Thursday was perfect. The sun rose with unusual splendor in a cloudless sky; no breath of wind marred the smooth surface of the ocean, and it shone like a thousand mirrors. It was a day when a man forgets he exists.

Being only a volunteer, I was consigned to the tender mercies of the post surgeon, who was excellent company; and by the liberal use of hospital stores, of which he had a large quantity on hand, he made me very comfortable. He had a liquid he called a "prophylactic," which, under his direction, I consumed in such quantities as kept up a steady appetite. He said it cured the sick and made the well better. It had the further effect of belittling the strength of the enemy and increasing our own.

On land, during that night, the best glee-songs were sung, and tales told around the camp-fires. This is always the case before a battle; when about to leave this world, we would recall only the pleasant, happy times in it. A soldier has much more fear of defeat than he has of death. The companionship involved in death in battle relieves it of that lonesome feeling which surrounds the ordinary deathbed. Neither are there any tears to sadden its last moments; it is surrounded by the joy and excitement which made Nelson say, "Kiss me, Hardy!"

The sun had just risen above the ocean when the ships were seen in motion. One by one the big black men-of-war drifted out of the crowds slightly inland for perhaps a mile, when, at a blast from the flagship, method grew out of disorder. Speed was increased and flags hoisted as each ship fell into her place in the line of battle as they approached the battery. On the line came, the flagship leading, men in the topmast, Dupont, glass in hand, on deck; the hulls looming up black out of the clear water, flying flags of every color, shape, and size; no smoke. They did not seem to be separate things, but each ship part of one whole, ruled by the one man in front. Flags carried his orders, and flags returned answer. It did not look like war;

it was a picture—a glorious pageant, filling one's soul with a sense of awe and the sublime.

Down, low down, four feet above the level of the ocean, 1,500 untried brave men watched the majestic spectacle. The historic bravery of the foe, the silence of their approach, inspired the Confederates with keenest desire to grapple with the gallant men who seemed courting death and destruction. Not a man in the battery would miss that day nor his part in it, let the end be what it may. Every gun loaded, every man at his post ready for the word "Fire!" A wreath of white smoke from Battery Beauregard, and a solid shot ricocheting across his bow, tells Dupont that he is about to cross the line of the Confederacy and the authority of the great ocean. There was no necessity to fire this shot across the bows, but the commandant of the battery acted on the chivalric courtesy with which the South Carolinian always treated his foe. It was a challenge and an acceptance, and a fight between gentlemen.

There was a lull of two or three minutes to let the ships get nearer, when this battery opened with all of its guns. There is a blast from the pipes of the flagship, and on they come, spite of shot and shell, until the distance between the combatants is about half a mile, when, with the roar of an earthquake, the "Wabash" opens with a broadside of thirty-two guns; then another roar, and another, down the line, until thirteen ships have poured a shower of near 700 shots at the little battery. One or two men senseless and a gun or two off its trunnion is the damage so far. "Keep clear of the muzzles, men, and aim carefully," cried Elliott, as the young soldiers cheered answer to the broadside. A tall, bearded man mounts the parapet, waves his hat, and points where the "Wabash" stands. He is Montague, the Yankee, fighting with the boys from Beaufort. The line occupied by the ships was nearly one-third of a mile in length, and there were not guns enough in the battery to give one to a ship, but the flagship bore the brunt of the shots. Every effort was made to sink her.

The scene at this stage was grand beyond description. Roar after roar, as broadside followed broadside in almost continuous successsion; the ground trembled as in an earthquake. The smoke hid the combatants so effectually that it was impossible to strike but by guess, and Commodore Dupont, seeing the futility of continuing his fire at an object he could not see, signaled his fleet and ceased firing. The fleet, now in a large curve, approached the battery at Hilton Head, when the same scene we had just gone through was enacted over there until the smoke again became so dense that a second attack was made on Bay Point.

By this time a slight current of air, enough to partially clear the smoke, gave both sides a better chance, and we could see our shots as they would strike, but they made little or no impression on the ships. The roar became furious and continuous; great volumes of sand were hurled into the air, nearly burying our gunners in its fall. Now a shot would strike one of our big black guns and knock it clean off its carriage. Sometimes it would careen it only a little, but so long as the muzzle could point toward the enemy it was loaded and fired by the begrimed gunners.

The casualties were too few to keep our friend the doctor busy. He carried his yellow flag wherever he went, and declared that no civilized nation would fire on a hospital. One or two very close shots made him use some strong and inelegant language, but he got through safely, and after the retreat was ordered he told the colonel that he (the doctor) was the only one he had met except the colonel who had shown real, true courage during the fight. He had still

on hand a little "prophylactic," which he shared with us.

The naval forces, at about one P. M., withdrew, and made a second attack on Hilton Head. By this time the tide was at ebb, and while engaged in this attack one of the ships had her propeller broken by a shot, and drifted aground. A large hawser was hitched to the stranded vessel, and two others tried to pull her off, but they failed, and it looked as if that ship would be entirely destroyed, for the battery, seeing the fix she was in, had turned all of its guns on her.

Then it was that the fighting qualities of the ships were seen as they closed in almost on the battery, and poured such a fire on it that in a quarter of an hour every gun had been dismounted and silenced. The garrison, seeing that it was useless to stay longer, retreated in confusion across an open field in the rear, when they were terribly cut up. The ground was literally plowed up with the shots. This ended the fight, for on the other side the commander saw the uselessness of holding a fort on an island where retreat could have been entirely cut off; so, after spiking all the guns, the troops were, during the night, safely taken away, and within two days reached main-land.

AN INTERRUPTED CAVALRY CHARGE.

Rev. J. R. Keyes.

THE last days of March, 1865, found Sherman's army encamped in and around Goldsboro, North Carolina. There it rested and refitted for what was confidently believed to be its last active campaign, and the subsequent events fully justified this confidence. By the 10th of April all preparations had been completed, and that mighty army was once more in motion. It was not known to us that on the day preceding the beginning of our march the army of General Lee had actually been surrendered to General Grant at Appomattox, and that the only hostile forces in our front were those of General Joseph E. Johnston, known to be at Smithfield, North Carolina, and supposed to comprise about 40,000 men. It was a general impression among the troops that we were marching to meet the combined forces of Johnston and Lee somewhere beyond Raleigh, in a final struggle for victory.

About ten A. M., April 12th, our cavalry encountered the Confederate rear guard, which was

intrenched across the road near a forest some miles south of Raleigh. This guard was soon dislodged from its intrenchments, and a running fight was kept up until about five o'clock in the evening. We halted in line of battle along the Raleigh and Wilmington Railroad, some six miles south of Raleigh, and by daylight the next morning, without any breakfast, were in the saddle and on the march to Raleigh, the only capital of a Confederate State that had not already been honored with a visit from the boys in blue.

About eight o'clock in the morning the head of our column entered Raleigh, and after some considerable fighting on the north side of the city, moved on to Morrisville, some ten miles distant, pushing the Confederate cavalry before us. On the 15th, in a drenching rain, we moved on to Durham Station, fifteen miles distant, where we went into camp. On the following morning, with five of my comrades, of Company L, 5th Ohio Cavalry, I was sent on a special mission in a direction eastward from Durham. We rode about five miles, when we came to a river—probably the Neuse—which was a raging torrent, having been swollen by the recent rains. We rode into the murky waters and happily reached the opposite shore without accident. Immediately thereafter we were informed by citizens that a detachment of Wheeler's cavalry was encamped a mile or two east of the river. We had no particular desire to renew acquaintance with Wheeler's bold riders, and therefore turned southward, down and oblique from the river. Desiring to obtain some definite information as to the exact location of the force above named, we rode down a ravine, through an open field toward a farm-house which we saw in the distance. When within about 200 yards of this farm-house, we were not a little surprised to see a squad of Confederates in the road just beyond the house. We did not stop to count them, but judged that there were about twelve of them. The mind works rapidly in the presence of real or supposed danger, and we instinctively concluded that the men we saw were the pickets of the aforesaid cavalry forces. At that time we were not aware that General Johnston had actually opened negotiations with Sherman, looking toward the surrender of his army, and having recently had reason to know that there was still a good deal of "fight" in the gallant boys in gray, we regarded them as our lawful prey, providing, of course, that we could capture them. We could not well retreat in any direction without drawing their fire, so we hastily got under cover in the rear of the house, and, after a moment's consultation, concluded that we were in for it, and that there was no alternative but to fight. I dismounted and threw down the heavy rail fence, remounted, and we drew our weapons and rode through the gap into the yard. As we drew out from the cover of the house, I cocked my Colt's navy revolver and leveled it at the first man that came in sight. As I was about to press the trigger I saw his hands go up in the air, and at the same instant several hats were thrown high above their heads. We saw immediately that they were not armed. We recovered arms

and rode up to the men who were in the road on the opposite side of the yard fence. They were terribly frightened. Poor fellows! They were naturally worn and pale from insufficient rations and the hardships they had endured. Their teeth chattered as if they were shaking with the ague. They could not speak and tell us who they were, so great was their fright. I spoke to the one who appeared to be their leader and told him that we had taken them for a Confederate picket, but we saw that we were mistaken, and that they need have no fear, as we were not engaged in shooting down unarmed and helpless men. Presently they became somewhat calm and told us their story. They were some of Lee's men, paroled at Appomattox, and were on their way home. About a mile from the farm-house they had passed through the camp of Confederate cavalry before mentioned, where some of Wheeler's troopers—presumably in the spirit of mischief—warned them that the Yankees were on the opposite side of the river, and that they were to be avoided, as they would not respect their paroles, but would shoot them down at sight, wherever found.

We could then well understand the reason they were so terribly frightened at our sudden appearance and our hostile demonstration toward them. To us it was an illustration of the suddenness with which the hostile feelings of the soldier may be transformed into sentiments of fraternal sympathy toward his former enemy. It was a great pleasure to assure these men that they were perfectly safe anywhere within our lines, and that there was not a brave soldier in the army that would not gladly divide his rations with them. We insisted that wherever they should find any Federal forces they should freely make their wants known and they would be supplied. We dismounted and put them on our horses, and allowed them to ride as far as we went in the same direction. Although we had not then heard of the utterance of the hero of Appomattox when he requested his men to abstain from all signs of rejoicing over their fallen foes, yet somehow we felt that "the rebels were our countrymen again."

THE STORY OF A FLAG

AND THE STRANGE BRINGING TOGETHER OF ITS CAPTORS AND DEFENDERS, AS RELATED BY ONE OF THE FORMER.

Frank P. O'Brien.

APRIL 12, 1864, the Confederate forces evacuated their intrenchments on Rodman's Point and at Fisher's Hill, below Little Washington, North Carolina, where they had lain in siege fourteen days, and took up their line of march for Hamilton, where they were directed to report to General Hoke, whose division was being strengthened for the purpose of marching on Plymouth. At break of day, April 16th, the long roll was sounded and orders to march were given; word was passed down the line that Plymouth was the objective point, and every officer and man was given to understand that our job was not an easy one, and that possibly before twenty-four hours would pass many a poor fellow would hand in his checks and have them cashed in full by the eternal Banker above.

The artillery company of which I was a member was attached to General Matt. Ransom's brigade of North Carolinians, as brave a band of " tar heels " as ever shouldered a musket. A bond of sympathy soon sprang up between our battery and Colonel Wortham's regiment, and " our Alabama boys " were cheered on all occasions by their " tar heel " admirers and supporters. On the morning of April 19th two brigades were thrown into line and ordered to move on Block House No. 2, near a point known as Warren's Neck. After a hard fight, in which our forces were several times repulsed by the heavy discharge of hand-grenades, the blockhouse was captured and its guns turned on the intrenched town.

General Hoke ordered General Matt. Ransom, after the capture of Block House No. 2, to march his brigade to a point below the town, and there to co-operate with the Confederate gun-boat " Albemarle," under command of Captain James W. Cook, C. S. N. This brave officer had already destroyed the " Southfield," crippled the " Miami," and captured two small boats. That morning orders were given simultaneously to move on the town from all land sides, and, with the assistance of the iron ram on the water front, the place was taken within three hours of first moving. General Wessels

and his brave band made it rather warm for us, and many a poor fellow lay with his face to the skies before capitulation. Even after we had gotten within the outer line of breastworks, they fought us hand-to-hand from the various bomb-proofs they had erected, anticipating a siege similar to the one of Little Washington, which had taken place on the 1st of April.

During the hand-to-hand encounter referred to, a bomb-proof was captured by Private G. M. ("Mortie") Williams, two others, and the writer. When we entered the mouth of the bomb-proof we discovered five lieutenants, a color corporal, and Major John H. Burnham, all of the 16th Connecticut volunteers.

Mr. Williams was in front, and on discovering the color corporal, he caught the staff and dragged the flag out of the hands of its bearer. The brave fellow begged for possession of his colors. It proved to be the battle-flag of the 16th Connecticut, and when this was denied him, he asked that a piece be given to him as a memento. This Mr. Williams cheerfully accorded, and himself cut a corner from the bottom and gave it to the color-bearer.

All prisoners captured at Plymouth were sent to the rear, some going to Salisbury, North Carolina, and some to Andersonville, Georgia.

Major Burnham was among the number sent to the former place. Immediately after the capture of Plymouth, I was assigned to scouting duty, and was instructed to report to Captain Cook, of the " Albemarle," who ordered me to go down the river and learn, if possible, where torpedoes were being placed. I was permitted to select my own comrades on all my trips, and was frequently accompanied by Signal Officer Arthur Chalk and Pilot James H. Hopkins, of the " Albemarle," also by Private G. Mortimer Williams, of my own company, the Montgomery True Blues.

Another attempt to capture Newbern was contemplated, the plans being to send the " Albemarle " down Albemarle Sound, through Croatan Sound, thence to Newbern by Pamlico Sound, to co-operate with the ram " Neuse," which had been completed at Kingston, on the river Neuse.

The troops were to move on Newbern as soon as the "Albemarle" had reached Croatan Sound. The result of the engagement in Albemarle Sound between the sturdy old Confederate ram, with nine of the largest double-enders in the Federal navy, on May 5, 1864, will never be forgotten by those who to-day are able to describe it. The "Merrimac" engagement in Hampton Roads is often referred to as the greatest naval engagement of the nineteenth century, and comparatively little has ever been written of the engagement of the 5th of May. As a member of the famous old 3d Alabama, I witnessed the "Merrimac" fight from Sewell's Point, but I participated in the latter as a volunteer, and in my judgment the "Merrimac" engagement compares to the "Albemarle" fight as a skirmish to a pitched battle. But to my story:

During one of my scouting trips over on the Chowan and in and around Elizabeth, I learned that two mail-boats made regular semi-weekly trips between Roanoke Island and Norfolk, and that on a certain day the United States paymaster would go to Roanoke Island from Norfolk on the mail-boat "Fawn." I returned to Plymouth and reported my information, which was perfectly reliable, to Captain James Maffit, of "Florida" fame, who, soon after the engagement of May 5th, had relieved Captain Cooke of the command of the "Albemarle." Captain Maffit organized a crew to carry out my idea of capturing the boat. Master's Mate James H. Long was placed in command, but on the eve of leaving he was ordered not to go, as he had but recently recovered from a severe spell of sickness. Mr. Shelley, sailing-master, took his place.

My plan was to go to the draw-bridge on the road leading from Windsor, in Bertie county, capture the draw-bridge keeper, force him to respond to the signal of the "Fawn" as she approached, and when within a short distance to close the bridge. Orders were given to the men that at a given signal, which was to be the firing of a pistol, the men who were concealed in the bushes on both sides of the canal were to rush forward and board the vessel. This was easily done, as in many places along the bank a man could step from the shore to the boat.

Everything was carried out to the point of opening the bridge. Engineer Disher was detailed from the "Albemarle" to take charge of the prize when captured. His orders were to run her from the canal into Pasquotank River, thence to the Sound, across to Roanoke River, thence to Plymouth. Engineer Disher, becoming greatly excited, discharged his pistol too soon. This gave the alarm, and precipitated the attack. All our men boarded the boat immediately. If there was a paymaster's mail on board the "Fawn," it was the first thing to be destroyed, for when we boarded her we found that the crew had thrown a number of mail and other bags into the furnace. Among those captured, to my great astonishment, I found Major John H. Burnham, of the 16th Connecticut, whom I had assisted in capturing at Plymouth. This brave officer had been exchanged, and had reported at Norfolk for duty. On account of bad health he was given a furlough, but before leaving for home he decided to go to Roanoke Island on the "Fawn," and see his old comrades who were on duty at that place, but, unfortunately for him, the boat was captured, as set forth in the foregoing.

Just here came a struggle between duty to country and sympathy for the unfortunate soldier, broken in health caused by confinement in prison, who had been looking forward to a speedy reunion with loved ones whom he had not seen in over two years. I would gladly have liberated him, but duty forbade, and poor Burnham was again an inmate of a Confederate prison.

Nothing of moment occurred for several weeks after the destruction of the "Fawn." I made frequent trips to Edenton and Chowan county, bringing back such information as I could gather of interest.

The last trip I made was October 20th. This time I entered the little town of Edenton. I was the bearer of several letters from parties on the outside. I was informed by a Mr. Gregory that he had information of a movement of some kind that was on foot for the capture of Plymouth. I returned to the garrison and reported to Colonel George H. Wortham, who was in command of the point. On the night of the 27th, the culmination of the plan of attack was reached by the daring feat of Lieutenant W. B. Cushing in the blowing up of the "Albemarle" and the capture of Plymouth after eight hours of hard fighting.

The war ended the following spring, and the overpowered fragments of a once glorious army went sorrowfully to their respective homes. Time passed on and the scenes and incidents described in this sketch passed into history, and were things to be thought of and spoken of when old comrades come together or meet at long intervals.

In July, 1884, in company with Major Frank Wadsworth, of Birmingham, Alabama, I was stopping at the Union Square Hotel, in New York City. One morning a friend joined us in the café, and, during the interview with him, a gentleman was introduced, who proved to be Mr. John H. Burnham, formerly major of the 16th Connecticut, and at that time postmaster of Hartford. Mutual recognition followed, hands were clasped, old incidents were gone over, and the time lang syne was referred to and greatly enjoyed by several persons seated at various tables around us. These latter had witnessed the meeting and listened to the expressions of unfeigned delight at the *rencontre* of two men who had been thrown together under vastly different circumstances twenty years before.

The first question asked by Major Burnham after the greetings were over, was, "O' Brien, where is my flag? I would give a thousand dollars to get it back. Do you know what was done with it?"

I informed him that the flag was in possession of its captor, Major Mortie Williams, of Montgomery, Alabama. "He is in Birmingham often," I continued, "and the next time I see him I will tell him of our meeting and of your great desire to obtain possession of the flag, and I can safely say that he will send it to you."

Burnham expressed great delight at the prospect of recovering his flag. We met daily for two or three weeks, and passed many pleasant hours together, and at the end of that time, Major Burnham kindly invited my friend and me to accompany him to his home as his guests. Matters of a business nature prevented our acceptance, and we parted, never to meet again.

Soon after my return South, in September, I met Mr. Williams and related the meeting, also the promise I had made Burnham about the return of the flag, and his desire to get possession of it. Mr. Williams readily promised to gratify my request, saying that on his return to Montgomery, which was then his residence, he would look up the flag and send it to Hartford. I saw Mr. Williams in December, 1884, and he told me that he had been unable to find the flag, but would continue to search for it. It was finally found in 1888, and Mr. Williams turned it over to Colonel Thomas G. Jones, of the 2d (Alabama) State Troops (now Governor of Alabama). Colonel Jones sent the colors to the Governor of Connecticut with the statement that it was the battle-flag of the 16th Connecticut, captured by Private G. M. Williams at Plymouth, on April 19, 1864. The flag was received by Executive Secretary McLean, of Hartford, and the following lines appeared in the *Hartford Times* of the next day:

Secretary McLean to-day received from General Jones, of Montgomery, Alabama, one of the flags of the 16th Connecticut Volunteers, captured at the surrender of Plymouth, North Carolina, 1864. The flag is not the United States flag furnished by the government to each regiment, nor the State colors furnished by Connecticut, but one of the guidons, and has been identified as the one presented to the regiment by the Hartford City Guards. It is about two by three and a half feet in dimensions, of heavy blue silk. The State coat of arms and the inscription, "16th Connecticut Volunteers," are embroidered in silk, and the edges are trimmed with yellow silk fringe. The guidon is in an excellent state of preservation, and the colors almost as bright as when the flag was new; one corner was missing. Although this is not a battle-flag, the good feeling of the Alabama veterans in returning it is as greatly appreciated by the 16th as if it were a flag which had been torn by shot and shell in the rage of battle. It is the fraternal feeling, not the flag alone, which is appreciated.

Thus by pouring balm upon old wounds, returning trophies such as this, proves that in the hearts of old soldiers of the late war all bitterness has died out. Politicians may rant about "solid South" and "bloody flag," but when old soldiers who have braved the dangers of the battle-field get together, all bitterness disappears, and they talk calmly and dispassionately of the great Lost Cause; regretfully, too, maybe, but laying aside all resentment, knowing themselves brothers of a common nation, and uniting in the belief that "whatever is, is right."

THE BEGINNING OF SHERMAN'S ADVANCE.

ROCKY FACE RIDGE.

Robert Shackleton, Jr.

THE winter that intervened between the battle of Missionary Ridge and the advance of Sherman toward Atlanta, was to both armies a time of earnest preparation. Jefferson Davis, in an address to the Confederate army, assured the soldiers that the Union campaign of 1864 must necessarily, from exhaustion of resources of men and money, be far less formidable than those of the last two years. At the same time, however, the Confederate government was making tremendous efforts to increase the forces in the field, and about the close of 1863 a law was passed that was depended upon to develop the entire Southern strength.

Every white man in the Confederacy, between the ages of eighteen and fifty-five, with the exception of those belonging to a few necessarily exempt classes, was to be considered in the military service, and subject to the articles of war and to military discipline and penalties. If any such man should fail to report for duty within a specified time, he was liable to arrest and execution as a deserter.

During the winter of 1863–64, there was much of scarcity and suffering among the Confederates at Dalton. The horses were poor and weak from insufficiency of food, while the men themselves were short of supplies of all kinds. They did not have enough food. They did not have enough blankets. They did not have enough clothing and shoes.

"Were many of the men actually barefoot that winter?" we recently asked a Confederate soldier, who was one of the army there.

"Yes," he replied, "there were many of them." He paused a moment, and then added, quietly: "I was one of them myself."

It is very pleasant to find, in conversation with Southern men, a very general absence of boastfulness or conceit. They speak just as readily, for instance, of how they went down the wrong side of Missionary Ridge, "twenty feet at a jump," as they do of how they sent Rosecrans hurrying to Chattanooga, and they rarely, unless the turn of conversation specially calls for it, tell of their individual happenings.

One colonel, indeed (a real colonel he was, too, and not merely one who has been given the

MILL CREEK GAP.

title since the war), began with his personal history the instant he commenced talking to us, and within a very few moments explained very fully what a mainstay of the Confederacy he had been, and what a thorn in the side of the Yankees. He talked so rapidly and strenuously that we could scarcely find time to wonder how it actually happened that Lee ever surrendered while he had such a follower as this. But the colonel was an exception. The Confederate veterans are mostly modest and unassuming in the extreme.

While Johnston's men were awaiting, under circumstances of such privation, the advance of Sherman, that general was preparing to move forward with forceful vigor. "Now that I insist on war pure and simple, with no admixture of civil compromises," he wrote, "I am supposed vindictive." And again: "I would make this war as severe as possible, and show no symptoms of tiring till the South begs for mercy. The end would be reached quicker by such a course than by any seeming yielding on our part."

With about 100,000 men and over 250 cannon, Sherman prepared to advance, and Johnston, with a force which has been variously estimated as being from 43,000 to some 60,000 men, and which was probably nearer 50,000, confronted him. The Confederates had about 125 cannon, but it is said that about half could not be used because the horses were too starved and weak by the wintering at Dalton, to manœuvre them.

GENERAL JOHNSTON'S HEADQUARTERS AT DALTON.

Frequently, however, it has happened that the quantity of cannon with an army has had but little to do with its success or failure. General Grant, at one time, in Virginia, sent a large number of cannon away from the army rather than be encumbered with them. Napoleon, with forty or fifty pieces of artillery, conquered Italy. With 1,000 pieces, thoroughly equipped, he invaded Russia and failed.

The problems of food and forage that Sherman had to solve, were extremely difficult. He was to advance into a country that had already been largely stripped of supplies, and was to maintain a line of communication that was constantly to increase in length.

A soldier needs about three pounds of gross food per day. A horse or mule needs twenty pounds. Such amounts as these, multiplied by the number of men and horses that were to be fed, and supplemented by the immense quantities of necessary stores of other kinds, prepare us for the statement that 1300 tons of supplies were needed by his army every day.

Sherman met the question with characteristic vigor. The railroad which connected Nashville with Chattanooga, and the railroad from Chattanooga southward toward Atlanta, were to be devoted exclusively to the carrying of supplies. Private traffic, whether passenger or freight, was forbidden. The people might travel, and ship goods, in any other way they could, but the use of the railroads was not allowed. Even the soldiers had to march, except when, in cases of emergency, they were specially ordered to go by rail.

These stringent rules were from time to time, as circumstances permitted, slightly relaxed, but in the main they were sharply adhered to. The army was not allowed to carry any tents, except some for the sick and wounded, and one for each headquarters as an office. The officers, however, were allowed to have tent flies, without poles, but with no accompanying tent furniture. The flies were used by being spread over saplings or fence-rails.

Early in May, the forward movement of the Union armies began, and from Chattanooga and Ringgold the troops, leaving their camps, advanced toward the Confederate army.

At Tunnel Hill, there was some sharp skirmishing, but no strong resistance, and the Confederates fell back to Dalton.

It was with a feeling of profound relief that Sherman learned that the enemy had retreated without destroying the tunnel, for its destruction would most seriously have hampered and delayed the Union advance, dependent, as it was, upon the use of the railroad. Surprise has been expressed that Johnston omitted the destruction of this tunnel, but to us the explanation seems very clear and reasonable.

He occupied a position at Dalton which he considered impregnable. He felt positive that Sherman would be defeated there. Then, as the Federals retreated, he wished to use the tunnel himself, and to leave it intact for future army operations and for the use of the railroad in forwarding supplies. Of course, the Federals might destroy it as they themselves retreated, but that was no reason why he should by his own act an-

BATTLE OF MILL CREEK GAP.

ticipate the calamity. Besides, he could fairly hope, by an active dash as the Federals fell back, to make it impossible for them to complete the tunnel's destruction.

Later in the campaign, it is said, when Sherman was rapidly nearing Atlanta, and when the Confederates had learned to their cost that he had an almost marvellous faculty of repairing any loss and supplying any need, a group of Confederates were told that a cavalry raid had destroyed the tunnel, and that, as the railroad was thus rendered useless, the Federals would have to retreat.

"Oh!" exclaimed one, bitterly and with an oath, " *Don't you know that old Sherman carries a duplicate tunnel along ?* "

The news of the destruction, it may be added, was erroneous.

The position occupied by Johnston, at Dalton, was wonderfully strong. General Bragg, while still in command, had selected it as the most favorable location for defence, and Johnston, realizing at once the possibilities of the position, had fortified it with all the splendid skill of which he was such a master.

The town of Dalton, now containing some 4,000 inhabitants, is pleasantly situated among low rolling hills. A little to the westward the view is hemmed in by the long line of heights known as Rocky Face Ridge, while far to the eastward rise the blue Cohutta Mountains, majestic and beautiful.

We had occasion to forcibly realize, in this neighborhood, what we afterwards found to be

the case at other localities still farther south, that many of the rising generation know and care but little about the late war. If one, at the locality of some battle, meets a Confederate veteran, he is sure of ready and full and courteous information ; if, however, he meets the Confederate's son or daughter, he is not unlikely to find only ignorance.

"I've heard my father talk about it; *he'd* know where they fought ;"—or (if it is a family of less education), "I reckon pap 'ud know. The Fed'rals went clar to Atlanty, I've hern tell, but I dunno ef thar war any battle hyar ;"— while their own home, perhaps, stands where events took place that are world-famous.

Surely the spirit of the " Lost Cause " is itself lost when the children of those who struggled for it care more to know about present union than past dissension.

The lofty and rugged ridge which rises as a barrier between Dalton and an approach from the direction of Ringgold, is known as Rocky Face Ridge. Part of the ridge, indeed, was once known as St. John's Mountain, and later and more prosaically as " John's Mountain," but the entire length of ridge is now commonly referred to as Rocky Face.

At Mill Creek Gap, four and a-half miles above Dalton, the railroad passes through the ridge. Dug Gap is about as far south of the town as Mill Creek Gap is north. The ridge runs due north and south. The Federals, following the railroad, approached from the west.

Harker's brigade tried to effect an advance at the northern end of the Confederate position, about a mile and a-half north of Mill Creek Gap, but the difficulties of the land were too great to be surmounted.

At Dug Gap, too, an effort was made, and the daring Geary, who could be fully depended upon to make a desperate assault, was chosen to lead the attack.

Unlike Mill Creek Gap, Dug Gap is not really a break in the ridge. It is merely a place where, the ridge being a very little lower than at some other points, a road has been laid out which, running over the top of the ridge, connects the valleys on either side. To reach the summit,

BATTLE OF DUG GAP.

the road winds and twists, following long sweeps to take advantage of the ground. The woods all along on the Dalton side of the ridge, and especially, of course, on the easy slopes near the base, were full of camping-grounds, and little hillocks and depressions are still pointed out as places where the soldiers had huts and cooking-places.

A plain little cabin, too, is passed, which is still termed the "Widows' Retreat," for there, it is said, seven women, whose husbands were all in the Confederate army in Virginia, waited and watched for their return. They worked the field about the hut and lived as best they could, suffering hardships and poverty and enduring heartaches that were embittered by misery. And then the Confederates retreated, and the poor women "refugeed" farther to the South, and what became of them, and whether they

and their husbands hopelessly lost each other, or whether the men returned from the war and found their weary, waiting wives, or whether the husbands were placed hastily in some ditch in the Wilderness or beside the Chickahominy, no one can tell. The sufferings and trials of the women of the South can scarcely be appreciated by the people of the North, for, besides partings and death, there were invasion and burning and starvation and hurried flying from before the enemy's advance.

We reached the summit of Dug Gap, and found there a most remarkable and stupendous formation. The top of the ridge is covered with immense stones and solid masses of rock, which, running in a continuous line along the summit, form a natural barrier of unsurmountable strength. The rocks present sharp angles and slippery faces, and all shapes and formations, and from behind them a force, with bravery and resolution, could make it impossible for even the most devoted troops to carry the ridge.

We went down the road by which and by the side of which Geary's men tried to advance, and it twisted so much that at one time we were facing back directly toward the gap, although, of course, the road still trended downward.

Geary, finding the road itself blockaded and fortified, had his men charge right up the side of the ridge, and, that we might the better realize the difficulties of that charge, we clambered back to the summit up that very slope.

A long and tedious climb it was, over fallen trees and rocks, and among the forest trees and through bushes and underbrush. Geary's men, as they climbed up, met a withering fire from a protected foe, and fell before great stones and bowlders which came crashing down the steep incline upon them.

After clambering up the long slope, and nearing the summit, Geary's men found the greatest difficulties of all, for there, fronting them, was the rock barrier, and the most heroic attempts could not carry it. The attack, very wisely, was given up as soon as it was seen that it was utterly hopeless, and before there was too serious a loss of life.

By the pass, on the summit, being very thirsty, we dug out a spring of pure, clear water, and, as we drank it, could feel that perhaps we were the first to do so since the soldiers occupied the post. Then, climbing along the ridge, over the great rocks, we looked forth over the fine panorama of fields and hills and homes, and tried to fancy what the Confederate garrison must have thought as they gazed far below them upon the marching columns and waving flags of those whom they considered to be unjust invaders of Georgia soil.

A favorite maxim of one of the greatest of European generals was that an army can pass wherever a man can put his foot. After all, though, it makes a good deal of difference whether or not another man has got his foot there first. The Federal army passed Rocky Face Ridge easily enough after the Confederates retreated from it.

At Mill Creek Gap the Federals made some efforts to pierce the line, but there, too, they were unsuccessful. There the ridge is cut through by a stream, named Mill Creek, and the lofty heights on either side are termed Buzzards' Roost. In the centre of the gap is a rounding knoll. On one side of the knoll runs Mill Creek. On the other side are Little Martin Creek and the railroad. The two creeks unite just behind the knoll, to the eastward.

The hamlet of Rocky Face is just outside of the entrance to the gap, and is a place of, perhaps, a dozen one-story little houses, two small stores, and the inevitable blacksmith-shop. Earthworks may still be seen along the ridge and on adjoining hills just inside of the gap.

"Sherman couldn't 'a' rid over us," observed a Confederate veteran whom we met there, and whose home is close by, "we was too well heeled." He added, however, with that admiration for Sherman's ability which is universal among Johnston's men, that if Sherman had not flanked them in the way he succeeded in doing, "he'd 'a' found some other way o' doin' of it."

It is an attractive region inside of the gap, for the heights stretch off in irregular and picturesque sweeps, and the valley winds beautifully onward.

Mill Creek Gap, with the railroad and the creek passing through, was the most vital and at the same time the weakest point in the Confederate line, and Johnston, with the determination of genius, had set himself to make it impregnable. He not only placed commanding batteries, he not only constructed breastworks, and carefully posted his men, he did more, and it was a master stroke.

The creek flows through the gap from west to east, and about a mile from the entrance Johnston constructed a strong dam. The water then flooding back, made the valley into a lake, with only narrow stretches of dry land along which to advance. These stretches, too, were commanded by works on the hills above, while, more than this, strong works were constructed near the dam itself.

It is not surprising that Sherman, after some demonstrations against this position, and a sharp fight which is generally termed a battle, gave up any serious intention of breaking through there and again turned his attention to assaulting other points along the line.

"They couldn't 'a' got through unless they'd 'a' swum. Ef they'd a tried 'twould 'a' ben murder," said the veteran to whom I was speaking.

Part of the dam may still be made out, although, of course, the work was long since destroyed.

Within the central portion of the town of Dalton there is nothing now to show that contending armies struggled for its possession, but on the two Fort Hills, immediately overlooking the railroad tracks, there still remain extensive works, and on picturesque Mount Rachel, but a mile or so away, there are also carefully constructed lines. On Little Fort Hill, too, there still stands an old tree which was used as a signal tree. A platform was built in the top, and strips of wood were nailed against the tree for a ladder. Some of the spikes are still in the tree, and are plainly to be seen. Strictly speaking, perhaps, we should not have said that there is nothing within the town that tells of war, for the building still stands there which is pointed out as having been the headquarters of General Johnston.

"And he often used to tie his horse to that post," is added, but as the post is on the other side of the street, we may be permitted to doubt this additional point.

The house is now used as a boarding-house. It is of quite a good size, with a pleasant porch in front, and has the appearance of having been quite a mansion in the time of the war.

The people of Dalton, while they still retain certain Southern prejudices and opinions, heartily welcome Northerners, and seem to have almost forgotten that there was ever a war. Their reminiscences are not war reminiscences. Their stories are not war stories. But they will tell you with gleeful appreciation of the Dalton lawyer who, retained by the defendant in a certain case, unfortunately came to the trial under the influence of liquor, and, considerably befuddled, made a telling speech against his client. The poor fellow pulled him by the sleeve. "I say," he whispered hoarsely, "*you're on my side!*" The lawyer, with drunken gravity, gazed at him a moment and strove to collect his wits. Then he slowly turned again to the jury: "Now that I have brought up every point that can possibly be urged against my client," he said, with slow deliberation, "I shall now proceed to explain what is the actual truth and justice of the case."

Long ago, years before the war, the Indians were forcibly, and under circumstances of atrocious cruelty, compelled to leave Northern Georgia, the discovery of gold having rendered the land valuable in the eyes of the whites. The Indians so loved the beautiful mountains and valleys that they could not bear to go away, and they were fiercely hunted from their hiding-places and dragged off, great numbers being even killed.

It was made a penal offence, so it is said, for any white man to assist an Indian in eluding the officers, but John Howard Payne, who was then in the neighborhood of Dalton, was so deeply moved by the removal of the savages from their homes, that he did what he could to help them.

He was arrested, and while in charge of an officer, began to sing a verse of "Home, Sweet Home," thinking, doubtless, of the homeless Indians.

The officer listened and was touched.

"Who wrote that song?"

"I did."

The officer urged him to sing some more, and was so affected by the emotions that it called up that he at once, although with danger of reprimand and punishment to himself, released the man whose only offence was to sympathize with the Indians in the desire to live in the homes that they so loved. At that time the song had not been given to the world. The story, whether true or not, is believed in this region, and is given for actual truth, so far as can be ascertained.

Sherman himself, years before the war, was at Dalton, when he was a lieutenant in the army. His remembrance of the country made him, doubtless, the more ready to understand the impossibility of breaking through the Confederate lines when so well intrenched and defended, and he realized that he must depend altogether upon manœuvring Johnston out of his position by a flank movement.

IN MEMORY OF THE BRAVE.

COMRADES, through storms and clouds, down in the valley,
  So none could tell where the long march might end,
You've seen the darkness, dawn, repulse, and rally;
  We're reunited now—not foe, but friend.

Your arms are grounded and your ranks are broken,
  The brazen bugle sounds the charge no more;
We're "waiting orders," till the word is spoken
  To join our comrades on the other shore.

AN ARTILLERY FIGHT AT SHORT RANGE.

WILLIAM BYRNES.

ON the 9th day of August, 1862, was fought the battle of Cedar Mountain, in Virginia. The Confederate forces were commanded by General T. J. Jackson, better known as "Stonewall" Jackson, and the Union army by General John Pope. Our regiment, the 107th Pennsylvania Volunteers, had lain the greater part of the day between Culpepper and Cedar Mountain. The distance between the two points is about nine miles. In the afternoon we moved slowly up in the direction of the conflict. About sunset we turned off the main road and went into camp without pitching tents. No mail had been received for several days—two weeks as nearly as I can recollect—so when it was announced that one had arrived there was excitement and rejoicing among the boys. Those who got letters were elated, and those who did not, the writer among the number, were correspondingly depressed. By the time the mail had been distributed it had grown dark, and some stumps of

candles were lit in order to read. Hardly had the lights been struck until orders to put them out went hurriedly around. Our first lieutenant, who was eagerly reading a letter, was a little slow in obeying, when the major rushed up and kicked out the candle, which, I think, the lieutenant held in his hand, although I am now not sure, notwithstanding that I was within a few feet of them. (The usual way was to stick a bayonet in the ground and put the candle in the socket.) Just then there was a boom from the direction of the enemy, and away over to our left a curved streak of light showed the track of a shell. "Pretty," "beautiful," and similar remarks were heard all around. Another, and then another followed, each nearer to us. Some one said that they came from the mountain three to five miles away, and they must have siege guns. The observations were made as if we were disinterested spectators. The next shells went immediately over our heads. They had gotten the range with surprising quick-

LETTERS FROM HOME.

"THE CAISSON EXPLODED, MAKING A RED FLASH ON THE NIGHT."

ness. Within a few yards of the writer was the regimental ambulance, and under it was curled a small "contraband," a boy the surgeon had picked up somewhere. A shell struck the ground between us and exploded. The little fellow sprang up and struck his head against the axle of the wagon and fell down dazed, with a scalp-wound. He always insisted that he had been hit on the head by that shell. The order, "Fall in," was responded to at once, and we found ourselves formed, I think, in close order, company front. A battery came galloping by us to the rear, and some one gave the order, "Left flank, march." Very slowly a few paces were taken to the rear, when a "halt" was ordered, and Lieutenant-Colonel McCall rode up and demanded to know "by whose order was this march?" Among the men it was generally understood afterward that the order was given in a moment of excitement by a captain of one of the companies on the right of the regiment, who resigned a day or two subsequently. The exact facts I never knew. In a few minutes we were marching on the main road in the direction of

the firing, in regular order, Company A on the right and B on the left. The shelling had ceased. We had reached the top of a rise in the road, when the moon came out and revealed us to the enemy. Immediately a Confederate battery on the left of the road opened on us. In a wonderfully short time Thompson's battery (Union), on the right of the road, replied. Which was Union and which was Confederate at that time our company, B, at least did not know. The distance between the two batteries was 400 yards, and we were half-way between. We had halted and were lying close to the ground. Even to sit up was to take a great risk of having our heads knocked off. The battery on the right fired lower than the other. Both of them were on ground slightly lower than our position, which, as may easily be understood, was not the most comfortable to be imagined.

After a time Second-Lieutenant Gist called my attention to the fact that the battery on the left was slackening fire a little, while the one on the right was, if anything, increasing its fire. We could plainly hear the voices of the officers on our left, commanding and entreating the men to stand their ground. One of their caissons was struck by a shell and exploded, making a red flash on the night.

Suddenly there was a tremendous roar from the rear, as another battery opened up. Every gun seemed to speak at once. They were ten-pounders, and had been brought into action without our knowledge. We knew this must be our own artillery, and the direction of the shells indicated the enemy. The Confederate battery held on bravely for a little while, so that from the rear and the right and the left shells went hustling and shrieking over our heads, and there was plenty of "music in the air." Soon the firing from the Confederates on our left ceased entirely; both the artillerymen and their supports were compelled to retire, leaving the guns on the field. The fire from the Union batteries stopped shortly afterward; the fight was over, and our boys began to breathe easier.

Our command filed off into a corn-field on the right and lay down. With a corn-hill for a pillow, in a few minutes the writer was fast asleep, and so was nearly every one else. There we rested until morning, when we went back to our original position of the night before when the shelling commenced. Sometime after the firing had ceased, the Confederates returned and recovered their pieces.

This engagement was certainly one of the most unique artillery duels of the war. It was fought at less than point-blank range and directly over the heads of our regiment.

THAT OLD FLAG.

CALEB DUNN.

BRIGHTER than ever is that old flag that smiles on us to-day,
And brighter still its stars shall grow as ages pass away;
Their light the brightest light of hope for man shall ever be—
The glory of the grandest flag that waves on land or sea.
It has ever been the symbol of our greatness in the past,
Its spirit shall be our hope and guide as long as time shall last,
For the souls that reared that standard, and first raised it toward the sky,
Resolved that long as freedom lives that "banner shall not die."

O grand old flag! fraternal love thy glory e'er shall crown,
And from the ramparts of our land no foe shall tear thee down!
There thou shalt ever wave, as thou art brightly seen to-day,
The pride of all true hearts that beat beneath the blue and gray!
Thou smilest on the noblest blood the world has ever known,
Whose signet of nobility is simple nature's own;
The blood of all the people who to liberty are true,
Though they be rich, or they be poor, or high or lowly too.
'Tis found within the cottage where the toiler's baby lies,
As well as in the cradle of the richest 'neath the skies;
'Tis not the blood of arrogance, that seeks its power to win
By pride of birth or caste—that superannuated sin.
No hostile power can ever change the color of that blood,
That bears the seal of nobleness, stamped by the hand of God.

Beneath thy starry gleams we see pass in a grand review,
George Washington, and Stark, and Knox, and Francis Marion, too;
We see bold Captain John Paul Jones, and plain Ben Franklin, too,
With Jefferson and Adams, and Charles Carroll, staunch and true;
We see stern Andrew Jackson, and brave Phil. Kearney there,
With blunt old "Rough and Ready," who had will to do and dare;
We see the spirits of the dead—the martyred soldiers true—
The patriots who for freedom died, pass on in this review.
Beneath thy folds, old flag of stars, while we renew the vow,
That long as hearts shall beat, and thought shall dwell within man's brow,
We'll hold thee e'er aloft, though storm and danger threaten thee,
And with our lives defend thee, thou loved banner of the free!

Oh, dark indeed would be our hope for future liberty,
If that old flag of stars and stripes should ever cease to be!
For it alone, unsullied there, with all its folds unfurled,
Is Freedom's dearest gift to man,—the safeguard of the world.
It symbolizes genius, and the work that it has done—
The grandest, best achievements that God's sun e'er smiled upon;
It tells of splendid palaces that people ever see,
Where'er the white-winged birds of universal commerce be;
It tells of mighty threads of thought that with electric band
Girdle the earth—the wondrous work of men born in this land.

And as the ages roll apace, that flag shall brighter grow,
With the lustre of new triumphs that our genius shall bestow;
And glorious as its record is—a monument sublime—
It shall e'er increase in glory with th' increasing years of time,
For when that flag was first unfurled, 'twas with this stern decree:
That long as man be true to man, in this Land of the Free,
Those stars shall be our hope, that flag shall never cease to be!

GENERAL ULYSSES SIMPSON GRANT.

BORN APRIL 27, 1822, AT POINT PLEASANT, OHIO.   CADET AT WEST POINT, 1839–1843.
SERVED IN MEXICAN WAR FROM SPRING OF 1846 TO AUTUMN OF 1847.
COLONEL 21ST ILLINOIS INFANTRY, JUNE 17, 1861.   BRIGADIER GENERAL, AUGUST 7, 1863.
LIEUTENANT GENERAL, MARCH 1, 1864.   APPOMATTOX, APRIL 9, 1865.
GENERAL OF THE ARMY, JULY 25, 1866.
PRESIDENT OF THE UNITED STATES, 1869–1877.
DIED AT MT. McGREGOR, N. Y., JULY 23, 1885.
ENTOMBED AT RIVERSIDE PARK, NEW YORK CITY, AUGUST 6, 1885.

THE GENERAL.

SEYMOUR HERBERT RANSOM.

NOT many years ago I had the pleasure of making an extended tour through the western part of North Carolina. My companion was a very stern though genial man of fifty-five years, whom I had known from my earliest recollections. At home every one called him "General," without paying any attention whatever to his name. I could understand the appellation, for General Malcolm was a veteran of the late war; but I confess I was somewhat surprised, in our travels, to learn that he was so familiarly known. He was much beloved by the old soldiers in the State, and at the reunions the "General" was a prominent personage. On his right arm he bore the scars of three wounds, and everywhere throughout the State he had won the reputation of having been a dauntless man on the field of battle, and a strict disciplinarian in the camp.

On our journey the General told me many old stories about the war, and I soon became so delighted with his pleasant, modest way of relating these incidents, that I vexed him, I fear, with impertinent questions. However, he was patient with me, and did much to make our otherwise tedious journey agreeable.

About nine o'clock one evening our train rolled into a little station where we had to change cars. The quiet hamlet of B——, consisting of perhaps fifteen or twenty houses, lay in the heart of the Blue Ridge, and a clear half-moon, ascending the vault of the heavens, lighted up the surrounding mountains and valleys with peculiar beauty. To me it was a

271

strange sight, just having left my home by the sea, and I stood on the platform for some time, enjoying the magnificent scenery around us.

"Come, Gampillo, we must go in now. You'll catch cold here," and the thoughtful old man took me kindly by the hand, and together we walked down the platform and entered the waiting-room of the little station. In an adjoining room we heard talking, in which the deep voices of men were plainly audible. We sat for a moment—the General and I—in silence. Then one of the voices asked,—

"At Malvern Hill?"

"Yes," replied another, "just as the sun went down the command was given to charge."

That was enough. The General rose, and beckoning to me, crossed over to the little room on the right. The two men, who were the only persons in the room, looked up as we entered, but appeared scarcely to notice us, as they continued their conversation.

"You remember," said one, who was the older of the two, "we'd been fighting all day. It began early in the morning, and I'll never forget one thing that happened that day, John, as long as I live."

"What was it?" asked John, shifting in his chair and becoming interested.

"Well, as I said, the firing began early in the morning, about seven o'clock. I was then in the 36th North Carolina, Colonel Montgomery commanding. You knew Colonel Montgomery, didn't you? No? Well, sir, a braver man never lived. When the Yankees began to shell us across the Chickahominy, Colonel Montgomery ordered the regiment to the rear, where there were some fortifications, which would protect us from the shelling. We'd been there about half an hour, when we saw the 27th North Carolina marching across the field with old Colonel Green at their head. On they went—across the open field—down the little hill by the river—never firing a shot. We stood there watching them. Colonel Montgomery told us to wait for the command before we charged. Twenty minutes passed. We looked over the breastworks again, and, John, it was a sad sight. A few hundred straggling, limping, wounded men—all that was left of the brave 27th—came up over the little hill by the river, and we knew then that the remainder were bleeding on the field of battle, or their dead bodies floating down the Chickahominy. Some of the boys in the 36th were crying, and Colonel Montgomery clutched his

sword in a nervous way and started to say something. Just at that moment a horseman dashed up to the works, dressed in a Confederate uniform, his face red as fire. Waving his sword defiantly, he asked, in a most excited manner,—

"'What troops are these?'

"Colonel Montgomery stepped forward, and coolly replied,—

"'This is the 36th North Carolina, Colonel Montgomery commanding.'

"'The 36th North Carolina!' thundered the officer, who wore two stars on the collar of his uniform. 'You miserable coward! Here you are skulking behind these works, and your comrades are out there bleeding on the field,' and the officer pointed his sword toward the river. 'If you have a spark of manhood, you'll go to their assistance at once;' and ripping out several uncomplimentary oaths, he turned his horse and galloped across the field.

"No sooner had he gone than Colonel Montgomery gave the command. 'Charge, boys, charge!' he cried, and leaped over the embankment. The boys followed his example. Just as we cleared the breastworks, 'Double quick' ran down the lines, and the 36th answered with a yell and started for the Chickahominy. There we met the Yankees. For two hours the two sides advanced and fell back—one gaining an advantage only to lose it—until the 14th Virginia came on the field, and then the Yankees withdrew across the Chickahominy, destroying the bridges behind them.

"As we were coming back, I heard the voice of some one moaning and sobbing aloud. I thought I recognized it. I had heard the voice many times before. I climbed over the fence and waded through the mud in the direction the sound came from. As I drew nearer, the sound grew more distinct, and I thought I heard mutterings. Yes, it was, indeed, too true. There lay my colonel, outstretched on the ground, with his head in a little pool of water, pressing his forehead with his hand. The blood was trickling down his face and besmearing the gold stars on his shoulders. He beckoned me to him. I hated to speak to him, John, for the colonel had been just as kind to me as he would have been to his own boy. I didn't want to see him die, and so I almost turned away; but he called me back and said, 'Won't—you—please—give—this—to—Julia?' and he took from his finger the ring he had worn at the Military Academy. 'Tell—her—Bob,' he said,

'I—died—blessing—her.' He moved as if in mortal agony, and I begged him to let me carry him to the hospital; but he waved me aside with his hand. And then, John, happened the saddest thing I ever saw. He suddenly became delirious, and began to strike his head violently with his hand. Then he would fall back in my arms and rave like a maniac. Oh, John, it was a piteous scene! I can't tell you how it was. He cried out for the man who had called him a coward. 'Oh, God! Am I a coward? *Am I a coward?* General, tell me I die a man—just tell me *I die a man!* My God, my God! I'm lost! I'm lost!' He turned his head from me, covered his face with his hands, and there, beside the quiet stream, John, he sobbed out his brave young life.''

General Malcolm drew his large slouch hat over his eyes, and passed out into the other room. I followed him; our train was due in a few minutes. We were standing on the platform again. The General looked off to the mountains, pulled his beard nervously, and muttered to himself,—

"It was too bad—too bad. War is an awful curse. But I had to do it.''

SUPPORTING A BATTERY.

Edward P. Tobie.

"FOURS left—march! Halt! Right dress. Front!'' and we find ourselves in line, sitting on our horses, looking about us with more of anxiety than curiosity, to see where we are, and what we are here for. We know well enough we are here to fight, and the moments before going into a fight — before we know what sort of a fight we are going to get into, and what sort of a position we are going to occupy—are moments of anxiety. After we get fairly at work, it is a different matter. At this time, my company, which is on the right of the regiment, is behind some woods, and the regimental line stretches away to the left across a field, with woods at the distance on the left and in front. At the right of the centre of the regiment is a large, old-fashioned Virginia chimney, where once stood a mansion, now destroyed. Just beyond that, a little to the front, is a slight rise in the ground, and on this rising ground a battery takes position. There is intense, earnest action, interesting and exhilarating to soldier and civilian alike, in light-artillery drill on the muster field, but wonderfully intensified are these emotions when watching a battery getting into position under the excitement of battle when every nerve of men and horses is strained to the utmost and it seems as if the very guns themselves are anxious to get into play as quickly as possible. It is a sight well worth seeing; but the feelings of the soldier vary, according to whether the battery is of his own force, and is about to pour shot and shell into the enemy, or belongs to the enemy, and is about to play upon him and his comrades.

The interest is as strong in either case, but there is an entirely different tinge to it, and this tinge makes all the difference in the world. In the one case, it means assistance; in the other, it means resistance—only a slight difference in the sound of the words, but a vast distinction in the meaning.

But on this particular day there are still other emotions as we see this battery galloping into position. We watch their rapid manœuvres, and are pleased with the promptness, precision, and business-like air with which they are performed; but there is an anxious dread as we realize the fact that we are to serve as support for that battery in the coming fight. That means more severe strain upon our nerves and our courage than a soldier has to endure in any other kind of fighting. It means that the minutes are to drag into hours, with every second full of danger, while we are to do nothing; that we are to have all the danger of battle, with none of the activity and excitement, or the forgetfulness of self and of danger which excitement and activity bring; are to be under fire without the privilege of returning the fire; are to be quiescent while the enemy is exceedingly and offensively active. But such is the fortune of war, and we must submit as cheerfully and with as stout hearts as we can.

The battery is in position, and ready for action; but we can see no enemy; can hear no artillery fire; can hear nothing but a slight skirmish fire in the distance; can see no reason for the battery going into position. There is no excitement about the battery. The men are calmly awaiting orders, and are, apparently, unconcerned, though all are in their places. The caissons and limbers have been taken to the rear; only the guns and the men are on the little hill. The carbine fire in the distance grows more continued and more heavy, but is still in the distance. A staff officer suddenly rides out of the woods, gallops diagonally across the field to the commander of the battery, salutes, says a few words, and gallops back into the woods. The resonant tones of command are heard, and the artillerymen spring to their work. A moment more, and the guns have spoken in unmistakable tones, and sent messages to the enemy which they can readily interpret. There is no response, and our battery fires again. Still no response, nor does the carbine fire seem to be affected. So far as sound can tell us, it is neither increasing nor diminishing. Suddenly the roar of cannon comes to us from a distance, and at the same instant, almost, shells come screaming over our heads, and we are sure the enemy is near, though we cannot see him, and that he has a good range of our position. Being acquainted with the country, being on his own ground, he knows, by the direction from which our shells come, where our battery is probably posted; knows also the approximate distance from his own battery, and thus can elevate his guns, and aim them with a good degree of accuracy. The battle has begun, and we are in for a season of "supporting a battery," with all the suffering in spirit which such duty involves. We are in line in rear of the battery, sitting on our horses, wishing, oh, so much! that we could dismount. We know, by experience, that the greater portion of the shot and shell thrown at our force will go over the battery, some will go over us, and some will just reach us. We remember another engagement when we supported a battery, where the first few shells sent over by the enemy were shrapnel, and striking, some in the midst of our battery, and some between the battery and our own line, sent the iron bullets rattling in amongst us, until it was a wonder that any of us escaped. We are in quite as much, yes, more, danger than are the artillerymen, who are doing so nobly in our front. How tall our horses seem, and how high we seem to be in the air, as the shot and shell come screaming over us, threatening to strike some of us. Oh, why do we not get the order to dismount? It is cruel, it is wicked, to keep us mounted under this fire! At least, that is the way we look upon it just now.

The firing has hardly got well under way when a shell strikes into the company at the left of my own, wounding two horses, and of course dismounting their riders, who start for the rear, one of them wounded. The shell rolls leisurely along a short distance, directly under the horse of the lieutenant-colonel, who is a few yards in rear of the right centre of the regiment, and there stops, with the fuse still burning. The lieutenant-colonel realizes his danger and strikes both spurs vigorously into the horse's flanks; but the horse has seen the whizzing thing under him, is frightened, and, instead of bounding away, as he ought to under the spurs, he dances about, whirls around and around in his endeavors to keep his eyes on the shell and the sputtering fuse, and remains right there. We look with awe upon the scene, for we expect the shell to burst any instant, and if it does it seems that nothing can save man or horse. And there is a hint of selfishness in this awe, for the pieces of shell may fly in our direction. The look upon the face of the lieutenant-colonel, as he gazes down upon the shell and tries to get his horse out of the way, is beyond description. There is a mixture of anxiety and dread, and of a determination to meet whatever comes bravely. He tries to laugh, but the laugh is a failure. The agony is but for a moment. The shell bursts, and, somehow, we cannot tell how, horse and rider are unharmed. But a piece of the shell flies back toward the regiment, another horse is disabled, and another rider starts for the hospital. The injured horses are killed to put them out of their misery, and again we rest quietly under the artillery fire, with nothing to take our thoughts from the danger of flying shot and shell. Shells never scream so fiercely or sound so wickedly as under such conditions as these, when we are doing nothing, and there is none of the noise of our own carbines, none of the noise of battle, to drown the sounds of the flying missiles, except the steady "boom" of our own battery.

In a little while comes the welcome order to dismount. There is remarkable promptitude in obeying this order. We leave the horses in the line, and sit or lie down on the ground in front of them. There is a feeling of relief all along the line. We are in danger yet, but it seems less as we come down from our elevated position in the saddle. As we dismount, the first sergeant of my company stops by his horse a moment to get some tobacco from the saddle-bags, and then takes his place with the rest of us. As he sits down, a shell or solid shot comes along and takes off both nigh legs of his horse, where he was standing but an instant before. This gives us a thrill of horror. A little delay in giving the order to dismount, or a bit longer time at the saddle-bags, and the sergeant would have been severely wounded, perhaps killed. We have learned to look upon such incidents, not as accidental or arising from chance, but as the direct interposition of a Higher Power. We feel that "narrow escapes" are simply protection afforded those who come so near death, and thus, though used to all the cruelties and roughness of war, and at times to harshness and even profanity in the men, we have as firm belief in God and His goodness as the most devout worshipper in civil life; aye, more, for we see His hand almost daily in these stern times. The sergeant shoots his horse as a kindness, though the tears spring into his eyes as he does so, for that horse has been his best friend; distributes as much of his worldly goods among his comrades as he cannot conveniently carry with him, and starts for the rear. We bid him good-bye sadly, for we are all more or less affected by the incident, and we know not when we may see him again—some of us perhaps never. In half an hour or so he returns, having procured another horse somehow; gathers up his belongings, and takes his place in the line as though nothing unusual had happened. Some of us wonder at this, for we think we could not have obtained another horse so quickly. But it is of such stuff that the American soldiers are made.

The change from the saddle to the ground is a relief for a time; but we soon begin to feel as unsafe as before. We who are on the extreme right of the line do not fancy those woods close in our front. To the ordinary mind it might seem that trees are a protection from shot and shell; but we have learned otherwise from experience. We remember another engagement, when, as we were changing position under a heavy artillery fire, we halted behind a hill, where we felt as safe as at home, for the shot and shell were flying high over our heads, and we thought could not by any means get down behind that hill, which was as good as breastworks; but a shell struck the top of a dead tree on the hill, and was lowered into our midst, killing two men by cutting them in two, and, going a little further along the line, exploded and wounded four or five more, taking a comrade into eternity with an unfinished sentence on his lips. We remember also another fight, where we were

supporting a battery which was getting into position close to some woods, when a shot struck a tree, was lowered in like manner, and killed one of the drivers. We think of these experiences, and have no faith in trees as protection from shot and shell. Then, a little to our left, is that old chimney, looming up so tall, as we look at it from our humble positions on the ground. A shot or shell may strike that, sending the bricks in all directions, and possibly changing the direction of the shell itself, so that it may come down among us. It would seem that it were enough to be exposed to the artillery fire without the possibility of having bricks thown at us or a chimney tipped over upon us. We consider all these possibilities as we lie on the ground; and they do not serve to reassure us. All the time the shot and shell are flying, our own battery is keeping up a lively fire, and in the distance we can hear the carbines rattling merrily; and we wish that we were at the front with something to make us forget the danger for a time.

A comrade near me is busily engaged in reading his Testament. This is a peculiarity of his. Just before we were going into the fight before this one, we were marching along, when the advance found the enemy, and skirmishing began. We were drawn up by the side of the road in readiness to go promptly whenever and wherever we might be wanted; and there we waited as the fire grew hot and hotter. As soon as there was a possibility that we might be called upon, I saw him reading his Testament. He reads it now, under like circumstances, because he finds some consolation in it and it takes his mind from what is going on around him—from what is before him. He is a better soldier for this. When the time comes for action, he is as brave as any one. He knows the danger, but has the courage to face it; and this is his way of keeping up his courage until the excitement of action destroys all thought of danger. Other men have other ways of doing this. Here is the captain. He is a little apart from the others; is saying nothing, but is apparently thinking deeply, and is industriously whittling twigs, which he puts into his mouth as if they were tooth-picks, throwing one away every moment to put in another one. Here is another comrade who has no desire for conversation; whose thoughts are evidently far away. He is busy picking up twigs and breaking them into bits. Like the captain, he is keeping his fingers busy as a relief to his thoughts—as a balm for nervousness. Here is a man whose face is "white as a sheet." He is afraid, but not more so than most of those around him. He knows that he may be killed at any moment, but is possessed of that higher kind of courage which enables him to go calmly wherever duty calls, or to meet any danger nobly which may lie in the path of duty. Here is one who shows no sign of anxiety or of fear; but he is no more brave than the others. When we first took this position he was very sick, but is now ready for any duty. The excitement or the dread was too much for him at first, and "went to his stomach"; but that is over. It was only physical, to be sure; but the cause was mental, and the removal of the physical disturbance has relieved the mental cause. This internal disturbance is no uncommon thing under the first excitement of going into battle; and ofttimes in these circumstances the soldier fears that he is going to prove to be a coward; but this feeling overcome, he is as brave as he could wish. Another comrade is reading a letter,—the last one received,— and he is well aware that it may be the last one he will receive. Ah, well we know where his thoughts are; and we sympathize with him, for are not our thoughts all on our homes and our loved ones there? Every man here understands to the fullest extent the danger he is in; but he is brave enough to remain here; to go further, if need be, for country and flag; and yet just now his thoughts are with the loved ones; and from many a heart goes up a silent prayer for God's blessing upon them, whatever may happen to him. His thoughts are for their happiness, not for his own welfare. Thus, in various ways, do the comrades show their peculiarities under this terrible artillery fire. Some are trying to keep their thoughts busy by conversation; some by joking; some are silently smoking; some are in deep meditation.

The time drags slowly on. We cannot tell which side, if either, is getting the better of the fight. At times the carbine firing sounds nearer, as if our boys are being driven; and again it appears to recede, as if our boys are driving the enemy. At times we hear cheers, as if a charge were being made, and we try to distinguish by the sound of the cheering from which side it comes, and whether or not the sounds are coming nearer. Our battery keeps up a steady fire, with intervals of rest, and the enemy's battery does the same, but we see no enemy. All we have to do is to lie flat on the ground, count every shell that goes over our heads as one less chance of disaster, consider all the unwelcome possibilities, wait patiently and trust, and be all the time in readiness to repel a charge by the enemy. It seems as though the watches have stopped, so slowly do the minutes pass. A shell burst over our heads, and a piece as large as a dollar strikes the ground between two comrades, one of whom coolly picks it up and puts it in his pocket to send home as a souvenir of the fight. A shot or shell strikes the commander of the battery, and the officer next in rank takes command. A man in our line, down on the left, is killed. A shot or shell strikes the ground in front of our line, and comes bounding along through the line so slowly that it seems one might easily stop it, and as it nears the line the men scatter in all directions. A comrade a little way off laughs at them and shouts, "Are you afraid of anything you can see, and which is coming no faster than that?"

"Oh!" says one of the boys, "but the blarsted thing may be rotten."

That is something the first speaker did not think of; it may be a shell, and if so, it were well to be as far away as possible. All these are but incidents that momentarily relieve the long, anxious, terrible monotony. Still we remain here, some of us almost crawling into the ground in our endeavors to "lie low" and get out of danger, until we are inclined to wish the enemy would charge upon that battery to give us something to do; fighting is far better than this waiting under fire. The charge, mounted or dismounted; the fight on foot—anything would be preferable to this, except the retreat. Or if our battery would only change position; any change would be welcome. So passes away all the long afternoon, and not till after sundown do we leave the field.

We have been in one of the most hotly-contested cavalry fights of the whole war, but have lost only three or four men, have not seen an enemy, have not fired a shot; yet we have done our whole duty, have won another name on our battle-flag, have been under more severe strain and had our courage more severely tested than the men in the thick of the fight at the front, and there has been no time during the day that we would not have gladly changed places with them.

A REMINISCENCE OF FIRST BULL RUN.

Captain Charles E. Dilkes.

WHEN it became a certainty that the initial struggle of the late war would take place at Manassas and the probable date had been made known, the occasion was looked forward to by the citizens of Washington and the strangers within its gates as an opportunity for the enjoyment of a free and altogether unique show, and a general exodus of sight-seers followed. Vehicles of every description, crowded with parties of pleasure, with hundreds of equestrians, crossed the long bridge into Virginia, on the road to the scene of action, and the Alexandria boats were also well patronized.

The writer, in company with the lieutenant-colonel of the 79th New York Regiment (Highlanders), who was returning to his command, took the latter route, trusting to the chance of securing a conveyance of some kind from Alexandria, but on landing could find nothing available. I had about concluded to abandon the enterprise when, passing the station of the Orange and Alexandria Railroad (now the Virginia Midland), I noticed a group of gentlemen on the platform in which I recognized the Assistant Secretary of War, Colonel Thos. A. Scott, and, on speaking to him, was introduced to General Cameron, Secretary of War, and Bishop McIlvain, of Ohio, the latter a prominent divine of that day. A train, composed of engine, tender, one flat, and one box car, with a passenger coach, stood on the track, the flat bearing a large closed carriage and the box car containing a pair of fine horses. Colonel Scott, under whom I had formerly served in Pennsylvania, asked me if I knew anything of the road, stating that he had learned that the track had been torn up at a point some ten miles out from Alexandria, but that the exact location of the break was unknown to any of the employés about the depot; that it was his intention to proceed as far as possible with the cars and finish the journey to the battle-ground with the carriage and horses.

I had never traveled over the road in my life and knew nothing of it, and so informed him, when he requested me to accompany the party and look after the train, as he knew nothing of the men who were running it. I was glad of the opportunity, and in a short time we started,

running cautiously until we had neared Burke's Station, about ten miles out, when the train was halted by a picket of the 3d New Jersey Regiment, which was stationed at that point, and we were informed that the track had been destroyed a few rods beyond.

This ended the railway trip, and, as night was approaching, the matter of supper and lodging was next in order. A comfortable looking farmhouse on the brow of a neighboring hill seemed promising, and I was deputized to look up the proprietor and, if possible, secure quarters for the party. The lady of the house informed me that her husband was an officer in the Southern army, that the staff officers of the 3d New Jersey were her guests, and that she could not possibly accommodate us. I could make no impression, not even when I named the rank of those craving her kind offices—the Secretary and Assistant Secretary of War and a bishop. She smiled and looked as if about to ask me why the President, the Czar of Russia, and the Pope had been left behind; but the arrival of Colonel Taylor, of the New Jersey Regiment, who soon overcame her objections, made all pleasant, and she agreed to make our party as comfortable as possible.

After a capital supper we adjourned to the sitting-room of the mansion and engaged in conversation with our hostess. Her views were naturally intensely Southern, and she was not backward in the expression of them. One of the party, disposed for a little amusement at her expense, remarked:

"Mrs. ——, I notice you have removed all carpets from the floors as well as curtains from the windows; did you fear that you would be driven from your home by the Yankees?"

Quick as a flash she replied: "Not at all; but I was told that Yankees would steal anything they could lay their hands on, and I took the precaution of placing my valuables in a place of safety."

Our friend was satisfied and asked no more questions. He seemed to lose all interest in the conversation.

Toward ten o'clock Colonel Scott informed me that the bishop proposed to offer up a prayer before retiring, and suggested that I mention the fact to our hostess, as she would probably wish to call the members of the household together, but when I approached the lady on the subject, she informed me that she would not consent to have the President prayed for publicly in that house. I reported the failure of my mission to the bishop, who was much amazed, and requested me to assure her that nothing objectionable to her personal feelings would occur. With this understanding her consent was obtained, and we moved into the large par-

CAPTAIN CHARLES E. DILKES.

lor, which, like the other rooms of the house, was carpetless, and which in a short time presented a most impressive appearance. The members of the family, with the colored servants, the staff, with many of the line officers, and several privates of the 3d New Jersey, with its gallant Colonel (later General) Taylor (who lost his life at the second Bull Run battle), and the Secretary and Assistant Secretary of War, all kneeling in the dim light, while the good bishop offered a prayer which for beauty and fervency I have never heard excelled, together made an impression on my mind which will always remain.

After prayers our hostess stated that she had two rooms at her disposal, and it was arranged that the bishop should occupy one and General Cameron and Colonel Scott the other, I being accommodated with a "shake-down" on the parlor floor.

We were all up betimes in the morning, and I fully expected to soon be on the road to Manassas, but after an early breakfast Colonel Scott

called me to one side and observed: "I suppose you don't care particularly to see the battle, do you?" I assured him that that certainly was my object.

"Oh," said he, "you'll see plenty of them before long, and I wish you would take our train back to Alexandria, as I don't like to leave that crew without some one in authority."

I of course consented, although much disappointed, and soon after the party left in the carriage, and I remained behind, grumbling at what I then considered as my bad luck, but the event proved that I was most fortunate after all.

The train started on its return to Alexandria about noon, and on arrival, I concluded to visit the camp of the 4th New Jersey, near the Virginia terminus of the long bridge, opposite Washington. Having many friends among the officers and men, I remained with them several hours, when, learning that the approaches to the bridge were in charge of an old friend—Captain Perrine—I determined to look him up. I found him with his company in comfortable quarters, which he insisted I should share for a few days.

In the early morning of the second day the advance guard of the stragglers from the battle-field arrived, reporting the total defeat of the Northern army, and before noon the scene was beyond description. A panic-stricken mob of soldiers, with civilians of both sexes in carriages, as well as on horseback, came pouring into the enclosure and on the bridge, all convinced that the "rebs" were just behind them and would be in Washington in a few hours. About noon orders were received from General Runyon to "keep vehicles ten feet apart," as the bridge was old and weak; but if he had ordered the flow of Niagara checked, the task would not have been more difficult. The guards were knocked over promptly as they attempted to control the fugitives, and the rush continued in an unbroken stream. The bridge stood it nobly, and the stampede continued until late in the evening, when the rush gradually subsided. Bidding my friends good-bye, I crossed over to Washington.

I found that city in a state of panic. Wild stories were afloat of immense slaughter, with total annihilation of some regiments, and the arrival of the Southern army with the terrible Black Horse Cavalry hourly expected, the sacking and destruction of the city to follow. The excitement subsided, in a measure, during the next twenty-four hours, as reliable reports came to hand, but some days elapsed before it entirely quieted down. Some of the stories told of the Black Horse Cavalry, their prowess and subsequent defeat, would have taxed the genius of a Munchausen. Many of the narrators had, according to their statement, been actively engaged with this formidable troop, as proof exhibiting bowie-knives, pistols, etc., captured in hand-to-hand conflict. I learned that my late traveling companions had returned safely by way of Alexandria, and as I turned over the events of the past few days, arrived at the conclusion that although I had not witnessed the battle I was rather better off than many who had.

In the summer of 1878, thirteen years after the close of the war, I enjoyed, in the company of Colonel John S. Mosby, quite an extended trip through that portion of Virginia on and near the line of the Orange and Alexandria Railroad. We traveled in the private car of the late Honorable John S. Barbour, president of the road, as his guests, and were not restricted to time or special trains, but were privileged to have our car switched off at any station, and to resume our journey at will at the rear of any following train. The trip was made through a section of country thoroughly familiar to Colonel Mosby, and from first to last was most enjoyable, as it could not fail to be in the opportunity of listening to a narrative of stirring incidents of the war from the lips of the chief actor on the spot on which they occurred.

The colonel was much amused at the recital of my adventures in search of a battle-ground, and remarked that I should, as the trains all stopped at Burke's Station returning, call on my late hostess, which I promised to do. He left me at Warrentown, his home, I continuing on toward Alexandria, and on arrival at Burke's Station, finding that I had abundance of time for a visit, walked over to the farmhouse referred to, and on being admitted was ushered into the presence of a stately matron in whom (time within the past seventeen years having dealt very leniently with her) I at once recognized our entertainer of the night before Bull Run. On making myself known she fully recalled the circumstance of our visit, and seemed much amused at the recollection. Replying to my question as to exactly what she thought when she first met the distinguished party to whom I introduced her, she said that " at first she was rather suspicious, but that we all improved upon acquaintance."

Her refusal to grant the bishop's request for prayers until assured that her loyalty would receive no shock, the episode of the carpet, and others, were all referred to, and after a pleasant visit of some fifteen minutes' duration I retired, boarded my car, and was soon in Washington.

TO COLUMBIA.

A VALENTINE FROM THE ARMY AND NAVY.

WILBUR N. HEDGES.

O BEAUTEOUS Columbia ! thy knights will ne'er neglect thee,
  Sons of the brave who fought to save, shall evermore protect thee !
Thy fond admirers faithful are, on land and on the ocean :
In war, in peace, they never cease their valorous devotion.

We love thine eyes of heavenly blue, thy lips of sweetest scarlet,
Thy brow so white that ne'er a blight can ever cloud or mar it !
Each cherished hue shall wave for you, in harmony unbroken,
O'er ev'ry camp and fort and fleet, the patriot's true-love token!

Columbia ! Columbia ! thy gallant knights adore thee,
And vigilant the watch and ward they constant shall keep o'er thee !
Above thy form, 'mid sun and storm, our guardian Eagle hovers,
While at thy feet, in homage sweet, kneel hosts of loyal lovers.

And, whether in the ball-room gay or on the field of battle,
When duty calls us to the fray, 'mid martial roar and rattle,
We're ever thine ! and thou shalt twine bright laurel wreaths of glory,
To crown each brow, while list'ning to the patriot's true-love story !

BELEAGUERED PETERSBURG.

Col. William H. Stewart.

IT was the beautiful spring-time. The sun shone brightly, the young leaves were trembling in the gentle breezes, the wild flowers were blooming and scenting the air with delightful aroma, the birds were singing merrily and sweetly in the surrounding groves, when our tents on the north side of the James River were struck, and we took up the

COL. W. H. STEWART.

line of march for the beleaguered city of Petersburg, Virginia.

We crossed the river on a pontoon bridge at Drewry's Bluff, marched over the battle-field on which Beauregard had recently routed the Federal forces under General B. F. Butler, and bivouacked near Chester Station, on the Richmond and Petersburg Railroad.

Early next afternoon, on the 19th day of June, 1864, we reached Pocahontas, the northern suburb of Petersburg.

The Federal artillery was bombarding the city from Blandford Heights, and solid shot and shells were crushing through the buildings. The sounds that reverberated from their deserted halls were solemn and fearful evidences of the destructiveness of men. Many families had been compelled to desert their homes and seek shelter in church buildings, barns, and tents beyond the range of the great guns. It was to all appearances a doomed city, and the soldiers felt that its rescue from destruction depended upon their efforts and exertions.

Late in the afternoon we marched through the city, and took position in the breastworks on Wilcox's farm. This was in the open field, exposed to the sun, and the only shade-trees near

were those in a small graveyard, a few paces in the rear of the left of the line of our regiment, and there the field officers pitched their tents and made the headquarters of the 61st Virginia regiment over the graves of the dead.

A singular fatality prevailed in the army about this time, for which even medical science failed to account. Many soldiers became perfectly blind after dark, and required to be led whenever on a march at night. The experience of these poor fellows on the march caused many amusing incidents. How it was caused or how cured no one knew, but some believed it was brought on by sleeping in the open air, with the eyes exposed to the moonlight.

About half a mile to our left the lines of the two hostile armies closely approached each other, and the artillerists and pickets were fighting constantly, day and night. At night the mortar shells were continually darting through the air, and made a much grander display than some of our holiday pyrotechnics. They often fell and exploded in the trenches, and in order to sleep securely the soldiers were compelled to burrow in the ground, which was a perfect honey-comb of dens and chambers all along the line of breastworks.

The opposing pickets could converse with each other, though not permitted to expose themselves above their pits. A private was on one occasion basking in the sunshine, with one foot exposed above the earthwork, and when asked what he was doing replied, "I'm only fishing for a furlough."

Where the earthworks came nearest together, the soldiers carried on a considerable traffic by means of long strings. There it was instant death to raise a head above the works. They would attach a brick or stone to the end of a string and throw it over into the Federal trenches, then tie a piece of tobacco in the middle, and notify the "Yank" at the other end to draw it over, and presently "Johnny" would haul back a little bag of coffee, over which there would be great rejoicings. In this manner quite lively trading in various kinds of small articles was kept up, as well as the exchange of newspapers.

The 2d division of the 3d corps, Army Northern Virginia, under command of Major-General

William Mahone, made a brilliant record by its dashing achievements during the eventful campaign of 1864. So frequent and rapid were its movements that the soldiers named it Mahone's Foot Cavalry Division. It was composed of one brigade from each of the States of Alabama, Florida, Georgia, Mississippi, and Virginia, commanded respectively by Brigadier-Generals Forney, Finnegan, Girardy, Harris, and Weisiger.

The Confederate authorities seemed to have been oblivious to the qualifications of our little general as a leader, and did not make him a major-general until May 6, 1864, although he was one of the oldest brigadiers in the Army of Northern Virginia. Yet late as it was, he soon won the admiration of the army and the confidence of General Lee, and it was generally conceded that the mantle of Stonewall Jackson had not unworthily fallen on the shoulders of Mahone. His foresight and dash were the great characteristics which gained for him the unyielding confidence of the soldiers he led to battle.

I believe there is no better criterion by which to judge the merits of an officer than the opinion of the soldiers under his command. They always admire those officers who display courage and efficiency, and have supreme contempt for blunderers and cowards.

On the 22d day of June, 1864, our brigade was ordered to advance from our earthworks on Wilcox's Farm to check a movement of the Federals to extend their breastworks to the left. We crossed the open field in our front through a deep ravine to a thick woods, which covered our movements and prevented their detection. After reaching the woods, the column was faced to the left and formed in line of battle.

The order "Forward!" was given, and as the men leaped a worm-fence, which divided the farm from the woods, they immediately struck the enemy's pickets. These fought in retreat very stubbornly, but our soldiers pressed them back and marched forward as rapidly as possible through the underwood and bushes.

Our regiment about the colors, or centre, struck the end of the enemy's newly-made breastworks, and by wheeling to the left we were in their rear and front, fighting hand to hand with bayonets, butts of muskets, swords, and pistols.

This pell-mell fighting lasted only a few minutes before the bluecoats surrendered and our people were in charge of their works, facing on the reverse side. The manoeuvre was so rapid and secret that the Federals were almost completely surprised. They were caught enjoying their dinner, and we were just in time to share their hardtack, pork, and beans.

Ashwell Curling, the gallant file-leader of Company A, 61st Virginia regiment, which I commanded, was shot through the head, instantly killed, falling very near me just as the regiment was wheeling. John Wills, of the 16th Virginia regiment, who was mortally wounded, offered Philip Miller, one of our ambulance corps, twelve dollars in gold to take him off the field; but Philip, true to his orders, told him that it was his first duty to take off the wounded of his regiment, after which he would return and take him off, but that he would not accept his money. Philip, faithful to his promise, did return, but then poor Wills was dead.

After the works were captured, we re-formed and were moving forward, when one of our own batteries, on the main line of our breastworks, opened fire on us, forcing us back to the captured line. We then marched to the right flank, to receive the enemy, who seemed about to attempt to retake their line; but they did not get near enough for another hand-to-hand fight.

About night, we were marched to the left and reoccupied the works we had captured. The enemy opened on us with artillery and infantry, but did not dispossess us. The charge was made by the Alabama and Virginia brigades of Mahone's division, Virginia on the right of Alabama. The captures, I then understood, amounted to 2200 prisoners, 1500 small arms, eight stands of colors, and a battery of four Blakely guns.

General Grant, in his despatch to Major-General Halleck, dated City Point, June 23, 1864, nine A.M., says: "Yesterday and this morning have been consumed in extending our lines to the left, to envelop Petersburg. The 2d and 6th corps are now west of the Jerusalem plank-road. Yesterday, in moving to this position, the two corps became separated. The enemy pushed out between them and caused some confusion in the left of the 2d corps, and captured four pieces of artillery. Order was soon restored, and the enemy pushed back." And in his despatch, dated June 24, 1864, 2.30 P.M., he reports: "I find the affair of the 22d was much worse than I had heretofore learned. Our losses (nearly all captures) were not far from 2000, and four pieces of artillery. The affair was a stampede and surprise to both parties, and ought to have been turned in our favor." *

General Grant was evidently misinformed about "pushing us back," for we were not pushed one inch, nor were we in any manner surprised. We surprised and pushed the Federals all the time. About ten o'clock at night, after all the trophies had been removed, we evacuated the position from which we had driven the enemy, and marched to our place on the line of our fortifications.

Official Records above cited, p. 454, journal of Major-General G. K. Warren, United States

army, commanding 5th army corps, Wednesday, June 22d, says: "Second corps had a bad fight. Got flanked and lost 2300 prisoners and four cannon." Captain George F. McKnight, commanding 12th New York Independent Battery (p. 437), reports: "Four three-inch rifled guns, four ammunition chests, and three limbers lost."

Major-General William Mahone, with two small brigades, directed the charge in person. The manœuvre was brilliant and successful in every respect. The engagement is designated as "Jerusalem Plank-Road," and was a victory for the Confederates.

* Official Records, Series I, Vol. XL, Part I, pp. 13-14.

SECRETARY HERBERT'S TWO BOY HEROES.

I NEVER saw more glorious conduct than that displayed in these two instances, by two youths in their teens, one wearing the blue, and the other the gray. The first was in the second day's fight. My regiment had charged right up among the guns of the Union battery, whose men and horses had nearly all been killed. There was one gun to which four horses had been attached. The two rear horses had been shot down in harness. The two leaders were apparently unhurt, and on one of them sat a lad, head erect, vigorously plying his whip on the other horse, and striving to save his gun. He was devoting his whole soul to that purpose, utterly unmindful of our men, who were surging about him. He was literally like the Casabianca of the flaming deck. I could have touched him with my sword, and was just about to beg him to surrender, when shots rang out from behind me, and he dropped from his horse, dead as he fell. He might have saved himself, but he seemed determined to save that gun or die.

It was sublime, but I can never think of it without a shudder at the horrors of the sacrifices of that war. The other instance was on the third day, in the height of the terrific artillery duel that was preliminary to the great charges. Our men were in line awaiting the word to advance. In front of us, riding deliberately up and down the line, was a handsome youth in gray, mounted on a fleet-looking iron-gray horse, and bearing a bright new battle-flag, whose vivid stars and bars shimmered in the sunlight. The boy sat erect, looking as proud as any Rupert, and his horse as spirited as an Arabian. The flying bullets and shrieking shells never phased his superb bearing, as he rode to and fro, up and down the long line. Now and then he would disappear in thick clouds of powder-smoke, but he would be seen riding back, his face actually beaming with what O'Hare calls the "ardor of the fight." Before the word came to move, he had gone again down the line, and had not returned.

I never knew whether he was killed or not, but I thought involuntarily of how that Yankee boy had died the day before. These were indelible pictures caught in a gleam of light in shifting battle-smoke, and have always been to me anything but counterfeit presentments of Northern and Southern courage.

WINCHESTER, VIRGINIA.
AN HISTORICAL REVERIE.

LEILA MECHLIN.

VIEW OF WINCHESTER, LOOKING SOUTHEAST FROM MILROY'S FORT.
In the distance the Blue Ridge ; Snicker's Gap near centre, and Ashby's Gap to the extreme right.

THE Winchester of to-day is a lazy, little Southern town, little beauty in itself but vastly much in the surrounding country. Shut in from the outside world by the Blue Ridge, Masanuten, Little and Great North Mountain Ranges, it rests in the beautiful valley of the Shenandoah.

There is little modern architecture to be seen, the most of the houses are built directly up to the sidewalk, plain, straight façades, regularly set windows one above the other with outside green shutters. Here and there through the town we find fine, old, stately mansions, surrounded by large grounds. To the southwest,

land has been booming, streets have been cut through, and new and modern houses have been and are building, as well as a new hotel, probably one of the finest of its kind in the country, which has just been completed. Electric lights have taken the place of the old street lamps.

The principal street, now Main, once Loudon, is lined for about three squares with stores of all kinds, and such queer little stores as they are, too! You find dry goods, books, and carpets in one, as well as pots, pans, dishes, and groceries in another. Here the court-house stands, a large, square building, broad porch across the front with great pillars to the over-reaching

"STONEWALL" CEMETERY, WINCHESTER, VIRGINIA.
Monument. with figure of Confederate soldier.

roof. Above is the odd belfry and old bell by which the court is still summoned. In front is Court House Square, inclosed by a high iron fence. Here the town loafers congregate (here and at the tavern opposite), in quiet, little groups. To the right and left are the lawyers' offices, those to the right tiny, little, one-roomed, one-story buildings on the ideal doll's house plan. The street itself has lately been improved, and, like many of the others, it sorely needed it. The sidewalks of brick are all dolefully hobble-de-hoy, and the gutters, which are necessarily deep, are almost dangerously so.

The conveyances are of every sort and kind, yet all, from the lightest phaeton to the clumsiest mountaineer's wagon, is termed a "fix." At first you might find it confusing, but you will soon fall into the habit and find it convenient, ceasing to be lost in wonderment when you hear you were seen in "a mighty pretty fix yesterday." For "fix" will mean as plainly to you anything on wheels that you chose to fancy (unless otherwise directed), as if you had lived there all your life. There is one exception to this rule: they do have "'buses," for in 'buses the many pleasure seekers every summer go from the depot to Rock Enon Springs, fifteen miles in the Great North Mountain.

The two cemeteries—the old and the new, the Confederate and the Union—are side by side to the east of the town; here the Blue and the Gray have found, within a stone's throw of each other, their last resting-place. In the Stonewall Cemetery stands the ruins of an old, gray stone church, half overgrown with vines, yet adding

HOTEL WINCHESTER, ERECTED 1893.

strangely to the terrible solemnity of the spot. The soldiers' graves, row upon row, bring vividly to mind the horrors of war, for many of the simplest inscriptions are the saddest. In one great mound under one monument, are buried 828 unknown dead. This is the old town burying ground, the home as well as the soldiers' cemetery. The other, the Federal, is entirely a soldiers', the brave men who fell for the Union.

OLD STONE MILL, TORN DOWN IN 1889.

To the west still stand the earthworks left by the Civil War. The valley pike over which Sheridan took his poetical ride, is much the same as then. In the town it merges into Braddock Street, over which General Braddock passed so many years before on his way to Fort Duquesne. Not far from this, on Water Street, is the Episcopal Church, another relic of the past, though a much modernized one; the same Lord Fairfax founded, and in which rests his ashes. Away up at the extreme end of Main Street, "on the hill," are still a few remnants of old Fort Loudoun, built by Washington, and the well dug at the same time is still in use.

Beyond, to the other end, gurgles a little spring, Shawnee by name, recalling the time when Winchester was not; and around it yet, though near by is the railroad trestle, hovers the old Indian superstition, that he who drinks of its waters will return sometime to drink again; and each year many of the summer visitors go to its brink and invoke of its magic power. Not one but many are the romances in which it has played a mystic part.

Let us wander back to-night to that earliest time and follow, o'er the fields to be trod no more, that quaint town in weal and woe, in the

VIEW IN FEDERAL CEMETERY, WINCHESTER.
The bodies of 4400 Federal soldiers rest here.

two hundred years that have passed since the bright little spring played part in its first romance. Here is the easy chair, before us the crackling blaze; and truant thoughts can but wander backwards, for there is some faint unknown yet felt communion between the flames and time—the wood and the years

———

Yes, we are standing now in the beautiful rolling country of the upper Shenandoah, fine grass land, interspersed with forest patches. But what are these? Not houses—no, you may well rub your eyes—but wigwams, a veritable village of them, the home of the Shawnee In-

put on the war paint, I knew that he must go, so I prayed the Great Spirit for a charm to bring him safely back. Three nights, just at sunset, I prayed, and the third night I dreamed; and in my dream I was near the border of the 'happy hunting ground,' when at my feet I saw a tiny, star-eyed flower, and as I stooped and plucked it a voice cried, 'Put this blossom in the crystal spring, let it stay there till sunrise, and henceforth and forever this charm will be upon it: Whosoever drinks of its waters will some day return to drink again.' And I awoke, and found close in my hand the star-eyed flower; and I arose and did as the voice had spoken and

SHAWNEE SPRINGS, WINCHESTER, VIRGINIA.
The principal spring, mentioned in legend, is situated under the willows, to the right.

dians. Tradition has told us that the present site of Winchester was first occupied by a large and powerful tribe of Indians called the Shawnees or Shawanees, and now we see them seated around their camp-fires, in all their paint, recounting the tales of their adventures on the great war path just completed. The great chief is telling the eager-eyed Indian maid of the bravery and marvelous escapes of her own young warrior, gone for the first time as chief, to earn by his valor this fair Shawnee. But hark! she is speaking, telling in the low, flickering light, how dauntless was her heart while waiting for his return. "For surely," says she, "had I not the promise of the Great Spirit that he should go through all unscathed? When the great council

had *faith*, for it was the voice of the Great Spirit, who never breaks His word."

———

The lights burn dimmer and lower, the voices farther and farther away—they are gone. The tents, they, too, are gone, the Shawnees, where are they? Gone on beyond the mountains. The years? They, too, are gone. The beautiful country, the gurgling spring, these still are here, yes, and two houses are built near the "town run."

It is 1738 and civilization has entered the valley; nor does it stop with two houses. One after another creeps in until 1752, February, in the twenty-fifth year of the reign of George II, the General Assembly passes an "Act for the

Establishment of the town of Winchester." More houses are built and a tavern; while out of town we find the home of Colonel Hite, and most notable "Greenway Court," the home of Lord Fairfax. One of the first of Virginia's manors, it stands thirteen miles southeast of the town, a tiny village in itself, with it quarters, smoke-house, tenantry, etc. Here is the long, low gray stone building occupied by his lordship's steward, while

OLD STORE AND LOG HOUSE, CORNER CORK AND BRADDOCK STREETS.
Occupied by Colonel George Washington while building Fort Loudoun, in 1752

he, when at home, lives in yonder tiny stone cabin. Here we see the young surveyor, Washington, welcomed and entertained on his first expedition across the Blue Ridge.

Later we see him as he stops in Winchester to procure baggage, tents, etc., in November, 1753, on his celebrated mission, by order of Governor Dinwiddie, to the French authorities on the Ohio. We watch him off, yet tarry in one of those odd houses built so strangely, yet so strongly, of the rough unsorted stones. We look through the tiny window off over the country, (our neighbors as yet are not so many as to obstruct the view), and scan the landscape with anxious eye and strained ear, fearing and dreading the approach of red men.

These are anxious, anxious years. Washington's headquarters are fixed here. Wild tales of Indian maraudings are brought in from time to time; much is feared, but little happens.

Braddock marches through the town; all rush to see him pass. The brave men in their bright uniforms, so hopeful, so sure of success. None

PRESENT INTERIOR OF FORT LOUDOUN.
On the left, the ascent formed by the southwest bastion of the fort; Female Seminary on the right.

less are we who wait behind. The warfare will be over, the Indians conquered, all again safe. But no! again the road; are these the same troops who, but a few months since, marched so

WASHINGTON IN 1756—FROM AN OLD PAINTING.

proudly over it? A mere handful of them, worn and ragged. "The news, the news!" we cry. "Defeat," we hear, and turn again with heavy hearts to our homes.

In September, Washington comes again, this time as "commander and chief of all the forces raised or to be raised in the colony." Lord Fairfax, lord-lieutenant of the county, organizes a troop of horsemen and goes for cavalry parade with all the gusto that he once entered on a fox-hunt. All is astir. Washington has started for Williamsburgh on military business, but scarcely has he left when an "express" rushes into town, sent by Colonel Stephenson, of Fort Cumberland, declaring a body of Indians are ravaging the country. All is again the wildest confusion. An express is sent after and overtakes Washington at Fredericksburg. Lord Fairfax calls for militia, and we of the town see the women going around with white faces, children cowering from view, and men talking in excited groups. One horrible account follows another. All is nightmare, butchery. The

militia does not come; the troops from the outposts cannot. Washington at last sends a brigade, and they find, to the amusement of all, that the Indians, whose firing has been heard all night and so alarmed the neighborhood for miles around, are but three drunken men whose carousing has taken the form of wild whoops and firing of a small cannon. The troops arrive. It is ascertained that the real Indians, but about one hundred and sixty-five in number, have retreated over the mountains, and quiet, comparative quiet, again reigns.

Though the life is one of expectancy, living fearfully on the brink of some anticipated catastrophe, yet, like all other anxious times, it is not one of continual woe, and we may look in on as bright a picture as one could wish to see, at the tavern, where to-night Lord Fairfax is holding a levee. The room is filled. All the fair dames for miles around are there in their dainty silks and satins, while they seem to smile and look as exceeding pleased as I have seen the maids of nigh a century and a half later. 'Tis a gladsome picture, those gayly decked men and women, forgetting, for the time, the day of anxiety, while they tread with almost solemn precision the mazes of a minuet. The young Colonel Washington is here, and happy is the partner chosen by him. Proudly she steps through the dignified dance. The older participants are gathered in little groups, talking over

WASHINGTON BESOUGHT BY THE PEOPLE, 1756.

the "home" affairs and the latest news from old England. In yonder corner sits the evening's belle. Can she be flirting? Impossible, for that is unheard of; yet, 'tis strangely like it.

Another Indian panic occurs in 1756. The town is truly terrified. This time it is not a foolish fancy or idle talk, but the enemy have come almost to our very borders, murdering—worse still—butchering. Horrors accumulate, until the women and children confront Washington on every side, weeping and beseeching him to save them from the threatening terrors. To accomplish this a fort is built, for which purpose the General Assembly vote one thousand pounds. It is situated at the centre, where the principal roads meet, and named Fort Loudoun in honor of the General lately appointed to command all the colonial troops. It is an odd old fortress but it serves its purpose, and the well dug then remains in use long after it has crumbled away. The governor is inefficient in furnishing militia, so in time all, who are able to, leave and go to the larger settlements, and we once more see the Shenandoah almost deserted.

———

The French and Indian war is over ; the Revolution has come and gone ; the young colonel that we knew then has been the great general and the first President of our country, and he now is no more. The years have sped past us as a flock of pigeons. We watched them by in a listless way, seeing here and there a characteristic. We are too far off to see each feather, though perchance we single out one and another bird almost without mentally noting it. They are gone, the white and the black, the good and the bad, the brown and the gray, the prosperous and the unfortunate. 'Tis the time of the great statesmen. Clay and Webster are in their prime. We take a bird's-eye view of the whole country and marvel at its vastness, its thrift. We turn to the little deserted town of those many years ago, and we see instead a great town surrounded by a greater country. It is Virginia's palmiest day. We see the town laid off in regular streets, the paved walks, the great queer gutters, the stores and factories, the churches. We see the court-house, and we look curiously at the taverns, with their odd pillared porches all across the front and signs hung out

flag fashion. There is a bustle of business about it all, an air of progress. But the "wealthy and aristocratic" are not found here. Only the doctor, clergyman, and lawyer can live in town and still retain their social position. They are "country gentlemen," not town "citizens."

The houses are dotted all through the country, and such houses ! Veritable mansions ; see them, the long, low house itself, with its inviting broad porch, surrounded by its flower-garden. Beyond, the funny little kitchen, the negroes' quarters, the granary, the barn, while down in that hollow yonder we see the roof of the spring-house and dairy. At the door we find the renowned Virginia gentleman, hospitable, courteous beyond measure, welcoming all as befits the first in the land. Courtly

OLD STORE AND LAND OFFICE OF LORD FAIRFAX.
Built in 1752, and now standing at "Greenway Court," Clarke County, Virginia.

to the verge of pomposity, generous, almost reckless, little knowledge of the value of money, fond of social pleasures, devoted to "family." Society is represented by the one word—aristocratic. The "Springs" are crowded every year by pleasure-seekers, banquets and balls are ever recurring.

But to-day the town is in a stir, everybody seems to be on the verge of expectancy. "What is it?" we ask of an old man at the corner of the post-office, and it is with a genial smile he replies: "Massachusetts' great man, Webster, sir, comes to-day on the two-ten train. He'll have mighty hard work to leave the station without a speech. I reckon it will be a rouser, up to the times." We join the crowd assembled at the depot, watch the approach of the train, and listen with eager interest to the speech. It

THE VALLEY PIKE, ONE MILE SOUTH OF WINCHESTER.
Scene of Sheridan's Ride.

is a "rouser," and we gladly mingle our voices with those of the town-folk in cheering him on.

We meet him next day at the banquet given at Capon in his honor. Around this board are assembled some of Virginia's finest gentlemen. The *menu* is extensive and elaborate; as the wine goes round the talk increases, politics are discussed with less reserve, the wit is sharper and more poignant. Toasts are drank and a speech called for. Webster, never more eloquent than now, responds. Words flow from his lips as a mighty river in its course, no hesita-

tion, no lax sentences or thoughts,—power, gigantic mental capacity, unfathomed ability. The speaker ends with a glorious compliment daintily paid to his hosts and listeners, and, after more toasts, the dinner is over, and we will tarry no longer.

———

Again we find ourselves rushing onward, dashing ahead with greater speed than ever steam-engine or electricity accomplished, and yet we do not feel the haste. It is more like one huge leap, without the jar at the last, for it is years we have flown over. A cloud blacker than night hangs over the little town, a shadow darker than all others, for it is the shadow of death. The mighty Civil War is raging, the little town that we last saw in the light of prosperity and gayety has been plunged into the deepest mourning. Many of her bravest sons lie buried there on distant hill, not a household that has not sent son, brother, husband, or all to fight for . hearth and home.

THE LOGAN HOUSE, WINCHESTER, VIRGINIA.
Headquarters of General Sheridan in March, 1864.

Battle, bloodshed, pillage, and devastation have all been seen and felt.

We cannot live those years, and—thank God for it—even those who lived them cannot again. It is only a glimpse here and there, the horror of the whole, but to live the days again is impossible.

As all know, it was the very centre of the combat, the Federal and Southern armies played a great game of "Prisoner's Base," with its outskirts for boundary lines. We scarcely know from day

HOUSE ONCE OWNED BY GENERAL DAN. MORGAN.
The left half, of stone, was built by Hessian prisoners. In the lower room (shutters open) General Morgan died, July, 1802.

to day which army will hold the town the next; scant news comes from the front. The first few years are of the anticipation that the Federal army may gain possession, the last in the realization. All is doubt, anxiety, weary, hopeless waiting, constantly on the *qui vive* of terror and wildest excitement. Hark! how plain is the sound of guns! another encounter is taking place. For which will it mean victory? Who will tell? Strange mixed accounts come to us, first one and another, the last always contradicting the previous one, with a successor

to call it false. What can we believe? The worst always. "The Yanks are coming! the Yanks are coming!" resounds through the town, and we all flee as from so many demons. Blinds and doors are secured, valuables hidden, and children, fancying all sorts of fairy-tale horrors and bravery, speak in awed whispers and are very quiet. Sure enough, here they are, blue coats everywhere; they seem to fairly swarm all over the town, but, presto! they are gone, and we catch a glimpse of the gray coats in hot pursuit, more firing, then silence.

VIEW OF LOUDON (OR MAIN) STREET, WINCHESTER.

The great battle of Kernstown has been fought. The still of death is over us all. Many of the houses are turned into hospitals; the wounded and dying are being brought in. Here is the women's work, and they do it nobly. The work of burying the dead goes on for even longer; it is a terrible time!

Again, the town has been held for months by the Northern army. All have retired for the night, fearing and looking for nothing unusual. Many nights have passed in quiet, but toward midnight all are aroused. Tumult and confusion, smoke fills the air, the sky is glorified by the great fire. Eight large warehouses are burning, other buildings in all parts of the town are in conflagration. Is the town doomed? Men, women, and children rush screaming through the streets; all is dire confusion, din. The clanging of the court-house and fire-bells only serves to heighten the awfulness. The negroes believe it to be the Judgment Day; their mistresses themselves know not where to turn or what to look for next. That all will be destroyed we firmly believe, and, with trembling haste, are making most hurried preparations to leave when the last and greatest terror is added. An explosion so violent that our houses are shaken to their very foundations, every pane of glass in the whole town is shattered, all feel deafened. What does it mean? Are we to be blown up, as well as burnt alive? How that frightful night was lived through but few can tell, a nightmare of nightmares. When morning dawns we find ourselves again in the hands of the Southern army, our Northern friends having beaten a hasty retreat the night before, after kindling the great bonfire and setting match to the store of powder. Their last act cost them one brave life, for he who "touched it off" in some way was too tardy in retreating, and thus played the part of his own executioner.

———

But the war with all its horrors, the war that left behind it such a sweep of barren land and houses, and took with it the very cream of the manhood of the South, and much of the North, too, is over. Slowly the valley that served as the stage for the great panorama has recovered from the waste it was made. Years have served to lighten the shadow it left, to soften the blows it dealt, until now when we look in on Winchester we would say the sun was shining on it as brightly as it did thirty-five years ago.

The last flickering blaze has died away, only a heap of ashes remain. We glance from them to the pile of fresh logs at the chimney-side, the years to come. Here the page is still blank, and so we must leave it.

EPISCOPAL CHURCH, WINCHESTER, VIRGINIA.
Under the chancel rest the remains of Lord Fairfax. Memorial tablet on left wall of entrance.

RECOLLECTIONS OF AN ARMY SURGEON.

J. O. HARRIS, M. D.

"BOYS, there is a battle on up yonder, as sure as guns!"

"Nonsense; it is only them confounded gunboats blazing away, as usual."

"I tell you it's so; come out here in the timber a little way, and you can hear the volleys of musketry."

This conversation was heard in the camp of the 253d Illinois Infantry, on the morning of April 6, 1862.

Our regiment had been landed at Savannah, Tennessee, some seven or eight miles below Pittsburg Landing, on the opposite side of the river, and we were encamped near a beautiful grove, in what had evidently been the Fair Grounds, where we were waiting to be supplied with wagons, ambulances, teams, tents, etc., when we expected to be sent to the front, which in this case was not far away.

But the necessary supplies were slow in arriving; it was almost out of the question for us to move without transportation for our camp equipage, commissary stores, etc., and without any kind of tents or shelter for the men, and so we were taking life easy, enjoying the mild temperature and balmy air of the Southern spring, content to wait until those in authority over us should be able to fit us for active duties in the field. At least this was the feeling among the non-combatants, although it is quite possible that our field officers and the men felt differently. I know that some of the men expressed themselves as being quite anxious to have an opportunity of "popping away at a secesh!" But none of us had ever seen an actual battle, much less been engaged in one, and these men did not apparently recognize the fact that the "popping away" might be reciprocal, and that a battle, or even a skirmish, meant wounds and death to some of the participants on both sides.

General Grant had his headquarters at Savannah, and from the fact that he went up daily in a steamboat to Pittsburg Landing, and from the further fact that additional troops were frequently arriving, and that some of the gunboats at the Landing were firing more or less every day, we were confident that a movement of some consequence was contemplated, though when it would take place, or what its nature would be, none of us knew.

But on the morning alluded to, we were suddenly awakened; in a short time the sounds of battle were distinctly heard, and soon after our colonel received an order to have his regiment ready to move at a minute's notice, the men to have three days' cooked rations in their haversacks; ammunition to be supplied after reaching the field.

Then all was bustle and activity. The commissary supplied the food, the company cooks went to work preparing it, the men packed their knapsacks and filled canteens with coffee or water, the officers put on their fatigue uniforms, got out their side arms and sashes; woolen and rubber blankets were rolled or folded, ready for use, valuables and extra articles not supposed to be needed were bundled up and placed in charge of the sutler, and within an hour we were waiting and ready for the expected order to march to the boat.

While all of this was going on, the colonel ordered "one of the surgeons to remain and take care of the sick, the other to march with the regiment," and left it with us to determine which one should go and which stay. My wife had often said that she did not think I actually desired to get hurt, but she was confident that I was always ready to put my foot "just over the danger line." However this may be, it is certain that I earnestly wished to go with the regiment, and it was soon decided that I should.

But no orders to march came. Meantime, after the preparations had all been completed, many letters containing messages to loving friends at home were written and placed in charge of the sutler, who, of course, was to stay at Savannah until it should seem safe and desirable for him to join the regiment.

And still we waited. The steamboat was constantly going and returning, taking up regiments which were fully equipped and which had seen some active service, and, after a trip or two, returning with wounded men.

Our regiment, one thousand strong, was well officered, and the men, almost without exception, were eager for the fray, but we had seen no actual service, and through the fault of some one, certainly not of our colonel or other officers, we had not been furnished with the indispensable *impedimenta* of a regiment for active duty, and therefore others, which had been under fire or had seen active service, were first sent to the battle-field.

As the day advanced, the sound of the conflict became more distinct, but the sensation produced by the cannonading was very different from that experienced on the 4th of July and on other festive occasions. Then it meant rejoicing, hilarity, exultation; now it meant death, perhaps, to some of our warmest friends, possibly defeat. It produced in me a strong feeling of regret and depression, and an ardent wish that men might learn to live together in peace and harmony.

The battle raged on, fresh troops were constantly going forward, hundreds of wounded returning, though we were not sent for. Our time had not yet come, but we were taking a military lesson often not fully learned—that of waiting for and obeying orders, and if inactive, were as fully performing our duty as though engaged in battle. Just before night, a portion of Buell's army arrived at Savannah, and the remainder of it rapidly followed, a portion of it, under Nelson, continuing the march up the river to a point opposite Pittsburg Landing, where they were to be ferried over by the steamboats. This so increased the demand upon the boats, that it was clearly apparent that marching orders would not be received by our colonel that day or night, and although there was no little excitement in and about our camp, the usual routine was observed, except perhaps that the men not on duty did not indulge quite so much in card-playing and other amusements as they formerly did. With the approach of darkness, the sound of battle ceased, but all that night the gunboats continued firing once in five minutes, which, as we afterwards learned, had but little effect, further than to demoralize the enemy and prevent them from approaching too near our own forces, which had been driven back nearly to the river.

None of us knew much about the results of the day's fighting, but rumors of all sorts were thick and diversified. Some of our boys had been down near to headquarters, and on their return to camp were certain that "we had been whipped like blazes"; that "nearly all of the commanding officers had been killed, whole regiments had been annihilated, at least ten thousand captured, nearly all of the batteries taken"; that "the 'rebs' were to make a night attack and gobble up the rest or drive them into river"; but on the other hand, the optimists declared that ll of these rumors were "fairy tales." originating with and disseminated by a crowd of cowards, who, when they found that the enemy also knew how to shoot and fight bravely, deserted from their commands and sought safety behind the river bank or on the boat with the wounded. The truth, of course, was between the two extremes. Thousands of gallant soldiers on both sides had fallen; our men had fought like heroes, but there were equally brave men on the other side, and our army, though stubbornly resisting, had been gradually driven back, and apparently nothing but the approach of night had saved us from total defeat. With the dawning light of the next day, the battle was fiercely resumed, and during the forenoon the conditions in our regiment were substantially unchanged. Our preparations for the conflict had been fully completed and we were ready to march at a minute's notice. By this time quite a number of soldiers, too slightly wounded to remain in hospital, were strolling around the town and into our camp, and a few of our own men had in some way smuggled themselves aboard the boat and gone up to the Landing; these men, on returning, were surrounded by those who had remained in camp, and eagerly interrogated. They, of course, had heard the din of battle much more distinctly than we had, but they had not been far from the Landing and knew but little more than we did as to what was going on or had actually taken place. One man declared that our army had been "cut to pieces; was terribly demoralized; entire regiments had left the field and were crowding behind the river bank, out of reach of shot and shell; the 'Johnny rebs' would soon gobble them up, seize the steamboats, and be down after us and our army supplies before night." Another was equally confident that we had them whipped; they were trying to skedaddle, but we "would bag the whole lot of them in an hour or so," and pointed triumphantly to a small number of prisoners who had been sent down to Savannah.

Meantime the battle continued unabated, and we were waiting, some with dread, some with anger. Most of us by this time were extremely anxious to be sent to the front, where we might have an opportunity of avenging the death of the gallant Wallace and other brave soldiers whom we knew had been killed. But it was not until long past noon when the orders to march finally came. We were not long in getting on board the boat, the battle still raging, the sounds of strife becoming more and more distinct as we approached the Landing; then the roar of cannon grew fainter and fainter and entirely ceased by the time we arrived.

We had both a regimental and a brass band, and on the way up the colonel placed all these men under my charge to carry the wounded off the battle-field and to assist in every way possible. I managed to get them all together to instruct them in their duties and assign various places for each, so that when my work actually began there would be no confusion, and that our assistance to those needing our services should be prompt and efficient. Among the musicians was a pale, bright-looking young fellow, named Williams; and learning that he was a medical student when he enlisted, I selected him as my immediate assistant, gave him a tourniquet and some bandages, and told him to keep with me constantly, and that I should rely upon him more than any of the rest, to whom I assigned positions as stretcher-bearers, water-carriers, etc., giving each man a definite place and something to do.

Not doubting that wagons would be assigned me as soon as we reached the Landing, and having no knowledge whatever (except what I had learned by reading) of the actual requirements of the battle-field, I had very foolishly taken on board the boat a large box containing medicines, instruments, bandages, and all sorts of dressings; also a case of brandy, stretchers, leather water-buckets, and other hospital stores; almost enough, in fact, to make a wagon-load. I did not then know—I had not even stopped to think—how extremely unwise I was, although I realized my mistake very clearly within a half hour or so, and never repeated it.

When we arrived we saw that the river bank was high and precipitous; there was no wharf or wharf boat, no buildings except a solitary log-house, which was utilized by the surgeons as an operating hospital. Behind the bank and along the river were crowded in the greatest confusion hundreds of soldiers, some slightly wounded, others badly frightened, and still others whose officers had been killed or wounded, or who had in some way strayed from their regiments and lost all trace of them for the time being. Mingled with the men were perhaps 500 wagons and teams, army stores, camp equipage, a cannon or two with its carriage partially wrecked, caissons, etc.

Our regiment at once marched off the boat, up the hill, and I saw it no more until the next day, as I waited with the musicians for the wagon which never came; but momentarily expecting it, I had our hospital stores taken off the boat and carried on the bank.

We waited a half hour (which seemed to be several hours), and not seeing a team arrive for us, I went down the bank and endeavored to persuade one of the teamsters to take our stores to the regiment, but although the firing had entirely ceased, not one of them would go. I think I have never seen men so thoroughly frightened as they were. I appealed to an officer standing near, but he could do nothing with them. Soon after our own quartermaster came down; I told him that it was almost impossible for me to join the regiment without transportation for our hospital stores, and made an urgent appeal to him; but he, having no authority over any of the teamsters, was unable to induce any of them to move. In about a half hour our major rode down to the Landing, and I solicited his services in procuring a team; he made the attempt but failed. I then asked him where the regiment was, and he said he didn't know precisely but he thought not more than a mile in front, so I asked the musicians if they could not carry our stuff that distance. They thought they could, and we started. From the top of the bank the ground was seen to be uneven, sparsely covered with trees, here and there a valley or ravine, occasionally a cleared field and a log-house, one larger log building being called Shiloh Church; in one place a small peach orchard, no roads, but numerous wagon-trails winding irregularly through the battle-field.

We had not gone far before one of the men exclaimed, in startled tones, "My God! there is a dead man." "Yes," said another, "there's some more," and as we moved on the more numerous they were and the less surprise and horror was manifested.

We were in a sort of transition state; but a few weeks before we had been engaged in peaceful avocations in office, shop, or farm, reading of marches and battles but not fully realizing the conditions; then came enlistments, with stirring music, sword and flag presentations, speeches, orations, sermons, all going to show what a noble thing it was to devote one's self to his country; but little or nothing was said about wounds and death, of actual suffering to be endured, of marching, or of picket duty in the mud, and of other horrible and disagreeable features of actual warfare; all of this was yet to be learned, and now our small fraction of the regiment was taking its first lessons and learning something of the "stern realities of war." Some of the orators had made use of this phrase when urging others to enlist, but somehow its meaning seemed materially different when used to "round a period" from what it did when we were learning how to define it by actual experience.

Slowly we moved on, over and around the *débris* of battle, making frequent inquiries of officers and men whom we met as to the whereabouts of the 253d; but none knew or could even guess, further than that it was "somewhere out in the front." Not a trace of it could be found by any of our party. Our commissary sergeant (a jolly good fellow, by the way) had been attending to his duties, and in doing so had lost the regiment and accidentally found us, but he could not tell us which way or how far we had to go. Night overtook us as we were still painfully and slowly moving on, for by this time the men were tired out and the most of us were excessively hungry, so I said :

" Boys, drop that stuff right where you are ; you have carried it far enough, and if our Uncle Samuel wants it, he will have to send a team and wagon for it. We will camp here for the night and make the best of it. In the morning I will get you out of this scrape in some way."

A fire was built by the side of a log, the "cooked rations" were produced, and the boys made a hearty supper out of the contents of haversacks and canteens ; and it is more than probable that the case of brandy contributed more or less to their repast ; mine consisting principally of hard-tack and coffee, dashed with brandy.

After supper some of the men picked up more than a hundred muskets and stacked arms near the fire, in the most approved style. Others smoked their pipes and told stories. A few expressed regrets for the fallen now sleeping so thickly all around us, and sympathy for their friends, especially for their mothers, wives, or sisters, then all unconscious of the terrible fate which had befallen their loved ones ; but all of us were more or less startled and benumbed and before long we were lying down to sleep. I had made use of one of the stretchers, and by placing one end of the poles on a log and propping up the other end, had made quite a comfortable cot. The fatigue of the afternoon, together with the excitement of the day, caused me to fall asleep almost immediately. I do not know how long I slept, but I do know that I was awakened by the rain falling on my face ; as there was no improvement to be made in my lodgings, I went to sleep again, only to be awakened once more by the rain, which came down in heavy showers, and by finding that there were several quarts of water collected in the stretcher. Too worn-out and sleepy to think that by punching a hole or two in the stretcher with my knife, I could easily get rid of the water, I baled it out with my cap, and again went to sleep, only to be awakened long enough to bale out the water. This continued until daybreak, when I arose, replenished the fire, attempted to dry my clothes and get warm once more, for the night had become cool and my clothing was thoroughly saturated with moisture.

As soon as it became light enough to see well, I observed a log-house not far away, and proceeding to it learned that it was General Hurlbut's headquarters. I explained the situation to him, when he very kindly said :

"If you had reported to me last night, I could have sheltered your men."

"But I did not then know where to find you or any one else, general ; and besides, my men were so completely tired out that they could go no further."

"Well, get your men in that sutler's tent— our friends the foe have thoroughly emptied it —and come in to breakfast with me."

After my night's experience, the warm log-house seemed a palace, and the breakfast a banquet, although it consisted only of warm "soldier's biscuits," baked sweet potatoes, fried salt pork, and coffee ; but having eaten but little for twenty-four hours, I enjoyed it as he only who has been deprived of food for a time can appreciate a warm meal, in pleasant company.

After breakfast, the general ordered a wagon and team to be placed at my disposal, told me where and how to find the regiment, and was about to wish me good-morning, when suddenly were heard three heavy volleys of musketry from away out in the front, followed by utter silence again. General Hurlbut's manner changed in an instant ; from being a courteous host he became the brave and efficient commander. He ordered his men out in line of battle, and they responded as promptly and coolly as though summoned for dress parade. He then sent a company of cavalry out to the front, with orders to ascertain what the firing meant and to return immediately. All over the battle-field were hundreds, if not thousands, of men, strolling around.

Some were brave soldiers, who had gallantly fought for two days, but whose regiments had been cut to pieces or their officers killed or wounded; others were men who had arrived too late to be engaged; still others were cowardly wretches, who, now that all danger, as they supposed, had passed away, were in search of mementos of the battle, and did not scruple to rob the dead. When the firing was heard, all of those men fled toward the river, like frightened sheep, some capturing stray horses or mules, two or three mounting one animal; others, less fortunate, running as though pursued by demons, all seeking a place of safety from anticipated danger. But this humiliating spectacle had one bright spot; just in front of the general's headquarters, a second lieutenant stopped, soldiers began to gather around him like a swarm of bees, and in less than a minute more than a hundred men had halted near him, the number being increased every second.

General Hurlbut, who had, of course, witnessed the disgraceful stampede, became indignant and cried out, angrily, "Shoot the infernal cowards; drive them into the river!" An aide responded, "They are not cowards, general; they are brave men, who want to fight, and now they have an officer to command them."

"Well, let them form in my rear then, and I will give them all the fighting they want, if there is to be any more of it."

Our civilian readers may not know that men trained as soldiers and accustomed to having all their actions controlled by orders or signals, even to "turning in" or "turning out," going to bed and getting up, become like little children, in the absence of officers and commands; but place some one over them having due authority, and they instantly become brave, valiant soldiers, ready and willing to fight as long as they live, or until the close of the battle. This was finely illustrated in the case cited, and had there been a battle, it is certain that all of those men who had behaved like frightened children, and who had halted at the command of the officer, would have fought as bravely as any other soldiers on the battle-field.

The cavalry soon returned, and reported that "the firing was done by the new regiments which had been sent to the front the night before, after the close of the battle, and having lain out in the rain, fired off their pieces, so as to be able to put them in good order." Whereupon the men were ordered to stack arms and get their breakfast. Soon after this, General Grant and staff came riding by, and he sent an aide to General Hurlbut to say that we were attacked again and to instantly get his men out in line of battle. General Hurlbut, of course, obeyed the order, at the same time saying to himself, "Humph! I know more about that than he does," and as soon as Grant was out of sight, repeated his order to his men to stack arms and get their breakfast.

I had been a deeply interested spectator of the stirring events just described; it was my first experience of anything looking like actual warfare, and the scenes and incidents which had been witnessed made an indelible impression on my mind, vivid pictures as it were, like photographic views, which are recalled as clearly to-day as when this bit of history was being enacted. While it is now well known that further fighting then was impossible, none of us had that assurance at the time. We had been largely reinforced; it was not impossible that the enemy had also been as fortunate; and, if so, it seemed more than probable that they would attempt to regain what they had just lost. If there was to be another battle, there would, of course, be much work for me, and I carefully considered what I should do and how I should do it, if occasion required. Meantime, it was manifestly proper for me to remain just where I was, until after further developments had been made. But the excitement soon subsided; the fugitives stopped running, on hearing no more firing; the general strolled listlessly around, and his men resumed their ordinary and usual duties, as though nothing out of the common had occurred. Not long after, a team and wagon were provided for me, our hospital stores were loaded, and we started again on our search for the 253d, which we found encamped in the woods, near where the battle had begun on Sunday morning.

The arms were stacked in line of companies, but there was no camp equipage, no tents except one badly perforated with bullet-holes, which our colonel occupied. The men had full cartridge-boxes and empty haversacks, but nothing to do; they were simply there, officers and men, ready for duty, and if it had not been for the *débris* of battle and dead men lying around on every side, a stranger would have supposed that they were a body of soldiers out in a pleasant grove on a picnic. The regiment had not yet been placed in any brigade; it was simply there, at a point supposed to be nearest the enemy, had been furnished with ammunition and nothing else, and the colonel was instructed to await orders.

Nor was this at all surprising under the circumstances, for one of the most hotly contested battles of the war had just been fought; all of the regiments first engaged had been decimated, some almost completely cut to pieces, some captured entire, and regimental and brigade organizations destroyed. Those regiments which, like ours, had arrived too late to participate in the action, had been thrown out in the front; and, had occasion required, would have been quickly provided with brigade and division commanders. But it was now the lull after the storm. Ours and other regiments were in the place where they would do the most good, and General Grant, while protecting his army, was reorganizing it as rapidly as possible.

None of our men were sick; the wounded had all been picked up and taken to the field hospitals near the river. I was without employment and therefore availed myself of the suggestion of our colonel, and taking a detail of men went to the camp of one of the regiments near, which had been badly cut up and which had an abundance of good tents—provided for the men who were now sleeping unburied upon the field. The only officer left in the regiment was a second lieutenant, who very kindly gave me my choice of the tents. I selected an excellent Sibley, which I had pitched in the rear of our regiment, and later had the gratification of knowing that this tent not only afforded me protection from cold and rain, but also enabled me to contribute largely to the comfort of some of our officers who soon after became seriously ill.

Having established my home, as it were, and taken care of my hospital stores, I strolled over the battle-field and witnessed the devastation which the last two days had wrought. The field, as I have before said, was principally covered with a moderately thick growth of trees, among which there had been a dense growth of underbrush, with here and there a cleared field, which had been cultivated. I observed two striking peculiarities, one of which was that the underbrush had been cut off almost as completely as a field of grain is cut with a sickle, and the other, that there were innumerable marks of bullets, and occasionally a cannon-shot, on the trees at distances of from six to fifteen feet or more above the ground, showing that the aim of the combatants, in part at least, had been wild and inaccurate. Had there been greater precision, the casualties would have been much more numerous and the results of this terrible battle far more dreadful than they actually were.

The evidences of the terrible conflict which had taken place were numerous and deeply impressive. Strewed all over the field were broken caissons, wagons, dead horses, boxes of ammunition, arms of all description, haversacks, canteens, articles of all kinds for warfare or for comfort; but worst by far of all were the poor, mangled remains of the brave men of both sides, which so thickly covered the ground and whose sudden, awful death would surely cause the deepest grief and mourning in many a household, both North and South.

All around, in every direction, lay the bodies of those who had but recently been brave and valiant soldiers, some wearing the blue and some the gray, but who now were sleeping their last sleep, many of them unrecognized and unrecognizable, many without means of identification and who must be included in that plaintive list "missing," always made up after a battle. It is no exaggeration to say that I could walk across the cleared field, on the edge of which was my tent, by stepping upon the corpses of the dead, so thickly were they strewn in that fatal spot. In one place I counted the bodies of nine horribly mutilated men, lying almost in a heap together, who had evidently been killed all at once by an exploding shell. Some had been killed by a single bullet, the wounds scarcely perceptible and the features as placid as though the tired soldier had calmly lain down to rest. Some had met with a painless death, others had evidently suffered the greatest agony, some had lost a leg or an arm and had other wounds besides. One had lost a leg, and the other leg was hanging by a shred of flesh; wounds of every description, by bullet, shot and shell, had been made, and this sight was so sickening and horrible, that I, although used to scenes of suffering, had seen more than I could well endure, so turned away in sadness and retired to my tent.

THE FIRST GUN IN VIRGINIA IN 1861.

William L. Sheppard.

GLOUCESTER POINT, VIRGINIA—1861.

IN the year 1861 the man who had smelled the gunpowder of combat was a rare individual. There was here and there a veteran of the war of 1812, but his experience was generally that of camps, with an occasional false alarm. One old gentleman there was who had walked all the way from Richmond to Plattsburg, New York. I forget whether he had ever been in an engagement or not, anyhow he had seen active service in a real war, consequently was an object of great interest to the boys. The Mexican war recruited temporarily the diminishing ranks of the veterans, and with real fighters too, some bearing the marks of battle upon their persons, and at least one wore a sword of honor presented him by the State.

But when war was actually upon us, the average young man had derived his knowledge of it from books only, and mostly from those of the "Charles O'Malley" type.

So, with their notion of military life derived from sources of this kind and souls aglow with patriotic fervor, it may be imagined that men of the command to which the writer was attached heard with enthusiasm, one May morning of this portentous year, that there was a detail to go to the front.

The battery, now swelled to a battalion of 300 men, was composed mostly of Richmond material, and I do not suppose that the ages averaged twenty-two. It was subsequently observed in the recent war that men from nineteen to twenty-two—in the Confederate army, at least—made the best soldiers; that is, if they stood the first campaign.

We had been in barracks at a college in the then environs of Richmond, which its students had deserted for the ranks. We were getting deadly tired of the monotony of drill and camp routine; especially worn out with the restraint and surveillance which kept us fastened to this dull spot when we were in sight of the comfortable homes of our parents and the delectable abodes of our sweethearts.

The detail was for about fifty men, as I remember, but pretty near the whole battalion requested to be sent. The fortunate ones, as we considered ourselves, were marched away to the York River Railroad depot to be transported to some threatened point, we knew not where; but we had surmised, as we soon learned, correctly. It was a mystery, by the way, throughout the whole war, how movements intended to be conducted with perfect secrecy got to be whispered about amongst the private soldiers, without any betrayal of trust being traced to headquarters.

The enthusiastic "God-speeds" and tearful "good-byes" of those we left behind us were soon forgotten on the train. It would probably be impossible to check the exuberant spirits of half a hundred young men left to themselves under any circumstances, but when you have them associated under some common excitement the attempt to repress is almost hopeless; so we sang and joked as if we were going to a picnic, played practical jokes and munched our lunches, many of them really luxurious. From an accident to the engine we were forced to spend the night on the road and found ourselves a good deal cramped and our ardor a little damped next morning on our arrival at the then village of West Point at the head of York River. Here discipline was resumed and we were given the choice between drawing free rations and cooking them ourselves, and paying for our breakfasts at the hotel. The latter alternative was seized by the whole detail and was the only "option" on breakfasts in the field that ever offered itself to us in the whole four years.

Our battery, a boat howitzer and a three-inch rifle-piece of the same dimensions and having a similar carriage, an alteration from the boat carriage, were placed on the deck, and we steamed away, leaving the inhabitants of West Point in a comfortable sense of security. This had been much disturbed of late by the news that a "Yankee" gunboat was patrolling the lower river and threatening to come up higher. Works were being thrown up by our people at Gloucester Point, opposite the historic village of Yorktown, and the authorities at Richmond had heard that an armed craft was to be sent from Fort Monroe to order the work to cease and to prevent its resumption. This was considered an unwarrantable interference, and we were sent to forestall or resist it.

In order to deceive the anticipated foe into the belief that the steamer was going on her ordinary trip (which was to the wharves on the river), the uniformed men were kept out of sight, and we found ourselves parties to a proposed naval ambush. The steamer kept on without getting sight of any other craft except those of peaceable fishermen, and we landed uneventfully at the shaky wharf at Gloucester Point. Here we found quite formidable works in process of erection under the orders of Colonel (afterwards General) Taliaferro and the direction of Lieutenant Clarke, an engineer. Swarms of negroes were digging earth for the battery from a hillside, the foot of which ran to a swamp, which, with the river on the other side, incurving here, formed a sandy peninsula, expanding at the outer end, upon which was situated a storehouse and from which the wharf ran out some fifty feet into the stream.

We found the garrison to consist of a local company, over-uniformed with felt hats and plumes. They had brought from somewhere a six-pound iron gun of the pattern of the last century, having a double trail, with a place upon the end for an ammunition chest and a "linstock," a wooden rod about three feet long, around which the match was to be twisted with which the gun was "touched off." This ancient weapon had been in use during the war of 1812 and in disuse ever since. It was suspiciously honey-combed by the long action of the elements, but had evidently been furbished up and made the best of for this occasion.

As "ramps" and platforms for the guns had not been completed, they were not in a condition to receive our artillery. We were therefore directed to throw up a little "lunette" in the space on the beach between the larger works and the water. When finished, these were masked with cut bushes. With the aid of the negroes this work was quickly accomplished, and the two brass pieces were put in position. The detachment assigned to the iron gun, and to which I was detailed, placed their piece in battery to the right of the lunette and under the wharf. I do not know why we were not accorded a place in the breastworks—a misnomer, by the way, as they were not more than knee high—but in the sequel we congratulated ourselves that we had gone through the ordeal without any extraneous protection and trusting solely to the bulwark of manly breasts.

We were now called off for dinner, which we felt that we had earned, but by no means enjoyed the prospect of having first to cook. We were divided into several messes; but little had been accomplished, however, when the officer in command, who had been "sweeping the horizon" with field-glasses, announced that a steamer was approaching, and we were ordered to our guns. Our steamer must still have been in sight of the approaching stranger, who probably had come up in hope of finding her at the wharf.

We had plenty of time for speculations and grumbling before the suspicious craft was near enough for us to discern with the naked eye that she was low in the water, had high paddle boxes and a single smoke-stack. She kept well to the further side of the river and was now somewhere nearly abreast of us and a thousand yards (at a guess) away. We had been standing expectant at our guns sometime and now gladly, at the colonel's command, fired across the bows of the steamer.

The shot from our little rifle ricochetted some distance ahead of the still moving vessel, and still she moved without slowing down—she was already going very slowly. After a reasonable time had elapsed for them to consider our well-recognized military or naval warning to stop, the colonel said: "Let her have it, boys!"

The steamer's wheels ceased revolving. We saw that our shot had struck the water near her and had ricochetted either aboard or over her. She slewed a little to bring her more broadside on, her flag flying gayly out. Then a puff of smoke rose from her bow, and in an instant the first shot from the enemy struck the water short of us, but in good line. We were now ordered to fire *ad lib.* The old six-pounder joined in now, and we found that she carried as far as the others; indeed, further than the smooth-bore howitzer, whose missiles fell short every time. The six-pounder detachment claimed to have struck the vessel at least once.

Meanwhile, the steamer kept up fire from her long thirty-two-pounder, the only gun that she had, apparently, though there may have been others that could not be brought to bear. We ascertained the calibre from a shot which we recovered.

Either because she thought the odds too much against her, or because she had completed an intended reconnoissance, she sheered off after a few shots and retired, evidently with her chain boxes to port, as she had a big heel to that side.

We read in a paper, subsequently, that she had received three shots between wind and water. We also learned that she was the sea-going tug Yankee, and considered it no bad augury that a craft bearing the concrete name of our enemy had been discomfited in the first engagement of the war north of South Carolina. By counting our ammunition left, we found that we had fired thirteen shots. I do not remember that there was any cheering or other demonstration when the steamer left us.

At our gun, we now had leisure to observe that the wheels and ourselves were standing in the water. The tide had not made an exception in our case.

It being apparent that the fight was over for the time being, we were allowed to break ranks and resume our preparations for dinner, and found, on coming somewhat to our normal selves, that we were very hungry. We were not long in discovering that whilst we had been occupied in upholding our honor at the front, we had had an enemy in the rear. Our camp had been raided by the pigs, our mess kettles and frying pans overturned, and everything eatable within reach either consumed or spoiled. There was nobody to interfere with the pigs, as our attention was, of course, engrossed elsewhere, and every negro and non-combatant had retired to the bluff, or out of sight.

I think from this incident sprang our future uncontrollable desire to kill a pig wherever we encountered him, especially if the provost-guard was not around.

But true soldier-fashion, we made light of this accident and went to work on another dinner. The memories of this and one or two subsequent dinners stood by us for some time, and were subjects of much mirth to us as we increased in knowledge of military mess cooking.

That night, in our Sibley tents, with guards posted at every possible point to secure us from interruption, we went through the scenes of the day, and gradually the accumulated experiences pieced out a tolerably complete *resumé* of the incidents and sensations growing out of our first smell at gunpowder. It was evident that the shot were very dangerous if they *should* strike anybody, as they dug holes in the ground fully as large as graves and very suggestive of the same. So it was unanimously concluded that we had been *in danger.*

We, at the six-pounder, had another escaped peril to report. The old piece had such a recoil that at the first shot she came near wiping out all the gun squad except numbers one and two, who were opposite the muzzle. The next shot we stood clear. We also came to wonder why we had been placed under the wharf, where our position was a much more dangerous one, from the possibility of flying splinters, had the wharf been struck, than if we had been in the open, to say nothing about the risk of being driven off by the tide. Everybody remembered one incident, however, and the hero, though a total stranger that morning, immediately became an object of great attention. He was a big brindle nondescript dog, who leaped and capered in front of the guns, jumping all four feet off the ground at the smoke, and then rushing frantically into the water, looking in vain for the traces of our shot, swimming out to where he saw the thirty-two-pound balls make a great splash, and diving for them, remaining so long under water that we several times thought him drowned.

There have been many things written about men's feelings when the first time under fire. The consensus of opinion with us, under similar circumstances, was that we hardly had time to think of the danger. As for myself, I do not think I realized that we were being shot at with any intention of hurting us. Later on, I think that we all took in the risk much more thoroughly, for it soon became apparent that we were being shot at with serious intent to hurt, and saw fearful evidences of that intent.

HOW THE 164TH NEW YORK LOST ITS COLORS.

CAPTAIN JOHN McANALLY.

CAPTAIN JOHN MC ANALLY.

IN a recently published article, among other things Gen. Horatio C. King referred to a very happy reunion of the blue and the gray in which he participated on the Fourth of July, 1883, upon which occasion " the cadets of the Virginia Military Institute at Lexington visited New York for the purpose, among other things, of returning the flag of the 155th Regiment of New York Volunteers, which had been captured by cadets during the war when they were suddenly called into the Confederate service."

Had General King looked closely at the lettering on that flag, he would have found that it had belonged to the 164th Regiment and not the 155th; and the flag was one of those generally known as a State flag, such as each regiment carried in addition to the national colors. The flag in question was taken from me, while commanding a company of the 155th Regiment, N. Y. V., and under rather peculiar circumstances, which I will relate.

The 155th, 164th, 170th, and 182d Regiments of New York Volunteers were known as the Corcoran Legion, and during the month of November, 1863, were encamped at Fairfax Station, Virginia. An order came directing the

164th and 182d Regiments to go to Fairfax Court House, while the 155th and 170th Regiments were instructed to guard the Orange and Alexandria Railroad from the Bull Run Bridge to the bridge across Accotink Creek.

After the 164th Regiment had departed, their colors were found standing near a sutler's tent, close to the station. How they came to be left behind I have never known. The colors were found by a member of my company, who brought them to my tent. I made diligent inquiry, but could learn nothing as to the reason for leaving the colors behind; but I supposed they would soon be missed and sent for. Shortly afterward I was ordered to go with my company to Sangster Cross Roads, about three miles west of Fairfax Station, and, having had no inquiry for the flag, I took it with me.

Arriving at our new post of duty, we found a quantity of timber that had been taken there to build a block-house, and this I at once used in the construction of breastworks, extending across the highway close to the railroad. On each side of the road was a ditch nearly ten feet deep, and by extending the timbers over the ditches, I secured a position where we were comparatively free from danger from a sudden attack or a dash by the enemy's cavalry. I had some sixty-five men, who were sheltered by four Sibley tents, while the first sergeant occupied a wall tent. The three officers were quartered in the county house near by, with the consent of the keeper, who was a fine old Virginia gentleman. We expected to remain there all winter, so the officers sent for their wives, who happened to be three sisters, to come and spend the Christmas holidays in camp. We were far in the rear of the army and felt quite secure; but we reckoned without our host, as subsequent events proved.

About half-past six o'clock on the evening of December 17th, I was standing near the first sergeant's tent, listening to a very good amateur minstrel performance which the boys were giving for their own diversion, when our post was suddenly attacked from the south, and I presume no show was ever broken up more quickly. Of course it was dark, and we could not make out the numbers or the exact character of our assailants, who speedily dashed up on the railroad track and opened fire upon us at not more than one hundred feet distance. They could not get to us on account of our substantial breastworks and the equally impassable ditch, and I think they must have been somewhat surprised to find that they had struck a foe that, though suddenly assailed, did not intend to run away or dodge the issue. Our men promptly and vigorously returned the fire, and the air was soon filled with singing bullets, traveling in both directions.

The Confederate leader quickly saw the impossibility of dislodging us from that point of attack, so he sent a column to my left, which worked around over another road and came up behind our works. Our first lieutenant, with one-third of the company, engaged the enemy in our rear, and kept them at bay for about forty minutes, killing one of our assailants and wounding several. In front, where we were still fighting behind the timbers, we killed Captain Cartwell, of Company D, 12th Virginia Cavalry, a brave officer who was leading his men in a charge. His body fell into a little run which they were crossing. It is an awful thing to shoot down a brave and dashing soldier, though he be an enemy, but such is war.

All this time I suppose neither commander knew whom he was fighting nor how many men were before him. I know I didn't; but after things became serious, and our enemy began to crowd us, front and rear, with blare of bugle, clash of steel, beat of hoofs, and that blood-curdling "yell," I began to think it had fallen to my lot to "do up" the entire Confederacy. We cheered back and kept up all the show we could, but it was "no go." The first lieutenant was forced back, and our tents were fired, which exposed our position and our weakness, so the only thing left for us was to "get out," which we did, through the railroad ditch to the west— the only line of retreat left open.

Nine of my men failed to get away, and every one of them subsequently died at Andersonville. One of my sergeants had a narrow escape. He was disabled, and instead of attempting to escape, he crawled under the timbers, where he could see nothing but could hear considerable. Among other things he could hear a surgeon addressing a Sergeant Myers, from whom a bullet was being extracted. We had a Sergeant Myers

in our company, and so our man crawled out of his hiding-place only to see that all the uniforms were gray. He speedily crawled back again but did not have to remain long, for the Confederates made a very short stay and were soon out of sight and hearing.

One of my men hurried down the railroad track toward Fairfax Station and, by means of a fire-brand, stopped all trains, so that the chief object of this cavalry dash was frustrated.

When I returned with reinforcements I found our camp in ashes, but to my intense relief the county house was all right, and so were the ladies. The flag of the 164th Regiment, previously mentioned and which had remained in my possession up to that time, had been taken from my quarters along with some other things, and that is the way it was captured by the Confederates.

The ladies of our party were cared for, during the fight, at the county house, and they were much affected by the courtesy of the Confederate officers, who showed them every attention. After the fight they went over the field and picked up one poor fellow in gray, shot through the abdomen and fatally wounded. His name was Van Meter, and he belonged, I believe, to Captain Cartwell's company, of the 12th Virginia Cavalry. We did all we could for him, but he died the next morning, and we gave him a soldier's burial. His brother-in-law subsequently obtained a permit and removed the body to his home.

Our assailants proved to be General Rosser, with his brigade of cavalry, the 7th, 11th, and 12th Virginia, and the 35th Battalion. It may seem strange that a single company could make so good a stand against a greatly superior force, but our position was strong and the darkness was so great that our assailants were in a quandary as to our strength. Poor Van Meter told me that they had heard that we had seventy-five men, but that it seemed to him we had 300 at least.

Colonel McMahon, of the 164th Regiment, came looking for the missing flag, but was too late. He said he didn't care so much about the flag, but he didn't like to have Rosser go off with the idea that he had been fighting his regiment when it was only a company and from another command.

THE LAST VICTORY OF THE LOST CAUSE.

Colonel William H. Stewart.

COLONEL LAUNCELOT MINOR—1894.

ON the night of the 6th of April, 1865, Mahone's Division, the rear guard or left wing of the Army of Northern Virginia, slept on its arms at the High Bridge, on the Norfolk and Western Railroad, near Farmville, in Virginia. Early on the following morning the unmounted officers and privates crossed over the Appomattox River on this bridge and the mounted officers forded the stream. The close pursuit of the Army of the Potomac prevented the destruction of this great structure; but our soldiers succeeded in burning a barn near, to prevent the capture of a large quantity of tobacco stored therein.

After a march of a few hours, our division was halted at Cumberland Church and formed in line of battle across the highway. The right was connected with another line of troops, that extended away toward Farmville, and its left, entirely unprotected, rested a few hundred yards in rear of the church.

It was my fortune to be assigned to the command of the division picket line, which was barely established before the hostile sharpshooters were seen advancing in front, and the contest began, to continue hotly the live-long day. The men in line of battle had hurriedly thrown up a slight earthwork, with bayonets and

bare hands, which afforded scant protection from the duel that raged fiercely between the pickets.

The Rockbridge Artillery, Captain Archie Graham, was posted on the line of battle near the public road and rendered valuable service throughout that long day. Robert E. Lee, Jr., son of General Robert E. Lee, our commander-in-chief, was a private in this battery.

In the afternoon my pickets were forced back by a strong column of troops, which made a dashing charge upon our left, with the view of turning our flank. The galling fire from my pickets impeded the charge, and the advance brigade halted for protection in a deep ravine only a short distance from the flank of our crude earthworks. The pickets were quickly reinforced by a regiment of Georgians from General "Tiger" Anderson's Brigade, and held the enemy in check until the gallant Anderson, with the remainder of his command, swept around the left of our position, struck the enemy in flank, capturing an entire brigade with its colors.

This magnificent manœuvre was directed by the dashing Mahone and performed under his eyes, as I can testify. It was the quick conception of one of the greatest military leaders of the war between the sections—of a soldier well worthy of the mantle of Stonewall Jackson. After the brilliant feat of the glorious Georgians, our picket line was soon re-established; but not without the sacrifice of some brave men.

Conspicuous for gallantry was a handsome young artilleryman, not out of his teens, who, when not engaged with his cannon, would borrow rifles from the infantrymen, stand up, while others were protected by breastworks, and with deliberate aim fire at his man, regardless of the continuous shower of bullets to which he was exposed. Finally he was shot down, desperately wounded, and borne off the field to the residence of Mr. Hogsden, which was made a field hospital.

Subsequently Adjutant Griffin F. Edwards, a youth of twenty years, of our 61st Virginia Regiment, Infantry, while gallantly rallying his men to recover the lost picket line in front of his regiment, was also severely wounded. After dark he was taken to the field hospital. The yard was strewn with the wounded and dead, the kitchen, out-houses, and even the stables were full of bleeding men. There was one vacant place in the parlor of the old mansion where a blanket was spread for Adjutant Edwards. The soldier nearest happened to be the brave artillery boy who had been shot down

PRIVATE LAUNCELOT MINOR—1865.

while acting as a voluntary infantryman, as above stated, and he appeared to be in the agonies of death. Although severely wounded, the chivalrous Edwards ministered all in his power; and as he gave him a drink of water from his canteen, the boy whispered: "My name is Minor." For three days these wounded sufferers remained without surgeons or nurses. Then the wounded companions were separated and unknown to each other, until recently, after twenty-nine years, Adjutant Edwards, now a prominent lawyer in Virginia, by accident ascertained that the comrade whom he believed dead is living, in the person of Launcelot Minor, colonel of the 2d Regiment of Infantry, Arkansas State Guards, and a prominent lawyer of Newport, in that State.

When Private Minor recovered consciousness he found a note pinned to the inside of his shirt, requesting that in case he died some one would give him a decent burial, and a five dollar gold piece was enclosed in the note to pay the expense. He still has the gold coin and wants to know from whom it came.

The shadows of evening found our weary and starving soldiers in full possession of the battlefield at Cumberland Church and rejoicing over their last victory. The only rations which could be issued on this retreat were a few ears of corn to each soldier, but these men were of that pure metal which yields neither to danger nor hunger.

Soon after dark the troops were withdrawn from this line of battle, and proceeded on the march toward Appomattox, where Mahone returned the silken trophies, which were so gallantly won at Cumberland Church, to his released prisoners. I was left to cover the retreat, with orders to withdraw my pickets from the line at three o'clock A. M. and follow the army.

The long hours of darkness and anxiety dragged heavily along, while the ever watchful pickets experienced the unpleasant anticipations of being killed or captured. On the hour and the minute we quietly withdrew from the field of the last victory of the lost cause. About eight o'clock next morning, the 7th of April, 1865, we overtook the army, and though desperately tired, rejoiced with a "rebel yell" over our escape from capture, for which we received the congratulations of General Mahone. The following night we built our camp-fires on the brow of a hill and rested on our arms in line of battle for the last time. Before another sun gained the meridian our arms were stacked and our battle-flags furled forever on the hills of Appomattox.

GRIFFIN F. EDWARDS, ESQ.—1894.

WITH PICKETT AT CEMETERY RIDGE.

Lieutenant G. W. Finley.

SCENE OF PICKETT'S CHARGE AT GETTYSBURG.
(*View from right of " High Water Mark."*)

I WAS in the charge on Cemetery Ridge, July 3, 1863, and was taken prisoner at the stone fence on the ridge and behind which the first Federal line waited our attack. I shall limit what I write to what I heard and saw at the time.

Our division pickets reached the vicinity of Gettysburg—near where the prisoners captured in the battle of July 1st were held under guard about or a little before sunset on the 2d. Longstreet's fight on our right was then raging, and we could hear its roar and crash and rattling musketry that told of stern work on both sides. We bivouacked in some woods near us and rested after our long and hot march from Chambersburg. Early next morning we were marched to the right and, I think not later than eight o'clock, reached a point on what I have since learned was Seminary Ridge, where we were halted under cover of the ridge and a piece of woods some two or three hundred yards in rear of the position we took in line of battle just before the assault. Our artillery was just outside of the woods in our front in the edge of open fields. Here we rested, and from some cause, I never knew what, the morning was permitted to wear away without movement on our part. An oc-

casional shell passed over us, or a minié ball sang among the tree-tops, but few or none of us were hurt.

While in this position a group of officers, among whom I recognized Generals Lee, Longstreet, Pickett, and others, remained dismounted in our rear for a good while. Staff officers and couriers were coming and going, but no orders were issued to us.

The division—that is all of it that was at Gettysburg—comprised the three brigades of Kemper, Garnett, and Armistead, and had in line that day about 4500 muskets.

About twelve o'clock we were moved up to the edge of the woods and just behind our artillery. In my immediate front we were so close to the guns that I had to "break to the rear" my little company to give the men at the limber chest room to handle the ammunition. The caisson, with its horses and drivers, was just in my rear.

The order of battle for the division was: Kemper and Garnett in the front line and Armistead in the rear or second line. Kemper on the right and Garnett on the left. Garnett's five regiments took their usual order from right to left as follows: 8th, 18th, 19th, 28th, and 56th

Virginia regiments. This, you see, threw my regiment (the 56th) on the left of the first line, and my company (K) was second or third from the extreme left of the division. After

THE BLOODY ANGLE, GETTYSBURG.

we got into position we were ordered to lie down and wait for the order to advance after our guns had bombarded the position we were to assault.

The day was intensely hot, and lying in the sun we suffered greatly from the heat.

About one o'clock P. M. our batteries opened, and the Federals promptly replied. For more than an hour the most terrific cannonade any of us had ever experienced was kept up, and it seemed as if neither man nor horse could possibly live under it. Our gunners stood to their pieces and handled them with such splendid courage as to wake the admiration of the infantry crouching on the ground behind them. We could see nothing whatever of the opposing lines, but knew from the fire that they must have a strong position and many guns.

Our loss was considerable under this storm of shot and shell, still there was no demoralization of our men in line. They waited almost impatiently for the order to advance, as almost anything would be a relief from the strain upon them.

When the fire slackened and had almost ceased, I saw General Longstreet, attended by a single officer, whom I took to be his adjutant-general, Colonel Sorrell, riding slowly from our right in front of our line and in full view of the enemy's skirmishers. He did not seem to notice

the Federal lines at all, but was coolly and carefully inspecting ours. We looked for him to be hit every moment. As rifle balls whistled by and a shell now and then ploughed up the ground close to and startled the splendid horse he rode, the general would check him and quietly ride on. Many a voice from the ranks remonstrated with him on his reckless exposure, in terms more emphatic than elegant, told him "to go to the rear," "you'll get your old fool head knocked off," "we'll fight without your leading us," etc. Not a word fell from his lips, and when he had passed our left he rode into the woods behind us. In a few moments General Pickett dashed out from the woods where Longstreet had entered them, and called his division to "attention!" In a few brief words, which I failed to hear, he told us, as I subsequently learned, what was expected of us, and then ordered us forward. He rode to the right of the division, and I never saw him afterward.

The orders to us were to advance slowly, with arms "at will," no cheering, no firing, no breaking from "common" to "quick," or "changing" step, and "to dress on the centre."

A few steps and we had cleared our guns, and the fatal field was before us. Where I marched through a wheat field that sloped gently toward the Emmittsburg road, the position of the Federals flashed into view. Skirmishers lined the fences along the road, and back of them, along a low stone wall or fence, gleamed the muskets of the first line. In rear of this, artillery, thickly planted, frowned upon us. As we came in sight there seemed to be a restlessness and excitement along the enemy's lines, which encouraged some of us to hope they would not make a stubborn resistance. Their skirmishers began to run in, and the artillery opened upon us all along our front. I soon noticed that shells were also coming from our right and striking just in front or in rear of our moving line—sometimes between the line and the file-closers. I discovered that they came from the high hills to our right, which I have since learned were the Round Tops. This fire soon became strictly enfilading as we changed the point of direction from the centre to the left while on the march, and whenever it struck our ranks was fearfully destructive—one company, a little to my right, numbering thirty-five or forty men, was almost swept, "to a man," from the line by a single shell. We had not advanced far beyond our guns when our gallant Colonel Stuart fell, mortally wounded. (He was taken back to Virginia and died in a few days after.)

We had no other field officer present, and the command devolved upon the senior captain.

Still on, steadily on, the fire growing more and more furious and deadly, our men advanced. The change of direction threw Kemper's brigade closer to the Federal line (which was oblique to ours) than Garnett. So he was hotly engaged before our left was in musket range. I could hear and see a part of his fighting before my attention was absorbed by my own front.

As we neared the Emmittsburg road the Federals behind the stone fence on the hill opened a rapid fire upon us with muskets. But as they were stooping behind that fence, I think they overshot us. When my regiment struck the road the board fences were still mostly standing, and there was a momentary check until our men went against and over them. Men were falling all around us, and cannon and muskets were raining death upon us. Still on and up the slope toward that stone fence our men steadily swept, without a sound or a shot, save as the men would clamor to be allowed to return the fire that was being poured into them. When we were about seventy-five or one hundred yards from that stone wall some of the men holding it began to break for the rear, when, without orders, save from captains and lieutenants, our line poured a volley or two into them and then rushed upon the fence, breaking the line and capturing many of the men, who rushed toward us crying: "Don't shoot!" "We surrender!" "Where shall we go?" etc. They were told to go to our rear, but no one went with them, so far as I saw, and I suppose the most of them afterwards made their way back into their own lines.

The Federal gunners stood manfully to their guns. I never saw more gallant bearing in any men. They fired their last shots full in our faces and so close that I thought I felt distinctly the flame of the explosion, and not until we had crushed their supports did they abandon their guns. Just as I stepped upon the stone wall I noticed for the first time a line of troops just joining upon our left. Springing to that flank I found they were from Archer's Tennessee brigade and part of Heath's division. This gallant brigade had been terribly cut up in the first day's fight, and there was but a fragment of them left. Some of them with us seized and held the stone wall in our front. For several minutes there were no troops in our immediate front. But to our left the Federal line was

still unbroken. This fact is impressed upon my mind by my taking a musket from one of my men who said he could not discharge it and firing it at that line to my left and obliquely in front, and further by seeing our brave Brigadier-General Garnett, who, though almost disabled by a kick from a horse while on the march from Virginia, would lead us in action that day, riding to our left, just in my rear, with his eyes fastened upon the unbroken line behind the stone fence and with the evident intention of making such disposition of his men as would dislodge it. At that instant, suddenly a terrific fire burst upon us from our front, and looking around I saw close to us, just on the crest of the ridge, a fresh line of Federals attempting to drive us from the stone fence, but after exchanging a few rounds with us they fell back behind the crest, leaving us still in possession of the stone wall. Under this fire, as I immediately

SPOT WHERE CUSHING AND ARMISTEAD FELL.

learned, General Garnett had fallen dead. Almost simultaneously with these movements General Armistead, on foot, strode over the stone fence, leading his brigade most gallantly, with his hat on his sword and calling upon his men to charge. A few of us followed him until, just as he put his hand upon one of the abandoned guns, he was shot down. Seeing that most of the men still remained at the stone fence, I returned, and was one of the very few who got back unhurt.

Again there was comparative quiet for a while in our immediate front, but bullets came flying still from the unbroken line to our line. During one of these pauses, I took a rapid but careful look at the ground over which we had advanced, and was surprised to see comparatively so few men lying dead or wounded on the field. Doubtless many of the wounded had gotten back before I looked. But the fact was that the loss did not seem to be anything like so great as I had supposed it must be. But we were not left long at leisure to survey the field. We were in plain view of the Federal officers, and they saw that we were but few in numbers and well-nigh exhausted by what we had already accomplished. The death of General Garnett and the fall of General Armistead left us on that part of the line without an officer above the grade of captain. While we were lying there and the Federals were completing their disposition of forces to repulse and capture us, some one ran rapidly along our line calling out to the men, "General Lee says fall back from here!" Many of the men attempted to obey, but a few of us, not recognizing the order as authentic, held our men in line and encouraged them to look for support. Just then the Federals advanced in heavy force. The bullets seemed to come from front and both flanks, and I saw we could not hold the fence any longer. I again looked back over the field to see the chances for withdrawing. The men who had begun to fall back seemed to be dropping like leaves as they ran, and in a very few moments the number on the ground was four or five times as great, apparently, as when I had looked before. It seemed foolhardy to attempt to get back. The Federal line pressed on until our men fired almost into their faces. Seeing that it was a useless waste of life to struggle longer, I ordered the few men around me to "cease firing" and surrendered. Others to the right and left did the same, and soon the sharp, quick huzza of the Federals told of our defeat and their triumph. As we walked to the rear, I went up to General Armistead, as he was lying close to the wheels of the gun on which he had put his hand, and stooping, looked into his face and thought from his appearance and position that he was then dead. I have since learned that he did not die until some time during the night. As soon as the Federal cheer announced our repulse, our batteries opened a brisk fire upon the hill, on friend and foe alike, to check any advance that might be contemplated. And so, under the fire of our own guns and the guard of our enemies, we passed away from that now historic hill and ridge to a long and dreary imprisonment, from which I was not released until May 14, 1865.

Lest I may do unintentional injustice to some troops who, though not Virginians, were as gallant as they or any others and who nobly did their duty that day, permit me to add a few words of explanation, showing why the line behind the stone fence, to our left, was not broken or dislodged. The formation of the Federal line, where the left of Garnett's brigade struck it, was peculiar. It ran obliquely across the face of Cemetery Ridge from the right. I was posted behind one of the substantial stone fences common in that section. In order, as I supposed, to get position for a battery or two, that fence had been pulled down and thrown forward down the slope of the ridge, some seventy-five or one hundred steps, and rebuilt loosely to about three feet in height. On the left it retained its original position and height—say four and one-half to five feet—and afforded fine shelter against infantry. The left of the 50th Regiment and some of Archer's men struck it at the salient. The rest of Archer's men and those on their left when we were in possession of the stone fence, while in line with us, were, as you see, still seventy-five to one hundred yards from the stone fence in their front. Every soldier knows how vast a difference this made in our favor on such ground and in face of such a line. Those brave fellows, led by Pettigrew, Trimble, Lane, and others (as I have since been informed), went as far and suffered as heavily as we did, and many of them were captured on the ridge when we were, with whom I shared the long imprisonment that followed.

As to the effect of the fire from the Federal line upon ours, as we advanced, I can only say that it did not seem to check it in the least. There was no pause in the slow and steady movement, save the momentary one at the Emmittsburg road, caused mainly by the fence that inclosed it. There was a little "huddling" of the men when we were ordered to dress to the left rather than to the centre, as at first commanded. There was, so far as I saw, no skulking or straggling, but a quiet, determined advance. Our loss, I am inclined to think, was greatest in the three combats at the stone fence, where we broke first the line that held it, and second repulsed the attempt to retake the fence, and third resisted the effort that overwhelmed us. The lines were so close, the fire was unusually fatal. And then the men who attempted to run back to our original line suffered dreadfully.

COOPER'S "BATTERY B" BEFORE PETERSBURG.

By One of Its Members.

IT may be said, without disparagement to the artillerists of any other Federal command, that the Lawrence County (Pa.) company, known as "Cooper's Battery," performed hard and faithful service, the value of which cannot be easily estimated. It participated in every important engagement of the Army of the Potomac, from Drainsville to the capture of Petersburg. Our first captain was Henry T. Danforth, a soldier who had seen service with Bragg's Battery during the Mexican War, and had later been in the cavalry service on the frontier under General Albert Sidney Johnson. Isaac A. Nesbit was our first lieutenant. Captain Danforth was killed at New Market Cross Roads, on June 30, 1862, and was succeeded by James H. Cooper, who is now a resident of New Castle, Pennsylvania. Captain Cooper had been first sergeant of the battery; he was one of the bravest men in either army, and was acknowledged one of the best battery commanders in the Army of the Potomac by his superior officers, Generals Reynolds and Meade, both of whom, as well as General Ord, had the honor of commanding that grand body of men known as the Pennsylvania Reserves, the pride of the Keystone State.

On the 20th of December, 1861, all original members of our battery who had not reënlisted were honorably discharged, and the company was recruited until it again had its full complement of 152 men to man the six guns. Captain Cooper was mustered out on August 8, 1864, having served two months beyond his term of enlistment. He was commissioned major and had General Meade's endorsement for a colonelcy, but pressing private business compelled him to part company with the men he had so long led, and whose confidence he fully possessed. Lieutenant William C. Miller, a brave and competent officer, succeeded to the command, and was mustered out November 22, 1864, from which date until the close of the war the battery was commanded by Captain William McClelland, who had risen from the ranks by gradual promotion. At the time of which I write, April 2, 1865, the other commissioned officers were: First lieutenants, Thomas C. Rice and James A. Gardner; second lieutenants, J. M. Pennypacker and John Geary.

We first saw the church spires of Petersburg a little before noon, June 17, 1864. For nearly a year thereafter we were seldom out of sight of them, and our work was constant, although confined to a small radius. We had our winter-quarters about a mile in the rear of our main line of works, of which Fort Sedgwick was the most advanced. Our battery served its turn at the front, first at Battery 22, then near the Yellow House or Globe Tavern, in which action we took part; then in Forts Hays and Howard, and in Batteries 24 and 26. Later we had two guns in Battery 22 and four in Fort Davis. The numbered batteries, both Union and Confederate, were strong earthworks, generally a part of the main line and located between the larger forts. They were designed for one or more field guns and were open at the rear. Battery 22 was on the right of the Jerusalem plank-road, some 300 yards to the rear of Fort Sedgwick, the Union line having been sharply swung back on account of the formation of the ground. Fort Davis was on the other side of the plank-road, about 100 yards to the left and rear of Battery 22. Fort Sedgwick—better known in those days as "Fort Hell"—was built across the plank-road.

The nearest point of the Confederate works, perhaps 600 yards distant, was a strong earthwork, also built across the road and known as Battery 27; and on the right of this (our left) was Fort Mahone, which was about the most pert and combative earthwork on the Confederate front, this part of which was commanded by General John B. Gordon, the dashing Confederate leader.

Early in 1865, the last grand movement, "by the left flank, march!" was inaugurated. Sheridan had rejoined the army, and the comparative monotony of life in winter-quarters gave place to bustle and excitement. Soon the army was on the march, and in front of Petersburg, where our front had been manned by double lines, with heavy reserves at hand, there remained a force hardly larger than a strong picket guard. The Confederate line was correspondingly weakened, the troops being re-disposed to meet Grant's flank movement. Each of the departing Federal corps was allowed five four-gun batteries; the remaining artillery remained in the works before Petersburg, subject to the orders of

General J. C. Tidball, artillery chief of the 9th Corps.

Our winter camp was finally abandoned and we moved to the front on March 25th, the day Gordon captured Fort Steadman, which he held for so brief a time. On Saturday, April 1st, came the great Union victory at Five Forks, and preparations were at once made to force an entrance into poor, beleaguered Petersburg, before whose hitherto impregnable defences we had been halted for so long.

There was a meeting of all the battery commanders at General Tidball's headquarters that night about ten o'clock, and orders were issued for a general bombardment which was intended to cover an advance of the infantry line. The Confederate defences were to be attacked at or near the Jerusalem plank-road, from which point the lines were to be taken in reverse, right and left, as soon as a lodgment could be effected and enough troops thrown forward to execute the design. This attack of the infantry was to be made under the guns of our artillery, which were to open fire all along the line at a given signal from a battery near the Avery House. General Tidball also gave us orders to be ready to move in any direction at a moment's notice.

Captain McClelland returned to our quarters and transmitted the orders to Lieutenant Gardner, and our boys were soon on their way to the front. Reaching Fort Davis, the command "Cannoneers, to your posts!" found every man ready for duty, with Lieutenant Rice under orders to open fire as soon as the signal should be heard. Our captain rode away to Battery 22, to see that the boys there were all in shape for action, but he had only reached the bridge leading from Fort Davis when, with a flash and roar, the signal gun turned loose the dogs of war. Long experience had given us the range and indicated the proper length of fuses, and in a moment the guns of Cooper's Battery were once more dropping masses of shrieking, splintering metal upon the heads of our heroic adversaries. Corporals John A. Heasley and James McChage, half dressed, as the signal found them, were serving two guns in Battery 22 as though they had a special spite against Fort Mahone, to which they seemed to give their whole attention; all the members of the battery were working with the energy born of four months' desire for such an opportunity. Meantime, our friends the enemy were returning our attentions with no little interest added, and, as usual, the most

wicked, deadly shots seemed to come from Fort Mahone and Battery 27.

This bombardment was kept up for several hours, and at last came the order to cease firing. We took advantage of this cessation to replenish our stock of ammunition, giving each gun an extra supply for future use. Shortly after three o'clock in the morning (Sunday, April 2d), the order came to reopen fire, which we did with cheerful alacrity. The sight was one long to be remembered. From countless muzzles on either side there seemed to flow a constant stream of living fire as the shells, with burning fuses, screamed and hissed through the night in a semicircle of lurid flame. The constant roar of the field guns and mortars was punctuated by the sharp detonations of exploding missiles. Dense banks of smoke hung in the air, pierced by shafts of light from fiery muzzles and traversed by arching curves of spiteful, hissing fuses.

At four o'clock the infantry movement began, and we were compelled to stop our fusillade. We could discern the movements of the combatants only by watching the lines of opposing fire, which gradually approached as our troops pressed on through and over the obstructions which barred their pathway. At last we heard a mighty shout, which meant the triumph of our forces, and then we knew the gallant defenders of the works before us had at last been overpowered by our own victorious host. The shout was taken up and carried to the rear, where all the wagoners and camp followers waited in breathless expectancy.

Shortly after six o'clock an aide-de-camp came from General Parke with a verbal order to Captain McClelland, directing him to send a squad with one officer to man two guns that had been captured from the enemy. Lieutenant Rice was promptly detailed with a selected squad of men, who at once set out for the front. The orders were urgent, and in the hurry there was little time to record details, but I am quite sure the detachment was made up as follows: Lieutenant Thomas C. Rice, Sergeant Isaac T. Grubb, Corporal Andrew J. Gilkey, Privates William Scott, Alexander Campbell, Jacob Copenhaver, George M. Dopp, George Hurst, Samuel Jones, David Lloyd, Timothy O'Brien, A. B. Oliver, John Q. Stewart, Jacob E. Smith, and Ezekiel N. Tracey.

When General Parke's order was received, it was not contemplated that Captain McClelland should accompany the detachment; every confidence was placed in Lieutenant Rice, who was an exceptionally capable and careful officer. It was well understood that the duty to be performed was one of great peril, and some of the boys gave their valuables to Captain McClelland for safe keeping. By the time we reached Fort Sedgwick, our captain's martial spirit was so thoroughly aroused that he determined to go with the detachment, which he did, leaving the guns and remainder of the battery, as well as the aforesaid valuables, in the care of Lieutenant Gardner. Sergeant Grubb also joined the detail at this point.

Each man was given full instructions as to his proper place and duty, and then the detachments started on a lively run over the plank road for the designated post. This trip was in no sense a pleasure excursion. Although dislodged in our immediate front, the Confederates were still well posted on both right and left, and had a converging fire on the plank-road which they raked vigorously with both cannon and musketry, making our trip one of considerable interest and excitement. Luckily, none of our party was hit, and when we halted in front of Battery 27 for a few moments' breathing spell we found the ditch thronged with our infantry, who were not a little demoralized by their early morning experience. Many of the troops had never been under fire before, but the dead and wounded were plentiful enough to attest their valor when the assault was made. Shortly before our arrival the Confederates had been reinforced, and our line had been pressed back upon the works. To us unarmed artillerymen the prospect at that moment was not particularly inviting or encouraging. Through the embrasures we could see the guns we were expected to man, but beyond them the Confederate sharpshooters were well intrenched in the traverses and had a good range on the guns, unprotected as they were at the rear. It looked like a veritable death-trap, but there was nothing to do but go ahead.

Our progress through the embrasure and to our places would have been ludicrous under less serious circumstances. It was a series of jumps and rolls and short runs, seeking any protection that might offer from the enfilading fire from all around and from the second line of works.

There were six guns in this battery: four brass twelve-pounders and two heavy iron field pieces. One of the latter was still pointing its grim muzzle toward the Union lines, and the other had been run back a short distance outside of the works and spiked. The magazine contained about 600 rounds.

No sooner had we got inside the fort than a fragment of a mortar-shell clipped the first two fingers off Captain McClelland's left hand, while Private Oliver was momentarily stunned by the explosion. Nothing daunted, the captain ordered his men to their places, which order they promptly obeyed, although the air seemed alive with flying metal. We were not used to smooth bores, but soon mastered that trouble and began to serve up Confederate shells out of Confederate guns that a few hours before had been directed at us. Our detachment was serving two of the brass guns. No other Federal artillerymen had been in Battery 27 before our arrival, nor for two hours after, but during the day Captain Ritchie, of Battery C, First New York Artillery, came over and for a short time had charge of a squad working the other two brass pieces.

During the afternoon several attempts were made to drive us out of Battery 27. On one occasion a Confederate battery was brought up at full gallop into a position just back of their second line and in full view of our position, but a few well-directed shots caused it to disappear very rapidly. At three o'clock a most determined attack was made upon our position. It began with a murderous fusillade from guns of all descriptions, followed by a gallant charge, with the customary dash and "yell." Our troops were visibly "rattled" for an instant, but quickly recovered their senses and repelled the attack. It was at this time that the boys of Cooper's Battery showed their mettle. Although almost entirely unprotected and with the enemy's sharpshooters filling the near-by traverses and firing constantly at short range, they stood gallantly by the guns, firing double charges of spherical case, solid shot and canister at point blank range. The fuses were cut down close and the shells exploded with terrible effect, making it a physical impossibility for the Confederates, with all their dash and daring, to retake the works, which I do not hesitate to assert they would have succeeded in doing had our boys flinched for a moment in the performance of their duty. It was a case where Greek met Greek.

At the height of the engagement we received reinforcements, conspicuous among which we saw the red caps and trousers of the 114th Pennsylvania—Collis's Zouaves—who had come up from City Point and were most welcome. The fresh troops went into position on our right, but no further effort was made to dislodge us. Every man in the detachment bore marks of the encounter, either on his person or clothing. Sergeant Gilkey was shot through the heart, dying in the arms of Stewart, who caught his falling body. Almost at the same moment Sergeant Grubb fell, pierced through the breast; he died a few hours later in the field hospital. We buried Gilkey near the plank-road, in the rear of Battery 22, this sad duty being performed under fire. He was a young man of fine promise, a good soldier, and exemplary in every respect.

During that Sunday night additional troops came up, and dispositions were made to advance the whole line at daybreak, the *abatis* and *chevaux-de-frise* being moved around from the front to the rear of the works, in accordance with the change in ownership. During the early part of the night the moon shone brightly, making this work and the removal of our dead and wounded perilous in the extreme, for the musketry firing continued all evening. About ten o'clock Captain McClelland returned to the captured works, where our detachment still remained. Lieutenant Rice, exhausted by his hard day's work, was snoring lustily on a bunk in the Confederate officers' quarters, and the others had disposed themselves in various ways to get rest and sleep, except Hurst, who was a provident chap and had taken possession of a half-cooked mess of beans, kettle and all, that had been left behind by the former occupants of Battery 27. The beans had been put on to boil before the works were captured, and Hurst was only finishing the job for his own benefit.

The next morning, to our surprise, we learned that the enemy had departed from our front, and this ended the great struggle so far as Cooper's Battery took an active part in it. After ten months' hard and patient work, we at last had the privilege of marching into Petersburg, a city that had been most gallantly defended. The Confederates fought valiantly and even desperately, and the same must be said of their opponents. We were all glad when the end came.

In due time we marched to Washington, over ground that had become perfectly familiar to us, and at the national capital we gave up our guns and other property, and proceeded to Camp Curtin, Harrisburg, where Battery B, or Cooper's Battery, was mustered out on the 8th of June, 1865, after a service of four years and two days.

Most of the men who formed the detail to man the guns in Battery 27 have answered the last roll-call. Captain McClelland became Adjutant-General of the State of Pennsylvania, and died while holding that office. Those who have since died are Lieutenant Rice and Privates O'Brien, Campbell, and Smith. Those who survive are: William Scott, of Scranton, Pa.; Jacob Copenhaver, George Dopp, of Susquehanna County, Pa.; Ezekiel N. Tracey, of Allegheny City, Pa.; Samuel Jones, of Pittsburg; A. B. Oliver, of Dunmore, Pa.; George Hurst, of Lycoming County, Pa.; John Q. Stewart, of Harrisburg, and D. Lloyd, of Beaver Falls, Pa.

I think all of these survivors will recollect one incident that occurred while we were working those brass guns in Battery 27. Jacob Copenhaver was acting as No. 3, and while holding his thumb over the vent, a minié ball came whistling along and passed through the sleeve of his blouse. Stewart was ramming a charge at the time. Oliver, No. 4, of the same gun, shouted to Copenhaver to stand his ground, and hold his thumb steady on the vent, which he did, and the loading was finished without further accident.

At the last reunion of the survivors of this gallant band, held at New Castle, Pennsylvania, June 8, 1894, thirty-eight members were present at roll-call, and more than three thousand of their friends participated in the festivities of the occasion. The oration was delivered by Captain Cooper, and addresses were also made by Professor P. F. Rohrbacher, Lieutenant Gardner, John Q. Stewart, and others. Letters and other information received indicate that there are some fifty survivors scattered throughout the country. The association elected Captain Cooper president for the ensuing year; D. W. Taylor, vice-president; and James A. Gardner, secretary.

SOCIAL CONDITIONS DURING THE WAR.

DELILAH TYLER.

I AM often asked by my own children and others the question : " When the war was going on did not persons in the same community, some loyal and some secessionists, feel very bitter toward each other ? " or, as one little one expressed it, " Didn't you just 'spize each other ? "

I think it right that these of a succeeding generation should understand the social as well as the warlike conditions of those troubled times. The cause, conduct, and results of the late unpleasantness have been recorded by numerous historians, but the social life of that period has seldom been touched upon.

That there was some bitterness of feeling, some things said and done that had better been left unsaid and undone, cannot be denied; but there was less of this than one would imagine, considering the intense excitement of the times. Communities did not often, if ever, divide into cliques, secessionists on the one side and loyalists on the other ; friendly and kindred ties were too strong for that. Social pastimes, marrying and giving in marriage, and other forms of neighborly intercourse continued among people of different political proclivities as much as the exigencies of the times would admit of.

During the war I lived in a town on the extreme Northern border of a Southern State. There were secessionists on both sides of the line dividing my State from the free State, and numbers from our families—fathers, sons and husbands—joined the army of their choice, Union or Confederate. Singular as it may seem, I know of some instances when persons truly loyal to their government assisted in equipping a soldier friend for the Confederate army, and quite as often, secessionists lending aid to a relative or friend preparing to join the Union forces. Each believed the other honest at heart, but misguided.

About July 1, 1862, a proclamation was issued by the officer in command of the Union forces then in possession of our section, announcing that a grand Fourth of July celebration would take place in a grove adjoining our town, at which time it was expected that every one able to leave home would be present. Noted orators would speak, and a feast of good things to eat would be provided, the proclamation stated.

Excitement and party spirit at that time was at fever heat, and when it was rumored that the Federal authorities intended to take that time and occasion to administer the oath of allegiance to the Union, there was consternation among us, for this oath was an ironclad compact, binding one not only not to take up arms against the government, but exacting as well that he aid not, in any way, disloyal persons.

Now there was scarcely a man in our community, even the most loyal, who had not either kindred or friends on the other side, from whom he felt he could never turn in their hour of need. They felt that if they took this oath they must sometime perjure themselves, or act against nature and humanity. Later on we understood that a terrible conflict was upon us, and, realizing that extreme measures were necessary, looked at this thing in a different way.

On the morning of the memorable Fourth, an uncle of mine, at whose country home I was then visiting, said to us:

"I will not go into town and subscribe to an oath which I think unjust and which I cannot keep. I know, however, that soldiers will be sent to scour the country in search of delinquents, so I and the others here of the *genus homo* must hide. Let us all go down to Minnehaha and have a celebration of our own."

Minnehaha, named for Longfellow's dusky heroine, was a beautiful spring which gushed from a rock on the side of the bluff in a sequestered spot among the trees, about a hundred yards from the house. The place was so sheltered from observation that one might pass within twenty feet of it and never know of its existence unless the sound of its waters rushing over the rocks should reveal it.

My uncle's scheme was agreeable to us, for while we never expected to commit any flagrant acts against the government, we all had some near and dear to us in the Southern army, and if one of these had asked us for bread we could never have given him a stone.

We went to work and filled hampers with cakes, ham, pickles, and other picnic accompaniments, then clambered down the steep hillside to the " boundless contiguity of shade " in whose depths Minnehaha's sparkling waters gushed, gurgled, and rushed over the precipice below. We sat down in the cool shade, and

314

after we had discussed matters and things in general, and inconvenient oaths in particular, we began to spread our lunch. In the midst of our preparations our attention was arrested by the sound of stealthy footsteps above us. Presently a low voice called: "Mr. S——!"

My uncle in reply advanced cautiously in the direction of the sound to reconnoitre, and directly laughingly greeted some one, saying:

"Come down and join us in celebrating the glorious Fourth!"

Immediately a well-known citizen of our town and his wife joined our party. "I am no rebel," said this man, "but I cannot take the oath, so wife and I slipped away with our lunch, and knowing of this retired spot, concluded to celebrate in a quiet way here."

Before very long footsteps were again heard, and almost instantly a merry party rushed down upon us, thinking they had the field to themselves.

"Well, well! What means this gathering of the clan among these trees?" asked one.

"It is a new species of *trea*son," replied a ready-witted one, "we are dodging the oath."

We spent the day very pleasantly, notwithstanding our uneasiness for fear of detection and a slight feeling that we were not acting exactly fair and square, certainly, at least, not open and above board.

Toward nightfall we crept cautiously back to the open ground, found all serene, and returned in peace to our homes. The strange part of this unique affair was the fact that of that Fourth of July party, so averse to taking the oath of allegiance, two-thirds were natives of free States—Ohio, Illinois, and New Hampshire; the others, Southerners by birth. Perhaps some who were members of that party may read this sketch far away from the brink of limpid Minnehaha; others of us are still near this scene, and often recall the events of that day and those times, and feel, with Franklin, that "there never was a good war nor a bad peace." The big celebration in town went off to the satisfaction of the originators of it, and the oath was administered to hundreds loyal and disloyal. Our little party was not missed and for the time being enjoyed immunity from a compact so distasteful, but their time came later on when they understood better the exigencies of war, and the pill was not so bitter to swallow. After 1862 the Fourth of July was scarcely celebrated at all with us until the cruel war was over. Then kindred and friends, Union and Confederate alike, a reunited band, celebrated a glorious Fourth not far from Minnehaha's sparkling fountain. Some hearts would ache, some tears would flow for missing ones who "slept the sleep that knows no waking," but all tried to be cheerful and content; no resentment was felt, or, if felt, was not manifested. Our flag, the banner that

"Waves o'er the land of the free and the home of the brave,"

unfurled its folds in the summer breeze, over those lately foes, now friends, with a common interest—"the Union, one and inseparable."

One instance illustrative of the condition of affairs social during the war was in some respects peculiar. This was the marriage of a young lady, a ward of a loyal citizen and a member of his household, to a Confederate soldier. The groom slipped within the Union lines to be married. The loyal guardian of the young bride gave a sumptuous wedding feast, to which he invited friends of both parties, Union and Confederate alike.

Another instance of the better feeling that prevailed at that time was an affair most touching. A young man, indeed a mere boy, belonging to one of the best families, enlisted in the Confederate army. He was killed, poor boy, soon after his enlistment. When his father heard of his death he procured a metallic coffin and traveled two hundred miles in a wagon to bring home for burial the body of his son. He supposed, of course, that the remains had been thrown into a ditch, with no covering but his army blanket, as the stern necessities of war often rendered necessary. He found, however, that of the sixteen killed in the company, his son alone was buried in a coffin, and his grave was marked by a wooden slab bearing his name —"Spencer McCoy."

The father was deeply moved. He inquired of some one standing near by whom this act of kindness was performed, and was told that Captain T——, then in command of the Union forces in possession of the place, had bought the coffin, had the young Confederate decently buried and his grave marked. The father sought Captain T—— and thanked him warmly, at the same time asking him why he had selected his dear boy, from the many who fell that dreadful day, for this mark of kindness.

"My wife wrote me," replied the captain, "that during the severe weather of the past winter she was at one time entirely without fuel or money to buy it, and that a neighbor across the street, hearing of her condition, took a wagon and team, drove to the country, procured and brought her a load of wood. She said the man's name was M——; that he was a Confederate, and had a son in General S——'s command in the Confederate army. When this battle occurred between General S——'s corps and our forces, the Confederates were defeated and driven from the field, I noticed in the reports of the slain who were left within our lines, one named M——. Upon inquiry I found he was the son of the benefactor of my family. I was gratified that I was here to do what I could for your son." This was in the fiercest of the conflict.

War is a dreadful thing, and while it often furnishes opportunity and excuse for lawlessness, and develops vicious natures, yet it calls forth the noblest traits in humanity—unselfishness, forbearance, and the greatest of all, charity. When

> "Withered was the garland of war
> The soldier's pole was fallen,"

when hearts were sore, when triumph dwelt in the hearts of some and defeat humiliated others, that so little was said or done to offend or distress, is to me a wonderful thing. It was the victory of the better nature.

> Peace hath her victories,
> No less renowned than war.

HOW VALLANDIGHAM CROSSED THE LINES.

CAPTAIN S. F. NUNNELEE.

I KNOW but little of the circumstances which led up to the banishment or expulsion of Clement L. Vallandigham from the Federal lines, except what I had from his own lips the day he was ushered into the Confederate lines near old Fosterville, the advance picket post of the Confederates.

CAPTAIN S. F. NUNNELEE.

I was a private in Company H (Captain Kirkpatrick), 51st Alabama Cavalry, Colonel James D. Webb commanding. One bright morning in May, I think it was, Colonel Webb sent for and ordered me to go to the outpost and escort a flag of truce between the lines, and to put on my best "bib-and-tucker." I changed my wool hat for a new, home-made gray jeans cap, or bonnet, which my wife had made, and proceeded, having a very indefinite idea as to the purpose of my mission.

Arriving at the outpost, I soon saw a wagon coming down the pike, two men being seated therein and driving like Jehu. When they pulled up under a large oak on the side of the pike, I advanced and told the two officers, a colonel and a lieutenant, that I had been ordered to protect their flag between the lines. One of them replied: "All right, come on!" Turning their wagon they started back, and their trotter kept my horse in almost a full gallop to keep up. Coming in view of their outpost, the colonel asked me to remain there until his return. You may imagine what I thought. I was protecting his flag, which he bore away, leaving me without one, and I asked myself, Who is protecting me? Of course, I had no arms and didn't know the fellow who was posted a hundred yards ahead of me. In less than half an hour I saw the flag returning over the ridge, and the wagon had an additional passenger.

Returning at the same break-neck speed, we halted under the oak, and the third man was told to alight. As he stood up in the wagon, he said: "In the presence of this gentleman I protest against being forcibly taken from my State and my family." The colonel (I think his name was Gibbons or McGibbons) said that they were simply obeying orders and that he must get out. He did so, and I advanced and helped him lift his trunk out. As the colonel turned, the prisoner handed him some letters which he requested should be mailed to his family, and again protested against his forcible ejectment from his country. Approaching, I gave him my hand, telling him who I was. Having sent him my paper while he was in Congress, he at once remembered my name, and with some surprise asked what I was doing there. I told him that I was playing soldier, and was trying to keep Rosecrans and his men from running over us. With surprise he asked what position I held, and being told that I was a high private in the front rank, he asked if many of my sort were in the army. I told him that nearly all of us were there. He then said: "They can never whip you." I told him I did not think they could, but that it was possible they might over-power us.

He then gave me a brief account of his arrest, condemnation, and expulsion from home. The day before he had asked General Rosecrans for the freedom of his camp, but was denied, and intimated that if he could have addressed the troops, he believed that a large number would have mutinied; that many of them were opposed to the war, and would not fire a shot at us if they could help it.

I helped with his trunk into a cabin on the side of the pike, and left him to report to Colonel Webb, with whom I rode back to where I had left my protégé. Having no instructions as to how I should act, I was in an embarrassing position, and determined to "wait for something to turn up." Mr. Vallandigham was also a little embarrassed, but in a moment, addressing Colonel Webb, he said: "I am Clement L. Vallandigham, a citizen of Ohio, in the United States, and for my political opinions have been arrested, and without a fair trial for any offence, have been forcibly driven from my State and family, and am seeking an asylum in the Confederate States of America." Colonel Webb replied, very coldly at first: "As a citizen of Ohio, in the United States, you are my enemy, as are all of your people who have combined against my people to destroy their homes and property. But as Clement L. Vallandigham, a citizen of Ohio, driven from his home and

seeking an asylum in my country, I give you a cordial welcome and true Southern hospitality until I learn what is the mind of my superiors in office." The two shook hands most cordially, and soon I was ordered to report to Colonel Hagan, commanding our brigade.

A company from the 8th Confederate, and my own company from the 51st, proceeded to the front, escorting Mr. Vallandigham to head-quarters. I and my horse, not having had any breakfast, were excused from the six or eight mile ride that would complete the courtesy to the distinguished "foreigner," who, when reaching our camp, was given a scattering cheer —of course without orders.

That was the last I saw of Mr. Vallandigham, but not the last I heard of him; for when he reached Richmond, a sort of "tempest in a teapot" was gotten up by the critics of Mr. Davis, who found, in the course of a few days, that he had "an elephant on his hands," and I believe arrangements were made to send him to Nova Scotia or Canada.

The end of Mr. Vallandigham was most tragic. After the war he resumed the practice of law, and in a criminal case was showing the jury, with a pistol, how the man might have been ac-cidentally killed. The pistol was discharged and the ball entered his bowels, from which wound he died.

Mr. Vallandigham was a man of splendid physique; about five feet ten in height; light or auburn hair; florid complexion; sharp, thin nose, and handsome features.

On the 14th of June I was wounded and cap-tured at Shelbyville, and spent fifteen months in prison at Camp Chase and Fort Delaware. At the latter I spent eight months, and on account of extreme illness was sent to the hospital, where Dr. Eagle, of Ohio, was assistant surgeon. In conversation with him I told about Vallan-digham, whom the physician knew well, and he was very much interested in the account I gave of his induction into the Confederacy. Dr. Eagle was a very clever gentleman and treated me quite differently from the medical directors I encountered at Shelbyville and Louisville. If he is alive or has any relatives living, I wish to say to them that he was a gentleman far above the aver-age of those I encountered in Northern prisons.

WHO WERE THE BRAVE?

CHARLES A. FORD, 6TH CORPS.

WHO were the brave—
    The bravest of the brave?
Were they men, who at the call of country, gave
Their strong manhood; who 'mid the whirlwind of the strife
    Laid down their lives?
Were they the mothers, who, in time of direst need, gave
Husbands, sons? who in the stillness of a broken home
    Lived, and pressed back the moan?
Or noble sisters, grown gray with faithful waiting for
Father, brother, lover; and who still wait on,
    Till death shall come?
Mother, sister, dear one, who gave your heart of hearts, yet
Still lived on, to bless and comfort others,
    Ye were the brave—
    The bravest of the brave.

A NIGHT WITH BUSHWHACKERS.

*FROM A SOLDIER'S DIARY.

ATLANTA having been captured by General Sherman's army, and my three years' service having expired, I called upon Lieutenant Tracy, commissary of musters, to muster me out of service on October 3, 1864. He began to do so; but before the blanks were half filled up, a squad of men belonging to my regiment drew up in front of the commissary's tent for the same purpose. I told Lieutenant Tracy I was in no hurry, and at once waived my claim of priority in favor of the dozen or more of my comrades in waiting. These were mustered out in due form, and the commissary was about to finish my papers, when the order came, "Pack up everything instantly, and prepare to move to the rear."

There were rumors a day or two before that General Hood had moved his army around Atlanta, and was tearing up the railroad at Big Shanty, north of Marietta, with a view of cutting off Sherman's supplies. The rumor proved to be true.

After a tedious march of ten days north from Atlanta, we reached Rome, Georgia, where I received my final muster-out and discharge from the army; but General Hood still being in our rear, I was requested by General Carlin to remain on duty, and assist in the transportation. This I did for five days more, when we camped, on the 18th, on the Lafayette road, near the little town of Villanow.

Here it was that Sherman ordered all the discharged soldiers, all convalescents, men, mules, and horses, all unnecessary or unserviceable commissary and quartermaster stores, to be removed to Chattanooga, while he made his grand march through the very centre of the Confederacy.

Our army of discharged and convalescent soldiers was not so large as Sherman's, by long odds, and yet we were a caravan of no mean dimensions, and, I suppose, occupied a mile or more in length, marching in as close order as the officer in charge could keep so heterogeneous a command.

Being no longer a soldier, I did not care to carry my sword, so I had it locked up in one of the feed-boxes; and there being presumably no enemies in the vicinity,—and if there were any, the boys were all armed,—I had disposed of my revolver by locking it in my mess-chest, which I was taking home with me as a souvenir of the war.

The day's march was a tiresome one, and it was near sunset before we reached the farm of Henry Mack and parked.

---

*This narrative is taken from the private diary of the late Lieutenant J. M. Johnston, 79th Pennsylvania Volunteers, by courtesy of his son, Herbert Johnston, of Lancaster, Pa.

The farm appeared to be well stocked, and "the boys" at once helped themselves to what they wanted. Chickens, ducks, geese, and turkeys were confiscated by whoever could catch them. Pigs, sheep, and calves were shot and slaughtered and cooked; the mules and horses were fed from Mr. Mack's stack, and every one connected with the caravan appeared to be gay and happy. I was among the last to get into camp, but reached it in time to see that the boys were making themselves comfortable.

Mr. Mack's house was on the south side of the road, and stood back from it more than a hundred yards, and was reached by a lane leading to it from the road. I strolled down the lane toward the house, and met Mr. Mack, a tall, lean, elderly man, with a rather woe-begone expression on his face.

"Colonel," he said (nobody down South at that time was supposed to rank lower than a colonel), "can't you save what little there is left of my property? Your soldiers have taken almost everything I own. I am a Union man, and have a protection paper signed by General Thomas," and he pulled it from his pocket and showed it to me. It was genuine.

I told Mr. Mack that I was not a colonel, nor even a soldier; that I had been discharged; and though I wore an officer's uniform, I had no more authority over the men who had appropriated his property than he had. Most of the men, also, were discharged soldiers, belonging to many different regiments, and were probably without officers to restrain them. About the only consolation I could give Mr. Mack was to hold on to his "protection paper," and if he was a good Union man, Uncle Sam would some day make good his losses, perhaps. In the meantime, if my shoulder-straps could be of any service to him in keeping the boys out of the house, I would give him the benefit of them.

He thanked me, invited me into the house, and introduced me to two or three of his daughters, who were as lean and almost as tall as himself. He told me all he had left was his beds and bedding, some cooking utensils, table cutlery and queensware, and a barrel of sorghum sugar.

I asked him if he could give me a bed for the night, and he said he would be only too glad to do so.

Mr. Mack's house was a peculiar structure, unlike any I have seen North, though I saw a number of them down in Dixie. It was a double two-story frame, about forty feet front, without

cellar, and there was a wagon-drive right through the middle of it. It had windows, but no doors, either front or back; but on either side of the wagon-drive were doors leading into the respective apartments.

Mr. Mack's few remaining valuables were soon stored in the room on the west side of the wagon-drive, and I was given charge of them. The room had a good bed in it, and three or four chairs. I talked with Mr. Mack and his family until quite late, though orders had been given that the troops and train would move at three A. M.

It was not until the family had bade me good-night, and retired to the other side of the house, that I noticed there was no door to my room. The opening was there, but the door had never been hung, and any one could step from the covered wagon-drive right into the room. For a moment I wished I had my revolver; but when I came to think that I was surrounded by Union soldiers, the wish vanished, and I resolved to have a good night's rest, taking the precaution to place three chairs, turned over on their sides, one above the other, in the open door-way, so that if any foragers should happen to come around, they could not get in without making a noise that I would be apt to hear.

I had not slept in a bed for a long, long time, —a year or more. I pulled off my coat and boots only, and tumbled in. How I did revel in that bed! I stretched my arms apart and clasped the rails on either side! What a luxury compared with sleeping in a wagon, or under a wagon, or on the lid of a mess-chest, or on two rails, or on the frozen or muddy ground, as I, in common with hundreds of thousands of others, had so often done! And there was a pillow to the bed,—a feather pillow! I was so delighted with my quarters that I could not get to sleep for a long time. I crawled all over the bed, so that I might enjoy every square inch of it; and fancy carried me to even a better bed that awaited me at home, and which I would reach in a very few days! And in this blissful frame of mind I fell asleep.

And I slept soundly—and long.

I was awakened by the clatter of hoofs, as a horseman galloped down the lane and reined up his horse in the wagon-drive, almost at the doorway of my room.

"Wasn't there a Yankee officer stopped here last night?" asked the horseman, sharply.

There was a momentary pause, and then I heard Mr. Mack say, very slowly, as if he would rather not say it:

"Yes, sir, there was; and——

"Yes, there were several of them here," chimed in one of the daughters, interrupting her father, "but they have done gone; they went off with the other soldiers, toward Chattanooga."

I had crept noiselessly out of bed the moment the horseman had reined in his steed. Instinctively I believed him to be an enemy, and was convinced of it when I heard the words spoken by the old man and his daughter. I had overslept myself, and all my comrades had left the premises, and were miles ahead on their way to Chattanooga, and I was alone, unarmed, and in the clutches of bushwhackers.

These thoughts passed through my brain in a twinkling, as I pulled on my boots and coat, and grasped as my only defence a light cane, which I had used the day before as a walking-stick.

"Yes," the girl repeated, "there were several of them here, but they have all done gone; went with the other soldiers at three o'clock, toward Chattanooga."

"God bless that girl!" was my mental prayer.

"That's hard luck," said the horseman, and then added, "Are there any other houses near here?"

"Yes," said the girl; "there is one a very short distance down the road, and I think some of the officers stopped there."

Wheeling quickly around, the horseman dashed off at full speed, and was soon out of the lane and galloping down the road toward the other house.

Then Mr. Mack leaned over the chairs with which I had barricaded the doorway, and said to me, in a whisper:

"Stranger, you had better be getting out of this; that man means you no good."

"Is he a Confederate soldier?" I asked.

"He is not one of your people," replied the old man, "and means you no good; and he is not alone—he has companions."

"It won't be safe for you to take the road," said the daughter. "Go through this field and through the woods beyond. You will not be far from the road, and will be out of sight of the men who are looking for you."

Thanking the Macks for the kindness shown me, I emerged from the room and entered the field. It was overgrown with rank weeds, many of them towering above my head. A very heavy dew had fallen, and every weed in my path shook down the pearly drops upon me. Before I was half way through the field, which was a very large one, I was wet from head to foot and shivering with cold. At last I reached the woods and hurried through it for some distance. In the darkness I was impeded by undergrowth, and every now and then I would step upon rotten boughs, which, breaking under my weight, made a cracking report that sounded to my strained ears as loud as pistol shots.

Oh, how disgusted I was with myself! To think I had passed through three years of service, almost without a scratch; had been honorably discharged, and was within a few days of home,—within arms' reach, almost, of wife and children and friends, when, like a fool, I had laid aside my arms; had been stupid enough to act as policeman over a lot of household truck; had dallied in the luxury of a bed, overslept myself, and was now shivering and shaking with cold, and wandering in the woods through thorns and brambles and briers, trying to save my precious throat from being cut or my brains blown out by bushwhackers! I knew I richly deserved such a fate, but I couldn't bear the thought of it. Had I died of disease, or been killed in battle, I thought I wouldn't have minded it much; but to have lived through the perils of legitimate skirmish, battle, and siege for three long years, only to fall into the hands of bushwhackers, in the midst of a forest, where my remains would never be found—this was too much! Then the horrible thought came into my mind that if the bushwhackers shot me, and my body was not found, I would be suspected of having deserted my wife and family! The very thought made me shudder.

My firm resolve was at once taken. "Better die on the road than in the midst of a big woods," and I struck out in the direction in which I thought the road lay.

I had a long walk before I reached it, and day was now beginning to dawn. Not a sound was heard except that made by my own feet. Keeping as much as possible in the shadow of the woods, I peered up the road and down the road, and seeing nothing, hurried forward on the run, and had perhaps placed two or three miles between the Mack farm and myself, when, through the mist of the morning, I espied two horsemen just going over the brow of a hill in front of me. They and their horses appeared to be of gigantic stature; but that I knew was only an optical illusion, caused by the vapory mist of the morning. As soon as the horse-men disappeared behind the brow of the hill, I hurried forward, cautiously, until I also reached the top of it, when again the horsemen were in view, leisurely ascending a hill beyond. I did not doubt then, and do not doubt now, that they were the men who expected to capture me at Mr. Mack's house.

While secretly watching them from the edge of a copse by the roadside, I was startled by hearing voices but a short distance off. I hid myself behind a tree, took a very long breath, and looked and listened.

"How did you make out?" asked one of the party. There were eight or ten of them, each dressed in blue uniform and carrying a rifle.

"I got along first-rate," was the reply. "I took the old reb's mare and colt, had a good ride all day, and then sold them for $25. Not long afterward I picked up a mule and sold it for——"

"Hello, boys!" said I, stepping out into the road. "You are on your way to Chattanooga, I suppose, and, like me, overslept yourselves. The rest of the boys are not far ahead; we'll soon overtake them," and I promptly made myself one of their party. They eyed me rather sus-piciously, but saluted me in true soldier style.

They were a band of stragglers, and had been out on a private foraging expedition. Not one of them belonged to my regiment; but as I looked into their faces I thought they were the handsomest men I had ever seen, if, indeed, they were not angels sent to rescue me from the hands of the bushwhackers! No matter who they were, or what they had been doing, I was glad to claim them as comrades. I knew the bushwhackers had no business with that party. Right cheerily we marched on together, and ere long overtook the train, and before noon reached Ringgold, the same night Chattanooga, and next day Nashville, and next Louisville, and on to Pittsburg, and next day "home, sweet home!"

"FRATERNITY—UNION."

J. NORRIS.

NO color-line divides us now,
    The battle-smoke has passed away;
No scornful eye nor frowning brow
    Mars the face of blue or gray.

The victor now has sheathed his sword,
    Peace again resumes her sway;
Sable wings of fell discord
    No longer flap o'er blue and gray.

Taunting words are heard no more,
    Except by cowards who pursue
Hapless victims as of yore.
    They are neither gray nor blue.

"THE BATTLE ABOVE THE CLOUDS."

WILLIAM E. HORNE.

HON. WILLIAM E. HORNE, 1893.

I LINGERED once, as if in dream,
    'Mid climbing vines that round me grew,
While through the leafing oaks was gleam
    Of star and moon in sky of blue.

It seemed as if the vines that hung
    From bowers above were listening, when
The bird of song a carol sung,
    For there was hush and silence then.

"O night of stars ! bright stars, that shine
    In yonder vault of heaven's blue,
Wilt thou not lend to mate of mine
    The light of love—of love that's true?

"O moon ! of magic power and light,
    Flood forest, field, with rays of thine ;
And then with song I'll lull the night
    Till she shall come, loved mate of mine.

"Shine out, O stars ! with jewelled ray,
    While for my mate Love's song I sing ;
Gild mountain, stream, and Love's pathway,
    While Love takes flight on Love's young wing.

"Though winds may chill, and night may gloom,
    I'll wait, love, wait, and for thee sing ;
Though leaves may fall, and fade the bloom,
    My love shall know, for you, but spring !"

Above me arched o'erhead a zone
    Of azured clouds, with isles of light
In sea of blue, where brilliants shone
    In coronet of queenly night.

The risen moon was silvered o'er
    With films of light, and from it hung
A necklace of some gems that wore
    The gleam of pearls on silver strung.

Far out were isles of forest shade,
    As isles that rise amid the main,
Whose shoreways in the gloaming fade,
    These shadow isles, decked distant plain.

A silver band the river seemed,
    Engirdling rocks of gray and green,—
Great rocks that climbed where lamplights gleamed,
    And lent enchantment to the scene.

For miles and miles there stretched away
    A valley that was opaline ;
Where city, radiant, jewelled, lay,
    A gem of fire and furnace sheen.

Beyond the glinting lamps of light,
    And fires that burned with angry glow,
From Lookout Mountain's throne, the night
    Had mantled all the vale below.

And now, to me, the mountain seemed
    A scene of war, where peace had been ;
For bayonets and sabres gleamed,
    And lines were formed of marching men.

Advancing legions—phantoms they—
    By regiment, battalion, corps,
Now climbed the heights to meet the gray,
    Who still aloft their banners bore.

I saw unbroken lines of gray,
    In lines unbroken came the blue,
With steady tramp, till dawn of day,
    And then they met, these armies true.

For with the morn the shielding night
    Withdrew her veil, and then the two
In carnage met, in deadly fight,
    From crag to crag, the gray and blue.

As waves from angry seas will pour,
    On, up, o'er cliffs, came on the blue
To meet the gray, 'midst cannons' roar,
    And deadly aim of veteran true.

From cone of mountain, gray and hoar,
    Some great huge rocks now tottering fell—
Went crashing on, 'midst cannons' roar
    And bursting bomb and screaming shell.

And every rock seemed stained with gore,
  Where men would die, and where the dead
In heaps would lie, and more and more
  Would wounded fall, where duty led.

I saw these phantom legions meet
  In point-blank range of shotted flame ;
I saw them charge, and then retreat—
  Brave men, who fought for honor—fame !

Where one had fallen, passion's glare
  Was fixed in deadly, icy eyes ;
Cut short, unshriven, lying there,
  As when some fiend, incarnate, dies.

On one, as when the dews congeal
  To answer back the kiss of heaven,
Were fresh-formed tears, that made appeal
  To Him who rules, to be forgiven.

A mother, in deep mourning, came
  To climb the rocks, and hunt for one
Who, dying 'midst the battle's flame,
  Was her last hope,—an only son !

And here and there, and everywhere,
  Were those who fell upon that day—
Who knew no fear, and, dying there,
  Were heroes, both—the blue and gray.

In that weird scene I heard the scream
  Of bursting bomb—heard hissing rain ;
Saw phantom legions, as in dream,
  Emerge from clouds, unseen, again.

Above the clouds ? Oh ! yes ; they fought
  With bayonets, and breast to breast,
Till few were left, and then they sought
  The rifle-pits on mountain's crest.

Though Lookout Mountain's famed to-day
  For legions of the phantom slain,
Thank God ! the blue 'll ne'er meet the gray
  Above the clouds to fight again.

For now o'er all there's peaceful reign—
  A common country—common aim ;
A treasured trust for living, slain ;
  For all the gallant fallen, Fame !

Raise shaft of marble, pure and white,
  And freedom's flag float from its height,
That stars—the brightest stars of night—
  May flood it with their purest light.

Oh ! Union, that our fathers gave,
  Where man should break the bonds of slave,
May freedom's flag through æons wave—
  A flag of peace, where all are brave !

A DOG ON THE BATTLE-FIELD.

IT was near Spottsylvania Court-House, Virginia, on the morning of May 18, 1864. General Grant wished to pierce our line, and had massed some ten thousand troops for this purpose. Many of these were reserves from the camps at Washington. The point at which the attack was made was a strong one, and the storming columns were subjected to a deadly cross-fire. The first advance was repulsed with fearful loss. Again did the Federal troops gallantly charge our works, but their lines melted away under the storm of musketry, grape, and canister that swept the intervening space. They then fell back in confusion, leaving their dead and wounded on the smoking field. Immediately our skirmish line was thrown out to watch their movements, and was established at a point where the slaughter had been greatest. The smoke had scarcely cleared from the field and the random shots were growing fewer. A member of the 4th Virginia Infantry, " Stonewall Brigade," who was posted on this line, on looking around him, saw a small white spaniel, with black ears, standing with one foot on the breast of a Federal lieutenant who had been killed a short time before. The dog commenced barking furiously at the skirmisher, whose first impulse was to shoot the animal ; but, on second thought, he took in the situation, and admired the fidelity of the little beast, guarding, with its own life, the dead body of its late master. The scene touched the soldier's heart, and he tried to pacify the faithful creature. Getting a sash from a dead Zouave near by, he succeeded, after many attempts, in throwing it over the dog's head, and claiming it as his prisoner. The dog was loth to leave the dead soldier, and continued to lick the wound upon his cheek.

When the line was relieved, the Confederate brought the little dog back to the regiment, and gave it to our major, who sent it back to the wagon-train. For two days it would eat but little, seemed dejected, and at night would whine most piteously. On the morning of the third day hunger had conquered, and new life had come to the poor animal. It ate greedily, was cheerful, and frisked around as if reconciled to its new friends. We supposed that this faithful little creature had been the pet of some soldier ; had followed him closely in all those terrific charges, was by him when he fell, and guarded his body with tender devotion when all had fled.   A. S. P.

HELD BY THE ENEMY.

OCTAVIA DOCKERY.

"Halt! Halt!"

Only at the second command did the old negro coachman tighten the reins over the splendid bay horses, and then partly because the animals seemed to scent the danger, when the straight-laced blue-coat picket stepped in front of them, and clapped his musket to his left shoulder.

"I tell you, sah, le' go dat bridle rein."

"You are prisoners of the Federal army," said the guard. "Dismount."

"Sit still, mistiss. No Yankee lives who can outrun Bay Tom and Stonewall."

The keen whip came down upon the satiny bays with all the strength of the driver's arm, and the unusual treatment caused them to spring like steeds of fury into the air, carrying the Winston family coach, with its two occupants, a young woman and a child.

"Halt!" A bullet whizzed from the musket of the second guard.

"Well, Mistiss Laura, dat Yankee has done shot Stonewall."

The strong horse trembled violently and sank groaning to the ground.

"Get down off that box, you black scoundrel! Get that woman and child out of the carriage. Egad, I believe she is a spy attempting to pass through our lines, and she shall be dealt with accordingly."

"Dat's a lie! My mistiss am de most beautiful lady in de Souf," retorted the old slave, whose pride in the fame and beauty of his aristocratic young mistress was instinctive. The great grandfather of Laura Winston, during a visit to Jamaica, had paid the sum of three thousand dollars for a priceless negress and her child. In the service of descending generations of Winstons the slave child had grown gray. No tie of blood could have made a heart more loyal than that which beat beneath the old negro's bony chest for his master and his descendants, a sentiment not fully understood by younger generations in the South.

"Put the negro into service, and take the woman and child to camp," said Captain Joe Wilks to the soldier who came to the assistance.

"Don't you lay your finger on my mistiss, soldier!" and as the Federal officer's rough hand grappled the negro's wrist, a sharp knife glistened in the light, and the blood spurted from the white man's face, flowing rapidly over his blue coat.

Fatal bravery! A heavy carbine barrel descends swiftly upon the negro's head, and gallant old William lies prostrate on the ground.

In vain the Southern beauty resented this detention and the loss of horse and servant. Captain Wilks was a soldier in whose breast but little sense of chivalry had ever found a place; and now, with the blood from faithful William's knife still streaming from a ghastly wound upon his forehead, he was in no mood for leniency. His orders were imperative: no one should pass the lines, and all suspected persons should be sent at once to headquarters.

Poor little sister Flossie, unused to such wild scenes, had fainted. Laura knelt beside her limp form, in an agony of sorrow and despair. "Water!—water!" she said; "in mercy's name, water, before it is too late!" and her eyes were superbly eloquent in her grief.

"Wait, laidee; I know of a stream near by," and a spare-built soldier ran across the picturesque meadow, as his broad Scotch accent floated welcomely to the ears of the grief-stricken girl. With her hand on the feeble pulse of the delicate child, Laura listened, in that moment of suspense, to the booming cannon and bursting shells, and she saw in the direction of Vicksburg a dark cloud of smoke.

The heavy thunder of artillery fairly shook the earth. Three hundred men in General Dockery's Arkansas regiment were fighting bravely, nobly suffering death-wounds on the battle-ground of Champion Hill. Even in that extreme moment she saw familiar and well-loved faces upturned in agony. Stout hearts she knew would throb last for her, perhaps were being trampled upon by horses maddened with the fight.

Those were long days that dragged wearily onward, while Laura and her sister were held by the enemy. Twice a week they went in a common vegetable-cart, driving a mule, to headquarters, where their plain rations were given them. It was always "first come, first served," and often they were compelled to wait for hours before their turn came.

It was on one of these days that the fair-haired child, weary of her cramped position in the cart, ran across to where a white spitz dog was rolling on the grass. The dog was very cordial in his greeting, and soon the two became fast friends.

Romping and scampering around the yard, his excitement made him rough in play, and he barked so fiercely, the child ran, partly from fright, to a group of gentlemen who sat talking near a doorway. With a half-friendly, half-angry growl, the dog caught the thin material of her dress, as the little one sprang into the arms of one of the men, who was smoking, and her flowing hair caught the cigar from his mouth.

"Down, sir!" said the smoker, in fierce tones, and the spitz dropped in a fluff of white at his master's feet.

"You are captured, little miss. Where did you come from?" said one of the group.

With wide-open blue eyes she looked from one to another and at the dog. Then, with all stoutness and confidence, she nestled closer to her captor.

"Where did you come from, missie?" he inquired.

"I live in Alabama, and I want—oh, I want so much to go home!" the child said. The friendly voice had awakened afresh the longing for home.

"Well, you are a long ways off," and he stroked his thick, short beard, and looked interestedly at the dainty child on his lap.

"Yes, I know it. We been visiting grandmamma. We were going to Vicksburg to buy some things for our soldier cousins, and—and the Yankees stoled us."

The innocent eyes filled nearly to overflowing. But the serious face of the man who held her was a check to the others, who were smiling at the childish talk, so unconscious of her listener's identity.

"There was one bad one. He killed William and shot Stonewall, and I fainted, sister said; and we may never, never get back home any more. Yankees are bad people, and do nothing but kill, kill, kill. I am going now. You are the only nice man in this place. My name is Flossie Winston. Good-bye."

After flinging two short, dimpled arms about his neck, she sprang away, and went skipping off to her sister, waiting for her in the cart.

General Grant, for it was he to whom she had been talking, looked after the child wistfully, and, stepping inside the door, sat down to write. He seldom wrote passes. But he wrote one then.

A few lazy clouds, like snow-drift, floated in the infinite blue of the sky. The warm sunlight sent long shadows across the lawn at Bellemont. Busy spiders, unmindful of the times, stretched their gauzy webs about, blending silver in the weave of nature's carpet. Crowds of bees, grown giddy with clover, kept up a musical thrumming in the orchard. Old Bellemont, the Winston homestead, in North Alabama, stood grandly on the mountain-slope, surrounded by nature in her happiest musings.

"That is a broad statement, my fair coz, that you 'would marry any Confederate soldier who would kill Yankee Joe Wilks.' It savors of a challenge, and from the lips of the 'Belle of the Confederacy' is enough to fire Southern gallantry to deeds at which Don Quixote himself would stagger."

"I know the words sound harsh and wicked, Arthur. But when I think of poor old William, and the torture little Flossie suffered at the hands of that man, I cannot curb the feeling of revenge my words express. I mean all I said; for I am sure my gratitude would grow to real affection for the man who would avenge that horrid wrong."

That light told its own story—the light that sprang into the young man's eyes, as he lay stretched at length on the grass, near the hammock, where Laura Winston swung. She was offering a reward for which he would gladly risk his life.

"My furlough's at an end. My horse, Sam. To war! To-morrow think of me, Laura; for when the sun goes down either Joe Wilks will have paid the penalty for his cruelty to you, or I will have given my last glance at yonder sky, and my last thought to you."

When the setting sun glinted through the woods on the hill back of Bellemont, the ladies stood watching Arthur's vanishing youthful figure, outlined against the ruddy sky. They saw also several horsemen pass him, advancing toward the house. Were they friends or enemies? There was a cry of joy when the gray uniforms came clearly into sight. One of the riders was slightly in the lead of the others, —a man of splendid physique and military bearing.

"How superbly he rides!" said Laura, and unconsciously she caught her mother's hand, who noticed the color deepen in the fair girl's cheek, though neither understood why.

Hospitality found its true meaning at Bellemont. All the famed splendor of its manner of entertaining shone forth this night when the several Confederate soldiers were the guests.

"And it was you," Laura said, entering the spacious supper-room upon the arm of Captain Champion, "who rode ahead down the mountain-slope?"

His handsome face showed pleasure, that she had noticed him apart from his companions.

"Well, Captain Champion is about the only one of us deserving of this feast to-night," said Lieutenant West. "He did a service to the whole army when he cut down that burly Captain Wilks."

Laura's fork dropped jingling from her grasp. Was it Fate, this meeting with the man who had rid her of her *bête noir?* But we are all baubles in the hands of Fate, and only wait for her to turn the stream of our destiny.

———

Not many months later a handsome couple stood beneath a marriage-bell in the elegant parlor, and Arthur was the first to greet the bride as the wife of Captain Champion.

The happy, unclouded honey-moon was one week old. One day when the bright, sweet sunshine flooded the country, several Confederate officers were riding along through North Alabama scenery.

The day was perfect. The three horsemen in gray rode gaily on to join their comrades on the field. Captain Champion, radiantly happy, threw back his broad shoulders and drank in the exhilarating mountain air. "What a glorious morning!" said he. "It almost makes one want to live forever."

A sharp bend in the road, and the three Confederates were almost in the midst of a score of blue-coated cavalrymen who wore the insignia of Joe Wilks' regiment. The fight lasted but a minute. A Federal lieutenant bent over the prostrate form of Captain Champion. "Brave soldier he was," said the trooper; "too gallant to die this way. But it served him right. Poor Joe!"

A HERO OF MANASSAS.

Col. W. C. Elam.

A NICE young man joined our battery a few days before the first battle of Fredericksburg. He had fitted himself out with a fine new uniform, from head to foot, with a great deal of gilt lace and red about it. His cap was particularly flashy, and he wore it with a jaunty and devil-may-care air. In a belt around his waist, he habitually carried a five-shooter and a large bowie-knife—weapons with which he had already done good service for the Confederacy, as he boasted. According to his story, he had been amongst the earliest volunteers for six months, and had captured a Federal battery at Manassas, if he had not really won that battle. Beauregard had complimented him on the field, and would have promoted him at the same time, but that he had declined office,—preferring the careless and irresponsible life of the private soldier.

He was enrolled as Augustus Forbes, and he lightly declared that every time he was wounded the blood of all the F. F. V.'s was shed. He showed us some of his wounds. They looked like briar-scratches, but he said his flesh healed with remarkable rapidity and smoothness, the most fearful gashes leaving small marks behind

them. He was soon pretty well known as "The Hero of Manassas."

"I tell you, fellows," said he to us, who had seen no greater battles then than skirmishes and affairs of outposts, "it's a little ticklish making your first charge on a battery in full play; but you get your blood up, you know, and then you feel like you are waltzing to the band with your best girl. It's so with me, anyhow. Most fellows always feel somewhat scared; but after my first fight, I've been cool as ice, but eager to be in the thickest of it."

Our junior lieutenant, Mitchell, was standing near by, and he heard Forbes.

"You are the man for me, Forbes," he said, "and I'm glad you are on my gun. You'll set myself and my other men a good example and keep us to our duty if we flinch."

"All right, lieutenant," responded Augustus, assuringly. "You may rely on me. I trust it won't be long before we have a battle, as camp-life is mighty dull without plenty o' fighting."

On the strength of his alleged record, Private Forbes assumed all the privileges of the veteran, and largely shirked his duties, even including his share of the mess-work. But he was tolerated by the boys in this shirking, not only on account of his accredited prowess in battle, as well as in personal brawl, but because he was the most skilful and successful forager in our part of the army. Some carpers declared that he must be a trained sneak-thief; yet we all regarded him very highly as we partook of the dainties he had purveyed from smoke-house, sty, hen-roost, dairy, field, orchard, and garden.

Meanwhile, December 13, 1862, arrived. Burnside had crossed the river at Fredericksburg, and the desperate struggle for Marye's Hill was in progress. We had been engaged in long-range firing Friday, and also Saturday morning; but about noon, Saturday, we had been sent to the rear, where some of us contrived to get a few dry beans to boil. So far, Forbes had shown us no feats of daring, and had kept carefully under shelter, as far as possible, as we all had done. While we were still absorbing the beans, Lieutenant Mitchell came up and informed us that our battery, with others, was ordered into the trenches on Marye's Hill, to relieve the Washington Artillery (of New Orleans), and that we must get ready immediately.

"Oh! these horrid beans!" suddenly exclaimed Forbes. "They have given me a dreadful colic."

"You don't mean you have no stomach for this fight, eh?" asked Lieutenant Mitchell.

"Unfortunately," replied Forbes, "I fear I shall be obliged to look up a doctor. These half-cooked beans have given me awful cramps."

"Pshaw!" said the officer; "there is nothing like gunpowder for colic, and we can't risk losing the battle by leaving you behind. Mount the limber-chest, sir; and, Sergeant Brown, see that he doesn't stay back."

Forbes had to mount the chest, with Sergeant Brown on one side of him and Corporal Faxter on the other.

"I'm in dreadful pain!" he moaned; but he couldn't get away; and there he had to sit until we had galloped a mile or more, amidst shrieking shells and singing rifle-balls, to a deep ravine, behind Marye's Hill. Here we were under shelter for a while, waiting for the trenches at the front to be cleared for our reception. We had all dismounted, and many were lying down. Forbes was groveling, face downward, in feigned spasms of colic. We had to make the rest of the run on foot, beside our guns and horses, across the plateau that crowned the hill; and it was indeed a frightful scene to traverse,—every inch of ground continually

struck, apparently, by bullets or fragments of shells. The hurly-burly, too, was terrific. It looked like certain death, or ghastly wounds, at least, to venture on that storm-swept plain. Nevertheless, at the order to move, the guns were carried at a gallop, and we did our level best to keep up—all except the hero, Forbes.

"I won't go!" he yelled. "I can't! I know I will be killed!"

"Fetch the infernal coward along, Sergeant Brown!" shouted Lieutenant Mitchell.

Brown and Faxter seized the demoralized wretch, and dragged him up from the ravine to the level.

"Now, go on, you dog!" cried Brown, giving him the kick of a battering-ram.

And go Forbes did, on all fours, howling every jump, the sergeant following him closely, and giving him a swinging kick for every howl. Brown's well-directed kicks carried Forbes to the trench to which his gun was assigned, and he tumbled in, lying flat on the earth, and still bellowing. He could be heard even above the din of artillery. The rest of us unlimbered the guns, and took off the chests; but before we could place them in position, two men at Forbes's gun were hit pretty severely, and word was despatched at once for help from the ambulance corps. We who were able were speedily working our guns with all our souls and bodies. The wounded men sat still and quiet, patiently awaiting succor. Augustus Forbes writhed in the dirt, as if suffering excruciating agonies, and his shrieks and screams rose high and higher with the tide of battle.

The first men who arrived with a stretcher, of course, saw Forbes—and Forbes saw them. Up went his hands and heels, as signals of distress, and a piercing wail came from his wide-open mouth. They took him up tenderly, and placed him on the stretcher. The wounded men sought to prevent the blunder, but the noise, confusion, and excitement were too great. Then, in a moment, Augustus Forbes was borne off to the rear at a double-quick step. The really wounded had to wait until later.

The ambulance corps had established a station behind the brick walls of the cemetery that stood on Marye's Hill, overlooking the deep ravine already mentioned. The bearers of Forbes, at a trot, brought him safely to shelter; but no sooner was he behind the walls, than he leaped from the stretcher into the ravine, and dashed away like a wild deer, leaving the stretcher-men agape with unbounded amazement. He fled swiftly out of sight, and we never heard of Forbes again during the war.

In October, 1872, I had some business at a court-house, on a court day, not far from home, and when I was through I went on the green, where a great crowd was listening to a number of political speakers. One of these particularly attracted my attention, both by his voice (which seemed familiar) and his relentless temper. As this orator proceeded, not only abusing the North and the Federals with old-time fury, but also denouncing the incapacity and cowardice of leading Confederates as the causes of Southern defeat, vowing that all issues were yet alive while a brave man still survived at the South, some one touched me on the shoulder. I turned, and saw my old fellow-soldier, ex-Sergeant Brown.

" Don't you know that red-mouthed knave ?" he asked.

" If I do," I replied, " it can be nobody in the world but Augustus Forbes, the hero of Manassas and Marye's Hill."

" That's the hound," said Brown, " and I mean to speak to him."

We chose our opportunity after the speaking was over, when we caught Augustus somewhat apart.

" Hello, Forbes," said Brown.

Forbes gazed at him haughtily.

" You remember Marye's Hill, eh ?" Brown suggested.

" Why, yes, to be sure," replied the unabashed scamp, " where I had that severe attack of colic. I should have died, if I hadn't got to the rear and received prompt relief. How are *you*, Brown ? Shake hands."

" Now, Forbes," said Brown, impressively, as he put his hands behind him, " there is only one sort of greeting that I can give you, and that I will extend to you with the greatest pleasure, and with all my might, if you will just turn around," and he lifted his right foot and drew it back significantly.

As Forbes did not turn, but kept silent and seemed to grow more haughty, we moved off. He didn't appear to recognize me, and I have never heard of him again. Yet, as he was a fellow who took very good care of his health, he is probably still alive, and still posing and ranting not only as " The Hero of Manassas," but also as " The Hero of Marye's Hill."

ROUND TOP—A VISION.

T. C. HARBAUGH.

I STOOD on Round Top's rocky height, the night was soft and still ;
In beauty lay the calm starlight upon that historic hill.
I longed to hear the bugles blow afar upon the plain,
Where in a summer long ago fell fast the leaden rain.

The snowy shafts that mark the scene where struggled Gray and Blue,
Stood in their loveliness serene with crowns of star-kissed dew ;
But still methought that I must see two armies 'neath the stars,
The blue of Meade, the gray of Lee—" Old Glory " and " the bars."

Beyond the summer's fragrant bloom that decked the silent glade,
I looked in vain for Hancock's plume and Longstreet's shining blade ;
I looked to see the solid shot cut down the stately pines
Where raged the battle fierce and hot between the surging lines.

But sudden from among the trees a white-robed figure came,
Her hair the sport of nocturne breeze, and " Peace " her holy name ;
In stately mould I saw her stand where death had held the plow—
A wreath of flowers in her hand, a crown upon her brow.

Methought the starlight softer grew as vanished far away
The battle-smoke that hid the blue, and crowned the ranks of gray.
And Peace in matchless beauty stood beneath the vaulted sky,
Wherein the battle-haunted wood I saw the stricken lie.

I looked again ; O blessed sight ! two figures, side by side,
Were touching elbows in the light, star-scattered far and wide ;
The form of one was robed in blue, the other wore the gray,
As once like heroes tried and true they met amid the fray.

They halted where the angel stood, as if their march was done ;
The smile she gave was sweet and good ; to each she said, " My son !
To union o'er her children's graves Columbia plights her troth,
And 'neath the fairest flag that waves to-night I crown ye both.

" In love and peace together stand the men who met as foes ;
Where once they battled hand to hand blooms now the gentle rose.
I reign to-day from sea to sea, where stretched the battle line,
From frozen lakes to orange tree, from lofty oak to pine."

I looked once more, the angel blest was gone ; beneath the blue,
Where soft her sacred feet had pressed, a snow-white flower grew ;
And soft on Round Top's summit fell the first fair flush of morn ·
And in each hero-haunted dell a newer love was born.

RUNNING THE BLOCKADE—ESCAPE OF THE "FOX."

JOHN F. MACKIE,

Late of U. S. Marine Corps (U. S. S. "Seminole")

ONE of the most magnificent displays of fine seamanship, cool courage, and daring that I ever saw, took place off Galveston Bay, Texas, on the morning of April 1, 1865. Having participated in most of the important naval battles during the entire war, I witnessed many gallant acts of devotion, but none ever exceeded this for heroic conduct.

The "Fox," an English Clyde-built side-wheel steamer, commanded by Captain S. A. Adkins, which had successfully run the blockade several times, left the Bahamas in the latter part of March, with a valuable cargo for the port of Galveston, Texas, expecting to make the port on the evening of April 1st, and run through the Federal fleet, which was closely guarding the entrance with twelve large steam sloops-of-war.

The fleet was busily engaged on Saturday morning, April 1st, as usual, when the weather permitted, cleaning ship, holystoning the decks, scraping the masts and spars, painting the iron work, scrubbing the paint work, and performing the thousand and one things necessary to cleaning the ship from keelson to main-truck, fore and aft.

About ten A. M., when we were up to our eyes in dirt, sand and water, and the general confusion incident to such occasions, with a fresh breeze blowing from the southeast, with hazy weather, which usually prevails in those latitudes, the sea perfectly smooth except a heavy ground-swell setting in from the eastward, the mast-head lookout reported, "Sail O."

"Where away?" demanded the officer of the deck.

"Two points off the weather-bow, sir."

All eyes were turned in the direction, and a faint line of smoke lay along the eastward horizon, showing a steamer apparently coming toward us. This fact was reported to the flag-ship "Ossipee," Captain Guest, who ordered the "Penguin" to get under way and interview the stranger. In a few minutes the "Penguin" was off and steaming rapidly to the eastward. She had not gone more than a couple of miles when the lookout at mast-head again reported, "Sail O."

"Where away?" again demanded the officer of the deck.

"Right abeam, sir."

An officer sprang into the weather rigging with a glass, and, taking a good look at the visitor, reported a long, low steamer about eight miles to the eastward, burning black smoke, steaming rapidly to the northward and westward. The flag-officer ordered the "Seminole" to get under way at once and overhaul her.

Captain Clarey ordered the cables to be slipped, and in less than five minutes we were rapidly steaming four bells to the eastward. "Call all hands to quarters." Buckets, brooms, holystones, and swabs were quickly thrown down the forehold, and the decks "cleared for action." The strange steamer, which proved to be the "Fox," sighted us at the same time, and instantly changed her course from west to northwest, and steamed directly for the Texan shore, distant about eight miles, which trends rapidly to the northeast above Galveston. By this course the "Fox" would strike the shore in about an hour, unless prevented by us from so doing. If successful, she could reach an inner channel which runs between the shore and a sand-bar, which runs along the Texan coast, distant about a mile from the mainland; but on this bar there is only about six or eight feet of water, while on the inside there is twelve and fifteen feet. But in order to do this she would have to run the gauntlet of the whole fleet, all heavily armed. That she could escape by so doing seemed impossible. As this was the apparent object of the "Fox," and as she was going ahead full speed, sailing much faster than we were, Captain Clarey sent for the chief engineer, Mr. Stephenson, and asked him:

"Can you get any more speed out of the ship? The blockade-runner is getting way from us."

"I will do the very best I can, sir."

In a few minutes the "Seminole" fairly shook with the throbbing pulsations of the engines, as they were doing the very best that could be got out of them. We were now speeding along at the rate of ten knots an hour, the best I ever saw her do under steam alone. The "Seminole" was gaining rapidly on the "Fox," when the latter suddenly changed her course to the northward, set her jib and foresail, and was getting away from us again in fine style.

Just as soon as she did this, Captain Clarey seized a trumpet from the officer of the deck, sprang into the horse-block and shouted:

"Stand by the fore and main-top sail sheets and halliards—lead out the jib sheets and halliards—lead out the fore and main sheets—are you all ready there?"

"Aye, aye, sir!"

"Let go, sheet home, hoist away!"

In a minute the "Seminole" was staggering under a cloud of canvas trimmed well aft—every rope drawing as tight as a fiddle-string—causing the sea to boil like soapsuds under our bows as we fairly flew through the water.

Let us board the "Fox" for a few minutes. When the chase opened, her pursuer was about eight miles astern; after a short consultation with her pilot, Harry Wachsen, Captain Adkins decided to make a run through the fleet for Galveston. But here was the difficulty of running from one foe: she must run through a dozen more, all dogs of war of a most savage breed. Her course was instantly taken for the coast sixteen miles to the eastward, to get as far away from the fleet as possible. She was carrying a very heavy cargo—seventeen hundred barrels of beef and pork, besides a large quantity of miscellaneous articles, such as saltpetre, lead, hardware, and other heavy freight. It was just such a chase as Sir Walter Scott so beautifully describes:

"Nor nearer might the dogs attain
Nor further might the quarry strain."

But in this case the friends of 'the "Fox" might have repeated the advice given the flat-boatman by his friend—"Go it, old man, he's a-gaining on you."

The "Fox" began to obey the Bible injunction, —to lay aside every weight that might retard her progress,—and, stripped for the race, made directly for the beach, closely pursued by her fleet antagonist, sanguine of her capture or destruction, which seemed just within his grasp.

The "Seminole" was overhauling her rapidly. Captain Clarey ordered the quartermaster to "heave the log." "Aye, aye, sir!" "Well, sir, what are we making now?" "Twelve knots, sir." "Good, good; is that the best we can do?" "Yes, sir, with the present breeze."

The distance was being rapidly closed between the two ships, now about three miles off, running full speed for the shore. For the first time

the "Seminole's" men got a good look at the "Fox,"a long, low side-wheel steamer, schooner rig, with a fearful rake in the masts and smoke-stacks, all painted a grayish white, common to all blockade runners, so as to make them undistinguishable against the foggy horizon which prevails in the Gulf. The "Fox" was now within range of our guns.

"Fo'castle there!" called out Captain Clarey, "do you think you can reach her with the rifle?"

"Yes, sir."

"Try it."

In a few seconds a flash and a puff of smoke announced that a thirty-pound Parrott shell was flying toward the "Fox," but it went over and exploded in the water beyond.

"Try it again, sir," and a second shell exploded in the air above her.

"Very good, sir, but try it again," and a third shell exploded under her bow. But she paid no more attention to these than if she had been going on about her regular every-day business, and we were amusing ourselves with a little target practice.

The ships were now within less than two miles distance, when we opened on her with our eleven-inch pivot, exploding a shell right under her bow, nearly deluging the ship with water, but doing no further harm.

While we were reloading the pivot she suddenly put her helm "hard-a-starboard," and ran right across our bow, heading directly for the shore, distant about a mile and a half, apparently intending to run herself ashore.

While this was being done we were not idle. The change compelled us to "shorten sail." I have often seen our men do some handsome work in "fleet exercise," but never before in my life did I ever see such quick work or more splendid seamanship than our officers and men exhibited on this occasion. The fore and main-top-sails, the fore and main-sheets and the jib were hauled down, clewed up and stowed, and the men back to their stations at the guns in less than five minutes, without the least confusion, but amid the most intense excitement.

As soon as the last man reached the deck, Captain Clarey shouted:

"Put your helm hard-a-starboard, sir."

"Hard-a-starboard, sir," answered the officer at the wheel, putting the wheel sharply over, and the ship turned on her heel as if she knew what was expected of her, and started directly for the shore, with the "Fox" now right abeam starboard side, about a mile off. Bringing our whole battery of five guns to bear directly upon her, Captain Clarey called out:

"For'ard rifle there, fire as soon and as quickly as you can, without further orders, but don't waste any ammunition. Pivot there, fire carefully; aim at the wheel-house; sink her if you can. Go ahead now, and show us what you can do. Quarter-deck battery (six 32-pounders), fire as rapidly as you can; aim at the wheel-house; don't let her get away from us."

All this was done in less time than I have taken to describe it, and we were now rapidly nearing the "Fox." It seemed impossible that she could escape us. A shell from the rifle exploded over the "Fox"; a shell from the 11-inch pivot burst close alongside, and the 6-inch guns were sending their compliments thick and fast as hornets when enraged. Yet, strange to say, not a single shot had hit her in a vital spot; she seemed to bear a charmed life. We were only about half-a-mile distant from each other, and about a mile from the shore, when the "Fox" suddenly changed her course to south-southwest, and started to run down along the beach, running directly across our bow.

At this moment the leadsman in our fore-chains called out:

"By the deep three fathoms."

"Hard-a-starboard, quartermaster," shouted Captain Clarey; and as the ship's head swung to port he remarked, "By God, we'd been ashore in another minute!" The "Seminole" was drawing sixteen feet, and deep at that.

It was now nip-and-tuck. The "Fox" was going to run for it, and had the bar between us. Our only chance was to sink her, if we could, before she got out of range.

Apparently nothing now could save the "Fox." The "Penguin" and the "Ossipee," with all the other vessels of the fleet, had joined us, and opened fire upon her, with no better success than ourselves, all shots flying wide of the mark. The most tremendous excitement prevailed on board each vessel. Captain Clarey raved and stamped about in an intense but subdued tone, swore like a pirate, and directed in as cool a manner as if we were having a race for a purse, but all to no effect. Shot after shot went over her and exploded on the beach beyond. Some exploded short of the steamer and covered her with spray; some in the air over her deck; others cut the water just ahead of her; one just grazed her stern, but not one touched her, so far as we could see. It seemed impossible to hit her. The men worked the guns as if they were toys; in their excitement loading and firing as if their lives depended on the accuracy of each shot. So rapidly did we fire that we had to wait frequently for the smoke to lift before we fired the next shot.

We were now rapidly approaching Galveston harbor, and it seemed as if the "Fox" was going to get away from us in spite of all our efforts. Since changing our course the last time, we were sailing, or rather steaming, dead to windward, but the "Fox" was the lighter draught and was slowly but surely getting away from us.

Her captain for the last hour had been walking the bridge between the wheel-houses, with both hands in the pockets of his pea-jacket, smoking a cigar as unconcernedly as if there was nothing going on that should cause any uneasiness on his part. But there was evidently a feeling that their lives and property hung only on a single thread, as was manifest in the way those wheels flew around, leaving a track of boiling, foamy sea far astern; and the thick, huge volumes of black smoke that poured out of the funnels told a story that did not need a trumpet to announce it.

The channel now began to widen, and if she could only hold her own for twenty minutes she would escape. What must have been the thoughts of that captain as he walked to and fro on that bridge, with the air full of flying missiles, now hid in their smoke, the next minute drenched with spray, again, in a second or two later, one flying a few feet above his head! He never flinched an inch or changed his manner, but kept quietly on, directing his ship as if it were an every-day affair.

But let us board the "Fox" and hear what the pilot thinks about it.

The "Fox" was now in the condition of poor Reynard, as described by the poet's hero, glorying already in anticipation of his prize, closely followed by his friends, eager to be present at the closing scene:

> "For the death wound and death halloo,
> Mustered his strength, his whinyard drew,
> The wily quarry shivered the shock,
> And turned him from the opposing rock;
> And dashing down the darksome glen,
> Soon lost to hounds and hunters' ken."

So our "Fox," when apparently about to dash herself on the beach, suddenly turned square off to the southwest and made for the pass as if all the fiends who fell from heaven had joined in the chase; and in fact, the whole squadron was belching fire, smoke, steam, shot and shell, as though they would tear the fugitive into more shreds than even poor Reynard was rent into by the largest pack of hounds. The "Fox" kept close in to the shore, while one or two of her pursuers, forced to remain in deeper water, kept alongside, firing broadsides as fast as they could load, and the whole fleet fired up and joined the chase, trying to intercept the fugitive vessel.

Shot, shell, grape, shrapnel, and every other missile known to mankind were thrown with the rapidity of lightning and the abundance of hail at, around, over, and into the water beneath the doomed victim; elongated shot and shell shrieked before, behind, and over her, or struck the water and ricochetted over her decks like a flock of sheep over a pair of bars. Strange to say, although hundreds of shot were fired at her, but four took effect. An ugly shell about two feet long exploded a few yards from the ship. A portion of it struck a forward sheet plate and burst it in about two feet above the water, but beyond making a rent in the bow did no further damage. A ten-inch shell came over the rail and passed out on the other side, doing no harm, while the wind took the breath of two persons who stood near it. The shrouds were cut under another man as he was ascending the rigging, but he suffered no other injury. A piece of shell cut the escape pipe above the deck, but nobody was hurt by it.

There were a number of old veterans on board who had seen service in several closely-contested engagements on Confederate vessels, who pronounced the affair a very gallant one, but took it as a matter of course that was to be expected on occasions like this, and paid a high compliment to the officers and crew for the admirable manner in which they handled the ship. As they passed out of danger they were received with three cheers, which they took with the utmost composure, like a man answering a fulsome toast.

As we viewed the scene at this moment from the deck of the "Seminole," it was one of the most picturesque that I ever saw. The fleet all around was looking with eager eyes to see us sink the flying steamer, the bay gradually widening, with the white sand hills in the distance, the city of Galveston to the south, and its piers filled with sympathetic spectators; the fort in the bay, with the Confederate flag flying, and its ramparts crowded with men watching and praying for the success of the flying steamer; the three warships leaping through the water like hounds, oftentimes hid by the smoke of their own guns. But fate decided in favor of the "Fox." In spite of every effort that could be made to prevent her, she reached Galveston Bay, which is nearly three miles wide, and, as the channel is very dangerous to vessels drawing more than ten feet of water, we were rapidly getting into less than three fathoms again. So with intense chagrin we were obliged to give up the chase, sending as a parting compliment an eleven-inch shell with our regrets.

As the "Fox" passed out of range, her captain hoisted the Confederate flag and dipped it three times, at the same time taking off his cap and waving it toward us, bowing gracefully in our direction his adieu, steamed in under the guns of the fort at Galveston, and dropped his anchor safe at last.

We returned the salute, and returned to our anchorage for the night, as it was nearly sundown, after one of the most exciting days we ever spent, with less credit to ourselves than could possibly be supposed under the circumstances, showing that

> "The best-laid schemes o' mice and men
> Gang aft aglee"—

at sea as well as on shore. The "Fox" discharged her cargo, reloaded with cotton, successfully ran the blockade again through the gauntlet of ten warships, at night, and reached Havana in safety. The war by this time happily had ended. Her pilot, Harry Wachsen, was the commander of the steamer "Buckthorn," at Galveston, for several years, and as he passed in and out of the port had no occasion to hurry, as he did on the occasion when his "Fox" was so harried.

ANTIETAM—A REMINISCENCE.

Col. A. H. Nickerson.

WHEN, immediately after the second battle of Bull Run, McClellan was reassigned to the command of the Army of the Potomac, he conducted his advance through Maryland as though he believed that Lee intended to fight the great battle of the war before he returned to the South bank. On each day's march the several corps were always within striking distance of the others. To do this, some were marched through the country and some distance off the main roads, with the heads of the columns about parallel to each other.

After leaving Frederick City, Maryland, Sumner's corps was some distance off to the right of the turnpike upon which the main column was marching. I was in command of the skirmish line in front of the corps, and as I had but recently been placed in command of the color company of my regiment, the 8th Ohio, although only a lieutenant, I had great pride in being in this so-called post of honor. I felt decidedly elated that I was in command of the very vanguard of that superb body of men which was afterwards immortalized as the old Second Corps. The woods and tangled undergrowth seemed almost impenetrable, and yet we pushed on through the brush and brambles until Sunday, September 14, 1862, when we emerged from the thickets, and looked down upon our comrades already fiercely engaged in the battles of Crampton Pass and South Mountain. When we presently made our way down to the main road to reinforce our comrades, those battles were over, and the troops were already marching through the passes that the Confederates had so strongly contested.

On reaching the main road, I found that the thorns and brambles through which we had been skirmishing had torn my uniform to shreds. As the coat was a uniform, it might be considered honorable rags, but they were certainly very disreputable looking. While we were halted to allow a battery of artillery to pass us, my covetous eyes rested upon an extra artillery jacket, which a soldier belonging to the battery had strapped to his saddle, and I asked him if he would not sell it to me; at the same time calling his attention to my ragged uniform. He seemed to regard the matter with favor, and told

me I could have it at the regulation price at which it was charged to him. The price was not large, but as we had not been paid for several months, I came very near not being able to raise the required amount. However, by negotiating a loan, I succeeded in accumulating the necessary sum, and soon discarded my bundle of rags for the somewhat jaunty jacket of the amiable artillery-man.

The jacket was quite pretty and had some bell-buttons on it, which, though small in size, were decidedly immense in the importance of their influence upon my future career, as we shall presently note. We soon passed over the mountain through Boonesboro, and Tuesday evening found us on the high ground beyond Keedysville, overlooking Antietam Creek and the rolling valley in which it wended its way. Here our brigade was posted in support of our batteries that had opened up an argument with the Confederate artillery, which was posted on the other side of the creek and just back of Sharpsburg.

Supporting batteries is always irksome, and when the enemy has found your range, and occasionally drops a ten or twenty-pound shell in your ranks, it is both disagreeable and dangerous. My servant was a colored boy, who rejoiced in the name of Joe White, and that evening it seemed as though he was about to gainsay the scriptural aphorism in regard to the impossibility of an Ethiopian's changing his skin. He came very near turning white in person as well as in name. My men had stacked arms and were taking things as comfortably as possible under the circumstances. I was leaning against a caisson of one of the batteries and facing the company. Joe, looking very uncomfortable, shifted his position every time a shell came unusually near. Presently a man started to run across the open space that separated the battery from the infantry, when a conical shell came swooping down upon him, taking off one of his feet just above the ankle. He was going so fast that he took two or three steps on the mangled stump before he fell. The sight was not a pleasant one, and "Joe" could hardly be blamed for turning pale and changing his location.

The color guard, which, of course, was attached to my company, had made some coffee and were sitting in a little group near the colors, which were laid across a stack of muskets. A conical shell, which from its size must have come from one of the enemy's twenty-pound cannon, came wobbling through the air, its force almost spent, and turning over just as it reached the color guard, it plunged into the ground in the midst of the group. The dust flew in a cloud as the men, apparently, jumped to their feet. When the cloud floated away I saw that one man, the color corporal, named Farmer, had not arisen. I ran to him and raising him gently saw that the seemingly harmless shell that had not exploded and lay there, an innocent looking chunk of iron, had torn away the man's whole side; he was dead almost as soon as I reached him. This awful sight made "Joe" look whiter than ever. I had scarcely had the body removed when another shell, evidently from the same gun, struck the ground in our front, ricochetted over us, and striking in the regiment immediately in our rear, killed several men at one fell swoop. This was too much for "Joe." He ran to a pile of rails which the men had stacked for the evening fires and lay down behind them. He had barely gotten snugly ensconced in his new location, before another shell came screaming through the air, struck the ground as the former had done, and glancing up, took the top of the rail pile off, sending the rails in every direction and bringing Joe to his feet as white a looking negro as was ever seen. Finding that he was not hurt, he started at full speed to the rear, and I saw him no more that night. About this time General Hooker's corps commenced their assault upon the enemy's left, and I stood for at least two hours watching the long lines of infantry fire that writhed and rolled in and out, as one side or the other gained a temporary advantage. When the battle slackened its fury, I lay down, drew my overcoat cape over my head, and slept the sleep of a tired soldier.

The next morning, Wednesday, September 17, 1862, our corps, then known as Sumner's, moved to the right, forded Antietam Creek, and forming *en echelon* by division, Sedgwick's on the right, ours (French's) next, and Richardson's on the left, advanced to the support of Hooker's and Mansfield's troops, already warmly engaged. As military readers will see, our formation brought Sedgwick's troops into action first. On reaching an orchard near the Roulette House, our brigade, Kimball's, was ordered to be held in reserve; but probably no "reserve" was ever "reserved" for so short a time as were we

on this occasion. Our alignement was hardly complete when it looked as though all the troops between us and the Confederates had given away, and were pouring back with a shower of bullets, hurtling through the branches of the trees over our heads. Immediately we heard the voice of our stalwart Indiana Commander, General Nathan Kimball, ordering his grand old brigade—ever afterward to be known as "The Gibraltar Brigade of Antietam"—forward!

We had gone but a very short distance when we met the enemy in strong force. Their fire, both infantry and artillery, was so heavy that we were brought to a stand on a sort of side hill, immediately in front of what is variously termed Bloody Lane or the Sunken Road. Its condition, immediately after the close of the battle, bore a striking resemblance to Victor Hugo's description of the sunken road of Ohaine, at Waterloo. It was filled with Confederate dead. In this road the enemy were almost entirely hid from sight, while we stood exposed to a sweeping fire, totally unprotected. The range being so short and the fire therefore so deadly, I thought we should capture the position and not remain there and be wiped out of existence. Springing to the front with the colors of my regiment in the hands of as brave a man as ever fluttered the eagles of Cæsar's Tenth Legion, Sergeant Conlin, I called upon my men to follow me into what I then supposed was a ditch. I believe that nearly the whole regiment followed, and we had gotten so near that the Confederates put up on their muskets and ramrods all the old dirty white clothes they could find, in token of surrender. Just then an order came, from whom I do not know, for the colors to return to the main line of battle; I directed Conlin to take the colors back; but as we, in our new position, commanded the ditch or road, and completely silenced the deadly fire of the men in it, I and my men remained where we were. Looking back I could still see the brave color sergeant swinging the regimental colors like a mad-man, and calling at the top of his voice: "Come on, you —— ——" etc. "You can't take these colors!"

Why he was not hit and killed by the bullet from some of the hundreds of rifles that were leveled at him is one of those mysteries "no fellow can find out"; but I believe he escaped without a scratch.

A reinforcing column soon came up in the cornfield back of the sunken road, and I could plainly see the Palmetto flag of South Carolina, side by side with the Georgia State colors, as the Confederates deployed into line of battle and opened upon us. At this our friends (?) in the ditch pulled down their white flags and reopened their fire, and altogether they swept the hillside where we stood very much as a stalwart mower cuts a swath in a meadow. It seemed that everybody near me was killed. A waif of a boy named Johnny Cummins, whom I had enlisted in the company with which I came out, had, with a large number of men from the company, followed me when I first started for the ditch, and, though his arm was broken by a rifle ball, he would not leave me. Handing me his musket he said: "Do the shooting, lieutenant, and I'll furnish the cartridges." There did not appear to be much else to do, so I used all the cartridges he had; and as I was putting down the twelfth and last, I felt the whizz of a bullet that came very close to me and drove the splinters from a little sapling standing partly on my right rear. I saw the tall Confederate who had apparently paid me the compliment as he slowly put down his gun and looked to see if he had hit me. Then he dropped down, and was evidently reloading his piece. I could see the crown of his hat, in which I thought about four inches of his head might be exposed. The musket I had was an old-fashioned Springfield, and the cartridge a buck and ball, i. e., nine buckshot and one large round bullet. There was but one sight, the forward one, a small hollow at the butt being all there was for a rear sight. I drew as close a bead as I could; but knowing that by reason of my being on higher ground I was likely to overshoot my mark, I drew it, as the saying is, a little too fine. A little cloud of dust flew up from the edge of the bank as I fired, and the man's head, unconsciously popping up, showed me that I had missed him. I looked around for Cummins, but he had disappeared. A dead soldier lay across my feet, and stooping down, I hastily drew a cartridge from his box, bit off the end, poured in the powder, and forced the bullet in. It proved to be an elongated bullet, and, of course, unfitted for a smooth-bore musket. When it was about half way down it turned in the barrel and there stuck. My adversary raised and very deliberately drew a bead on me. I knew that I was gone. He was so close that I could see the brass bands on his rifle, but it was of no use to run. Had I tried to run away I should certainly have been shot in the back and almost as certainly killed. There was only one thing to do, face my man

and take my medicine, and that was what I did. It might perhaps not have been quite so bad if he had been the only one. But "he was not the only one" who was paying me special attention. "Oh! dear, no." At least one or two bullets went ploughing through my hat. All the time, however, I was trying to force the bullet in my musket home. My arm was upraised in this position when my Confederate antagonist fired. I felt the sharp jab of the bullet, a blur about the eyes, and the warm blood running down my right side as that arm fell helpless. His shot had been a centre—a bull's eye—but the bullet had caught the second button of my little artillery jacket; it was a bell button, shaped something like a California grape, and it saved my life. The deflection kept the bullet from entering the body just above the heart, and instead it struck the shoulder joint, and continuing its glancing course, came out between the shoulder and elbow. On looking around it did not seem that there was a living man left near me, till my eyes rested upon the captain of the company to which I belonged, but from which it will be remembered I had been detached. His name was Allen, and beside being my own captain he was a devoted friend. On duty he was Captain Richard Allen, and I Lieutenant Nickerson, but when we were off duty he was "Dick" and I "Nick." He was evidently watching me then, and as I turned, still holding the half-loaded musket in my left hand, and growing paler every minute from the loss of blood, he saw that I was badly hurt, and calling out, said: "Nick, go to the rear!" And then, as I still clung to the old musket and looked wistfully back to the spot where my duelistic enemy was safely posted, he put his command in more positive official form, and said: "Lieutenant, go to the hospital immediately." The "hospital" on the field of battle is anywhere that the surgeons happen to be. In this case it was the barn-yard of the Roulette House, and when I reached it the sight was appalling. It seemed as though nearly the whole of my regiment was there: three of my lieutenant comrades, with their eyes shot out, and poor Lieutenant Barnes, with an awful wound in the head, from which a portion of his brain protruded. Singularly enough, Barnes lived till the next day, and appeared well enough to be moved, but when he got up to walk to the ambulance and took a few steps, he dropped dead.

I could not remain there, but wandered along in a half-dazed manner till I came to Antietam Creek, where an officer of McClellan's staff, who was accompanying Franklin's corps to reinforce us, took me across his saddle in front of him and ferried me over. When I reached the opposite bank I was much rejoiced to find my servant "Joe" quite recovered from his fright, and delighted to see me alive. With his aid I reached the Keedysville Church Hospital. The wounded were lying in the little grove that partially surrounded the church, each poor wretch waiting his turn for examination. When my turn came, they took me up to a seat that stood facing the pulpit, but perpendicular to the others and near which was an open window. As we walked up the aisle we splashed along in the blood that had run down from the amputations that lay on boards placed on the pews on either side. The operating surgeons were in their shirt-sleeves, which were rolled up, leaving their bare arms exposed and covered with blood, giving them the appearance of a bevy of butchers in a Chicago abattoir. While sitting awaiting the surgeon, every few minutes an attendant would bring past me, to the open window, an arm, a leg, or a mangled hand, which he pitched into a little trench dug under the window for the purpose.

Pretty soon a young surgeon came up and, grabbing me by the shoulder, said interrogatively: "Shoulder smashed?" A sickening feeling came over me as I replied that "it certainly would be if it were not." "Bring this man some whisky," said he, as I reeled in my seat. A glass of whisky, nearly full and drank down neat, did not seem to affect me any more than would so much water, the pain was so intense. Then the young surgeon thrust his finger into the hole where the bullet had entered, and with his other fore-finger plunged into the place of its exit, he rummaged around for broken bones, splinters, etc., until I swooned away again. Fortunately I knew no more about what transpired until I found myself again under the trees outside and Joe fanning me with his old slouched hat. The next two days were occupied with walking, riding on horseback, or on an old army wagon or ambulance, as we could catch opportunity, till we finally got to Hagerstown. Here, stretched on some clean straw in a box car, with hundreds more, we were transported to Harrisburg. While waiting in this railway station, a Philadelphia physician, named Stroud, who carried his own hospital supplies in a basket on his arm, gave my wounds a much-needed dressing. He also made me take a few mouthfuls of soup, though the fever had commenced

and took away my appetite. As I had not a cent of money, I was trusting to my luck to get through to Pittsburg, but I confess that after we had gotten under way, and I saw the conductor coming, and every few minutes giving that awful warning, that fell like a chunk of lead on my ears, "Tickets!" my courage, or cheek, nearly gave out.

Finally, however, when he came and I had told him how I was wounded and ill, and wanted to get home and would send him the money for our tickets immediately upon my getting there, he gave me his address and the amount, and refused, absolutely, to take my name, though I assured him that if he had it, and I failed to pay, I would be dismissed from the service.

When we reached Pittsburg, we found that our train did not leave until one o'clock that night, it being Sunday. So we wandered around all the afternoon, I with a burning fever, and Joe with a hunger common to a healthy negro. But I had no money to get him anything to eat; for myself I did not want anything. In the evening, as we stood on the sidewalk, I heard the familiar tap of a drum corps as it gave the step to a body of troops I saw marching by. A strange thing about these men was that though they looked like soldiers from the front, they had no arms. I finally inquired of a passing file closer who they were. He told me they were a part of an Ohio regiment that had been captured by Jackson at Harper's Ferry and paroled. The colonel was an old friend, formerly a captain of the 4th Ohio, Col. H. B. Banning, afterward an M. C. from Ohio. As soon as I learned this, I hastened up to the head of the regiment, and, finding Banning, told him the trouble I was in. He had no money himself, but said if we wanted anything to eat, to join him, as they were on their way to a supper that was provided for them by the ladies of Pittsburg. We accepted, and Joe soon had a square meal. We then went to the station, and as it was nearly time for the train to leave, I started to go on it as I had done at Harrisburg, when I was thunderstruck to find that our entrance was cut off by a picket fence at least ten feet high. At the gate a keeper examined the tickets. I think I never before had such a feeling as came over me then, while I stood and saw the passengers going aboard that train. It was of no use to approach the man at the gate; and to ask the man who was selling tickets to trust me for them was equally absurd.

Already so weak that I could hardly stand, with a fever burning up my very brain, this unforeseen dilemma nearly paralyzed me. It was almost time for the train to start, when I saw a large man come bustling down from the ticket office. He had a tall, old-fashioned hat pulled well back on his head; his black frock-coat showed several inches below his linen duster, and he carried a flat, old-fashioned oil-cloth grip-sack. As he came near me, I caught him by the arm and asked him if I could speak a word with him. How my heart went down into my boots as I thought of the hundreds of worthless tramps who had said almost those identical words to me! "What do you want?" he replied, almost gruffly. I could not speak, but something in my face or expression caught his eye, and, coming closer, his manner changed, and he asked me in the kindliest way possible what he could do for me. It seemed like an age before I could recover myself sufficiently to explain what I wished. My voice choked; the tears filled my eyes, and if he had spoken one harsh word, I am sure I should have given up and fallen in my tracks. The unkind word was never spoken. He proved to be a man with a heart as large and old-fashioned as the grip-sack he carried. Would I have money, and if so, how much? But I didn't want money; all I wanted was two tickets to Cleveland, for which I would repay him as soon as I arrived there. Where did I stop when in Cleveland? At the Weddell, and that was where he stopped; but I must have some money for food *en route*. I was too ill to eat, and Joe must wait, I explained, and I positively would not take a cent of money. With this he purchased the tickets, wrote his name in my diary, "A. Hoag, Minneapolis, Minn.," and still demurring at my alleged stubbornness in not accepting any money for incidentals, gave me the tickets, and we went aboard the train. When we reached Cleveland, I jumped from our train and ran across to the Sandusky train, where I knew the U. S. mail agent, a man named Ingersol, who had a brother in my regiment. Finding him, I simply assured him that his brother was alive and uninjured, and begged him to let me have what money he had with him, if less than a hundred dollars. He gave me all I wanted, and, as his train moved out, I ran over to where the carriages were and made a bargain with a hackman by which he agreed to overtake and pass the regular omnibus that was already on its way to the Weddell House. We got to the hotel first, and after I had registered I went immediately to the curb, and stood there waiting when the omnibus pulled up and my benefactor alighted. When I met him with the money I owed him in my hand, the tears that rolled down his rough cheeks showed that he must have felt that exquisite pleasure which comes to a man who has done a good and charitable act and finds that it is appreciated.

The next day found me at the little village twenty-five miles from Cleveland that I called home, where, in a comfortable bed and surrounded with every care that devoted friends could give, I passed through the weeks of delirious fever that always accompanies the healing of gun-shot wounds like these. Many times during that weird period did I, in imagination, fight again my duel with the butternut-coated Confederate in the sunken road. And when at last the fever had gone, and with it the fantastic unrealities which had filled my brain, I rejoiced to remember that I had missed my aim. I afterwards learned that when our troops had finally captured that bloody lane, they found a few of its occupants alive and uninjured. I sincerely hope that my antagonist was one of the fortunate few, and that he still survives. If he is living, it is not too much to imagine that, as he sometimes sits in the shade of the magnolias which surround his Southern home, he tells his children and grand-children how, on that September day, now more than thirty years ago, he stood in that appalling death-trap, "The Sunken Road of Antietam," and with his trusty rifle shot a "Yankee" officer who stood under the folds of the old flag, as it were, on the bank above him.

BRIGADIER-GENERAL W. E. STRONG, GENERAL McPHERSON'S INSPECTOR GENERAL, ORDERING A COLONEL TO PLACE HIS COMMAND IN ACTION.

WHAT A NORTH CAROLINA BOY SAW OF THE CIVIL WAR.

James Eastus Price.

DOWN on the coast of North Carolina, where the Cape Fear River makes a bend, forming a fine bay four miles wide, just before rushing into the sea, the town of Southport (formerly Smithville) lies amidst a beautiful grove of live-oak trees. Here I found my little world, bounded on one side by pine forests, and on the other by the great Atlantic Ocean, over which I often longingly gazed and wondered what was beyond the line where sky and sea seemed to meet.

Across the bay, on the north side of the river's mouth, was old Fort Caswell, built many years before I was born. My grandfather had assisted in superintending its construction; and the old place, with its citadel, long brick galleries, drawbridge, and moat, was at once a pleasure and a mystery to me. In the late war this fort, and one on Smith's Island, forming the southeastern boundary of the river's mouth, served to intimidate the too venturesome blockading steamers that lay off the port to prevent the entrance of ships which brought supplies for the Confederacy.

When President Lincoln, on the 19th of April, 1861, issued his proclamation for the blockading of the coast of the Southern States, the Carolina coast was not included. It was not until the following July that this, the most important port on the Southern coast, was declared blockaded, and the Federal steamer "Monticello" sent to intercept the venturesome traders.

Being dependent on England for most of its foreign supplies, the large production of cotton in the South was a source of much wealth to the English traders, who, owing to the immense profit, took great risk in running the blockade. As the neutrality law prevented direct trade with England, the cotton was taken to intermediate ports, and there transferred to its true destination. The principal intermediate points for the neutral trade were Nassau, Bermuda, Havana, and Matamoras. Nassau was the most important of these; but Bermuda, though second in extent of its trade, was nearest to the Cape Fear port, which was—especially in the latter part of the war—the place most sought by the blockade-runners, and became the scene of stirring events, some of which were indelibly impressed upon my youthful mind.

When war was declared, I was too young to fully appreciate the situation; but when my father told me he was going away on the ocean to get a ship at Nassau, I was uneasy, and said that he might not come back again. I was an unconscious prophet; he never returned. When his ship arrived at Nassau, he was stricken with yellow-fever, and died soon after getting on shore. The vessel on which he went (the steamer "Kent") returned, and was destroyed by the blockaders. For years the framework of her walking-beam, sticking out of the water in front of our town, was a continual reminder of my great loss.

The clouds of war thickened; our little town was enlivened by some of the pageant of military display, and the bright uniforms and bands of music made a pleasure for the boys (who always dearly loved a soldier) that was only lessened by the continual expectation of the enemy, who, to our youthful imaginations, were monsters with horns. This belief was somewhat lessened when a Yankee prisoner was brought to Fort Johnson, located in the town. We did not look upon the poor, lonely fellow, far away from his friends in the North, as an object of pity. He was a curiosity, and although we saw he was as other men, we still doubted.

Never before nor since has the town Southport—although over a hundred years old—experienced such prosperity as came to it in the blockade-running days. Danger from capture by the blockaders and the possibility of yellow-fever abroad were outweighed, in the minds of numerous pilots of the town, by the golden harvest their services brought. Nearly $4000 were paid a pilot for each round trip, and the gold so quickly obtained was lavishly spent. Money was plentiful, and, although many communities in the South were suffering for the necessaries of life, the people of the ports of entry were well fed and clothed.

This gold was gotten at an enormous expense to the English people. Hundreds of vessels were destroyed by the blockaders, and it is said that, in two years after the war began, $10,000,-000 were distributed by relief committees in England on account of the closing of the Lancashire cotton-mills, which, owing to the impossibility of securing the raw cotton, were compelled to shut down. For many years on the Carolina coast, for miles on either side of the Frying-Pan shoals, could be seen the wrecks of blockade-runners which had been run aground to escape capture.

Among these was the steamer "Condor," the pilot of which was my uncle. Although it was night, the low gray hull of this ship, which was difficult to see, even by moonlight, was detected, heading for the bar, by the blockader. Both vessels crowded on steam, and an exciting chase began. It did not take my uncle long to see that his charge was in great danger, and the solid shot tore up the water all around. Heading straight for the nearest land, which was near Fort Fisher, the "Condor" was driven at full speed and struck bottom, unfortunately, quite a distance from the shore. The enemy was pressing hard, and, being unable to use the boats, the "Condor's" crew were compelled to swim for life. Uncle had with him a Newfoundland puppy, which, though only a few months old, swam ashore through the breakers with his master. My uncle escaped the blockaders only to fall a victim to the malice of the Confederates, who accused him of uselessly running the ship ashore. He was unjustly imprisoned at Fort Johnson; then taken to Wilmington, and from there to Salisbury, while awaiting trial; and, but for the timely cessation of hostilities, no doubt he would have suffered a great wrong at the hands of the people he was honestly serving.

Another of my uncles had a very narrow escape. He had taken his vessel out, the profitable cargo of cotton had been disposed of, and, with the much-needed load of stores, the swift steamer was again nearing the Carolina coast. As usual upon these occasions, the night was dark, and they were creeping in with not a light showing, until near enough for the grand dash for the bar. Suddenly a rocket shot through the darkness, then another, and in a moment they were surrounded by the enemy. All was excitement on board the blockade-runner.

"We must surrender the ship," said the captain. "No, we will not," said uncle, and he rang the signal, "Full speed, ahead!"

The blockaders, seeing their supposed prize rushing through the water regardless of their presence, brought their guns to bear; and, although it was quite dark, they made it ex-

ceedingly unpleasant for the bold craft. The shot screamed over and around the flying ship, and one entered the cabin and knocked a man's head off. But superior speed and daring courage won, and the blockade-runner anchored safely behind the guns of Fort Caswell.

For a time the presence of the armed blockaders, so near our town, was a source of much uneasiness to us; but the blazing rocket and the boom of cannon soon failed to alarm. We had three forts near us, and, after much hurried labor, the iron-clad ram "Raleigh" was built, and steamed down from Wilmington, making us feel doubly secure. This iron-clad security ere long went to the bottom of the river,—a veritable "sinking fund"; and in after-years, at low tide, I sat upon the double-ended hope of war and caught fish. She had never won a battle, but she made an excellent fishing-place for flounders and sheepshead.

———

Although feeling, in the strength and number of our defences, secure from attack, we were rudely awakened one morning, as to the courage and ability of the enemy.

Captain Cushing, the daring commander of the "Monticello," determined to make us a visit. Though his ship was some miles from the river's mouth, on a night in February, 1864, he took a cutter, and, with several seamen, pulled quietly in around Fort Caswell, and up to the town two miles across the river. He captured a colored man, who willingly led the way to the commander's quarters, located within a stone's throw of the garrison. The commander was not in, having gone to Wilmington that day; but there was an officer in charge, who, upon learning that the enemy were after him, ran off to the woods, *sans ceremonie et sans cullotte.* He was so badly alarmed himself that he did not take time to alarm the garrison; and when Cushing's presence became known the latter was pulling away as hard as sailors could work an oar. Signals were made to Fort Caswell to "intercept an enemy," but the darkness and the smallness of his cutter enabled the daring Federal to escape. He took one prisoner from the general's headquarters, but the object of the expedition was the capture of the general himself. It is needless to add that the citizens of our fortified village thereafter felt somewhat unsafe. They knew not at what time they would be awakened by the prod of a bayonet, accompanied by a command to get up and start seaward. But this alarm did not weigh upon my youthful mind very long; the camp, with its white tents, bravely-clad warriors, and glittering weapons, claimed my fancy to the exclusion of future fear. Above all, the dashing cavalry officers, with all the accoutrements of their positions, on dress-parade, were to me the perfection of beauty and romance.

Among the latter was Lieutenant D——, a tall, broad-shouldered gentleman, who owned a large, splendid black horse, which attracted me even more than his master. This animal was as fiery as any fighting cavalryman's charger should be, and it delighted me to see the *debonair* officer on his back. I saw him often, for he visited our house, where there was a young lady with whom he seemed much pleased—much, indeed. Upon one of these visits he hitched the black charger to our front fence, and while the master was basking once again in the sunshine of smiles, the war-horse was receiving the close attention of my elder brother and his chum. The chum proposed to my brother that they should mount the steed and see how it felt to be a mounted soldier; and John, though more accustomed to boats than to fiery steeds, willingly accepted a back seat on the animal. The chum got on first and took the reins, and John climbed up and put his arms around his companion. Until the adventurers got seated the horse acted as if he had been a plow-horse, accustomed to being clambered over, but when he felt the urchins wriggling on his back and had his bit jerked suddenly by the leading equestrian, the noble animal "rose to the occasion." I may say the boys rose with him, while his hind feet shot out in various directions, as if feeling for some flying object. The chum sawed on the bridle in the vain endeavor to stop his speeding mount; but a mixture of John's arms and legs in the unstable air was followed by a substantial landing that took from the youth all desire to be a cavalryman. The chum managed to land safely, and the horse was recovered. But when the lieutenant went courting after that, he never endangered his matrimonial prospects by letting his sweetheart's brother mount his fiery war-horse.

As the war progressed, the large government hospital, situated about two hundred yards from my mother's house, was a great attraction for me. The soldiers who had faced cannon and shed blood on many a hotly-contested field, were here suffering from wounds and disease. Sometimes I stood by when the surgeon was dressing a poor fellow's wound, full of curiosity

to see how it was done. I remember one case where the glory of war was mingled with the beauty of romance.

Early in the struggle Captain B—— had been a frequent visitor at our home, and it was understood that he was to wed a certain young lady residing there, when the strife was over. To me he was a great hero, and, when he came to be treated at the hospital for a gunshot wound, my imagination placed him among the immortals. I stood by once in mute sympathy while the doctor dressed his wounds; and through his convalescence he was the object of my youthful but tender solicitude. My experience did not tell me that the pain of his not dangerous wound was more than offset by the pity of love from her for whom he cared most, and the glory of military renown which raised him so high in her estimation. Promotion followed restoration to health, and my hero went back to the tented field, where, after another great battle, in which he had performed deeds of bravery, he was made a major. Again we heard he had been promoted, and then, after a fierce and bloody fight, we heard he was dead. They found him on the field of battle with his handsome face turned toward the sky, as if watching the flight of his intrepid spirit as it sought the warrior's paradise. And over his faithful heart they found the picture of one we both knew and loved.

———

If there is one bright spot around which the memory of other days centres and regilds the halcyon hours of youth's fleeting dream, that place is the riverside, where, with bare feet and rolled-up trousers, I felt the waves swirl around my sun-burnt legs, wetting my clothes, but giving new pleasure with every unlucky splash.

It was there, one eventful morning, I stood with other adventurers, superintending the launching of the "Ben Cipi." She was not a great craft, with graceful lines, whose bilge felt the supporting stocks that would soon glide her into the anxious water, where the waves would lap her sides, and the sea-breeze blow out gallantly the pennant from the lofty truck. She had lain prone upon the drifting sand for many days, with the summer sun widening the cracks in her garboard streak, when my delighted glance fell upon her. Benjamin Cipio, a gentleman from Africa, had owned and navigated this craft upon river and creek; had burdened her frame with oysters, fish, and crabs for many years, and now, when the ravages of time had made her unseaworthy, she was abandoned.

It took but little effort to get possession of the forlorn vessel, and soon the surrounding air was redolent of boiling pitch, while the sound of the caulking-iron was heard filling up big cracks with strips of worn-out pantaloons. A piece of tin secured the shaky stern, a strip of board gave stability to the keel; and then we turned her over, put in the thwarts, made a mast-hole, and stood off, contemplating with pride, mingled with unspeakable emotions, the consummation of a cherished hope.

What visions floated through my mind! The marshes were teeming with marsh-hens' nests, the sheepshead and trout were waiting for me at Nancy's Rock, and the terrapin were laying their eggs for me at Caswell Beach, where the wild plums hung in mellow readiness for my unsatisfied lips. I longed to be away on the bosom of the deep.

With repeated instructions to my companions, who had gathered with covetous feelings to assist at the launching, to be careful about the stern, and not to pull too hard on the starboard side, we slowly pushed the ancient craft into her native element; and as she rose to the gentle swell of the waves, I named her the "Ben Cipi."

What cared I that the water oozed in where the pantaloons did not fit a seam? Were not an envious throng watching me from the shore? Columbus never felt greater than I, as I sat in the stern, while the breeze caught the small piece of thin carpeting used for a sail, and wafted me over the bosom of the Cape Fear River. I knew naught of Jason, Perseus, Andromeda, Charybdis, or Scylla; but never did the Argonauts sail forth more eagerly in search of the Golden Fleece, than I in quest of pleasure, with a ship at my command.

My acquaintance with the beautiful thoughts of Thomas Buchanan Read had not begun at that early day; if it had, I surely would have said,—

> My soul to-day is far away,
>   Sailing the Vesuvian bay;
> My winged boat, a bird afloat,
>   Swims round the purple peaks remote.

When I had gotten into this poetically satisfied state, with the shore about three hundred yards astern, my delight was suddenly changed to fear by a booming sound from the ocean. "The Yankees!" I exclaimed. Hardly had the words escaped me, before a whistling sound

high overhead told me that a long-range gun had sent its shot over the town. The enemy were not shooting at me; but I didn't know this; and the yells of my companions on shore added to my terror. Without thinking of the crankiness of my boat, I jumped up, and frantically tried to turn her around. In doing this, the "Ben Cipi" was overturned, and I found myself hanging to her bottom.

To say that I cried for help is putting it mildly. I yelled with all my might, and my lusty effort brought an old gentleman in a boat to the rescue. My craft drifted away, and I went ashore, but not to receive the congratulations of the boys.

————

The government hospital, for my visits so conveniently near our house, caused the town to be almost depopulated. An enemy we were not looking for came upon us in shape of the yellow-fever. When this dread visitor made its appearance, all who could get away went into the pine country, into which it is said the fever will not go. But my mother, full of sorrow for her lost husband, could not be persuaded to leave the village, and only moved into another part of the town. Indeed, it seemed as if we were under divine protection, for, although the disease was so near us, and we could see the smoke rising up from the burned clothes and bedding of the dead, not one of the family was sick. The gloom of desolation brooded over the place and intensified the shadow of war that was continually over us.

We had our Christmas, celebrated New Year, and were congratulating ourselves on the absence of the enemy, when, on the 13th of January, 1865, we were startled by the appearance of General Terry before Fort Fisher. We were not long in doubt as to his intentions, for the booming of a cannon, that soon turned into a continuous roar, told us that a battle had begun in earnest.

Although several miles from the scene of action, I climbed upon the top of a house and saw the smoke of the war-ships' guns rising in great clouds, while the windows in the town rattled as if a storm were beating against them. All day the fight went on, and we became in a manner accustomed to the thunder of battle. Our anxiety was great; we knew that if Fisher fell the enemy would, soon after that important event, be among us. The cannonading continued through the 14th and until in the afternoon of the 15th, when a decrease in the sound of firing gave hope that the Federals had gotten tired of the fight. But we were undeceived by the news that came in the night, telling us that Fort Fisher had fallen, and that the Yankees would soon be with us. It indeed had fallen, after a terrible fight, and around it the pallid blue and gray were silent witnesses of the struggle, which Admiral Porter said was the most terrific he ever saw.

I wasted no time meditating on the fate of Fisher; to me the all-important question was the coming of the Yankees. Some of the citizens left town; but our family had successfully defied the yellow-fever, and people who could defy yellow-fever were not going to run away. As for my part, I would heartily have favored a vacation. I only needed a little encouragement to cause me to run off to the woods.

Late on the night of the 15th I heard the tramp of feet. "Is that the enemy?" No. I soon learn that our own troops are evacuating the town.

Everybody is full of the excitement of the hour. The troops are marching to the support of Fort Anderson.

"Good-bye, Jimmie!" cries Adam Corcoran, the hospital steward, who sees me standing on the piazza in the dim light. "Don't fall in love with the Yanks!" he continued, as gayly as one going to a picnic.

"Good-bye, Ad.!" I cry. And in a moment he and all my soldier friends are out of sight.

When day dawned, we looked out over the water, expecting to see the victorious war-ships sail into the harbor. But the peaceful river flowed on as if it had not swept the bloody beach at Federal Point before coming to us, and the harbor was yet all our own.

The day passed in ominous suspense, and when night—that ally of fear to the youthful mind—came, we were treated to a spectacle that shocked us mentally and physically.

Our house was near and facing the river, and directly across the harbor from us was Fort Caswell. While I was trying to pierce the darkness over the water in search of approaching lights, I looked toward this fort and beheld the most astonishing sight I have ever seen. As I looked, a vivid flash of light shot through the darkness and traveled with lightning rapidity toward the fort; and then, as if a mighty volcano had sprung its blazing contents from the sea into the sky, a great light flashed up from Caswell, accompanied by a roar and a jar that smashed the glass in our house like the wave of an earth-

quake. Fort Caswell has been evacuated and blown up. When I visited it some time afterward, it presented a scene of ruin and desolation I had never imagined could come to it. To me it was an ideal spot before its destruction; it seemed the perfection of strength and the embodiment of defensive skill.

A deep structure of brick formed a hollow square in which were buildings whose tall chimneys towered above the works; from the square a wide passage opened on a drawbridge which spanned the moat when down, and was to be raised from within when the enemy had carried the outer works.

When the drawbridge was up, huge doors studded with spikes, were closed by a portcullis, like those of an ancient castle. Long galleries ran through the outer brick wall which flanked the moat; and in the sides of the galleries were openings, commanding all approaches, where the soldiers, with crossed guns, could shoot the opposers while they were trying to cross the water. A high earthwork surrounded the inner structure, and was the only thing that presented a likeness of its original shape after the awful explosion. The beauty, the grandeur of the place had fled, and the long stretch of bare beach, near which the wave-torn frames of the blockade-runners "Spunky" and "Agnes E. Fry" lay, intensified the lonely aspect of the surroundings; even the waves that beat upon the shore below seemed to sing the requiem of the Lost Cause.

Afterward I found pleasure in strolling amidst the ivy-crowned ruins of the old fort, and in hunting on the beach near for the eggs of the great sea-turtle and riding on her back to the water's edge; but the military glory of the camp and the splendor of our sea-coast defence were not replaced in my mind while I remained a boy.

After the night of terror and tragic events, day dawned upon the town deserted by its defenders and still unoccupied by the foe. It was a period of uncertain calm that we thought was the forerunner of the certain storm which would come in glittering array and despoil us of our little possessions. But with all our fear we remembered that the Confederates had left a great quantity of food and clothing stored in a large building near Fort Johnson. As the fortunes of the South waned, food had gotten scarcer and dearer, and although we did not actually suffer, we had not an abundance of the creature-comforts.

It seemed that the thought "commissary" occurred simultaneously to every man and boy in the town. It came with equal force to my older brother and me, and never did prospectors seek a gold field more eagerly than we sought, with flying feet, the house of plenty. From all directions the throng crowded in; some with carts and wheelbarrows, but the majority with backs and hands. John and I were among the majority. I cannot imagine my feelings as I stood in the big building surrounded by a seemingly inexhaustible store of provisions; just what to grab first I knew not. Men were scrambling for and quarreling over choice articles, and the goods were rapidly disappearing through the doors. I knew that my undeveloped strength was not equal to a barrel of pork, a box of "canned horse," or a sack of meal; a box of "hardtack" was too heavy for me; in fact, for a time I was "athirst at sea with the water all around me." I was not long idle, for a broken box of canned beef furnished me with a load, and I was soon on my way home, lugging two large cans. Depositing my spoil, I ran back for more, and kept working while there was anything to get, winding up with a load of Confederate-gray soldier's clothes. John worked like a Trojan, and together we managed to get quite a respectable quantity of provisions.

With plenty of food, clothing, some gold, and the Yankees not yet arrived, we felt more at ease, and I with my companions started out to explore the soldiers' quarters. To our delight we found a number of muskets and swords, and plenty of ammunition, which had been left behind in the hurried evacuation. We were not long in appearing upon the streets, each bearing a gun with its glittering bayonet attachment which made us look like sawed-off militiamen. Guns were useless unless we could shoot them; so, like old veterans, we tore off the paper end of the cartridge with our teeth, rammed the charge home, pulled from our little leather boxes the percussion-caps, and blazed away.

No boy on the Fourth of July was ever more hilariously happy than I, and I cannot imagine what injury would have befallen me, or some one else, if an old gentleman had not appeared upon the scene of action and interrupted my fun.

Without ceremony he seized the weapon of my young "defender" and broke it off at the stock. I mournfully picked up the iron ramrod, and departed, exploding caps on its end.

My cousin was more unfortunate than I. Unable to get shining arms like mine, he had found a crooked musket and beguiled the time by popping caps on it. He had exploded several and was getting down to business in satisfied earnestness, when the gun, which had two or three loads in it, went off with a deafening roar, and a kick that gave its possessor a fine idea of the horrors of war.

Many of the boys made their gun-barrels shorter and used them for fowling pieces, and for years after the war these sawed-off guns were the treasures of the village youth.

Among the other deserted buildings which received our inquisitive attention was the hospital. There was but little within the solemn building to satisfy our curiosity, and the thought of friends that were once there and now gone, perhaps forever, deepened the gloom of the place.

Our adventurous band had explored the house, and were cutting up pranks in the yard, when some one shouted, "The Yankees are coming!" I have seen many boys frightened, but I have never seen a more panic-stricken crowd than that which scampered from the old hospital yard. My younger brother took the lead and ran straight in the direction of an old well, the top of which was close to the ground. Too frightened to notice his surroundings, he ran on, and before I could warn or catch up with him I was horrified to see his feet disappear over the side of the well. In a second I was to the rescue, and found him standing in the midst of oyster-shells, broken bottles, tin cans, and other rubbish which almost filled the well. He was pulled out without having received a hurt of any consequence. But he has never been able to tell which terrified him most: the thought of the advancing Yankees, or the sudden plunge down the well.

At last, after much looking for the ships that were sure to come, the Federals cast anchor before our town. With mingled curiosity and fear I watched a large cutter, full of men, pull away from the ship for the shore; watched her until her bow struck the land; and then I ran home to await developments.

Among the anxious watchers were many colored people, whose emotions were altogether different from mine. They saw in our foes deliverers from bondage; and, with demonstrations of joy, they were not slow in proffering their services for anything that might be asked of them. Not the least officious in that negro crowd was a boy who belonged to my uncle. His mother—a woman of fine character, who was loved by my people, and whose memory is still dear to me—was called "Aunt Mag," being, as in the case of most colored people then, without a family name of her own. We called her boy "John Mag," the latter part being the nearest approach to family distinction we could give him.

When the Yankees had landed, John Mag immediately offered to conduct them over town, in their search for firearms at the houses of the citizens. To the envy of his companions, and the anger of the whites, he sat on a horse, the embodiment of untrammeled mischief, and piloted the foe from house to house.

Contrary to our expectations, the enemy behaved like a well-brought-up antagonist, and let us off with little trouble. After collecting all the deadly weapons that could be found, they went back to their ships. After their visit I had a better opinion of them; and when, later on, troops were stationed at Fort Johnson, I became a regular visitor to see the soldiers on dress-parade and hear the band play.

The first troops which were stationed in our town after the fall of Fort Fisher were badly in need of tobacco, and—as most soldiers, like most sailors, are as restless as fish out of water without the "weed"—they sought diligently for it. Among other things which my brother secured from the government storehouse was a large box of North Carolina plug-tobacco, of a fine quality. In some manner the soldiers learned that we were in possession of the luxury for which they longed; and their knowledge of this was followed by their presence at our house. John had his "tobacco store" in a small back-room on the second floor, where he received the enemy gladly; and, in a business-like manner, stripped off the beautifully-mottled plugs, which were eagerly carried away. Up and down the stairs tramped the once-dreaded foe, with only the thought of satisfying the cravings of a tobacco appetite, until the last plug was sold. "We had met the enemy, and their cash was ours."

It was strange how quickly my brother developed the instincts of a sharp trader, and yet more strange to me was the coolness with which he dealt out his stock in trade to the bronzed veterans, who stood thickly around. But he had found them just like other mortals, and saw that they did not wish to harm us.

He also saw the opportunity to make the best trade in tobacco that had ever been made in his town. How his eyes did sparkle as he stowed away the money paid by the enemy for tobacco that would have been a part of the spoils of war, had he not gotten ahead of them.

With the throng of buyers came an old man who was plainly in the service of King Alcohol. He looked as if he had suffered much in life's moral battle, as well as in the ones of blood he had passed through. But the stamp of the warrior was upon him, although he was foolishly drunk. He, too, was much in need of tobacco, and strove to force his way to the front. This did not suit the first-comers, who, when the old man insisted on the right of way, put him out into the yard. I looked out of the window to watch him, as he went away shouting something about blowing up the town. I was very uneasy at this; and, without asking permission, I snatched up a plug of tobacco, ran down to the angry man, and gave it to him, saying, "I hope you will not blow up our town, sir." He took the gift, and said he guessed he would spare us.

When the news of Lee's surrender ran through the town, we were greatly shocked. But the situation did not appear to my youthful mind as forcibly as it did to the older people. The struggle had ended, but the hoped-for victory did not perch upon our banner. The gloom of defeat hovered over us, and the uncertainty of our future made us unhappy indeed.

We could not look into the future years, and see the South, phœnix-like, rising, beautiful and grand, out of her baptism of blood and fire. Our saddened hearts could not feel the great heart of human brotherhood beating through the future years. The consolidated, invincible Union was to rise triumphant out of the chaos of war; but, through the tears of sorrow and disappointment, hope gleamed for us as a dimly-distant star. The tragedy was over, the curtain rung down, and the audience were silently weeping for the pity of it all.

MY RECOLLECTIONS OF SHILOH.

George W. McBride.

IN SEASON and out of season there has always been a conflict of opinion as to the facts regarding this great battle. I do not pretend to know, nor have I a desire to express an opinion in regard to the matters in dispute. I only ask to tell what a boy sixteen years old saw one day, on that historic field.

Our regiment, the 15th Michigan Infantry, arrived at Pittsburg Landing, by the steamboat "War Eagle," on the afternoon of April 5, 1862. We were tired, hungry, and impatient because of the cramped conditions of our voyage. We disembarked, moved up onto the bluff, and went into camp just back from the river. We were allowed to move around, and found ourselves amidst the wild whirl of an army in the field—men, camps, tents, wagons, mules and swearing drivers, cannon, sutlers, drummers, darkies, and the flag. Men were everywhere: some were in a pavilion playing cards, and in one corner of the small enclosure lay a dead infantryman, whose presence seemed unknown to the boys who were hazarding all they had on a full hand ; while just outside was the carcass of a dead mule, giving evidence of a not very recent demise. I can see that wild scene now, clear and sharp. It was my first real experience with soldiers in the field, and, boy-like, I saw many things to remember. Around the landing were grouped a multitude of war munitions, and on the river, with their prows pointing up stream, were moored a fleet of river steamboats. All was activity and bustle and change. We were fed, and lay down on the ground to sleep. Having been excused from duty because of the mumps, I tried to find a warm place, but was finally content to roll up in a blanket, and make Mother Earth my bed for the first time. Early the next morning, at what time I cannot say, the bugle-call aroused us. We came to life and activity, got something to eat, and our command moved out of camp. I was still excused from duty, but went along to see what was coming next. The air was balmy, the roads were good, the birds were singing in the trees, and a strange, profound stillness fell about us. The camps we passed through on our way out were alive and in motion ; proceeding on our way we heard the firing of guns in our front ; inquiring the cause of the firing we were informed that the boys in

advance were " shooting squirrels." Soon the shots became more frequent, and seemingly nearer us ; and for some reason our column moved with quicker step. When we had passed out and beyond Hurlburt's division, whose men were forming, and whose battalions were mustering fast as we passed them, we met three men, one of whom, in the dress of the 54th Ohio, was being helped to the rear by the others. He was holding in one hand the other, bleeding and crushed by a rifle shot. We spoke to him about "shooting squirrels" ; his answer was that they were the " funniest squirrels we ever saw," and that the enemy was attacking us in force. The excitement had reached us, and soon an officer, riding up with the order, " on the left by file into line," was quickly obeyed, forming the regiment's first line of battle. We were moved to the left, halting in a peach orchard, and constituting the extreme left of Prentiss's division, we were told. Near to us, on our right, were the 18th Wisconsin and the 18th Missouri, like ourselves new regiments and just arrrived. We unslung knapsacks, fell back three paces, fixed bayonets, and stood to attention at order arms

The ground we occupied was a clearing around a log house ; the house was old and somewhat dilapidated. Before us the ground sloped down to a small creek, where the clearing ended. Across the creek the hillside was covered with a growth of scrub oak and bushes ; the ridge ran obliquely to our right and beyond our view. The crest of the ridge was in plain sight from our line and higher than where we stood. It seems to me now that we were there but a moment, when there appeared over the ridge in front a column of men, some of them dressed in blue, some in gray, some in bright-colored uniforms. Who are they ? We do not know. They come down the hill, through the underbrush, with closed ranks. Behind comes another line similar to the first, and further back still another. The first line moves down the hillside, crosses the little creek, enters the clearing, halts and fires into us. We stand at an order arms and look at them as they shoot. No reply on our part—not a man in our command has a cartridge to use, and there are none to be had. Again comes that blinding line fire ; a few men fall. We are ordered to shoulder arms, about face, and move back, which we do; but as we go the regiments on our right answer the challenge with a terrible volley and the fight is on.

It seems ridiculous to think of men going out to fight, and when the time comes to find they have no cartridges for their guns, and in the face of the enemy turn and march away; but that is just what we did, and in good order. Back into the openings we went, remaining inactive until we met the 23d Missouri infantry, who were armed with guns of the same calibre as ours; we were given sixty rounds of ammunition, about-faced, and started back for our place in the line.

The Shiloh battlefield was a series of clearings and oak openings, with now and then a clump of underbrush and occasional ravines. We return through the thin woods, and as we ascend a sharp rise we see, out in the front and on the flanks, the struggle.

The roar of the fight rises and falls, ringing along the line in war's wild, grand sweep. We are hurriedly formed into line on the crest of the ridge, and ordered to load. I get down on the ground, close to the roots of a large oak tree, and fire my first shot at a human being. In a moment the regiment is engaged: the enemy, in unbroken columns, comes like the waves of the sea, pitiless and in grand form upon us; batteries swing into position, and the hissing shells fall like hail about us. We are new men, but we are firing at short range, and the line in front melts away. Yet it closes up and on it comes, sullen and determined; batteries are increasing their fire—the line on our right breaks, and we are flanked by the enemy. I can see the fight now as I saw it then.

To its credit be it said, our green regiment stood like a rock in the pathway of our opponents, and checked and held them at bay until they flanked us out of our position; but repeatedly were they driven back and repulsed in their assaults upon us. We went in recruits; we came out veterans.

I said I could see the fight now as I saw it then; the enemy had pushed back Sherman, McClernard, and Prentiss; officers had fallen and the day seemed lost, but to the boy it was war's wild splendor—overhead the smoke of battle, all around the busy, active, fighting comrades mingled with the silent dead, the wounded, and the dying. There was the crash of musketry, the roar of artillery, the yells of the combatants, the smoke, the jar, the terrible

energy. Why should it not remain a picture on my memory? In our front is the coming line, tipped with fire and flame. The white smoke, leaping out in front, slowly rises, forming a curtain that unites the line of fire and the cloud above. At intervals we can see the faces of the foe, blackened with powder, and glaring with the demoniac fury of battle, lost to all human impulses, and full of a fiendish desire to kill; they are no longer men, they are devils incarnate. Here lies, stands, or crouches a line of men, opposing this rushing and advancing foe; but in the body of that regiment abides the iron of Michigan, and with slow, cool movement the guns are loaded and fired with awful effect. The men before us fall like leaves in autumn. The line vanishes, a new one takes its place, the rattling roar blends into a continuous sound, and scores of men fall dead. Guns grow hot to the touch, the iron heats in the blood of the green regiment, and the ground grows rich with our fallen heroes' gore.

The enemy flank us and are moving to our rear; some one calls out, "Everybody for himself!" The line breaks, I go with the others, back and down the hill, across a small ravine, and into the camp of the 11th Illinois cavalry, with the howling, rushing mass of the enemy pressing in close pursuit.

When I arose from the roots of the tree, where I had lain and fired as fast as I could, I was as cool as one could expect a raw recruit would be in his first fight. I was partially dazed, and the full force of the situation did not impress me at the time. As I reached the bottom of the hill and entered the camp of the cavalry, the artillery seemed to have a cross fire, and at short range was sweeping the ground with canister. The enemy was active, and the musketry fire was awful; the striking of the balls on the Sibley tents of the cavalry camp gave out a short, cutting sound that terrified me. The striking of the shot on the ground threw up little clouds of dust, and the falling of men all around me impressed me with a desire to get out of there. I recollect that the hair now commenced to rise on the back of my head, and was soon standing straight up, and I felt sure that a cannon-ball was close behind me, giving me chase as I started for the river. In my mind it was a race between me and that cannon-ball. For the first mile I traveled, I won. I was never so frightened before, and trust I may never be again; I never ran so fast before, and know I never will again. I was never in such a storm of bullets before or since ; it seemed as if the trees were casting them. Out of that fire that killed, I came alive and unharmed, but it was a marvel that any of us did, for an examination of the field afterwards showed the ground plowed with shot, and the smallest twig told of the storm of death that had swept over it. " Chaos had come again," and the slope was slippery with blood and strewn with the dead.

I succeeded in escaping the cannon-ball, and soon found myself in company with a stalwart young Irishman, belonging to the 15th Iowa, who was blackened with battle-smoke, and his gun showed that he had been in the fight. I asked him where he was going. He replied : " Back, be jabers ! " He said there was too much mixing of the gray with the blue at the front for him.

We together passed on toward the river. Soon we came to a line of men who were acting as guards. A man on horseback, with the cleanest uniform and the brightest sword I saw that day, rode pell-mell upon us, and in a loud voice called us cowards, cravens, and the like. He was out of reach of either bullets and cannon-shot. He ordered us to fall in with his men. We did not, but suggested to him that if he would move to the front he would find something that would take the brightness off his sword. He let us pass.

You ask me what time of day this was. I don't know. It was when Wallace fell back, sometime in the afternoon. The fight at the " Hornet's Nest " was ended.

I went to the river and drank of its waters, the first I had had for hours. Turning, I saw an army of skulkers hiding under the bank of the river—men from all commands, officers of all grades. It was a pitiable sight ; men with the fear of death upon them, some thoroughly demoralized and ready to throw themselves into the river, some wounded men, and some, thank God, ready to fight it out !

An officer whose appearance indicated he had been in the fight came and called on the huddling mass to rally and follow him. I was simple enough to do so ; why, I cannot say, unless it was my utter contempt for those great, burly creatures wearing boots and hiding in shelter out of danger, while their comrades were out yonder, breasting the storm. I went out and found Dan Clark, a member of my company, the only person I knew in all that crowd. The officer placed us on a slope of a hill, facing the

enemy. There were earthworks on the top, behind which was a battery of artillery and some siege-guns, all under the command of Colonel Webster. We lay down with our feet higher than our heads.

While waiting for the final struggle, I saw the grandest sight, except one, I witnessed during the war. It was nearing sundown ; the heroic legions of Sherman and Prentiss had practically ceased to be, Hurlburt had been shattered, McClernard was in pieces ; Wallace was mortally wounded, but his division remained invincible. The proud army of Donelson was crouching like whipped curs in a small circular line, whose two ends rested upon the Tennessee River. Thousands of men were hiding below the bluff, unable to get farther away. The enemy, terribly battered, but determined, was assured of victory. Regimental organization had disappeared ; the dead were lying out along the ridge, in the valleys, everywhere ; but with all the wreck of retreat and attack, there was within that line that unconquerable heroism afterwards shown on so many fields. The man who tells you that without Buell, Grant would have lost at Shiloh, did not see the last grand grapple on Sunday night.

I said we were placed head downwards on a hillside, with a battery or more of guns at its top. We are facing the West. Looking out through the openings, the sunshine falls bright and clear on everything. Looking to the right or left, we see battalions forming and artillery getting into position. A lull in the crash and roar of battle ; its stillness is oppressive. Look away out yonder—see the flashing, gleaming sunshine on the polished steel in front and on the flanks—it is the coming of the enemy ! In close columns by division, with flags fluttering, and its army moving *en echelon*. See how distinct every rifle-barrel, bayonet, and sabre, like the gleam of silver and shimmer of brass ! In the very front is a regiment of Zouaves. A grander sight no man ever saw than this coming of the Confederate army. We see the swinging motion noticeable when great bodies of men move together. Thus comes this human battering-ram, with artillery trailing in its ranks, presenting the appearance of a huge monster clothed in folds of flashing steel. On comes the enemy in its grand, full pride, sure of crushing the beaten, broken Army of the Tennessee, in perfect step and with arms at right-shoulder-shift, seemingly conscious of its might. With blare of band and bugle the line advances ; we see it coming and wonder if some one will raise a white flag. I load my gun and lie flat on the ground, head downward; with teeth tightly closed I await what seems our sure defeat. Behind the front line comes another, and still another. The woods are alive with them. On they come; soon their lines begin to unfold and develop; these movements are executed with exact step, and arms still at right-shoulder-shift.

I live an age in a moment. We are startled by a cannon-shot above us—a signal for more. It is answered by a blinding flash—a mighty roar. The earth trembles; something strikes me; a darkness falls about me; smoke, and leaves, and twigs, and gravel, and earth fill the air. I start up affrighted, wondering if the heavens and earth are coming together. It is the "good-evening" of Webster's great guns above us to the bold, defiant Confederate host. Artillery along the line opens, and the final struggle has begun.

No white flag there! Our cannoneers are planting their shrapnel where it will do the most harm, and it falls amid the crowded mass of the enemy, as true as if it had been carried by hand. The smoke before us lifts, and we see beneath it the lines of the enemy with great gaps torn in them, closing up and still advancing. We open upon them a line-fire, the guns behind us are still throwing case-shot, the roar deafens and the smoke blinds us for a time. Again it lifts and we see the gray line staggering under the awful fire it faces. The gunboats take up the fight, but on comes that determined line until only a corporal's guard remains. We look again. It has vanished—gone! Another pushes on, to disappear like the first. Our line is a blaze of fire —it is a volcano. It hurls defiance with its shots at the proud, splendid bravery of the enemy, who die but refuse to retreat.

The fight becomes fiendish; the enemy concentrates his fire, and brings into action every available man and gun. Arms are no longer at the right shoulder, but are being used by experienced men. The stubborn resistance of the seemingly beaten Federal army is a surprise to the legions of Beauregard, who can neither crush nor dislodge the blue. The gray line trembles, almost, as it halts, wavers for a moment, and then sullenly falls back, the few that are left firing as they go, until the supporting line is reached. Then we see real discipline in battle. The retreating line halts, closes up, reforms on its support. See how deliberate and full of action it becomes, maddened at the repulse, and burning to avenge their fallen comrades! The fiery sons of the South are again in perfect form, ready to hurl themselves with their angry impetuosity against their tired but undaunted foe. For a moment the gray line is motionless; then all at once it leaps forward with a mighty yell, and sweeps across the bloody space separating the blue from the gray. Following the yell comes a storm of leaden hail full into our faces. It is a battle of the giants. A wild cheer from our line is hurled back upon them, and shot answers shot. The roar of artillery is incessant. The crash of musketry is deafening, and the earth trembles from the concussion and shock. Watch the play on the faces of the men! The eye flashes, the face grows wild and grand, the form rounds out to its fullest limit, and the plain, dull soldier boy rises into the grandeur and glory of an Homeric god as he springs to his feet, with no thought of white flag or defeat, full of a desire to meet and destroy the coming enemy. All individuality is lost in this wild dance of death. The gray line again halts, trembles, and is gone, followed by a wild cheer that bursts from the heroic line in blue, telling in its own glad way that they are victors on that bloody field.

You may point to the skulkers that line the river bank, with a flippant expression of disdain. I answer by pointing to the heroes who met the shock of Beauregard's battalions on that Sunday night, and rolled them back in bloody rout and defeat. No braver men ever faced an enemy.

It now became apparent that the hill, bristling with batteries, could not be carried by assault, so the splendid line of the enemy moves to the right, looking for some easier point of attack. They crowd into the valley of Lick Creek, and find that the boats are still in the river, and are pouring their deadly shells into their crowded mass. I did not see that; I was engaged elsewhere.

Let me say to those who question the result of the first day at Shiloh, that in our front the enemy were beaten and driven back by Grant's army, and before the arrival of any of Buell's men. We held on until the enemy let go. It was terrible: the field strewn with dead and wounded men, broken implements of war, horses, cannons, guns, and wagons. Soon the ambulances and night came together; the sun sank on that ghastly field, leaving the two armies about even: ours driven from their camps, theirs hurled back and beaten from their last grand rally and attack. I left our shattered line and rejoined my regiment, or a portion of it, finding it in camp on the same ground where we were the night before. We went out in the morning with fully six hundred men; we had one hundred and fifty in line that night. All dead, wounded, or prisoners, you ask? No; there were enough of them dead and wounded, but many had strayed away, and came to us later. The orderly-sergeant of our company lay out there, front face to the stars; a brother and comrades were motionless and still where the storm had struck them.

The day is history's; its tragedies ended, its foemen are friends; its magnificent bravery on the one side was matched by splendid courage on the other. It was a stand-up fight on an open field for the supremacy of American manhood. On one side was the prestige of victory with the army in gray; on the other was the gloom of defeat. On that awful Sunday night the two civilizations struggled for the mastery amidst the grandest settings of war. The broad, cultured, stalwart, sturdy sons of the Northwest stood amid the wrecks that strewed the field, and beat with a Titanic hand the gallant chivalry of the South. Each found a foeman worthy of his steel.

OUR UNION.

Mrs. E. E. Brown.

L AND of our boast and pride! Home of the free!
   Proudly we own our allegiance to thee.
Thou art our birthright. Thy power and thy worth
The dearest possession we treasure in earth.
Beloved is each mountain-top, fair is each vale;
Sweet every sea-breeze that floats on the gale.
The North boasts of grandeur, the South of her bowers—
We honor no section —the country is ours.
    God of our fathers, almighty and just,
    Lord of all nations, in thee is our trust;
    Keep our loved country unspotted and bright,
    Banish the wrong and deliver the right.

Here is the wanderer's haven of rest;
Here is a home for the poor and oppressed.
Under our banner no despot is found,
Freedom and peace in our borders abound.
Our country! Oh, fonder that aught upon earth
Is the soil that we claim as the place of our birth!
Where's the kingdom or crown that could tempt us to stray
From the land that so proudly we honor to-day?
    God of our fathers, almighty and just,
    Lord of all nations, in thee is our trust!
    Keep our loved country unspotted and bright,
    Banish the wrong and deliver the right.

Say, on our soil shall a tyrant e'er stand?
Shall traitors conspire to dishonor our land?
Shall "America" ever be coupled with "shame,"
A blot ever tarnish her story of fame?
Ah, no! By the blood which our ancestors shed;
By the hallowed dust of our patriot dead,
Shall the flag of our country wave proudly o'er all;
Thus united we stand, but divided we fall.
    God of our fathers, almighty and just,
    Lord of all nations, in thee is our trust;
    Keep our loved country unspotted and bright,
    Banish the wrong and deliver the right.

THE STONEWALL BRIGADE AT BULL RUN.

D. B. Conrad, M. D.

THE CELEBRATED BRIDGE AT BULL RUN.

WHEN in May, 1861, General Joseph E. Johnston arrived at Harper's Ferry to command the unformed, disorganized mass of men and muskets there assembled, he found five Virginia regiments and two or three from Alabama and Mississippi, all in nominal control, simply by seniority, of a colonel of the "Virginia Army." Soon order grew out of chaos, and we of the Virginia Army found ourselves brigaded one May day on Bolivar Heights. Five regiments in all assembled, and were called the "Virginia Brigade"; they were the 2d, 33d, 5th, 27th, and 4th. Our senior colonel was a man who never spoke unless spoken to; never seemed to sleep; had his headquarters under a tree; the only tent used was that of his adjutant. He walked about alone, the projecting visor of his blue cap concealing his features; a bad-fitting, single-breasted blue coat, and high boots covering the largest feet ever seen; this completes his picture. Cadets from the Virginia Military Institute called him "Old Jack"; told us that he had been of the United States Army in the Mexican War and had resigned; was then chosen professor of mathematics and had mar-

ried a professor's daughter. He was as exact in the performance of his duties as a mathematical proposition; his only pleasure was walking daily, at the same hour, for his health; strict, grim, and reticent, he imagined that the halves of his body did not work and act in accord. He followed hydropathy for dyspepsia, and after a pack in wet sheets every Sunday morning, he attended the Presbyterian church, leading the choir, and the prayer-meeting every night during the week. He ate the queerest food, and he sucked lemons constantly, but where he got them during the war—for we were often many miles from a lemon—no one could find out; but he always had one. In fact, no one knew or understood him. No man ever saw him smile, and but one woman—his wife. But he stood very high in the estimation of all for rigid moral conduct and the absolute faith reposed in his word and deed. Soon it was observed that every night there was singing and praying under "that tree," and every Sunday morning and evening he held prayer-meetings, which, I regret to say, were attended by only a few; always, however, by his staff, who seem to have been chosen or elected because they were of his way of life. When thrown with him on duty he was uniformly courteous to all. He always kept his eyes half closed, as if thinking, which he invariably did before answering; but his replies were short and to the point. Not many days elapsed before the officers found out that when he gave or wrote one of his short orders it was always to be obeyed, for suspension at once followed neglect. In May many regiments arrived from Georgia, Mississippi, Alabama, and Tennessee. They were brigaded by their States, and there was some semblance of discipline, as an immense log guard-house, always well filled, gave evidence.

One Sunday morning in early June the long roll was beaten, and we soon were in line, marching out between the high hills toward Shepherdstown bridge on the upper Potomac, accompanied by a long procession of carriages, filled with our mothers and sisters, escorted by our middle-aged, portly fathers on horseback. We could not go to them, so they daily visited us in our camp, and that evening, for the first time in our lives, it looked and felt like war. For were we not on our way to keep the "Yankees" out of Virginia? Were they not in force somewhere in Maryland, intending to cross over the bridge which we were marching to defend and burn? This was the feeling and belief of all of us, and as in the narrow country road, winding around the many high hills, our long line of bright bayonets glinted in the setting sun, our five full regiments, numbering near four thousand five hundred, the brightest and most joyous of Virginia youth, stepping out quickly to the shrill music of the drum and fife, with its accompanying procession of vehicles, carrying weeping mothers and sisters. It was my first and most vivid sight of what war might be. As darkness fell apace all were left behind but the soldiers. It was our first night march, and by two o'clock we were "dead beat." Many fell asleep by the roadside, and were only aroused by the rattling of muskets as the foremost regiment fired a volley without orders and swept across the bridge, only to be sternly ordered back by "Old Jack, the Sleepless," who reprimanded its colonel, and then personally superintended the firing of the wooden structure.

During the next week we marched over several counties, and by the time we reached Winchester, where General J. E. Johnston had established his headquarters, we were in perfect physical trim, and knew each other well and felt like soldiers. In Winchester we were re-galed day and night with the speeches of "fire-eaters" and "original Secessionists."

I recall the following: I saw a crowd listening eagerly with arrested attention to an orator (he was both corpulent and crapulent) who had "just come from Washington," which was his present glory and distinction. He announced that he would redden the Potomac with the blood of every Yankee who crossed to invade the sacred soil of the South. One Southern man with a bowie-knife was the equal of any two Yankees, and the war would be over after the first fight, when they would be driven out and away forever. Another orator drew a large audience. His chief distinction and glory seemed to be that he was and had been a "Nullifier"—an original Secessionist; he had a brother fighting in Italy with Garibaldi, who he announced was expected daily, the looked-for "military Messiah!" and finally that he was a South Carolinian and came here to assist in fighting Virginia's battles. Then there were groans and derision from the assembled Virginians.

For a week, ending July 2d, we were encamped near Martinsburg, some four miles from the ford of the Potomac leading to Hagerstown, called Falling Waters, watching the Federal army under General Patterson. At sunrise the alarm was given, "The enemy is crossing!" and we were under arms on our way to the ford. Emerging on the turnpike, we were halted to support a battery; skirmishers were thrown out, and soon we were all engaged. We tried hard to hold Patterson until General Johnston could come up from Winchester, but were forced back, and here we saw Colonel Jackson under fire for the first time; stolid, imperturbable, undisturbed, and as he was watched by every eye, his example was quieting and of decided moral effect. There, for the first time, we saw the long line of blue, with the United States flag in the centre, and both sides exchanged shots—the first of the many fights in the old Valley of Virginia. We fell back through Martinsburg—it was occupied by General Patterson—and at a small hamlet called Bunker Hill, some seven miles away, we were in line of battle during the whole of July 4th, expecting Patterson hourly. The next evening we fell back upon Winchester, and, after our arrival, there happened an episode which I will relate briefly, as it was the only attempt at mutiny ever heard of in the Confederate army:

About three o'clock on the afternoon of the 17th of July the long roll was beaten, and we were marched to an adjoining field, crushing under our feet, in our haste as we moved along, the stone fences bounding it. There we found our five regiments surrounding a number of tents, and when the "hollow square" was perfect we became aware that we enclosed a battalion of troops, who had refused positively to further obey their commander, General Joe Johnston's adjutant. Colonel Whiting, with Colonel Jackson and the colonel of the refractory troops, rode up into the square; the drums were ordered to beat the assembly, and, to our infinite relief, the battalion, under the command of its several captains, fell into line at once. Then there was a dead silence; this was a mutiny. What came next? How was it to be punished? Was every tenth man to be shot, or only the officers? As I rode along I heard these questions asked by both rank and file. Colonel Whiting then rode to the front with a paper in his hand, and when he arrived at the head of the troops he read aloud, with marked emphasis, in substance as follows: That General Johnston had heard with regret and surprise that on the eve of an action both men and officers had refused to obey the orders of their commander. He could only say that it was the imperative duty of all soldiers to obey orders; that their grievances would be redressed in time, but such an example would and should not go unpunished. He therefore expected of them instant obedience of their colonel's orders; that Colonel Jackson with five regiments was there to enforce, if needed, his commands.

Their own colonel then put them through their evolutions for so many minutes, and they were ordered back to their tents and all was quiet. It seems hardly necessary to state that those were the last orders ever given by that colonel, as he was removed from the command.

All of General Johnston's army was encamped around Winchester, when, on the 18th of July, at three o'clock in the afternoon, the long roll was again sounded. From the number of mounted officers and orderlies galloping off to every encampment, it was evident that there was important news. General Patterson was known to be at Charlestown, twenty miles to the northeast, but nearer to the passes of the Blue Ridge than we were. General Beauregard was known to be at Manassas Station, far to the east, eighty miles by direct line, with the Blue Ridge and the Shenandoah River between him and us. Soon the news came; it was not an order, but simply a message from Colonel Johnston to each brigade, regiment, and individual soldier, that General Beauregard had just notified him from Manassas Junction, on that morning at daybreak, that he had been attacked by an overwhelming force of the enemy at Centreville. He was holding his own, but needed help. General Johnston had started, and would go, day and night, to his relief; and he expected every man who wanted to fight the enemy would up and follow. There is no man living of all that army to-day who can ever forget the thrill of rage which took possession of us all when the news was understood, and General Johnston's inspiring message was repeated along the line. We were to help General Beauregard drive the enemy back; then return to the Valley; would hurl General Patterson back across the Potomac and end the war. For had not Secretary Seward proclaimed that in sixty days it would be over?

Every man sprang to his place, and in an incredibly short time we were rapidly moving through the dusty streets of old Winchester, there only to be the more inspired and encouraged, for there was not a mother or sister there who had not in the ranks a son or a brother, and who, through tears and wails at being left undefended and alone, told us it was our duty to go.

Our Virginia Brigade took the lead, and to the eastward, making for Ashby's Gap. We footed it fast and furious; it was at first like a run, but soon slacked to the "route-step," and now we wondered at the old soldier's puzzle: Why is it when the leading files of a mile of soldiers are only in a walk, that the rear files are always on a run? As we passed through the rich and fertile Clark County, the road was lined with ladies holding all manner of food and drink, for General Johnston's staff had passed at a sweeping gallop an hour before, giving tidings of our coming. At sundown we came to the cool, swift Shenandoah, and with two and three to every horse, the rest stripped of trousers, crossed, holding aloft on muskets and heads our clothing and ammunition. This was the severe test, for it was a long struggle against a cold, breast-high current, and the whole night and next day witnessed this fording of men, guns, and horses. I did not see my mare for two days; nearly a dozen cousins and brothers or other relatives had to use her in the crossing. Luckily, the road beyond was hard, dry, and plain in the dark night as we slowly climbed the Blue Ridge, which rises precipitously from the river, and in a straggling line passed by the big

BATTLE OF BULL RUN, JULY 21, 1861.
From a well-known painting.

poplar tree that crowns the summit and is the corner of four counties—Clark, Warren, Fauquier, and Loudoun.

Coming down the mountain by the hamlet of Paris, and there leaving the "pike," we took the country road, soft and damp, to the railroad station of Piedmont, where, sleeping on the ground, we awaited the arrival of the train to carry us to Manassas Junction. At sunrise it came; a long train of freight and cattle-cars, in which we packed ourselves like so many pins and needles, and as safely, for the engines and cars were more precious than speed, since we had only one engine on that part of the old Manassas Gap Railroad. We slowly jolted the entire day past the many country stations, warmly welcomed by the gathered crowds of women and girls with food and drink; and when, at sunset, we arrived at Manassas Junction, we sprang at once into line and swept out into a broken country of pine forest. Four miles brought us to the banks of Bull Run, where we slept. That was Friday night, the 19th, and it had taken twenty-four hours to bring four thousand men to the expected field of action.

Bright and early on Sunday, the 20th, we were up and examining, with a soldier's interest, the scene of conflict of the 18th. A line of fresh graves was rather depressing; the trees were lopped and mangled by shot and perforated by minié balls; the short, dry grass showing in very many spots a dark, chocolate hue, spreading irregularly like a map, which the next day became too familiar sight. We could not make anything out of the fight except that here was the ford and here they came down to cross in force. They were simply repulsed from the ford; there was no pursuit, the artillery remaining on the hills beyond, and it was agreed that here, any day now, we were to fight against a direct assault. The enemy's object, we supposed, was to get to Manassas Junction, murder every one there, and destroy buildings and stores. The art of war was so simple and so well understood by all in those early days of the war that the opinions of high up college graduates and successful lawyers were even sought for; and in all cases, I must do them the justice to say, were given with the utmost freedom and liberality. Every man who had been in the Mexican war, or had seen fighting abroad, was a colonel or a brigadier at once, and they swelled and swaggered around, disposing willing information of tactics and grand strategy in the most profuse and generous way to a listening and absorbent crowd.

The whole of Saturday, the 20th, we lay in the pines resting and surmising, greeting each new regiment as it arrived at all hours of the day and night, fresh, eager, and panting for the fight. The general questions asked were: "Had the fighting begun yet?" "Are we too late?" "When is it to be? Let us get some place where we can kill every Yankee, and then go home." Not a sound or shot disturbed the quiet of that long Saturday, and we slept peacefully in the pines that night. As the next day (Sunday, the 21st) broke, we were jumped out of our lairs by the loudest gun I have ever heard, fired right at our heads, as we supposed, and from just over the bank of Bull Run, only a hundred yards distant. But it proved to be the single gun from Centreville, four miles away, in the encampment of General McDowell. At the double quick we were in line along the bank of the stream, momentarily expecting the enemy to appear and open on us; and thus we waited until the sun got over the tops of the trees, when a mounted officer rode up, and, after a hurried interview with Colonel Jackson, we were, to our surprise, wheeled to the rear, and at double quick, over the fields and through the woods, we went to the extreme left of our army. It then turned out that at the same day and hour, General McDowell had decided to attack us on our left, and General Beauregard had decided to attack the Federals on their left, so, had it not been discovered in time by the Confederates, each army would have followed the other in concentric circles.

GENERAL S. P. HEINTZELMAN, U. S. A.

Born at Manheim, Pa., September 30, 1805. Graduated from West Point in 1826. Served with distinction in Florida and Mexico, and through the Civil War. Died at Washington, May 1, 1880.

For two long, hot hours did we move toward the rattling of musketry, which at first was very faint, then became more and more audible. At last we halted under a long ridge covered with small pines. Here were the wounded of that corps who had been first engaged; men limping on gun or stick; men carried off in blankets, bleeding their life away; men supported on each side by soldiers; and they gave us no very encouraging news to new troops as we were. They had been at it ever since sunrise. The enemy were as thick as wheat in the field, and the long lines of blue could not be counted. Up the narrow lane our brigade started, directly to where the musketry seemed the loudest, our regiment, the 2d, bringing up the rear. Reaching the top, a wide clearing was discovered; a broad table-land spread out, the pine thicket ceased, and far away over the hill in front was the smoke of musketry; at the bottom of the long declivity was the famous turnpike, and on the

hills beyond could be seen clearly Griffin's and Ricketts's batteries. In their front, to their rear, and supported on each side, were long lines of blue. To our right, about one hundred yards off, was a small building, the celebrated "Henry House."

As ours was the last regiment to come up, and as the brigade, as it surmounted the hill, wheeled into line sharply to the left into the thickets, we were thus thrown to the extreme right of the line and of the entire army. Halting there and mounted on a gate-post, I could see the panorama spread out before me; the brass pieces of Griffin's and Ricketts's batteries were seen wheeling into line, caissons to the rear, the horses detached and disappearing behind the hill. The glinting of the morning sun on the burnished metal made them very conspicuous. No cavalry were seen. I do not think that McDowell had any in action that day. Both batteries soon opened on us with shell, but no casualties resulted, for the reason that in their haste and want of drill none of the time-fuses were cut. I picked up many which fell into the ground with a dull sound, and found that to be the reason they did not explode.

The infantry was engaged on the side of the long, gradual slope of the hill on which we stood, and in the bottom below, out of our sight, we could hear the sound and see the white smoke. At this time there rode up fast toward us from the front a horse and rider, gradually rising to

A SOLDIER'S DREAM.

our view from the bottom of the hill. He was an officer, all alone, and as he came closer, erect and full of fire, his jet-black eyes and long hair, and blue uniform of a general officer made him the cynosure of all. In a strong, decided tone he inquired of the nearest aide what troops we were and who commanded. He was told that Colonel Jackson, with five Virginia regiments, had just arrived, pointing to where the colonel stood at the same time. The strange officer then advanced, and we of the regimental staff crowded to where he was to hear the news from the front. He announced himself as General B. S. Bee, commanding South Carolina troops. "We have been heavily engaged all the morning, and, being overpowered, we are now being slowly pushed back. We will fall back on you as a support; the enemy will make their appearance in a short time over the crest of that hill." "Then, sir, we will give them the bayonet," was the only reply of Colonel Jackson. With a salute, General Bee wheeled his horse and disappeared down the hill, where he immortalized himself, General Jackson, and his troops by his memorable words to his own command: "Close up, men, and stand your ground. Colonel Jackson, with five regiments of Virginia troops, is standing behind us like a stone-wall, and will support you."

Thus was the name of "Stonewall" given to General Jackson and his famous brigade. General Bee was killed the next moment.

Our entire line lay in the pine thickets for one long hour, and no man, unless he was there, can tell how very long it was to us. Under fire from the two batteries, throwing time shells only, they did not do a great amount of killing, but it was terribly demoralizing. Then there was a welcome cessation, and we were wondering why and when the fighting would begin for us. After nearly half an hour the roar of the field-pieces sounded louder than I had yet heard, and evidently very near. This was the much-criticised movement of Ricketts, who had ordered his battery down the opposite hill, across the pike, and up the hill we were on, where, wheeling into battery on the level top, opened with grape and canister right into the thicket and into our exposed line. This was more than Colonel Jackson could stand, and the general order was: "Charge and take that battery!" Now the fight of Manassas, or Bull Run, began in earnest, for the position we held was the key of the field. Three times did our regiment charge up to and take this battery, but never held it; for though we drove the regiment supporting it, yet another was always close behind to take its place. A gray-haired man, sitting sideways on horseback, whom I understand

stood to be General Heintzelman, was ever in one spot, directed the movements of each regiment as it came up the hill, and his coolness and gallantry won our admiration. Many fragments of these regiments charged on us in turn as we retreated into the pines, only to be killed, for I do not think any of them went back alive. The green pines were filled with the 79th Highlanders and the red-breeched Brooklyn Zouaves, but the only men that were killed twenty or thirty yards behind and in the rear of our line were the United States Marines. Many of these I sailed with, and they called on me by name to help them as they lay wounded in the undergrowth. "Water! water!" "Turn me over!" "Raise my head!" and "Pull me out of this fire!" were their cries. I then saw what was afterward too often the case—men with wounded legs (unable to move out of the fire) mortally wounded while lying helpless!

Our entire brigade thus fought unaided and alone for at least an hour, charging, capturing, retreating, and retaking this battery, resisting the charges of each fresh regiment as it came forward at quick-step up the slope of the hill, across the table-land at its top, and into the pine thickets where we were, until we were as completely broken up into fragments and as hard pressed as men ever were. It had gotten down to mere hand-to-hand fighting of small squads out in the open and in the pines. There was no relief, no reinforcements, no fresh troops to come or to fall back upon. Luckily for us, the enemy was in the same disorganized condition as we were.

General Johnston seized the colors of a regiment and on horseback led a charge, excusing it afterward as necessary at that moment to make a personal example. Our Colonel Jackson, with only two aides, Colonels Jones and Marshall (both subsequently killed), rode slowly and without the slightest hurrah frequently along our front, encouraging us by his quiet presence. He held aloft his left, or bridle-hand, looking as if he were invoking a blessing, but in fact to ease the intense pain caused by a bullet-wound that had badly shattered two of his fingers. He never alluded to this injury, and it has been forgotten. It was the only time he was ever wounded until his fall in action in 1863.

Thus the fate of the field hung in the balance at 3.30 P.M. At this moment Mr. Davis and his staff made their appearance on the field, but not being known attracted no attention. Both sides were exhausted and ready to say,

"Enough!" The critical moment which comes in all actions had arrived, when we saw to our left a cloud of dust, and out of it emerged a straggling line of men with guns held at a "trail." Slowly they came onto the field, not from want of spirit, but tired out by double-quicking in the heat and dust. As they passed through and by our squads there were hurried inquiries; the enemy were pointed out to them, and, when seen, from out their dusty and parched throats came the first "rebel yell." It was a fierce, wild cry, perfectly involuntary, caused by the emotion of catching first sight of the enemy. These new troops were Kirby Smith's delayed men; the train had that morning broken down, but on arriving at the station near, and hearing the sound of the fighting, he had ordered the train stopped and, forming in line and rapidly marching, guided only by the roar of the guns, had arrived on the field at the supreme moment.

The "yell" attracted the attention of the enemy, surprised and startled their lines. Inspired by the sight of the Federals, the new Confederate troops, in one long line, with a volley and another yell, swept down the slope of our hill and drove before them the tired, broken enemy who had been at it since sunrise. Kirby Smith was shot from his horse, but onward they went, irresistible, for there was no opposition. The enemy stood for a few moments, firing, then turned their backs for the first time. As if by magic the whole appearance of the field was changed. One side was cheering and pursuing in broken, irregular lines; the other a slow moving mass of "blue-backs" and legs. Guns,

caissons, and ammunition wagons swept down the hard, white pike. Our batteries, with renewed vigor and dash, had again come to the front, and from their high positions were opening with shot and grape.

One solitary bridge was the point to which the fleeing Federals converged, and on that point was our fire concentrated. The result was at once seen: a wheel or two knocked off a caisson or wagon blocked the passage, and the bridge became impassable. The men cut loose their horses, mounted and rode away; others plunged into the mud and water, and the retreat became from that moment a panic, for the god Pan had struck them hard for the first and last time. There was never again the like to be seen in the subsequent four years of the war.

Our pursuit, singularly, was by artillery, our infantry having become incapable of further motion from sheer exhaustion. Stuart had only a few companies of cavalry out of his one regiment on the field, but they did good work in keeping up the rout until late in the night, when they were brought to a standstill at Centreville, where there was a reserve brigade that had not been in action.

So ended the part taken by the "Stonewall" Brigade in this their first fight. I may add here that our regiment was not gathered together for four days, and the brigade not for one week. We, as well as the rest of our victorious army, were as much disorganized and scattered by our victory as the Federals by their defeat, and pursuit by us would have been simply a physical impossibility.

MENDING THE OLD FLAG.*

IN the silent gloom of a garret room,
  With cobwebs around it creeping,
From day to day the old flag lay
  A veteran worn and sleeping.
Dingily old, each wrinkled fold
  By the dust of years was shaded ;
Wounds of the storm were upon its form,
  The crimson stripes were faded.

Three Northern maids and three from glades
  Where dreams the Southland weather,
With glances kind and arms entwined
  Came up the stairs together ;
They gazed awhile with a thoughtful smile
  At the crouching form before them ;
With clinging hold they grasped its folds,
  And out of the darkness bore them.

They healed its scars, they found its stars,
  And brought them altogether
(Three Northern maids and three from glades
  Where smiles the Southland weather) ;
They mended away through the summer day,
  Made glad by an inspiration
To fling it high at the smiling sky
  On the birthday of our nation.

In the brilliant glare of the summer air,
  With a brisk breeze round it creeping,
Newly bright with a glistening light
  The flag went grandly sweeping ;
Gleaming and bold were its braids of gold,
  And flashed in the sun-rays' kissing ;
Red, white and blue were of deepest hue.
  And none of its stars were missing.

*Recited by General J. B. Metcalf, C. S. A., at " Blue and Gray " Reunion, at Seattle, October 30, 1894.

HOW NORTH CAROLINA WENT INTO THE WAR.

Colonel H. C. Graham.

ONLY those who lived in the stirring days of '61 can form the faintest idea of the intense excitement that prevailed throughout the land at that period, or of the frenzy of military spirit that manifested itself.

North Carolina was regarded as one of the most conservative of the Southern States; indeed, it was the fashion among her more fiery sisters south of her to characterize the State as a "Rip Van Winkle," to illustrate its slowness of action. It would have been more appropriate

the heaviest during the war, promptly responded: "I always found more dead North Carolinians on the Virginia battle-fields than from any other State." This statement from the distinguished general, himself a Georgian, who had such abundant opportunity for observation, is borne out by the official records of the United States government, published in its great history of the struggle, compiled from the archives of the Federal and Confederate War Departments, and which has now reached its eightieth volume. There was not much Rip Van Winkle-

MARKET SCENE IN A CAROLINA COUNTY SEAT.

to have likened the "Old North State" to a sleeping lioness, for when once aroused she knew no end to her efforts, manifested by the endurance and bravery of her heroic sons, who went to the front until the State had sent over 170,000 soldiers to Lee's army; and there was not a battle-field in Virginia where the "Tar Heels" were not buried by the hundreds and thousands.

General James Longstreet, next to Lee and Jackson the most prominent general in the Confederate army and one of the most stubborn fighters and thorough soldiers ever produced by any country, when recently interviewed by a newspaper correspondent as to which State lost

ism about this business, but it was characteristic of the State—slow to move until convinced, but a fight to the finish when she entered in earnest into the combat.

Secession was not popular in North Carolina. The State was loath to pass an ordinance of separation; so reluctant, in fact, that a proposition, submitted to the voters of the State, whether a convention should be called to consider the question of secession at all, was voted down. But the war spirit grew apace.

After the secession of South Carolina, which took place in December, 1860, the military spirit began to manifest itself in earnest, and a number of new companies were organized on a really military basis.

The old military organizations of the State might, with truth, up to this period have fairly been entitled to the sobriquet of "holiday soldiers," for their principal labors had consisted of an occasional target-shoot, picnic, or Fourth of July jubilee, when each private was encumbered with a gold-laced, aiguleted, and epauleted uniform, and plumes that would have done credit to a field marshal of France in the days of the Napoleonic Empire, and where profuse perspiration was the certain torture inflicted on the warriors that wore them. At these military junketings nearly every man in the company was accompanied by a negro servant, bearing hampers of refreshments, the liquid portion of which at the target-shoots was, perhaps, responsible for the wretched marksmanship, which, with the old smooth-bore musket, rarely came, by accident, within three feet of the "bull's-eye." Heigh-ho! but those were happy times. Different days, however, were soon to dawn on the peaceful "Old North State." The black clouds of war were rapidly gathering on the political horizon, and the distant mutterings of the thunder gave token of the terrific storm that was to follow.

I bear in mind, at this moment, the appearance of the Warren County Guards as they came into the first camp of instruction at Raleigh. This county (Warren), by the way, was named after the grand Revolutionary hero, of Boston, who laid down his life at Bunker Hill, and it was one of the most aristocratic counties in the State, thoroughly permeated with old English ideas and customs.

When this company arrived in Raleigh and came into the camp (which was commanded by D. H. Hill, brother-in-law of Stonewall Jackson and afterward one of the ablest lieutenant-generals in the Confederate army), it came with a train of wagons that would have sufficed, a few years later on, to transport the baggage of Stonewall Jackson's corps, and the quality of the baggage was remarkable. There were banjoes, guitars, violins, huge camp chests, bedsteads, and other material startling in amount and unique as to quality, while the soldiers, a number of them large landed proprietors, were uniformed in a style of magnificence, as to gold lace, plumes, and epaulets, that would have required the genius of Sir Walter Scott to describe with proper effect. There was something really pathetic in the nonchalance and *naivete* exhibited by these Warren cavaliers, who could see no incongruity between camp life and the luxuries of home.

But gallant heroes they proved themselves to be, for they formed part of the celebrated First Regiment of North Carolina Volunteers, commanded by D. H. Hill, which fought and won the first battle of the Confederacy at Bethel, near historic Yorktown, where the gallant Major Winthrop, of Boston, fell—probably the first Federal officer killed in the war—and where the first Confederate killed in battle—Wyatt, of Edgecombe County, North Carolina—gave up his life, and in honor of whose memory there now hangs a life-size portrait in the library of the beautiful Capitol at Raleigh.

These same fine Warren County soldiers soon learned the sad realities of war and nobly performed their duty. The handsome gold-laced uniforms were soon exchanged for the regulation gray blouse. The bodies of many of them were placed beneath the sod on Virginia battle-fields, and the little remnant came back to the old homesteads in rags from Appomattox, to fight bravely the battle of life under the new *regime*.

Governor John W. Ellis, of Rowan County, was North Carolina's distinguished war executive, one of the ablest men who ever occupied the gubernatorial chair and who was confronted with the gravest issues that had ever presented themselves for the consideration of a chief magistrate of the State. He was a States Rights Democrat of the old school, was exceedingly popular with his party, and was serving his second term when the Civil War commenced.

While Governor Ellis was naturally in deep sympathy with his Democratic *confrères* in the far Southern States, yet neither by word nor deed did he compromise North Carolina beyond the law and the expressed will of the people on the secession question. On one occasion, when a number of over-zealous soldiers took possession of Fort Johnson, at Wilmington, he immediately ordered them to evacuate the fort and turn it back to the United States government, and this, too, at a time when the war spirit had commenced to boil over.

It was not until President Lincoln's proclamation, calling for 75,000 troops and on North Carolina for her quota, that the people of the State became a unit and her secession a certainty. Governor Ellis declined to furnish the quota. Relations with Washington were immediately broken up. Never was there such a transformation of political sentiment wrought

in so short a time. Raleigh, the capital of
the State, where strong Union sentiment prevailed and where the Stars and Stripes were
conspicuously displayed before the proclamation,
was instantly metamorphosed.

The writer of this article was, at the time of
the intense excitement, a student in the senior
class at the University of North Carolina at
Chapel Hill. There were over 600 students
at "The Hill," from all parts of the South,
and a military company had been formed
there, known as the "University Blues," who
promptly offered their services to the Governor,
but they were declined because, as *ex-officio*
head of the University, he deemed it unwise to
take any action that would disorganize this
time-honored institution of learning. But the
inevitable was near at hand.

Ex-Governor David B. Swain was at this time
the president of the University—"Bunc," as
he had been affectionately known by the students for years, so styled because he was from
the celebrated Buncombe County, of North
Carolina, which was also the home of the late
lamented Senator Zebulon B. Vance. He had
been twice Governor of the State, was the intimate friend of many of the most distinguished
historic characters of the country, and the University made wonderful progress under his
administration. He was a man filled with the
milk of human kindness, dearly loved by the
young men under his guidance, and every one
of whom, surviving to-day, reveres his memory.
The old man dearly loved his country, mourned
deeply over the disruption that took place, with
tears in his eyes witnessed the departure of the
ninety-five members of the senior class before
the commencement, and sent them their diplo-
mas in camp.

The writer was a member of an artillery company in Raleigh, in which he had been enrolled
a short time before President Lincoln's proclamation. Immediately after the proclamation a
military camp of instruction was ordered at
Raleigh, and a State Convention assembled.
The writer received an order from his commanding officer to report at the camp, and responded thereto.

What a wonderful change had come over the
"Old North State"! Arriving at Durham,
twelve miles from the University, then a mere
station on the Central North Carolina Railroad,
but now a thriving city, the writer awaited the
arrival of the train. When it came in sight it
was decorated with the then Confederate colors,

MAJOR WINTHROP, U. S. A. (KILLED AT BETHEL).

the three bars and stars, from the engine to the
rearmost car, and had three military companies
on board. The first sight that greeted us, as we
came in sight of Raleigh, was the Confederate
flag flying from the dome of the Capitol. Many
of the citizens wore the red cockade, the old
Revolutionary symbol of the State, and the city
was alive and active with military preparation.

The Convention soon assembled, composed of
the best material of the State, with Hon. Weldon
N. Edwards, of Warren County, as its president.
This body at the Capitol, with the military camp
established at the Fair Grounds of the North
Carolina Agricultural Association, were the two
great points of attraction, while the city was
crowded with visitors from all parts of the
South. The camp bore off the palm for its
large and constant flow of visitors. There
were nearly 2,000 infantry in the camp, with
Ramseur's superb artillery company. This
company, when completed, numbered over
120 stalwart men. It had been raised in
Raleigh, and many of its members were
prominent society young men. To it was
given the only complete battery in the State,
which had been captured with the Fayetteville
arsenal. It was entirely new, consisting of six
brass field-pieces, four six-pounders, and two
howitzers, and when fully equipped had six
matched horses to each gun, caisson, the battery
wagon and forge, and it was one of the finest
batteries in Lee's army. Its commander, Captain David Ramseur, had just resigned his commission as a first lieutenant of artillery in the
United States army. His ancestors were of

Revolutionary fame in Western Carolina. He afterward became a distinguished major-general in Lee's army, and was killed in the valley of Virginia.

The battery was afterward known as "Manley's," being commanded by Captain Basil Manley, afterward major, a son of an ex-governor of the State, and, after the surrender, mayor of Raleigh. One of the sad duties of the battery, before it left for Virginia, was to take part in the funeral pageant of Governor Ellis, in Raleigh. The Governor, broken down by his arduous duties, went to the Red Sulphur Springs, in Virginia, to recuperate his health, and there died. His remains were brought to Raleigh and interred with imposing military honors. There were also two regiments of infantry in the procession (on their way to Virginia), one of them, the 6th, commanded by Colonel Charles Fisher, who, a few weeks afterward, lost his life at the battle of Manassas.

Governor Ellis was succeeded by Governor Clarke, of Edgecombe County, who took the gubernatorial chair by virtue of his office as president of the State Senate.

The camp of instruction presented special attractions. The Raleigh ladies, always noted for their beauty and accomplishments, were strongly reinforced by numbers of fair visitors from other portions of the State and from the South, and every afternoon, at dress parade, a long line of carriages, filled with fair occupants, were in attendance to witness the ceremonial. A fine band of musicians was in the camp, which added greatly to its attractiveness.

Finally the day came when the ordinance of secession was to be passed. The whole city was early astir. A great crowd gathered in the Capitol grounds. Ramseur's battery was ordered down from the camp, to fire a salute of 100 guns in honor of the event, and a fine military band was stationed in front of the Capitol to add inspiration and *eclat* to the occasion.

The hall of the House of Representatives, where the Convention was held, was crowded to overflowing, and as each member affixed his name to the ordinance, he was loudly applauded. Outside, on the Capitol grounds, the crowd was so great it overflowed in every direction, and sentries marched beside the artillery to maintain sufficient space for working the guns.

It had been arranged that a handkerchief should be waved from a window of the convention hall when the last signature was placed to the ordinance of secession, as a signal to the artillery. Captain Ramseur and his officers and men stood by, their guns ready, and when the bit of embroidered cambric, in the hands of a fair daughter of the State, waved the signal, the guns thundered their salute as rapidly as they could be loaded and fired by the well-drilled artillerymen. And let me tell you they were good ones. If you have never listened to the music of a full battery, well served, you can form but little idea of the racket it makes. At the moment the salute commenced, every bell in the city rang out, and the band struck up North Carolina's inspiring anthem, "The Old North State":

> Carolina, Carolina,
> Heaven's blessings attend her;
> While we live we will cherish,
> Protect, and defend her.
> Hurrah! Hurrah!
> For the Old North State forever.
> Hurrah! Hurrah!
> For the good Old North State.

This martial hymn was composed by the great Gaston, one of North Carolina's most distinguished and beloved sons, and the music is most inspiring. It was, and is to-day, the Marseillaise of the State, and has a power to arouse to the highest pitch of enthusiasm the heart of every true son of the "Old North State," whenever and wherever he hears its inspiring strains. It is related that on one occasion in Virginia, at night, after a bloody conflict, when the armies were resting on their arms, preparatory to renewing the battle next morning, a band of one of the North Carolina regiments struck up this anthem of the State. There were a large number of North Carolina regiments that had participated in the battle bivouacking along the line, and as far as the strains of music could reach them cheers went up that made the welkin ring.

When that memorable event in the history of North Carolina which I have attempted to describe took place, amidst the thunder of the cannon, the ringing of bells, and the inspiring music, the assembled multitude went wild. Old men rushed into each other's arms; young men, soldiers, and civilians yelled themselves hoarse, and all sorts of extravagances were indulged in.

And so the momentous deed was accomplished. Then came the serious duties and sad realities of the great conflict. The First Regiment of volunteers left us for Virginia, with band playing, colors flying, and handkerchiefs from fair hands waving adieu. The regiment left in the early morning, about seven o'clock, and notwithstanding the early hour, all Raleigh was on the *qui vive* to give a grand send-off to the first soldiers to leave the State for the seat of war in Virginia. At the head of the regiment rode D. H. Hill, as its colonel. Charles C. Lee was the lieutenant-colonel, afterward colonel of the 37th North Carolina Infantry. He was killed the day before the battle of Malvern Hill, in the seven days' battles of Richmond. James H. Lane was major of the regiment. Major Lane was afterward colonel of the 28th North Carolina Infantry, and after that one of the most gallant and distinguished brigadier-generals in Lee's army. He is now professor of civil engineering at the Agricultural and Mechanical College, at Auburn, Alabama.

When the first volunteers marched down Fayetteville Street, the principal avenue of Raleigh, on their way to the cars, to the lively strains of "The Girl I Left Behind Me" and "Dixie," amid the waving of handkerchiefs by the ladies and the cheers of the men who lined the sidewalks, the scene can be more readily imagined than described, if I may use the trite saying in recording what was indeed a most inspiring sight.

But it was not long before the glamour and novelty of first military experiences passed away, and the stern realities of the great tragedy faced the Confederacy. North Carolina's legions were poured rapidly into Virginia. Several camps of instruction were established, and from these went forth regiment after regiment, well drilled and equipped. Excellent service was rendered in these camps by West Point cadets, who had resigned and come home, and by the cadets of the Virginia Military Institute, which was looked upon as the leading Southern military academy. These young officers drilled the raw recruits, and did their work well. Many of them reached high rank in the army afterward. It was found that their services could be dispensed with as mere drill masters, for "Hardee's Tactics" soon became as familiar as Webster's spelling book in every branch of the service.

Nearly all of North Carolina's troops were sent to Virginia, and formed part of Lee's Army. From Bethel to Appomattox they participated in every important battle, and their losses were enormous. Take, for instance, those of Branch's brigade of A. P. Hill's "The Light Division," in the seven days' battles around Richmond, as shown by the official records. This brigade was commanded by General S. O. B. Branch, who was afterward killed at Sharpsburg (Antietam), and it was composed of North Carolina regiments, with Captain Marmaduke Johnson's Virginia battery attached, for at this time the artillery had not been placed in a separate corps, but each brigade carried its own battery.

The 7th Regiment, in which the writer was serving as a lieutenant (and he may as well state here, was wounded at Gaines' Mill, where the two other officers of his company were killed, and which regiment was commanded by Colonel Haywood, after the fall of Colonel Campbell, who was also killed at Gaines' Mill), in its official returns, shows that out of 450 officers and men carried into action, 253 were killed and wounded. (See Government Records, Vol. XI., page 890.)

These same records show that Colonel Cowan's regiment, the 18th, lost sixty-eight killed and wounded; the 28th, Colonel Lane's, ninety-one; the 33d, Colonel Hoke's, seventy-five; Colonel Barbour's, the 37th, who took command after Colonel Lee was killed, 138. Captain Johnson's battery lost twenty killed and wounded and ten horses.

At Gettysburg the losses were frightful to the North Carolina troops, and so on every battlefield they laid down their lives by the score.

But the end came at last, and the battered fragment came back to the old home in their ragged jackets and with ruined fortunes, ready to commence bravely anew the battles of civil life. And what a splendid record they have made! Look at the "Old North State" to-day, with its constantly increasing population and growth in manufacturing, mining, and agricultural development, largely brought about by its old Confederate soldiers, and say if these brave followers of Lee and Jackson are not worthy of their Anglo-Saxon lineage and of the name of Americans.

TO THE MEMORY OF GENERAL ROBERT E. LEE.

LET glory's wreath rest on the warrior's tomb,
  Let monumental shaft surmount his grave,
For all the world yields homage to the brave,
And heroes dead have vanquished ev'ry foe.
The earth is strewn with storied slabs which tell
That manliness is born of every clime.
Each sword is drawn to guard a seeming right,
Each blow is struck to crush a fancied wrong ;
For war proclaims sincere consistency,
And victory but seals just heaven's decree.
O Western World, what noble men are thine,
How brave their hearts, how steadfast to the end !
The pride of empire is of valor born,
The soldier shapes the destiny of man.
Look, then, ye tyrant kings that rule by fear !
Behold, ye nations of the earth !   Our sons
Are warriors born: Lee was our son ; he sleeps—
Our son, a soldier, an American.

—Geo. M. Vickers.

This poem was forwarded to the Lee Monument Association by General Buckner, in the following letter :—

FRANKFORT, KY., May 15, 1890.
To President Lee Monument Association, Richmond, Va.

DEAR SIR:—I enclose a communication from Mr. Geo. M Vickers, of Philadelphia, who was a soldier in the U. S. Army during the Civil War, transmitting a poem written by himself in honor of the memory of our greatest Southern leader It was my purpose to have handed this poem to you in person, if I had been able to be present on the occasion of the unveiling of the statue of General Lee.

As official engagements will probably preclude the possibility of my attendance, I do not feel at liberty longer to withhold from you a literary production which does honor alike to the memory of the great American soldier and to the patriotism of the writer of the poem.

Respectfully,   S. B. BUCKNER.

A BOY AT SHILOH.

JOHN A. COCKERILL.

SHILOH CHURCH, Sunday morning, April 6, 1862. Here is a date and a locality indelibly burned into my memory. At sixteen years of age, I found myself an enlisted fourth-class musician in the 24th Ohio Regiment, in which my elder brother was a first lieutenant, and afterward captain and colonel.

I had campaigned in Western Virginia, and had seen some of the terrors and horrors of war at Phillippi and Rich Mountain, and some of its actualities in a winter campaign in the Cheat Mountain district. During the winter of 1861, my command was sent to Louisville, Ky., where General Buell was organizing his splendid army of the Ohio for active operations against Bowling Green and Nashville. My regiment was assigned to General Nelson's command, and the early spring found us on the left flank of the army, on the north side of the Green River. With unexpected suddenness, Nelson's division was one day in March sent hurriedly back to the Ohio River, where it was placed on transports and headed for the Cumberland River, to participate in Grant's movement against Fort Donelson. Before reaching that point, intelligence was received of the capture of that stronghold, and our flotilla proceeded to Paducah, Ky. At that point, General W. T. Sherman was organizing his recruits from Ohio, Indiana, and Illinois, for the forward movement up the Tennessee River. I had been taken ill on board the steamer *en route*, and my father, who at that time commanded the 70th Ohio Regiment, stationed at Paducah, found me and took me in his personal charge. Two days later, my regiment sailed up the Cumberland river, and was with the brigade first to enter Nashville. When I reached the convalescent stage, I asked permission to rejoin my command, but General Sherman said that the armies of Grant and Buell would form a coalition some-

363

where up the Tennessee River, and I might as well remain where I was, for the reason that my father could give me better care in my feeble state than I could have with my own command.

Thus it happened that I was with the army of General Sherman when it felt its way up the turbid Tennessee River as far as Pittsburg Landing, and so it happened that I was at Shiloh Church on the morning of that terrible onslaught by General Johnston's army upon Sherman's division, which held the advance of Grant's army operating against Corinth.

I have often wondered what sort of soldier in blue I must have appeared at that time. I can remember myself as a tall, pale, hatchet-faced boy, who could never find in the quartermaster's department a blouse or a pair of trousers small enough for him, nor an overcoat cast on his lines. The regulation blue trousers I used to cut off at the bottoms, and the regulation overcoat sleeves were always rolled up, which gave them the appearance of having extra military cuffs, and that was one consolation to me.

The headquarters mess of the 70th Regiment had finished its early breakfast, and I had just taken my place at the table on Sunday morning, 6th of April, when I heard ominous shots along our adjacent picket lines. In less than ten minutes, there was volley firing directly in our front, and from my knowledge of campaigning I knew that a battle was on, though fifteen minutes before, I had no idea that any considerable force of the enemy was in the immediate front of our cantonment. The 70th Regiment and the brigade to which I was attached, commanded by Colonel Buckland, of Ohio, formed on its color lines under fire, and, although composed of entirely new troops, made a splendid stand. At the first alarm, I dropped my knife and fork and ran to my father's tent, to find him buckling on his sword. My first heroic act was to gather up a beautiful Enfield rifle, which he had saved at the distribution of arms to his regiment, because of its beautiful, curly, maple stock. I had been carrying it myself on one or two of the regimental expeditions to the front, and had some twenty rounds of cartridges in a box which I had borrowed from one of the boys of Company I. By the time I had adjusted my cartridge-box and seized my rifle, my father was mounted outside, and, with a hurried good-bye, he took his place with the regiment. By this time, the bullets were whistling through the camp, and shells were bursting overhead.

Not exactly clear in my mind what I intended to do, I ran across to the old log Shiloh Church, which stood on the flank of my father's regiment. On my right, the battle was raging with great ferocity; and stretching away to my left and front, one of the most beautiful pageants I have ever beheld in war was being presented. In the very midst of the thick wood and rank undergrowth of the locality, was what is known as a "deadening"—a vast, open, unfenced district, grown up with rank, dry grass, dotted here and there with blasted trees, as though some farmer had determined to clear a farm for himself and had abandoned the undertaking in disgust. From out the edge of this great opening, came regiment after regiment and brigade after brigade of the Confederate troops. The sun was just rising in their front, and the glittering of their arms and equipments made a gorgeous spectacle for me. On the farther edge of this opening, two brigades of Sherman's command were drawn up to receive the onslaught. As the Confederates, marching regimental front *en echelon*, sprung into this field, they poured out their deadly fire, and, half obscured by their smoke, they advanced as they fired. My position behind the old log church was a good one for observation. I had just seen General Sherman and his staff pushing across to the Buckland brigade. The splendid soldier, erect in his saddle, his eye bent forward, looked a veritable war eagle, and I knew history was being made in that immediate neighborhood. Just then a German field battery from Illinois, which had been cantoned a short distance in the rear, came galloping up with six guns and unlimbered three of them between the Shiloh Church and the left flank of the 70th Ohio Regiment. This evolution was gallantly performed. The first shot from this battery, directed against the enemy on the right opposite, drew the fire of a Confederate battery, and the old log church came in for a share of its compliments. This duel had not lasted more than ten minutes when a Confederate shell struck a caisson in our battery, and an explosion took place, which made things in that spot exceedingly uncomfortable. The captain was killed, and his lieutenant, thinking that he had done his duty, and, doubtless, satisfied in his own mind that the war was over so far as he was concerned, limbered up his remaining pieces, and, with such horses as he had, galloped to the rear, and was not seen at any other time, I believe, during the two days' engagement.

By this time, the enemy was pressing closely on my left flank, and Shiloh Church, with its ancient logs, was no more a desirable place for military observation. I hurried over to the headquarters of the 70th Ohio Regiment, taking advantage of such friendly trees as presented themselves on the line of my movement, and there found a state of disorder. The tents were pretty well ripped with shell and bullets, and wounded men were being carried past me to the rear. As I stood there, debating in my mind whether to join my father's command or continue my independent action, three men approached, carrying a sorely wounded officer in a blanket. They called me to assist them, and as my place really was with the hospital corps, being a non-combatant musician, I complied with their request. We carried the poor fellow some distance to the rear, through a thick wood, and found there a scene of disorder, not to say panic. Men were flying in every direction, commissary wagons were struggling through the underbrush, and the roads were packed with fugitives and baggage trains, trying to carry off the impedimenta of the army. Finding a comparatively empty wagon, we placed our wounded officer inside, and then, left at liberty, I started on down toward the Tennessee River. I had not proceeded more than a mile when I encountered a brigade of Illinois troops drawn up in battle array, apparently waiting for orders. It was General McArthur's Highland brigade, the members of which wore Scotch caps, and I must say that a handsomer body of troops I never saw. These fellows had been at Fort Donelson, and they counted themselves as veterans. They had their regimental band with them, their flags were all unfurled, and they were really dancing impatiently to the music of the battle in front of them. As I sauntered by, a chipper young lieutenant, sword in hand, stopped me and said:

"Where do you belong?"

"I belong to Ohio," was my reply.

"Well, Ohio is making a bad show of itself here to-day," he said. "I have seen stragglers from a dozen Ohio regiments going past here for half an hour. Ohio expects better work from her sons than this."

As I was one of Ohio's youngest sons, my state pride was touched.

"Do you want to come and fight with us?" he said.

I responded that I was willing to take a temporary berth in his regiment. He asked me my name, and especially inquired whether I had any friends on the field. I gave him my father's name and regiment, and saw him make a careful entry in a little pass-book which he afterward placed in the bosom of his coat, as he rather sympathetically informed me that he would see, in case anything should happen to me, that my friends should know of it. Thus I became temporarily attached to Company B, of the 9th Illinois Regiment, McArthur's brigade. Several other men from other regiments who had been touched by this young officer's patriotic appeals also took places in our ranks.

Rather a strange situation that for a boy—enlisting on the battle-field, in a command where there was not a face that he had ever seen before; only one face, indeed, that had the least touch of sympathy in it, and that belonging to the young officer who had mustered him.

We waited here for three-quarters of an hour before receiving the command to move. During that time, one of the regimental bands played "Hail Columbia." It was the first and only time that I heard music on a battle-field, and soon afterward I saw that heroic band playing "Over the Hills and Far Away." That is to say, they would have gone over the hills if there had been any in that neighborhood. Finally, the order came to move to the front. By this time, the stream of fugitives on the road rendered it almost impassable, but we forced our way through them, and in due time reached the point where our men were being severely driven. At first, we were sent to strengthen the line from point to point, and twice that morning our brigade was moved up to support field batteries, which service, I must say from my brief experience, is the most annoying in modern warfare. These batteries drew not only the artillery fire of the enemy, but they furnished a point for the concentrated fire of all the infantry in front. To be in supporting position was to receive all the bullets that were aimed at the battery, and which, of course, usually vex the rear. The shells intended for the battery in your front have a habit always of flying too high or bursting just high enough in air to make it pleasant for the troops who are held in comparative inactivity. Under these conditions, we hugged the ground very closely, and fallen timber of every kind was most gratefully and thankfully recognized.

It is amazing how rapidly time flies under these circumstances. I am sure there were occasions that morning when twenty minutes' exposure to fire behind these field batteries seemed to me an entire week. Everything looked weird

"ERECT IN HIS SADDLE, HIS EYE BENT FORWARD, LOOKED A VERITABLE WAR EAGLE."

and unnatural. The very leaves on the trees, though scarcely out of the bud, seemed greener than I had ever seen leaves, and larger. The faces of the men about me looked like no faces that I had ever seen on earth. Actions took on the grotesque forms of nightmares. The roar and din of the battle in all its terror outstripped my most fanciful dreams of Pandemonium. The wounded and butchered men who came up out of the blue smoke in front of us, and were dragged or sent hobbling to the rear, seemed like bleeding messengers come to tell us of the fate that awaited us.

It was with the greatest sense of relief that orders came for us to move to the left, to face again that awful wave of fire, which seemed to be all the morning moving toward our flank. The Confederate divisions came into action at Shiloh Church by the right, with a view to penetrating to the Tennessee River, and taking us in flank and rear. It was along in the afternoon sometime, that we were pushed over to the extreme left of the forward line. I had no watch, and could have no idea of the hour of the day, except as I saw the shadows formed by the sun. Up to this time, our command had suffered but little, but a dreadful baptism of fire was awaiting us. For a moment, I realized that we were on the extreme left of our army; that my regiment was the left of the brigade; that I was temporarily attached to Company B of the regiment, which practically placed me on the left flank of that heroic army. I know all this because there was no firing in our front, and no sound of battle to our left, but steady, steady, steady from the right of us rolled the volleys which told us that the enemy was working around to our vicinity. I saw General McArthur, our commander, at this point, and as I remember, his hand was wrapped with a handkerchief, as though he had been wounded. By his orders, we pushed across a deep ravine which ran parallel with our front, and in five minutes we had taken up a position on the bank of this ravine, facing the enemy. Everybody felt that the critical moment had come. The terrible nervous strain of that day was nothing compared with the feeling that now the time had come for us to show our mettle. The faces of that regiment were worth studying at that moment. Not one that was not pale; not a lip that was not close shut; not an eye that was not wild; not a hand that did not tremble in this awful, anxious moment. Presently the messengers came—pattering shots from out the dense growth in our front, telling of the advance of the skirmish line. On our part, no response. No enemy could be seen, but the purple wreaths of smoke here and there told of the men who were feeling their way toward our lines. A nervous man, unable to stand the strain, let off his musket in our lines. This revealed our presence. With a suddenness that was almost appalling, there came from all along our front a crash of musketry, and the bullets shrieked over our heads and through our ranks. Then we delivered our fire. In an instant, the engagement was general at this point. There were no breech-loaders in that command, and the process of loading and firing was tedious. As I delivered my second shot, a musket ball struck a small bush in my front, threw the splinters in my face, and whistled over my shoulder. I may say that I was startled, but I kept loading and firing without any idea whatever as to what I was firing at. Soon the dry leaves, which covered the ground about us, were on fire, and the smoke from them added to the general obscurity. Two or three men had fallen in my vicinity. At this moment, the young lieutenant who had my descriptive list in his coat bosom, and who was gallantly waving his sword in the front, was struck by a bullet and fell instantly dead, almost at my feet. Then it was that I realized my utter isolation, and shuddered at the thought of the fate impended —"Dead and unknown."

By this time, the fire from the enemy in our front—it was the division of General Hardee turning the flank of the Federal position—became so terrible that we were driven back into the ravine. Here we were comparatively safe. We could load our pieces, crawl up the bank of the ravine, and fire and fall back, as it were. But many poor fellows who crawled up this friendly embankment fell back, dead or wounded; and in one instance, as I was crouched down loading my piece, a man who had been struck above me, fell on top of me and died by my side. It was here in this terrible moment that I, boy-like, thought of the peaceful Ohio home, where a loving, anxious mother was doubtless thinking of me, and with the thought that perhaps my father had been killed, came a natural desire to be well out of the scrape. Notwithstanding, I kept firing as long as my cartridges lasted. These gone, a fierce sergeant, with a revolver in his hand, placed its muzzle close to my ear, and fiercely demanded why I was not fighting. I told him that I had no cartridges.

"Take cartridges from the box of the man there," he said, pointing to the dead man who had just fallen upon me. Mine was an Enfield rifle, and my deceased neighbor's cartridges were for a Springfield rifle. I had clung to this beautiful Enfield, with its maple stock, which my father had selected as his own, and I was determined that it should not leave my hands. While this scene was passing, the enemy came upon us in full charge, and, looking up through the smoke of the burning leaves and beyond a wash-out which connected with our ravine, I saw the gray, dirty uniforms of the enemy. I heard their fierce yells, I saw their flag flapping sullenly in the grimy atmosphere. That was a sight which I have never forgotten; I can see the tiger ferocity in those faces yet; I can see them in my dreams. For what might they not have appeared to me, terrified as I was!

It was at this point that our blue line first wavered. Out of this ravine, over the bank, we survivors poured, pursued by the howling enemy. I remember my horror at the thought of being shot in the back, as I retreated from the top of the bank and galloped as gracefully as I could with the refluent human tide. Just by my side ran a youthful soldier, perhaps three years my senior, who might, for all I knew, have been recruited as I was. I heard him give a scream of agony, and, turning, saw him dragging one of his legs, which I saw in an instant had been shattered by a bullet. He had dropped his rifle, and as I ran to his support he fell upon my shoulder and begged me for God's sake to help him. I half carried him for some distance, still holding to my Enfield rifle, with its beautiful curly stock, and then, seeing that I must either give up the *role* of good Samaritan or drop the rifle, I threw it down, and continued to aid my unfortunate companion. All this time, the bullets were whistling more fiercely than at any time during the engagement, and the woods were filled with flying men, who, to all appearances, had no intention of rallying on that side of the Tennessee River. My companion was growing weaker all the while, and finally I set him down beside a tree, with his back toward the enemy, and watched him for a few moments, until I saw that he was slowly bleeding to death. I knew nothing of surgery at that time, and did not even know how to staunch the flow of blood. I called to a soldier who was passing, but he gave no heed. A second came, stood for a moment, simply remarked, "He's a dead man," and passed on. I saw the poor fellow die with-

out being able to render the slightest assistance. Passing on, I was soon out of range of the enemy, and in a moment I realized how utterly famished and worn-out I was. My thirst was something absolutely appalling. I saw a soldier sitting upon the rough stump of a tree, gazing toward the battle, and, observing that he had a canteen, I ran to him and begged him for a drink. He invited me to help myself. I kneeled beside the stump, and, taking his canteen, drained it to the last drop. He did not even deign to look at me during the performance, but he anxiously inquired how the battle was going in front. I gave him information which did not please him in the least, and moved on toward the point known as the Landing, toward which all our fugitives seemed to be tending. But my friend on the stump—I shall never forget him. How gratefully I remember that drink of warm water from his rusty canteen! Bless his military soul, he probably never knew what a kindness he rendered me!

A short distance beyond the place where I had obtained my water supply, I found a squadron of jaded cavalry drawn up, and engaged in the interesting work of stopping stragglers. In the crowd of fear-stricken and dejected soldiers I found there, I saw a man who belonged to my father's regiment; I recognized him by the letters and number on his hat. Inquiring the fate of the regiment, he told me that it had been entirely cut to pieces, and that he had personally witnessed the death of my father—he had seen him shot from his horse. This intelligence filled me with dismay, and I then determined, noncombatant that I was, that I would retire from that battle-field. Watching my opportunity, I joined an ambulance which was passing, loaded with wounded, and by some means escaped the vigilance of the cavalrymen, who seemed to be almost too badly scared to be on any sort of duty. When through this line, I pushed my way on down past the point where stragglers were being impressed and forced to carry sand-bags up from the river, to aid in the construction of batteries for some heavy guns which had been brought up from the transports. I passed these temporary works, by the old warehouse, turned into a temporary field hospital, where hundreds of wounded men, brought down in wagons and ambulances, were being unloaded, and where their arms and legs were being cut off and thrown out to form gory, ghastly heaps. I made my way down the plateau, overlooking the river. Below lay thirty transports at least, all being loaded with the wounded, and all around me were baggage wagons, mule teams, disabled artillery teams, and thousands of panic-stricken men. I saw, here and there, officers gathering these men together into volunteer companies, and marching them away to the scene of battle. It took a vast amount of pleading to organize even a company of fifteen or twenty, and I was particularly struck by the number of officers who were engaged in this interesting occupation. It seemed to me that they were out of all proportion to the number of fugitives in the vicinity. While sitting on the bank, overlooking the road below, between the beach and the river, I saw General Grant. I had seen him the day before, review his troops on the Purdy road, while a company of Confederate cavalrymen, a detachment of Johnston's army, watched the performance from a skirt of woods some two miles away. When I saw him at this moment, he was doing his utmost to rally his troops for another effort. It must have been about half-past four in the afternoon. The general rode to the Landing, accompanied by his staff and a body-guard of twenty-five or thirty cavalrymen. I heard him begging the stragglers to go back and make one more effort to redeem themselves, accompanying his pleadings with the announcement that reinforcements would soon be on the field, and that he did not want to see his men disgraced. Again I heard him proclaim that if the stragglers before him did not return to their commands, he would send his cavalry down to drive them out. In less than fifteen minutes his words were made good. A squadron of cavalry, divided at either end of the Landing, and riding toward each other with drawn swords, drove away every man found between the steep bank and the river. The majority of the skulkers climbed up the bank, hanging by the roots of the trees, and in less than ten minutes after the cavalry had passed, they were back in their old places again. I never saw General Grant again until I saw him the President of the United States.

While sitting on the high bank of the river, I looked across to the opposite side, and saw a body of horsemen emerging from the low cane brakes, back of the river. In a moment, I saw a man waving a white flag with a red square in the centre. I knew that he was signaling, for I had seen the splendid corps of Buell's army, and I recognized that the men with that flag were our friends. Sitting by me were two distracted fugitives, who also saw the movement on the other side of the river. Said one of them to

his companion: "Bill, we are gone now. There's the Texas cavalry on the other side of the river!" The red square had misled him. Fifteen minutes later I saw the head of a column of blue emerge from the woods beyond, and move hurriedly down toward the river's edge. Immediately the empty transport moved over to that side of the river, and the first boat brought over a figure which I recognized. The vessel was a peculiar one, belonging in Southern waters, and had evidently been used as a ferryboat. On its lower forward deck, which was long and protruding, sat a man of tremendous proportions, upon a magnificent Kentucky racehorse, with bobbed tail. The officer was rigged out in all his regimentals, including an enormous hat with a black feather in it. I knew that this was General Nelson, commonly known as "Fighting Bull Nelson." I ran down to the point where I saw this boat was going to land, and as she ran her prow up on the sandy beach, Nelson put spurs to his horse and jumped him over the gunwale. As he did this, he drew his sword and rode right into the crowd of refugees, shouting: "Damn your souls, if you won't fight, get out of the way, and let men come here who will!" I realized from the presence of Nelson that my regiment (the 24th Ohio) was probably in that vicinity. I asked one of the boat hands to take me on board, and, after some persuasion, he did so. The boat recrossed, and as soon as I got on shore I ran down to where the troops were embarking, to cross the river to the battle-field. I soon found Ammen's brigade and my regiment. Hurrying on board one of the transports, I climbed to the hurricane deck, and there found my brother with his company. He was looking across the river, where the most appalling sight met his vision. The shore was absolutely packed with the disorganized, panic-stricken troops who had fled before the terrible Confederate onslaught, which had not ceased for one moment since early that morning. The noise of the battle was deafening. It may be imagined that my brother was somewhat surprised to see me. I made a hurried explanation of the circumstances which had brought me there, and gave him news of my father's death. Then I asked him for something to eat. With astonishment, he referred me to his negro servant, who luckily had a broiled chicken in his haversack, together with some hard bread. I took the chicken, and as we marched off the boat, I held a drum-stick in each hand, and kept by my brother's side as we forced our way through the stragglers, up the road from the Landing and on to the plateau, where the battle was even then almost concentrating. Right there I saw a man's head shot off by a cannon-ball, and saw immediately afterward an aide on General Nelson's staff dismounted by a shot, which took off the rear part of his saddle and broke his horse's back. At the same time, I did not stop eating. My nerves were settled, and my stomach was asserting its rights. My brother finally turned to me, and, after giving me some papers to keep, and some messages to deliver in case of death, shook me by the hand and told me to keep out of danger, and, above all things, to try and get back home. This part of his advice I readily accepted. I stood and saw the brigade march by, which, in less than ten minutes, met the advance of the victorious Confederates, and checked the battle for that day. It was then that the gunboats in the river and the heavy siege guns on the bank above added their remonstrating voices as the sun went down, and the roar of battle ceased entirely.

But that night on the shore of the Tennessee River was one to be remembered. Wandering along the beach among the rows of wounded men waiting to be taken on board the transports, I found another member of the 70th Ohio Regiment, named Silcott. He had a harrowing tale of woe to relate, in which nearly all his friends and acquaintances figured as corpses, and together we sat down on a bale of hay near the river's edge. By this time, the rain had set in. It was one of those peculiar streaming, drenching, semi-tropical downpours, and it never ceased for a moment from that time until far into the next day. With darkness came untold misery and discomfort. After my companion had related the experiences of the day, I curled myself up on one side of the hay bale while he occupied one edge of it, and soon fell asleep. Every few moments I was awakened by a terrible broadside, delivered from the two gunboats which lay in the centre of the river a hundred yards or so above me. They were the "Lexington" and the "A. O. Tyler," I believe; wooden vessels, reconstructed from Western steamboats and supplied with ponderous columbiads. These black monsters, for some reason, kept up their fire all through the night, and the roar of this cannonading and the shrieking of the shells, mingled with the thunders of the rain-storm, gave very little opportunity for slumber. Still, I managed to doze very comfortably between broadsides,

and my recollection of the night is that from these peaceful naps I was aroused every now and then by what appeared to be a tremendous flash of lightning, followed by the most awful thunder ever heard on the face of the earth. These discharges seemed to me to lift me four or five inches from my water-soaked couch, and to add to the general misery the transports which were bringing over Buell's troops had a landing within twenty feet of my lodgment. All night long they wheezed and groaned, and came and went, with their freight of humanity, and right by my side marched all night long the poor fellows who were being pushed out to the front to take their places on the battle line for the morrow. By this time, the roadway was churned into mud knee-deep, and as regiment after regiment went by with that peculiar slosh, slosh of marching men in mud, and the rattling of canteens against bayonet scabbards, so familiar to the ear of the soldier, I could hear in the intervals the low complainings of the men, and the urgings of the officers: "Close up, boys, close up," until it seemed to me that if there was ever such a thing as hades on earth, I was in the fullest enjoyment of it. As fast as a transport unloaded its troops, the gangway was hauled in, the vessel dropped out, and another took the vacant place and the same thing was gone over again. Now and then a battery of artillery would come off the boat, the wheels would stick in the mud, and then a grand turmoil of half an hour follow, during which time every man found in the neighborhood was impressed to aid in relieving the embargoed gun. The whipping of the horses and the cursing of the drivers was less soothing, if anything, than those soul-shattering gunboat broadsides. There never was a night so long, so hideous, or so utterly uncomfortable.

As the gray streaks of dawn began to appear, the band of the 13th Regulars on the deck of one of the transports, came into the landing, playing a magnificent selection from "Il Trovatore." How inspiring that music was! Even the poor wounded men lying in the front on the shore seemed to be lifted up, and every soldier seemed to receive an impetus. Soon there was light enough to distinguish objects around, and then came the ominous patter of musketry over beyond the river's bluff, which told that the battle was on again. It began just as a shower of rain begins, and soon deepened into a terrible hailstorm, with the booming artillery for thunder accompaniment. I was up and around, and

"I BURST INTO A REGULAR BOO-HOO, AND STARTED ON."

started immediately toward the front, for every-body felt now that the battle was to be ours. Those fresh and sturdy troops from the Army of the Ohio had furnished a blue bulwark, behind which the incomparable one-day fighters of Grant and Sherman were to push to victory. The whole aspect of the field in the rear changed. The skulkers of the day before seemed to be im-bued with genuine manhood, and thousands of them returned to the front to render good ser-vice. In addition to this, 6,000 fresh men under General Lew Wallace, who had marched from Crump's Landing, ten miles away, and who should have been on the field the day before, had arrived, during the night, and the tide of battle was now setting toward Corinth. I met a comrade drying himself, out by a log fire, about a quarter of a mile from the landing, who had by some process secured a canteen of what was known as Commissary whiskey. He gave me one drink of it, and that constituted my breakfast. Cold, wet, and depressed, as I was, that whiskey, execrable though it was, brought me such consolation as I had never found before.

I have drank champagne in Epernay, I have sipped Johannisberger at the foot of its sunny mount, I have tasted the regal Montepulsiano, but, by Jove! I never enjoyed a drink as I did that swig of ordinary whiskey, on the morning of the 7th of April, 1862. While drying myself by this fire, I saw a motley crowd of Confederate prisoners marched past, under guard. As they waded along the muddy road, some of the cow-ardly skulkers indulged in the badinage usual on such occasions, and one of our fellows called out to know what company that was. A proud young chap in gray threw his head back, and replied: "Company Q, of the Southern Invinci-bles, and be damned to you!" That was the spirit of that day and hour.

At ten o'clock, the sound of the battle indi-cated that our lines were being pushed forward, and I made up my mind to go to the front. I started with my companion, and in a very short time we began to see about us traces of the terri-ble battle of the day before. We were then on the ground which had been fought over late Sunday evening. The underbrush had literally been mowed off by the bullets, and great trees had been shattered by the terrible artillery fire. In places, the bodies of the slain lay upon the ground so thick that I could step from one to the other. This without exaggeration. The pallid faces of the dead men in blue were scattered among the blackened corpses of the enemy. This to me was a horrible revelation, and I have never yet heard a scientific explanation of why the majority of the dead Confederates on that field turned black. All the bodies had been stripped of their valuables, and scarcely a pair of boots or shoes could be found upon the feet of the dead. In most instances, pockets had been cut open, and one of the pathetic sights that I remember was a poor Confederate lying on his back, while by his side was a heap of ginger cakes and

him bore the number of a Georgia regiment, embroidered, I am sure, by some tender fingers, and his waxen face, washed by the rains of the night before, was that of one who had fallen asleep, dreaming of loved ones who waited his coming in some anxious home. He was about my age. He may have been a drummer! At the sight of that poor boy's corpse, I burst into a regular boo-hoo, and started on. Here beside a great oak tree I counted the corpses of fifteen men. One of them sat stark against the tree, and the others lay about as though during the night, suffering from wounds, they had crawled together for mutual assistance and there had died. The blue and the gray were mingled together. This peculiarity I observed all over the field. It was no uncommon thing to see the

"I REALIZED THEN HOW DEEPLY HE LOVED ME."

sausage, which had tumbled out of the trousers pocket, cut by some infamous thief. The unfortunate man had evidently filled his pocket the day before with the edibles found in some sutler's tent, and had been killed before he had an opportunity to enjoy his bountiful store. There was something so sad about this that it brought tears to my eyes. Further on, I passed by the road the corpse of a beautiful boy in gray, who lay with his blond curls scattered about his face, and his hands folded peacefully across his breast. He was clad in a bright and neat uniform, well garnished with gold, which seemed to tell the story of a loving mother and sisters who had sent their household pet to the field of war. His neat little hat lying beside

bodies of Federal and Confederate lying side by side as though they had bled to death while trying to aid each other. In one spot I saw an entire battery of Federal artillery which had been dismantled in Sunday's fight, every horse of which had been killed in his harness, every tumbrel of which had been broken, every gun of which had been dismounted, and in this awful heap of death lay the bodies of dozens of cannoneers. One dismounted gun was absolutely spattered with the blood and brains of the men who had served it. Here and there in the field, standing in the mud, were the most piteous sights of all the battle-field—poor wounded horses, their heads drooping, their eyes glassy and gummy, waiting for the slow coming of death, or for some friendly hand to end their misery. How those helpless brutes spoke in pleading testimony of the horror, the barbarism, and the uselessness of war! No painter ever did justice to a battle-field such as this, I am sure.

As I pushed onward to the front, I passed the ambulances and the wagons bringing back the wounded, and talked with the poor, bleeding fellows who were hobbling toward the river along the awful roads or through the dismal chaparral. They all brought news of victory. Toward evening I found myself in the neighborhood of the old Shiloh Church, but could get no tidings of the 70th Regiment. Night came on, and I lay down and fell asleep at the foot of a tree, having gathered up a blanket, soaked with water, which I could only use for a pillow. It rained all night. The battle had practically ended at four o'clock that evening, and the enemy had slowly and silently withdrawn toward Corinth. Next morning I learned that my father's regiment had been sent in pursuit of the enemy, and nobody could tell when it would return. I found the camp, and oh, what desolation reigned there! Every tent had been pillaged, and in my father's headquarters, the gentlemen of the enemy who had camped there two nights before had left a duplicate of nearly everything they had taken. They had exchanged their dirty blankets for clean ones, and had left their old, worn brogans in the place of boots and shoes, which they had appropriated, and all about were the evidences of the feasting that had gone on during that one night of glorious possession. I remained there during the day, and late that evening the 70th Regiment came back to its deserted quarters after three days and two nights of most terrible fighting and campaigning.

At its head rode my father, whom I supposed to be dead, pale, and haggard, and worn, but unscathed. He had not seen me nor heard from me for sixty hours. He dismounted, and taking me in his arms, gave me the most affectionate embrace that my life had ever known, and I realized then how deeply he loved me. That night we stayed in the old bullet-ridden and shot-torn tent and told of our adventures, and the next day I had the pleasure of hearing General Sherman compliment him for his bravery, and say, "Colonel, you have been worth your weight in gold to me."

*   *   *   *   *   *   *   *

Speaking one day to General Sherman, the last and the greatest of our warriors, I asked him, "What do you regard as the bloodiest and most sanguinary battle of our Civil War?"

"Shiloh," was the prompt response.

And in this opinion I most heartily concur.

John A. Cockerill

[To Mr. Allan Foreman, the able editor of *The Journalist*, is due the credit of giving to the public what General Sherman pronounces the best war story ever written, and the best account, because the truest, of the battle of Shiloh. It is not surprising to the personal friends of John A. Cockerill that anything written by him should be the best of its kind ; but when Colonel Cockerill tells the story of a battle in which General Sherman took such a prominent part, and the story shall be pronounced the best account of that battle, by one who is so capable of judging as was General Sherman, it adds to the admiration of even those who so earnestly believe in the genius of John A. Cockerill as a journalist. Cockerill's tears, shed while standing near the boy who wore the gray, are more valuable to-day to a reunited nation than any act of bravery done during that dreadful day in April at Shiloh.

John A. Cockerill records none of the deeds which the spurious article (the warrior in time of peace) so delights in telling. But, between the lines, all through the article on Shiloh, one can read the mile-stones on which are written Courage, Honesty, and Principle.]

HIS SWEETHEART'S FACE.

WALTER LeRoy Fogg.

THEY found him, when the musket rattle
    Had died away,
Lying where the fiercest battle
    Raged all day ;
Unknown his name,—they only knew
    He fell in strife
But where the breast-blood trickled thro'
    They read his life ;
For there his cold hand held a face
    Serene and fair,—

Features in mold of virgin grace
    Framed in gold hair,
And stern eyes then grew soft with tears
    To think that they
Had held the same hope thro' those years
    As he that lay
With life-light put in sad eclipse
    By bullet's hiss—
So near the sweet and waiting lips
    He longed to kiss !

A NORTH CAROLINA CAPTAIN'S BREAKFAST.

CAPTAIN WALTER A. WHITTED, Co. G, 55TH NORTH CAROLINA REGIMENT.

I HAD only one day's fighting at Gettysburg. Two wounds, one in the foot and another in the face, received during the little excitement in the railroad cut on the first day, relegated me to the field hospital in the rear. Here I remained until the Army of Northern Virginia began its retreat southward. By that time my injuries were repaired to such an extent that I could hobble around fairly well, and could take a little solid nourishment instead of the soups and thin stuff to which my wounded mouth had confined me for three days. When we commenced our retreat, on the evening of the 4th, I was decidedly hungry, but in the hurry and confusion of loading up and stowing away our wounded I found no chance to go through my slow process of eating. The result was that after I had ridden all night across a spur of the mountain I found myself, at eleven o'clock next day, still without food and nearly famished.

About the hour named our column was halted, and not knowing the orders, I assumed that we would at least be given time to get a bite to eat. To my dismay the wagon-drivers said they had nothing, and I was informed that our brigade, rations and all, was " a long ways ahead." I was further informed, upon authority, that as soon as our horses could graze and rest a little we would continue our retreat, " rations or no rations."

This did not suit my ideas very well. I began prospecting on my own account. Looking to the left of the highway I saw a substantial farm dwelling about half a mile distant. The very appearance of the houses of the thrifty farmers of Pennsylvania suggests abundance, and I felt an irresistible desire to find out what good things that house contained for me. Could I go there and return in time to keep up with my comrades? Are we near the end of the column, and who is covering the retreat? Are there any " Yanks " in those woods near the right of the house? These and similar queries flashed through my mind. But that silent monitor within me—not conscience this time, but hunger—cut short my dilatory musings. At any cost my hunger must be appeased.

I reined my horse up to the fence and threw off the top rails. In a moment I was galloping across the field, over hedges and ditches, through fields of wheat and corn. Approaching the house from the rear, I halted at a distance of about a hundred yards and took a quick survey of the premises. In the front yard were half a dozen cavalry horses tied to the cherry trees. This was far from cheering, as I had no means of determining whether those horses represented Union or Confederate troopers. My aforesaid inward monitor urged me forward, however, and I rode rapidly into the yard and looked through an open window at the end of the house.

My boldness was rewarded by the welcome sight of three gray coats. Leaving my horse in company with the others under the cherry trees, I entered. On the piazza I encountered a fine-looking old gentlemen, apparently the owner, whom I saluted, but who neither returned my salute nor bid me welcome. I was too hungry to stand upon ceremony, and passed on toward the kitchen end of the dwelling. I met two of our officers coming out, one of whom assured me that the young lady in charge was "as mad as a wet hen," adding, "if you get anything to eat in there you will have to take it!"

Upon entering the room I found three more of our officers—a captain and two lieutenants—comfortably seated at a table, stowing away buckwheat cakes and fresh country butter. A nice-looking young lady bent over the stove frying the cakes, but with evident reluctance. Her face was flushed with anger, and the tears were falling down her cheeks, while her eyes flashed fire. And she was certainly giving my hungry comrades a piece of her mind. She was evidently a hearty, good-natured girl, who felt that she was being greatly imposed upon, and our boys, under the genial influence of her buckwheat cakes and golden butter, were inclined to chaff her good-naturedly.

"I'll be glad when you're all gone, and I hope the good Lord will never let you live to come back here to take and carry away everything you can lay hands on. Why don't you go on back to that 'Dixie,' as you call it? You are the most hateful, ugly——"

"There, now, madam, you are greatly mistaken; and if you will come down in Dixie we will prove to you that we are nice people, courteous, polite, and not always hungry. Besides, we will give you a nice little 'reb' for a sweetheart."

"No, indeed, you won't! I wouldn't have one of you 'rebs' if he was the last man on this green earth! Our men gave you fellows a good whipping," she went on, "and now I hope you will go back where you came from and stay there. I don't want to see another one of you as long as I live!"

As the young girl thus rattled on, her tormentors leaned back in their chairs, patiently awaiting, knives in hand, another instalment of the luscious cakes, and eyeing a large bar of fresh, yellow butter.

"There, now, that is all you will get in this house. You can go on farther and rob someone else. I have nothing more for you."

While listening to this little spat I had been standing near the stove warming and drying myself, and enjoying, in anticipation, my share of the cakes. I had ridden all the preceding night in the rain, and although it was the 5th of July I was actually cold.

A moment later I found myself alone; my Georgian comrades had departed, the little cook had gone, and even the cake of butter had disappeared. I was sadly disappointed, and hungrier than ever. I looked into the tray which had contained the buckwheat batter; sure enough, it was empty. Just then the young lady returned, seized the tray, and abruptly left the room again. I began to reflect upon the advice of my brother officer, given me as I entered, and looked about to see what I could "take." Nothing whatever, of an edible character, rewarded my search. I was beginning to grow desperate, for I knew my time was short, and I was growing actually faint. Just then my fair tormentor came back again to the kitchen. Planting herself defiantly about six feet from me, she said:

"Do not stand here thinking I will give you something to eat, for you heard me tell those men that we have no more buckwheat flour, and ——"

She had a pleasant, hearty countenance, despite its mask of unwonted wrath. I determined to try a little diplomacy.

"My dear young lady, have you any relatives in the Federal army?"

"Yes, I have; a brother and two cousins."

"Were they in the first day's fight, do you know?"

"I know they were in General Reynolds' Corps, but I have not heard a word from them since the battle." And the look of wrath began to fade into an expression of deep anxiety.

"What regiment do they belong to?" I asked.

"The —th Pennsylvania," she responded.

"Why," said I, "our fellows fought that regiment at the railroad cut."

"Perhaps you can tell me something about my brother, then," she said, eagerly.

"No, miss," I replied, "I only know that one of the colonels in that brigade was wounded and captured at that place, and that he was with me at our hospital. The surgeon of my regiment treated both of us, and our own cook prepared our food. My wound was such that I could not eat my share of the good things, so the wounded colonel took my place at mess."

I remembered the name of this colonel at the time, and mentioned it to her, but I have now forgotten it.

This incident was strictly true, but I have often wondered since that she believed it at once. There was a marvelous change in her manner. She actually smiled, and asked me to be seated, then, hurrying from the room, returned directly with a tray and some buckwheat batter. In a few moments I was in the midst of luxury—golden brown cakes and golden yellow butter. As the girl bent over her work I could see her eyes fill again with tears, and her manner was kindness personified. Speaking in an earnest, sorrowful tone, she said:

"You seem to be a gentleman, and I hope I have not been rude to you. I heard that Colonel —— was wounded and captured. Didn't he tell you anything of my brother?" mentioning his name.

"No, I regret to say that he did not. But we talked of the war, its cause, its progress and probable conclusion, and recounted our experiences of that first day's fight. I asked him why he did not hold his position, posted as he was behind a rail fence, when we first struck him. His reply was: 'You fellows fight like wild cats, just as if you had not a particle of sense or fear. You would run over the devil himself at that rate. There is not a particle of sense in such fighting as that.'"

By this time my first instalment of buckwheat cakes had disappeared. My! my! Like the old negro, I was not able to "'spress myself." My long fast, the rain, and the low temperature of my body had reduced the fever and the soreness of my face, and I ate with a will. While I ate, the young lady stood with her hands resting on the back of my chair, asking me many questions about the war and the people of Dixie. I assured her that a large majority of the Confederate soldiers were high-toned, Christian gentlemen, many of them highly cultured graduates of colleges, chivalrous and refined, having at home humble Christian mothers whose prayers were constantly ascending to heaven for the protection of their sons; that we were fighting the Union soldiers, and were not making war on women and children; that we were fighting for what we conceived a just cause, though that cause might be hard to define; that we had no animosity against any Union soldier—as an example, I had, while at the hospital, divided with two Union soldiers, lying wounded under a tree, the last particle of tobacco I had, knowing that I could not get any more for perhaps a week; and after having assisted in the amputation of my own colonel's arm, I hobbled out to a shade tree near the house, and found a little boy suffering very much, a grape-shot having penetrated about two-thirds its own diameter into the top of his foot, crushing its way through and embedding itself among the bones. He asked me to see the surgeons and ask them to "please put him on the table next." Though it caused me considerable pain to walk, yet I knew the kind, sympathetic heart of the surgeon of my own regiment, and begged him to attend to that little Yankee boy. He stopped one moment, raised up, turning his benevolent, sympathetic face to me and said: "Captain, I have been watching that little boy for the last six or eight hours, giving him all the stimulants he will bear, but he does not revive. He has never recovered from the first shock, and I fear never will. In his present condition he would certainly die on the table. I shall continue to watch him, and if he revives I will put him on the table immediately." I went back to the house by another path. I could not look upon that pale, boyish face again and tell him what the surgeon had told me.

After I had eaten the cakes she once more left the room and returned, bringing a dish full to the brim with large, luscious raspberries. I asked her to place in another dish the part she wished me to eat, warning her that if they were placed in my hands in their present condition I should eat them all. She assured me that I was welcome to all. I ate all. They had been gathered early in the morning and sugared.

Before I left the house, this hospitable young woman placed in my hands a generous slice of delicious dried beef, neatly wrapped, saying, "You will need this, perhaps." I thanked her, and rejoined the retreating column, but left in her hands, as a memento and not as a reward, the last piece of silver I possessed.

ON THE RAPPAHANNOCK—SEPTEMBER, 1862, TO APRIL, 1863.

By Yvan.

OUR vessel was a side-wheel steamer, and was formerly a New York tug-boat. She was large and very powerful, and was purchased by the Federal Government to be converted into a gunboat for river service. She proved to be admirably adapted to the purpose : a heavy battery consisting of two nine-inch Dahlgrens, which were pivoted, one forward, the other aft ; two thirty-pounder Parrott rifles, and three or four howitzers. She was detailed for the "Potomac Flotilla," then guarding the Potomac, York, and Rappahannock Rivers. Our story has to do only with the above-mentioned period, on the Rappahannock. We were constantly obliged to be on the alert, and to keep a bright and sharp lookout. Our boats patrolled the river by night, in order to prevent supplies and despatches from being carried over. We often were fired on from masked batteries, but as a rule had no trouble in silencing them.

All our officers were volunteers. There was not one regular officer on board. Our commanding officer was an old Fulton Ferry pilot, and, of course, knew nothing about the service. He knew as well, however, how to handle a steamer as any one in the flotilla, and was as brave as Julius Cæsar. He was ready and willing to fight on all occasions, and the name of the opportunities he had was legion. The enemy was very troublesome and kept us constantly moving. We occasionally captured a boat at night, attempting to cross, but they generally managed to destroy their despatches, if they had any, before being captured.

One night we saw the enemy making signals across the river, just above us. We were about to fire upon them, but desisted at the earnest request of one of our officers. He was a young man who had been in the army, and was very fond of adventure. There was nothing too hazardous for him to undertake. He begged the captain not to fire on them, stating that he was sure he could capture the whole party. He then unfolded his scheme, which was as follows : To let them continue their signals for that night unmolested. The next night, he said, if the captain would give him a couple of boats with their crews, he would promise to capture the whole outfit. The captain reluctantly con-

sented, and we dropped down the river so as not to be seen by the enemy.

The next night we returned as quietly as possible, and there was the enemy, sure enough, making signals as before. Everything had been prepared during the day for the expedition—the boats' crews selected and instructed. The crews were then armed, and the boats quietly lowered away. We had, of course, taken the precaution of muffling the oars. We were wished all manner of good luck, and away we went. We landed about a mile, I should think, from the place where they were making signals. We anchored the boats a short distance from the shore and put two boat-keepers in each. We then started for the signal station, very quietly and cautiously. No one was allowed to speak but the commanding officer of the expedition. We had no idea as to the number of the enemy, and, indeed, no one appeared to care. After about fifteen minutes' march, we came in sight of the house from which the signals were being made. It had evidently been a negro cabin. We could see about a dozen men around the hut.

When within about fifty yards of the house, our commanding officer ordered us to charge. We did it to such good purpose that we captured the whole party without firing a shot. They were the most surprised people imaginable. They had no idea an enemy was anywhere in the vicinity. We secured the prisoners, took them back to the boats, and got them safely on board ship.

While ashore, and just before starting from the house, the most bizarre looking negro I ever saw came marching into the place, never dreaming of any change in the condition of affairs. We at once seized him. On questioning him he informed us that he had just returned from the big house, where he had been all day with "Massa Charles." On questioning him further we discovered that "Massa Charles" was Captain Charles Lawson, of the 55th Virginia Cavalry, and had a recruiting station in the neighborhood of his house. Judging from what the negro told us we concluded his house must be about four miles inland.

After seeing the prisoner safely on board, we concluded to try and capture "Massa Charles"

377

as well. So we started off, taking the strange negro with us as a guide. We told him very plainly that should he in any way attempt to deceive us we would certainly blow out his brains. He was terribly frightened, and made the most extravagant promises to be faithful and true.

It was a very rough road, and we made haste slowly. We again left two boat-keepers in each boat and anchored them as before, giving them orders that in case they should hear any firing, and we should fail to return within a reasonable time thereafter, they were to pull off to the ship. The guide told us the enemy had cavalry pickets out, but that they were very far apart and not very vigilant, as no enemy was expected. We got safely through, and finally reached the captain's house.

We were at once ordered to surround it as quietly as possible, and proceeded to do so. The commanding officer of the party then, taking two men with him, entered the house through a window. The negro had given him a complete plan of the house, describing the position of the rooms, halls, stairs, etc. He also told him the exact location of the captain's bedroom.

The captain awoke just as the party burst into his room. He was a very large, powerful man, but as he saw three revolvers pointed at him, and had no arms himself, he concluded to take "the better part" and surrendered, saying: "Great Scott, this is too bad!" It did seem mighty hard, but such is the fortune of war.

Our commander told the captain that we would treat him with the greatest kindness and consideration if he would go along with us quietly, but if he attempted to escape or make any outcry we would certainly kill him. He also told him he had no desire to humiliate him by binding him, and that if he would give his word of honor to go along peaceably with us he would leave him untrammeled. He gave his parole, and we started for the ship.

We again got safely through the pickets (if, indeed, pickets there were) and reached the boats, got aboard of them, and pulled off to the vessel. We had, we felt, accomplished a good night's work, and all without the loss of a single man.

A few nights after this, while one of our boats was patrolling the river, a large boat was discovered just ahead. Our boat immediately gave chase, when suddenly another large boat appeared, and the two at once attacked our boat with great vigor. We were doing our best, but were very much overmatched. Those on board the vessel, hearing the firing and seeing the flash of the guns, at once came to our assistance. Relief came none too soon. One of the enemy's boats escaped in the darkness, but we succeeded in capturing the other. They were out on a raid for the express purpose of capturing our patrol-boat. In this encounter we had one man killed and three wounded.

We now had more prisoners on board than we could accommodate, so we ran down to the mouth of the river to intercept an army transport steamer. We saw one next day, and put all our prisoners, including the Confederate captain and our own wounded, aboard her. The prisoners were soon safely housed in the "Old Capitol Prison," in Washington.

We again ascended the river and went to work as usual. We steamed up just beyond where we had broken up the signal station. We paid for our temerity. A masked battery (Stuart's) opened upon us with destructive effect. They killed two of our men and wounded seven. We returned the fire briskly, and after about an hour's fighting we silenced the battery. We then dropped down the river a short distance for the purpose of burying the dead, attending to the wounded, and repairing damages. All our machinery was above the water-line, but fortunately, as by a miracle, it all escaped without injury.

The enemy from this time on kept us very busy. We formerly used to have "a day off," when we could go oystering and amuse ourselves. But these halcyon days were gone forever. We could have a fight now any time we wanted one. It was only necessary to go up the river a few miles to get it.

We now had less trouble with the enemy, and it had become very quiet, indeed, rather suspiciously so. Our young officer again came to the fore. He, in common with the rest of us, felt there was "something wrong a-brewin'." He had another scheme on foot. He proposed on the first dark night taking a captured skiff we had, disguising himself and escaping (?) to the enemy. We were to chase him and keep up a brisk fire. He said he would have some important information to give the enemy, and would endeavor to get some in return. Since his last adventure the captain had such confidence in him as to be ready to accede to any proposition he might make.

So he made all his preparations, and on the first dark night he took the skiff and was followed by our patrol-boat. After a little while the crew began firing rapidly, and he rowed for dear life, and just managed to make his escape and reach the shore in safety. He was received by the Confederates with open arms. He told them he had been sent to inform them that General Stuart was about to make a raid, and wanted them to make a demonstration on the gunboat so as to keep her busy and away from him. It was a very clever ruse. They immediately told him they had already made their plans to capture the gunboat, and revealed the whole scheme to him. This, it appears, was just what he suspected, and took that method of finding out. He said he must get back before sun-up; they were afraid he would be captured by the Yankees, but he said he had no fear ; he had "fooled them coming over" and could do it again.

A couple of hours afterward he was back safely on board ship.

The attack was to take place on the night of the 11th, should it prove to be a dark one. This was the 9th of the month. We made no change whatever in our movements, but acted as though we suspected nothing.

The night came and it was dark as Erebus. We had a slip on our cable and "heavy banked fires." Our guns were loaded with grape and canister, and every man was in his place. About half past eleven we heard them coming; fires were spread and we were all ready. On they came, and as soon as we could see them we got under way and began firing into them. Not one of the boats reached the ship. As soon as they saw we were prepared for them they separated, after giving us a volley, and made for the shore. We never knew what damage we inflicted on them, but it must have been very great. This was the first time they had attempted any very bold movement. Of their next attempt more anon.

Shortly after this, the first battle of Fredericksburg took place, in which, as all know, the Union forces were defeated, with terrible loss. This made the Confederates still more bold and defiant on the river, and they certainly made matters very lively for us. We were obliged to keep in the middle of the river. When we approached either bank, we seldom failed to get one or more shots. After enduring this state of things for some little time, our captain determined to go up the river as far as possible, and do all the damage we could. He heard that Stuart had a very strong masked battery some distance up the river, and had received very accurate information as to its locality. He arranged to reach the place about midnight. The site was admirably selected, and had we not known the exact position of it, I very much doubt if any of us would have been left to tell the tale. It was on a little bend of the river, just above Port Royal. We arrived there about midnight, as intended, and notwithstanding all our precautions, the enemy discovered us all too soon, and we both began firing at almost the same moment. Our guns were of much heavier calibre than theirs, but they had the advantage of a plunging fire.

I think both sides were glad when the fight was over. It was a long way the most severe one I had yet been in. Our machinery was somewhat disabled, and we were obliged to drop down the river. We kept firing as long as we were in range. Our loss was four killed and nine wounded. We never knew how many they lost on the other side. We went back to the vicinity of our old "stamping ground" to repair damages, bury the dead, and take care of the wounded. We were getting very short of coal, and were looking very anxiously for the arrival of our regular coal-schooner. These schooners were sent us from the Washington Navy Yard, at stated intervals, in tow of a tug-boat. They also brought us supplies of all kinds. It was three days before she appeared, and we were really in great straits when she arrived. Haply the enemy didn't know of our condition. We couldn't leave the river, and to remain, in our then condition and without coal, seemed sure destruction. *Mais, la fin couronne l'œuvre.* The schooner arrived all right and gladdened our hearts.

This was also our principal means of communication with the outside world. We got all our supplies, and the schooner left for Washington. Shortly after this all the officers were detached, and an entirely new set of officers ordered to the vessel. The new arrivals were given all the information in our possession ; were told that "eternal vigilance is the price of safety," etc.

They were also told of the attack that had been made upon us; of the most dangerous parts of the river, etc., etc., etc. It is probable that, finding nothing extraordinary occurring for some time, they relaxed their watchfulness in some degree. The new *regime* had not been long in existence when the vessel, together with another gunboat, which had been sent on the river, was attacked one dark night by a number of boats under Captain John Taylor Wood, and, after a brief resistance, were both captured.

Captain Wood had formerly been in our service, and was a very gallant and accomplished officer. His expedition was skilfully planned and brilliantly executed. His men attacked with the fury of demons. Our people were caught napping, and made but a feeble resistance. The manner in which the whole affair was managed reflected great credit on Captain Wood.

Our officers and men all spoke in the highest manner of the way in which they were treated while prisoners. They had plenty of good food to eat, the wounded were tenderly cared for, and all hands, on giving their parole not to attempt an escape, were allowed to roam about as they liked until they were exchanged.

What ultimately became of the captured vessels is a matter of history.

THE OLD THIRTEEN.

MARY H. LEONARD.

I

FEEBLE, yet mighty in courage, along the Atlantic shore,
With the Old World's past behind them, the wilderness dark before,
They flung off effete traditions, resolved to succeed or fall,
And builded well for the future, while hazarding their all ;
But when the incompetent rulings of despots would hold them fast,
They rose in their stalwart manhood, and liberty triumphed at last.

II

They planted on virgin soil a Republic of iron strength—
Behold it now in its glory, its fertile borders, at length,
Stretching in proud expanse from the ice-bound Pine-tree State
To the coast where the calm Pacific unbarreth its Golden Gate ;
From the dashing Northern cataract, roaring in thunders deep,
To where, in tropic breezes, the Gulf-locked islands sleep.

III

So, now, as the Twentieth Century comes hurrying on apace,
Back over our wondrous history we turn a reflective face :
The little one truly a thousand hath now in its might become,
In a myriad populous cities we hearken to industry's hum,
And unto our land all nations look over with worshipful eyes,
As the country where grandest hope for weary humanity lies.

IV

But away from the elder Statehood the centre of power hath passed
To the fertile inland plains, the dominion of prairies vast.
O Land of the West, the rainbow of hope thy horizon doth span—
The hope of the cause of the toiler, the heritage sacred of man ;
Thy freshness is like a spring morning, thy strength is the strength of ten,
And the richest wealth of thy garners is found in thy women and men.

V

But yet, O West, remember that the life in thy veins was drawn
From the East, thy nursing mother ; her blood into thine has gone ;
Over mountain and valley and prairie the sons of the Old are spread,
Where the truths that the Fathers fought for have peace and prosperity shed ;
Your lusty youth hath its glory ; your heritage, hold it fast,
Yet turn sometimes to the record of the stern and struggling past.

VI

To-day on our Nation's ensign nigh fifty stars are found,
In brilliant constellations, to illumine the azure ground,
And every star of them all hath peculiar lustre, I ween,
But belike the New seem different from the Old war-stained Thirteen.
Yea, while its priceless glory each several State doth hold,
Yet the Red and White of the emblem must still belong to the Old.

VII

So forget not, ye Western brothers, the font where your infancy fed,
The Eastern States, whose borders with the patriots' blood were red ;
Remember the thrilling story of our country's natal morn,
And tell it again in triumph to children yet unborn ;
May you keep your escutcheon as stainless as that of your sires hath been,
And never belie the manhood you drew from the Old Thirteen.

THE SUTLER.

WALDO CAMPBELL HIBBS.

SUTLER! What a world of reminiscence that title (for was it not a title?) brings to the mind of the volunteer soldier of the American Civil War. All attempts to find his like have failed. The Sutler of to-day is not he. The Sutler of the Revolution had not even the prerequisite of sex, for in her we find also the camp-washerwoman; and no woman could have ever risen to the dizzy heights of inglorious eminence in such a vocation (or shall we call it art?) to which he aspired and reached. He was *sui generis;* his species is extinct.

Of any nationality was he, yet no nation acknowledged him. What was his status? He was a volunteer; no sutler was ever drafted. He entered into the cause—of Mammon—with an eagerness to serve which, had it been one tithe as intense in some other cause, must have won him laurels such as would have sunk into oblivion the deeds of all heroes in times before or after. But for meed of praise, crown of fame, honorable scar or storied bust, he cared not; nay, despised. He professed no patriotism, though among patriots; he pretended to no bravery, though brave men surrounded him; he cherished no war-like ambitions, though he existed only in time of war. Of money he risked all he had; for money he suffered or rejoiced.

Subject to military discipline, he ranked a trifle higher than corporal, a fraction lower than army mule. In theory, his position was impregnable, secured by official mandate; in practice, kicks, curses, and wanton spoliation were his dues; yet his revenge was keen.

Men's food is their spirit, their nature—within limitations. Who shall not say that upon his shoulders rests much of the responsibility for battles lost, for inglorious retreats, for disaffection among generals, for ignominious guard-house incarcerations, for untimely sojourns in gloomy hospital? Would not the sum total of the ills devolving upon the warrior have been less but for the insidious presence of a sutler? A glance at the stock in trade of any one of him forces one irresistibly to this sad conclusion; or, at best, grave doubt must arise. Such fare as rancid sardines and petrified bologna, gall-tasting pickles, cough candy, potatoes hardened to a leaden consistency, and soft bread six months old, topped off with exiled bourbon, streak lightning in liquid form, and Havana onion leaves for

smoking purposes, was not calculated to produce heroes. These and an hundred other prime necessaries of luxurious military existence were here, side by side with such articles of the toilet as wooden combs, wrinkled pocket-mirrors, eyeless needles, pointless pins, lip salve, razor soap and plasters.

With more or less capital and credit, usually the possession of some mistaken and always unknown personage who secured his right to exist as sutler, he set forth on his mission of extortion. His vocation was indeed one of vicissitudes. The end of a campaign might find him with a balance sheet that would not balance, a tattered tent, a battered wagon, hundreds of pounds of scorned "sundries," and a ledger full of charges against the killed and mortally wounded and missing of the great host that he followed and who were his largest "customers." But again, his venture successful, the bloated bondholder, at whose head so much vituperation has been hurled, were but a groveling worker compared to this Prince of Mammon.

And yet it has been said that the Sutler was greatest at a "charge." His was indeed always the post of danger. In the rear during an advance, in front while on retreat, encompassed about with perils, his deeds in defending his traveling treasure-house of perishables were marvels of intrepidity and generalship. A rallying point in battle was his vehicle, a position contended for by friend and foe alike, when the vicissitudes of combat left it between them. But he was not in the midst of carnage; not he. From some point without the beleaguered citadel he anxiously watched the desperate contest over things despised yet loath of relinquishment by those who struggled. Not until his armed companions, victorious, would turn upon and rend his treasures with mouths made hungry by the mortal conflict, did his smile of "trust" give way to the horror which spread o'er his once gloating visage.

If ever a volunteer warrior fell upon the neck of his regimental sutler and embraced him, history does not record it. Suspicion, not affection, was the sole sentiment that distinguished their intercourse. Always was the stock in trade of the sutler suspected and sneered at, yet was it coveted and—bought. And when pay-day came, Suspicion again made her appearance, stalking ominously at the elbow of the dispenser of depreciated greenbacks. The motto, "Base is the slave that pays," though mayhap written in the heart of many a soldier-boy, ne'er found utterance. With wisdom born of close study of military human nature, the Sutler made himself thoroughly "in it" with the regimental paymaster, and he who had reveled in the effete luxuries of the Sutler's stock found himself in possession of a bill to settle with a despatch that ill comported with martial dignity.

Not only have we seen cavalrymen strapped on their horses, but infantrymen "strapped" on the ground. The one who furnished the material for the "strapping" was the Sutler, and he who paid for it was the individual soldier. The preparatory command was not "Prepare to strap on," but "Prepare to be strapped." The feat was common and not very difficult of accomplishment, for when one received greenbacks with gold at 240, he was pretty well "strapped" already. All that was necessary to complete the job was to walk up to the Sutler's tent or wagon—always placed in an easily seen or convenient spot—square up arrearages, and order "erplugerterbacker" or "ercaneroysters."

There was grim humor about the Sutler, his ways and his means. Time mars our bliss, yet soothes our sorrows, and to say "Sutler" in any gathering of old soldiers is now almost certain to set the story-telling mill going. Many "good ones" are related at the expense of both sutler and his victim.

The writer remembers an Englishman who was appointed sutler of an Ohio regiment, the members of which were noted for their cunning, their duplicity, and their valor. The sutler was one of those early on the ground, for he appeared in May of the first year of the Civil War. A few days after he had set forth his stock, the colonel of the regiment met him and asked him how he liked his new "business."

"Ho, first-rate," said the embryo highwayman.

"The 'boys' patronize you, then?" asked the father of the regiment.

"Yes, hindeed; hit's the best and liveliest trade Hi 'ave hever struck."

The colonel then queried as to what companies dealt with him most liberally.

Said Ezekiel, "They hall do, but Company J buys the most."

"Company J!" exclaimed the officer; "I guess you mean Company I."

No, he didn't mean Company I. "Company

Hi don't buy nothink, scarcely. Hi means Company J."

The colonel tried hard to explain, but the sutler would not have it. He triumphantly exhibited his book, showing the orders on the paymaster. An inspection revealed strange names for that extravagant Company J, and the colonel assured his sutler that not a man of Company J belonged to the command. As soon as he mastered the situation, Ezekiel pulled a long face and remarked confidentially to the colonel:

"Why, blawst them Company J fellows! They've hup-heended me, 'aven't they?"

And the upshot of it all was that he resigned soon afterward, and was succeeded by one who was known as "the apple-butter man," and who was "consid'ble hard" to "hup-heend."

Another sutler, this one the purveyor to a New York regiment, kept in his stock a barrel of really very fine whisky. The price of it was a little high for patriots wearing corkscrew caps and getting (on the books) $13 a month, but they wanted some of that whisky. A smooth-faced, boyish young fellow proposed a plan. A crowd of his companions in wickedness got into the shanty and kept the sutler busy. Even that usually respectable personage, the orderly sergeant, sat on the barrel and joked and laughed in his loudest key. Into the cellar under the shanty went a few of the "boys" with camp kettle. The instigator of the plot had an auger, and the orderly sergeant's voice above told him where to locate the cask. It was the work of a few moments to bore through the floor and into the keg, and draw all the precious fluid into the kettles. As the thieves sneaked back into quarters they could hear the other folks quarreling with the sutler about some mistake in giving change to one of them the day before. And it was several hours later, when a darky brought a flask from the colonel to be filled, that the this-time victim discovered the outrage. It was too late then, but doubtless he "got back on 'em" before he was through with that regiment. Incidentally, I may say that the chief robber on this occasion is now the much-loved pastor of a church out in Iowa.

While located in forts or other permanent garrisons, the Sutler had things much his own way, but while campaigning he was compelled to "look a leetle oudt." It happened one day that a New York battery attached to the Third Corps turned from the road into a meadow to feed their teams, and while waiting the men disposed of the few fragments in their haversacks and called them "dinner." There was still, as was often the case, considerable air-space left under the belt, and some of the men, seeking what they might devour, spied a sutler's tent, and at once "made tracks" for it. But they had no money; and when they joined the crowd around the tent and witnessed the things there set forth in appetizing array they groaned in spirit. Cans of lobster and condensed milk and gingersnaps tempted the hungry palate. But the aforesaid impecunious volunteers soon discovered something in the wind. Going around to the back of the tent they saw about a hundred men engaged in quietly watching the gathering of a cyclone destined to sweep down upon and envelop the unsuspicious sutler. Some of the ropes of the tent had been loosened; men held them taut, awaiting the signal for catastrophe. Suddenly, with a wild yell, the crowd surged against the side of the canvas, the ropes were let go, and over it went with a rush. The sutler, oh, where was he? Before

that bewildered individual could extricate himself from the hopeless entanglement in which he found himself the crowd had dispersed, and with it the treasures he so dearly prized.

And so, "goin' through the sutler" was a favorite pastime indulged in with enthusiasm and dexterity by all within reach, upon the slightest pretext that promised success. But here again the suave dispenser of *in*edibles enjoyed revenge. After a successful wrestle with and consumption of stolen toothsome morsels many a doughty private was fain to lie down in his rubber blanket and wish he might even die unhonored and unsung could he be rid of the direful agony that possessed him.

But enough. The Sutler is no more. Of all the unique characters upon the stage in the great drama of the Civil War none played their part so well as he nor became so intimately woven into the lives (and stomachs) of the soldiers whom he fed and bled. He came from no one knows where; he departed without a sign into the misty vale of the past.

FORAGING IN THE KANAWHA VALLEY.

H. S. FORD.

THE incidents here related occurred during the Kanawha campaign, when the Federal forces, under General J. D. Cox, were pursuing the Confederates, under Generals Floyd and Wise, up the valley. There had been a few engagements, which in those early days we called "battles," but which, measured by the tremendous struggles of the later years of the conflict, were but unimportant skirmishes. At the time of which I write, we were pushing the enemy very close; in fact, it was no uncommon thing for our advance cavalry boys to eat the hot breakfast prepared for the rear-guard of the Confederate army—an opportunity which our people never neglected, for who ever saw a soldier who was not ready for a square meal, and scheming all the time to get something to eat outside of the regular rations?

The last I saw of Wise's army was at a place called Hawk's Nest. The rear-guard of the enemy brought on a "spat" with our artillery, which lasted only a short time, and which ended in the premature discharge of one of our guns, from which the swab or rammer had not yet been removed. This novel projectile went whistling across the field and into the ranks of the enemy,

creating great consternation. They were not accustomed to missiles of this character and jumped to the conclusion that we were giving them the much-dreaded "chain-shot." Well, I have since seen batteries limber up and get out with considerable celerity, but I don't recall any greater expedition and rapidity of movement than our opponents exhibited that day. Both sides were comparatively green at the business at that time. I have no doubt that the survivors of both blue and gray who were in that campaign will recall this incident, for it was the talk of our camp, and also that of the Confederates, according to the stories of some prisoners who were captured soon after.

Like most mountain regions, the Kanawha Valley was largely loyal. The old flag was frequently seen displayed above the cabins of the woodsmen, and our approach was hailed with delight by blacks and whites alike. There were also many gangs of bushwhackers—that contemptible class of semi-brigands who were hated and despised by both Confederates and Federals. They had no general organization, but preyed upon whoever came in their way. Capital shots were these long, loose-jointed outlaws, and their rifles were often of the best quality and range, being effective at a thousand or twelve hundred yards. These men were perfectly familiar with every nook and corner of the territory, and their rifles would crack and their bullets sing from all sorts of unlikely places. Many a poor straggler dropped dead with a bullet hole in his back before he could turn and see his skulking murderer slip into the bush. The soldiers had no love and less pity for the bushwhackers, and lost no time in "wiping them out" whenever the opportunity offered.

After the little fight at Hawk's Nest, our army, about 5,000 strong, gave up the pursuit of Wise, who had disappeared from our front, and went into camp. After a time, camp life and rations became monotonous, and the boys conceived and executed various plans for killing time and adding to the variety of our bill of fare. Foraging was strictly forbidden by general orders, but the prohibition did not "go" with all the boys, as was proved by the frequent appearance on our tables of fat little pigs and plump turkeys. Our officers were on the alert, and frequently inquired the source of our undue supply of fresh meat, but their inquiries always elicited the short, sharp, and decisive reply, "Bought it!" which answered every purpose, in the absence of controverting testimony.

One morning, in company with my side partner and comrade, Ben, I started on a little raid of my own, the object being "fresh meat." All went well until we reached our outer pickets, but after considerable dodging and crawling we at length found ourselves outside the lines. The country was hilly and broken, with here and there a cabin or clearing. Numerous by-paths diverged from the few roads. Following one of these paths for a mile or two, we came upon a substantial log-house in the midst of a clearing. Upon our approach a pack of hounds came tearing to greet us, making a terrible noise and causing us to pause a moment for consideration. Just then the cabin door opened and a venerable old darky made his appearance. He stood and gazed at us for some time in silent wonder, then clasped his hands and shouted: "Bress de Lawd! Am you some of Massa Linkum's men? We hab been waitin' fer you eber so long, an' here yo' is now, shuah!"

Calling off the dogs, the old man rushed to greet us most cordially. "Come right in hyar, right in dis yer cabin, an' de ol' 'oman'll hab yo' sumfin to eat."

Everything about the cabin gave evidence of neatness and thrift. The old "aunty" busied herself with getting up a first-class "feed" for us, being assisted by her daughter. The old man plied us with questions about the war, asked us whether we ever knew John Brown, and a hundred other inquiries of a similar character. At last he unearthed from some corner a little brown jug, which he handed to Ben, saying: "Try some ob dis yer peach brandy. Dat ar was made by my ole massa, way down in ole Kaintuck." Ben says it was good.

Then we had a veritable feast of slapjacks and honey, hoe-cakes, pumpkin pie, and lots of other good things—a feast fit for the gods, or at least we thought so. After dinner we took leave of our kindly host, receiving from him a warning to "look out fur dem 'fernal bushwhackers—heap o' dem 'roun' dar."

Ben and I were out for a tramp. Four days we traveled over hills and valleys, across creeks and rivers, living on the fat of the land. We knew we were in hourly peril, but this excitement only lent zest to the sport. We were in danger of being gobbled up at any minute by the bushwhackers, or of being taken into camp by some remaining straggling detachment of Wise's command. But luck was with us. Not only were we unmolested by enemies, but we were not discovered by our own guards, and the people we encountered fed us bounteously.

The afternoon of the fourth day found us back within two miles of our own picket line, at a point where two roads branched off from the main road, which led directly to our camp. Here we sat down to rest and consider. We had an immense sack of edibles which we had "bought," and we were anxious to get the goods into camp. We also wanted to get back ourselves without attracting too much attention or receiving an ovation from the corporal of the guard. While this "committee of safety," so to speak, was in the midst of an executive session, a mounted Federal officer suddenly made his appearance around a sharp bend in the road only a few rods away. We knew at once that we were in for it, for he saw us quite as soon as we saw him, and it was useless to try to hide. I am not sure he was glad to see us, and I know we were not overjoyed at his coming.

We quietly awaited the officer's approach. He rode directly to us, and proved to be Captain W——, of an Ohio regiment belonging to our brigade. Ben and I stood at "present arms," which salute he courteously returned. Then started in pursuit. An instant later we saw the captain assumed a most dignified and ultra-military attitude, and in a voice almost tragic in its severity demanded our names and the cause of our absence from camp; also upbraided us for foraging, saying that General Cox's orders were imperative, forbidding all depredations, etc. For several minutes he lectured us, saying that we had subjected ourselves to trial by a drumhead court-martial, and stood a good chance of being "shot at the head of the regiment," etc.

This all sounded wonderfully solemn and serious, but somehow it didn't seem to impress us very deeply. I do not know how long the officer would have kept up the harangue, but it was cut short by a sudden and irrelevant exclamation from Ben:

"Look! There he goes! There is one of them!" pointing down the road.

Sure enough, there was one of the hated bushwhackers, mounted on a powerful bay horse and armed with one of those long, deadly rifles which lay across his pommel. When Ben first caught sight of him, he was just coming out of the brush into the road; he did not see us until he reached the middle of the road, about 300 yards away. Evidently the surprise was mutual.

The bushwhacker instantly turned his horse and galloped away like the wind. The captain, taking in the situation at a glance, made one grab for Ben's Enfield, secured the weapon, and started in pursuit. An instant later we saw him raise the rifle and take quick aim. A flash, a sharp report, and the fleeing bushwhacker, now fully 400 yards away, threw up his arms and fell to the ground, his left foot catching in the stirrup, so that the rider was dragged fully fifty yards before his foot become disentangled, when he lay prostrate on the dusty road, while the big bay horse soon disappeared in the distance.

The captain coolly returned the rifle to Ben, remarking: "One more rubbed out. How was that for a flying shot?"

This all occurred in an instant, a mere flash, and it was the best shot I have ever seen before, during, or since the war, with a musket. We found the bushwhacker as dead as a hammer, with a ragged bullet hole in the middle of his back. I picked up his rifle, upon the stock of which were eleven notches, which, I suppose, represented the number of his victims. We dug a hole by the roadside, and covered him up, with no prayers, and I fear no sorrow. The captain remarked: "That fellow will do no harm, for I have mustered him out."

Captain W—— was a pretty good fellow, and let us go our way. We dodged the pickets that night and got safely to camp, and up to the present time neither of us has been court-martialed or "shot at the head of the regiment," nor experienced any other evil effects from our pleasant and exciting foraging expedition in the Kanawha Valley.

THE VICTORY OF PEACE.

FRANK H. SWEET.

An old battlefield
  In the sunny South,
And a sparrow's nest
  In a cannon's mouth;
The cannon buried
  Under leaves and dust,
And scarred and broken
  By its years of rust;
But the sparrow sings
  Through the livelong day,
And clambering vines
  Make the cannon gay

THE BLUE AND THE GRAY.

MARION JULIET MITCHELL.

THE blue and the gray took their muskets one day,
   To settle a little dispute ;
Each said they were right, and declared they would fight,
   As long as they had a recruit.

With looks that were surly, they started out early,
   And thought it might take them till noon ;
But if as intended, by night 'twas not ended,
   They'd fight by the light of the moon.

Now, when these great powers had fought several hours,
   The battle had scarcely begun ;
And when time for dinner, lo, neither was winner,
   Nor was at the setting of sun.

On, on went the fight, both by day and by night,
   For neither were cowards nor meek ;
Till some dared to say, that to end the affray,
   It possibly might take a week.

But time travels fast, and the weeks and months passed,
   Till cold weather came with its snows ;
Then each, thinly dressed, soon concluded 'twas best,
   To send for their old winter clothes.

With hopes and with fears, thus had passed weary years,
   Since that morning battle begun ;
But neither would yield, nor abandon the field,
   And neither the contest had won.

And though long ago, as the records will show,
   At length smiling peace was restored ;
'Tis grievous to say there are many to-day,
   Who this happy fact have ignored.

Although not in style, and the critics may smile,
   A moral I here would append :
Don't fight o'er the laurels, nor keep up your quarrels,
   When war hath once come to an end.

THE BATTLE OF NASHVILLE.

R. B. STEWART, Co. E, 15TH OHIO VOLUNTEERS.

"NASHVILLE" is the last of a long list of names inscribed on the banners of the "Army of the Cumberland." On Brentwood Hills was positively the last appearance of that magnificent army whose acquaintance we made at Shiloh, and with whose fortunes we were so intimately connected during the long three years that followed.

At Donaldson, at Vicksburg, at Appomattox, and at Goldsboro large armies were surrendered. But to General Thomas alone and the army that he commanded must be given the honor of having completely destroyed one of the largest armies mustered during the war, and we who had so often met it face to face know that it was not the least gallant of them all.

The battle of Nashville was decided at Franklin two weeks before it was fought, and it was only the wreck of an army that lay siege to the capital of Tennessee. If it were not the sublimest faith and most exalted courage on the part of the Southern army, it was the blindest credulity and most reckless bravery that compelled its action. It was no doubt faith and discipline on the part of the men, but to my mind it could not have been anything but blind presumption on the part of their leaders.

The prize was a rich one and worth all that could have been paid for it had the prize been won, but it was a prize not to be had at any sacrifice. We who were shut up for two weeks within the defences of the city had a good understanding of the situation, and a full assurance of what the result would be. It was true that we had retreated from Franklin, but that was on the program, and it did not humble us in our own estimation at all.

We had reached the limit of our backward march and now were ready to fight, and somehow we all had the impression that whatever the fighting would be in character, it was going to be our last. We spent two weeks of solid soldierly comfort in Nashville. The freedom of the city was given to us, and our going and coming was unrestrained by either pickets or provost guards. We lived on the fat of the market and crowded the theatres and playhouses every night, and it is pleasant to record that this liberty was never abused except by those who would not have been restrained by all the guards that could have been mustered.

The enemy gave us no trouble after the first day or two, though they were only a few rods away. General Stanley's headquarters were in the Acklin house, a fine large mansion near the Granny White pike. On a low hill not far away was posted the first brigade, third division, fourth army corps. It was a position from which could be had a fine view of the field in front. It was here that the two armies were nearest together. It was also a favorite resort for many of the aristocracy of Nashville. They came in crowds to get a view of their Southern friends. For a few days they were tolerated, when some of their actions not being pleasing to the Federal soldier they were given a gentle hint to stay away. Being slow to take the hint, picks and shovels were put into their unwilling hands, and an hour's work in the trenches satisfied their curiosity and they came no more to camp.

The days passed on, with the weather becoming more and more disagreeable. Our breastworks were completed, our picket duties light, and our camp required but little care. There was nothing for us to do but wait. What the next move would be we could not tell, but the longer we waited the more evident it became that we would have to begin the movement.

On the morning of the 15th of December we were under arms by daylight and awaiting the command to march. A heavy fog was hanging over the country, hiding everything but itself from view. The hours passed away and everything remained quiet. The sutler, foreseeing a lack of customers, rolled out his beer kegs and invited us all to drink. We heartily accepted his invitation, all of us except perhaps the chaplain, and I am not sure about him. Whether it was the beer or the rising sun or both together that drove the fog away I will not pretend to say, but about ten o'clock we began to see things clearly, and looking from our hill away off to the right we saw that something was going on. Groups of horsemen were riding over the hills and disappearing in the valleys. It was Wilson's cavalry moving to the front. Soon the reports of carbines and the boom of cannon came to our ears and we knew that the battle had begun. We kept our eyes upon the open fields across which we knew the enemy's lines were formed. By and by the cavalry reappeared upon the borders of those fields, and as they advance, squads of men rise up suddenly from the ground, wait only long enough to empty their rifles, then start for the South with all possible speed, or, laying down their arms quietly, wait to be gathered into the United States.

As we watch with all our eyes, the scene grows more and more interesting and the situation somewhat reveals itself. Our position is a pivot upon which the whole right wing of our army is turning. The bugles upon the extreme right of the infantry sound "Forward," and the command passes down the line. One by one the regiments and the brigades join the movement, and we can see the enemy's line crumbling and breaking to pieces before the sweep of that mighty arm. Impatiently we wait our time. At last the bugle sounds, and at the first note we leap over the breastworks, then with a wild rush and shout down the gentle slope of the hill and across the narrow strip of neutral ground, we reach the Confederate line only to find it deserted except by those who were willing to fight no more, and the guns of a battery that they were unable to get away. These were soon turned upon their retreating owners and added noise and interest to the occasion.

We were not expecting any serious resistance but were surprised at the weakness of the enemy and the heartlessness of his defence. It was like striking a hard blow at some object when no object was there. The pursuit was continued until night came on and compelled us to halt.

The next morning we were up bright and early and ready for work. During the night Hood had rallied his broken army and concentrated it along the crest of a low range of limestone hills. Directly across these hills ran the Franklin pike on its way to the South. The place was well chosen and its natural strength increased by a hastily constructed line of breastworks. Behind these logs and rocks and brush the Southern army was waiting to fight its last battle. Their prospect was a hopeless one, as Hood himself must have seen; but he was a fighter and not a retreater, and he thought to gain time if nothing more.

Two companies of the 15th Ohio were sent around to the extreme left of the line to feel after the enemy's flank. We found it, but there did not seem to be much of it. However, we let it alone and quietly awaited events. Our army was being concentrated and made ready for a last grand charge. Steedman's brigade of colored troops was moved up and put in position on the left. Our two companies were thus left without anything to do except look on and enjoy the show. We might have taken this as an insult, but we did not. Our colored brothers were welcome to the place of honor, and we were satisfied to be left in the rear, and glad to be lookers-on for once.

When all was ready, or supposed to be, the word was given, and the line of black and blue moved steadily forward until they were lost to view in the fog and smoke of battle. The grapeshot began to rattle uncomfortably close to the lookers-on, and we retired to a safer if not a better place of observation.

It soon became evident that the charge was a failure. The firing ceased, and back out of the smoke came hundreds of struggling and wounded men, followed by the broken and dis-ordered regiments. But there was no rush, no panic. The officers soon had the men under control. The regiments were reformed, the stragglers gathered up, and the wounded sent to the rear. Only some one had blundered. The command was given too soon, and the black bri-gade fought its battle alone.

All was ready once more and the command given. This time the whole line moved forward, and sooner than was expected the works were carried, and the enemy, or all that was left of an enemy, was sent back through the woods and down the road toward the land whence they came.

Night came on with fog and rain and put an end to the pursuit. But it began early next day and continued through rain and mud as far as Lexington. Here Hood's army disappeared forever from our front and we were left without an occupation. Already we had heard of Sherman's march through Georgia, and the capture of Savannah. In a few days we went into winter-quarters near Huntsville, fully as-sured that our work was over and our warfare ended.

A RECONSTRUCTED REBEL.

J. M. WADDILL.

BESIDE the road I traveled, on a sultry day in June,
  A little farm lay baking beneath the noonday sun ;
The owner, gray and grizzled, plow'd the thin and thirsty soil,
His face and hands an index to his life of constant toil.

I noticed as he nearer came, that with an only hand
The plow was guided steadily in turning up the land.
Assured that in that empty sleeve a gallant story lay,
I paused to say a kindly word, and hear its history.

"Yes, stranger, up to Gettysburg, I can't now rightly tell
Just whar it were, but think they call it Cemetery Hill ;
The orders was, that not a man should stop to fire a shot
While rushin' up the slope. I tell you, sir, 'twas hot.

"A few of us got nigh enough to count ther noses, plain,
The grape an' minnies spatt'rin' like a summer show'r o' rain,
When all at onct I felt myself a-whirlin' round and round,
An' never stopped untwel I tumbled back'ards on the ground.
I s'pose it must have been a shell, the way the job were done,
For when I reach'd to git my gun, I found one arm were gone.

"Was I captur'd ? Yes, you bet ; they did that quick enough,
An' soon ther doctors had me. Ah, you'd better b'lieve 'twas tough !
I didn't mean to say but what they toted fair and square,
For wer'n't there thousands of ther men a-lyin' ev'ry-where ?

"Lee blunder ? Well, when first I heard we had the charge to make,
I thought that maybe old Mars' Bob had made a slight mistake ;
But when I thought it over good, I know'd the move was right,

And ever since I've thought the same, altho' we lost the fight.
If thar was any blunder made, it wer'n't by Gin'ral Lee ;
For such as that wer'n't possible—the thing just *couldn't* be.
A Higher Power was rulin', tho' we done the best we could
To smash the Union, but He sav'd it up for something good.

"Hard work a-plowin' ? Well, not now, but when I first-begun it,
I found it pretty rough, but tried the trick and won it ;
A rock or stump would jerk the plow an' pitch me 'cross the row,
But now I've learnt to dodge an' jump, but has to do it slow.
I've work'd this farm for thirty year, in cold as well as heat,
An' saved enough to buy the land, an' made enough to eat.
I feel as big as any man, altho' I'm short an arm,
But now I've got to braggin', but I didn' mean no harm.

"Would I like to try it over ? No ; this Union's here to stay ;
It b'longs as much to me as them ; leastways, I feel that way.
But if I had my other arm a-swingin' in its place,
I'd like to stand up with them fellers what we us'ter face,
An' fight some kings or emperors, or maybe try the czar,
Or anybody, just to show 'em how to run a war.
I'm not a-goin' to criticise the fight the Yankees made,
Ther men was jest as good an' brave as ever lived or died ;
I mean I'd like to show 'em how, with little bread or credit,
To march and fight for months an' years, and see the way we did it.
But here I am a-talkin' 'twel the sun is down a'most,
So good-bye, stranger. Git up, Beck, an' make the time we've lost !"

A BRAVE MAN'S SENSATIONS IN BATTLE.

J. M. WADDILL.

CAPTAIN MORROW is a quiet, matter-of-fact man, who came home from Virginia in '65 with little or nothing of worldly goods to his name except the worn suit of gray in which he stood. Twenty odd years of industry finds him now with a good share of taxable property, an unsullied name, and a warm welcome to such as find pleasure in his society.

It was a fact known to all in his neighborhood, that the old captain made a fine soldier in his day, cool, steady, and reliable. We therefore selected him as a suitable and competent witness to testify in a dispute between myself and a friend concerning the sensations of a brave man in battle, and it was settled that his experience should be taken as evidence by which the question at issue should be finally decided.

We found him seated on his piazza after supper enjoying his pipe, and the question in dispute was laid before him.

"The testimony you wish, boys, involves a wide range of condition, varying very much in accordance with the circumstances; the state of one's liver, stomach, and temper having a large bearing in the matter. I guess I can do no better than to try and give you my experience in one battle (and a very trying one to me) as in a general way illustrative of my sensations in others.

"This fight took place late in the war, in February, '65, to the right of Petersburg, Virginia, where Grant was continually stretching his lines around our right wing in the effort to reach and destroy Lee's railroad communication with the States of the further South. History has but little to say of this battle, though it was bloody for a brief time. We were in pretty good winter quarters, behind a line of low earthworks which extended continuously to and around Petersburg.

"On a cold, bleak morning in February, the long roll startled me from a sound sleep just before daylight. I seemed to hear the rattle of the drum for some seconds before I could awake; at least, that was my thought as I bounded off my bunk and felt around in the darkness for my clothing, sword, and belt. As I stepped out of my hut, half clad and shivering with the cold, I heard my orderly sergeant storming at the men to 'fall in.'

"In a few seconds the company was formed, and we took our place in the regiment. It was too dark to see, but the colonel's voice could be heard as he gave the command, 'Forward, march!' and we moved off in rear of the earthworks in the direction of Petersburg. It was an intensely cold, misty morning, and it seemed as if daylight would never come. We stumbled on for half an hour in the darkness, over stumps and logs, until there were some signs of daylight, when the regiment was halted at a narrow opening in the works. Here we found some pieces of artillery, the horses harnessed, and the artillerymen sitting motionless in their saddles and on the caissons.

"In a few minutes we filed through the works into the open field beyond, where there were other bodies of troops waiting in silence, apparently for orders. As these were passed, one of the men said to a comrade:

"'So we're to be the advance, it seems.'

"'Of course,' replied the other, in tones of disgust, 'ain't it always so?'

"'Fold up your tongue, Williams, and pack it away till next summer; where's your thirst for glory?'

"'I thirst now for a warm bed and a good breakfast later,' answered Williams.

"'Don't you know Mars' Bob can't make a mistake?'

"'That's so,' replied Williams, 'but some of his couriers made a whopper in waking us up too early.'

"With such chaffing we passed out of the open into a wood. The talking ceased, and the silence was broken only by the hurried tread of the men and the clanking of the canteens.

"A few hundred yards further on, and the column is again halted.

"'Load your guns, men,' is the order, and the ramrods are ringing in the Enfields as the cartridges are pressed home.

"The first command to load always gave me a slight shiver. The order is suggestive of blood. I have known of but few jests circulating among the men while obeying it, and now the wag of the company is as solemn as a judge.

"A short distance further, and the line of battle is formed. Scarcely a word is spoken, save the quick, sharp word of command, as the companies file into their places. Some of the men seem confused, though all are veterans, and appear to have partially forgotten the usual company commands.

"'Skirmishers to the front!' is passed down the column, and the thin line of sharpshooters trot away and in a few seconds are lost to sight.

"It is a solemn moment, and I find it necessary to keep my teeth clenched to keep them from chattering with something else besides the cold. I also have an involuntary 'catch' of the breath occasionally, such as you may have experienced or noticed in others, when by a fall the breath is for a moment lost.

"'Forward!' is the order, loudly repeated down the line, and the long double column, neither end of which can be seen, moves rapidly to the front. Soon it is broken and in disorder from the obstruction of the trees and leafless undergrowth, and the order is passed to halt and reform. As the ranks are closed up, scattering shots are heard in front and to the right and left, which by the time we are again moving forward have rapidly increased in number. Our skirmishers have struck those of the enemy. We press on, and in a few minutes our sharpshooters are in sight, popping away at the bluecoats, who seem disposed to stand their ground. Minié balls are whistling about us by this time, and the men involuntarily dodge.

"An opening in the distance can be seen through the trees as we hurry on, crowding too near upon the skirmishers, who, with a yell, charge the opposing line, which, seeing our column, retreat toward the open.

"A gray-coated skirmisher passes through our line to the rear, with blood streaming from a wound in his face, over which both hands are pressed, and I step over a fallen body clad in blue.

"We are near the opening now, in the edge of which is our skirmish line, banging away at the enemy, who have taken possession of shallow rifle-pits, further out in the opening. Something rises in my throat, producing a choking sensation, and I can plainly hear my heart beat. Pallor may not be felt, but I think I must have been very pale.

"'Great God, captain, look up there!' exclaims one of my lieutenants, as we reach the edge of the open ground, halting to again reform amid the whistling bullets from the enemy.

"I grow faint and weak, as I gaze at the sight before us. A long hill, smooth and bare. In front, to the right and left, as far as the eye can reach—the crest crowned with a long line of red earthworks dotted at fearfully short intervals

with black-mouthed cannon, while above the red ridge are thousands of bayonets glistening in the sunlight as it breaks through the morning mist. All eyes are fixed upon the unwelcome spectacle, and the faces of my veterans blanch as they read the task before them. The suspense is terrible. The men appear paralyzed, for it seems to everyone useless, hopeless slaughter.

"Without orders, firing has begun to our left, and my men are beginning to follow the example.

"'Steady, men! hold your fire!' I yell. 'Don't you see our skirmishers right before you?'

"'Keep your men well in hand, captain, and hold your fire till we mount the works,' says the colonel in passing, in a voice so cool and collected, and free from excitement, that for the moment I feel that I am, beyond doubt, the worst coward in the regiment. But his manner does me a world of good, and I ask the adjutant, as he hurries past, who our support is to be. 'Archer, I think,' he answers, and at that moment the command, 'Forward!' rings out above the din.

"Forward we go, helter-skelter! no time for reflection! It is death to which we hasten. Flesh and blood cannot accomplish the task assigned us, if those are men behind the works on the hill-top; but on we go. As the line shows itself in the field, the earth fairly trembles under the explosion of artillery and small arms from the crest of the hill, which disappears from view in the cloud of smoke. Onward we go, stooping and crouching from the tornado. The rush of shells and hiss of bullets is continuous. Right in our faces the shells are bursting. Men are falling in every direction, and those in the scattered line seem dazed, but on, on we go, up the incline, hurrying to our graves. All formation is lost in the headlong rush and by the gaps made by those who have fallen. The very earth seems as if it were swept by the rain of missiles.

"We haven't fired a shot. It were death, seemingly, to pause for the aim. All depends on reaching the works as quickly as possible. Our column seems little more than a scattered group of skirmishers. On we scramble, and we are momentarily expecting the clash of bayonets when the works are reached. Now all fear is gone; it is horrible, but it is exhilarating. We are not men now; animals, beasts of prey, blood-thirsty devils we are. Desperation has routed fear, hope, and mercy.

"My sabre swings high in the air, and the yell of a fox hunter first at the death rises to my lips. Onward we go! Will the crest never be reached?

"'It's no use, captain. There's nobody to our left,' yells old Klutts, my orderly sergeant, in my ear, and the handful of men see it in a moment. True it is; there is no use in going further. My little remaining reason says plainly it is no use. The fire has slackened slightly; doubtless they are getting ready with the bayonet. Nothing remains but to get back as quickly as possible, and that means death for the few survivors.

"'Back, men! back for your lives!' and the dread retreat commences. The men in the works have heard the shout, and their fire is redoubled. Surely none can escape the storm of lead beating upon us. There is a slight ravine in our path, a mere wash in the hillside, barely deep enough to hide our bodies. With a common impulse, each one falls despairingly into it, lying prone in its bottom to escape the steady rain of the bullets. The less-favored portion of our decimated column, which formed our right, continue the fearful retreat, and we lose sight of them as we flatten ourselves in the ravine's bottom. For some moments not a sound escapes our lips, each one realizing that a few brief minutes will decide whether death or a prison awaits us, for certainly the Federal line will soon advance.

"It was yet some 400 yards to the wood whence we had advanced to attack, and perhaps 150 paces to the enemy's works. Momentarily I expected the shouts of the victorious Federals as their advance began. This meant a prison for us. Little time there is for consideration, yet I cannot make up my mind to risk further retreat. It seems madness, for I well know that our first appearance will be the signal for a hurricane of fire, which has just now greatly diminished.

"The thought of a Northern prison decides me, and in a moment of desperation I cry to the men, 'Get ready! We can't stay here! Be ready at the word to move, one at a time!'

"Either the order was misunderstood, or the men lost their heads, for when the man nearest me rose to go, every man followed instantly, and I joined them.

"In a moment a perfect tornado of fire opened on us. Man after man tumbled headlong as we ran at the top of our speed for the woods. On we flew over the ground, over the fallen bodies of those of our comrades who fell as we advanced, down the long hillside, seemingly surrounded by a swarm of bullets.

"A fearful price we paid in the alternative we had accepted, for more than one-half of those who started on the retreat lay on the frozen hillside to rise no more.

"As we entered the friendly shelter of the woods, a portion of our force lying flat on the ground, thinking we were the advance of the enemy's skirmishers, opened fire on us, and before their mistake was discovered, two or three of our little handful fell, wounded at the hands of friends. Out of forty-seven men in line at daylight, eleven only of my company remained. The others were dead or wounded on the field in our front. The Federals did not advance, and the miserable affair was over."

"Captain," said my friend, "do we understand you to say that you were scared and fearful on that occasion, or that you simply dreaded the work of the day?"

"Yes, sir," replied the old captain, vigorously, "scared and fearful both." And he knocked the ashes out of his pipe. "And I wouldn't believe a man on his oath who says he is not frightened under such circumstances."

The captain's verdict settled the dispute between us, and we bade him "good-night," leaving him with a yet higher regard for a man who could and did gallantly do his duty on many bloody fields in spite of his fears.

"IN FORO CONSCIENTIÆ."

G. H. BLAKESLEE, 129TH ILLINOIS VOLS.

"THE Southern people, as a mass, never understood the Federal soldier. A majority of them looked upon the Federal soldiers as unprincipled hirelings, cowardly defamers of womanhood, thieves, and murderers!" said the old man, pausing in his whittling long enough to give his knife a vigorous strop upon a well-worn boot-leg. " I

G. H. BLAKESLEE.

tell you, sir, they never understood us. Now, I'm not saying that there were not some cases that fully deserved the execration of the Southern people, and the roughs of the service were abhorred, as they should have been, by all good and true comrades. It could hardly have been otherwise in gathering up two millions of men for an army in any age or any part of the world. But during nearly three years of service, I cannot call to mind a single instance of abuse to a Southern woman by a Union soldier, even when taunted and inflamed, as they sometimes were. It is possible that this was so, because our service was, from the beginning, mostly at the front. Of course, there were individual cases where the Southern people came to know us as we were.

"One particular occurrence, as it comes to mind, makes me almost forget the months of pain I endured, and a limb crippled for life, but

I don't care to speak of it, because I got mixed up in that matter somewhat."

But, on my solemn pledge not to divulge his identity, the veteran told me this "ower true tale."

"You see," the old man commenced, "it happened on the Atlanta Campaign, in '64. We had been keeping things hot for nearly two months, and our ranks were sadly thinned by the fearful storms of lead and iron that had swept our lines all the way from Chattanooga. Day and night the roar of guns, without an hour's cessation, had kept up their fearful work, charging here, flanking there. The Confederates had been forced back a hundred miles through the mountains of northern Georgia, and in those last days of June—

> Kenesaw frowned in its glory,
> Frowned down on the flag of the free,

and 'Uncle Billy' said we would go at that old mountain in front and quit flanking for awhile. Well, you know the results. Two thousand of as brave boys as ever followed 'Old Glory' went down into the cold shadows under the towering cliffs of 'Old Kenesaw.' Those boys, disciplined until they were actually machines, though not of brass and steel, could not accomplish impossibilities, and were swept back, down the steep declivity. Far above them, grand and sullen, were lifted the precipitous battlements of the foe. No bravery, no gallantry, no sacrifice of human victims could secure the prize for which 'Uncle Billy's' boys so grandly struggled.

"Then God let down a fold of his pavilion and darkness covered the mountain—a kindly mantle covering the dead and dying boys in blue and gray.

"Our wounded lay there all those weary hours of pain—unrepining and content. Our dead lay there, and surely they slept well. Some thousands of us stayed there helpless, yet alive, until near morning, when searching parties, under cover of darkness, moved us to the rear.

"Brought back with others was Fred W., a lad scarcely more than seventeen years of age, of the 79th Ohio (of our brigade), shot through the lungs. With us, also, was brought a young Confederate soldier, mortally wounded, for in such times there was no difference in the care given to the suffering ones on account of the color of the uniform. This Confederate soldier was laid on a cot adjoining mine, and Fred W. on the other side.

"Fred died a glorious death about eleven o'clock A. M., the next day. The surgeon had just finished examining his wounds, and had informed him he had but a short time to live. Fred called his chum, a boy who had brought him off the field, and taking a letter and a picture from his pocket, he kissed them and gave them to his 'pard,' with the request that they be forwarded to his mother in Ohio. Then he said: 'Charlie, the doctor says I must die; that I have but a few moments to live. Now, before I go, I want to give three cheers once more for the old flag,' and raising himself upon one elbow, and swinging his old tattered cap around his head, his lips moved, as if forming a cheer, when the crimson tide burst in jets from those patriot lips, his head drooped upon his manly breast—the cheer was unspoken, he fell back upon his couch dead—great—grand—glorious! A boy in years, his last words, his last thoughts, were for the old flag.

"My other neighbor, the young Confederate, lying on my right, suffered untold agony. He was evidently of good family, intelligent and educated. The long campaigns in which he had been engaged had reduced his wardrobe to a low ebb; but through the torn and tattered raiment shone the reflection of the gentleman.

"In mortal agony, low moans would now and again escape his faltering lips; recovering himself and turning to me he would apologize for having disturbed me. At every request I made for the attendant to bring him some relief, he turned gratefully to me with a gentle 'thank you'; every cup of water brought, or dose of medicine administered, the kindly 'thank you' followed.

"Knowing that his wound was mortal, that his time was short for this earth, he gave me his name, company, and regiment, and requested that should I ever have the opportunity to communicate with his people—but before I learned their address or names he became flighty in his speech, and his mind evidently wandered back to his home in Tennessee.

"Again, he lived over the old home life, among his kindred and friends. He walked along the shady paths, and over the old fields; again he tasted the cold water, which he dipped up with the old gourd, as it flowed over the rocks in the dear old spring-house. Once more he romped with his sisters and talked with them of father and mother in heaven. Again his mind would revert to the war, would dwell upon the gathering gloom that was spreading over his dear Southland, would picture in feeling terms the loss of some brave comrade, and of the suffering borne by those who had been brought up in luxury; but for himself no sigh nor complaint ever escaped him.

"Again becoming a suppliant at the throne of grace, he thanked his Heavenly Father that it was his fortune to have fallen into the hands of those whom in prosperity he had looked upon as enemies, but in his adversity had proved to be friends. He fervently implored that God would be a father to his orphan sisters and protect them in the days to come. In feeling supplication, he asked the Great Ruler to bless his beloved land and the rulers thereof, and prayed that the days of danger and trouble would soon end in peace.

"Thus the moments slipped away, and during the dark hours of night his soul went back to his God, to join the father and mother on the shores of time. Thus passed from my presence through the portals of heaven the immortal spirit of William H. Parks, Co. K, 12th Tennessee, C. S. A.

"At my request young Parks was buried in a shady nook in a grave separate and apart from all others and his lonely resting-place marked. I also mapped the vicinity so that his place of burial could be found in the future, should his friends be discovered.

"In 1869 his remains were disinterred, and now rest with his comrades, in the Confederate Cemetery at Marietta, Georgia.

"Time passed on—weary months in various hospitals. The spring of 1865 opened; the war was virtually over, and the government, regretfully acknowledging that they could not patch me up to be of any further use to them, turned me adrift, a physical wreck, to begin life anew. I endeavored to forget the scenes of those four dark years, and I put as far away from me as it was possible all remembrance of those sad times, till one day, several years after, I came across one of my war-time diaries. It brought to my mind my promise to the dying Confederate.

"I wrote letters to a dozen postoffices in Tennessee but could learn nothing. I resolved to try another method, and advertised in the newspapers of Memphis and Nashville. In a few days letters began coming thick and fast, from comrades, friends, and relatives. No word had ever reached them regarding his fate. From these letters I learned that young Parks's home had been at Humboldt, Gibson County, Tennessee, and that his two sisters lived there. A correspondence followed with one of these sisters, that continued through several months, and I received some of the most beautiful letters from her, all breathing the most devoted Christian spirit, and a gratitude for the small service I had done, but which they felt was of inestimable value to the sorrowing ones. Those letters I cherish to-day with greater pride than any other relics I have of those sad days. Here," said the captain, reaching down from a shelf a little box, "I keep my treasures. You have been so kind as to listen to my story, I will show you them; they are sacred memories, and so must ever remain.

"To idle curiosity seekers, they are never shown; they form one of the links of friendship that bind the blue and the gray in bonds that partisans of North or South shall never sunder.

"Sometimes when my heart is sickened by the hollowness of apparent friendships, I take them down and with dimming sight read over these mementos, and I wander back to that June night in '64, on the banks of Noses Creek in Georgia, under that old hospital tent, and recall the scenes enacted there. I feel that should it ever be my fortune to meet on earth the writers of these letters, the comrades of Willie Parks would be my comrades, and his sisters would be mine also."

The old captain's bowed form straightened up, and clasping his hands behind his back, he walked to a window to conceal his emotion, in his mind evidently living over again those exciting scenes. While thus engaged, I copied the closing sentence of one of the letters; it reads:

May the God of all grace bless you abundantly and make you perfectly happy through eternity, is the prayer of your Southern friend,

MRS. —— ——

HUMBOLDT, TENN.

ANECDOTE OF GENERAL POLK.

A GOOD story is told of Bishop (then Lieutenant General) Polk, of the Confederate army, and another general, whom we will call "Blank," who now resides in Alabama. We cannot vouch for its accuracy, further than to say that we have full confidence in the veracity of the gentleman who related it:

During the Georgia campaign, and not long before General Polk was killed at Pine Mountain, he requested General Blank to accompany him to a hill in front of the lines which commanded an excellent view of the position of the opposing Federal forces. The figures of the two officers outlined upon the sky as they stood upon this eminence, offered a tempting mark for some Federal gunners, and in a few moments both lay on the ground stunned and senseless from the effect of Federal shells. The fortunes of war had brought together a most distinguished churchman and one of the bravest and most trusted of Forrest's officers. The latter, however, was not at the time noted for extreme piety, but was rather given to the use of vigorous language and forcible expletives, which fact the good bishop knew and regretted; he also knew that his present companion was one of the very best and bravest men in the Confederate service.

The two officers lay stunned for several minutes. General Blank was the first to recover. Looking about him in a dazed way, he soon discovered the burly form of his companion, who was breathing heavily but evidently coming around all right. In a few moments he heard General Polk mutter: "Oh, Lord! where am I, where am I?" General Blank, keenly alive to a sense of grim humor, whispered gently: "In hell, general." "Impossible," murmured the semi-conscious Polk. "Who is it that tells me so?" "It is I—General Blank," solemnly responded that practical joker. "Oh, Lord," groaned the good bishop, "have mercy on me! If Blank is here, I know it must be true!"

BOMBARDMENT OF FORT DARLING.

JOHN F. MACKIE.

EARLY in the morning, May 15, 1862, a small fleet of Federal gunboats appeared before the Confederate Fort Darling, on the James River, a few miles below Richmond, Virginia. It consisted of the "Galena," the "Aroostook," the "Naugatuck," the "Port Royal," and the "Monitor," which a few days before had battled successfully with the dreaded "Merrimac" in front of Newport News. Fort Darling was a very strong fortification, situated on a bluff nearly 200 feet above the river, which at this time was swollen to an unusual height. The bombardment commenced early in the morning, and it soon became apparent that the Federal vessels were at a serious disadvantage from inability to get sufficient elevation for their guns, and most of their shots were wasted. Besides, the Confederate gunners sent in the shot and shell too rapidly and accurately for the wooden vessels; and so, in a short time, all the boats had retired except the "Galena,"—Captain John Rodgers. This gallant commander held his position and maintained the fight as long as his ammunition lasted.

During this engagement the "Galena's" crew displayed great heroism, and several of the seamen and marines won the much-coveted "Medal of Honor." John F. Mackie, whose portrait is here shown, was one of the heroes of the occasion, as will appear later. He was a corporal in the marine guard aboard the "Galena." To him we are indebted for the following account of the engagement.

The "Galena" dropped anchor under the guns of the fort, about 400 yards distant. Above her were ten heavy guns in casemate, and a water battery mounting two more of large calibre. Owing to the narrowness of the channel, the "Galena" was forced to remain nearly stationary, which accounts for the great damage she sustained. Early in the engagement, Captain Rodgers was severely wounded, but he stuck to his post all day.

The "Galena" opened with her port battery of six 9-inch guns and two 100-pounder Parrotts, doing considerable execution and actually silencing the enemy's fire for a time. From the first, however, the Confederate gunners had her range, and poured down shot and shell without stint upon the gallant craft. About ten o'clock the fort reopened fire with great energy. Reinforcements of trained gunners said to be the crew from the destroyed "Merrimac," had arrived, and with a cheer that echoed across the James, resumed the battle, which now waxed hot and furious. Nearly every shot struck the "Galena" with terrible effect, and her decks were soon slippery with human blood and covered with the dead and dying and the splintered fragments from her sides. A solid ten-inch shot struck the after 100-pounder, killing and wounding a score of men. At the same instant an eight-inch shot struck her amidships, followed immediately by another which killed a gunner and several men. This same shot struck and exploded a nine-inch shell that was standing on the deck, the fragments of which killed a powder boy who was "passing" a ten-pound cartridge, which in turn was exploded, killing and maiming another score of men, and filling the ship with smoke so that it created the idea that the "Galena" was on fire.

Confusion reigned, and when the smoke drifted away the sight was appalling. The after 100-pounder was all right, but its entire crew of twenty-three men were *hors du combat*. This was Corporal Mackie's opportunity, and he was equal to the occasion. Summoning a number of his mates, the dead and dying were removed, the splinters swept away with a broom, and the gun, under Corporal Mackie's charge, was turned once more upon the Confederate works. The new gun's crew was selected from members of the marine guard, who had been stationed at various points as sharpshooters. The gun was cleverly handled until the close of the engagement, and did effective execution. Though unused to this kind of service, the marines got credit for several very fine shots, one of which blew up a casemate and did great damage to the Confederate works.

During the height of the battle a shot from Fort Darling struck the safety-valve of the "Galena's" engine; a young fireman, named Kenyon, rushed into the blinding live steam and repaired the damage, nearly losing his life in the effort—a most heroic action. A seaman prevented a serious accident by stopping a vent with his bare thumb, which was severely burned by the operation. A white flag, used in signaling the lower fleet, became fouled aloft, conveying the idea of surrender; but Quartermaster Reagan, heedless of the shells

NAVAL MEDAL OF HONOR.

from the fort and the rain of bullets from the sharpshooters who lined the river bank, sprang into the forerigging, ascended a hundred feet, and cleared the flag, throwing it, rolled up in a ball, toward the enemy's works. When he regained the deck after this perilous deed, Captain Rodgers asked him why he threw the flag away in that manner, and Reagan replied: "I wanted to show the 'Johnnies' that we have no use for white flags now or at any other time."

The "Galena" withdrew from the fight in a most pitiable plight. Her sides were riddled, her rigging cut to ribbons, and her smokestack perforated like a huge nutmeg-grater. Her dead had died the death of heroes, and the survivors were covered with glory.

Some time later, President Lincoln and his Cabinet visited the "Galena," and the ship's crew were formally introduced as "a band of heroes." On this occasion, Corporal Mackie and three other young men were called into the presence of the distinguished visitors and awarded Medals of Honor by Mr. Lincoln himself, who personally thanked them for their distinguished gallantry.

The Naval Medal of Honor differs very slightly, in design, from the army medal, as will be seen by the accompanying fac-simile illustration. It carries precisely the same honors.

John F. Mackie comes of good old Scotch stock, and his ancestry shows fighting blood all the way back. He is a native of New York, but at present a resident of Philadelphia, and in 1891 was elected Senior Vice-Commander of the Department of Pennsylvania, G. A. R. He was one of the originators of the strong Naval Post, No. 400, and is the champion of the old sailors and marines. His services during the war were continuous and highly valuable. Comrade Mackie is a staunch patriot, and believes in fraternity and union. He has hosts of friends in the South as well as in the North; knows all about naval history and warfare, and can make an off-hand address that will warm the heart of the most sluggish American, and set the "old vets" wild with enthusiasm. The accompanying portrait is an almost perfect likeness.

REMINISCENCES OF THE SANITARY COMMISSION

WITH THE ARMY OF THE CUMBERLAND.

Mrs. Sophia McClelland.

"A thousand million lives are his, who carries the world in his sympathies."

MRS. SOPHIA MC CLELLAND.

TO those who sit at a distance and read of the marching and manœuvring of a great army, the gay colors, the ringing trumpets, the splendid charge, the dramatic heroism—all these have a grand and pulse-thrilling effect. War is glorious in the abstract; in its details it is sickening and harrowing. The brilliant uniforms soon become faded and stained, and fall into rags or show great patches. The "splendid charge" is a mad rush of maddened men, mounted on strong horses urged to their utmost speed, riding down a mass of fellow-beings on foot. The reader is content with the information that "the enemy's line was broken and gave way." But when the "splendid charge" has done its work and passed by, there remains a spectacle of death and desolation in which grandeur and glory are forgotten and horror reigns supreme. The surgeon's note-book, rather than the flowery pages of the historian, tells the realities of the glories of warfare.

The Crimean War proved the efficiency of skilled women in the army hospital, and this experience led to the early employment of women as nurses during our late Civil War.

Being fully impressed with a sense of my duty, the writer devoted the years of the war to active hospital work.

It was in the early autumn of 1861; regiments of soldiers from the North and West were daily passing through Louisville, Kentucky, to points below on the Louisville and Nashville Railroad. I drove down to the depot, and on passing out of the yard from the train of cars, noticed several of the soldiers lying on the platform, some of whom seemed very ill; I had them removed to some vacant rooms over a warehouse on the opposite corner from the depot, Broadway and Ninth Street; then, driving as rapidly as possible to my residence, gathered up as many blankets, comfortables, and pillows as the carriage could hold, and returned to the newly-improvised hospital. In the neighborhood I procured provisions for the men's supper, and candles to give them light for the evening.

This was the beginning, and the general impression seemed to be that in three or four months the trouble would be all over. But every day added to the numbers in the hospital. Regiments were continually marching through and leaving their sick; skirmishes were frequent on the Nashville Road, and there were those coming to be cared for who were disabled by wounds as well as sickness. We were obliged to depend on soldiers taken from the convalescent wards for nurses, who, though most kind, were unskilled and in most cases illy adapted for their duties, requiring patient training and drilling to render them efficient.

After the battle of Fort Donelson, we took down a party of physicians and clergymen and six ladies as nurses, also a quantity of hospital stores from the sanitary rooms, for the use of the wounded and sick. The expenses of this company were borne by private funds.

General Wm. Nelson had his headquarters at Evansville, Indiana. It was necessary to obtain from him a pass to enter within his lines, which extended to Dover, the point nearest reached to Fort Donelson. He refused an audience to our messengers, though backed by credentials from his personal friend, Dr. Robert Murray, medical director of the department.

They called again, when he consented to see them for a few moments, but sent this message:

"You will say it is simply impossible to grant passes. I have refused every application, and mean to." At this report I decided to make a personal appeal, although my friends made every effort to dissuade me, using for argument Nelson's ungracious speech and gruff manners. He was sitting at a table at one end of the long parlor of the hotel. I approached him, supported on either side by my friends, the two gentlemen with whom he had had an interview only a few moments before. General Nelson was a man of commanding presence; he seemed not only tall but very large. He had black hair and eyebrows, with piercing eyes, which he bent on me from the moment we passed the sentry at the door. Indeed, his countenance was fierce and forbidding, as if to intimidate.

After the introduction he said:

"Madam, can you tell me what you want?"

"Yes, general, I have come to ask you for passes ——"

"Speak louder, I am a little deaf."

——"Passes for my little company within your lines; we desire to reach Fort Donelson. You have already been made acquainted with the object of our errand, to care for and bring the sick and wounded soldiers of Kentucky where they may have the attention necessary for their comfort and recovery."

"That is all very well, madam, but we have no place for ladies," said the general.

"General," said I, "we have not come to be entertained, but on a mission of mercy. All we ask of you is transportation and liberty within the lines to take care of our wounded."

"But, madam, there are no conveniences, no rooms you can occupy. All these boats you see coming down the river are filled with soldiers, besides officers and crew."

"General, we will only ask for a chair or two that we may place in some out-of-the-way corner."

"Madam, there are no chairs, no doors to the rooms, nothing but men; everything has been taken out to lighten the craft."

"But, general, we can stand——"

Then a fearful pause ensued, my heart beating audibly to my own ears, and I was trembling in every nerve so that I could scarcely stand. During this time General Nelson's face remained immovable, while he steadily and sternly gazed into my eyes. After what might have

been a few moments of time, though it seemed ages, he said:

"Well, you *are* a determined woman, and the first one I ever saw who knew what she wanted, and could tell it in a few words."

He then turned to his private secretary, who was sitting at his table, and made a remark in a low tone; then, recollecting for the first time his position as host, invited us to be seated. The secretary wrote a few lines on a sheet of paper, and placing it in a yellow envelope, touched a bell. The orderly on making his appearance was directed where to carry it. I received the pass, and was consigned to the care of one of the most courteous officers in the Federal service, Colonel Hazen, of the Forty-first Ohio.

In justice to General Nelson, I will say it was never my privilege to meet with greater consideration than he extended to our little company. During the two hours of waiting for our boat he seemed the graceful, polished gentleman; laughed and made merry over the sallies of wit and humor, and withal showed a sympathetic tenderness and solicitude for his sick soldiers that went far to remove the previous prejudice I had formed of his austerity. Poor fellow! his tragic death occurred a few months afterwards—the result of a quarrel with General Jeff. C. Davis. The circumstances of the difficulty are well known. We should judge leniently of those faults of character which, had they been curbed, might have been trained into virtues, and hold in remembrance only his lofty patriotism and undaunted courage.

We reached Smithland, Kentucky, but could get no boat to take us to the fort, nor could we obtain an overland conveyance of any description. We were looked upon with suspicion. Some even hinted that we were spies. We could not buy food. No one would sell to us nor give us shelter; even at the miserable place they called a hotel they refused to allow us to sit down. We walked all over the town, followed by one or two persons, who, by a motion or sign, indicated their supicions to any one who seemed disposed to favor us. Therefore, there was nothing for us to do but to leave the place, and, from the aspect of affairs, to do that as quickly as possible seemed most prudent. We applied for admission on the government boat, "Silver Moon," and shortly reached Paducah.

What a scene was there presented! The river as far up as the eye could reach was covered by a fleet of steamers, with gay colors flying and bands of music playing, laden down to the water's edge with soldiers.

Each regimental band played its own favorite airs, but all had a note for " The Girl I Left behind Me."

General W. T. Sherman was then in Paducah, to whom I reported for duty, and from him I received orders to go to Mound City and Cairo, take from the hospitals there all the sick and wounded, and leave them at the points nearest their homes. This would make place for others who were expected soon, as a battle seemed impending. He also directed us to draw commissary stores and other supplies at Cairo, and report on our return to Paducah, where we would then take aboard all the wounded prisoners for whom we could find place.

" And now, my dear madam," said General Sherman, " I desire to say to you that the prisoners are to receive the same attention as our own men; no distinction is to be made in the management or treatment of the prisoners by the surgeons or nurses."

Then turning to Dr. McDougal, the venerable medical director, he inquired of him what quantity of medical supplies would be necessary for us to take for the use of 150 sick and wounded, for nine days.

[Copy of General Sherman's order :]

HDQRS., DISTRICT OF CAIRO,
Feb. 22, 1862.

Mrs. Dr. McClelland, of Louisville, will take charge of two boats, "Hastings" and "Fannie Bullitt," going to Mound City for the wounded and sick. She will be assisted by Drs. J. H. Holister, Wm. Haydock, and T. McGregor, also Rev. F. M. Bushnell and a volunteer corps of five lady nurses. Male nurses will be taken from convalescent wards or from volunteers. These physicians will return immediately to their posts, or to their several homes as they desire.

I am, etc.,

W. T. SHERMAN, Brig. Gen. Comd.

We were obliged to wait at Paducah for our boats. Every available craft was used in the service, not only for the transportation of troops and supplies, but to convey a large number of people who were anxious about their friends, and also sight-seers who had curiosity to visit the scene of battle. We busied ourselves for two days in aiding the surgeons and citizens, who were untiring in their efforts to relieve the suffering. Churches, stores, and school-houses were hastily improvised into hospitals. Many private residences were filled. Some of the most frightful wounds of the war we saw here; and decidedly the worst surgery. One poor fellow was wounded in both of his legs. A round ball had

entered the fleshy part of one leg and flattened on the bone, where it lay imbedded. The ball entered the other leg in front and passed out at the thigh, shattering and splintering the bone. The surgeon laid him on the table and cut off one leg; after which he discovered that he had made a mistake and taken off the wrong one; he immediately turned the sufferer over on the other side and cut off the other leg. This piece of butchery was done by a doctor from a Western city. I have never revealed his name, though the memory of thirty years has not effaced it nor the incident. He may live to recognize himself. What became of the mangled body I never learned.

I was becoming impatient and restless in waiting, therefore determined to take the boat that first arrived, and trust to chance to have the other one overtake us. We brought on board about sixty prisoners; half of them were wounded men, the others were suffering from the effects of measles and colds from exposure. They coughed almost incessantly, and there was not an ounce of opiate or sedative to be found this side of Cairo. It was in the evening and nearly dark when we reached Cairo. We had very few provisions and our needs were extremely pressing. In order to get our order on the commissary honored it was necessary to report at headquarters at once. Then, to make matters still more desperate, our boxes of sanitary stores, containing bedding, clothing, and bandages, had gone astray; we had been placed in such straits for the bandages that some of us had taken our underclothing and torn it into strips to bind up the wounds of the suffering soldiers.

A long line of cars from Chicago had just come in, and for fifty minutes continued drilling back and forth until it was quite dark. There were no lamps or lights on the wharf, save here and there what seemed a flaming torch of some resinous substance, which only partially lighted up the vicinity. As soon as the cars stopped long enough, I climbed through and over them to the other side. The mire was knee deep. At every step I was obliged to extricate one foot before I could plant the other down. I lost one congress gaiter in the mire, and was obliged to present myself at headquarters with one shoe on and the other foot covered with a badly soiled stocking. I received a pair of heavy army shoes, and endeavored to hunt up the representative of the Sanitary Commission of the Northwest. I worked all that Sunday morning—war knows no Sabbath—packing boxes with needful articles that brought comfort and life to many who were well nigh ready to despair.

Crowds assembled at the wharves of the several towns as our boats passed, and we were greeted with cheers. Deputations of ladies were allowed to come on, who brought many needed delicacies—milk, fresh butter, and home-made biscuits. Oh, what a feast it was for the wounded and sick when the ladies distributed it to all, Federal and Confederate alike!

Surely it was a picture worthy of the skill of an artist of the realistic school. On reaching Louisville the military authorities took charge, and the sick were removed to the different hospitals.

II.

After the battle of Pittsburg Landing, the Military Board, co-operating with the Sanitary Commission, sent one of the largest and finest passenger steamers to go in search of Kentucky sick or wounded soldiers. With the prompt and cheerful aid of Dr. G. Perin, the assistant medical director of the district, the boat was equipped in a style worthy of the old commonwealth. The orders were given that if, upon the arrival of the boat at Pittsburg Landing, there was prospect of a battle, the boat should remain in readiness to take care of the wounded. A corps of able surgeons and a sufficient number of experienced nurses were selected to carry out the general design of relief.

At the suggestion of Attorney General James Speed, of Kentucky, who wrote to the Secretary of War, the following pass was sent to the writer:

Officers and guards will pass the bearer, Mrs. Dr. McClelland, through the lines unmolested, and her baggage undisturbed.   EDWIN M. STANTON.

We reached Pittsburg Landing a few days after the battle of Shiloh. Captain Scott, from an Ohio cavalry regiment, accompanied me over the battlefield some ten miles in search of hospital tents, and to give notice that all sick and wounded, both Federal and Confederate, were to be sent down to the hospital boat. We had previously directed our assistants to make all preparations to receive those who should be sent down, as we were well supplied with stretchers, cot-beds, and every necessary appliance.

The ground was loose sand and steep, and in some places ran in winding ridges. It was difficult to walk; here and there were chasms and hollow flats. There had been fighting in knots or groups. The Federals, coming up unexpectedly, had repulsed a charge of Confederate cavalry, and the foot-soldiers were lying about among the dead horses. Two men were found dead, foes locked in each other's arms. It was with difficulty the dead men could be separated.

We found many badly wounded men, who had not received attention since the battle, lying on the ground, begrimed with sand and dirt, faces blackened with powder, and hair matted in their own blood, delirious with fever, and not a drop of water to cool their parched tongues. Men were there who had been impaled upon their own bayonets; arms twisted wholly off, and legs smashed up like bits of firewood. Mere boys lay helpless and struggling in delirium, hoarsely raving of the conflict, shouting to their comrades, or calling the names of dear ones at home, while many others lay in that fatal stupor preceding death. I found one man shot through the breast, lying in a little thicket, groaning in great pain.

"Water," he moaned. "For God's sake, give me water!"

I placed my water-flask to his mouth, and as I knelt beside him I noticed that he wore the gray, and belonged to some Georgia regiment. He almost emptied the flask before he took it from his lips, and as he looked up at me gratefully the tears rolled down his cheeks, and he stretched his hands feebly out toward the flask, which I was about to replace in my belt.

"It's pretty good, isn't it?" I asked, when he had taken another draught.

"Good!" he repeated, between gasps. "I should say it was. I've been cryin' for it for six hours, an' I never thought I'd be cryin' for water—anyhow, not to *drink!* But this blamed war has upset things so that there ain't no tellin' what a man will do."

He said this between gasps, as if every word hurt, and when he got it out at last he lay back in a dead faint.

I called to Jack Norris, a stalwart six-footer of the Fifth Kentucky (Federal) Infantry, who had been detailed as a stretcher-bearer. Jack had him tenderly carried to the boat, and we brought him to the hospital at Louisville, where he recovered in three months. But he often said he never got a drink that did him so much good as those two swallows of water when he lay parched and dying, as he thought, among the dead.

Instructions from the medical director-in-chief advised not to take more than 150 sick or wounded on board, but we found many cases so urgent, and were so piteously importuned, even to tears, from these brave men who did not hesitate to plunge headlong on foot, in front of flying horses, and charged even to the cannon's mouth!

We held a consultation as to what was best to do. Drs. Bush and Chipley, of Lexington, put the question in this way: "It is for you to decide; shall it be room *on* the boat or room *in* the ground? There are at least 160 men here that will die within thirty-six hours if we leave them; take them, they have *one* chance for their lives."

"Gentlemen," I replied, "we will make room on the boat, and risk making it right with Dr. McDougal."

Forthwith we took on 225 men, principally wounded. We stowed them away on the lower deck, in bunks three stories high; we were obliged to ascend ladders to attend them. Fore and aft, the boat was packed full of cots. We brought carpenters and lumber sufficient for every contingency. The guards of the second story were full, besides the upper deck. We used canvas, blankets, and quilts, stretched to protect them from dampness and night air. All the staterooms were occupied by the wounded except six reserved in the ladies' cabin for physicians and attendants, who were only permitted to sleep or rest three consecutive hours in the twenty-four; when their time expired the watch called them, and their places were eagerly filled by other tired and weary ones.

We carried 110 prisoners from Louisiana, Mississippi, and Arkansas. Quite a number were over fifty years of age; and many were boys from sixteen to twenty. They were called "Beauregard's sixty days men." Most of them had only reached Pittsburg Landing a few days before the battle, and were wounded in the early part of the engagement.

We decided to leave without delay with our precious cargo, but determined to return as soon as possible, to bring all available succor for those whom we were compelled to leave. We had a remarkably favorable passage; no detention or accidents, but overladen as we were, we had to make slow time.

Many cases that were considered uncertain began to improve in one or two days, though we had several amputations and many peculiar and difficult surgical cases.

The Indiana and Illinois soldiers we landed at points nearest their homes. This in accordance with General Sherman's expressed orders. We took sixty of them to the hospitals of Mound City and Cairo, and supplied them with everything necessary to their comfort and recovery.

We found many of those who had enlisted at the first call for men, were now badly off for clothes. The materials of which theirs were made having proved worthless or of very poor quality, we were obliged to procure for them a new supply. The expense of this outlay was borne by private funds. Governors Morton, of Indiana, and Yates, of Illinois, in a subsequent interview, expressed their gratitude with the assurance that the States they represented would "never forget what we had done for their brave boys."

III.

About this time a battle was expected at or near Corinth, Mississippi. It was therefore decided to prepare another outfit and proceed at once to this point. The same steamer was placed in readiness, with a supply of medical articles needful and sixty boxes of stores from the sanitary rooms.

I also took a supply of articles from home for my personal use, having suffered on a former occasion from lack of suitable nourishment. I took the precaution to prepare a large trunk with all kinds of delicacies—cakes and biscuits, wines, jellies, and brandy, sufficient for any emergency that might arise.

When we again reached Pittsburg Landing it was in the month of May; I have forgotten the date, but the dogwood trees were in blossom. There was a most sickening spectacle to view on that hill. Many of the bodies had been buried only a few feet under the ground; the heavy rains had washed the sand away, leaving a leg or an arm exposed; the air was permeated with a nauseating odor; green flies swarmed everywhere, and the buzzards were swooping down.

There were about 600 sick men still in the field-hospitals. Some sutlers had their goods in the hold of our vessel, and we could not get out our supplies until theirs were first disposed of. Almost as soon as we landed, I had an application from the surgeon in charge. As we could not reach our stores, and the sick were dying for lack of suitable nourishment, there seemed nothing else for me to do but draw from my own private resources for their great needs.

The surgeon remarked that he had no doubt he had men whose lives could be spared if a few hours' timely assistance could be procured.

I gave him the contents of my trunk, requesting him to send an ambulance in the afternoon, when we hoped to reach our hospital stores. When the messenger called for them he brought a note, written in pencil. I will leave the reader to say if it did not more than repay me for all the sacrifice from hunger or exhaustion that might ensue from their personal loss and inconvenience.

CAMP STARTER.

To Mrs. Dr. McClelland, Steamer " Telegraph ":

RESPECTED MADAM : —We move five miles nearer Corinth to-day. We need bandages, lint, isinglass, plaster, and other comforts for wounded men ; please send by bearer. It would have done you good, dear madam, to have heard, as I did, repeated fervent "God bless dear Mrs. McClelland," from the lips of each suffering soldier to whom I ministered the delicacies from your trunk.

Respectfully yours,

W. LYMAN.

Surgeon in charge of hospital of 1st division.

Our provisions were becoming short, the weather very warm, and our supply of ice had failed. Our hospital boat standing under the bluff, using the water draining from the foul *débris* of the camps, it was no wonder that many of our corps were taken ill with dysentery and fever. Therefore it was determined to remain no longer, but to load up all the sick we could take—about 175 men. Many of the physicians and attendants on this occasion sickened and died after their return home.

At a field hospital at this place, an incident occurred which may interest the reader. We had just finished our last sad duties for a dying young Confederate prisoner, when my attention was directed to a man who lay opposite ; his appealing look, as if he would speak, induced me to sit down beside his cot with a word or two of friendly interest, when after awhile he related to me the circumstances of his early life in these words, as nearly as I can remember :

"I was a wild and wayward boy, impulsive, yet kind-hearted. My father was intemperate, and died while I was quite a little boy. My mother had a hard struggle ; she was a good woman, and taught me to pray. I went to Sunday-school until after she died, and then I drifted away. But I had a faithful Sunday-school teacher and often she hunted me up, and brought me once a book. In the first page she wrote my name with these words : 'Remember thy Creator in the days of thy youth, before the evil days come when thou shalt say, I have no pleasure in them. This is your teacher's prayer for you, John ;' and signed her name.

"But I got into bad company and drifted farther and farther away, and for years I had forgotten all that was good in my childhood, until once I came into a great temptation. Had I fallen, I fear I had fallen never to rise again.

"A companion suggested that we enter and rob a certain house ; that I should go in and conceal myself in some way, and open the door to him, who would be near on the outside, at a preconcerted signal. This I did, how it is unnecessary to state, but I entered the house and found my way unobserved to one of the upper chamber rooms ; was armed with a knife and a revolver, and concealed myself in a closet. Quite early in the evening, two little children came into the room with their mother. I had a full view of the group from the partly-open closet door, as they knelt with clasped hands beside their mother's knee and repeated their evening prayer thus : 'And lead us not into temptation, but deliver us from evil, for thine is the kingdom and the power and the glory forever. Amen.'

"Far back for many years it took my thoughts ; at my mother's knee thus I said nightly 'Our Father' that she taught me. I was yielding— the earnest, loving voice of a woman, the words, 'deliver us from evil' brought me back with a sudden bound through all the intervening years, and I was a child at heart again. The loving, tender prayer of the Sabbath-school teacher written in the book, so long forgotten, came back, and humbly and reverently I said over the holy words, with eyes uplifted to heaven. The hour and the darkness had passed, I was no longer standing on slippery places with a flood of waters ready to sweep me to destruction, but my feet were on a rock. I was saved—saved through memories. After the mother left the room, I noiselessly slipped out, told my confederate I could not carry out the plan, and left him.

"I soon after attended a prayer-meeting, was taken by the hand and encouraged by God's people ; was received on probation for a time as a candidate for membership, and am now a full communicant in the Methodist Church."

Upon inquiry I found that this man had been promoted for bravery, and bore an unblemished reputation in his company. A few years subsequently he called upon me on his way to Philadelphia, on a furlough, when I learned that he was then an officer in the regular army, on frontier service.

GENERAL LEE—THROUGH THE EYES OF A STAFF OFFICER.

Rev. John K. White.

A MAN'S ability can best be tested by extraordinary opportunities; his character by the every-day course of his life. As the natural family can best know the character of the man as a man, so the military family can best know the character of the man as a general.

I have been fortunate in securing some extracts from the diary of Major (now Reverend) Giles B. Cooke, who was inspector-general on

GENERAL ROBERT E. LEE.

Lee's staff during the latter part of the war. These notes are specially useful as showing how General Lee appeared to the eyes of those men who saw him "behind the scenes."

If the common idea of a commanding general's staff is that of a body of men galloping about in glittering uniforms during the heat of action and flirting with the ladies the rest of the time, a perusal of this diary would soon dispel the illusion.

General Lee's staff numbered twelve officers, and there was very little leisure indeed for any of them. A great part of the time of both a general and his staff is occupied with the making and examining of reports and a thousand other details of the dry routine work of army

life. It is during this time that a closer insight can be obtained by those about him into the *real self* of their commander. They see him then when not under the excitement of battle, when the gaze of the world is not upon him, when there is no occasion to pose or act a part for the sake of popularity, when he is most apt to say and do those things which his natural inclinations suggest. In this routine work a great many difficulties arise, in the settlement of which there can be no inspiration, but which have a tendency to vex and worry the man who has to deal with them. Sometimes it is one of the staff, sometimes the general himself. If the latter, his conduct under the circumstances is, of course, an indication of his character. If it be the former, and he display any irritation, the commander's treatment of him will probably show whether or not the power of the *general's* authority is used to manifest with impunity the harshness or passion of the *man*.

Now General Lee was a member of the Protestant Episcopal Church, and nothing was more evident in his daily life among the men of his staff than that he was a christian. He did not, like Jackson, lift his hand to heaven in prayer during the storm of battle, but a multitude of occurrences served to prove every day that his life was guided by the principles of christianity. It is also, doubtless, perfectly safe to say that no commander was ever more beloved by his staff than General Robert E. Lee. And yet even he has been known to exhibit temper or irritation more than once in speaking to those who formed his military family. At such times his words hurt the more because of the very fact that they loved him. But his efforts at reparation were so prompt and so persistent that none could long remain wounded by or offended at what he had said.

On one occasion, when he was deeply engaged in thinking out some plan or problem of great importance, an officer brought him a large bundle of reports to sign. This duty being among those most disliked by the general, he spoke rather sharply:

"Colonel A, *what* did you bring me those for?"

The hot-headed colonel fired immediately, and, throwing the bundle violently down on the table, was leaving the room abruptly. At the door the general's voice arrested him.

"Colonel A!"

The colonel saluted.

"If, with the care of the army on my shoulders, I sometimes forget *my*self, I hope you will not forget *your*self."

The gentleness with which these words were said completely overcame the colonel's anger.

At another time, while on the way to Falling Waters, the general was sitting conversing with a group of soldiers, when one of his staff officers, whom he had sent on some duty, returned, and, full of the result of his work, commenced blurting out a report. He was abruptly interrupted by the general.

"Colonel B, you had better report that to the whole army!"

The colonel was very angry and showed it as much as he dared. When again on the road, General Lee tried to pacify the irate officer. Some buttermilk, of which the general was very fond, being given him, he called an orderly and sent some of it to the colonel. The latter refused to accept it. Arrived at Falling Waters, the general and staff stopped to wait for the army to cross. Colonel B, utterly exhausted, threw himself on the muddy ground and fell asleep. When he awoke the rain was pouring down and—he was covered with General Lee's own cape!

General Lee's ordinary attitude toward the officers of his staff was that of a familiar and very courteous friend, and, if they desired it, a confidant and adviser, even in matters unconnected with their military duties. They seemed naturally drawn toward him in any time of perplexity. Soon after the war closed, one of the young officers who had been on his staff had a question to decide which would influence his entire life. He was sorely in need of advice, and, although he had great confidence in his own father's sagacity, yet the very first person he thought of going to was General Lee, whose opinion he afterwards followed to the letter.

General Lee's judgment of men was exceptionally good, and he thoroughly knew the general character and peculiarities of the members of his staff. This might not be so remarkable, as he was constantly with them, but his power of discerning character was often evidenced by stronger proofs than that. Although he may have seen General Grant before, yet they had never had occasion to make a special study of each other until their forces met in the battle of

the Wilderness. Toward the close of the tangled and continuous fighting there, General Lee said to General Gordon, "You will please take your command as rapidly as possible to Spottsylvania Court House and hold it until I come."

"But, general," replied General Gordon, "do you mean to say that you are going to Spottsylvania Court House? I thought that General Grant's lines were broken in many places and that he would probably retreat to-night."

"His lines may be broken, but he will not retreat. The best thing for him to do is to go to Spottsylvania Court House, *and General Grant will do the best thing.*"

This was after only two days of contact!

This remark was forcibly impressed upon General Gordon's mind by the fact that, when he arrived at the Court House, he was met by the vanguard of the Federal army.

This clearness of judgment, prompted by his kindness of heart, enabled him to give more than one useful hint to his officers concerning matters affecting their personal welfare. This was generally done privately, always with great gentleness of manner. But on one occasion, at least, he found publicity a necessary condition to give his admonition proper force. One of his best officers occasionally "tarried too long at the wine," and it was a matter of much distress to General Lee, who himself drank no alcoholic beverage. Whatever may have been his efforts in private to change this order of things, they had met with no success, although the officer in question was always ashamed after such an occurrence. One day the general and staff were invited to a dinner where they met a considerable number of people. Wine was passed, but the general shook his head, and, with a smile, remarked, "Colonel X, over there, is the only *drinking* man of our party." The colonel became crimson in a moment.

Many might think that, whatever the end desired, it was neither wise nor kind to use this means of attaining it. Its wisdom was proved by the fact that the desired end was obtained, and, as to the kindness of it, the thing to be decided is, whether it was kinder to save his feelings or to save *himself*.

Although his bearing was that of grave dignity, yet General Lee's disposition was genial, and even jovial. He was fond of a joke on one condition, namely, that no one suffered by it; and humorous jests and pleasant passages of wit enlivened the intercourse of general and staff. Any bright expression or pithy saying was sure to draw from the general an approving nod and a rewarding smile; nor were his own replies lacking in force or point.

Thus it was that this delightful familiarity, together with their mutual hardships and dangers, hopes and anxieties, bound commander and subordinates together in the strongest bonds of a most peculiar friendship, such as could not exist under any other circumstances. But there is one thing to be emphatically remarked: this nearness of approach and constant companionship did not in the smallest degree lessen in the minds of his staff the idea of General Lee's *greatness*. If there was any difference between their opinion and that of others in this regard, it is probable that the officers of the staff possessed the higher conception of his worth. An officer once said: " He (General Lee) is the only man I ever knew concerning whom it was *not* true that ' distance lends enchantment.' But in his case the better he was known the more towering his greatness appeared to be."

It is undoubtedly true that what the world *supposed* him to be his staff *knew* that he was.

It was General Lee's habit to frequently invite his staff to share with him the special delicacies sent from time to time by his many admirers. The scarcer these delicacies became the more certain was the general to ask his officers to help in disposing of them. When such things became so scarce in the South that the supply for the sick began to fail, he always sent to the hospital the little luxuries presented to himself.

This desire to fare no better than his staff, and in fact than his entire army, was most strongly shown during the retreat from Petersburg. He had ordered provisions to be sent to Amelia Court House, but a telegram from some authority in Richmond directed that all the trains on that line should be hurried forward to the latter place, and thus, before the army arrived, the car-loads of provisions were run right by Amelia Court House " on to Richmond." This mistake was fatal to the Army of Northern Virginia, for the troops had already been for some time without adequate food, and were weak in consequence of it, and this made it necessary to scatter half of the men as foragers, who when they were gone were unable to find anything to " forage," so that the whole army was compelled to subsist upon the young shoots of trees and whatever else could be found that would at all help to support life. The horses

and mules were no better off, and all these things combined to retard progress, besides necessitating a change in the route. Of course, even in this strait General Lee could get enough for himself, but he and his staff filled their pockets with parched corn which they munched as they rode along through the dark hours of the last march.

GENERAL LEE'S RESIDENCE IN RICHMOND.

Nor was this the only mark of self-denial and thoughtful care bestowed upon those about him during the bitter days of that retreat. He knew that the mother and sisters of one of his staff-officers were " refugeeing " at a house by which they would have to pass, and so he sent the officer on ahead to await the arrival of the army at that point. From four o'clock in the morning the refugees furnished to the soldiers all that could be had in the shape of food. About three in the afternoon the general himself arrived. Of course the ladies hurried out and insisted on his dismounting and partaking of their hospitality. With a sad smile, he refused, saying: " My men are starving, ladies; if you will do what you can for *them*, *I* will get on very nicely."

No amount of insistence could persuade him to have anything but a glass of milk brought out to him.

He left the son and brother in command of the extreme rear, so that he could be at home as long as possible.

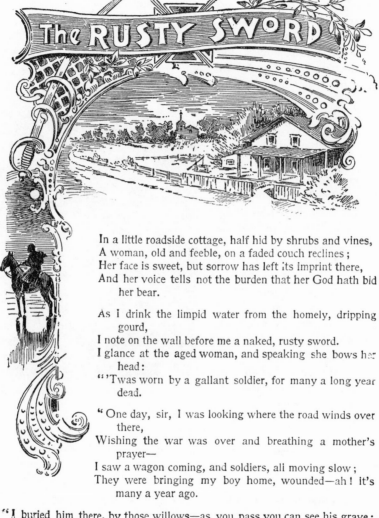

The RUSTY SWORD

In a little roadside cottage, half hid by shrubs and vines,
A woman, old and feeble, on a faded couch reclines;
Her face is sweet, but sorrow has left its imprint there,
And her voice tells not the burden that her God hath bid
    her bear.

As I drink the limpid water from the homely, dripping
    gourd,
I note on the wall before me a naked, rusty sword.
I glance at the aged woman, and speaking she bows her
    head:
"'Twas worn by a gallant soldier, for many a long year
    dead.

"One day, sir, I was looking where the road winds over
    there,
Wishing the war was over and breathing a mother's
    prayer—
I saw a wagon coming, and soldiers, all moving slow;
They were bringing my boy home, wounded—ah! it's
    many a year ago.

"I buried him there, by those willows—as you pass you can see his grave;
Oh, stranger, my child was a comfort, but his heart it was true and brave!"
Watching the pearls drop downward over her aged face,
I mount, and I ride in silence away from the lonely place.

But now I have reached the willows, and I leap to the shady ground;
I gather some wayside flowers to throw on his mossy mound.
I care not if Grant has led him, nor if he has fought with Lee;
I am an American soldier—and so was he.

GEORGE M. VICKERS.

PRAYER IN "STONEWALL" JACKSON'S CAMP.

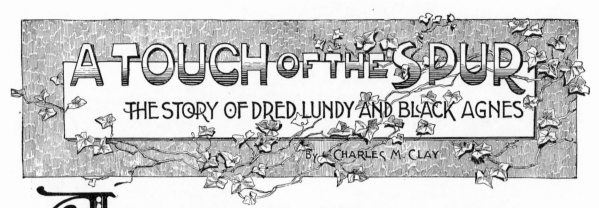

A TOUCH OF THE SPUR

THE STORY OF DRED LUNDY AND BLACK AGNES

By Charles M. Clay

A CLEAR, cold morning in November of 186–, two horses were ready for the riders who were saying last words to the family gathered on the broad piazza of a planter's residence near Hernando, Mississippi.

The hostess turned from the tall lady in the riding habit to the handsome young cavalryman standing on the steps, as she said:

"You think I am croaking, Dred, but you know it's a foolhardy thing for you to go so near the enemy's lines. You may meet a scouting party anywhere above Horn Lake."

"It is possible, but hardly probable. Henderson's scouts are close to the Yankee lines, and some one of them would have invited himself here to breakfast if a raid threatened. Those fellows have a nice thing of it up here on the border. They live on the fat of the land; but, to give them due credit, they do watch the enemy between meals. They get points from the cotton traders, who carry harmless bits of news to Memphis, and thus keep in high feather at headquarters. However they manage it, Henderson's fellows rarely fail to let Forrest know who to expect out from Memphis."

"But, Dred, you——"

"Oh, there is not the slightest risk in my morning ride. I could not let Mrs. Hamner go from here to Captain Edmondson's with so young a protector as Tom, when Cartwright's gang are known to be in the neighborhood."

"Cartwright's gang would rather capture Black Agnes than a cotton-train. If you tempt them with such a prize they may try a shot at you. Their patriotism is hardly strong enough to resist the reward which is offered for your capture; for that much money and Black Agnes they would sell the Confederacy."

"I do not think they will attack me, nor will they capture my bonny mare. A shot at one of Forrest's men would bring a swarm of hornets about their ears. They have a wholesome dread of 'Old Bedford.' But we must be off."

The blooded pony—a long, slender little gray, with quarters which told the "Autocrat" strain in his pedigree—had fretted himself into a lather. He seemed trying to knock out the glistening white teeth of the grinning little negro who was bobbing from side to side in constant effort to dodge the pony's head.

Of a very different temper was the thoroughbred mare which an old groom was leading up and down the avenue. She was a dark, dappled chestnut; so dark, under the shade of the heavy-leaved magnolias, that the name "Black Agnes" seemed no misnomer. Her small, beautifully-shaped head was gracefully poised on an arching neck, set into superb sloping shoulders. Of great girth, ribbed up almost to the point of the hips, her heavy quarters and the bone below the knees told at once the staying qualities of the racer. There was not a light hair in her silky, chestnut coat except a tiny white star in her forehead and a dash of silver floss from below the knee to the centre of the right forefoot. Not quite sixteen hands high, in perfect condition, with every muscle fully developed, Black Agnes was indeed a prize to tempt the border outlaws gathered in Cartwright's gang, which held a somewhat similar position in the debatable land between the Federals and Confederates below Memphis—from Nonconnah Creek to Horn Lake —to that which was held by the "Skinners" in the country above New York during the Revolution.

Cartwright's gang had been recruited from the deserters of both armies. Its captain, was a Tennesseean. Its first lieutenant was a deserter from Connecticut. Each of these worthies proved his patriotism by a fine scorn of mere sectional distinctions.

They robbed with a like readiness and good will the Mississippi planter of the cotton which he brought up to sell and the Yankee trader of the goods which he brought out to barter. With neither did they leave a greenback or a Confederate dollar.

Their impartiality was imperturbable. No entreaty ever shielded a pocket or got back a shilling; and, in a business-like way, they did listen to much entreaty while steadily going through with their work.

In their dealing with the Federal and Confederate cavalry the "gang" was equally unsectional. They hid in the swamps whenever Forrest came thundering through the enemy's lines in Tennessee, and with like prudence sought a secret shelter if a column of "Yankee Raiders" ventured down from Memphis into North Mississippi.

At the cross-roads above Horn Lake Mrs. Hamner and her escort met a squad of the "Home Guard," in which were several acquaintances of the young cavalryman. They stopped, as all travelers did then, to ask and tell news. The cavalryman had left General Forrest the previous morning at Panola. The "Home Guard" had later intelligence:

"Forrest is at Senatobia. Three of the Bluff City Greys came up from there before daylight this morning. Do you think 'Old Bedford' will go into Memphis?"

"He is the only man who could tell you. He has taught us to take no thought of the morrow. He says, 'Come!' and, no matter what are the odds or how difficult the path, we *come*. Is there any movement above?"

"Yes. Two of Henderson's scouts went down to Senatobia last night, and another fellow passed here two hours ago with despatches, sent out from Memphis to Forrest."

"We did not meet him!"

"He went the old road by Perkins's place."

"Are the Yankees this side of Nonconnah?"

"Yes; a regiment of Michiganders are camped on the hill beyond Nonconnah. Their pickets are two miles this side of the creek."

"Did Henderson's man say that a raid was coming out?"

"No; he thinks there is no sign of their moving. A company of their scouts came down as far as Major Anderson's yesterday. Are you going there?"

"No; we are expected at Captain Edmondson's at the rebel headquarters."

"Yes, his house is free to every Confederate. He's the gamest old man alive; and the young ladies are true as steel. A rebel's safer there than at any other place on the border. It's off

the road, and crossed with blind bridle-paths which puzzle strangers. Unless the Yankees have some runaway negro guide they would be bothered at each turn. That's to *your* advantage, Dred; you have hunted over every acre of the county, and I don't think the Yankees could stop Black Agnes if she was out of rifle shot when they sighted her."

"They may try it for any money they will put up."

"But, Dred, watch the swamp paths; look out for that red-headed lieutenant of Cartwright's. The scamp is somewhere over the bayou with the very worst lot in the 'gang.' The thief would risk his ears to get that mare of yours."

"I'll have his ears before he will get her. I promise you he shall pay his footing if he ever comes near my dainty Agnes."

The "Home Guard" rode on to Hernando, while the two travelers galloped eastward into a neighboring horse-path, which wound through deserted plantations, where broken columns of crumbling chimneys told of burned homes and of ruined and scattered families.

The lonely road that led through gloomy hollows and around silent pools, in which the melancholy cypress grew, disposed the cavalryman to confidential talk. With a quick look into the distant glades and over the neglected fields—the watchful look of a soldier who thinks an enemy may be near—the young cavalryman reined his mare to a walk, a walk in which Black Agnes kept up with the fox-trot of the pony— that easiest and most restful of gaits which is the peculiar inheritance of blooded southern horses. The bridle had fallen on Black Agnes's neck, and the rider, in an effort to steady himself for some speech which seemed difficult of utterance, plucked restlessly at every overhanging bough or vine, until looking at his companion he caught an amused expression, which gave him courage to say:

"Mrs. Hamner, I am going to ask a great favor."

"Ask. Unless it is impossible it will not be refused. Even then I should not refuse, but would try. You know, Dred, the favors have all come to me. Without your kindness and your sister's assistance I could not have reached Mr. Hamner when he was wounded; nor could I have sent clothing or shoes to my barefoot brothers in Virginia. It will be a great pleasure, Dred, to do anything I can for you."

"If your Cousin Lillias is not at Captain Edmondson's——"

"Why do you think Lillias may be there?" interrupted Mrs. Hamner.

"I had a letter from her last week. One of Henderson's scouts brought it. Miss Belle Edmondson gave it to him for me. Lillias wrote she would be there this week. But if she is not I want you to take Miss Belle with you and go in this afternoon. I know you can' arrange for her to come back with Miss Belle."

"But, Dred, you must not stay at Captain Edmondson's to-night. Of course I will do what you ask. But Belle and Lillias could not come out until to-morrow. There may be some difficulty about getting passes to-morrow, and we would all be miserably anxious if you were so near the Yankee pickets."

"If you will promise me that if Lillias is not at the Edmondson's you will send her out to-morrow, I will go back to Hernando as soon as I see you safely under Captain Edmondson's roof. You must tell my sweetheart, Mrs. Hamner, that if she does not come out with Miss Belle I will ride into Memphis to see her."

"Oh, Dred, you will not be so reckless?"

"I have a week's leave of absence, and I give you my word I will see Lillias before the week ends if I have to race through the Yankee pickets at Nonconnah and back through their lines on the old Fort Pickering road. I can easily go in—that dash would be nothing at night-fall. They would think me a belated cotton trader chased in by Cartwright's gang. Why, I might send them out to catch the rascals. You know three of the 'Bluffs' are up here somewhere, and they would like the fun. They could personate the 'partisans' and lead the Yankees a wild-goose chase into the swamp. It would be capital if they got into Cartwright's camp." And the gay young soldier laughed at the possibility he pictured.

Half amused and half alarmed at the thought of the threatened ride into Memphis, Mrs. Hamner turned from her escort. Suddenly her face blanched; with a cut of the whip she started the pony into a gallop, as she called:

"Dred! look! over on the ridge path, coming this way, are two of Cartwright's men."

"I see no one," he said, as he rode up to her.

"They are in that bushy little hollow; but they are coming."

"It may be some of the neighborhood people going to Horn Lake."

"No. They had on Confederate uniforms."

"Then they are two of the 'Bluffs' who came up this morning."

"Oh, Dred, I am sure they are Cartwright's men."

There was a glitter of excitement in the cavalryman's eyes, but his voice was steady in tone as he answered:

"We will ride on and see. That bridle-path crosses this road further up the ridge. We will be on the high ground before they come to the crossing."

They galloped rapidly up the easy slope which led to the top of the broad, sweeping, billowy ridge that was dotted with a few sparse cotton-patches, which served to emphasize the desolation of the wide fields, where the rusty, brown stalks of the last year had fallen or were brokenly bent over the weedy furrows.

They were near the opening in the path which crossed the ridge when they caught sight of the two horsemen. The path crossed their road at an acute angle, running through the fields and then down into a densely-timbered hollow. With quick decision the young cavalryman took the only advantage his position offered.

"Go on, Mrs. Hamner; send the pony at his best when you cross the path. Ride slowly until then. After you cross they cannot see you for the thick undergrowth. It is a Godsend that the open fields are on this side. When you get to the old orchard you can draw rein. From that rise you will be in sight of the overseer's house. It will be safe for you to wait there to see what happens here. I must see these fellows, and not have them following us to Captain Edmondson's. If it comes to shooting, run the pony to Marshall's overseer. The overseer's family is there, and I think Marshall himself is up here. I will get rid of the fellows someway and follow you. There! I see them. They *are* Cartwright's men."

"I was *sure*, Dred——'

"Go on slowly till you cross the path. Then with a rush——"

"But you?"

"I must meet them here, Mrs. Hamner; it is the only way. Go, please!"

Mrs. Hamner understood that perfect obedience was the best assistance she could give. When she crossed the path the men were yet 100 yards away. She ran the pony at his topmost speed to the old orchard. Then she stopped, under shelter of the trees, and looked back. The young cavalryman had reined up below where the path crossed the ridge. His position was such that he could not be taken at a dis-

"DRED LUNDY, VERY MUCH AT YOUR SERVICE."

advantage. Black Agnes's head was turned toward the two men, who were coming up the wood-path from the left. Black Agnes's rider was watching their advance from below the mare's curved neck while apparently arranging some fastening of his stirrup-leather. Mrs. Hamner saw the men ride into the road and stop. They were between the cavalryman and her.

Something was wrong with Black Agnes. She had got her head between her knees and was backing down the road and then rushing forward in sudden dashes, which quite unsettled the little black cob upon which the red-headed lieutenant was mounted.

The two men glanced from the plunging mare to the lady who was waiting under the distant trees, and then at each other. There was a look of indecision in the sharp visage of the lieutenant and of surprise and doubt in the sleepy blue eyes of his follower. This division of forces was evidently confusing. The young cavalryman called out, as the mare settled into good behavior:

"You are Confederate soldiers?"

"We are guerillas,"—the tone was somewhat defiant.

"An officer, I see?"

"Yes,"—more of hesitation than defiance.

"To what command do you belong?"

"Cartwright's Partisan Rangers."

"Are you camped near here?"

"Over the bayou, in the swamp. Would you like to see our camp?" he added, in a ruffling, insolent tone.

"Yes. I was about to propose a visit. I belong to Forrest's command. Some of our fellows are up here. Did you meet any of them?"

"No,"—with an uneasy look up the road and a glance of warning at the man with him.

"Well, more are coming, probably 'Old Bedford' himself. As you fellows must know the swamp, Forrest will expect you to furnish guides."

"Is he going into Memphis?" The questioner was growing eager, excited, and a trifle more civil.

"No one can tell just what 'Old Bedford' will do; but I know he will expect me to be able to find your camp."

Again Black Agnes interrupted the conversation, backing down the road, madly flinging out her heels and then bringing her feet together in sudden jumps, which set the little black cob in a tremble. Apparently the young cavalryman had all he could do to quiet the mare. He did not seem to notice the rapid conference between the two Rangers.

"So, Agnes; steady." With a quiver of the ears, her head thrown up and the nostrils distended, the mare was motionless.

The situation had changed. The lieutenant, his curb bearing hard on the mettlesome cob, was waiting by the road. His follower had crossed the field and was rapidly vanishing around a little wooded knoll, from which there was a sudden descent into the heavily-timbered hollow. Rather awkwardly the lieutenant began:

"If you are going to our camp——"

The young cavalryman interrupted:

"I must first see the lady there to the next house, where she can wait my return, or until some of our command arrive. Does not that bridle-path this side of Marshall's lane lead into the old road over the bayou?"

"Yes; you seem to know the country pretty well?"

"I ought to know it. I was born and brought up in the near neighborhood."

"You are?"

"Dred Lundy, very much at your service."

The hazel eyes flashed and a mocking smile gave a glimpse of white teeth beneath the drooping, silky mustache, as the young cavalryman raised his hand to salute the utterly bewildered partisan, who exclaimed:

"Dred Lundy?—the devil!"

A clear, ringing laugh, which reassured Mrs. Hamner, did not provoke the lieutenant to mirth. He was inwardly cursing his folly in sending away the man he now knew he had sent upon a fool's errand. Together they might have captured the daring scout for whom a large reward had been offered. "Dead or alive"—the thought fairly possessed him, and he could scarcely keep himself from repeating it aloud. "Five thousand dollars, dead or alive. If I could only get a chance at him! If he does not suspect!" In a few moments his wits cleared and he said:

"I ought to have known the thoroughbred. I've heard all our fellows talk of her. Any other man of the Rangers except 'Fool Barnes' would have known her."

"So you did not recognize 'Black Agnes, of Dunbar'?"

"I did not know you, and I did not think of the famous mare. Yet I ought to have known the 'Border Queen'—why, she shows the born racer. Now this little horse of mine isn't a bad goer; yet in a four-mile race she'd double him up, though in a quarter stretch he's a flyer. I believe I'd back him to beat the mare in a quarter stretch."

The young scout looked the cob over as he said, musingly:

"Fairishly built, nervous, mettlesome, quarter bred, but lacks wind and bone. The horse might do it now, for I see that he is perfectly fresh and ready for work; and Agnes has been under the saddle constantly for a week. It's hardly fair for Agnes, but if you care to try, I'll not balk you."

"A hundred in greenbacks my horse will beat the mare from here to the mouth of Marshall's Lane."

"I'll take the bet." He called to the lady: "Mrs. Hamner, ride back here, if you please."

At the call she rode back to where they were waiting, looking with amazement at her escort as he handed her a roll of bank-notes and said:

"Will you please count them and tell us the amount?"

Twice she slowly counted the sheaf of bills before she said:

"Two thousand dollars in Confederate money."

"Which is twenty dollars to every one of your greenbacks, lieutenant," said the cavalryman.

There was a shade of dissatisfaction in the partisan's face, as the cavalryman continued;

"I have no greenbacks, but twenty to one is the cotton trader's price. Will you race for the Confederate money?"

"Yes." It was grimly said, but he thought of the $5,000 reward and the thoroughbred mare. One hundred in greenbacks was not too much to put up for the gains he was counting.

While he reckoned the chances, Dred Lundy was instructing the unlearned stakeholder.

"Ride on to the lane yonder. Leave the gate open and stop behind it. When I call 'ready,' wave your handkerchief. You are to give all the money you hold to the first man who enters the gate."

The lieutenant handed her ten crisp, fresh notes. She counted them, looked at her escort, and said:

"One hundred in greenbacks." Then holding the bank-notes closely, she sent the pony at the top of his speed to the gate. As she entered the gate, Dred asked the lieutenant:

"Are you ready?"

"Yes."

"Ready!" shouted the cavalryman.

The lady waved her handkerchief, and side by side the riders started. Neither seemed in haste to win. In fact, the cob showed that he felt the pressure of the curb. Black Agnes's snaffle held her easily; but the ears and the nostrils of the thoroughbred quivered with excitement.

Dred Lundy had readily guessed the tactics of the partisan. He had seen the revolver stealthily loosened from its hiding-place in the top of the long boot. He knew the lieutenant's curb was holding the cob for the mare to pass— her owner was to be shot in the back whilst riding a winning race.

At the pace they kept, conversation was easy.

" It seems, lieutenant, you are careless of your greenbacks ; or am I to understand that the last man wins?"

A smothered volley of expletives, and a vicious twist of the curb which cut the cob's mouth until it bled, was the only answer.

With a dextrous turn of the supple wrist Black Agnes was brought close up to the horse. Quick as thought the matchless rider drew his foot from the stirrup and raked the cob's flank with his sharp Mexican spur.

Only a touch of the spur ! At the quick roll of the pointed star the cob reared and shied. Dred Lundy's foot was instantly back in his stirrup and Black Agnes was falling behind in the race.

For an instant the lieutenant's hand had loosened its hold on the reins ; the horse caught the bit in his teeth and rushed forward in a mad run. His speed increased as the mare came sweeping up beside him in long, telling strides.

They were running neck and neck. The lieutenant pulled at the bit in vain. There was a factor in the race which he did not understand and which he could not master. The mare would drop behind a length and then come up with the bound of an antelope. At every spring she made, the cob swerved and again rushed forward. They were almost at the gate when the double disguise was dropped.

As the mare swept on to win the race, two revolvers were held fairly in view.

Black Agnes had *her* idea as to how the race should end. She flung her foot in the cob's face, which either touched his feelings or suggested a new use of that pointed spur. He reared and turned with a furious rush into the open field. The red-headed lieutenant was shot into the air like a rocket. The revolver dropped from the hand which was clutching at space and went off, grazing the cob's back.

When Dred Lundy passed the goal and drew rein upon Black Agnes within the gate, Mrs. Hamner gave him the double sheaf of banknotes, which he held aloft, waving them at the discomfited partisan, who was sitting in a soft, weedy furrow, filling the crisp air with strange oaths, while the cob was racing down the bridle-path to the hollow, where an ambush vainly waited to capture the daring cavalryman and Black Agnes, the " Border Queen."

A DRUM-HEAD COURT-MARTIAL.

CAPTAIN H. C. GRAHAM.

LATE CO. E, 7TH N. C. INFANTRY.

IN the spring of 1865, the Confederate forces in Southwestern Virginia, with headquarters at Wytheville, were put in motion, and marched to Abingdon, Virginia, near the Tennessee line, to meet one of the periodical incursions of the Federal forces in that section.

The force was about 3,000 strong, consisting of two batteries of artillery, about 600 cavalry, and the remainder of infantry. As a military division, this portion of the State was known as the Department of Southwestern Virginia, and was under the command of General John Echols. The command had been at Abingdon but a few hours, when orders were received to retrace its march with all speed, and hasten toward Lynchburg. The time was the closing hours of the Confederacy, but the troops composing this command did not then know that the end was drawing near. There was an undefined impression that momentous events were at hand, but nobody dreamed of surrender. This little army in the mountains of Virginia, isolated from the main body, had its special duties to perform, in guarding the great salt-works at Saltville, and holding the fertile valleys that extended from Jonesboro', Tennessee, to Lynchburg, Virginia. It was in this department that General John H. Morgan, the Kentucky cavalry leader, met his tragic death at Greenville, Tennessee, and the history of the command was dotted with some of the most dramatic incidents of the great struggle.

As soon as the orders were received to hasten back to Lynchburg, our forces were put in motion; the cavalry and artillery were ordered to march on the fine macadamized road that leads from Salem to Abingdon, and the infantry were packed on the few cars that could be gathered on the East Tennessee and Virginia railroad.

It is not the purpose of this article to describe all the dramatic incidents that attended the march of the forces in Southwestern Virginia in their efforts to reach the main body at Appomattox. For present purposes it is sufficient to say that after proceeding but a short distance the infantrymen were compelled to leave the cars, on account of railway communication with Lynchburg being cut in several places, and uniting with the cavalry and artillery, proceeded as a body toward their destination. Telegraphic communication had also been completely destroyed, and nothing could be learned of the momentous events that were transpiring at Richmond and Petersburg.

As our march progressed, the excitement and anxiety of the citizens along the route became every hour more manifest; the strictest discipline, however, was maintained with the troops, and, as a rule, the command, composed largely of veterans of many hard-fought battles, behaved with steadiness and soldierly bearing. It was while on this march that the event I am about to relate occurred.

During a temporary halt of a few hours, the writer was standing with a group of officers, discussing the probabilities of the campaign, when an orderly rode up and delivered him an order from headquarters, commanding him to act as the judge advocate of a general court-martial, ordered to assemble at once on the field. Under the guidance of the orderly, he proceeded immediately to the spot. When he arrived at the place where the court was assembled, a scene was presented that would have made a striking picture for an artist. Under the shade of a broad spreading oak, which stood alone in a large open field, ten officers, in full uniform, were seated in a circle on the ground; within the circle stood a drum, with ink and paper placed on the head; just without the circle, with two soldiers beside him with their muskets, stood the prisoner, a young man about twenty years old, charged with desertion. About twenty yards distant was gathered a group of citizens, among them a middle-aged woman, dressed in black, weeping and apparently in great distress. A few officers and soldiers scattered about on the ground, as spectators, completed the scene. The case was a clear one: the home of the accused was near the line of march, and as he passed his native heath, the temptation to quit his soldier life became too strong, and he left his company without leave; all the attendant circumstances indicated that he had no intention of returning. His absence was immediately discovered, a guard was sent in pursuit, and he was captured on the mountain a few miles from the camp.

The young soldier was apparently unconscious of his extreme peril; he gazed about him with a wild and earnest look, but it was not so much that of fear, as wonder at the stern court before him, with its attendant formalities. He was brought forward by his guards, and the order convening the court being read, the members were sworn, and without delay the examination of witnesses commenced.

The captain of the young man's company was first introduced. He testified to the prisoner quitting his command, without leave, while on the march. The orderly sergeant's testimony was the same; the two guards sent in pursuit testified to the flight of the accused, his capture, and his attempt to conceal himself when they discovered him. This completed the evidence for the government.

The duties of the judge advocate of a court-martial differ from those of an ordinary prosecuting officer in a civil court, in that while he represents the government, he likewise represents the prisoner, and it is a pleasant duty he performs in bringing out any evidence that the accused may have to offer in his defence. In other words, it is the duty of a judge advocate simply to bring out *all* the facts of the case *pro* and *con*. In this instance his deepest sympathies were enlisted for the unfortunate young man, who had been summoned for swift judgment, for he well knew what the stern sentence would be unless some strong defence could be offered. He was about to take the prisoner aside to consult with him as to his defence, when the orderly in attendance approached and informed the judge advocate that a citizen desired to speak with him. The colloquy was a short one, for drum-head courts-martial, when an army is on the march, brook but little delay. The substance of the citizen's communication was, that the young man was not responsible for his act, as he was not of sound mind; that he had been "foolish," as he expressed it, since he was a child, and that he did not know the extent of the military crime he had committed.

Here, then, was a faint hope. "Who can prove this?" asked the judge advocate.

"I can testify to facts in the case," replied the citizen, "and if I am given an hour's time I will produce other witnesses who will do the same; but that lady standing there," said he, pointing to the weeping woman, "can give the best testimony."

"Who is she?"

"She is the young man's mother," replied the citizen.

All this was reported to the court, and messengers were quickly despatched to bring in the witnesses.

The young man's mother was then introduced. A more affecting scene was never presented before a court, military or civil, than when this weeping widow gave her testimony. Every member of the court was deeply affected; tears ran down the furrowed cheeks of grim and grizzled old Colonel H., the president of the court and a veteran of many battles, as he listened to the young soldier's mother. The other witnesses were examined, and testified to peculiar conduct on the part of the accused in his past life, which led them to believe that he was not of sound mind. By the order of the court, the captain of the young man's company and the orderly sergeant were then recalled, and several of his comrades were examined. These testified that while the accused was not particularly bright, his conduct while with the company had indicated an average knowledge of right and wrong. The case was then submitted to the court, after all the spectators had been removed out of hearing. Commencing, as is always the case in a court-martial, with the lowest officer in rank, in this instance a first lieutenant, the opinion of each was asked, and the case was discussed. The tone of argument was the same with every member of the court.

Colonel H., the president, addressing the judge advocate, and greatly moved, said: "Ah! captain, our sympathies are all deeply excited in this case, we are all moved with the scene we have just passed through, but we must perform our sworn duty. The discipline of this army must be preserved. Release this soldier, and there would be 200 desertions from our ranks before morning. The evil must be stopped right now." The vote was then taken, and it was unanimous that "Private ——, charged with desertion," should be shot to death with musketry. The court then adjourned; the record of the testimony, taken on the head of the drum, was sent to headquarters, and in an hour we were on the march again; but it was a sad march to those who had participated in the dramatic scene of this trial. To the judge advocate the tearful face of the widowed mother, who accompanied her son to the last, was ever present, and he thought of her anguish as she contemplated the fate of her boy that would follow swift on the judgment passed against him by the inexorable law of military rule. The command in its march was now nearing Christiansburg. There had been no delay beyond that absolutely necessary in the short rests required for the refreshment of the troops, and these at long intervals.

.   .   .   .

It was within four miles of Christiansburg, Virginia, and about two days after the court-martial mentioned, that the news of the surrender at Appomattox was received by the little Army of Southwestern Virginia while on its march in obedience to orders. Arriving in the town, great confusion and excitement was found prevailing among the citizens, who had also heard the news. Couriers had come by circuitous routes and brought the intelligence. It was soon apparent to our commanding general that the end of the great struggle had come. The minds of all were now occupied with the stirring events of the present, and forgetful of the past. A hurried council of war was held to decide what should be done. An appeal was made to the troops to decide whether they would stand by the last of the Confederacy, and cross the mountains to join General Johnston in North Carolina. Two

or three hundred responded, but the great body of the Army of Southwestern Virginia was here disbanded, with orders to go home and be ready to report again for duty if properly called on by the Confederate authorities.

Then came the general confusion attendant upon the breaking up, the sad farewells spoken by old comrades, and the disappearance of all discipline which follows the disintegration of a military force.

The writer happened to meet Major J. Stoddard Johnson, the adjutant-general at headquarters. "What was done, major," he asked, "about the finding of the court-martial that was held on the field day before yesterday?"

"The general reviewed the proceedings," said Major Johnson, "disapproved the finding of the court, and the boy is now on his way home with his mother."

"Thank God for that," said Major C., who overheard the conversation, and who had been a member of the court. "But, captain," said he, as we walked away, "somehow I think the general had got some news from Lee's army before he set our verdict aside."

And thus ended the last court-martial held in the Confederate army.

REMINISCENCES OF POINT LOOKOUT.

THAD. J. WALKER, 2ND MARYLAND CAVALRY.

AMONG the many incidents of prison life at Point Lookout, Maryland, during my nine months incarceration there, I can recall some very amusing ones which the "boys" played upon each other. There were about 12,000 Confederates in the prison at the time, from all parts of the South, and the beach fronting on the Chesapeake Bay, where we were allowed to go in limited numbers during the day, presented quite an animated appearance with the "graybacks" sunning themselves, some washing their clothing, some bathing, some making bricks for the chimneys of little "cracker box" prison houses, and others fishing and crabbing. Now there were many there who had never seen a crab; many who had seen salt water for the first time, and were enjoying, in open-mouthed wonder, the scene of ships plying the bay; particularly one verdant specimen from away back among the mountain districts of North Carolina, who approached a

Georgian busily engaged in catching crabs, when the following conversation ensued: says Tarheel: "Mister, what are you 'uns doing thar?" "Catching sweet-bugs," says Georgia. "Sweet-bugs," says Tarheel, "they are the biggest bugs I ever seed. What are you 'uns going to do with 'em? Will they bite?" approaching closer for a better examination. "No!" answers the not very truthful representative from the "Goober" State, catching up the crab in a safe way for himself, for the poor Tarheel's inspection. "We sell them outside the prison to make cologne and sweet-scented extracts. Come and smell this one"—a fine large specimen he had just caught. Unfortunately, Tarheel's curiosity and innocence were so great that he was induced to do so, when the struggling crab caught him by the nose. It is scarcely necessary to add that a piercing "rebel yell" rent the air, which could be heard far away. Only those who have been bitten by a lively crab, freshly captured, can appreciate the poor fellow's sufferings, and his pitiful pleading to the Georgian to make him let go. Finally, becoming frenzied with pain, he yelled out: "Mister! Mister! make him let go or *I'll knock his brains out!*" Finally the crab loosened his hold, and the poor Tarheel, who had doubtless bravely faced the music on many hard-fought battlefields, hurried from the scene a sadder and wiser man.

Another incident or joke perpetrated upon a North Carolina sergeant who was himself a practical joker, occurred during the winter of '64 and will be remembered by many of those who were prisoners at that time, as the occurrence occasioned much excitement as well as amusement.

Tobacco was a very scarce and valuable article at Point Lookout, and happy was the individual fortunate enough to secure any. I have often seen men following a lucky chewer and waiting for him to finish his chew and beg it for himself. The poor fellows would daily hunt for the "old soldiers," as they termed discarded chews, and consider themselves lucky if they found one —a fact easily verified by any prisoner at the above-named place.

To retaliate upon Sergeant D— for some joke of his, the following placard (as nearly as I can remember it) was written and posted conspicuously about the camp:

NOTICE, NORTH CAROLINIANS.

The Governor of North Carolina having sent me twenty-five boxes of fine chewing tobacco for distribution among the troops from his State confined at Point Lookout, Maryland, all such will call at once at my quarters and obtain their share.

SERGEANT D—, Co. H, 2D DIVISION,
PRISONERS' CAMP.

The news soon spread like wildfire, and was not confined to Carolinians by any means, and very soon a large crowd, numbering at least 500 tobacco-starved graybacks, were clamoring and crowding excitedly about the tent of Sergeant D—, some of whom, in their disappointment, wanted "tobacco or blood." Finally the prison guards arrived on the scene and dispersed the poor disappointed fellows, and soon all was again quiet along the Potomac.

There are many sad memories connected with prison life and camp life which we gladly forget. Let us remember only those scenes on the bright side of the picture.

How vividly the old veterans of the Army of the Potomac can recall a "night after the battle" with the Army of Northern Virginia, how tired nature would seek any spot of hard ground, no soft couch, no covering but the star-spangled heavens, and remember how quickly silence came upon the scene, only a stray shot, the quiet tread of the sentry keeping guard! But all is over now, and the two armies of Grant and Lee are brothers again, fully realizing the happy peace that culminated in the hearts of "Our Chieftains" in the surrender on that eventful day on the historic hills of Appomattox.

COMRADE JOHN.

MATTHEW H. PETERS.

ALL day we two stood side by side, the fury of the foe defied,
    My Comrade John and I.
All night we two lay side by side upon the field our blood had dyed,
    My Comrade John and I.

'Twas in the dead of night, as we
Were lying wounded, helplessly,
    My Comrade John and I,
A voice broke forth in agony,
"Oh, Matt, if I could only see
    My wife before I die!"

Poor Comrade John, 'twas of his bride
He thought, as on that field he died.
    Alas, poor Comrade John;
And pity for the sweet young bride
For whom the brave young soldier sighed—
    The last ere he was gone.

Poor Comrade John, that night he died,
The last wish of his heart denied,
    My noble Comrade John;
He fought and fell, and he fought well.
Thank God that I survived to tell
    The tale of Comrade John.

They buried him upon the hill
(Where at my side he stood and fell)
    Beneath an old pine tree;
But his last words yet send their thrill
Through misty years from that far hill
    To widowed bride and me.

THE NEW RECRUIT.

Louis Goddu.

I WAS deeply in love. My sweetheart was a very pretty French-Canadian school-teacher of La Prairie, opposite Montreal, whom I had met in the latter city. I was only eighteen years old. She was six years my senior, but at that age a young man often forms attachments for women older than himself. It was not her age that troubled me—it was my own. I remember how I wished myself a man of thirty, instead of the stripling that I was. How this feeling changes when one is nearing the half-century mark !

LOUIS GODDU.
1862

I wanted to marry this lady, and my deep affection for her often aroused my courage almost to the point of telling her so. I more than once resolved to ask her hand at our next meeting, but, somehow, when I was in her presence, I could not make up my mind to do so. An indefinable something seemed to tug at my coat-tail every time I opened my mouth to make the proposal.

"Don't be an ass," I fancied I heard that something say. "You young fool, you do not know the gravity of the step you are about to take. Don't you know you have not yet carved out your career ; that you have not yet made a position for yourself in the world ; that your earnings as a printer [I worked at the " case " then] are not sufficient to maintain this woman in the way that both of you would desire ; that you may have five or six children to support ere you have become a man ; that you have not yet begun the fulfilment of your mission in this world—have not even discovered what that mission is? Before you think of marriage, you young insensate," continued the voice, " go and make a position for yourself ; go and win honors, distinguish yourself, that your wife may be proud of you, and that you may be proud of yourself !"

This caused me to reflect and hesitate. Finally I resolved to make a clean breast of it, and tell my sweetheart of the varying emotions that were at war within me, and were harassing me beyond further endurance. On the following Sunday I went to La Prairie. We meandered through her father's vast garden. She plucked flowers for me, and gathered a handsome bouquet, which she bound together with a tiny blue ribbon, and which she presented to me with words that are still deeply graven on my memory. Love shone through her every action, her every word. It was indeed Elysium ! Had I then been able to see what was in store for both of us, owing to my future actions, I would not have left the garden unaccompanied by my —wife. But fate here interposed.

"Artémise," I at last ventured to say, " you know I love you enough to make you my wife. Tell me, do you reciprocate my love ?"

She looked deeply into my eyes, took both my hands into hers, and with a gesture that more than corroborated her words, she said :

" You *know* I do."

" Well, then," said I, " I came to ask you to make a sacrifice."

" I will make *any* sacrifice for you," she said. " What is it ?"

" You are aware," I continued, " of the disparity in our ages. You are not too old for me, Artémise, but I am too young for you. I want to get old quickly. I want to do something that will make an old man of me. I want to shape out my career, distinguish myself, accomplish something that will make me feel I am in a position to marry, and enable you to preside over such a home as you are deserving of."

" What do you mean ?" she asked, surprised at my rather incoherent, though earnest, language. " You have already accomplished what no man has ever been able to do—enough to make me eternally happy—the happiest woman in the wide world. You have absolutely and unreservedly won my love ; and if, as I believe, I have won yours, cannot we consider our achievements of sufficient greatness ? Need we care for aught else? Have we not what gold cannot purchase—the most precious kind of riches ?"

" Yet," I replied, " something tells me we should not marry ere a year or two have elapsed —not before I have——"

" I will wait for you as long as you desire," she interrupted.

" Well, then," I said, " I want to go away for a year or so. I want to go to New York, and thence, perhaps, to some other place, where I think fame, and possibly fortune, await me. Ask no further questions. Trust me. I will write to you as often as circumstances will permit, but if you do not hear from me for a month, two months, or even six, do not for one moment harbor the thought that I have forgotten you, for what I propose to do is all for your sake. To-morrow I shall leave for New York. In one year from to-day you will find me in this garden plucking the prettiest and most precious flower Nature has ever adorned this world with—I shall come and claim you as my own, for I shall feel then that I have not merely won, but *earned* you.''

After mutual vows of eternal love, we reluctantly parted. On the following day I came to New York. That was in August, 1864. I sought and obtained employment on a French newspaper, which has since joined the silent majority, and which I shall refrain from naming, out of respect for its memory. It has simply gone the way of most French newspapers in this community.

I was born of French parents, knowing no more English than what I had been able to acquire in a French college, where Latin and Greek (taught by an Irishman, by the way) were considered more useful languages than English. I continued to set type for a few weeks, meanwhile frequenting English-speaking people. Finally I was asked to translate war despatches, and therein lay the germs of my destiny. I became an enthusiastic Abolitionist. The Union army was meeting with reverses. Gold had taken a tremendous upward leap. In three days prices of the necessaries of life had doubled. Salaries remained at a standstill. A thought flashed through my mind. I went to the proprietor and told him I had decided to enlist in the army, and would do so on that very day. He told me I would rue it, but I would not be dissuaded.

Fabulous sums were offered as bounties, but that was not the main inducement, although I acknowledge it did not altogether act as a deterrent. I saw an opportunity of mayhap winning honors on the battle-field, also some $600. What if I came out unscathed, or even wounded —better still!—with a rank well-earned, epaulettes on my shoulders, a sword at my side, and $600 or $700 in my pocket? Could I not then go and claim my lady-love, not only with the assurance of a man who had earned what he asked for, but even with *éclat?* Chimeras and romance easily find their way into the brain of a youth of eighteen in love up to his ears.

So I forthwith sought a recruiting agent. He took me to Elizabeth, New Jersey, promised me $600, and gave me $150 when I signed my enlistment, telling me I would get the balance at the Trenton barracks after passing final examination. Being as unsophisticated as I was enthusiastic, I believed him. Instead of getting $450 after successfully passing the examination, I got $33.33 and a note for the balance.

I felt I had been deceived, and that was a blow to my enthusiasm. It was too late to retrograde. So I made up my mind to do the best I could out of what began rather inauspiciously.

Meanwhile, I had written to my sweetheart and my father that I was starting on a long voyage, and that several weeks, perhaps months, would elapse before they would hear from me, but told them not to be alarmed, as I was all right.

A few days later, we were put on a train and taken to Baltimore. Thence we took a steamboat for City Point. I will never forget that trip. When night came, I found there was not even room to lie on the floor. It was a question of either standing up all night or lying so close to the open gang-plank space that no one ventured to do so. I became so tired of standing in a few inches of space, unable to move, that I resolved to take the risk, and I lay down on the edge of the boat, with nothing between me and the deep sea. Fortunately, a kind Providence had evidently riveted me to the floor, and I got to City Point, Virginia, without having had to swim the distance.

For some unaccountable reason we were kept in the barracks at City Point for several days. Occasionally, at night, we would hear the booming of cannon. There were skirmishes at Petersburg, about twelve miles distant. I cannot say that that sound was as pleasing to the ear as that produced by the uncorking of a bottle of champagne. Still, I did not cry " Mamma!" nor *"Peccavi!"* I chafed, after a time, under the restraint of the barracks and court-yard, where I had to sleep for several nights. I began to yearn for a chance of earning those epaulettes and that sword. I knew, from the despatches I had translated, that Grant was preparing an attack on Petersburg and Richmond, and I wanted to participate in the capture of the Confederate capital.

Finally the order came to get ready to start for Petersburg. I began the journey with mingled feelings of joy and an apprehension I could not repress, try as I may. I believe almost everybody went through the same experience at first. " Twelve miles!" said I. " Well, that's a mere jaunt. It will take the kinks out of my joints.'' Off I went, with elastic step and jaunty air. To my surprise, in about an hour I found my knapsack getting heavy. Then my haversack and even my canteen accrued enormous weight, and so it went till they felt like a load of lead. We reached Petersburg at nine o'clock that night. I was perhaps the " worst used-up " Frenchman in the American continent. But I forthwith began to derive sustenance from the thought of my sweetheart and a piece of salt pork, which tasted delicious for obvious reasons.

For the first time I learned that I was to be assigned to Company K, 14th New Jersey, 6th Corps of the Army of the Potomac. Early the next morning we were given muskets and cartridges. Then we were drilled for an hour, and, *presto!* I was a full-fledged soldier!

That night the order was given to attack Petersburg. Again that overpowering feeling of mingled joy and apprehension seized hold of me. Finally I shook off the latter component part. Had not the opportunity I had yearned for come at last? This was the very night Petersburg was captured. Then on to Richmond! I will not here repeat the events compassing the fall of the capital, the burning of bridges and block after block of business houses; the desperate fighting on both sides amid the glare of appalling conflagration—events which the historian and the war correspondent have made familiar to the entire world. But I may here record the emotions of a new recruit. I must say that at first I hated the idea of killing a fellow-man, but after several bullets of said fellow-man had whizzed past my head and one had struck me in the left leg, all compunction left me and I began to fight with the desperation of a man attacked by a footpad. And I believe that also is the experience of all.

After taking Richmond, we remained encamped on the other side of the river for several days. Occasionally I would get a pass to go to Richmond, crossing over the pontoon bridge. My wound had been dressed. I refused to go to the hospital, as it gave me no very great inconvenience. I rather welcomed it. From Richmond —where I remember paying fifty cents for a pony glass of bad whisky—I wrote to my friends in New York, telling them of my experience. I mention this because of the part it plays in my narration later.

Finally we were ordered to Danville, in pursuit of General Johnston, who had not yet surrendered. As war has its horrors, it also has its comedies. And the most ludicrous, as well as pathetic, portion of my military career was the march from Richmond to Danville. Although I had passed through two desperate engagements, I was not yet inured to the hardships of a long march. We started at four o'clock in the morning. The first day, evidently to break us in, we were given fifteen minutes' rest every hour. I could stand that. We marched till nine at night. My bones ached so, I could not sleep that night until I had had a good rest. The next day we were given half an hour's rest every two hours. That began to tell on me. I stood it till four o'clock in the afternoon, when I became so exhausted that I could not put one foot before the other. I had to incline my body forward and let my feet follow my body. Finally I told a friend who had enlisted with me (his name is Joseph Matha, and he is now in the Newark Asylum, totally blind) that I couldn't go any farther, and was going to stop, regardless of consequences. I crawled outside of the line and lay down on the ground, more dead than alive, with my head on my knapsack, my haversack still across my shoulders.

Presently a thief stepped up to me and deliberately took my haversack from my shoulder and walked off with it. I had not the strength to resist, nor even make a protest. He saw this, and took advantage of it. Anyhow, I did not think I would ever leave that spot alive, and did not believe I would have any further use for my haversack.

When the entire column had passed, the provost guard stumbled across me.

"Hello!" said the officer in command. " What'r' you doin' there? Get up!"

" I can't get up," I said, faintly.

"What's the matter with you? "

" I am so exhausted that I cannot stand," I said.

" Oh, no you ain't! I'll show you that you ain't."

And he jumped off his horse and gave me a kick in the ribs, not noticing that I was almost dead, "just to show me." I could make no resistance.

" If you don't get up I'll kill you right on the spot!" he cried.

I did not move. I *could* not. So he elevated his sword and brought it down on my head. Seeing I did not move, he stopped as it reached my skull. I had not cared if he had struck me. I had begun to think I would die ere long. I had gone too far. For the only time in my existence I did not care for life. I felt it ebbing away, and my mind was made up. All thought of sweetheart and honors had left me. I was almost unconscious.

"Smell his canteen," suggested one of the aids.

He did so. I had nothing but water.

"———— you!" cried the officer. "If I can't make you walk, I'll put you on my horse and take you along."

He picked me up, put me on my feet, and tried to put me on his horse. He could not do so, and released his hold. I fell in a heap. Then he turned to his aids and said:

"I'll be ———— if I can do anything with him. I guess we'll have to let him stay here. Guess he ain't shamming, after all."

Then, turning to me, he said:

"———— you! Stay there and be d—d!"

I obeyed the first injunction. The second is yet to come.

Then they rode off. My friend had hidden behind a tree and had not been noticed. He rejoined me shortly afterward. He was in better condition than I was. After about two hours' rest, I began to gain a little strength. With his assistance we reached a farm-house near by. I asked them, after telling them of my predicament, to sell me some food. All they had was sour milk and corn bread, for which I paid liberally. Having obtained their permission, we prepared to camp in their yard. Half an hour after we had put up our tent, another provost guard came along and ordered us to join our regiment. I told them of my condition. This officer was more humane and gave us permission to camp out in the woods, for we were, he said, in danger of being killed in that yard, either by guerillas or perhaps the very people of the house, as the Southerners' hatred of "Yanks" at that time was intense. So we camped out in the woods, and did not put up our tent, so as not to attract notice.

The next morning I was surprised to find myself so recuperated. The column was only three or four miles ahead. We could see it defiling at the foot of a hill. My friend did not share his pork and hardtack with me, simply giving me coffee, of which he had a good supply. Coffee has a wonderfully stimulating effect on me. So we started in pursuit of the column, taking a short cut whenever possible. But in doing so we got badly fooled. We came to a river and had to swim across it—that is, I swam with one hand and with the other dragged my friend along, as he could not swim. He thought *his* last day had come. A few miles farther we had to cross a swollen stream on a tree that had been blown down. Both these experiences were more thrilling than romantic. Still, we were gaining on the column.

At about ten o'clock I espied a mule on the wayside that had been thrown aside as "played out." He seemed in fairly good condition. A thought suddenly struck me. I gave him some water, grass, and a little hay I found near by. When he had partaken of this, he seemed to revive wonderfully. So I proceeded to utilize him. I tied my musket and my friend's together, and placed them astraddle of the mule's back. I did the same with our two knapsacks, and then fastened my friend's haversack between the two knapsacks. In his haversack (as there was in the one stolen from me) were three or four chunks of fat pork, hardtack, bolivars, cheese, cigars, and a deck of cards in juxtaposition with each other, as there is but one compartment in a haversack. I bought a rope from a farmer, and improvised a bridle, and off we went.

Thus relieved of a burden of twenty-five or thirty pounds, walking became a comparative sinecure. The mule had had all the friskiness knocked out of him by hard work on a train wagon, and was quite tractable. Finding, after two hours' walk, that we were gaining too rapidly on the column, and fearing that if we caught up with them our idea of army discipline might not coincide with that of the commanding officers, we halted. While we were sitting in the shade, complimenting ourselves upon our good fortune, the mule suddenly threw himself upon the ground, and began, as mules are wont to do when they want to rest their muscles, to roll over several times, still with our accoutrements upon his back. I quickly jumped up and grabbed the haversack. But it was too late. The mule had accomplished his fiendish work. Somehow one of the muskets was discharged in the rolling-over process. The mule jumped to his feet, and started on a gallop. I started in pursuit. I did not want to lose my musket and haversack, nor the mule, for that matter. Besides, I feared that if he reached camp thus equipped, he would create a sensation that would have led to a disastrous investigation.

Knowing a mule's nature, I did not coax him to stop, so he stopped sooner than I had anticipated. It was only when my friend opened his haversack that the full extent of the mule's guilt was discovered. The pork, cheese, hard-tack, cigars, bolivars, and pack of cards had been ground into one concrete mass! I always thought my friend had been punished for refusing to share with me, inasmuch as the cigars, cheese, and bolivars had been bought with my money, for Matha had lost all of his in a sort of bunco game at City Point. The contents of the haversack had to be thrown away.

In a few minutes we resumed our journey. We met a farmer who offered me $300, in Confederate money, for my mule, but he was worth more than that to me, and I refused to sell. Half an hour later the provost guard who had threatened to kill me, with his party, again overtook us. Severe as he had been on the previous day, he burst into loud laughter, as did his aids, as he caught sight of the mule, rigged up as he was.

"Well, by —— ! Frenchy, I'll be —— —— if you ain't a h—— of a soldier!" he cried, and again burst into laughter. "If they were all like you in the army, we'd just raise h——, wouldn't we?" he continued.

I told him I thought he could do his full share of that, judging by my experience of the previous day with him.

"Where in h—— did you get that mule?" he asked.

"Found it on the road," I answered.

"H——! that's a good mule," he said.

"Of course it's a good mule," I replied. "Just refused $300 for him."

He again laughed. The ludicrous sight had completely divested him of harshness.

"Well," said he, "I'll have to take him away from you. We take these farmers' horses from them, and it's nothing but right we should give them these mules."

And so saying, despite my protests, he called a farmer, and gave him my mule, and again I saw hardship before me.

"What was the matter with you yesterday?" he asked.

"You seem able to understand that a mule can become played out, but you cannot understand that a human being can become exhausted," I retorted.

"Humph! How much bounty did you get?"

"I was to have received $600, but got only $183.33 cash," I answered, "but bounty is no factor with me. I——"

"Oh, no; patriotism, I suppose. Well, anyhow, I see you are not inclined to desert, and I'll let you straggle behind, but don't let the column get too far ahead of you. Where are you from?"

"New York."

"What is your business?"

"When I enlisted, I was translator of war dispatches for the —— ——, and have since acted as its war correspondent."

"Oh, indeed! Why didn't you tell me that yesterday? I would have been easier with you."

"I was too weak to speak, and, besides, you didn't give me much of a chance," I said. "See here," I continued, noticing he was good-humored, "I had my haversack stolen, and the mule made an awful mess of the contents (which I enumerated) of my friend's, by rolling over it. Can you not get us other haversacks, and something to eat?"

After another laugh, he said, "Well, come up to the commissary to-night at nine o'clock. I'll be there, and I'll see what we can do for you. So long."

And the party galloped off.

About an hour later we reached a farm-house, which bore evidences of comfort, if not of wealth and luxury. I approached the front door. A very pretty girl of about seventeen soon appeared. I asked her if she would sell us something to eat, telling her I had money (greenbacks, of which she knew little), and would pay her liberally. As she was inclined to chat and ask questions, I related my experience. She became sympathetic forthwith, and seemingly much interested in my welfare. She wanted to know when "this awful thing" would stop. I said, now that Richmond was captured, the war was practically over. She was highly pleased, and very affable. She became more so on learning I was French, and not a "Yank," as she had at first thought. Then she said they had nothing but corn-bread, sour milk, and coffee to subsist on. Her father and brothers had all gone to the war, and they had raised no crops for over two years.

"We were rich once," she said, "but now we are very poor, and I am told all our property will be confiscated. My father was killed, as were also two of my brothers. I only have one left now. Ah me!" she sighed, with tears in her eyes. "Why was this war ever begun? Whoever is responsible for this has assumed a terrible responsibility. But, stay!" she said, vivaciously, making an effort to suppress her sorrow. "I'll go and make you each a fresh cup of coffee, and bake you some fresh corn-bread and give you some strained sour milk and some cream, and you can come right into our dining-room and eat there. I suppose you haven't eaten in a dining-room in some time. Now, take off your things,—I hate the sight of 'em,—sit down on the bench there, and make yourself comfortable. I won't be long."

In less than twenty minutes she called us in to eat. It was plain that the tenants of the house were people of taste, refinement, and education. The lovely little maiden waited on us as if we had been princes, instead of foreigners ranged on the side of their foes. Then she sat beside me and made me relate to her the origin of the war from a Northern standpoint, and my experience at the battles of Petersburg and Richmond. I began to feel as if I were talking to a loving and beloved sister whom I had not seen in a long time.

"Can't you stay here till to-morrow?" she asked. "You are so different from those who passed by here before. I wish you could stay here all the time. I told mother about you, and she'd be willing to have you stay. We are *so* lonely," she said, ingenuously.

The warm-heartedness and sympathetic nature of this little maiden was really beginning to embarrass me. I did not know how to express my gratitude.

"Were I in a position to reciprocate your kindness and amiability in a more fitting manner," I said, "I would not offer you this money; but take this, and whenever you buy anything with it, think of the stranger you have been so good a Samaritan to, and who will never forget you."

She took it reluctantly and asked for my name and address in New York, saying I would hear from her if I would let her know when I returned there.

When we parted, I felt I was leaving a very precious gem behind me. She remained at the gate as long as we were in sight, then waved us a farewell.

That night we went to the commissary's tent for provisions. The provost-guard officer gave me a haversack, but said all he could do for us was to give us a supply of coffee, as the wagons with provisions were far ahead, the men having that morning been given three days' rations. The march lasted for six days, and for six days I subsisted on nothing but coffee, as none of the farmers I met thereafter had anything to eat for themselves.

The Southern Confederacy was not only subdued by force of arms, but by a still more potent foe,—Starvation!

When we reached Danville, my stomach was so weak that I could not eat even chicken, a can of which I managed to buy in a suburban store. It was only after an afternoon's and a night's rest that I felt I could take food. When I looked for my canned chicken, I found that my "room-mate" had eaten it all, as he had also a can of condensed milk! To add to my plight, through some unpardonable mismanagement, we were left for thirty-six hours without a distribution of rations. At the expiration of that time all we received was a chunk of beef that had just been killed and was still warm—not a bit of fat; it was impossible to fry it. So I whittled a stick to a sharp point, and, passing the point through the meat, I held it over the company's fire and "broiled" it. Everybody had to follow my example. We looked like a lot of weather-beaten fishermen fishing in a seething crater.

When we had reached Danville, General Johnston had surrendered; and, as everybody knows, that ended the war. We were, notwithstanding, kept encamped near Danville for about three weeks. Finally we learned that on the morrow we would start for Richmond. Another six days' march, we thought; but, to our surprise,—and it was the only pleasurable one I had ever had in the army,—we were placed, some on top and others inside, of freight cars. Even that we appreciated as a great luxury. I was one of those who were placed on top of the cars. We started in the afternoon. The train ran all night—when it ran. The small locomotive was more than a match for a tramp as to thirst. It had to be stopped every half hour for a fresh supply of water. The Richmond and Danville Railroad in those days was a rickety affair, built on curves and embankments. Now one side of the car would be down, now way up. I had to stretch across the convex centre of the car to establish something like an equilibrium. When night came, despite my efforts to keep awake, I fell asleep in that position, and more than once I narrowly escaped being hurled down embankments. Still we were grateful for being spared that long march, which had been so eventful for me.

On the next day the thirsty little locomotive landed its human freight in Richmond. We marched thence to Washington—from one capital to the other. We encamped in a field at

Alexandria. We remained there for several weeks, waiting to be mustered out. Meanwhile the 5th and 6th corps were "reviewed,"—that is, marched through the principal streets of Washington. Everybody agreed that that was the worst experience we had all had. It was a very hot day, and clouds of dust (for the streets had not been sprinkled) smothered the men, who began to fall by the wayside so fast that the officers had to order us to disband.

A few days later mustering out began. Those who had been longest in service were mustered out first. Though I was as anxious as anybody to return to New York, and thence to my sweetheart, I was glad to see such a considerate act of justice. Finally my turn came. I received the remaining $416.67 due me, plus $42 salary.

And the day I returned to my friends in New York was the happiest of my life.

There I learned that my father and my sweetheart, not having heard from me for so long, and having become suspicious, owing to the letter of warning I had sent them before enlisting, had written to the proprietor for information concerning me. He very foolishly answered that I had gone to the war, and that from letters he and my friends had received he knew I had participated in the battles of Petersburg and Richmond, and had been wounded, and that nobody had ever heard of me since, adding that the general supposition was that I had been killed!

With a stroke of the pen he had spoiled the plan I had so carefully laid and divulged the secret I had so jealously guarded.

I immediately wrote to both my father and sweetheart, telling them it was true I had gone to the front, and relating my experience, but that I had returned safely and would visit them in a few days. When I saw my father, he told me I had caused him the greatest sorrow and the greatest joy of his life. Then I went to La Prairie, post-haste.

The moment I entered the house I saw everything was not right.

"You have killed my daughter!" exclaimed Artémise's mother, in a paroxysm of rage and sorrow.

"My God! what do you mean?" I asked.

"Come into this room and see what you have done, *misérable!*" cried the frantic woman.

I was led into a room adjoining the parlor. Oh! that I could have been spared the pitiful sight that confronted me! There lay my sweetheart in the throes of death! Still beautiful, but, great God! how changed! Pale, emaciated, scarcely able to speak audibly, she extended her beautiful white hand and drew me nearer. I kissed her with all the ardor born of love and despair.

"Now I will die happy," she said, faintly, and in an instant the Angel of Death had fulfilled his mission.

It was the letter of my former employer that had struck the death-blow.

* * * * * * * *

I returned to New York. There I found a parcel awaiting me. It contained a beautifully-framed portrait of my little Southern Samaritan, painted by herself, and, to my astonishment, one of myself, which she said she had also painted.

"You see," the letter said, "that your features have left a great impression on my mind. It was with your money I bought these frames."

I was invited by the little maiden, her mother, and brother to pay them a visit. I did so. We formed a strong attachment for each other, but my sorrow haunted me constantly. I was finally induced to tell her everything. She appreciated my situation. I said I must travel for some time, and when I returned, if she was still of the same mind, we would get married. I went to California, where I remained for six years, engaging in various pursuits, and finally re-entered journalism. Then I returned to my little Samaritan, and she has ever since been making my coffee and baking my corn-bread.

A SOLDIER'S STORY.

WALKER Y. PAGE.

SITTING in the office of a friend, on an evening not long ago, our conversation turned, as it had often done before, upon the late Civil War, its constantly varying phases and remarkable episodes. He had, I knew, entered the Confederate army as a boy, with all the enthusiasm of a boy of sixteen, and had fought it out to its bitter end. I had often listened with pleasure to his graphic descriptions of battles lost and won, his hairbreadth escapes, together with his prison experiences, which tallied with singular exactness to my own. To his extreme youth (at the time) is due his vivid memories of that four years' struggle, which, in the excitement of narration, seemed constantly rising to the surface like the floating debris of the " wreck " that then went down forever. On the evening referred to, this was his story. My only fear is that it may lose much of its original coloring in the process of reproduction.

He said:

It was in the summer of 1863, memorable for General Hunter's raid through the valley of Virginia. We had just lost our commander, the gallant General Jones, in the battle at New Hope, and Generals Lomax and Imboden were conducting the retreat of our war-worn and decimated band. I was but a boy, then, of eighteen, though I had even then become inured to the horrors of war by an active service of two years.

This may read strangely to the uninitiated, but it is nevertheless true, that not only in every brigade and regiment of our army, but in nearly every company, were boys ranging from fourteen to eighteen years of age, as brave fellows as ever led a charge or stormed a forlorn hope, and though thirty years have come and gone since then, the memory still lingers with me of the dying messages of love and devotion of some of those gallant fellows who fell in that retreat, whom not even the prayers of anxious, grief-stricken mothers could save from untimely death.

Day by day, and step by step, we retired before the advancing foe, too few in numbers to hazard the result of a general battle, yet covering our retreat by daily skirmishes, sometimes lasting far into the night; our pathway, illumi-nated by the lurid light of burning barns and homesteads, revealing to us the onpressing squadrons of the enemy, and our own to them, as with the light of day.

We had received orders to hold the enemy in check, at all hazards, until we could be reinforced by Early, who, to aid us, would be obliged to make a considerable detour to the left in order to reach us in the rear. This detour had been necessarily lengthened by our daily retreat of from ten to fifteen miles, and not until we had left Lynchburg in our rear, and the hope that had animated us in all those days of blood, and nights of unrest, had well-nigh settled into despair, did we hear that that thunderbolt of war was with us, and was about to fall in all his fury upon the harassing and exultant enemy.

Hunter was still pressing upon us, with all his characteristic energy, when the glad tidings reached us, and spread from rank to rank of our belabored and shattered host. Then, all at once, a shout went up that seemed to rend the skies above us, " Early! Early! hurrah! hurrah!!" Had a meteor dropped from that clear summer sky into the midst of Hunter's hosts, it would not have more completely paralyzed it, but this was only for a moment. Flushed with victory and the dear-bought success of the unequal strife, he soon brought to the front his serried ranks, and, as though he had heretofore only dallied with his enemy as a cat would dally with the helpless mouse it had doomed to destruction, he seemed to think it now high time to crush, at one decisive blow, the enemy which had so long impeded and harassed his onward march.

It is little to the purpose to detail the incidents of that hard-fought battle, or to tell of the dying and the dead who strewed that field like sheaves when the harvest is done.

Truly the grim reaper had been there, and this was the ingathering of his spoils. Let it suffice, that a decisive victory crowned our arms, purchased with the blood of many of our bravest and best. And now the invaders became the invaded, followed closely and pressed hard by our victorious troops, until what had commenced in an orderly retreat, soon became a disorderly rout, where (as often happens) men from the retreating hosts detach themselves in squads of five, ten, or even twenty, from the main army, and seek safety for themselves outside the line of march of the retreating army. These are the fellows who are the disgrace of the army to which they may belong; these are the base insulters and plunderers of defenceless women and children; marauders, which would be a happy riddance to either army, could they be caught and hung, or shot, by drumhead court-martial.

And this brings me to the singular (but o'er-true) narrative of the "Diamond Ear-rings," which can lose none of their lustre, either from the lapse of years or my poor recital of their history. I was serving in the cavalry, under General Imboden, in that day's fight; we had lost heavily, and it was found that two officers of our command had fallen. I had acted as the general's courier during most of the fight, his regular courier having been killed early in the action.

After the battle was over and the enemy in full retreat, as I sat on my horse near by, awaiting further orders, I was called to him, and as I saluted, he said: "Young man, I have seen you to-day executing my orders in the very thickest of the fight, with a coolness and precision remarkable for one of your years. You now have my orders to take command of a squad of twenty men from your command, to hang upon the line of retreat for the protection of the women and children, and homes of those living within the distance of a mile or two from the probable route of the retreating army. You have witnessed what disciplined soldiers have done in their advance; what may not an undisciplined, lawless, and reckless soldier mob perpetrate on their retreat? Go; I trust to your courage and gallantry to protect innocence, and to your firmness to bring to swift and condign punishment the perpetrators of crime. If prisoners fall into your hands, spare those who can establish their innocence, but hold the guilty for punishment."

Elated with this mark of approval and confidence of my commander, I did not tarry in the execution of his orders, and long before the close of the day, was hovering upon the flank of the retreating foe. We had reached a point nearly opposite the town of Lynchburg (for though the battle has since been known as the "battle of Lynchburg," it was in reality some distance beyond), when we saw in the distance a sudden burst of flame, as from a burning building. Putting spurs to our horses, we soon became convinced of the truth that some large building had been fired. On our nearer approach, we discovered a large barn to be on fire, which, from the combustible nature of its material and contents, was now burning furiously.

A little way from the barn, and surrounded and protected in a measure by the dense foliage of the encircling trees, stood an old-time Virginia brick mansion, evidently the home of some former landed proprietor, and, even in the present neglected condition of its out-buildings and surrounding grounds, giving evidence of its former, but now faded, splendor. Seeing nothing about the burning barn to indicate the presence of an enemy, if such there had been, and feeling sure that the fire was the very recent work of some incendiary, I called to my men to follow me, and rode rapidly toward the house.

An elderly lady and, as I supposed, her two daughters, were standing upon the veranda as we rode up. They were evidently in a state of great distress and alarm, as from some recent disturbance, nor were they reassured until they realized that we were friends, and not enemies. They had all been weeping, and the traces of tears were yet upon their cheeks. I observed that the youngest of the group, a beautiful girl of not more than sixteen, seemed to be more overcome than the others, and besides, was bleeding from wounds about the head or face.

"For God's sake, ladies," I exclaimed, "tell me, and tell me quickly, what all this means!"

The mother was most composed, and was the first to speak. She said:

"Sir, I am a widow. My husband, a Confederate officer, fell in the first battle of Manassas, and I and my daughters have lived here unmolested until now. This evening a squad of Union soldiers came upon us, burning my barn and demanding all the money we had, as also our watches and jewelry. Unfortunately, my youngest daughter had a pair of diamond ear-rings in her ears, and he who seemed to be the leader of the gang, snatched them from her ears, tearing the flesh, as you see!" "And oh, Mr. ——," interjected the excited and indignant girl, "I hope, if you come up with them, you won't take a prisoner!"

"Not so, my child," said the calmer mother. "It is true you have suffered a grievous indignity and a great loss, for those diamonds, in addition to their intrinsic value, have been an heirloom in our family for several generations; but you are wrong, my child, to wish for vengeance. Remember, 'Vengeance is mine, saith the Lord.'"

"How long have they been gone, and which direction did they take?" I inquired, "for we must see that they commit no more depredations. We will see that you have protection for the night if you can give five of my men accommodation until the morning. By that time the stragglers from the army will have passed."

She gladly accepted my offer of protection, and after detailing five of my men to protect the mansion and its defenceless occupants, and just as we were saying our adieus to the ladies, the young and still bleeding girl stepped to my side and said, in a hesitating, broken voice: "I am sorry I said to you what I did. It was wrong, and I did not really mean it, captain!"

I stooped low from my saddle-bow and gave her my name, *sotto voce*, adding that if I should be so fortunate as to recover her diamonds, she should assuredly have them again; that I needed no greater incentive to do all my duty than those bleeding and lacerated ears, for I was maddened at the sight. I read in the countenances of my men that they fully entered into my feelings, and that woe would betide the perpetrators of this dastardly outrage, should they be overtaken. True, they had nearly an hour's start of us, but I had conjectured rightly when I supposed that they would go slowly, thinking themselves safe from pursuit, and taking all the chances for despoiling the unprotected farmhouses in their route.

Counting their horses' tracks, we found they numbered fourteen, while we, on the other hand, numbered fifteen. In every other respect they would, most probably, have greatly the advantage of us. Still, that cowardly outrage was a spur which even our horses seemed to feel, and our riding (if not exactly "Jehu-like") was by no means slow.

We had ridden thus for more than an hour, with no sign of the miscreants, except that their horses' tracks appeared fresher and more recently made than at first, when, suddenly, Lieutenant R. rode to my side and said: "Captain, I think I see them just in the skirt of yonder wood. They have halted and dismounted, perhaps waiting until nightfall to perpetrate even worse deeds than burning barns and robbing defenceless women. I see a large farm-house there away to the left, and those fellows, no doubt, see it too, and are deliberating what they intend to do. If I am not greatly mistaken, we will have something to say in protest to their little game!"

I had called a halt, and my men were gathered around me. We had come upon them suddenly, at the distance of not more than 300 yards, having been concealed from them by the hill, on the brow of which we now stood. We were now in full sight, while they were, as yet, partly concealed, with their horses, behind some undergrowth which skirted the road.

In a moment, one rode out from his fellows a little way as for reconnoissance, then hastily moved back to his companions. I took him for their captain, as he rode a fine, large black charger, and appeared to have the accoutrements of a non-commissioned officer—as savage-looking a fellow as one would care to meet anywhere, with a face almost entirely enveloped in a long, black, bushy beard, which reached nearly to his saddle-bow. As he turned, he brandished his sword in defiance.

Hastily addressing my men, I merely said: "Remember that poor bleeding girl, and act as though she were your sister who had suffered the cruel wrong. Now follow me, and let every man do his duty. Charge!" "Charge!" came in thundering tones from my hirsute adversary, who had singled me out as the first victim of his glittering sword, which he waved high in air as he rushed upon me, and with a blow that would have cleft me to the chin, had I not parried it with my trusty old basket-hilted sabre.

Our horses had been in full charge, and could not be checked at once. When I turned he had drawn his revolver, and now his eyes were ablaze with fury as he rushed again upon me. When within ten feet of me he raised his revolver, saying, "Now, d—n you, take this!" but his pistol snapped. I turned in my saddle and fired, when he threw up his hands, swaying to and fro, and when about fifty yards away, fell with a heavy thud to the ground, his noble horse coming to a full stop as soon as he missed his master's guiding hand.

I had been so occupied in my encounter with my furious and powerful adversary, that I had not had a moment to give to my brave fellows who were fighting hand-to-hand with the desperadoes around me. I had heard the clash of swords mingled with the quick and sharp reports of revolvers, but knew nothing of how the fight was likely to end. Suddenly the thought came to me that if I could exchange my jaded steed for the noble black, which still stood as though waiting for his master, I could carry more efficient aid to my comrades who might be too hardly pressed, never thinking, for the moment, that in the hurry and excitement of the fight I might be mistaken for the former owner of the horse. This was verified a few moments later, when one of my own men rode furiously down upon me, with his revolver raised, and only when on the point of firing did he recognize me.

"Thank God, captain, that I didn't shoot you," exclaimed he, "for I thought it was surely that other fellow who had killed you, and I had sworn to avenge your death."

The clash of steel here arrested our attention, and looking in the direction of the sound I discovered my gallant lieutenant in deadly peril from the sabres of two of his adversaries, and powerless to do more than ward off the blows, which came thick and fast upon him.

Riding rapidly forward, and realizing that a moment might end the conflict in the loss of my bravest and best man, we each singled out our foeman, and as we passed in full charge, the simultaneous report of two revolvers brought the unequal conflict to a speedy close, two empty saddles telling how sure our aim had been.

The hand-to-hand fight (which had not lasted more than ten or fifteen minutes) was over, except here and there, the report of revolvers growing more and more indistinct in the distance, as though the fight had become a flight. Who were the pursuers and who the pursued, we could but conjecture. A hasty survey of the field revealed the fact that four of the enemy and two of my men had fallen in the fight, either dead or mortally wounded. How many more, it was impossible to tell, as the night was fast settling in darkness over field and wood, rendering further search impossible. We could only tether our horses and wait for the return of morning and our scattered band.

As I have said before, I had become somewhat inured, young as I was, to the sight of blood and carnage and death, but that lonely night, with its silent stars shining down upon me, and the dead lying around—two of whom, at least, had fallen by my hand—gave me a feeling of awe and unrest I had never experienced before. Heretofore I had never, in the thick of the fight which raged around me, been certain that any human being had come to death by my hand, but now the certainty that my hand had shed human blood, though in self-defence, aroused a feeling akin to remorse, which drove sleep from my eyes until almost the dawn of day.

Morning brought with it sad duties and responsibilities. We could not leave our own dead unburied, and common humanity dictated that we should not leave our fallen foes to rot upon the field. The night had brought to me thoughts of mother, home, and friends, and I could not but conjecture that these men, debased and reckless as war had made them, had perhaps homes and mothers and friends also, who even then were watching for their coming. But how to accomplish this. The only feasible plan which suggested itself was that one of us should ride to the farm-house which we had seen in the distance the evening before, and procure the necessary implements for digging the graves. In the course of an hour the messenger brought the tools, accompanied by a youth, the only male representative of the family then at home, bearing an invitation from his mother to breakfast. Just as we were preparing to dig the grave of our own men (for we could only bury them side by side in one vault), the five men who had been detailed to guard the mansion on the evening before rode up, with a message of thanks from the ladies, and an additional one from her who had lost her ear-rings, that "if I ever recaptured her diamonds, I should keep them safe, and some day, when the war was over, bring them to her in person."

Just then I remembered her hasty description of the man who had committed the assault, and, calling one of my men, we walked to where the dead man lay.

I ordered the soldier who accompanied me to search the man's pockets and person, if, perchance (being the leader), he might have the stolen valuables upon his person.

As pocket after pocket was searched, nothing came to light but a miscellaneous collection, consisting of a knife, a spoon, a soiled handkerchief, and cartridges, mixed in indescribable confusion with pipe, tobacco, matches, etc., but no jewelry of any kind or description. I felt disappointed, and was about turning to leave, when suddenly it occurred to me to examine his inner clothing. Opening his coat, the side pockets were found to be empty, but the vest disclosed two large side pockets, and here we found the objects of our search—two gold watches, the diamond ear-rings, with the blood dried upon them, and a few other articles of jewelry, evidently all kept together for the purpose of future distribution.

I knew my men too well to doubt but that they would with one voice determine that this property, though recovered from an enemy in battle, should be regarded as a sacred trust, to be returned intact to its rightful owners as soon as an opportunity presented itself. With one accord they determined that I should keep it on my own person until such time as it could be returned to its owners, and with the further understanding that if I should fall in battle, my survivor or survivors should perform in good faith what we all considered a solemn duty.

The work of burying our dead, as also those of the enemy (six in all), had just been completed, when those of my command who had been absent all night returned, bringing with them three riderless horses, but whether their owners had forsaken them in their terror and anxiety to escape, or whether they had fallen victims to the bullets of their pursuers, they could not tell, as the night was too dark to determine.

Two or three of my men had received slight sabre-cuts in the hand-to-hand fight of the evening before, but the brave fellows had nevertheless followed the routed enemy far into the night, and not until their jaded horses could carry them no further had they relinquished the pursuit.

Whether the result of this skirmish with the marauders from Hunter's retreating army had been communicated to others who might be in like manner disposed to depredate or not, the fact is remarkable, that during the rest of that retreat we were troubled no more by mounted marauders from the retreating army until we reached Covington, in West Virginia, where I reported to my commanding officer, no longer a "captain of cavalry," but relegated to the post of courier to the general who had honored me with his favorable notice and clothed me with a little brief authority.

It would be a poor recompense for the generous hospitality received at the farm-house, not to mention the breakfast, such as none of us had tasted since we left our homes. The only return we could make was to leave upon their hands five worn-out specimens of horseflesh, which we sincerely hoped would in time prove useful.

The one redeeming feature of war is, that in the nature of things *it cannot last long*, and this war, which is still, after the lapse of thirty years, designated by some as the war of the "rebellion," was a thing of the past, and I, with the remnant who survived, had been for three years busied in recuperating from the disastrous financial condition in which "grim-visaged war" had left us, when it became necessary, in the course of business, that I should visit the James River country, taking the city of Lynchburg in my route.

I concluded that now was the time, if ever, to perform my promise and discharge the duty which had been imposed upon me, not only by my companions-in-arms, but by that suffering girl whose lovely, tear-stained face had haunted me in many a sleeping and waking dream, until it had become to me as a beckoning angel.

"Business first, and pleasure afterwards." Fortunately for the young men of the South, this was the lesson taught them by the war, and a salutary lesson it was, though written in blood and conned in poverty and privation, but peace had come to the land once more, and prosperity as the result of honest, earnest, well-directed toil, and the country, which three years before had been furrowed only by shot and shell, was now smiling in plenty, with waving corn and wheat fields and pastures clothed in living green.

My business mission to Lynchburg accomplished, I hired a horse to carry me to the scene of my first experience as "captain of cavalry," and I soon fell into the road which I at once recognized as the one over which three years ago I had led my troop. If I admit that my heart beat somewhat faster on this occasion than when an enemy was in front, let it be remembered that I was *then* only twenty-two years of age, and, like the knight of old, whose duty to his "liege lord" was only equaled by his devotion to his "lady love," I had sheathed forever a sword which had never been disgraced while in the service of the one, leaving the duty to the other paramount to all else.

I was not prepared for the change that met my eye as I neared the spot. The barn had been rebuilt, the fields had been fenced, and were in a high state of cultivation, while the house and surrounding grounds evidenced that some master hand had wrought a wondrous change.

What if the girl of the "diamond episode" had been changed also into the wife of some gallant soldier, who even now was restoring this old-time homestead to its former beauty and grandeur? As this unwelcome thought came over me like a chill, I put spurs to my horse and galloped up the long avenue. My approach must have been observed, for no sooner had I reached the door, and before I had time to knock, than it was opened by a tall, handsome, soldierly-looking man of about thirty, as well as I could judge, of a youthful face, while his hair and beard indicated full fifteen or twenty years more. I at once introduced myself, giving my full name (Bradford Chester), as I had done to Miss Carrington on that memorable evening.

" Ah !'' he exclaimed, as he heard my name, holding out his hand in cordial greeting, " I am happy, Captain Chester, to make your acquaintance, and I am sure the ladies will greet you gladly. Your name, captain, is not an unfamiliar one, I assure you, in our home circle. Your well-timed protection of defenceless women, and your gallant charge on the men who insulted them (for we have heard of it all), has been the frequent theme of our conversation. But if you will excuse my absence for a moment, I will go and inform the ladies of your arrival.''

I could no longer keep my seat, but as the door closed behind him, I arose, and was pacing the room with excited strides, when, turning suddenly in my walk, I was conscious of a presence. It was that of a lady.

She detected my look of wonder and admiration, and holding out her hands to me, I seized them both, though still uncertain that I recognized her.

"Don't you know me?'' she asked. "Look here at the scars,'' and the whole scene passed vividly before me, as it had a thousand times before.

"Remember you?'' I said, in an impassioned but most unjustifiable tone and manner, considering our casual acquaintance. " I should as soon forget the mother who bore me !'' Seeing her blushes and evident embarrassment, occasioned by my hasty speech, I exclaimed, " Miss Carrington, forgive me ; I have offended you by my impulsive manner.''

"Oh, no ! no ! I am not offended, only a little startled.'' " And now,'' I said, "to make some amends for my impulsiveness—but, excuse me, am I addressing the wife of that handsome gentleman who left me a little while ago, or have I the pleasure of speaking to her sister, Miss Carrington ?''

"I am a maiden, sir,'' she said, with a rippling laugh and a coquettish toss of her queenly head. " It is my sister who is married.''

"Then it is to you that I must return these,'' I said, as I took from my breast pocket a box, which I handed over to her.

"And what am I to do with this ?'' she asked, in wonderment, as she took it from me.

" Open it, if you please.''

With a glad cry, as she lifted the lid, she exclaimed, " Oh, Captain Chester, you have really captured my watch and diamond ear-rings.''

"Yes,'' I said, " and but for your message by one of my men, that if captured, they should be returned in person, they would long ago have reached you.''

" Oh, I am so glad that you did not send them,'' and blushing deeply, as though conscious that I might put a too flattering construction on her hasty exclamation, she added, "that I might have the pleasure of telling you how grateful we all are for your timely protection—but tell me, please, how you managed to get them.''

" That is one of the incidents of the war which I must withhold even from you,'' I replied. " The recital would only give you pain, while its only pleasurable feature to myself is, that I have it in my power to return those valued trinkets to their rightful owner.''

Just at this moment, Mrs. Carrington and her daughter, together with Colonel Hopkins, the husband of the latter, came into the room, and after the usual courtesies and formal introductions, the conversation naturally drifted to the war and its incidents, many of which were familiar to both Colonel Hopkins and myself, and thus the hours were beguiled until the setting sun reminded me that I had exceeded the bounds of conventional visiting. But upon my rising to leave, and apologizing for the length of my visit, they all, with one accord, protested against my going, except the one whose voice I most wished to hear ; she was silent.

I turned to her, and waited for a moment, hoping to hear her words added to the warm and earnest invitation that I should stay, but it did not come. I then extended my hand, and said, in as steady a voice as I could command, "Goodbye ; I shall carry back with me to my mountain home the memory of one of the pleasantest episodes of my life.''

"Oh, no, no ! Captain Chester, you must not leave us so !'' she said, as she took my hand, and blushing all over neck, and face, and brow, repeated : " You must not leave us so soon. You will stay all night, won't you ? Brother has had your horse taken, not dreaming that you would leave us. See, it is getting dark already, and it is a long and lonesome road. Stay until tomorrow, or—longer.''

I did stay, and not until the evening shadows began to fall, did I leave the next day, and then not until I had promised to repeat my visit, which I did on the next day, and the next, and next, until I ceased to reckon their number.

To bring a soldier's long yarn to an end—my wife still wears her diamond ear-rings, notwithstanding our oldest daughter, who considers herself a grown-up young lady, and protests against the impropriety of a matron of forty bedecking herself in " diamond ear-rings.''

CORPORAL KING'S TRIP TO WASHINGTON.

J. M. WADDILL.

"CORPORAL KING, you are wanted at the captain's quarters, right away," said our orderly-sergeant to me, immediately after roll-call, one morning in December, '62, a short time previous to the great battle of historic old Fredericksburg.

Thinking over my more recent misdeeds, and wondering which particular one was the cause of my summons to company headquarters so summarily, I took my way to the captain's tent, the same being two blankets stretched over a rail, supported by a forked stick at each end driven in the earth.

"Corporal," said the captain, as I gave the regulation salute, "how would you like a little trip of, say, two or three weeks?"

"It would fit me exactly, captain."

"Do you think you could discontinue your deviltry for that length of time?"

"I'm perfectly sure of it, Cap," I replied.

"There would be a good deal of business and some hazard in the matter."

"I think I could manage both, sir."

"There might be a hanging bee, in which you would be the central figure," he said, looking me steadily in the face.

"Suppose we hear the facts in the case, Cap," I replied; for while I would not have cared so much for Enfield rifle risks, I did not relish his tone of voice as he referred to hanging, such being an unusual method for a respectable soldier to meet his death.

"Sit down, King, while I give you the whole story. Several men are wanted for a dangerous trip across the lines, and you have been selected as one; that is, if you accept the appointment cheerfully. If you return safely you may be pretty sure of finding a pair of shoulder-straps waiting for you; if you are captured the probabilities are that you will be hung instead of being shot. You would perhaps be back here (that is, if you *do* get back) in three weeks—say in time for your Confederate Christmas dinner. Now, go off and sit down by that fire yonder, by yourself, and consider the matter for full five minutes, after which I will receive your decision."

I was about to decide the matter at once in the affirmative, but the picture of a human body swinging from a cross-beam at the end of a rope rose up before me, and I concluded to take the five minutes.

Seated by the fire, I reflected over the possibility of seeing, across the lines, a pretty little Yankee girl, dearer than all the world to me, who would ere that time have been my wife had not some hundred thousand Federal bayonets forbid the banns, and kept them forbid, for something like eighteen long months.

The prospect of seeing her would have at once decided the matter had I not disliked the idea of appearing before her as a spy, for I felt that such was the duty required of me. However, I decided to take the bodily risk, as well as the chance of being degraded in her eyes, and returning to my captain gave my assent to the proposed work.

"I know, as well as you, what influenced your decision, and I never would have sent up your name but for the hope and belief that the cause would lead you to exercise the greatest care and discretion," said the captain. "Remember, if you arrive at the distinction of a 'gallows bird' you will lose her. I know of no stronger incentive to prudence. Report to General —— at noon, and receive your instructions," he added, and soon I was *en route* to headquarters.

Captain B—— had known me from my boyhood—knew of my love scrape and doubtless considered my opportunity of seeing her in selecting me for what he pretended was an extremely hazardous duty, the dangers of which I fully believed he exaggerated.

Reporting to corps headquarters, I found eight others waiting the orders of the general. Very soon we were summoned into his presence, and the name of each called by his adjutant-general.

Said the general: "You have each and all been recommended as suitable men for an expedition beyond the enemy's lines. Upon your coolness, intelligence, and discretion rests the success of your undertaking, as well as your personal safety. You will each operate independently, have no communication whatever one with the other while in the enemy's lines, make record of all information received as quickly as possible, leaving nothing whatever to memory. Report to me, in person, about three weeks hence, but that is left largely to your good judgment. You will receive definite written instructions from the adjutant-general, which you will memorize and destroy before leaving our lines. I enjoin upon each coolness and prudence; your courage I do not doubt."

We then received our written instructions, together with a cipher code, which we were also to memorize and destroy, and a goodly-sized memorandum book, in which our daily reports were to be entered in cipher. We were furnished with orders on the quartermaster for such clothing outfit as we needed, and a sum of money sufficient for our expenditures while absent.

With a kindly word from the adjutant-general, and wishes for our safe return, we departed with solemn forebodings for the future. I never saw any of my comrades afterward, but as I heard of no military executions while in the enemy's country I presume they all returned safely.

It is unnecessary, in this writing, to state what our duties were or how our work was accomplished or what tools we used. Some of the tools being yet in the land of the living might object to too much publicity in such matters. This history relates alone to my experiences, aside from the duties assigned me, but it is not amiss to say that the probable result of our work was a fairly accurate knowledge beforehand, at Confederate army headquarters, of a certain great Federal expedition, involving much money and material, which came to naught, so far as actual results go.

That night, arrayed in the garb of a respectable young farmer, with sundry items in my memorandum book, in plain but not elegant English, relative to various farm matters, prominent among them being estimates and calculations pertaining to a certain lot of pork to be sold, I left Dixie, to make my way "beyond the lines." Within three days I found myself in Washington, at a cheap boarding-house, not far from where the Potomac depot now stands.

My first work, for two or three days, was to make sale of my pork, stored away up about Harrisburg, but somehow we could never seem to agree on the price.

Having made a few acquaintances, I set to work on my mission, which, though little to my taste, had to be accomplished, in the meantime planning as to how I should manage to see my darling Rozelle, who resided in a village in the vicinity of York, Pennsylvania.

She was a "high-strung" little bundle of feminine attractions, had exalted notions of honor, etc., and I knew was loyalty itself to the Union. This latter fact I had learned from various affectionate political quarrels with her down in the Palmetto State, where I had met and wooed her two years before. I had no fears of her betraying me, of course, though she knew I was in the Confederate ranks, but I did have very grave apprehensions as to how she would receive a spy.

I thought over every conceivable story I might offer, but abandoned each and every one, as I felt she would see through their flimsy fabric, leaving her to believe that she alone was the cause of my visit, though this, to her sensible eyes, would, I feared, look very "thin." Finally, I made up my mind to go, trusting to chance and her affection for a kindly reception.

More than thirty years have passed since I was ushered into the parlor in that quaint little old Pennsylvania town, but I can never forget the welcome of my promised wife, whom war had separated from me for so many months, nor can I fail to remember the love-light in her great black eyes as, sitting by me, she told of her thousand anxieties concerning me, and deplored the long intervals between my uncertain letters. Greater pleasure than was mine on that happy evening falls to the lot of few men; but there was a weight on my mind, for I dreaded the explanation which I felt was sure to follow. I was brought from the little hotel at which I was stopping, and duly installed in the house of my loved one, an honored guest.

We sat late that night, after her old father and mother had left the parlor, and as the hours sped by, I realized that I must get over the terrible explanation if I was to perfectly enjoy my visit. I could stand it no longer. Taking both her hands in mine, and gazing steadily into her eyes, I asked:

"Why do you not ask how and why I am here?"

Very slowly she replied, as if weighing each word: "My love for you and the esteem in which I hold you will not permit me to think of you as a deserter; still less can I imagine you a spy. I do not try to account for your presence, and am content to ask no questions and be happy with you, having no thought other than that you are with me."

If I pressed the dear little woman to my breast and almost smothered her with kisses, I could not help it. The act came spontaneously, and would have been prolonged indefinitely, but she promptly "called the house to order," and quiet was restored.

The next day, for appearance's sake, I showed myself on the streets for a time, and was not over-much pleased to find that a company of cavalry was quartered in the outskirts of the village, although, so far as I knew, there was no special cause for anxiety on my part. I had not extended my walk very far, when I noticed a little urchin gazing very intently at me, as if I was an object of considerable curiosity. Pretty soon he approached, and in a timid sort of way, said :

"Ain't you a rebel?"

The sudden and unexpected nature of the inquiry threw me off my balance for the moment, but realizing that there might be much of grave interest to me in the youngster's question, I determined to know, if possible, what had inspired it.

"Why, bub, the rebels are all down South, are they not?"

"That's what I told Billy Watkins when he said you were a rebel," he answered.

"What made Billy Watkins say such a silly thing?" I asked.

"He said as how Miss Rozelle's sweetheart from down South had come to see her, and that all Southerners was rebels."

"Well, you go and tell Billy Watkins that he is very foolish to talk such nonsense," I replied, leaving the boy gazing after me, but *not* leaving my apprehensions that very grave events might soon come to me.

Considering the matter in all its phases, I retraced my steps toward what I shall call home, and going up to my room, vainly sought to settle in my mind the best course to pursue. It was evident that I was being discussed as a rebel! To walk out of the village was but to invite further suspicion, and there was no train until the next day. I concluded to confide my fears to Rozelle and take counsel with her. In response to my request, she soon met me in the parlor, and as soon as I saw her face I knew she was in distress.

"Oh, Will!" she said, all in a tremble, "I am dreadfully uneasy about you."

"And I am somewhat dreadfully uneasy about myself," I replied, in as cheerful tones as possible.

"Do you know that your presence here is the subject of comment, and that it is known that you belong to the Southern army? Oh, I shall never forgive myself if you fall into trouble on my account."

I told her of my apprehensions, resulting from my interview with the boy, and together we discussed the situation, gravely. She had received her information from her father, and though the family, one and all, stood ready to befriend me, neither they nor myself had an idea of what could be done, except that I should take my departure by the first train if, perchance, I might be my own master on that occasion.

Rozelle despatched her father into the village, as on vidette duty, to learn of any talk or movement looking to my arrest. An hour or two after tea he returned, reporting no news whatever, and we began to breathe more freely.

Late that night we sat in the cozy parlor, she and I. Oh, the blessedness of those hours! Fears for my safety banished much of her maidenly reserve, and in her every word and act I read of a love the depth of which I never knew before. It was worth the risk and danger in which I stood, to know of her devotion and constancy, of her hopes for the future, and of the fairy air castles dwelling in her thoughts, each and every one with my unworthy self enthroned therein, her lord and king. Plans were laid and programme arranged in detail, of what I should say and not say in case of arrest. Loving "good-nights" were spoken and I ascended to my room, but not to sleep. My ears were too keenly alive to any sound about the house which might be the tramp of men coming to take me and lead me to —— ah, I dared not think of where or what!

I threw myself, half clad, across the bed, waiting and listening. Suddenly, the sound of heavy footsteps on the porch below, followed by the rattle and clash of dragging sabres, announced that my time had come; that I was to be arrested. There was no escape for me, and I rapidly conned over what account I should give of myself when the time came.

There is a gentle rapping at my door. I listen, and it is repeated, while my name is spoken in a whisper. I open the door, and in the dim light Rozelle is standing, with her fingers on her lips, to bespeak silence; her loose, flowing hair frames a face white as marble. A wrapper is thrown about her form, evidently to conceal the night-dress in which she is attired. In a whisper, between little gasps of fright, she says:

"They are at the door below. You must come into my room for concealment; they will not dare search for you there."

"No, I cannot do that. I will not compromise you for my safety," I whispered in reply.

"Come, oh, come at once," and seizing me

almost savagely, and, with pleading eyes and quickened breath, she drags me to the door, and I am hustled into the room with her and the door is locked.

"If discovered here you are lost, and—*I am ruined*," she whispers through the ashy lips. "So be it," she adds, in a tone of decision.

I am "stood up" in a wardrobe, apparently full of white, dainty garments of muslin and lace, and the door closed. The tramping of the troopers can be plainly heard in the hall below, and very soon they are ascending the stairway to the floor on which the bedrooms are located. As they near her door I hear her open it and ask, as if in a voice of indignation, what the commotion means. There is a reply, and she continues: "Mr. King left his room some time since, having heard that the officer in command desired to see him," and her door closes with a bang.

It appears that the troopers are not so easily satisfied, for I hear doors opening and closing as if rooms are being searched. After awhile they take their departure, but I am kept in my narrow prison for more than an hour. Then there is a slight noise of light footsteps in the room, the door opens and closes and the key is turned in the lock, and again all is quiet and darker than the proverbial hinges of hades.

Another apparently interminable time elapses, and the room door is again opened and I hear the sound of bare feet moving about—and still no light. Now the door of my prison is opened, and, speaking in a whisper, she says:

"Father is here. We must make no noise, and there must be no light, for they may be watching. Father will remain with you, and you two can plan for the best. You will write to me, Will, but you must address your letters to Billy Watkins. Now, kiss me good-bye, and may a merciful God be with you in your peril!"

That embrace and kiss through the wardrobe door was worth far more than double the hazard I was in, and the same would have been prolonged until a much later hour but for the presence of "father," and a vigorous dig by fairy hands in the vicinity of where my cravat was tied and she was gone, as I felt my way out of the wardrobe.

For some moments there was silence, broken at length by the old gentleman whispering: "We had better lie down here until toward daylight—maybe by that time the soldiers will give it up, and you can get away."

We groped our way to the dainty bed and lay down. Between us it was arranged that a short time before dawn I was to make my way from the rear of the house across the garden to the stables, and taking one of the horses was then to choose my own course for safety. The chances and possible mischances were carefully considered, the various available routes discussed until about four o'clock, when, guided by the old man, I found myself outside the building, making my way stableward. I had gone probably fifty paces when, from behind a bit of shrubbery, a tall figure arose and, in a low voice commanded "halt."

I was in the act of drawing my revolver when there was a crash of something against the side of my head, which may have been a twenty ton aerolite, to judge by the force with which it came. More than eighty thousand stars instantly appeared, though the night was cloudy.

When I regained my scattered and dazed faculties I found myself being led or dragged along by two stalwart cavalrymen, and in a few minutes was hustled through a door into Egyptian darkness of arctic temperature, while the grating of a rusty bolt as it shot into its place told that I was locked up; where I did not know. Having no means of amusing myself, except that of rubbing a very sore and aching cranium, I sat down, and as I rubbed endeavored to take a general survey of the future, which at that moment was quite as dark and gloomy as were my surroundings. In half an hour or thereabouts the door was opened and a pile of blankets thrown in, as a voice said: "I guess you can find a use for these." The proposition needed no discussion, for the cold struck clear through to the very marrow.

When daylight came I found myself in a room about eight feet square, ceiled with heavy oak boards, one small window secured with iron bars, the door plated over with iron, and not a vestige of anything in the "apartment" except my miserable self and scanty belongings. In due course my breakfast was brought by a soldier, who bade me a civil "good morning" and took his departure before I had time to make any inquiries or suggestions.

My appetite being wanting, I left the food untouched and gave myself to the task of thoroughly investigating my surroundings, determined that no effort should be spared to get myself out of a "fix" which, if not rid of, surely meant an ignominious death. Every board in floor and ceiling was sound and fast, and not less than two inches thick. The window, even had it been unprotected, was above my reach, while the door, in its massive strength, would have defied a dozen men. True, there was a small opening in the ceiling over my head, something more than a foot square, placed there, doubtless, for ventilation, but it was just then as inaccessible as the North Pole.

All that day I thought and planned and schemed, but there was literally no loophole for escape and no suspicion of one, unless it was the open ventilator, and though I could figure on nothing beyond, I fixed my thoughts on that as the only possible factor in the case. Late in the afternoon, without warning, my door was opened and a Federal captain ushered in Rozelle. The officer evidently knew how the land lay between us, for, with cap in hand, he said, with the utmost politeness:

"Now, miss, my prisoner is in your hands. I cannot parole him, but I can leave him for a short time in your hands," and he proceeded to retire.

"No, captain," she said, hastily, "please remain. I wish to explain my visit."

She made a clean breast of the matter—telling him of our engagement, entered into in happier times—that I was a Confederate soldier, come at the risk of my liberty or life to see her, and for this only, concluding by asking his kind offices in my behalf. I knew by her confession that she regarded my case as a desperate one, and that she deemed it best to rid me of any suspicion of being a spy, even though she consigned me to a prison in doing so.

Acting upon her words, I made known my name, company, and regiment, hoping to be sent to Point Lookout without any unpleasant investigations concerning my presence. The young captain, whose name was Rand, I could see was on my side, and I felt satisfied of his personal feelings, but he was a gentleman and a patriot also, and I knew he would do his duty. He assured her that he would be glad to make my position as pleasant as possible, but that he had already reported my capture and was then awaiting instructions concerning me.

He then withdrew, telling her, with a twinkle in his honest blue eyes, that he held her responsible for my safe-keeping. My first move was to steal a kiss without any "smack" to it, lest the captain should hear it, and my second was to place my tell-tale memorandum book in her keeping.

Our interview was brief, both of us deeming it best, but before she called my jailer I had pointed out to her the open ventilator, and it was agreed that she should ask permission to bring me a loaf of bread and some delicacies the next day, and that the loaf should contain a stout twenty-foot cord with an equally stout iron hook attached. Another kiss, and the officer came, and, with a smile and some pleasant words to me, I was again left alone.

All that night I dreamed of a white-winged angel, with rosy cheeks and a fairy figure, remarkably like my Rozelle. She appeared to me under many and varied circumstances: sometimes in palaces of wondrous beauty, then in vine-clad cottages, in the forest, in flower-carpeted fields, on the mountain side, or in deep, shadowy valleys, always hovering about me, with tender, loving smiles, but always with a good stout rope, with hook attached, clasped in her little dimpled hands.

The next evening she was again admitted by the gallant captain, bearing in her hands a well-filled basket, whence came odors most appetizing, chief among them being the smell of warm loaf bread. From that day to this I have delighted in the smell of bread, and take pleasure in hanging about our village bakery, reveling in the fragrance which lingers about the place—but this is aside from my story.

I politely offered to share my loaf with the captain, but he declined, saying the village baker furnished a very fair article. I cannot say what I would have done had he accepted my offer. It was very foolish to tender it, but he was very good to me, and I did it.

Again he retired for our short interview. As I looked at her inquiringly she nodded, as much as to say, "Yes, it is there."

The golden moments sped by, but before she bade me adieu a signal was agreed upon by which I was to see her in case I should escape that night. A handful of gravel thrown against her window was to bring her to the door.

After dark I tore open my loaf and found coiled snugly in its centre just what I needed. That was the first time I can remember hugging and kissing most fervently a common manilla rope, but I did it then. At a late hour, after several trials, I succeeded in tossing the hook through the ventilator, and gently pulling in the cord found that the hook had firmly caught on the planking around the opening. Climbing up, I managed to squeeze through the hole, and found myself in an attic, the planking upon which the tin roof was laid being easily within my reach. Industry is a marked feature in Yankee character, which I think extends to their animals and even their insects, for I never, either before or since that night, have found so many cobwebs in the same space as those Pennsylvania spiders had placed in that attic.

Pulling my rope up after me, I began the heavy task of cutting through the pine sheathing and tin roof with a dull pocket knife, and though I worked with all my might I think I must have been two mortal hours in getting a hole large enough to get my body through.

I climbed out into liberty some eighteen or twenty feet from the earth. As I stepped on the roofing with my shoeless feet it seemed as if the popping and crackling of the metal made noise sufficient to arouse the dead in their graves. I crouched down and flattened myself on the roof, waiting to find out if everybody in town had heard the noise, but all was still.

Not daring to leave my rope, I firmly tied to the sheathing a line made from one of my blankets, cut up for the purpose, and by its aid soon stood on solid ground, a free man, with my shoes and rope in my hand, but I supposed then and still suppose, the very coldest man in all that great State. Gliding over the ground "like a thief in the night" I soon found "our house," and a moment after she was at the door through which I had made my supposed escape two nights before.

Time, however, was too precious to spend in love-making. Holding her in my arms, she hurriedly whispered of a certain uncle of hers a mile away, and how to know the house when I reached it; of how to find her said uncle's stables, which would be found unlocked; of how I would find a certain good bay horse ready saddled and bridled; of how I was to steal said horse, the uncle being privy to the theft; of how I was to take a certain turnpike and ride at breakneck speed until I reached a certain large, red-brick house, by which time it might be about sunrise; of how I was to enter and deliver to the lady in charge a certain little letter which was then and there put into my hands; of how the lady would keep me in concealment until night, and would then direct me on my way to Washington; of how I was to keep away from all villages, telegraph offices, and gatherings of every kind; of how I was to write very often, through Billy Watkins; and, finally, of how I was to go back "as straight as I could go" to Dixie and stay there until the cruel war was over, and then come at once and make her the happiest of women.

Three days thereafter I was safely quartered in Washington, again striving to sell pork, but still I could not seem to meet the market in price. I visited contractors for supplies for the navy but could make no sales, and even tried several times at the general commissary department, still no sales. I became very friendly with several army officers, and went more than once to the White House, though I did not offer my pork there.

My labors in Washington were lightened by several letters through our friend Billy Watkins, whom I had never seen, and who, by-the-by, when seen some years later proved to be a big, double-jointed, apple-cheeked boy of eighteen, with more curiosity in his composition than all the cats in Christendom.

Some two weeks later found me trying to make my way back to General Lee's army, *via* many devious paths, and much of the time *via* no path at all. The Potomac was forded at Point of Rocks, which crossing is hereby recommended to any and all persons seeking death by drowning, being particularly suited for that purpose when the river is a little "up" and the night dark, as was the case when I crawled out on the Virginia side, one half drowned and the other half frozen, that December night.

With no further adventure, except a narrow escape from a couple of shots fired at me by a Federal vidette as I passed through their lines not far from Fredericksburg, I arrived at our camp and reported at headquarters with my memorandum book nearly full, not of pork sales and quotations, but of every particle of information gleaned during my stay at the capital. I was warmly received by the adjutant-general and sent to the general commanding, who, after listening to an account of my trip, thanked me for my services and ordered me to report to my company.

"Did you see her?" asked my old captain, as he grasped my hand.

"This was her keepsake," I replied, exhibiting my rope with the hook attached.

"Kinder suggestive of a hanging, wasn't it?" he said, as he examined it.

"Still more suggestive of a pretty narrow escape from that ailment," I answered, and then following him into his cabin proceeded to give an account of my adventures.

Three days thereafter, at dress parade, the adjutant read general orders, number something or other, I have forgotten what, announcing that Corporal King, of Company B, —— Regiment, South Carolina Infantry, was hereby promoted to be second lieutenant of cavalry, with orders to report to army headquarters within three days. Cordial congratulations from my comrades followed, but from none more heartily than my old captain, who still survives and whom I see every court week on the streets of old Abbeville, limping from a wound received at Cold Harbor in '64.

The war ended, and Rozelle and I were married; our friend, the Federal captain, coming all the way from near Emporium to officiate as best man; we still correspond occasionally. Billy Watkins, with a red-haired girl, his sweetheart, was present, as was also the uncle, who, while wishing my blushing bride much happiness, explained to her with a wink that he never expected to live to see her marry a horse thief, to which she retorted that in law he was the more guilty, having planned the raid and made arrangements for its execution.

Sixteen years of happiness followed our union, marred by no sorrow, until my great sorrow came, which no words can measure. Since then the cares and duties of each busy day have, for the time, partly hidden from the world and from me this grief, but when the rest time comes memory instinctively goes back to the happy past, and I live over again the years spent with her.

Ah, me! may the time soon come when, in a yet happier sphere of existence, we shall be reunited, to be together forever, as I firmly believe we shall, in a life where each earthly faculty shall expand and develop eternally—grander and nobler as the years sweep by—not one power lost, but all purified and intensified in the sunshine of His boundless love.

* * * * *

Down in the Palmetto State, by a silently-flowing river, stands a giant water oak, from whose branches hang pendant long swaying masses of gray moss, so weird and solemn.

Beneath its sheltering arms is a small green mound—her last earthly resting-place, selected by herself in the long ago. The marble headstone bears these lines:

A TRUE WOMAN,

A LOVING WIFE, A DEVOTED MOTHER.

If she had a fault her husband never knew it, while her virtues were known of all. She sweetly sleeps until the

GREAT REUNION

HOW BLUE AND GRAY BLEND.

CHARLES S. BRACE.

"OH, mother, what do they mean by blue?
  And what do they mean by gray?"
I heard from the lips of a little child
  As she bounded in from her play.
The mother's eyes filled up with tears;
  She turned to her darling fair,
And smoothed away from the sunny brow
  The treasures of golden hair.

"Why, mother's eyes are blue, my sweet,
  And grandpa's hair is gray.
And the love we bear our darling child
  Grows stronger every day."
"But what did they mean?" persisted the child,
  "For I saw two cripples to-day,
And one of them said he had 'fought for the blue,'
  The other had 'fought for the gray.'

"The one of the blue had lost a leg,
  And the other had but one arm,
And both seemed worn and weary and sad,
  Yet their greeting was kind and warm.
They told of battles in days gone by,
  Till it made my blood grow chill.
The leg was lost in the Wilderness fight
  And the arm on Malvern Hill.

"They sat on the stone by the farmyard gate
  And talked for an hour or more,
Till their eyes grew bright and their hearts seemed warm,
  With fighting their battles o'er.
And parting at last with a friendly grasp,
  In a kindly, brotherly way,
Each asking of God to speed the time
  Uniting the blue and the gray."

Then the mother thought of other days—
  Two stalwart boys from her riven;
How they'd knelt at her side and, lisping, prayed,
  "Our Father which art in heaven;"
How one wore the gray and the other the blue;
  How they passed away from sight,
And had gone to the land where gray and blue
  Merge in tints of celestial light.

And she answered her darling with golden hair,
  While her heart was sorely wrung
With the thoughts awakened in that sad hour
  By her innocent, prattling tongue:
"The blue and the gray are the colors of God;
  They are seen in the sky at even,
And many a noble, gallant soul
  Has found them passports to heaven."

BATTLE BONDS.

David Lowry.

A MIST floated over the Tennessee Valley. It stretched up the "coolies" on either side of the valley, swept in banners near the hilltops, and dissolved into viewless air. The base of the hills was enveloped in a surging sea of vapor when the eastern slopes began to reflect the morning light.

Strange sounds echoed across the valley; the solitude was broken; the slopes faintly echoed modulated sounds that rose above. Now the sounds are more distinct; out of the confusion the neighing of horses is heard. There is a muffled sound like the rumbling of wheels.

The sound swells as the morning mists are rent and the clear sunlight penetrates the valley in rays, mere flecks of light that come and go as the thin films of mist floating in tattered shreds, like the remnants of a battle-flag, twist upward to the crest of the hills and fade away. A mere breath of air—the first sigh responsive earth gives to the kindly glow of the morning sun—stirs the leaves. The sigh expands; the foliage trembles as the air sweeps the slopes. By the time it surmounts the crest it has gained strength and volume; the early morning breeze blows wide open the door of a cabin on the ridge. The door swung back gently. The breeze stirred the ashes in the wide chimney-place—stirred the embers until they glowed again.

A young man sleeping in the cabin moved uneasily in his sleep. Then he sat bolt upright and inclined his ear in a listening attitude. The wind bore to his trained ear a confused murmur. The listener rose quickly and donned his clothes. Meanwhile, his set mouth and a peculiar expression in his sharp eyes—good, honest, gray eyes they were—bespoke resolution.

"It's the Yanks—they're movin'. Knew they'd git out! Takin' the back track."

He darted out of the cabin, and stood listening a few minutes, with a hand to his ear.

"They're movin' on, that's it—goin' to Corinth, 'stid o' gittin' out."

He strode into the cabin and struck the door with his hand as he shouted, "The Yanks er movin', dad!" Then he took from its place against the wall a double-barreled gun, slapped the stock, hunter-fashion, with his open palm, pulled the hammer back, and blew through both barrels.

"Be you goin' ter—ter——" began a voice, the voice of an aged man, in the other end of the cabin, when a woman's voice interposed:

"Gabe's got more sense. He knows he's ter stay to keep things straight with us, dad. Lem's gone, 'n Dick—that's enough."

Here another voice rose: "If Gabe goes, there's two goin'—I'm goin'."

"Gabe shan't go." Gabe's mother was fumbling in a fretful way as she hooked her gown. "I've p'intedly said so from the first. 'Tain't none o' our doin's, 'n they'd no business ter fire up Lem 'n Dick. I tell Gabe, 'f they must fight, there's no manner o' sense 'n leavin' us pore old people to the marcy o' the Yanks. Somebody's got to stop—that's Gabe."

Gabe was kneeling in the middle of the floor now, blowing the red embers beneath a small iron pot, into which he had tossed pieces of lead, which he would presently shape into bullets. When his mother looked at him, she shook her head angrily. Gabe's father now crossed the floor in his bare feet. He, too, looked angrily at the figure kneeling before the fire. Next, a young girl emerged seemingly from a corner—in reality, she descended from a loft—and stared at Gabe. Maria, Gabe's companion from childhood, was also his sweetheart. Luke Acker had assumed the responsibility of "raisin' her" when her parents died.

Gabe rose to get his shot-pouch and powder-horn. Then he reached up and grasped the bullet-mould, saying, quietly, "I mean ter fight the cussed Yanks. They're goin' right up ther road; you kin hear them all along ther valley. We'uns 'll never hev another chance at the blame fools—I mean ter hev a crack 'long 'ith the rest."

PREPARING FOR WARFARE.

Luke and his wife stood outside the cabin, listening intently; Maria did not move. She looked fixedly at Gabe. Luke entered the cabin again, slowly. His wife stood near the door; her grizzly gray hairs fluttering in the air added to the haggardness of her homely face as her lips moved. Was she praying for her sons "with Gin'ral Bragg's army"?

The little group took no note of the beauties of the morning, which was now matchless in the splendors only to be witnessed on the heights. The brilliant hues of the eastern horizon surpassed the crimson glories of the setting sun; the exceeding brightness of the golden tints, and the faint pink blushes that flashed vividly beyond and seemingly above the gold-tipped clouds all along the east, imparted to early dawn a kindlier and more cheerful spirit than attends the waning of day.

Suddenly, Maria grasped Gabe's arm. "Be you goin' ter fight?"

Gabe did not look up. He was eyeing the iron pot. He did not move a muscle; he was able to control himself at all times.

"Be you?"

"I be."

"You are plum sot on't?"

"Plum sot on't. They're p'ison sure of a lickin', 'n I'm goin' ter holp ter lick 'em. Hear 'em?"

The sounds that rolled up to the cabin now were distinct. There were shouts and sounds of laughter. The occupants of the cabin silently walked out, one by one, and advanced to a great shelving rock that overlooked the valley. Gabe Acker extended a hand to the left. Looking down the valley, his companions beheld strange flashes; the sun's rays on shining steel; they beheld bayonets flashing in the sunlight, horsemen riding to and fro, infantry toiling on past long trains of wagons. They could hear the heavy rumble of the artillery wagons. Flags floated airily in the breeze; the blare of bands and the sound of the fife and drums rose to the hilltops. A great army was in motion.

"They're goin' ter fight—a power o' them ther seems ter be, all headin' ter the south," said Gabe Acker, shaking his clenched fist at the army in full view. "An' they're goin' ter git a wallopin'—they're p'ison sure of a lickin', dad."

"Ther's a powerful lot," Luke Acker answered. A man of eighty, he trembled with apprehension as he looked at the sinuous lines stretching out in the valley, reaching far beyond his dim sight.

"Bragg's got ez many; anyhow, our side's goin' ter lick 'em, dad; two ter one, they'll come back a durn sight quicker 'n they're goin'."

"Ef I was sure on't, I'd like ter let you go, Gabe," said Luke Acker. "I'd like it fust-rate." There was a fire in Luke's eyes as he spoke. "But we ain't sure. No one can tell; 'n mebbe some of them may come up hyar, 'n rip 'n stomp 'roun' 'ith nobody but me 'n the wimmin——"

"That's jist the reason I'm goin' ter fight," interrupted Gabe. "I'm goin' ter stop it. The Yanks can't stomp 'roun' hyar, dad. We'll send 'em back—all we don't kill—where they come from."

Gabe walked back to the cabin again, leaving the others standing on the rock, looking down upon the Federal hosts. The metal was liquid in the iron pot. To pour it into the moulds occupied very little time. He was paring the rough bullets when Maria stepped into the cabin.

"Gabe, I'm goin' 'ith you."

Gabe gave her a look in which scorn mastered surprise. "Sech fool talk! Hev' sense, Maria."

"I might as well. Why can't I? I can't do no good if the Yanks come ter bully dad an' ma'm. If I had a gun——"

"Dad!" said Gabe suddenly to his father, who at that moment entered, "don't you let Maria make a fool of herself. You an' ma'm talk to Maria. I'm goin'—goin'—ter holp drive the Yanks back. It's my duty to holp ter drive 'em out. A passel o' thieves crowdin' us! I'm sot on seein' this yer fight, 'n I'm plum sot on holpin' ter smoke every last tarnal ijit clean acrost Kaintuck' if need be, but whut's girls talkin' about! You settle Maria, hyar."

He was moving from the table to the cupboard all the while, gathering up cold biscuit, a piece of cold meat, and some salt. The last he wrapped in a piece of brown paper and placed in his pocket first. Then he put the biscuit and meat in his coat pockets. Maria looked on with burning cheeks and flashing eyes. Gabe's

"HE PAUSED IN ANGER."

mother looked helplessly at her husband. Luke Acker shook his head in reply.

"I can't holp it,—how can I holp it? *You* speak to him."

"'T'aint no sort o' use, ma'm. I'll come right back jist ez soon ez we wallop 'em. We'll giv' 'em a blamed good wallopin', 'n then I'll come home. Don't you worry none now; I'll be back ter-morrer, like ez not."

Without pausing for any leave-taking—indeed he dreaded that much more than a battle—Gabe hastened from the cabin. His mother sat down helplessly with her hands in her lap; Luke Acker paced the floor, glancing through the open door whither Maria slowly passed out after Gabe. Gabe was a considerable distance from the cabin when he heard Maria's voice. He paused in anger. Maria was breathless when she overtook him.

"Gabe, it's killin' me. I can't seem ter bear it."

"You'll hev' ter," said Gabe, angrily. He spoke roughly; he was afraid to trust himself to speak as he felt. "You go right back ter ma'm, Maria. Whut's all this yer fuss about? Ha'nt I a right to holp Bragg ez much ez Lem 'n Dick?"

"I'll die if anything happens you, Gabe. I can't spare you!"

"Be you clean crazy? Now you act sensible. I'm comin' back ter-morrer—jest ez soon ez we wallop 'em I'm comin' back. I'm a man; I must holp ter wallop 'em. You go back now. You're wuss'n—wuss'n——"

Language failed him. He looked at her sidewise, then inclined his ear. The sounds rising from the valley seemed to call him, and here Maria was holding him back.

"See hyar, Maria. Every last one o' the men folks hez lit out 'ceptin' me—all holpin'; d'ye suppose I won't holp my sheer? Whut's ther ter be afraid of? Now make me ashamed, Maria, 'stead o' encouragin' me, tryin' to keep me back. I'm goin', I tell yer!"

Then without looking at her he hastened on. He did not dare to look back; he almost fell in his haste to get out of her view.

When Maria realized that she was alone on the hillside a change came over her manner. She dried her tears quickly, and sat down on a stone. She was revolving a tremendous project in her mind. She resolved to follow Gabe to the end of the world if need be. She would follow him into battle—to death itself. Nothing should part them—nothing. It was not so difficult after all. She was familiar with the roads. In ten minutes—less time—she had thought it all out.

She hastened to the little patch of grazing ground below the cabin, called the horse to her side, mounted it, and, stroking its mane, turned its head in the direction of the nearest neighbor.

The neighbor's only son was a captain in the Confederate army. The Acker boys were members of his company. When Maria rode up to the door and dismounted, her errand did not surprise the housewife. Gabe Acker was welcome to the loan of her son's clothes. They mightn't just fit. Gabe was taller and heavier than Tom. When did they hear from any of the boys?

Maria was in a fever of anxiety, but she exchanged the gossip of the neighborhood, repeated the contents of Lem's last letter from Corinth, and was careful not to exhibit undue haste when Mrs. Sturm wasted ten mortal minutes searching for a string to tie the bundle she made of her son's clothes. Gabe could have them as long as he liked, and quite welcome, only, if he was wise, he would not go where the Yanks could lay their hands on him. And with this parting advice, Maria rode away with the bundle.

* * * * * * * *

The rapid march of Buell's divisions to Savannah, General Nelson's forced march to the Tennessee River, and the aids he employed to reach the battle-field at Pittsburgh Landing, have been described time and again.

The booming of cannon reverberated along the crags early that Sabbath morning. The very air pulsed with war's alarms; forebodings brooded on the heights where Luke Acker paced his cabin floor like a restless spirit. His wife was prostrated with grief. She could only lift her hands up and let them fall helplessly, as she bewailed the strange absence of Maria. Her husband alternately cursed the Yanks, and deprecated the age that held him in bonds of inactivity, when he might be fighting beside his sons.

Meanwhile, brigade after brigade marched into Savannah; division, brigade, and regimental commanders swore roundly at the delay experienced in transporting them across the river to the battle-field as the battle infection grew, swelled, and permeated Buell's army.

Two great battle-fields, Gettysburg and Shiloh, will be referred to by future historians as illustrations of the prowess of the men who contested an hundred fields. Future artists will find in them representative pictures. No other battles supply so much to the artist and tactician. One was a sheer waste of human life, indecisive; the other was the Waterloo of the Confederacy.

The sound of the cannon was music to Gabe Acker's ears. He lost no time in speeding down the slope when he turned abruptly from Maria. When he reached the valley he found a score or more at the ferry preparing to cross the river. The Federalists were a considerable distance below them. The Tennesseeans he encountered at the ferry, like himself, expected and predicted a great battle. Many were eager to participate in it. The Confederate government impressed many into service in Mississippi, but there were numbers in Tennessee who volunteered and provided their own weapons. Gabe Acker found himself on the bank of the river in a group who were eager to "wallop the Yanks." The fresh recruits craved to be led forward. They did not know who was to command them; they did not inquire. They were impetuous, scorned delay, and were desirous of joining Bragg's army at the earliest moment.

The ferryman, an ardent secessionist, was leisurely preparing to take the volunteers across the river, when someone directed his attention to a group of horsemen half a mile further down the valley. The ferryman scanned them coolly and uttered one word, but that word produced a magical effect upon the Tennesseeans.

"Yanks!"

Every eye was fixed upon the horsemen; resolute hands grasped the guns. There was an alertness in the movement of heads, but no word was uttered. Possibly they would be granted their hearts' wish then and there. The horsemen were few, and they seemed to be mounted on well-fagged horses. At that moment one of the spectators directed his comrades' attention to a horseman picking his way carefully through a fringe of wood near the Federal cavalry. The horseman in the wood was riding straight toward the ferry; it was plain that he was trying to reach the ferry before the Federalists discovered him. The group at the ferry were powerless to prevent his capture if the Federalists perceived him in time to head him off. The horseman in the wood evidently appreciated the situation; he was striving to urge his horse on when the Federalists discerned him and suddenly gave chase.

The spectators wondered, now that he was discovered, that the horseman did not exert himself to escape. His horse did not increase his gait; it jogged along in a way that exasperated the witnesses of this strange scene. They cursed the stupid rider; some consigned him cheerfully to the mercy of the Federalists, when it was discovered that he was riding without saddle or bridle.

The horseman was in plain view now. The group at the ferry could see him pause beneath a tree. Their wonder was lessened when they perceived his horse shooting forward at a pace that promised escape. The rider was whipping his horse with a branch plucked from the tree.

Now it was a race for liberty, perhaps for life. The Federalists were shouting—calling upon the horseman to surrender. The fleeing horseman paid no attention to them. He was nearing the main road, nearing the ferry, when a puff of smoke rose, then the sound of a carbine smote the air. It was well for the pursued that the horses bestrode by the Federalists were fagged. He bid fair to reach a point where the Tennesseeans could assist him, when two of the Federalists suddenly spurted forward. They were so near the man pursued that their voices could be heard calling upon him to surrender.

Now the group at the ferry shouted also, and beckoned to the horseman. Two shots were fired in quick succession by the Federal cavalrymen. The fleeing horseman rose on his horse's back, and plied the branch. Toward him thundered the cavalrymen, until Gabe Acker and another Tennesseean stepped boldly out in plain view of the pursuers and fired at them. The shots were wide of their mark, but as the twigs cut above their heads fell, the pursuers reined in their steeds, and when the Tennesseeans moved toward them in a body, they turned their horses' heads and galloped back. Meantime, the horseman thus rescued, while urging his horse on, was thrown violently upon the ground. When he staggered, rather than walked, to the group at the ferry, his hands and face were covered with mud.

The ferryman coolly took him by the arm, led him on to the ferry-boat, and ordered some of those nearest him to shove the boat out, laughing derisively at the Federal cavalrymen who seemed to be debating whether to venture nearer. A volley from the occupants of the ferry decided them; they turned leisurely and rode back the way they came.

The horse that bore the man to the ferry stood irresolute a little while, then turned and trotted back through the woods and was soon lost to view. This incident, trifling though it seems, afforded much amusement to the volunteers that crossed the river early on that Sabbath morning. They stepped out of the boat cheerily and made their way toward a road seldom traveled, that led them to the rebel line.

Gabe Acker was among the foremost. He felt himself a man among men as he strode along with his shot-gun on his shoulder. It was a motley crowd, armed with Kentucky

"THE FLEEING HORSEMAN ROSE ON HIS HORSE'S BACK."

rifles and double-barreled shot-guns—all save the man who joined the party last, the man the Federal cavalry pursued; and he knew he would be provided for in due season.

A bugle sounding near the new-comers indicated a camp. Then the sound of fifes and drums put mettle into them. The volunteers moved forward, crossed a stretch of boggy ground, and emerged from the woods upon a camp.

The air was full of martial sounds. Drums were beating, fifes piercing the air, flags flying everywhere. Soldiers in couples, singly, in squads, in companies and regiments. An air of activity pervaded the scene Gabe Acker looked upon. Bugles were sounding in the distance; cavalrymen were riding hither and thither; there were loud commands, sharp and clear; the barred flag was waving everywhere in the summer wind, flaunting gayly; all nature seemed to pulse with the animation and high resolve the legions of the South displayed, as Gabe looked around with wonder and pride.

The pomp and circumstance of war made a profound impression upon the young volunteer.

The bustle, the blare of bands, the figures moving to and fro on the road, the squads forming into company lines in the distance, the wagons lumbering heavily along, instead of confusing Gabe, confirmed him in his resolve. He was proud that he was part and parcel of the group; that he was to participate in the action everything foretold. The sullen reverberations that they had mistaken for thunder earlier, that all now knew indicated terrific strife, were musical to Gabe, whose blood tingled in anticipation of the hour when he would mingle in the battle. The little knot of Tennesseeans stood looking on, unnoticed, until a regiment moved across a field.

Rub-a-dub! rub-a-dub! rub-a-dub, dub, bub!

It was a marvel that the drums did not burst.

Squeak, squeak!—the fifes almost pierced Gabe's ears.

Tramp, tramp, tramp! How well they marched! Heads well up, shoulders squarely held, looking neither to the right nor left, what a gallant air had those men in gray! How they stepped out! Gabe's eyes glistened as he gazed after them. The breeze blew the Confederate flag straight from the staff, toyed with it, waved it aloft, flirted it right and left. The men sloped their guns until the sun's rays slanting on them were reflected in a series of shimmering waves that almost blinded Gabe.

Now a horseman rides out of the woods and approaches the little group of Tennesseeans at a pace that alarms Gabe. The horse is blown; the rider's face is creased with dirt, his long hair disheveled; but he spurs his horse on, sinking his rowels into his sides until the blood flows, and suddenly reins up near the little group.

"Colonel Clayton, the general's compliments. You will advance through the woods to the right immediately, and charge the enemy on the left. Cross the open field, and form your line in the woods on the other side of it."

The aid turned his horse's head and rode away into the woods as fast as he came. Gabe now observed a man with a soft gray felt hat, a plain gray suit, and a gray beard—a quiet-looking man, separating himself from a group. The sound of his voice startled Gabe as he shouted, "Sound the long roll!" Then, as if by magic, a line was formed of men in brown and gray. The man with the gray beard rode half-way down the line, followed by another horseman, then returned, gave some orders that could be heard half a mile, and the wavering line became straight. Suddenly the colonel turned to the Tennesseeans.

"Who are you? What brigade do you belong to?"

A minute was lost explaining the matter; the colonel was impatient.

"You are armed! Hello there! You in the black coat, get a gun from that man there by the wagon. You will fall in, in a line back of us—there, go! Now, drummer, beat up. Shoulder arms! For—r—ward, march!"

The regiment cheered as it marched forward. But the enemy—where was the enemy? There was no living creature in view save the men in ranks far to the left, and those they left behind them. A cabin almost concealed by trees suggested peace and plenty. The smoke curled lazily up from the chimney. Three kittens tumbled over each other in the doorway.

On swept the regiment, drums beating, the fifes' shrill notes smiting the summer air. On, on, toward the heavy timber. Then the fife and drum suddenly ceased. The regiment was in the timber.

What was that continuous rattle—that crackling like the sound made by trees falling in the distance? Could that be the roll of musketry? Gabe Acker asked himself.

Hark! There was no mistaking that sound. That was heavy artillery. The scream of the flying shell that cut the top off a tree startled the mountaineer.

On, on, the regiment swept through the woods. Now the forest is suddenly tipped with flame. The scream of shells and the sharp crack of musketry greet the advancing line simultaneously. Men drop here and there. The colonel's voice is heard thundering his command; the line moves forward—bounds forward; the cloud of smoke veiling the trunks of trees lifts, and the advancing line discovers the woods are alive with men. A mass of glittering steel confronts them, but on, on, the men in gray press, in obedience to the command of the colonel. Again the woods are fringed with flame, and now the Confederates realize that they are in the very bowels of hell, as shot and shell tear, sweep, through their ranks. The forest is ablaze with musketry. Shells girdle great tree-trunks here, cut through others there, fairly mow the forest, and cut tremendous swaths in the heavy undergrowth. The shock of the battle fills the air. Neither blue nor gray swerves an inch. First the color-bearer fell; then Colonel Clayton and his adjutant fell, never to rise again. But the battle rages. This is the spot where men refused to yield—where they confronted each other until the fever of battle expended its strength; until the ranks of the blue and the gray became so thin that there was no longer food for powder or shell; until the rank and file on both sides discovered that they were bereft of the semblance of command, and then both sullenly retired. But there was no victory —only a slaughter.

The sounds of battle diminish. Rambling shots are heard, instead of volleys. The edge of the battle is turned in another direction. The chief sounds now are groans and soul-piercing cries. Men in mortal agony pluck their garments open and place their hands convulsively over gaping wounds. They wrench vest and shirt open with one clutch, look down at the wound from which their life's blood is flowing, then die without a sign. Others manage to crawl to a tree, a stone, or a log, sit upright by a tremendous effort, bring forth with infinite pain the picture of a wife, children, mother, or sweetheart they will never see again, and, looking at their loved ones, breathe their lives away.

*   *   *   *   *   *   *   *

It was the day after the battle. One of the

surgeons employed at an amputating-table in the rear of a rude cabin near the southern line of the battle-field, looking up, observed a boy regarding the surroundings attentively. The cuff of his right sleeve was turned up. His left arm was in a sling.

The sight was not an agreeable one for man or boy. There was a pile of arms and legs at the side of the cabin, almost as high as the boy's head. Several lifeless forms in blue and gray were lying at a distance.

"What are you doing here?" demanded the surgeon, roughly. Two of his associates turned and scowled at the boy, who was not discomposed in the least. "Sergeant," shouted the surgeon, angrily, "what do you mean by allowing people to come here?"

"He couldn' help it," said the boy. "I'm looking for a—a—friend."

"Humph!" The surgeons stared at the boy, then at each other. "So you were in the fight, were you? You ought to be in the cradle. Sergeant, take this boy away, and if you permit anybody else——"

"I'll go if you let me look inside." The sergeant had a grip on the boy's arm; the boy was striving to free himself. "He may be inside—let me look! Do!"

"Oh, let him look; it won't signify now," said the surgeon. "What do these rebels mean, forcing mere children into the ranks?"

The boy was now staring hard at the men awaiting their turn on the operating-table. Suddenly an ear-piercing shriek startled the surgeons.

"Gabe! Gabe! It's me, Gabe! Oh, Gabe, for God's sake, look up and speak to me!"

The surgeons bore him away forcibly.

"I must see him—I must speak—he's my Gabe!" He looked up at them with hollow eyes—dry, fever-lit eyes.

"Come," said the oldest surgeon, in a sympathetic tone, "who is it? Who is Gabe?"

"He's my—my Gabe, and he's dying. Do something for Gabe—holp, oh, holp my Gabe!" The boy was ringing his hands helplessly now.

"Let's look at his friend." The surgeon in charge of the cabin bent over Gabe, frowned, then ordered his assistants to lay him on the table in the clear light, muttering, "Take that boy away for the present." But the weeping boy frantically declared he would not move—he would die by Gabe's side.

"I'll be quiet—I won't cry. I'll be still as death—only let me be nigh Gabe."

In thirty minutes the trephining operation was completed, and Gabe was looking around

IN THE FIELD HOSPITAL.

him like a man aroused from a sound sleep. He turned his eyes first to one side, then the other:

"Whut's the matter? Which side whupt?"

The surgeons smiled.

"Will he live—will he get well?"

"He will be all right in six weeks, if he takes care of himself," the surgeon said.

"Whut's thet? Who's ther? Thet—thet ain't Maria?" said Gabe, as he closed his eyes wearily. But Maria had fainted dead away.

There were exclamations. The group of surgeons were equal to the emergency, however. They recovered from their surprise with their usual promptness, and, when Maria opened her eyes again, were very considerate.

"I followed Gabe," she said, falteringly, "and

I'm goin' ter take him home. He shan't fight you'uns no more. His brother Lem and Dick's enough to be fightin'. I've nigh lost my arm, too."

The surgeons talked in subdued tones. The one in authority addressed Maria in a deferential manner.

"We entirely agree with you, miss. I shall make it my business to see that you and your friend are conveyed out of the lines and furnished with transportation home immediately."

"Then," said Gabe, slowly, as he looked from one to the other, "we'uns got the worst on't?"

"You needn't cry over that," said the surgeon, cheerily. "If it's any satisfaction to you, it's a case of nip and tuck."

THE LAST SHOT.

By Violetta.

ALL through the day, since at first streak of dawn, the signal-gun had sent its grim, hoarse challenge down the silent lines, the thunder of a thousand cannon had mingled with the ceaseless rattle of musketry to create din infernal.

From the sulphurous vapor, which hangs like a gray pall about the crest of the hills, sweeps forth, now here, now there, a dense roll of smoke pierced by a sullen flame—a roar that makes the solid earth tremble; and through the air comes the screaming messenger of death, to fall among the toiling gunners to the right or to the left, to vanish in a cloud of smoke, leaving to those around but the memory of brave comrades gone—to desolate homes far away, but the canker of a lasting sorrow. Such is war. Such, a soldier's death.

The young Federal artilleryman who stood with thumb on vent, facing the hurtling shower of death, almost unconscious of its import, had risen with the first warning note of action to tireless service at his gun. So weary was the frame, so blunted the sensibilities, from incessant labor, that his duties were performed mechanically, almost without volition, while his whole attention was fixed on a spot directly across the valley, where an occasional rift in the cloud of smoke revealed the position of a Confederate battery and (what especially riveted his attention) a gunner, "number three," like himself, attached to a piece on the left of the line,

and whose object seemed to be to silence the gun which the young Federal soldier was serving.

A gleam of ferocity shone out for a moment from the grimy face of the boy in blue, as a shell tore a great hole in the earth a little to the right of him, scattering death all around.

Slightly changing the position of his gun so as to bear directly upon the Confederate piece, for he was gunner as well as "number three," on that memorable day, a day when Battery B was unofficered by death, the artilleryman trained "Destroyer" carefully upon his annoying adversary, and the shell was sent shrieking on its way.

"Too short," muttered "number three," as the messenger was seen to plow a furrow in the hillside in front of the Confederates and ricochet over their heads to explode in the woods behind.

Puff—and a demoniac return from the Confederates tore off the top of the sapling not ten yards away.

Again the Federal gun was trained upon the Confederate "number three," for the tall figures of both artillerymen could be distinctly seen across the narrow valley, and the erect form between the wheels became the target of each. This time the iron messenger tore through a veil of smoke wafted over a battery on the right, and its effect could not be seen; but the response was almost immediate, and as the shell buried itself in the earth and exploded a few yards in advance to the left, " number one " staggered to the rear, badly hurt. The eyes of the young Federal fairly blazed.

"Cut that fuse a little shorter," he shouted. " We'll explode it in his face this time."

On sped the fateful iron—Ah!—Ere it reaches the grim muzzle of the Confederate gun—a flash—and " number two " is seen to grasp at a wheel for support as he sinks to the ground, while an officer's horse drops in his tracks, carrying the rider with him.

A shout goes up from the tired men who seem now to be endowed with new life. But alas! two of them shout for the last time. The compliment is returned with interest, killing numbers two and five, and tearing a gun-wheel to pieces, necessitating a delay of ten minutes to adjust a new one. The Confederate waited in silence, letting his gun cool until the next shot from the Federals tore along through the lines, cutting up a great deal of dirt but doing no damage, when he responded, killing a horse and dismounting an ammunition caisson.

By this time both combatants were lost to all thought of what was going on about them, save the service of their pieces. From a wooded hillock about two hundred yards to the left a detachment of sharpshooters had found lodgment, who poured in an incessant fire upon the Federals. Their leaden messengers whistled constantly past the duelist in blue, now burying themselves in the woodwork of the gun-carriage, now splintering the spokes of the wheels, or flattening themselves with a vicious thud against the metal itself. Had it not been for the heavy curtain of smoke enveloping the batteries on the left and slightly in advance, he would certainly have been killed. It was seldom, however, that this curtain lifted sufficiently to reveal him to his enemies, who could only direct their fire at the lurid gleams of light piercing the cloud at every discharge of the cannon, and so locating the position of the men. Directly in front of the Federal, however, and around and about the small knoll upon which his Confederate *vis-a-vis* had planted his gun, for some reason the cloud, which enveloped both ridges and frequently swept down the sloping sides of the hills, had not settled ; so that the effect of each shot could be noted and the fire directed with such accu-

racy as the gunners might exercise—a question of skill, of superiority of ordnance and marksmanship. There had been no cessation, no rest. Yet now that an hour of light remained,—now that the sun hung like a great globe of blood just above the horizon,—the labor of the day was as naught, wounds were nothing. The gray artilleryman, still unconquered, waves a sarcastic defiance as he sends once more his hurtling challenge.

Again and again the cannon belched forth their angry flame. Again and again the screaming shells burst in and around the blackened fiends about the guns. Only three remained to man the grim " Destroyer "—*only three;* the others are scattered here and there, where they had fallen. The slackened fire from the Confederate side told an awful tale. Yet did these two demons of destruction stand face to face, unscathed, unconquered—the blue and the gray —erect, clear-outlined against the dark bordering of the forest behind them, as the great red sun sank down behind the hilltops.

"Once more ere the night is here!" cried the blue.

"Once more while daylight lasts!" cried the gray.

In mid air the last shots hissed past each other as they sped upon their deadly errand.

For a moment it seemed as though the earth had opened, emitting a scorching tongue of flame, which shot from hell to heaven, and—it was gone—and so were all the blue save "number three," who, crawling from beneath the splintered carriage, struggled forward and scanned with eager gaze the opposite hilltop, where a tall form was seen to totter and fall amid the wreckage of a gun. With a last supreme effort the dying soldier seized the ragged, shot-torn guidon, waving it defiantly, as he feebly gasped a faint " Hurrah!"—then came night and darkness— and rest. For the dead heroes, rest eternal; for the survivors, the sleep of utter exhaustion, dreamless and undisturbed even by ghastly reminders of the day's fierce struggle. On the morrow these will awake to glory—glory surpassing, abounding; piercing the clouds and smoke still hanging over the battle-field, its light shall fall with equal radiance upon the blue and the gray.

SISTER JOANELLE.

By "Dixie."

IN the distance, through the transparent, misty veil of blue and gray that shimmered over them, rose the green-crested mountains of the Blue Ridge. Here and there cascades of purest crystal, springing from their source up among the rocks, dashed down the mountain-side through fragrant shrubbery, catching the sunlight as it leaped over moss-grown stones and fallen cypress-trees.

A trodden pathway led up the mountain-side through dark evergreens and tall pines. Slowly sauntering up this mountain-path could be seen the slender, graceful form of a girl of nineteen. Half-way up she paused, and turned her dark eyes toward the scene below. Down deep in the valley was nestled the small city of S——; while guarding it, like faithful, sleepless sentries, stood the tall mountains of the Blue Ridge. Scattered near and far, dotting the green valley, were the pretty, comfortable homes, of white frame, with cool green blinds and roomy verandas, over which the honeysuckle and morning-glory vines trailed in rich profusion. How beautiful it all was, and how peaceful to look upon! Tears came into her eyes, and a sigh escaped from the lips of the young girl. How long would this beautiful picture remain? Not long, alas! for the merciless tread of the soldier and the boom of the cannon were already heard throughout the land. North and South were preparing for war. Everywhere was heard the cry "To arms!" and upon each side faithful and noble men responded. A hurried step behind her caught the quick ear of the girl, and startled her from her reverie. In another moment she was clasped in the strong arms of Edward Deane, and his ardent lover's kiss brought back the color to her cheek.

"True to your tryst, sweetheart. Have you waited long?" Then, noticing the unshed tear, "Still pensive, and unresigned to the inevitable?" endeavoring, in the cheeriness of his tone, to dispel the gathered gloom upon the face he loved.

"Oh, Edward, I cannot become reconciled to live in constant dread of the coming morrow,— the terrible restlessness that seems to be with me, sleeping or waking! Just now I was thinking of the happy homes lying so peaceful and contented to-day in God's beautiful sunlight,

doomed, perhaps to-morrow, to devastation and ruin; and hardest of all is the parting from you." A convulsive tremor passed through her slight frame, and involuntarily the white arms clasped themselves about his neck. "I cannot bear it all—my heart will surely break." Her voice ended in a sob.

"Natalie, my poor child, you must not give way to your feelings in this manner; it will only make you ill; come, be brave and hopeful for my sake. Do not predict the worst, which, after all, may never happen. Come, cheer up! I want to see you happy this last afternoon we are to spend together—for some time, at least." He led her to the trunk of a fallen tree, where they seated themselves. She was the first to speak.

"How much I still wish, Edward, you could feel that it was right to fight with the Southern army."

She said this pleadingly, with her large, earnest eyes fixed upon his face. There was silence for a moment, and a look of pain came into the tender face of her lover. Then he answered, gently, but firmly:

"Natalie, darling, I cannot. I could not do it now, had I the desire, as I have already entered my name in the regiment of Pennsylvania volunteers. It grieves me sorely to speak on this subject, knowing your sentiments in regard to the matter, but I cannot see my duty in any other direction than that which I have already taken. The North is the land of my birth and the home of my mother. It has cost me a severe struggle to decide this momentous question; but, darling, cannot you see that I would not be worthy of you, were I less true to my convictions of right? Besides, little one, think; I am only filling a position which duty demands. It grieves me, for your sake, to feel I am obliged to meet your countrymen as enemies. Nay, had I but the right to speak or advise, we should come to a far more peaceable understanding in place of this cruel war, which separates me not only from the one I love most, but compels me perhaps to shed the blood of some fellow-man." The young face had grown stern in these last few weeks. The two, but yesterday children, were now man and woman, facing one of the most vital problems of our so-called civilization. " Tell me, am I forgiven, darling ? I know your patriotic blood is fired, and naturally so, or you could not be the loyal little woman you are. And, Natalie, you will not, I know, deem me less worthy for fulfilling my duty by giving my services to those to whom I have pledged myself, will you?"

He had risen now, and was standing before her, his handsome, stalwart figure looking grander in the conscious righteousness of the cause he was pleading, his earnest blue eyes bent anxiously upon her while they gave no token of a surrender of his own conviction of the line of duty marked out for him. It was a trying moment in the life of the young girl, whose loyalty to the South was as fervent and sincere as was her lover's for the North. While it grieved her that he did not feel in sympathy with her beloved country, yet, despite it all, she honored the steadfastness of his character which forbade his sacrificing duty to love. Unconsciously the lines came to her mind, "To thyself be true, and it needs must follow as the night the day that thou canst not be false to any man." Gazing into his face, which had grown pale in its earnestness, she forgot all else than that he was her lover ; that he was suffering because they were soon to be separated, perhaps forever. She could not let him go thus. For answer, she threw her arms about his neck and kissed him, bravely striving to keep back the tears.

" Edward, I will not ask you to be disloyal to your country, nor will I ask you to choose between it and me. My love for you is the strongest factor of my being ; and it will be with you wherever you may go, whatever may be your danger or deprivation. Believe this."

" Spoken like the true, noble little woman you are, God bless you ! And may He make me worthy of the priceless treasure he has bestowed upon me, Natalie, my rebel queen." He drew her still closer to him, and kissed again and again the sweet face.

An hour later, when plans for the future had been quietly discussed, the two sauntered slowly down the quiet mountain-path, together perhaps for the last time. Natalie lived with a widowed mother, who had, but three short months ago, with joyful pride, given her consent to her daughter's engagement to the handsome and manly Edward Deane.

Reaching the cottage, Natalie went to a quaintly-carved little oaken cabinet and took therefrom a tiny French cup and saucer of purest china inlaid with gold, and having upon the front and outer surface of the cup a most exquisite likeness of herself. It had been a treasure of priceless value to Natalie, as it was the last gift of her dear dead father, three years before, upon his return from a foreign trip. The picture was executed in Paris from a photograph which he had subsequently lost, and to-day it dawned upon Natalie that there would be no other likeness of herself that Edward could take with him.

" It is the only picture I have, Edward. Is it not a pity, for I know you could never carry it." And she held toward him the fragile little bit of china.

" Trust me, love, for taking care of it. Knowing how much it is prized by you, it shall be all the more carefully guarded by me if you will consent to my taking it."

" Take it, Edward ; it is yours, no matter what befalls it."

" Thank you, my dear, generous girl. The little love-token shall never leave my hands or care ; and when this cruel war is past, sweetheart, I shall return with it in triumph to you, unless the dear Father in heaven wills it otherwise." His voice faltered as he continued, " And should I—I fall in the conflict, this little cup will be returned to you with a last message from me."

" Don't, dear, dear Edward ; I have evil forebodings enough. I cannot live without you. You will,—you must return. Surely, God will answer my prayers and spare you to me."

" Natalie, loved one, I want to live to see you again. I ask for nothing else. God knows how much I crave that this boon will not be denied me."

Slowly the great red sun sank behind the mountain. One by one the stars came out to keep their vigil, while Natalie and her lover whispered their last farewell within the little vine-covered porch. ___

The days went wearily by, while the war raged fiercely. At home, sad eyes and anxious hearts awaited each day's tidings from their beloved ones. At long intervals blurred and hurried scrawls would reach the home of Natalie, filled with tender, loving words of devotion and hope. A year went by, and still the war was not over, nor had Edward returned. In the meantime another great sorrow befell Natalie Earle, in the death of her mother, which left her alone.

Slowly the long, weary days dragged by in the desolate home of Natalie Earle. The pretty little peaceful valley, with its thrift and tokens of peace and plenty, was no longer a garden of Eden. Waste and devastation were everywhere. Weeds sprung up where beautiful gardens had been. Homes were deserted, or made desolate by the death of loved ones. Natalie walked among them all, giving comfort here and there, consoling and helping those whose affliction seemed greater than her own.

She had not heard from Edward for some time now, and her anxious heart would quicken its beating at every strange step, at every knock at the door, or message sent.

It came, however, one evening, when Natalie was alone: a knock, feeble and timid, upon the front door. She arose, with fear and trembling, to answer its summons. An aged negro stood without, holding in his hand a tiny package. Lifting his hat respectfully, in a trembling voice he asked if Miss Natalie Earle was within.

"I am Natalie Earle," she said. "You have brought a message for me?" The old man made no spoken reply, but mutely handed the package to the trembling girl, then turned slowly, and disappeared in the darkness.

Eagerly she tore away the wrappings, and there, before her eyes, lay the tiny cup and saucer. The cup was filled with earth, in which was planted a tiny blue forget-me-not, withered now and dead, for want of air and sunlight. About the handle was wrapped a small scrap of paper, bearing these words:

"Farewell, darling Natalie, until we meet in heaven. Am dying, with your name upon my lips. EDWARD."

Without a word she sank upon her knees, and pressed the precious paper to her lips. The worst had come. Then, for a brief space, unconsciousness came to her like the blessed balm of sleep.

———

The war was not over when Natalie again faced the world, feeling herself now utterly alone. But she did not die—grief seldom kills. She took up the burden of life once more; but this time in the hospitals of the army, and no wounded or dying soldier, in gray or blue, who received the sweet, pure comfort of her care, but blessed her.

To-day, if you, perchance, happen to be treading the streets of a certain Western city, and will take the trouble to call at the Hospital of the Sacred Heart, and will ask to see Sister Joanelle, a sweet-faced, dark-eyed woman will greet you, attired in the habiliments of a Sister of Mercy; and in that patient, waiting face you will recognize Natalie Earle. Her work is still unfinished; but, with each day's ending, as she kneels before the tiny altar in her room, gazing with tearful eyes upon a quaint bit of purest china, these words escape her:

"One day nearer heaven and you, my love!"

———

A CURIOSITY IN VERSE.

SHORTLY after the close of the Civil War, a soldier of the gray, finding himself still possessed of some Confederate paper money, presented a $100 bill of this then hopelessly depreciated currency to a friend who wanted it for a collection in process of making. Before transferring the bill, the donor wrote on the back of it an impromptu poetical commentary, in which humor and pathos are oddly intermingled. Copies of these verses have been published by various journals, and generally incorrectly; but through the courtesy of Mr. Edwin H. Marble, of Worcester, Massachusetts, who is the possessor of an exact duplicate of the original, we are enabled to give the poem in full, and exactly as first written:

Representing nothing on God's earth now
  And naught in the waters below it,
As a pledge of a nation that has passed away,
  Keep it, dear friend, and show it.

Show it to those who will lend an ear
  To the tale this trifle will tell,
Of Liberty, born of a patriot's dream,
  Of a storm-cradled nation that fell.

Too poor to possess the precious ores,
  Too much of a stranger to borrow,
We issued to-day "our promise to pay,"
  And hoped to redeem on the morrow.

The days rolled on and the weeks became years,
  But our coffers were empty still.
Coin was so scarce, the treasury quaked
  If a dollar should drop in the till.

But the faith that was in us was strong indeed,
  Though our poverty well we discerned,
And this little check represents the pay
  That our suffering veterans earned.

They knew it had scarcely a value in gold,
  Yet as gold our soldiers received it.
It gazed in our eyes, with "a promise to pay,"
  And every true soldier believed it.

But our boys thought little of price or pay
  Or of bills that were overdue.
We knew if it brought our bread to-day
  'Twas the best our poor country could do.

Keep it. It tells all our history o'er,
  From the birth of our dream to its last,
Modest and born of the angel Hope,
  Like our dream of success, it passed.

GENERAL THOMAS AND THE TELEGRAPH OPERATOR.

Jesse H. Bunnell.

JESSE H. BUNNELL.

PRIESTS, physicians and telegraph operators are, by reason of their peculiar professional position, in possession of more secrets of others than any classes of men. In fact, they more nearly know the people with whom they are thrown in contact as God made the people, than even the most intimate acquaintance or relation would admit of under ordinary circumstances in a lifetime. As sagely written, John is three persons : "John as he thinks himself," "John as he wishes other people to think him," and "John as he actually is." Now John to the telegraph operator involuntarily is "as he actually is."

John may write a message telling his absent wife of his deep dejection and grief, but John cannot disguise the merry twinkle of his amorous eye and the perfume of the grape with which his breath is laden from the man who shall transmit what "John wishes other people to think him." John may hand the modest and meek manipulator of chained lightning a message big with courageous words and boastful phrases, but John cannot conceal from the lowly servant of the wire company his blanched cheek and trem-

bling fingers. Because of the existence of the (often unwilling) confidences reposed in the tapper of the key, he could, if he would, in many instances, an interesting tale unfold and give to the world pages existing in the book of some lives, the existence of which is unsuspected, and would be incredible when revealed.

The telegraph operators of the grapevine wire during the Civil War were, of necessity, the depositories of many and important secrets, plans of campaigns, orders of march, objects and intentions of commanding officers, the co-operation and assistance sought and expected when and where. All came into the keeping of, possibly, a mere lad or boy, whose humble position only entitled him to moderate compensation, while the betrayal of the secrets which, of necessity, were placed in his keeping, would have produced such wealth as would have offered temptation to older, wiser, and far wealthier men. To the credit of the lads who served the Union in those days of trouble in flashing orders and commands, which have made the grandest chapter of our nation's history, be it recorded, that no Benedict Arnold was found in their ranks.

In that band of wire-tappers I had the honor to serve for four years. In 1863, I was appointed or employed as telegraph operator in the field, and assigned for duty to the Army of the Cumberland. In that year I was but eighteen years of age, and by reason of my lack of stature and youthful appearance, I am indebted for the proudly recollected honor of being addressed as "my son" and "my boy" by that grand "Rock of Chickamauga," the noble General George H. Thomas, with whom it was my privilege to be thrown in daily contact, by reason of my position as telegraph operator at his headquarters, during the campaign from Chattanooga to Atlanta.

General W. S. Rosecrans was another commander of Union soldiers who, appreciating in the highest degree the importance of the field wire and its uninterrupted efficiency, gave much attention to it and the service thereof. It was during the battle of Chickamauga that I saw the most positive evidence of this feeling of General Rosecrans. I was working my instrument, which

UNITED STATES MILITARY TELEGRAPH WAGON.

rested on a little table at one end of the porch in front of that memorable Widow Glenn's house on the knoll which was used as headquarters. General Rosecrans had stationed himself at the other end of the porch, where he received the reports of staff officers, issued orders, and dictated messages and orders for me to transmit to different commanders in various sections of the part of the attack commanded by him. To perfect the circuit of the wire, and because of the lack of moisture in the vicinity, I had "grounded" one end of the wire by running it down into a well that was in the yard, and near the porch upon which I was stationed. A company of cavalry passing halted near by, and the tired, thirsty troopers made a descent upon the well to cool their parched throats, but in dragging up the bucket, which worked at the end of the long, old-fashioned sweep, up came my wire, and the connection was at once broken. Upon my reporting the fact, General Rosecrans became greatly excited. He savagely ordered the cavalrymen to replace "that wire" and to leave "that well." Their thirst was forgotten instantly, and they scattered like a brood of chickens at the appearance of a hawk.

Respectful, loving memory recalls so many scenes before me enacted during that stirring period, in which my *beau ideal* of the soldier, George H. Thomas, is the central character, that I find it difficult to particularize; however, one occasion, will demonstrate how truthful was the assertion made in the beginning of this article, that priests, physicians and telegraph operators were in positions to know "John as he actually is." Without even at this late day revealing secrets coming into my possession by reason of my occupation, I do feel at liberty to state that when General Sherman was preparing to attack Johnston's army, entrenched in a position almost impregnable on Kenesaw Mountain, I operated the wire at General Thomas's headquarters, and was the vehicle, in conjunction with the magnetic current, by which the conversation between Generals Sherman and Thomas was carried on. And in one particular the modest lad, tapping the key of his instrument, was better able to judge of what was meant and desired by the great American soldier at his side than even the other grand old leader—Sherman—was. I had the advantage of catching the glance of the eye, the meaning of the slight frown which accompanied the words sent over the wire. The glance, the frown, was revealed only to me, and then I was only a boy, and in some kind of manner a sort of senseless speaking-tube, entitled to little attention save as the means by which the end—communication—was attained. There need be no hesitation in permitting the features to play naturally under the impulses of the mind. No iron mask of military etiquette need be held before my general's face, who, sitting by my side, felt himself alone. In military life I, the operator, was nothing ; but I did see and I did think and I did know that my honored general did not want to send his gallant soldiers against Johnston's position on Kenesaw's sides. The glance,

what Burnside failed to do at Fredericksburg and Lee failed to accomplish at Gettysburg—whip an equal number of entrenched American fighting soldiers by direct assault. The result could be, and was, but one thing—failure, attended by most direful loss of life, in the brave Army of the Cumberland. It was a repetition of Fredericksburg and Gettysburg. Such will it ever be in America. I watched General Thomas as the wounded men passed by *en route* for the rear ; as he would glance at the shattered forms

"I WATCHED GENERAL THOMAS AS THE WOUNDED MEN PASSED BY."

the frown, the compressed lips, told me a story not conveyed to General Sherman by the respectfully courteous words sent over the wire to the commanding general by his skilful corps commander. Thomas delayed, excused, and reluctantly was forced to make the assault. Yet, I doubt if the conversation in cold type would exhibit one atom of delay, excuse, or reluctance, but I know it and saw it.

Next day after the night when final orders had been given to assail Johnston's position, I was on duty at General Thomas's tent. The attempt was making, and had been made, to accomplish

of some of his brave fellows, I would catch the sound of his deep breathing, almost a groan. His hands were clinched, and, with frowning brow, he gazed upon the ground, whereon he was making marks and crosses with the toe of his boot. Nothing of this scene as I witnessed it is placed in the record, but boys (old men now) of the Army of the Cumberland, wherever you be, learn that your general was hurt in his heart for each of you hurt in body or limb at Kenesaw, and in your most sacred shrine of memory place in grateful recollection the name of George H. Thomas. When the knowledge of General Jos.

E. Johnston's removal from the command of the Confederate army facing us, and the appointment of General Hood as chief of the army of our adversaries, was flashed over the wires by we youngsters of Telegraph Brigade, the soldiers became aware of the change in the commanders of the enemy with a sigh of relief. While all knew that Hood meant hard fighting, still that was preferable to the fox-like cunning and military ability that marked every move of "Uncle Joe," as the Johnnies affectionately called General Johnston.

In the narrative of General Joseph E. Johnston, the author states many things, in the frankness of his nature, that makes plain much that at the time was displeasing to the Executive of the Confederate Government, as well as mystifying and disconcerting to our army confronting the forces under Johnston's command. Not the least important and frank statement made by that great strategist, is the following: "I had served with those men (referring to the Union army), and I knew that it was impossible to defeat them with the much smaller force under my command." Johnston was one of the best and most gallant of that magnificent body of United States officers who served in the Mexican War. He knew his countrymen, and appreciated in the fullest manner the courage and ability of the men against whom he was contending. This knowledge, derived from past experience of Johnston in the Federal army, was the keynote of the wonderfully able campaign conducted by him from the time he assumed command of the Confederate army after its defeat at Missionary Ridge. He never was led into the fallacy of "barring the size" as the disasters of other leaders attest they did; but whenever he fought he selected such favorable positions as to more than "equalize the size," and watched his flanks like the time-honored cat watches the rat.

Hood, immediately on assuming command, in like manner assumed the offensive, and in such an erratic and unexpected manner, that it often seemed to puzzle our wary "old Tecumse" to know where he would break out next. When the inexorable blue lines with resistless, tireless energy, encircled Atlanta in their steely embrace that summer of 1864, Hood had made such frantic and unaccountable movements as to cause some doubt in the mind of our general as to the exact position of Hood's artillery, and where his force was massed. One day I wired a message from the general of the army to the commanding officers along the line to the effect that the whole line at ten o'clock that night should be in position, with every cannon and musket loaded; that at the signal given by the firing of a rocket on the extreme left, the bugle should sound the charge, every cannon and musket should be discharged, the troops should cheer as if making a night attack and keep it up for twenty minutes, but instead of advancing they should remain stationary behind their breastworks. The object was to thus provoke a reply from the enemy, and by so doing obtain the desired information as the position of Hood's artillery, and the strength of the force holding the position in front of our line. Having become aware of the intended demonstration, I climbed to the roof of a high barn near the headquarters, and seated on the shingles waited for the pyrotechnic display that would soon be spread before me.

The night was still, with that peculiar hush that inclines one to speak in whispers. Not a breath of air stirred the foliage, the moisture of the Southern climate seemingly deadening all sound. Perched upon the roof of the barn, with an occasional star peeping from behind curtains of clouds to silently blink an indistinct eye at me, I felt as lonely as if the 150,000 men in the vicinity had been turned into stone. A point of light moving beneath my elevated station, might be either a fire-fly or the end of a cigar. One would move as noiselessly as the smoke of the other. The very mosquitoes that were letting Yankee blood in revenge for the invasion of their territory, did so with less noise and bustle about it that night than I recall them as doing on any other occasion, and my counter-attacks were conducted in a subdued and silent manner.

Suddenly the all-pervading stillness was broken by the whirring sound of the ascending rocket on the left of our line; the indistinct sound of the popping of the ball as the rocket exploded upon reaching the zenith of its flight, appeared the breaking of the cord that held in check the torrent of noise so long and effectually restrained. For far down on the left, faintly at first, but growing louder and increasing momentarily, the sound of exploding musketry, cheering, and booming of cannon came rolling and rumbling like some mighty billow of noise-creating character along the line from left to right. It seemed to gather material as it crashed its way onward, with lighting-like rapidity. Like some gigantic train of gunpowder laid along the line we occupied, that had been fired by the flight of the rocket on my left, it rushed through the blackness and stillness of the night, aiming in its

"PERCHED UPON THE ROOF OF THE BARN."

flight, seemingly at me and for me, that even expected by me as it was, I was so startled as to almost fall from my perch. As the firing rolled down toward me, it was accompanied by the wild cheering of the troops, until when it crashed its way through the darkness as some gigantic wild animal would through the jungle, and sprang before my startled vision at my very feet, as the line in my immediate front took up the awful chorus of fire, explosion, and cheering, I was impressed for an instant with the thought that perhaps the attack was real after all, and that I had been mistaken in thinking it merely a feint. It was only when the fire and noise traveled along beyond me toward the left of the line, leaving only, like the receding waves of the ocean, little spots of water in the shape of answering yells and replying fire of the enemy, that I was assured my first idea was correct.

I could hear the beating of drums, and the quick sharp words of command of the enemy calling their men into line. The bustle and noise of the aroused expectant gray soldiers was as if the soft pedal of storm had been pressed after the first crash of the martial music. Soon the Confederate batteries opened fire all along the line, and volleys of musketry were fired toward our breastworks, as if they expected immediate attack at every point.

Sherman's object was accomplished, the position of Hood's artillery was unmasked, and no further movement was contemplated. However, several over-anxious and impetuous bodies of the enemy's soldiers charged forward to meet the expected attack and were quietly gathered in by our men, to be added to Uncle Sam's guests at the guarded hotels north of Mason and Dixon's line.

I recall the meeting of the prisoners next morning after the demonstration, and hearing one of the "Johnnies" drawl out to his nearest guard: " What the h—l is you'uns up to any hea'aou? We'uns thought the whole d—n Yankee nation was comin'."

Never having seen published an account of this feigned night attack of Sherman on the enemy's lines around Atlanta, I think this paper may recall the scene to many of the participants.

·ALL QUIET ALONG THE POTOMAC TO-NIGHT.

"ALL quiet along the Potomac," they say.
　"Except now and then a stray picket
Is shot, as he walks on his beat, to and fro,
　By a rifleman hid in the thicket.
'Tis nothing—a private or two, now and then,
　Will not count in the news of the battle ;
Not an officer lost—only one of the men.
　Moaning out, all alone, the death rattle."

All quiet along the Potomac to-night,
　Where the soldiers lie peacefully dreaming ;
Their tents in the rays of the clear autumn moon, ·
　Or the light of the watch-fires are gleaming.
A tremulous sigh, as the gentle night-wind
　Through the forest-leaves softly is creeping ;
While stars up above, with their glittering eyes,
　Keep guard—for the army is sleeping.

There is only the sound of the lone sentry's tread,
　As he tramps from the rock to the fountain,
And thinks of the two in the lone trundle-bed
　Far away in the cot on the mountain.
His musket falls slack—his face, dark and grim,
　Grows gentle with memories tender,
As he mutters a prayer for the children asleep—
　For their mother—may Heaven defend her !

The moon seems to shine just as brightly as then,
　That night, when the love yet unspoken
Leaped up to his lips—when low-murmured vows
　Were pledged to be ever unbroken.
Then drawing his sleeve roughly over his eyes,
　He dashes off tears that are welling,
And gathers his gun closer up to its place
　As if to keep down the heart-swelling.

He passes the fountain, the blasted pine-tree—
　The footstep is lagging and weary ;
Yet onward he goes, through the broad belt of light,
　Toward the shade of the forest so dreary.
Hark ! was it the night-wind that rustled the leaves?
　Was it moonlight so wondrously flashing?
It looked like a rifle—"Ha ! Mary, good-by !"
　The red life-blood is ebbing and plashing.

All quiet along the Potomac to-night ;
　No sound save the rush of the river ;
While soft falls the dew on the face of the dead.
　The picket's off duty forever !

GENERAL WILLIAM McCANDLESS.

OF THE FAMOUS PENNSYLVANIA RESERVES.

THE author of the following poem was a private soldier in the Second Regiment, Pennsylvania Reserve Corps, when commanded by Colonel, afterwards General, McCandless, and in more than one desperate battle witnessed that brave warrior's heroism. He was as calm in action as though on drill, and his kindly heart won the love of all who served under him.

GENERAL WILLIAM McCANDLESS.

GEORGE M. VICKERS.

WHILE monuments and shafts arise
　The coming ages to apprise
Of daring deeds by heroes done,
Of hard fought battles lost or won,
None will mark truer soldier's grave
Than that where sleeps McCandless brave.

Close to each heart he ever stood,
Pride of our soldier brotherhood ;
Fresh to our minds he still appears,
Still honored as in bygone years :
Warm-hearted, thoughtful, constant friend,
Alert and loyal to the end.

Amid the storm of shot and shell,
Where right and left his comrades fell,
Like statue cut in bold relief,
Ever was seen our gallant chief :
What tribute soldier true deserves
Give him—he led the old Reserves.

THE PICKET IS OFF DUTY FOREVER.

NORTHERN WAR SONGS.

MARCHING THROUGH GEORGIA.

BRING the good old bugle, boys! we'll sing another song—
Sing it with a spirit that will start the world along—
Sing it as we used to sing it, fifty thousand strong;
    While we were marching through Georgia.

CHORUS.

"Hurrah, hurrah! we bring the jubilee.
Hurrah! hurrah! the flag that makes you free!"
    So we sang the chorus from Atlanta to the sea,
    While we were marching through Georgia.

How the darkies shouted when they heard the joyful sound!
How the turkies gobbled which our commissary found!
How the sweet potatoes even started from the ground!
    While we were marching through Georgia.

Yes, and there were Union men who wept with joyful tears,
When they saw the honored flag they hadn't seen for years;
Hardly could they be restrained from breaking out in cheers,
    While we were marching through Georgia.

"Sherman's dashing Yankee boys will never reach the coast!"
So the saucy rebels said, and 'twas a handsome boast;
Had they not forgot, alas! to reckon with the host,
    While we were marching through Georgia.

So we made a thoroughfare for Freedom and her train,
Sixty miles in latitude—three hundred to the main;
Treason fled before us, for resistance was in vain,
    While we were marching through Georgia.

THE BATTLE CRY OF FREEDOM.

WE'LL rally round the flag, boys, rally once again,
    Shouting the battle cry of Freedom;
We will rally from the hillside, we'll gather from the
    plain,
    Shouting the battle cry of Freedom.

CHORUS.

The Union for ever, hurrah, boys, hurrah!
Down with the traitor, up with the stars;
While we rally round the flag, boys, rally once again,
Shouting the battle cry of Freedom!

We are springing to the call of our brothers gone before,
    Shouting the battle cry of Freedom;
And we'll fill the vacant ranks with a million freemen
    more,
    Shouting the battle cry of Freedom.

We will welcome to our numbers the loyal, true and brave,
    Shouting the battle cry of Freedom:
And although they may be poor, not a man shall be a slave,
    Shouting the battle cry of Freedom.

So we're springing to the call from the East and from the
    West,
    Shouting the battle cry of Freedom;
And we'll hurl the rebel crew from the land we love the
    best,
    Shouting the battle cry of Freedom.

JOHN BROWN'S BODY.

JOHN BROWN'S body lies a-mouldering in the grave;
John Brown's body lies a-mouldering in the grave;
John Brown's body lies a-mouldering in the grave,
    But his soul is marching on.

CHORUS.

Glory, glory, hallelujah!
Glory, glory, hallelujah!
Glory, glory, hallelujah!
His soul is marching on!

He's gone to be a soldier in the army of the Lord!
He's gone to be a soldier in the army of the Lord!
He's gone to be a soldier in the army of the Lord!
    But his soul is marching on!

John Brown's knapsack is strapped upon his back!
John Brown's knapsack is strapped upon his back!
John Brown's knapsack is strapped upon his back!
    But his soul is marching on!

His pet lambs will meet him on the way !
His pet lambs will meet him on the way !
His pet lambs will meet him on the way !
    As they go marching on !

They will hang Jeff Davis on a sour apple tree !
They will hang Jeff Davis on a sour apple tree !
They will hang Jeff Davis on a sour apple tree !
    As they march along !

Now, three rousing cheers for the Union !
Now, three rousing cheers for the Union !
Now, three rousing cheers for the Union !
    As we are marching on !

Glory, glory, hallelujah !
Glory, glory, hallelujah !
Glory, glory, hallelujah !
Hip, hip, hip, hip, hurrah !

TRAMP, TRAMP, TRAMP, THE BOYS ARE MARCHING.

IN the prison cell I sit,
    Thinking, mother dear, of you,
And our bright and happy home so far away;
And the tears they fill my eyes,
Spite of all that I can do,
Though I try to cheer my comrades and be gay.

CHORUS.

Tramp, tramp, tramp, the boys are marching,
Cheer up, comrades, they will come,
And beneath the starry flag
We shall breathe the air again
Of the free-land in our own beloved home.

In the battle front we stood
When the fiercest charge they made,
And they swept us off a hundred men or more;
But before we reached their lines
They were beaten back dismayed,
And we heard the cry of vict'ry o'er and o'er.

So within the prison cell
We are waiting for the day
That shall come to open wide the iron door;
And the hollow eye grows bright,
And the poor heart almost gay,
As we think of seeing home and friends once more.

THE VETERAN'S TOAST.

GOD bless the Union's starry flag,
    God bless our happy land,
God bless the gallant blue and gray,
    United heart and hand.
                    —*Geo. M. Vickers.*

SOUTHERN WAR SONGS.

DIXIE.

SOUTHRONS, hear your country call you !
Up, lest worse than death befall you !
To arms ! to arms ! to arms, in Dixie !
Lo ! All the beacon-fires are lighted—
Let all hearts be now united.
To arms ! to arms ! to arms, in Dixie !
Advance the flag of Dixie !
Hurrah ! hurrah !
For Dixie's land we take our stand,
And live or die for Dixie.
To arms ! to arms !
And conquer peace for Dixie !
To arms ! to arms !
And conquer peace for Dixie !

Hear the Northern thunders mutter !
Northern flags in South winds flutter.
Send them back your fierce defiance,
Stamp upon the accursed alliance.

Fear no danger ! shun no labor !
Lift up rifle, pike and sabre.
Shoulder pressing close to shoulder,
Let the odds make each heart bolder.

How the South's great heart rejoices
At your cannons' ringing voices !
For faith betrayed, and pledges broken,
Wrongs inflicted, insults spoken.

Strong as-lions, swift as eagles,
Back to their kennels hunt these beagles !
Cut the unequal bonds asunder ;
Let them hence each other plunder !

Swear upon your country's altar
Never to submit or falter,
Till the spoilers are defeated,
Till the Lord's work is completed.

Halt not till our Federation
Secures among earth's powers its station.
Then at peace, and crowned with glory,
Hear your children tell the story.

If the loved ones weep in sadness,
Victory soon shall bring them gladness,
Exultant pride soon banish sorrow,
Smiles chase tears away to-morrow.

THE BONNIE BLUE FLAG.

WE are a band of brothers, and native to the soil,
Fighting for the property we gained by honest toil;
And when our rights were threatened, the cry rose near
and far :
Hurrah for the Bonnie Blue Flag that bears a single star !
Hurrah ! hurrah ! for the Bonnie Blue Flag that bears a
single star !

As long as the Union was faithful to her trust,
Like friends and like brothers, kind were we and just;
But now when Northern treachery attempts our rights to
mar,
We hoist on high the Bonnie Blue Flag that bears a single
star.

First, gallant South Carolina nobly made the stand;
Then came Alabama, who took her by the hand ;
Next, quickly Mississippi, Georgia, and Florida—
All raised the flag, the Bonnie Blue Flag that bears a single
star.

Ye men of valor, gather round the banner of the right;
Texas, and fair Louisiana join us in the fight.
Davis, our beloved President, and Stephens, statesmen are ;
Now rally round the Bonnie Blue Flag that bears a single star.

And here's to brave Virginia ! the old Dominion State,
With the young Confederacy at length has linked her fate.
Impelled by her example, now the other States prepare
To hoist on high the Bonnie Blue Flag that bears a single
star.

Then here's to our Confederacy ! Strong we are and brave;
Like patriots of old we'll fight, our heritage to save;
And rather than submit to shame, to die we would prefer,
So cheer for the Bonnie Blue Flag that bears a single star.

Then cheer, boys, cheer, join the joyous shout,
For Arkansas and North Carolina now have both gone out ;
And let another rousing cheer for Tennessee be given,
The single star of the Bonnie Blue Flag has grown to be
eleven.

MY MARYLAND.

THE despot's heel is on thy shore
Maryland !
His touch is at thy temple door,
Maryland !
Avenge the patriotic gore
That flecked the streets of Baltimore,
And be the battle-queen of yore,
Maryland, my Maryland !

Hark to an exiled son's appeal,
Maryland !
My mother state, to thee I kneel,
Maryland !
For life and death, for woe and weal,
Thy peerless chivalry reveal,
And gird thy beauteous limbs with steel,
Maryland, my Maryland !

Thou wilt not cower in the dust,
 Maryland !
Thy beaming sword shall never rust,
 Maryland !
Remember Carroll's sacred trust,
Remember Howard's warlike thrust,
And all thy slumberers with the just,
 Maryland, my Maryland !

Come ! 'tis the red dawn of the day,
 Maryland !
Come with thy panoplied array,
 Maryland !
With Ringgold's spirit for the fray,
With Watson's blood at Monterey,
With fearless Lowe and dashing May,
 Maryland, my Maryland !

Dear Mother, burst the tyrant's chain,
 Maryland !
Virginia should not call in vain,
 Maryland !
She meets her sisters on the plain,—
" *Sic semper !* " 'tis the proud refrain
That baffles minions back amain,
 Maryland !
Arise in majesty again,
 Maryland, my Maryland !

Come ! for thy shield is bright and strong,
 Maryland !
Come ! for thy dalliance does thee wrong,
 Maryland !
Come to thine own heroic throng
Stalking with liberty along,
And chant thy dauntless slogan-song,
 Maryland, my Maryland !

I see the blush upon thy cheek,
 Maryland !
For thou wast ever bravely meek,
 Maryland !
But lo ! there surges forth a shriek,
From hill to hill, from creek to creek,
Potomac calls to Chesapeake,
 Maryland, my Maryland !

Thou wilt not yield the vandal toll,
 Maryland !
Thou wilt not crook to his control,
 Maryland !
Better the fire upon thee roll,
Better the shot, the blade, the bowl,
Than crucifixion of the soul,
 Maryland, my Maryland !

I hear the distant thunder-hum,
 Maryland !
The old line's bugle, fife and drum,
 Maryland !
She is not dead, nor deaf, nor dumb ;
Huzza ! she spurns the Northern scum—
She breathes ! She burns ! She'll come ! She'll
 come !
 Maryland, my Maryland !

ON PICKET IN FRONT OF THE ENEMY.

Edward P. Tobie.

"MINGLING TOGETHER IN THAT FIELD OF WAVING GRAIN."

HE picket experience of Colonel John B. Weber, just related to me by a friend, recalls to mind an incident in my own experience in which, as in this case, Texans were the disturbing element. It was in the summer of 1864, after the Union army had settled down around Petersburg. A portion of our cavalry was doing picket duty on the left of the line, and about the middle of July the First Maine Cavalry, in which I was then a sergeant, was sent out to picket near what was known as the "Gurley Farm." I was detailed as sergeant of one of the reliefs, and was assigned to a line about two miles in length, with the Gurley mansion in the centre. This mansion was situated on a road which ran across my line, and directly into and beyond the enemy's lines. The custom had been for the sergeant of each relief to pay personal attention to the pickets from the mansion to the right of the line, while a corporal attended to the pickets on the left of the road, under direction of the sergeant. I followed this custom, remaining at the mansion, and occasionally riding along the line. The enemy's pickets

were not more than seventy-five yards away, in the edge of some woods, in plain sight, with an open field between the two picket lines. I had scarcely made myself familiar with the surroundings, when a man from the enemy's pickets came walking out upon the road a short distance, waving a paper. I knew what this meant from previous experiences, but as I had no paper other than an old copy of a religious weekly, I did not at first think it worth while to offer an exchange, especially as I knew it was against orders to communicate with the enemy. But as he continued to wave the paper, the comrade on post in the road wished very much to go down and talk with the picket in gray, so I finally gave him the paper and he went. I watched the meeting with a good deal of interest, half inclined to wish that I were a private instead of a sergeant, so that I might go myself. In due time my picket returned, bringing me a Petersburg paper of that morning, and a kind note from the enemy's picket, expressed in such a manner that I not only knew that he could be trusted, but that he and I were brothers. I was told that he objected to so unequal an exchange of papers, but finally accepted the religious weekly.

The second day I had pleasant communications now and then with my friend on the other picket line, we both happening to be on duty at the same time, during which I learned that the Ninth Virginia and Fifth North Carolina regiments were on duty in our front. While I was happy in so comfortable picket duty, and without a care or thought of trouble, matters became somewhat complicated on the left of my line, though I was unconscious of it until the story was told to me by the corpora after all was over. Between the two picket lines was a field of oats, and some one, from which side I never knew, suggested that the pickets of the two forces suspend duty and cut some of that grain for the horses. This was agreed to, and in less time than it takes to tell it, the men in blue and the men in gray were freely mingling together in that field of waving grain, chatting like old friends, trading coffee for tobacco, etc., while our officer of the day endeavored to trade horses with an officer in gray. But before this last bargain was arranged, one of the general's staff came to visit the pickets, and was, as in duty bound, very much "astonished" at the scene. The men of both sides resumed their proper places quickly and assumed a warlike appearance, and all went on as before. We supposed the matter would be reported to the general, of course, and we all felt uneasy, but the only official notice taken of the matter, so far as we knew, was the issuing of more stringent orders against holding communication with the pickets of the enemy.

———

The next morning after this commingling of the blue and the gray, as my pickets were being relieved, I was startled by the sound of rapid firing on the right of my line. The next relief had gone up the line, and some of my men had been relieved and had returned to the mansion. I, with others, was enjoying a morning wash at the pump in front of the house, and some of the men were taking a bath inside the house. We got ourselves together and started up the line as quickly as we could, but long before we got to the right the firing had stopped. We found that an attack had been made, one of my men captured, another's horse shot, and others of the pickets driven in. There was no further demonstration, and we returned to camp. I was mad clear through, and feeling very badly. I could not help believing that I was some to blame— that perhaps my friendly relations with the picket in gray had caused me to be less careful; that he

had lulled me into a sense of security purposely, that I might be less watchful and this attack be better made. If so, one of my boys was a prisoner through my carelessness. I was not happy that forenoon, and was feeling pretty ugly when it came again time for my relief to go on duty. Hardly were my men posted and I in my position near the mansion, when my picket friend in gray appeared, waving a paper, as if nothing had happened, and beckoning for some one to come down and see him. That was too much, and had I had a carbine, I think I should have fired on him, as for a moment my anger was beyond control. As it was, it was with difficulty that I refrained from ordering my picket to shoot at him. At last, seeing that he was uncommonly anxious, I allowed the picket to go down and see what he wanted. When he returned he brought me a note from my comrade in gray, expressing his sorrow for what occurred that morning, and explaining that his command had nothing to do with it; that the regiment on their left, which was opposite the right of my line, had been relieved the night before by a Texas regiment; that the Texans knew nothing about picket duty, and had made the attack. Confidence was restored, and I felt kindly toward my acquaintance on the opposite line again, and was sorry that I had doubted him at all.

———

I am reminded of another picket incident. This was on the Rappahannock River at Freeman's Ford, in the fall of 1863. The enemy's pickets were on the other side of the river, within conversation distance, and communication was frequent and good-natured. One day I rode to the lower end of my beat at the ford, and found there the picket in blue, a man in gray, and our officer of the day, in earnest conversation. I watched them eagerly, and in a few moments the picket in gray recrossed and returned to duty, and the officer of the day rode away. I learned from the picket that the soldier across the river wished to trade tobacco for a pocket-knife, and he invited him over, promising him safe return. Before the trade was completed, however, the officer of the day came along and took the visitor prisoner, but the picket in blue told the officer that he alone was to blame ; that the other came over on his promise that he should go back, and that the officer might punish him if he chose, but the "Johnny" must go back. Fortunately, the officer was captain of the picket's company, and knew him to be a true man and a good soldier, and after thinking the matter over for a moment, he said to the stranger, "Well, you may go back this time, but if I catch you over here again I shall keep you." In closing the story, our picket, with unfeigned pride and pleasure, remarked : "I wanted to shake hands with a real live reb before he had been tamed, and I did it."

———

Picket duty was not the worst duty of the service, by any means. In fine weather it was a pleasure, and even in bad weather we managed to get some comfort out of it. There were many duties that were much more unpleasant than picket. We did not feel that there was any special danger in it, and yet there was enough to keep us ever watchful. We had no fear whatever of the enemy's pickets firing on us. They wished to keep on good terms as much as we did, and we always had a good understanding with them, but it was necessary to keep watch for any movement which indicated an advance upon our force. If their pickets were in our front, we felt as safe as in camp, and often quite as comfortable. Even when campaigning outside of our lines and put on post in the enemy's country,

"A TINY SAIL-BOAT CROSSING THE RIVER."

where an attack might be expected at any moment, we had no special sense of danger in the situation. I remember one moonlight night, when we were three or four days' march from our lines, being posted on picket on the brow of a hill behind some thick woods. I thought it a strange place to post a picket, but did not argue the matter. I was left there alone —no friendly picket in sight. Those woods might conceal a regiment of the enemy and I not be aware of it, while they could see me plainly in the clear moonlight. I didn't anticipate any danger. I knew if the enemy's pickets were in the woods I was all right—the pickets of the two armies were friends always—and if our force was

to be attacked I should hear them coming soon enough to give the alarm and get out of the way. I remember thinking how worried my good friends at home would be if they could know just how their soldier boy was situated that night, and yet I was perfectly comfortable, with the exception of being somewhat lonesome, as the hours dragged slowly away, and was perfectly safe.

———

During the winter of 1862–63, when we were picketing along the Rappahannock, picket duty was better than remaining in camp or doing fatigue duty at Belle Plain Landing. Our quarters that winter were very poor, in some cases a shelter tent pitched on the ground, with the bed on the ground at the rear, and a hole dug in the ground in front so the soldier could sit comfortably on the bed and put his feet in the hole. The camp-ground was a poor one, the weather bad, fatigue duty was abundant, and camp duty, drill, etc., were uncomfortable and irksome. On picket, however, we were more free and easy. There was no drill, fatigue duty, or anything of the kind, no "poppycock" review or dress parade. Instead of being cooped up in uncomfortable quarters, we were all under one shelter, all clustered around one camp-fire, and everything was more social and pleasant, while the duty was neither hard nor unpleasant, save for an occasional spell of bad weather. Indeed, I remember instances where we asked permission to remain on picket after the time was out, preferring that to going to camp in the storm. After the battle of Fredericksburg the relations between the pickets were most cordial. We had plenty of good old army coffee and sugar and no money, the enemy's pickets had plenty of tobacco and no money. We wanted tobacco, for a cavalryman without his pipe was out of tune. They wanted coffee and sugar. Between us we demonstrated in a remarkable degree the truth of the saying, "A fair exchange is no robbery." We exchanged to the mutual benefit of both. So general did this trading and this communication between the pickets become, that orders were issued from the headquarters of both armies to put a stop to it. After that communication was carried on upon the sly, and of course there was less of it. I was on post one morning and noticed that the pickets on the other shore were very busily at work. Soon I saw what looked like a tiny sail-boat crossing the river toward me. I watched it with much interest as it came nearer and nearer, but as luck would have it, the wind and current carried it below my post, and the comrade on the next post got it. It proved to be a raft made of corn-stalks, with a newspaper set for a sail, and some good tobacco for a load. That comrade was happy enough, and for the next few days his pet saying as he filled his pipe was, "My ship's come in." While visiting in Riverside, Cal., last summer, I met a man who formerly wore the gray, and who to-day carries a Yankee bullet in his body. We became quite well acquainted, and swapped war stories to our heart's content. One day we were speaking of picket duty, when he said he was on picket on the Rappahannock that winter, and spoke of trading with our pickets with the aid of these little corn-stalk rafts. As we talked the matter over we found that he was on duty opposite our line at this time, and it was very likely that he sent over this particular ship on this particular morning. I promptly thanked him in behalf of my comrade who secured the cargo.

It was quite a common thing for the pickets to banter each other by singing out across the river such phrases as "How are you, Yank?" "How are you, Johnny Reb?" "How are you, Abe Lincoln?" "How are you, Jeff Davis?" "How are you, Bull Run?" "How are you, Antietam?" etc., but I was not prepared, one morning in the latter part of January, at the time of the attempted movement of the army, to have the enemy's pickets sing out, "How are you, Burnside stuck in the mud?" which was the first information we, who had been on picket all the time, received of the failure of that movement.

If memory serves rightly, the enemy's pickets badgered us more than we did them. They had the best of us. We were on horses, not allowed to dismount, and had a long beat to patrol, which kept us busy all the time. They were infantry, and at each picket post had their little tent, with a little fire, and three or four men. There they lived cosily, taking turns of duty and enjoying themselves the rest of the time. It was rather aggravating to see them taking so much comfort

while we had to watch them in the cold and storm, but there was no help for it. One morning, just at daylight, as I was shivering away in the cold morning air after nearly two hours' duty, and looking anxiously for the next relief, one of the pickets across the river sang out to me: "Come over here, Yank, and warm you; you are most froze, I know you are." I wasn't particularly good-natured at that fling at my discomfort, so I made no answer, but I got square with my more comfortable friend that night. It was a custom for them when they heard a shot along the picket line to put out their fires immediately and "lay low and keep dark," so as not to give any clue to their presence should the firing become general. I was aware of that fact, as I had many times seen them hastily putting out their fires under such circumstances. That night, while on post, I listened to the sounds of cheerful conversation and of laughter which were borne across the Rappahannock until it seemed to me the pickets were taking too much comfort, when somehow or other my carbine was discharged. I was much pleased to see them kick the embers in every direction and hear their voices go out with the fire. The corporal came riding down to see what was the matter, and called me pet names on learning that the fire was purely accidental, but I was satisfied.

I was so fortunate as to be appointed corporal that winter, and the first time I went on picket in that capacity an incident occurred which, if it was not the origin of a since familiar term, was the first instance of its use within my recollection, though the emphasis at the time was somewhat different than it was after the phrase became a slang expression. It happened that I was detailed with the first relief, and as we rode to the line the corporal of the old picket accompanied us to show me the line and the various posts, to explain the surroundings and transmit to me the orders, and to call in his own men. As we rode along he related a joke that was played upon one of his men while there. Not far from the upper post, and in rear of it, was an old grave. As the victim of the joke went on duty the first time, the man whom he relieved told him that at midnight the night before the ghost of a man was seen near that grave, riding around on horseback, without any head. This so frightened the man that he did not dare to go on duty on the midnight relief, but instead hired a braver comrade to stand his picket for him. When I posted my relief, between eleven and twelve o'clock that night, this story came into my mind, and I thought to have a bit of sport with the man whom I was to leave there all alone at that midnight hour, so I told him the story with all the awe I could put in to my tone and manner. But my picket didn't frighten so easily. He was just lighting his pipe, and replied between whiffs: "Well (puff), if there's a man (puff) comes round here (puff) to-night (puff) without any head on (puff, puff), I'll put a head on him." He wasn't disturbed during his midnight vigil.

It was my fortune last summer, while traveling, to form the acquaintance of a man who wore the gray for the State of Alabama, and we fraternized gloriously. In some of our many war conversations he related two stories of picket which came under his own observation, and which, as they were new to me, I will relate now, as proof from the other side of the line that the feelings between the pickets of the two armies—the men who were at the outposts and the closest together in war duties—were as cordial as though they were friends, instead of foes who would shoot each other ruthlessly did they meet on the field of battle. The scenes were located in front of Petersburg. During one of the lulls in the firing a party of the pickets of both sides, among whom was my Southern friend, met halfway between the lines for a social chat. Their conversation turned upon their rations, and there was the usual exchange of Northern coffee and sugar for Southern tobacco, when one of the Yanks happened to say something about the sutler and the good things that personage had for sale. This recital aroused the appetite of one of the Southern soldiers—a young recruit, not long enough in the service to really enjoy army fare—and he asked the Yank if he would go and get him some of these good things if he gave him the money. The Yank promptly agreed to do so, and the reb promptly handed a ten-dollar greenback to the Yank, who as promptly disappeared over the breastworks. Then Northern and Southern soldiers alike began to chaff the recruit by telling him it was foolish to give his money to the Yank, that he would never see Yank nor money again, and that the expected goodies were a myth. They succeeded in making the young Southron very uncomfortable, though none of the older Southern soldiers had any doubt that the Yank would come back as he agreed. In a short time the

Yank reappeared with the goodies, and the young soldier was made happy. After that the recruit could never be made to doubt the word of a Yankee soldier. At another time my Confederate friend, accompanied by an officer and two or three soldiers, accepted an invitation from the Union breastworks to "come over and see us." They were cordially received, and were chatting and looking over the fort, when the firing opened sharply from the other side. The Southern officer promptly stepped upon the embankment of the Northern fort, under the full fire, and ordered the firing to cease. This order was obeyed, and the visitors returned in safety to their own works.

PINE AND PALM.

Eugene Davis.

SAID the palm tree to the pine :
　　"God be thanked, the fight is o'er !
　Stormy skies have turned to calm,
　Peace is with us evermore ;
Brothers' blood, alas, was shed,
　Brothers' hand was raised 'gainst hand,
Graves were glutted with our dead,
　Carmine torrents stained the land ;
Rival banners on the breeze
Floated high from tow'r and town,
Where by sunlit southern seas
　Men would smite the Union down !
God forbad such rash design,
　God spoke out, and all was calm.
Let us thank the Lord divine,"
　Said the pine tree to the palm.

"Once the cry : 'To Washington !'"
　Said the palm tree to the pine,
"Was the shout of sire and son
　Heard beside the Georgian brine.
Hot the blood flowed in our veins,
　Fierce our passions glowed, and hence
War's battalions swept our plains ;
　But we've gleaned more wisdom since.
We have laid the Stars and Bars
　Wistfully beneath the clay,
And the glorious Stripes and Stars
　Are our standards here to-day !
Pledged to each by bond and seal,
　Brethren all, we now combine
For the self-same commonweal,"
　Said the palm tree to the pine.

"We are one—forever one—"
　Said the pine tree and the palm,
"One beneath one sky and sun –
　One in tempest and in calm.
Bending over the dead dust here—
　Heroes' dust from sea to sea—
We can shed a sacred tear
　O'er the graves of Grant and Lee !
Heart to heart and hand in hand
　We shall stand, and never fall—
One sole flag o'er this broad land,
　And Jehovah over all !
Fanned by freedom's fearless breath,
　Joined in love while planets shine,
North and South are one till death !"
　Said the palm tree and the pine.

GENERALS FIGHT AND FRATERNIZE.

W. H. CUNNINGTON.

 HE morning of the twelfth of May, 1864, opened dismally on the battle-field of Spottsylvania Court-House, during Grant's great flank march from the Rapidan to Richmond. A drenching rain set in before daylight, accompanied by a bleak and cheerless atmosphere that lasted until past the noonday hour. The fighting men of Grant's advancing army had little cause for exuberant spirits, and the lowering clouds, keen air, and drenching rainfall, through which the smoke of the battle, that had been resumed at an early hour, could be dimly seen from the point of observation occupied by the writer of this sketch, did not enhance the cheerfulness of the men who were fighting their way to the Confederate capital.

The Army of the Potomac, with General Meade in direct and active command, but with the taciturn, imperturbable, and sphinx-like General Grant the ruling spirit of the army, had crossed the Rapidan seven days before, 120,000 strong, with artillery in abundance, and a proud, confident, well-equipped host in all respects. When marshaled in battle array on the south side of the Rapidan, disaster commenced, and it continued during the three days' bloody battle in the Wilderness. Towards the end of the third day the order was given by Grant to prepare to march, and it was generally believed that the march would be a retreat of the army back across the Rapidan, and to the old winter quarters around Culpeper. Everybody was astonished when Grant did exactly the reverse, and commenced his historic and famous flank movement that plunged his discomfited army still deeper into the enemy's country, and showing that he meant business, when the day before he sent his famous despatch to Washington : "I propose to fight it out on this line, if it takes all summer."

A dreary night march brought the army to Spottsylvania, and here was almost a repetition of the equivocal scenes met with in the Wilderness, and lasted until the morning of the twelfth of May, when the "pelting of the pitiless storm," as mentioned, added to the gloomy forebodings of the troops ; but still a ray of sunshine was to come, in the way of the news throughout the army of the brilliant success of Hancock's great charge before dawn that morning, and which incident of the battle is the burden of this sketch, and enables the writer, who was an eye-witness of the scene, to advert briefly to an occurrence that went far to prove that even among the opposing generals the "blue and gray" would affiliate, and warmly greet each other, even while directly before the soldier's heart was steeled to deeds of blood, and while fighting and ready to die themselves, or kill each other in defence of the cause they separately espoused, these same men, though wading through blood, could grasp each other by the hand, and in a moment only remember that they were brothers at heart, and really belonged to a common country.

It was, perhaps, about eight o'clock on the morning of the twelfth of May, that a detail of soldiers built a large camp-fire on a spot that had been selected on the Spottsylvania battle-field. The spot was a knoll of ground somewhat removed from where the battle was hotly raging, and which the rain-pour did not check, but the place commanded a fair view of different parts of the battle-field, and was, in fact, a good point of observation of the operations going on all around. Around that, under the circumstances, cheerful camp-fire were gathered a little coterie of men, some of whose names are now historic, and are indelibly associated with the great Civil War, and are stamped on the pages of its history. Among those who stood there looking at the bright embers, and drying their clothes, were Major-General U. S. Grant, then the general in charge of all the armies of the Union ; Major-General George G. Meade, in command of the Army of the Potomac, but under the orders of General Grant ; Major-General Hunt, Chief of Artillery of the Army of the Potomac ; Major-General A. A. Humphreys, who was a prominent engineer and corps commander, and one or two others of lesser note, including the humble newspaper man who pens this sketch. I had pressed myself in between General Grant and General Meade, hoping to catch any words that might drop from them and be of service to me in my correspondence to the Philadelphia newspaper with which I was connected, but my eavesdropping did not amount to much, for both generals appeared to be wrapped in thought, and had little to say until General Grant, turning to Meade, remarked: "Well, I guess we're pretty dry now. Let's go over to quarters." Then Meade, who had been looking at a certain part of the field, said: "Wait a little while. I want to see how Warren develops himself." General Hunt then came up near me, and I said to him: "Not much chance for your artillery to-day, is there?"

of voice, "Bully!" he passed the note to General Meade. It proved to be a despatch from General Hancock, and read as follows:

"MAY 12, A. M.

"*General Grant:*

"I have finished up Johnson, and I am now going into Early. I have captured between forty and fifty guns, and a large number of prisoners.   HANCOCK."

This was the first cheering bit of news since the opening of the campaign, and when it became known that Hancock had captured Major-General Edward Johnson, the commander of a

THE CAMP-FIRE AT SPOTTSYLVANIA.

Hunt replied: "No; this has been a bad country for artillery ever since we entered it. I'll get a chance after awhile." The chance came when General Hunt had his guns planted before Petersburg, when they belched forth fire day after day, and week after week. *En passant,* I may say that once I met General Hunt between City Point and St. Petersburg, and reminded him of the Spottsylvania camp-fire incident, and he sighed and remarked, "Oh, my, how long ago that does seem to me!"

Before the camp-fire party had broken up, a non-commissioned officer hurried up to General Grant and handed him a note or despatch. Grant read the note without a change in his cast-iron countenance, but this relaxed into a pleased expression, and simply saying, in an audible tone

corps in Early's division, and Brigadier-General Stuart, who commanded a brigade in Johnson's corps, and also between 4000 and 5000 prisoners, the enthusiasm throughout the army was very great. Here was where the blue and gray fraternization took place.

While Generals Grant, Meade, Hunt, Williams, Humphreys, and other officers of lower grade, were standing around Grant's quarters later in the day, the captured Confederate general, Edward Johnson, was brought up, mounted on the horse of an orderly. As soon as he dismounted, General Meade advanced briskly towards him, and extending his hand, remarked in a tone of friendly welcome: "Why, Johnson, how are you? I am glad to meet you." Johnson grasped Meade's hand and said: "General

"GRANT SHOOK HANDS WARMLY WITH THE CAPTURED CONFEDERATES."

Meade, I am pleased to see you again." After a few more words of a salutatory character, General Meade led General Johnson forward, and going up to Grant said: "General Grant, allow me to introduce General Johnson to you." Grant shook hands warmly with the captured Confederate, and some pleasant words passed between them, and then the other Federal officers present were presented to Johnson, and a social confab ensued. General Johnson then took a seat on a large log near the trunk of a tree, and chatted freely with his captors; but the writer noticed that, on every opportunity, he eyed General Grant with an evident feeling of great curiosity. While sitting on the log, talking about the campaign, and perhaps alluding to his own capture, General Johnson remarked in an abrupt sort of way, "Well, this is a h—l of a country to fight in, anyway." The captured general was well cared for by the Federal officers during the remainder of that day, and in fact, the *entente cordiale* between the Northern officers and their Southern captive lasted until General Johnson was taken to Fort Delaware, there to remain a prisoner of war in theory, but practically a social sojourner on his parole, until such time as he was once again a free man.

General Edward Johnson was a graduate of West Point, but being a Southerner, of course he accepted a commission in the Confederate States service when the war broke out. At one time he commanded the famous Stonewall Brigade, and had the reputation of being a brave, thorough-going soldier. He was a stout-built, rugged-looking man, and at the time of his capture was perhaps about forty years of age. He had a peculiar blinking-like affection of one of his eyes, and it was pleasantly related of him at the time he was an enforced guest at General Grant's headquarters, that he was an inveterate poker player, and that when an opponent who knew him sat down to a game with him, he could always tell whether Johnson had a good, bad, or indifferent hand by the spasmodic and involuntary contraction of the affected eye.

As stated, Brigadier-General Stuart was captured at the same time General Johnson was, during Hancock's charge, and immediately after his capture General Hancock at once advanced and extended the hand of personal friendship to his recent Confederate opponent. General Stuart, who was a great stickler for military etiquette, at first kept aloof from Hancock and declined the proffered hand of his captor, but the instincts of the man and brother soon overcame the rigid discipline of the soldier, and Hancock and Stuart soon forgot the bloody chasm between them, and joined hands over it.

APPOMATTOX.

I BELONGED to Mahone's old brigade of the Army of Northern Virginia. The last reveille moved our brigade from the line of battle, where the night of the eighth of April, 1865, was spent, after the hard march from Cumberland Church.

After a march of a few miles, a halt was ordered on the now famous field of Appomattox, just as the sun was throwing his curtains of crimson and gold over the eastern sky and while the newly-born leaves were yet burdened with dew.

The country is undulating, and an elevated position brings a large section within view. On the west, the Blue Ridge rose in its morning garb, and on the east a broad plateau of green, here and there broken by gradual elevations, appeared under the morning mists.

The everlasting artillery was thundering in front. Gordon's shattered columns were struggling there, endeavoring to reopen the path of retreat, now closed by the Army of the James; Pickett's magnificent division, which had made the hills of Gettysburg tremble beneath its terrible charge, and the world stand with bated breath at its sublime courage and matchless heroism, had been overwhelmed and torn asunder at Five Forks and Sailor's Creek, and only forty-seven men remained for duty. Field's and Mahone's divisions, "staunch in the midst of all disasters," were the only troops ready to be brought into action against the combined armies of the Potomac and James, numbering probably 140,000 men.

The blue lines of the enemy, like a huge anaconda, were extending the coils to the right and left, but our troops were ignorant of how closely they were enfolded. General Gordon, in reply to a message, said: "Tell General Lee I have fought my corps to a frazzel, and can do nothing unless heavily supported by Longstreet's corps." On receiving this, the great captain exclaimed: "Then there is nothing left me but to go and see General Grant, and I had rather die a thousand deaths." He had only 7892 infantry with arms upon the field.

About sunrise, in this dire emergency, the commander-in-chief of the armies of the Confederate States summoned to him our division commander. General Mahone found him with the "Old War Horse," General James Longstreet, at his side. The staff were requested to retire, and the three held counsel together as to the situation.

Surrender was inevitable, but General Lee had before determined that the terms must be such as he felt were due to his army; that the soldiers should not be sent to prison, but be paroled to return to their homes; these terms, or fight then and there to death. He was determined to preserve, untarnished, the honor of the Army of Northern Virginia.

When the last council-of-war was over, General Lee mounted "Traveler," saying to General Longstreet, "You take care of the command," and rode off to see General Grant.

General Longstreet sent General Mahone to take command of the rear left flank. Afterwards, General Lee was seen standing alone in the direction of Appomattox Court House, near the celebrated apple tree, with his staff near by, and a few soldiers in the vicinity grouped here and there.

He was awaiting a messenger. Soon a Federal officer, with a courier, came galloping from the enemy's lines. The officer dismounted upon reaching within fifty yards of General Lee, then advanced on foot, and when within fifty feet took off his hat and placed it under his arm. Colonel Walter H. Taylor, A. A. G., advanced and bore from him a note to General Lee. A message was returned, whereupon the officer replaced his hat upon his head, made for his horse and rode off to his lines.

Shortly after he returned, and in like manner approached General Lee and delivered to Colonel Taylor another note ; upon reading this General Lee, with great deliberation, tore it into many pieces and threw it upon the ground, afterwards pressing the pieces into the earth with his foot; a message was delivered to the officer, who, in like manner as before, made his exit. Soon after General Lee mounted, and, with Colonel Marshall and a courier, rode off in the direction the officer had gone.

It was then that the two opposing commanders first met, after which they retired to the McLean House, where the terms of capitulation were committed to writing. The reverence displayed by the Federal officer who bore the messages to General Lee impressed all with the high sense of

APPOMATTOX—GENERAL LEE RECEIVING GENERAL GRANT'S DESPATCHES.

the true manly propriety of that officer. I have been informed that General Babcock was the officer who was so courteous to our commander.

When General Mahone returned from the conference the command was ordered in line of battle; the men took their position with cheerfulness, and words ran along the line, "Well, we will get a chance at Sheridan now, and supply Mahone's foot cavalry with horses." Mahone's men cherished an earnest desire to get hold of "little Phil;" they had driven his troopers handsomely at Amelia Court House, and felt that they could now finally wind up the fierce career of his soldiers. But it was not long before the spirit which had never, not even yet, failed this noble corps, was suddenly seized with suspicions of surrender. A cavalryman had galloped across the open field from the right and disclosed the startling news, but they had little faith in his tale. They were actively engaged in

"EVERY HEAD WAS UNCOVERED."

building breastworks, when the order was passed to stop. This was singularly contrary to the precaution which had always governed. The cavalryman's story was true, the men's heart sank with grief, and they wept like children over a mother's grave. They knew all was over, and these manifestations of sorrow and distress sublimely attested their fidelity to the Southern cause. There was not a man in the command who did not prefer fighting to surrender. Like the inhabitants of renowned Carthage, many of them would have preferred death rather than survive.

On that last march, they hoped to join their fortunes with General Joe Johnston's army and throw all in the scale of one grand trial at arms with the armies of Grant and Sherman, thinking by generous emulation and rivalry, and one determined effort, with Lee and Johnston clasping hands, they might crush the unwieldy column of the enemy; but Providence ordained that the Army of Northern Virginia should fall by the wayside, gradually worn out by attrition —and thus the last hope of the Southern soldier fled forever.

The tenth of April was spent by the soldiers in discussing their gloomy prospects around the camp fires, for it was chilly, and a drizzling rain was falling, and foraging the immediate surroundings for scant food, as their commissariat had been long exhausted, and the Federals were unable to supply them. Hunger was gnawing sharply in their breasts, and fortunate indeed was the owner of a few grains of corn or a small piece of stale bread. After all the preliminaries were arranged, and General Lee had issued his farewell order, the formal surrender was made. I have often seen pictures, in my school books, of the surrender of Lord Cornwallis, at Yorktown, but never dreamed that I should realize a like scene.

Crawford's Division was drawn up on a hill just in front of Appomattox Court House, Mahone's Division marched up within a few feet, halted, faced it and stacked arms, furling the proud old bullet-torn, battle-smoked flags across the stacks. It was truly a sad mission, as plainly depicted on every countenance in our ranks, but General Grant's chivalrous terms were awarded the highest praise from all the captured.

When General Lee took his departure the soldiers gathered about the roadside, and as he passed through the broken and unarmed ranks every head was uncovered and each man was bidding a silent adieu with bursting heart and overflowing eyes. Even in disaster and defeat, all his manly characteristics stood out in his very appearance, and he seemed created to inspire love, respect and enthusiasm. His soldiers loved him with a deep and sacred affection no disaster could dampen or defeat destroy. After receiving their paroles the soldiers formed in groups and marched in the direction of their homes, relying upon kind-hearted citizens to supply them with rations on their desolate journey—a journey as dreary as a fugitive's through dismal avenues shrouded in the blackness of midnight and curtained on either side with the sombre forms of full-foliaged shrubs and trees—all surroundings as black as death, terrible as a tornado, and almost as awful as the night of crucifixion.

THE AMENITIES OF WAR.

S. FISHER.

IT was Sunday, the first day of the battle of Shiloh, the first engagement of the Second Texas Infantry regiment. The regiment had entered the battle on the right-centre of the Confederate line, which had pressed back the Federal forces in its front until about three o'clock in the afternoon. After making a desperate charge across a running branch, where the killed and wounded of both sides thickly bestrewed the hillside, and we had made a lodgment on the crest of a hill that terminated on our right in a bluff overlooking the Tennessee River, and had halted to rest and rally our forces, Dan Smith and I were sent to the rear with the canteens of our company to fill them with water. The sun of that April evening was sweltering hot, as is often the case before a rain. On our way down the hill we passed many dead bodies of Federal soldiers, when our attention was attracted by the groans of one poor fellow in the uniform of a captain, who lay with one leg pressed out of shape under him ; we approached him and asked if we could do anything for his relief.

He replied that he would be grateful to us if we would straighten him out, as his leg was badly shot to pieces, and the pain was almost killing him. Another man lying near him desired water, and a third complained of the burning sun. We raked some dry leaves into a bed under the sheltering boughs of a neighboring tree, and placing the captain on it, asked what else we could do for his comfort.

He then asked if we would not place the other two men, who were members of his company, beside him, so that they might be able to assist each other. We enlarged the bed of leaves and placed the other two men on it by his side. In placing the captain in position, I observed that he wore a heavy gold watch-guard which extended around his neck ; I suggested that he had better allow me to take it off and put it in his pocket, as some plunderer might come along and rob him of it. He insisted that I should take it off and keep it, saying : "I am sure I cannot recover, and I wish you to keep it for your kindness to us." This I declined to do, but took the watch and guard and put them into his pocket ; and then we took their canteens with our own to the branch and filled them with water, and on the way picked up some well-filled haversacks, and on returning placed these with the filled canteens by their sides.

The three were profuse in their expressions of gratitude, and asked us to write our names in their memorandum-books, which we did. In returning their books and on their reading our names with that of our regiment, "Second Texas Infantry," they looked at us in astonishment, and asked if we were really Texans. When we assured them we were, they said they were astonished, for they had prayed not to fall into the hands of Texans, as they believed that if they did, they would be shown no quarter, and would certainly be butchered like beasts. But here they were in the hands of the very troops they so much dreaded, and were being treated by them like brothers, and now that they knew what troops they were fighting, they were not astonished that they did not stand.

To these remarks, I replied : "Did we fight you like men ? and are not the brave always kind ? "

They answered : "You fought more like demons than like men ; but surely your kindness cannot be questioned, and we cannot express our gratitude for it."

Just then we saw in the woods near by an ambulance of our corps ; hailing it and placing them in it, we sent them to the rear. They were of the Illinois troops, and, if I mistake not, the captain's name was Miller.

After this the Second Texas passed through the battles of Farmington, Iuka, Corinth, Hatchie Bridge, Chickasaw Bayou, and Fort Pemberton, and then was engaged in the siege of Vicksburg.

On the night of the twelfth day and the last day of May, about midnight a false alarm aroused to arms, and in a moment the sleeping lines became a blaze of fire from the throats of muskets and artillery, and the air groaned with the shrieks of shell and the whirring of "Minnies"; amidst the aimless firing, a ten-inch shrapnel exploded in the trench where I stood, and three of its pieces found lodgment in my form, one severing my left foot from the ankle, another grazing my left hip and lodging against my right hip joint, whilst the third grazed my backbone and lodged against my right shoulder-blade. I was borne by my faithful comrades through the rain of lead and iron that deluged the battle-field to the surgeon ; and after this through the remainder of the forty-seven days of the conflict, endured a struggle for life against the intense summer heat, flying death-missiles, starvation, maggot, and inexpressible pain until the surrender—the hardest of all to bear—came, and my brave and true comrades filed into my tent at the hospital, and with solemn mien and bowed heads and smothered "good-byes," laid half of their small supply of coin on my couch, and with warm press of the hand and hushed "God bless you," left me as they thought forever. All the wounded who were unable to go out of the city were concentrated into one hospital in the old Vick mansion on the hill, where they were under the supervision of a Federal surgeon and the surveillance of a Federal guard. My spirits ran low and my life-blood ebbed and flowed with feverish excitement as I thought, "There is not a friend that I know or a hand that will lovingly help me," when a guard who paced the old mansion hall, halted at the door of the ward where I lay and asked if there were any Texas soldiers in the room.

Jeff Dearbon, who lay on a cot by the door, replied that there was.

"Are there any of the Second Texas Infantry here, do you know?"

Dearbon replied that there was, and pointed to my bed.

He approached me and asked, "Do you belong to the Second Texas Infantry?"

I answered, "I do."

"Where you in the battle of Shiloh?"

"I was."

"Did your regiment wear white negro cloth clothes in that battle?"

"It did."

His rifle-butt came down on the floor with a thump, and from his shirt pocket, with a hasty twist and a surge, he drew a worn and blackened memorandum-book with leaves well gone, and turning to a page in it with nervous hand, he thrust it before my eyes, and said :

"Do you know the men whose names are written there?"

My eyes and arms were weak and uncertain, but adjusting the book as best I could to the focus of my eyes, I replied :

"I do ; the first name is mine, the other Dan Smith's, of my company."

His lips quivered. There was a sudden choking in his throat ; his sturdy form trembled, as with husky voice he asked :

"Do you know me?"

"I do not."

"Did you write that?"

"That's my hand-writing."

"D'you remember picking up three men an' putting 'em on a bed of leaves in th' shade, an' giv'n' 'em water 'n' something to eat, an' tak'n' a watch off 'n the cap'n an' puttin' it in his pocket, an' then put'n' 'em in an amb'lance an' send'n' off to th' hospital?"

"Yes."

"I'm one of 'em."

The tears flowed down his iron cheek; his form of battle-steel was convulsed with nervous emotion; his sturdy arms clasped my emaciated form to his convulsing bosom, which had braved bayonet and shot and shell unflinchingly on many a field of carnage, and I felt serenely secure in my enemy's embrace. A hero's tears fell on my face and were mingled with my own. With dallying reluctance I was released from his embrace, and then with sobbing utterance he gasped:

"You saved my life and that of my captain and comrade, and I have hunted for you or some of your command on every battle-field since, that I might prove myself as true to you; now, what can I do for you? I am ready to do anything under God's heaven that I can."

"Nothing," I replied.

"But I must do something. Do you need money? (his well-filled purse now in his hand.) You must, for you are in our lines now and your money is worthless."

"No, no, I have plenty of money, gold and silver, given me by my comrades when they left me."

"Well, you need clothing?"

"No, I cannot sit up; and though my clothes were torn to shreds when I was wounded, I have no need of others than I have until I am able to be up, which will doubtless be many months yet."

"Tell me how you are wounded."

I told in an ear not less sympathetic than a brother's how I had been smitten by three pieces of shell at one time in the night, and had been borne to the hospital; how there exposed to dangers almost if not quite equal to those of the trenches; how the hospital being only supplied with one nurse to ten patients—one-half of whom were on duty at a time, in order that the other half might get needed rest—they could not give us proper attention; and how in spite of their best efforts the maggot-fly would light on every damp spot on bed or clothing, and flying away would leave, scampering from the spot, numerous, almost microscopic maggots, which would find lodgment in any crease of the skin, broken or not, and eat its way into the flesh; and had eaten between my helpless fingers, behind my ears, and in the creases of my neck, as well as in my wounds, and from the latter had been picked one by one with forceps by a faithful nurse; how with the demands of three large wounds to feed, my system had cried for food and had struggled with starvation; how my bones at knee and hip and shoulder had cut through the skin, and for more than a month I had been compelled to lie on these, burning as with the fires of torment, because I could lie in no other position; how in all this time I had never been dejected or cast down until the surrender had come, and my friends had gone out from me, and with them all hope for the cause for which I had proudly suffered, being able to do no more.

"Are the surgeons kind to you?" he asked.

"Yes, they are. Every one is kind to me."

"They will be kinder and better still when I have told them who you are and what you did for me. How strange it is that we should meet again with our circumstances so reversed! I have never forgotten your kindness or your face, but you look so young—so much like a mere boy. You were a man when we met each other at Shiloh."

"Yes, I have lost my hair and my beard since I was wounded; all came out, and this new, short hair and beard makes me look young."

"But you need better food than you get here?"

"No, we are all well fed and cared for now. Since General McPherson has been made commandant, he treats us well."

"I must bring in some of our officers and tell them who you are, and hereafter you will be well treated; I know you will."

He then disappeared, but soon reappeared, and with him the Federal surgeon in charge of the Confederate hospital, a colonel and others, to whom this strange tale of another day and this was told. They pledged their undivided attention to the foe that lay there all shattered and torn, and their pledge was not broken, and many of my crippled comrades shared the kindness thus betokened.

Again he was gone, again returned and laid upon my bed tobacco, canned fruit, and many delicacies. He imagined there was not sufficient bedding, and had fresh new blankets, sheets and pillow-slips supplied.

At sunset guard relief came on, an affectionate "good-night" was spoken, and hopes expressed of meeting again on the morrow.

The morrow has not come as yet, but may it not be, in that good day when wars are not, we'll meet again—foe-friends, Johnny Reb and Blue Johnny?

A BOY'S MEMORIAL DAY.

T. C. HARBAUGH.

The wild rose shed her fragrance deep in Shenandoah's glen,
Where in the years agone was heard the martial tramp of men,
The skies of May were soft and blue, and birds were singing free
On many a drooping alder bush, on many a cedar tree.

A little boy with bright blue eye and youth's elastic tread,
Came tripping down a shaded path with greenleaf overhead.
It was the land's Memorial Day, and fast upon the blue
From shore to shore the flowers fell, as falls the crystal dew.

Beneath an oak's majestic spread he found a lonely grave,
A rotting cedar head-board told where slept some hero brave;
Some comrade true had carved his name and left him to his rest,
Where flowed the Shenandoah 'neath the mountain's lofty crest.

"I know not who is sleeping here," the kneeling urchin said,
"But I will decorate his grave with flowers white and red:
He may have followed Sheridan, who fills this forest tomb,
He may have rode with Jackson, or behind 'Job' Stuart's plume.

"For him no more the bugles blow, no more the camp-fires burn,
And to some waiting sister's heart he never may return;
Perhaps some mother watched for him when homeward came the men,
And none could tell her where he slept in Shenandoah's glen.

"The hands of Love have healed fore'er the crimson wounds of war,
And over all in beauty floats the flag of stripe and star;
With North and South in bonds of peace, we strew alike to-day
The graves of those who fought in blue and those who stood in gray."

He gathered in the forest's core the fairest flowers that grew;
He plucked the rose deep in whose heart still shone the pearly dew;
He took the lily from its bed; from cedar, laurel, pine,
He wove a wreath to decorate that soldier of the line.

He questioned not which cause he served; he was a soldier true,
"A wreath should always crown the brave," said little Jack McGrew;
And tenderly amid the grass he laid his wreath of love,
While overhead on cedared bough cooed soft a gentle dove.

He breathed a prayer, that little boy, and gently rose to go,
He heard the witching murmur of the river in its flow;
It seemed to bear to sunlit lands of beauty far away
The sweet and sacred story of the lad's Memorial Day.

And on the forest-guarded grave a ray of sunlight fell,
It bathed in beauty for awhile the dark and gloomy dell;
No matter what the sleeper wore—a coat of gray or blue—
An angel seemed to kiss the wreath of little Jack McGrew.

GOING INTO ACTION.

POINTS OF DISPUTE REGARDING CHICKAMAUGA.

GEORGE E. DOLTON.[*]

NOTWITHSTANDING nearly one-third of the troops engaged in the battle, on both sides, were placed *hors du combat*, and though the victory was conceded to the Confederates, who said that another such victory would leave them no army, the nation paid little attention to the battle of Chickamauga, hardly considering it worthy to be ranked among the great battles of the war, until within very recent years, when careful, thorough investigation proves that it was one of the bloodiest, if not *the* bloodiest battle of the war, in proportion to the number of troops engaged; that the percentage of loss to the two sides, by death and wounds, was considerably greater than Gettysburg, and that it was the real turning-point in the war when Lee's right-hand man decided that it settled the fate of the Confederacy, and that the result of the war was foretold on that field.

Although the battle covered but two days, it was a battle as of giants. Each side fought with a determination not to be conquered, and though many commands in each day's fight were so situated that the customs of war would have demanded a surrender, they rallied their strength and defeated their apparent victors. The two armies were numerically about equal, and each occupied equally advantageous ground, except on Sunday afternoon the Union troops on Snodgrass Hill were more favored than the Confederates charging upon the same.

But it is not proposed, in this article, to give even a sketch of the battle, but simply to call attention to a very small portion of the field. The battle partly covered about fifteen square miles of territory, while in this we cover only about 1,300 yards in length and less than 200 yards in width.

During the two days' battle, the Confederate loss was some 16,000. Of that number, nearly one-half was sustained in six hours on the short line mentioned. That line is indicated in the

accompanying sketch, extending from the figure 1 to No. 13, on what is known under various titles—Snodgrass, Horseshoe, Battery, Missionary Ridge, etc. But there was hardly sufficient fighting to the left of figure 4 or to the south of figure 12 to merit taking those portions into consideration, thus reducing the line of actual battle to about 900 yards. Within this distance and within six hours, the Confederate loss in killed and wounded was nearly one-half of its total loss of the two days in killed, wounded, and missing.

But still more marvelous, it is contended by many that until late in the afternoon—some official reports giving the hour as late as 3.30—there were no troops of either side west of figure 5, and certainly, until Granger's Reserve Corps of Union troops arrived on the field, there was no fighting to the west of figure 7. Taking the majority of the Confederate reports and many of those of the Union as true, Granger's reserves were engaged not to exceed two and one-half hours. The report of the losses of the regiments under Steedman actually engaged, will indicate somewhat how like bull-dogs both sides must have fought and the amount of blood that must have been shed within the short distance of 500 yards. Assuredly the Confederate losses must have been as great as Steedman's, as the Union forces had the advantage of ground from No. 7 to 10, and the Confederates were the attacking forces. From No. 10 to 11, the Confederates had about as good ground on which to fight as did the Union troops, as the land is almost level and the Union forces were entirely unprotected, no attempt having been made to erect any breastworks or defences of any nature to the right of figure 8. The Union troops from No. 8 to 10, being on a very high prominence of natural great defensive strength, had a decided advantage over their assailants; but almost the whole of the fighting to the right of No. 10 was a square, level, stand-up-and-take-it struggle, and there, truly, Greek met Greek, as is shown by the official reports of Bushrod Johnson and his brigade commanders and colonels and of Steedman and his men for that part of the line.

The only purpose of this article is to call the attention of the survivors of both sides who par-

---

[*] In this article I have studiously avoided making any statement that should wrongly prompt anyone, or in any manner mislead, my sole object being to elicit all possible that is reliable, in order to settle as far as may be the thousands of points of dispute.

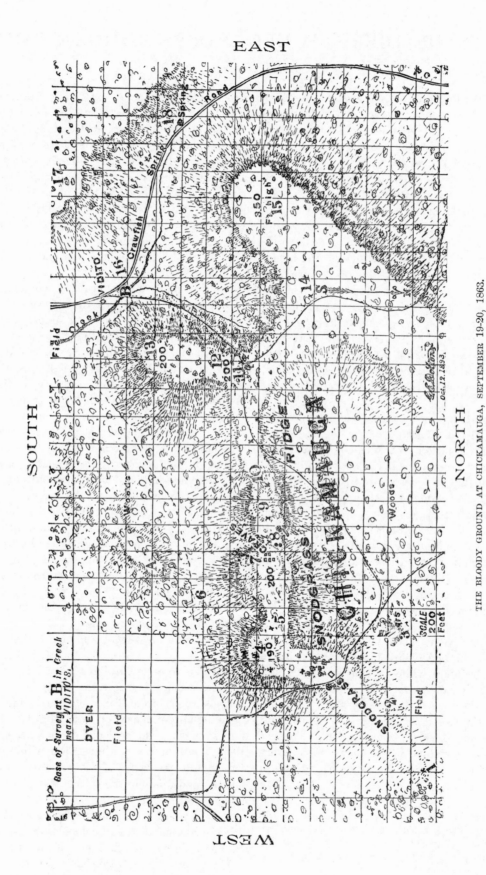

THE BLOODY GROUND AT CHICKAMAUGA, SEPTEMBER 19-20, 1863.

ticipated in the battle at any point covered by the sketch to that part of the field, and to request each and every one to carefully study the sketch, and, if possible, locate on it where he was at all times, showing the direction of his movements, determining as nearly as possible at what hour he was at each point, and what command he was with at the time; also what troops were on his flanks, and what regiment or brigade he was opposed to at each movement; also to note his line of advance to the ridge, and if he left it, by what route and at what hour. It is hoped that each participant who sees this sketch will do that, and then drop a note or postal to the writer, stating to what command he belonged that day, and giving his present address, and saying how many copies of the sketch he would like, and they will be sent him free, on condition that he mark one of them, and give on it all the above information that he can, and as much more as he will,—the more, the better,—and send the same to the writer.

It is not claimed that the sketch is absolutely correct, for the survey from which it is produced was made very hurriedly and under great difficulties; but it is hoped that it is nearly enough correct to enable each one to locate himself.

It is safe to say that there was no other battle of the war in which the troops of both sides were so frequently shifted from place to place, and so sadly confused or thrown into chaotic masses at various times, as Chickamauga; and no other part of that battle, in the faintest, compares with the state of affairs on and to the south side of Snodgrass Ridge, and it is with the hopes of untangling that jumble, that this work was undertaken and has been pursued for several years.

To somewhat assist in helping those there engaged to locate themselves, the following well-established facts are here given:

Beginning at figure 1, the most easterly extremity of Snodgrass Ridge, the 18th Ohio Battery was placed there for a short time in the afternoon. It was also the extreme left of Colonel Harker's brigade after it had fallen back to the ridge, its right resting at the Snodgrass house.

Figure 2 is where General Thomas took his position during much of the afternoon, and where the 18th Ohio Battery lay in reserve.

Figure 3 is where General Thomas had his headquarters the greater part of the day.

Figure 4 is the high prominence to the south of Snodgrass house, and on which the Confeder-

ates frequently charged, sometimes to the very summit.

Figure 5 is a depression in the ridge between Nos. 4 and 7, and down which several Union charges were made.

Figure 6 is near where a Union regiment encountered a Confederate command dressed in a bluish uniform—the first meeting of troops of the two sides after the gap in the Union lines was made to the south near the Brotherton house. It is especially desired to know what Union regiment that was, and what Confederate troops it met.

Figure 7 is the second prominence on the ridge going west from Snodgrass house, and on the top of which were some citizens' graves, well marked at the time and noticed by many.

The Confederates who were on the ridge on the 21st of September and later can doubtless remember what Union commands were represented among the dead and wounded around these graves and to the south of them, and if they can, it is hoped they will state the same.

Figure 8 is a depression between Nos. 7 and 9, and is noted for many incidents of the battle. At the time General Steedman was leading Whitaker's and Mitchell's brigades of the Reserve Corps on to the field,—Mitchell's brigade in the advance and following toward the west about where the wood road is indicated,—there was a body of Confederates, about 100 in number, a little to the east of figure 9, on the crest of the ridge. As Mitchell's brigade was well abreast of these, they fired down on it. The Union infantry that had been marching along at will, on each side of a battery near the middle of the column, immediately formed line and started in a charge up the ridge; but General Steedman, hearing the shots, galloped back and succeeded in halting the line before it was half way up the slope, and moved the column on to the west until the head rested at figure 11. It is important to know to what regiment the Confederates belonged, and to what regiment the flag belonged which General Steedman took at that time in his endeavors to halt the charging line.

The two prominent dots to the left of figure 8, represent two large trees standing close together, and behind which, it is claimed, two Union officers were on horseback at near dusk, one of the officers wearing large goggles. At that time, there was a Union regiment temporarily out of line, lying along the north side of the ridge, its centre being near a tree that inclines to the west at an angle of about 45 degrees, at the edge of the little ravine formed by the depression—the tree being indicated an eighth of an inch below figure 8. It is claimed that the two officers gave an order to the commander of the regiment to move it to the right, and which order being obeyed, delivered the regiment into the hands of the Confederates shortly after. It is very important to determine beyond question who those officers were.

Figure 9 is the third prominence west of Snodgrass house, and is where the Union regiments were captured about dusk. Here it is very important to know how far east the Confederate line extended on the north side of the ridge when it advanced up and received the surrender of the Union regiments.

Figure 10 is where General Steedman rallied a Federal regiment, and, holding its flag, led it up to the crest of the very low portion of the ridge at that point about dusk. It is also where the Confederate column passed over the ridge and moved around to the east in rear of the Union troops, at and near figure 9, whom they captured.

Figure 11 is the extreme right of the Federal line, and where there were three guns of a Union battery belonging to Mitchell's brigade.

Figure 12 is where the 22d Alabama Infantry left its flag.

Figure 13 is the most southerly point claimed to have been reached at any time that afternoon by any Union troops, and they were there but for a few minutes.

Figure 14 is where about 200 Union troops were seen lying on the ground, headed to the south, along the edge of the ridge, having a few stones thrown up in front of them as a protection in case of assault. To what regiment did those troops belong? They were there just at dark.

Figure 15 is the highest point of the ridge and is about 350 feet above the bed of the creek at the road near the Vidito house. At night, Deas' Confederate brigade bivouacked at the spring at figure 18, and posted pickets at figure 15.

Figure 16, on the Crawfish Spring road, is the gap where the Union wagon train, caissons, etc., were captured at the time when General Bushrod Johnson shelled them with one gun placed in the field below or south of the Vidito house. It is also the gap through which General Rosecrans is supposed to have passed on his retreat to Chattanooga.

Figure 17 is the large, long, high ridge to the west of the Crawfish Spring road, over which the right wing of the Federal Army passed when pursued by General Hindman's forces, and where the latter forces halted, and from which place they moved to the east and were placed under General Bushrod Johnson, and engaged later in the charges on Snodgrass Ridge.

A is the ridge to the south of Snodgrass, running down through the Dyer field, and on which the large pile of Federal knapsacks was captured, and to the north end of which the nine Union cannon were captured in the forenoon before Snodgrass Ridge was reached.

It is hoped that these explanations will enable each one there engaged to correctly locate himself on that part of the field; but, should any further information be desired, it will be cheerfully furnished by the writer, if in his power.

With the Evening Star

By Harriet E. McIntosh

IT was twilight; the sun had set, leaving a "golden west," in which clouds, beautiful in ever-changing tints and shapes, painted lovely pictures to the eyes of Lois Strong.

Just above them, in a space of pale-blue, shone the evening star, following its great predecessor, in serene beauty and magnificence.

Every evening Lois walked to the old gate between the lilacs and watched this star. It had become her confidant,—an integral part of her life. So many changes had come to her while Jupiter shone, that with it she felt was entwined her destiny.

At nineteen Lois was utterly unworldly; she had nobly taken the better part in life, in the giving up of an indulgent home to care for her invalid aunt, who was an aged widow. Her life was not one of sunshine, nor her path one of roses, at Edgewood Cottage. She was thrown much upon her own resources, and consequently was very lonely. For one who had no real beauty, she was singularly lovely, with her great gray eyes.

On this night, in her quiet dress, she seemed a Puritan maiden, as she stood at the little gate with her arms crossed upon the upper bar, gazing at this luminous star. It was Jupiter in all his greatest beauty.

"Oh, my star," she whispered, "my beautiful star; my friend, you have come, and are going. I shall miss you sadly until you return; I should love you too much, I fear, if you were with us always. Your sister star will be with us to-morrow, but I shall watch for you, and what you will bring. Shall it be joy or sorrow?"

She watched the changing lights and colors a moment longer, and then, like that glorious planet, passed from view. From her happy dreams she passed to stern reality,—the reality of her solitary life, with an old, irritable invalid. Here she knew nothing of youth; here she lived, brightening the last years of this invalid. Like the sun, she rose at dawn; and like it, sent brightening rays about her; even Aunt Jeanette ("Aunt Hornette" as Lois's brother Dick called her) would occasionally melt under the bright and cheery influence of this young girl.

Jeanette Wild was the only sister of Lois's father; she had been a spoiled and petted beauty in her youth, and, against her parents' wishes, she had linked her young life with that of a young officer, who had loved her with an adoration that proved a stumbling-block to his career; for, just when promotion was about to offer itself, he resigned his commission, and settled down on a small farm. Here four children were born, and their small fortune melted away.

Death at last claimed Herbert Wild, and the three older children soon followed him; thus Jeanette was left in delicate health with one daughter, Gertrude. Mrs. Wild gave her mind and energy to her little farm, and by careful management and judicious investments managed to retrieve her lost fortunes. When Gertrude was eighteen, she married, and the fretful invalid was left alone, save for the servants. Gertrude had married without her mother's consent, and then refused to again enter a home where her husband would not be a welcome guest.

Six months had passed since this marriage, when one morning the following characteristic letter found its way to the hands of Jasper Strong:

EDGEWOOD COTTAGE.

BROTHER JASPER:

My daughter Gertrude has seen fit to take unto herself a husband, who is quite as disagreeable as herself; therefore, by the rule of *simila similibus*, they may become cooing doves in time.

I offered her a home, but she has refused it; I am ill, cross, and lonely; I offer to one of my nieces the pleasant office of companion and lay-daughter to her aunt.

Once she comes, she is to stay; I will have no gadding. I shall expect to provide for her, as for a daughter, when she is with me. She may go home twice a year for a week, and, of course, she can see her family, should they care to visit her. I will have no changing hands; whoever comes stays,—or leaves.

Let my nieces think this enticing proposal well over before a final decision comes. My bark is frequent and loud; but my fangs are not often used, and it would be well that the prospective "she" and I try to pull together.

I shall expect an answer on this day month.

Your sister, JEANETTE WILD.

When the month had nearly passed, and a decision had to be made, all agreed that some one ought to go. Finally Lois said, "Father, I have thought it all over most carefully, and I will go to aunt; I am the youngest, therefore she will not expect me to know so much, and will have more patience with my shortcomings. I have not yet entered society, and therefore will not miss it as much as my sisters would; then, too, aunt thinks that I look a little like Uncle Herbert, and that may make her more lenient to my weaknesses. I will do my best to make her happy, and I will study hard to improve myself."

At first, Mr. Strong would not hear of it; but at last they all were persuaded to her view, that she was the best one to go, and take this trying office upon her.

That night a little note was written, which on its arrival caused Jeanette Wild to laugh to herself, and say, "That girl is clever,—she will do; and I will try not to let her feel my fangs." The letter was as follows:

MY MOST "CROSS" AUNT:

You have drawn so charming a picture of yourself, that it has become a bone of contention in the family as to whom the lot should fall to live with you.

The prospect of hearing you growl, and feeling your fangs, sounds so inviting, that I have persuaded father to let me be the happy mortal. Therefore, on Thursday next, I shall be with you about five P.M. Please have a delightful growl to welcome me.

Seriously, my dear aunt, I do truly intend to go to you, and trust you will have a little patience with my inexperience. Please let me learn to serve you in your own way. One motive that has helped to determine me to this course is, that you see in me a likeness to Uncle Herbert, and I have felt perhaps that would forge a stronger link between you and your affectionate niece,

LOIS STRONG.

Lois kept her word, and amid many ups and downs in her aunt's temper, she had kept her own; she had patiently heard many growls, had

seen the fangs, and almost felt them; yet never in her aunt's presence had she given way. Many tears had been shed in secret, but to the aged woman she had always been thoughtful, gentle, yes, even tender in her manner.

Poor child, how many were her weary hours, how much of her life was spent alone, apart from all that youth loves! Thus it had been that in the twilight she had come to watch for the evening star, as to the coming of a friend.

It happened to have been Jupiter that she first noticed; and in her childlike allegiance she would always watch for this same star; every night, while Jupiter held his sway, she would go to the old gate and watch him. She came to confide all her little woes and pleasures to him, as to a friend.

At the time we see her first she had been three years at Edgewood Cottage; it is the last night of Jupiter's reign, and on the morrow Venus will have taken his place, and each evening, until he comes again, Lois will write a few lines in her little journal, which she calls her "Star's book"; in it she confides in her star, just as she did in the great flashing planet, when he hung resplendent above the horizon.

Jeanette Wild is not all that she has painted herself. Behind the rough exterior with which she has been pleased to try to disguise herself abides a great heart. She has chosen to make trial of this young girl, and has been warmed, in spite of herself, by her unfailing cheerfulness and unselfishness.

She has tried to try Lois's patience, but is not quite sure of success. She has made her read for hours from Baxter's "Saints' Rest," a book she herself did not care for; and Harvey's "Meditations Among the Tombs," which she abhorred, just to try this girl's patience; yet it seemed never to be tried. Only once did there appear a flash on the horizon. Aunt Jeanette wished to name two cows which were to be registered, and as no name could be taken which had previously been entered, Mrs. Wild desired Lois to read the long list to her. Four times had this girl to read the seemingly endless list before anything was settled, and then she took two names suggested by Lois before the reading began. Then the tired girl said hastily, "Oh, aunt, why did you make me read all those names if you intended taking the two I had chosen? I am so tired reading all that for nothing." Then, a moment after, she exclaimed, "Forgive me, aunty; it was not for nothing, for it was to please you. I am sorry I was so rude."

Gradually, in spite of herself, Jeanette Wild was forced to admire and appreciate her niece's character; yet it did not belong to her code of proprieties to let Lois see that she was appreciated. "I will not flatter her, or let her see that she is unusual; it will spoil her," she said to herself.

Time passed, and the days were nearing when the beautiful star was to return. At last the night came, and once again Lois stood beside the gate, and gazed at the star with loving eyes.

"Dear star," she whispered, "you have been so long away. Have you brought any changes into my life? Have you brought any joys to me?" As she looks upward she fails to see an approaching figure, and is startled by a voice, which says, "I beg pardon, but can you tell me if Mrs. Wild still lives here?"

Lois returned to earth with the sound of the full, deep voice, and saw before her a tall, manly form in uniform, a noble face, with large, dark eyes, and a mouth shaded by a long mustache. He stood, hat in hand, and waited for her reply. "I beg pardon," she said; "I did not hear you coming. Mrs. Wild lives here still. Will you walk in? I do not know that she can see you; she rarely sees any one, and never strangers."

"Nevertheless," he said, smiling, "I think she will see me; I am her nephew, Jack Wild, Uncle Herbert's only brother's only son. I have seen two years of service, and have been on sick-leave. I am off again to-night, and have come to see Aunt Jean before I start."

When they reached the door, she went to tell her aunt, while he sat and waited in the old porch.

"Who can she be?" he said; "she is not Gertrude; that much I know. What eyes she has!—they absolutely make her lovely; yet she has no real beauty." He arose, and was leaning against the door, when she returned.

"You were right, Mr. Wild; aunty will see you at once. But I forgot to tell you who I am; I am Lois Strong; like you, I am an only brother's child, but not an only daughter. Father and Aunt Jeanette were only children; but I am only the youngest, and have been with aunt three years now. She needed some one with her when Gertrude married."

As she spoke they entered the old lady's room.

Mrs. Wild suppressed her real feelings, as usual, and exclaimed, "Well, Jack Wild! So you have come at last to see me. Do you ex-

pect me to die suddenly, that you seek me now to say good-bye?"

"Why, Aunt Jean, you know better than that. You know I went directly from the *Alma Mater* to the field of battle, with only a few hours at home. I have come now to see you, and ask your prayers for me while I am away. This time it is to be no child's play. It is to be a man's stern battle for the right and life. See," and the young man knelt reverently before her, "I ask your blessing."

The old lady pauses a moment, repressing a few sharp words, and gently places her hand upon his head, saying, softly and distinctly, "The Lord bless thee, and keep thee in all thy ways."

"Amen!" he responded, quietly.

"Aunt Jean," he said, rising, "I shall be the better for your blessing."

"You should have asked Lois," she said; "her pure heart's prayers are nearer Heaven than mine."

He turned to Lois, and said, softly, "And you—will you not add your blessing also?" and he knelt on one knee before her.

Lois hesitated a moment, and then held her hand out just above his head, and, with uplifted eyes, said, slowly, "Oh, most heavenly Father, guard this our soldier. In Thy good time, and in Thy mercy, lead him safely back to those who love him."

When the young man arose, she still stood with that divine light in her eyes, looking out into the unseen, praying for this brave youth, who was going out to battle.

As she stood thus, Jack Wild gazed upon her, and into his heart crept an image that was to be with him until his life's end; while to her came the realizing sense that something had changed,— that life was in some way different. The fact that she had so solemnly asked God's protection for this stranger, that he might be brought back safely to those who loved him, seemed to bring him into her life, as it were; for this man, for whom she had prayed, could never seem a stranger again, and she would find it hard to realize that he was of her life a thing apart.

Aunt Jeanette brought them both back to the present, yet it was a softened Aunt Jeanette. Lois could hardly realize that it was her voice as she said,—

"Lois, child, are you never coming back to earth? Do not ask that he may have too many wings about his head on the field of battle; it might make him conspicuous. Jack, do you

"SHE STILL STOOD, WITH THAT DIVINE LIGHT IN HER EYES."

feel that you must go to-night? Can you not wait until to-morrow? I have several things I would like to say to you, yet I would not have you neglect duty; only it would please me to see you a little longer."

"Yes, aunt, I will stay gladly. My one necessity is to be in Boston by one o'clock to-morrow; and I shall be glad, also, to see more of you before I go away, perhaps to return no more. I want to explain this sad separation from my family, of which you must, of course, have heard something."

"Lois, child," said Mrs. Wild, "just see that the west room is in order; and in the press you will find some things of your father's, which he left when here last, which Jack may find useful."

As Lois left the room, Mrs. Wild turned to her nephew, and said, "That girl is almost saintly; I have tried her and tested her in every way, and I can in no way disturb her serene exterior. A flushed cheek or a brightened eye are her silent betrayers. I wanted to tell you, nephew, that I have made my will. To-morrow, if I live to see it, Mr. Sergeant brings it to me to sign. In it I have given Lois this house and all that appertains to it, and fifteen hundred a year. To you I have left bonds amounting to about twenty-five thousand dollars. My other legacy is an old pearl pin, that goes to Jasper's wife. I have felt it to be simple justice to do as I have done. Since Lois has given up home, friends, and everything else for my sake, she should be rewarded. I have also made the contingency, that, should Lois die without children, this property goes to her brother Dick. I wanted to tell you this, that you should know my desires, should the Lord see fit to prevent my writing my name to-morrow. Those things do happen sometimes, when we are old."

"My dear aunt, you are most kind to tell me this; and, believe me, I will gladly further your wishes in any way I can. Mother wrote me, while I was at college, of Lois's devotion to you, and I, too, feel that she should have her reward. Just now it was almost the look of a saint that was on her face; it is one of the sweetest faces I have seen. I shall go away with your prayers always in remembrance, and I shall strive to so live that I may be worthy of them. If God spares my life to return to you, I trust it will be with honors to our name. I, too, am glad to be able to tell you something. I wish to truly explain the home matters. You know that I am forever separated from my family. It is the particulars regarding this of which I wish to speak. We have, as you know, a neighbor,—John Thurston,—and he has an only daughter, who is to inherit his millions. It has been his earnest wish, and the desire of my father's life, that I should marry this daughter, and manage this vast estate. Anne Thurston I could never love; and to marry without love to me would be impossible. She is highly educated, has many accomplishments, but has no natural refinement. She is handsome in a bold way, but to me is without attractions,—indeed, almost repellant.

"While I was at college, my father and Mr. Thurston both wrote me, pressing this matter, saying that Anne had always had an affection for the friend of her childhood, and that it would soon ripen into love, if I would only press my suit. I wrote, saying that it could never be; marriage without love was abhorrent; and I would never commit so great a folly, for it would assuredly involve us both in future unhappiness. Other letters passed between us, and the night I came home, after graduating, my father told me that I must go; I had refused to respect his wishes, and had shown no regard for his authority, and I could no longer be his son. He also said that he had placed a certain sum in the Farmers' Bank to my credit, and that after that night I was never again to know them. I passed that night in despoiling my old rooms, burning many things, and packing others; and when seven o'clock came, I had gone, leaving a long letter for my mother. One of the stable hands took my trunk to the depot, and by the night of the next day I had joined a regiment starting for the war. My trunk was left in the charge of the bank officials. I can take but little about with me; a fighting man can have no luggage. If I may, let me think of this spot as home, where you have always been so kind."

"Why, of course, my boy; let Edgewood Cottage be your home. Come when and how you will, only let it be 'coming home.' Now, I am tired with my unusual excitement; go and find Lois, and learn how sweet a companion she is, and how worthy she is of an old woman's love and favor. Good-night, my boy; you have been brave to take the stand you have. It was hard, but it was right, and 'God defends the right.' Surely he will reward you. Now go, and talk to Lois. I am sure you will find something to remember. She always has a way of saying things so that one cannot forget them."

As Jack passed from his aunt's room and down the stairs, he heard a sweet voice singing gently, and saw Lois sitting by herself, in the little porch, in the dusk. She sang very softly, and he paused just inside the door to listen to the words,—

> "Onward, Christian soldiers,
>   Marching as to war,
> With the cross of Jesus
>   Going on before.
>
> Christ, the royal Master,
>   Leads against the foe;
> Forward into battle
>   See His banners go.
>
> Onward, Christian soldiers,
>   Marching as to war,
> With the cross of Jesus
>   Going on before."

"Miss Lois!"

She started on seeing him, and said, "Mr. Wild, I did not know that you were there. I thought myself alone. Will you not join me? It is lovely here now."

"I was coming, but could not resist stopping one moment to hear you sing. You have no idea how sweetly it sounded. Do you know that I shall take that verse with me into battle? I shall never forget those words. The memory of this evening, and the prayers which have been made for me,—all are indelible. May I tell you a few words of myself? I want to tell you why I have now no home but this; Aunt Jean has made it mine also. I displeased my father, and he has disowned me. I am forbidden to enter my old home. I have sought his pardon, but that is only attained by what to me is dishonor; I have written him from 'the front,' on the eve of battle, only to have my letter sent back. Thus it is I have sought Aunt Jeanette's prayers, and I shall need yours, also, if you will give them."

"Oh, Mr. Wild, how sad this is! Is there no way by which you may win your father's forgiveness? Can you in no way take your old place? You are going away to-morrow, it may be to return no more. What will be his feelings if that should be?"

"Miss Lois, I have thought of that, and it has made me very sad; yet he has refused to consider, refused to even read my letter; as I just said, it was returned unopened. I can but submit. When I was sent back, wounded, I had no home; and as soon as I left the hospital, I felt that I must see Aunt Jean before I went again into battle. She is all I have left, unless you will let me count you as a dear friend, who will think of me as a 'Christian soldier,' and pray for a homeless man.''

Lois arose impulsively, and, with falling tears, stretched out her hands, saying, '' I will, indeed I will pray for you, for your safe return, and for your reconciliation with your father.''

Jack took the slender hands, and, holding them, looked into her face with deep emotion. ''I shall remember always,'' he said, three pictures I have seen to-night. First, a slender young girl, leaning on an old gate framed in lilacs; second, this same young girl, with eyes upraised, asking God's blessing on a lonely soldier; and, third, I shall see her again, with bedewed eyes, trying to forge a link between this soldier and the family who have cast him off. Sometimes, in singing that hymn, remember me. Would that I could feel that I was assuredly going out to fame and triumph. I may be gone before the triumph comes, but I shall have helped to gain it.'' He paused a moment, and then released her hands. '' Will you tell me what you were looking at when I came ?''

'' I was looking at my star, the wonderful Jupiter. How wonderful it was to-night! I love it dearly, and look for it every night while it stays. I—but you would laugh if I told you all I feel about it. Some day I may tell you more, but not now. It is the only friend I have here. I think it must be late. I must go. Stay here, however, as long as you wish, only when you come in please bolt the door, and bolt it loudly, too, for Aunt Jeanette is nervous, and likes to hear the bolt slide. If she should be asleep, she will not be disturbed; but if awake, she would be very much so, if she did not hear that sound. You will find the room at the head of the stairs ready for you. Good-night.''

Jack Wild drew out a cigar, and smoked it slowly, looking down the path and out over the old gate at the world beyond. Now and again a smile would come to his lips, as frequently followed by a shadow. At last he said to himself, '' I may never see them again, but I shall strive to win their love by gaining honor and distinction. Well, to-morrow brings my '.marching on to war.' '' Then throwing away his cigar, he arose and went in, and closed the door behind him.

As he does so, Lois, in her little room, takes her little hymnal, and, turning to the hymn 232, with a pencil draws a line about the first verse; then, with a tender flush suffusing her cheeks, she lets her lips rest on the words. She opens her journal, and writes, ''My welcome star, what have you brought us?. Watch over this 'Christian soldier.' He needs our care.'' She closes her little book, and, putting out her light, seeks repose.

Early the next morning she is astir, and in her fresh print dress is a charming little lady to look upon. Breakfast is soon over, and farewells said. Lois dwells upon a few words left in her ear alone. They were simple enough, yet brought a joyous sense of companionship. '' When you look up at your star, remember that I, too, will always watch for it. I shall take it as my guide, and for my motto, ' Ad astra,' for you know ' the stars point heavenward.' Good-bye; God bless you both !''

He was gone, and two forms stood in the doorway, watching his departing figure, with faces wet by falling tears,—one furrowed and lined, whose eyes are dim; whose aged heart is grieved at parting with this loved lad; the other, young and peaceful, whose heart is troubled for his peculiar loneliness. The thought that he may never again see his father, that death may claim him in his youth, strength, and beauty, seems very, very sad. She murmurs to herself, '' Oh, God, be merciful to this, Thy servant; guard him, we beseech Thee.''

Mrs. Wild seemed changed by this visit. She appeared to be.more gentle and more considerate than she had been. '' I have two children now,'' she said; '' my Lois and my Jack.''

'' Three, aunty dear,'' said Lois; '' Gertrude still lives.''

'' No,'' responded Mrs. Wild, sharply; '' she has turned her back on me, and refused to come to me, and she cannot expect me to claim her; nor can you expect me to claim so undutiful a child.''

Their daily talk was of the war, and the thousands of brave men who were fighting for their country. Each day Lois read the papers carefully to her aunt, seeking tidings of Jack's battalion, with fear for him, and earnest desires to hear of his promotion. One day came the news of a great battle, and they read of '' the bravery of Captain John J. Wild, whose heroic and gallant fighting had so influenced his men as to turn the tide of battle at a time when they were much influenced by the general discouragement.''

Weeks lengthened into months, and nothing had been heard from him, save a few shaky-looking words, written evidently by a feeble hand and addressed in another :

CAMP HOSPITAL.

LOVED AUNT AND MISS LOIS :

I have tried to do you credit, and have done a little good, I hope, to my country ; but I was "winged," as the boys say, by a bullet in my left arm, which has given me rather a bad time. I shall follow up the boys little by little, and by the time you get this, I shall be once more at the front. Pray for

Your loving boy,

JACK.

These watchful souls prayed for him nightly, and Lois would often think what change of thought had come with the advent of her star.

"I THOUGHT MYSELF ALONE."

"Oh, star," she wrote one night, "soon you will come again, and then—I hardly dare think what changes may come ere then ; what news may come."

Once again came the news of a great battle, and with it the list of the killed, wounded, and missing—that most awful of all reports ; keeping hearts in torture until fresh news can come. Among the names of this list of missing was that of John J. Wild, of Massachusetts, recently made Major of the —th Massachusetts regiment. For days they searched the papers for tidings ; searched them over and over for just one word which would relieve them of their suspense, but there was none. Weeks came and went, and drifted into months ; they had given up all hope, and with saddened hearts they tried to live their lives as if this man had never been taken within their narrow boundaries. But neither could disguise from the other that something had gone out of their existence.

Once again Jupiter has come, and Lois, in her plain black dress, has crept out to the little gate to see her luminous friend. "My star, you have come to find sad and sorrowing hearts. He bid me watch you still, and promised to watch you also. My soldier, who can no longer ——" Tears rush to her eyes, and she can no longer see. The fair face is hidden in the slim hands, and tears find their way through the little fingers. The more she thinks of the young life that had been taken in its manly strength, the more irrepressible become her sobs.

A hand is laid on her shoulder, and a trembling voice says, softly, "Lois, it is not Aunt Jean !"

With a stifled cry she raises her head, and looks into the face of Jack Wild.

"You," she said ; "you !—then you are not dead, as they said. Oh, I am so glad. I—I—I must tell Aunt Jeanette ; but I must tell her with great care, lest it be too much for her."

He had taken her hand in his, and said, gently, "This dress—what is it for ? I feared for Aunt Jean, when I saw you just now."

"No," said Lois. "I—we—we thought you had been killed—and we have grieved so ; but——"

"Lois, was this for me ?" and he put his hand upon her garment of black. "Could it be that those tears were for one so unworthy of your regret ? Why, child, I had hoped to find you, as I found first, looking at your star ; but when I saw you in this robe of black, I feared that we had met with a great misfortune."

"I had been looking at my star ; and as I looked, I could not help remembering that you had promised to look at it also ; then I thought I can see it ; but (a sob) he can never see it again (a sob) ; but that has passed. Come, sit in the porch while I break the news to aunty." Suddenly she said, "But you are wounded! How careless I am!" and her lips tremble afresh. "Your head and your arm, too. Oh, I am so sorry!"

"Do not worry about them; they are better now, and will soon be well,—at least I hope so. I have come home to be nursed; I feel sure you will cure me."

"I will do my very best; of that you may be sure. But I must tell Aunt Jeanette; it is selfish of me to be so long."

She went in, and quietly entered her aunt's room, put one or two little things in their places; at last she crossed to her aunt's side, and, kneeling by her, she said, softly, "Aunt Jeanette, I have something to tell you. Can you bear good news? There has been some news from the front; some news of the wounded. Aunty, dear, our Jack is alive; but he is wounded." She lays her cheek upon the aged hand. "He is to be allowed to come home to us; is not that brave news? and he will come very soon; he is coming to be cared for by us; so you must be very brave, dear, so that he will be very sure we are glad to see him. Aunty, can you be very brave,—brave enough to control your feelings? He may be here to-night; he must be almost here now—almost at the gate. May I go and look for him, and bring him to you when he comes? Remember he is wounded, and we must take great care of him, and must not let him find us weak and frightened."

"Lois, I thank God that his life has been spared, and that I have lived to see him again. Yes, child, bring him to me when he comes; my brave boy! Lois, let my door stand open, that I may hear his footsteps when he comes."

The girl slipped from the room and went quickly to the porch. "Aunty knows," she said; "her heart is almost breaking with joy and gratitude to God, who has brought you home again. We will go to her."

Together they entered the old woman's room, and he, with his bandaged head and arm, knelt before the old lady. She put both arms about his neck, and rested her cheek upon his forehead, while tears fell fast.

Lois gently closed the door, leaving them together, while she went back to her own favorite seat in the little porch. "Oh, star," she said, "for once you have been almost forgotten; he has come with you; we must care for him and his wounds; we must never forget that God has been with him in the hour of danger." As she mused, he returned to her side, and sat down beside her; he held out his hand, and she placed hers in it.

"Lois, are you glad enough to see me back, and not afraid of the trouble I shall cause you, now that I am such a miserable, semi-helpless fellow? I shall have to ask you to dress my wounds. I have learned to dress myself quite well with one hand; but you would laugh if you could see my contrivances to do so. Do you mind the trouble I shall be?"

"Oh, Mr. Wild, indeed you do not know the pleasure it will be to serve you; we are so grateful that your life has been spared. Please do not hesitate to ask for anything you want. Aunty and I would grieve to feel that you lacked anything."

"Well, Lois, I shall begin at once; first of all, you must call me 'Jack,'—indeed, I cannot be 'Mr. Wild' to you any longer,—and then I shall ask you to refresh my old head, which is very painful. I shall want only a little warm water from you. My valise is in my old room; it came while you were with Aunt Jean. In it you will find, in one end, all I want for head and hand. The doctor put in a lot of bandages; a lotion, with the proper sort of sponge. I'll go up with you and try to save you all the trouble I can."

Lois opened his valise and placed on the table all he needed, and then ran off for some hot water. When she came back, he said, "Lois, you must not mind if it seems an ugly spot, for it is not so bad as it looks. After it is washed, a little lint goes over it, wet with the lotion. You will see how when you take the old bandage off."

With trembling fingers she loosened the pins, and gently removed the bandage; and before her eyes was a deep sabre-cut, extending from the centre of the forehead to the left ear. It had partially healed, yet was very red and angry-looking.

This young girl, who had never seen a wound, caught her breath as she saw it, and her eyes filled with tears. Gently, but firmly, she went to work, and all went well until the end, when, just as she was applying the lotion, he winced sharply and tried to suppress a groan; instinctively she stooped and pressed her lips to the scar, while tears fell from her eyes. However, she quickly recovered herself, and bound up the wound. Then she loosened the sling which supported his arm, and, quickly taking off the bandages from his hand, she saw that the two middle fingers were gone. This proved too much for her, and, sinking on her knees beside him, she burst into tears.

"Lois," said he, "my little friend, do you really care? Are you sorry for me? Little one, I am the better for every tear. I am wounded, it is true, but when I am stronger, I am going to win my general's straps, if I can; dear child, do not cry, but tie up this old hand and keep it out of sight."

"Jack, you are brave, so brave! I am sorry I could not be brave, too. I will try now to make you comfortable; see, my tears are over, and I will not be so weak again. There, is that comfortable? I must learn to do it in the best way, you know."

"Yes, Lois; there is only one thing that it lacks," and he looked up with a mischievous smile; "it would be quite comfortable if treated as kindly as my poor head was just now. You have about cured that; I think that little kiss has made it well. Just now it has no pain, and it certainly has never been so comfortable since I was wounded."

Lois laughed. "Then, if the outer man is comfortable, I think I had better give my mind to the inner man; he must want some curatives also. Come to the porch when you care to, and we will have tea out there."

Going down-stairs, he found a little table on the porch, with a dainty tea, set out for two. "Aunty has been so excited and agitated by your return, she thought it best not to come down again to-night, and will have her tea up-stairs; I am sure that it is best. We will have our tea and toast brought out at once. We have only cold ham to-night, but to-morrow you shall have something more soldierly."

"Lois, do not think that I want anything else; remember I have been on 'short commons,'—hardtack, salt pork, an occasional cup of so-called coffee; but tea, never! So, you see, your buttered toast, fragrant tea, and boiled ham will be a treat, and those peaches should indeed make me content."

They sat laughing and talking over their tea, Lois helping him by cutting up his food for him, and teasing him about being a little boy again.

The meal being over, they walked down to the little gate while the maid removed the tea things, and they stand looking over the country before them.

"Lois, do you know that this lovely, peaceful scene makes me sad when I remember the scenes of desolation I have come from? Yesterday as peaceful and lovely as this, and to-morrow silent in death, and deserted by the living—ruin and destruction everywhere!"

"Jack, I have suffered, too; I have been in the midst of it all, even to the 'front.' You can never realize what it was to see your name among the 'missing,' and then to hear that there was no doubt that you were dead; to try and cheer Aunt Jeanette, to encourage her hopes, when I was hopeless. The dresses we wear were made for your sake. Aunty and I have mourned you deeply, and when you came to the gate I was overcome by the thought that you could not keep your promise about the star; do you remember telling me that you would look for the star also?"

"Indeed I do, Lois. Do you know, I think we must be the very best of friends always, and I shall have to put this friendship to the test for a while. In a short time my hand will be well enough to be freed from bandages, but my head will want longer care. If it troubles you, I will go over to the village and hunt up a doctor, so pray be honest with me."

"Why, Jack, can you doubt me? I shall be so glad to be of use. I am so proud of you that I would not give up to another my privilege of caring for you for any reason other than that they could make you more comfortable than I. To-morrow you will find me with a badge of office, for I believe all surgical nurses wear an apron. Now, sir, as head-nurse of this small hospital, I shall give my first order. You must go to bed early, until your head is better, especially to-night after your railroad journey. I am going to now see if your room is quite ready for you, and then go to Aunt Jeanette's assistance." They walked slowly to the door; there she pauses. "In thirty minutes you must go to bed. Remember you have had a long railway journey, and need rest. Will you obey?"

"Yes, dear little nurse, I will gladly go, for I am weary, and my head does ache more than I like."

Lois looked up with an anxious look, and smiled. "Well, then," holding out her hand, "good-night. Please call me if I can do anything for you; my room is next Aunt Jeanette's."

He took her hand and pressed his lips lingeringly upon it. "Good-night, little Lois; do not look so anxious, or I shall repent having come. I shall be better to-morrow; good-night, little girl."

The days passed very quickly, and the injured hand was at last set at liberty. After two weeks of practice he quite astonished the little household by his dexterity in using it. The wounded head required daily and watchful care; but as it healed he felt reluctant to admit that he would soon be able to start again for the front, and a still greater regret that the time had come when there was a question between inclination and duty,—a question he would not listen to for a moment. New chains were binding him to this place, yet he determined that they should not hold him from duty.

For two more happy weeks he lingered. At last one night they stood together at the old gate, and gazed at Jupiter in all his glory. Her hand rested upon the upper bar, and he placed his upon it. "Lois," he said, "it seems to me that you belong to me. I have twice come and once gone with your star. Will you take me as your star's gift? Will you let me be your 'Christian soldier' to my life's end? Will you once more bless my going and wait my coming?"

"Jack, with the evening star came my one happiness; if it please God, it will come one day to stay with me always. Jack, some day I will show you my star's book. No eyes but mine have ever seen it; then you will know more than I can *tell* even you. Jack, I shall wait for you when you come again, just here, where you first came to me."

He bent his head and kissed her gently, almost reverently. Together they enter the old house, and go up the stairs. At their aunt's door they pause a moment, and he puts his arm around her and kisses her. "That's to give me courage," he said.

"Aunt Jean," said Jack, "I have been in mischief. I—we"—"Yes, we," said Lois—"we," said Jack again—"have found out that we belong to each other, and that we are the happier for having come into each other's lives. Dear aunt, please tell us, if you can, that you do not think that I have violated your trust. We want you to think we have done what is best."

"Aunt Jeanette," said Lois, "forgive me, but I did not know I should be so tempted. I shall never leave you while you want me. I will keep my promise."

Jeanette Wild looked upon them with a smile. "The Lord is good," she said. "He has heard my prayer. I have longed for this, my children, since the first night Jack came to us, nearly two years ago; I have loved him as my own son. I shall die happy with my wishes consummated, and the old house will have a young mistress. I only wish I could see you married before you leave, but I suppose that cannot be."

"I fear not, Aunt Jean; I have but two more days, and I have much to attend to. I have made a long, and such a happy visit to you, that I am repaid for my wounds. Duty now calls me to the front; but may the day soon come when this terrible war will have ceased, and I can return to you to leave no more. I cannot tell you how rejoiced I am that you are pleased by my love for Lois. We will both strive to make your life happy."

"Indeed, Aunt Jean, Jack and I will always stay close to you so long as you may care to have us; we will be still more surely your children then than we have ever been; and"—with a mischievous smile—"I am so glad that you invited me to 'hear your growls, and feel your fangs,' otherwise I should have had no 'soldier laddie' to watch for and nurse."

Mrs. Wild laughed. "You little witch, you have long since cut the lion's claws, and even if I struck, you would not suffer. Now run away, both of you, for I have much to think of."

A little later Jack and Lois are both writing,—he to Lois's father, to ask him for his daughter; and she to her mother, to tell of this new joy which has come into her life.

"Jack, I cannot bear to think that you are going so soon,—only one more day; how much we must make of it. To-morrow we must go to the village and have some tintypes taken; it is the best we can do there, and I want to give you mine, that you may sometimes look at the girl you 'left behind you,' and not fall in love with any one else. I suppose I must give up that last day, as you have business to attend to, but I want every minute that does not belong to the army. I have never had a right to any of your time before, and it is very precious to me."

It was not a very talkative trio who sat in Aunt Jean's room the next evening. The thought of the morrow's parting was with them, and all the sad uncertainty of the future. Jack had purchased a plain gold ring for Lois, and she wore it proudly. "It is my corps badge," she said; "I belong to the Sixth now."

The morning came, all too soon, when these three loving hearts must part. With a force of character which was almost heroic, Lois walked with Jack to the station, and there made her last farewell. "I cannot lose one of the precious minutes," she said, "for who knows when you will return?"

WAR NEWS.

The tears fell fast as she slowly and sadly bent her steps homeward after the last farewell. On the way she purchased a small silver locket and chain, into which, on reaching her own room, she put the little picture of Jack. This she placed around her neck, never to be removed, there hidden from every eye,—the object of her constant prayer. Two days after Jack's departure she received a package enclosing a ring,—a tiny star of minute diamonds, and inside the inscription, "Ad astra."

Months have passed, and news of fresh triumphs for Jack, who has gained a colonelcy. His letters bring great pleasure and comfort to the watchers. Christmas is drawing near, and, though shadowed by Jack's absence, it has its bright side. Aunt Jeanette has invited Lois's sister, Margaret, to spend the holidays with them. The girls have been frequently to Boston, on shopping expeditions for themselves and their aunt. Two happy days were spent in filling a box to send to Jack.

It is now that she tries to execute a little plan of which she has thought much. She writes a letter, which she takes to Boston and posts. It is as follows:

DEAR MR. WILD:

The season of peace is with us, and I am sure it is in your heart to have "good-will unto men." On the birthday of "the Prince of Peace," can we not forget all who have wounded us?

I feel sure you cannot know how near death your only son has been; a little harder blow, and the sabre, which has marked him for life, would have killed him.

My life has been made very happy by his love, and, as your future daughter-in-law, I would beg you to reconsider your stand toward him. Oh, forgive what seems to you so great a fault, and let me convey to him your pardon, that Christmas Day may indeed be to you both a day of peace!

If I seem intrusive, forgive one who would do much for you, who are your son's father.

Very sincerely yours,

LOIS STRONG.

To this she received the following reply:

DEAR MISS STRONG:

Your letter does seem somewhat intrusive, as my son has long been dead to me. I no longer acknowledge him. Therefore I must beg to be excused from any further communications, either from, through, or for him.

Yours truly,

HENRY WILD.

Poor Lois! her little castle had crumbled into dust. She had so hoped to send Jack his father's forgiveness; but now she would never mention this, but bear her disappointment by herself.

Margaret Strong had come like a summer breeze, making great change in the quiet house. All is rippling laughter and music where she is. She would sing for hours, at the piano, the sweet old songs of long ago. In the twilight she sang her sweetest. One night she sang that sweet little English song, "Stars of the Summer Night":

"Stars of the summer night,
    Far in yon azure deeps,
  Hide, hide your golden light,
    She sleeps, my lady sleeps,—sleeps."

Lois, coming in softly, paused at the door; and, as the last words died away, she went to the piano.

"Why, Margie, dear, you should always sing songs like that; they suit your voice. No one can sing ballads as you do; do you know I found myself looking for 'my lady' that last 'she sleeps' was so softly uttered? Margie, I wish you had seen Jack before he went; I want you to know him. It seems strange to think that he is so much to me, and that you do not know him. If I could only know when he can come back—if I could know that he is well. I am worried, yet I know I ought not to expect letters. There can be but small chance of writing, and less of getting letters home; but lately there has been no news of Jack's regiment, and I cannot help being troubled."

The holidays had long since become a thing of the past. Spring appeared, and yet Margaret lingered; her aunt urged her to continue her visit, thinking that it was good for Lois to have her mind diverted.

Margaret had gone home for a few days, and since her return the girls had had many happy days together. Margaret had come to rejoice for Lois at the coming of her letters, and to feel for the deep anxiety caused by their delay.

Spring and summer passed and September came, and at last Margaret felt that she must go. The night before she was to leave, Lois stood at the gate watching her star, which had returned to her, and Margaret sat at the piano singing her sweetest. The refrain came through the open window, and reached Lois's ear; suddenly the words of Tennyson's exquisite song came to her, "Home They Brought Her Warrior Dead." Shuddering she hid her face in her hands, and burst into tears.

Suddenly came the sound of footsteps,—the martial tread of marching men. A thrill passed through her frame as Lois started nervously to her feet. A group of men approached the porch, bearing some heavy burden. Nearer they came, and nearer, with slow and measured step. Lois stood like one in a trance, while the sound of Margaret's pure voice came sweetly on the night.

One of the soldiers, a young officer, came forward, and approached poor Lois.

"I grieve to be the bearer of sad tidings," said he; "but such is my fate. We are bringing home the remains of General Wild. He was severely wounded two weeks ago, and at his earnest desire we were bringing him home. The journey has proved too much for him, and he died this morning on the train."

Lois listened as if turned to stone, and looked at him with unseeing eyes. Suddenly she sees the figure on the stretcher, utters a low cry, and falls upon the prostrate form at her feet.

Just then the sweet voice fell on the ears of the soldiers,—

"Home they brought her warrior dead."

The officer stepped quickly to the window, and, calling Margaret out, explained as best he could what had happened. Jack's body was carried gently to his old room.

"Tell your sister, when you think it best," said the officer to Margaret, "that Jack's last wish was that he should be buried under the lilacs, where he would be near her, and in sight of the star. She will doubtless understand his message. Tell her also, for me, that his general's straps and sword were given him on the field for one of the most gallant actions of the war."

———

Under the lilacs appears a simple white marble stone lying on the grass. It is in the form of a star. In its upper point are the words, "Ad astra," and in its heart, "J. J. W.—A Christian Soldier."

"SHE OPENS HER JOURNAL AND WRITES."

"STONEWALL" JACKSON'S LAST GRAND BLOW.

COL. W. L. GOLDSMITH.

COL. W L. GOLDSMITH.

THE battle of Chancellorsville was the most daring of all the brilliant victories of the Army of Northern Virginia.

When Hooker crossed the Rappahannock, and put himself directly on the left flank of Lee, the situation looked serious; but Jackson, acting under Lee's orders, went at Hooker with such startling vigor, that he pressed him back from the beautiful, open country into the gloomy wilderness around Chancellorsville. This was May 1, 1863. That night our brigade was formed in columns of companies by the right flank and ordered to charge. On account of the dense and almost impenetrable thicket, after moving some distance in this novel manner, amid the "zipping" of the Federals' Minié balls, we were halted, and returned. Next morning, the 2d of May, we started at daybreak to make the ever-memorable flank movement. Our division (A. P. Hill's) was not in the fight that day, but was held in reserve. After dark, our division was brought up, and formed the front line. Our brigade (Thomas's Georgia brigade) occupied the line to the left of the plank-road, looking east toward Chancellorsville. My regiment had formed line of battle, and we were expecting to make a night attack on the enemy, as he was in considerable confu-

sion. Going to the plank-road on some business, I was just in time to catch the full benefit of that fearful cannonade of the Federals, where, it is said, forty pieces of cannon were trained to sweep the plank-road, in order to check the victorious Confederates. Everybody vacated the road, and lay flat on the ground. I did the same; and, while thus "hugging the ground," four litter-bearers, carrying a wounded man, on account of that awful cannonading put the wounded man down so close to me that I could have touched him with my hand. I soon found it was "Stonewall" Jackson. He moaned frequently and piteously. When his friends proposed to move him out of the line of fire of the Federal batteries, he told them "not to mind him, but look out for themselves." When the firing ceased, I returned to my company (K, 14th Georgia regiment, Thomas's brigade), and spoke only to a few officers about what I had seen and heard, for we feared it would dispirit our troops, who loved Jackson so well; but in a very short time everybody knew it. The night attack was abandoned; and, as we lay down within a hundred yards of the enemy's line, I could plainly hear them cutting trees and building breastworks. It was impossible for Jackson's men to sleep that night. Engulfed in the midst of that gloomy thicket, surrounded with so much suffering and death, with the mournful and continuous cry of the plaintive whippoorwill, made the scene inexpressibly sad, and to many the poor night-birds seemed to be piping the funeral notes of the Confederacy's death.

Next morning, the 3d of May, the order came to "charge, and remember Jackson," given, it was said, by General J. E. B. Stuart, who had taken command of Jackson's corps. A. P. Hill was also wounded.

Instead of Jackson's death casting a gloom and damper on the troops, it acted just the opposite. I never saw our soldiers act so much like insane demons; they moved forward utterly regardless of the blinding rain of bullets. The Federals fought with great bravery. My company was the first to gain the breastworks, and I was the second man across them. Here I first saw hand-to-hand fighting. A young Federal soldier came at me with fixed bayonet. With sword in my right hand, I knocked up his musket, and grabbed it with my left hand. The tussle was a fearful one; but George Kelly, a sergeant of Company D, shot and broke the Federal's thigh. The poor fellow fell, but continued to fight game. I could have cleaved his head with my sword, and Kelly started to brain him with his clubbed musket; but I forbade it, and called on my brave enemy to surrender, or I would have him shot, which he did in broken English. He was a German and a brave fellow, and elicited our hearty praise. All this happened in a few seconds, and by this time fifty or a hundred men had crossed the breastworks of logs. These men I placed perpendicular to the works, and enfilading them both ways, which soon caused the Federals to vacate the entire works north of the plank-road. Our brigade reformed, and moved forward some two or three hundred yards, and within sight of the Chancellorsville House, and held that advanced position until the battle ended. This advanced position enabled General J. E. B. Stuart to do the bravest act I ever saw. He led in person several batteries down the plank-road, which was swept with the Federal artillery, and planted his guns on an eminence just to the right of the road, and in advance of our infantry line, just in his rear, and in a very short time after opening his guns the battle was won. Several caissons were blown up as the artillery passed down the road, and men and horses were torn to pieces.

I mention the above to show how quickly the demon can be transformed to an angel of mercy. As soon as the Federals gave way all along their lines, our army stacked arms, and, without a picket or skirmish line in front, gave our active attention to rescuing the poor fellows, whether in blue or gray, who were being burnt to death by the raging forest-fires, caused by the shells of both armies. Many dead and wounded were

burnt to a horrible crisp. Our loss was heavy. Our major, who was wounded and dreadfully burned, died. Captain Harmon, of Company G, was so burned that his friends could hardly recognize him. Captain Munger, with whom I slept that night, was killed. Water was very scarce, and we gave our scanty supply wholly to the wounded of both armies. I gave my canteen of water to a wounded Federal. After all had been cared for, I slaked my raging thirst from a sluggish wet-weather branch, in which lay three Federal corpses; the water was tinged with their blood. All enmity was broken down, and where pandemonium and destruction reigned a short time before, nothing but loving deeds of sweet mercy were now being enacted. Many a "God bless you!" rewarded our almost superhuman efforts to relieve suffering that awful day.

As soon as possible General Lee's army formed on and parallel to the plank-road, looking north, with full intentions to push the enemy, and reap the fruits of our hard-won victory. My regiment was near the burning Chancellorsville House, and General Lee was just behind us, when a courier rode up and handed him a despatch. He quietly and calmly ordered the line to remain where it was, and rode off down the plank-road toward our right. We soon learned that the General Sedgwick's command had broken our lines at Fredericksburg, and were coming up on our right flank. We were thus forced to remain inactive all that and the next day, listening to the fight going on around Salem Church, and which completely blocked our game of pushing Hooker into the river. On the 5th, Hooker recrossed the river, and we returned to camp near Fredericksburg.

Jackson's prompt execution of Lee's orders won the fight, and it was his last great blow for the cause he and his brave soldiers loved so well.

LEAVES FROM A SOLDIER'S DIARY.

RANDOM RECOLLECTIONS OF AN IOWA VOLUNTEER.

WHEN the fabled young artist drew upon his slate a figure, and then inscribed in characters clear and legible the inscription, "This is a Hoss," he surveyed his work with the greatest satisfaction, self-assured that there could now be no mistake as to the identity of the animal. Prompted, perhaps, by the same motive, I wish to say, at the outset, that this effort is "not a history," so there may be no mistaking its identity.

We who were participants in the great struggle of 1861-65, looking back now through the vista of the past, begin to realize that memory is treacherous. Our mental pictures of the realities of that period have lost the lustre of freshness, and we stand face to face with the fact that eventually there will remain but the stern historical truths established by the great conflict.

It is this thought that turns us frequently to the sacredly preserved diary,—that voluminous but unpublished history.

Here we refresh our recollection over the faithful record of the battle, of the march, and all the incidents of the soldier life in camp and field. It is true that history could not record all this. Perhaps it is no part of history to inform succeeding generations, when they go to war, how best to take advantage of given circumstances; how to devise for themselves all those little arts and contrivances which prepare them for the camp and the field and facilitate their efforts to become soldiers and captains.

The many volumes which tell us of the war, its causes and results from diverse standpoints, enlist our attention and interest for their eminence and worth. Horace Greely, after many years of onlooking, was qualified to write "The Great American Conflict." Alexander H. Stephens, from his seat in the Confederate Senate, could well write about the "War between the States." And who was better able to descant upon the "Rise and Fall of the Confederate Government" than Jefferson Davis himself?

History,—learned, able, profound,—all of these; but we find the authors respectively expounding his philosophy in his own way, dilating upon the motives of the actors, or the results of the struggle, according as his preferences directed his predisposition to be fair or otherwise. Yet

it is history; much of it of the "dry-as-dust" school, and but very little of it condescends to recognize the power and potency of the *real* sinews of war, that essential element in the defence of nations, the *private soldier*.

What follows here is essentially an "o'er true tale"; neither history nor fiction; simple war reminiscences, written down, for the most part, from day to day as the events transpired; uneventful it may be, but serving now to reflect the memories of that time when the country was divided against itself, when the legions of the North overran the "Sunny South," and, with fire and sword, laid it waste.

In 1863, the 14th Iowa Regiment of volunteer infantry was in garrison at Cairo, Illinois. It had assisted in the capture of Fort Donelson, and was in the engagement at Shiloh, where it was sadly decimated by capture and death. The survivors were gathered together at St. Louis, where the regiment was reinforced and rearmed for duty. We had been at Cairo several months when orders came to repair to Columbus, Kentucky, with all possible despatch.

General Asboth, the commander of the division, with headquarters there, was an Hungarian, and had seen service in his native country; a very excitable nature, however, and whom the dreaded Forrest sufficed to keep in a perpetual state of shivering apprehension.

Upon our arrival we proceeded immediately to the fort, where we found the little garrison in great uproar and confusion, with the general in the midst of it, the picture of contending apprehension and dismay. Forrest, the noted Confederate chief, was reported as bearing down upon them like a bird of prey. Our arrival was opportune, and sufficed to allay the unrest of the little band holding the fort.

How much our presence added to the sense of security of the old general is left to conjecture. We watched him, however, with amused interest, as he galloped here and there, booted and spurred with clanking sword and reeking steed, from town to fort, and fort to town, then upon a tangent, striking the main road at a dashing pace till halted by the picket a mile away, then back again to the fort, issuing his orders as best he could from the saddle in very broken English.

Our disposition was soon made. It devolved upon us to support the picket line, forming what was termed a grand guard. In this disposition our entire regiment was deployed into squads of six each, forming a line of detached posts in the timber about three-quarters of a mile beyond the main works of the fort, and provisioned for an indefinite period of constant duty.

We were cautious and alert, to be sure, not knowing what moment of the day or night Forrest would announce his approach. Thus, after four days of constant watch and no enemy, our vigilance was somewhat relaxed from the monotony of the situation. The weather was fine and very warm, being mid-summer, but the dense shade of the forest so tempered the sun's rays as to render our position a most enjoyable one, and aside from a certain sense of possible hazard to which we were in a measure exposed, we did, in fact, enjoy the season of retreat. But no matter what the hazard, our position presented such a contrast to the dull routine or barrack life at Cairo, that we were disposed to enjoy it, and so, after some days of undisturbed quiet at our respective posts, some of the more daring entered upon short incursions beyond the lines and to neighboring dwellings within. As events proved, these sallies were unattended with danger, but we were not aware of the fact at that time that neither Forrest nor any of the marauding complements to the Confederate army were in the vicinity or likely to be.

I recall an incident occurring during our grand guard duty at this time which serves to illustrate the chances assumed by the forager in search of plunder.

A very spacious farm-house was situated about a quarter of a mile to the rear of our line, just off the main highway which entered Columbus from the northeast. A comrade suggested a desire for some milk for the mess. Would I go with him in search of it? I would not go beyond the lines, but would go to the farm-house, where I had often been before. He acquiesced and we set out, taking each a vessel for the milk, but leaving our arms behind.

Arriving at the house and stating our wants, two very charming young ladies took it upon themselves to supply us generously, and received our thanks in return. We set out for the line, but had proceeded a short distance only, taking our way leisurely along the dusty road, when we discovered a squad of cavalrymen approaching in a cloud of dust. They were coming on at a smart canter, and from their gray uniforms we took them for a raiding band of guerillas.

Here was a predicament. What should we do? We were certainly seen by them, and our blue coats identified us. To be captured in that country at that time, with the evidence of plunder about us, by a band of guerillas, was a very serious matter. We must act quickly; there was a bare chance for escape.

Our post lay off to the left of the road in a diagonal direction; but, for some distance, skirting the road, there was a dense growth of young trees and underbrush. The latter was not high enough to conceal us standing or walking, but it was so thick and entangled as to almost effectually bar a passage through it. It was our only chance, however. There was no use in attempting to hide in it; we had been seen by the enemy and would be found. Our only hope was to work our way as rapidly as possible through the brush and get into the heavy timber, dodging their bullets, should they take it into their heads to open fire upon us. They never could ride their horses through the brush; we were safe if once we got beyond the range of their rifles. We dashed into the matted brushwood, and then came the exasperating difficulty to make any headway at all. What with watching the steady approach of the enemy, with an occasional glance at our milk as it wasted away from our mad rushes at the tangled undergrowth, and an unlucky fall when it gave way, we were in a sad plight. On came the enemy, while we were making little or no headway. Making a last desperate plunge into the obstinate brush, I fell prone, and lost the little that remained of my milk. Regaining my feet, I looked for the enemy. They had halted in the road and were apparently holding a council of war. I looked for a challenge to surrender at any moment now, and that might come in the nature of a whizzing bullet. My comrade was a short distance in advance of me. I called to him to stop for a conference. I was satisfied that there was no use in trying to evade them, but what should we do? He was at a loss. I suggested that we put on a bold front and make the best of it.

It was not bravery, perhaps, that induced us to halt and face our enemy. It must have been sheer desperation, for we viewed them with mingled dread and alarm. They had now resumed their march and were quite near us; still no summons to surrender, nor any sign of hostility on their part.

We began to reason and to think, when suddenly it occurred to me that this squad of daring Confederates had penetrated within the picket line; yes, even within the very line of our grand guard, and that without provoking a challenge from either. Their halt, in fact, had been at a point very near one of the posts of the grand guard. My comrade suggested, with a smile of hope lighting up his hitherto anxious face, that they might not be of the enemy at all.

Not fully reassured, however, we regarded their approach with some misgiving, notwithstanding they seemed to be wholly unconcerned about us. On they came, up the road, their horses at a walk, until they were within hailing distance. And now I discovered what appeared to be the yellow stripes of the blue uniform and forage cap, both vividly gray, to our perverted vision, with dust from the road.

Now came the long-deferred challenge from the leader: "Hello, boys, how are you making it?"

"Rather discouraging," I answered; "but who are you?"

"Just in from a scout," he answered.

"Looking for Forrest?" I inquired.

"Yes, but he's not about. Don't think he intends to molest you."

We were immensely relieved. The troop resumed their way, and we returned to the road and our post, without the milk with which we set out.

We told our experience at the post, as we felt called upon to account for our torn and tattered condition and spilt milk. It created some diversion at our expense, but we took it in good part as one of the ludicrous phases of a soldier's life, to be borne with tolerance.

———

These humorous incidents of life in the field are numerous, and result from various unforeseen causes. The sterner realities of war, thus interspersed, often make heroes and captains, while they frequently disclose the poltroon and coward. These latter are not always found in the *ranks*, for I remember well a certain captain of our regiment who could not face the enemy at Shiloh. The first volley was sufficient to drive him to the rear, and we saw him no more. This engagement was one of the realities of those times; there was no deception about it, and it required men of nerve to lead, as well as to fight. The following incident serves to illustrate the fighting qualities of those who may be superior in rank to the private soldier:

We were with the expedition under General Sherman, which set out from Vicksburg for a raid across the State of Mississippi. This was a sort of prelude to the "March to the Sea," and was known as the Meridian expedition. We had halted at Marion, preparatory to the return march to Vicksburg. While detained here, a grand foraging party was ordered and organized, consisting of a regiment of men, with the usual complement of officers, and a wagon train. During our march of some two hundred miles, we had been driving General Hood's army before us, and we now began to realize the effect of this double drain upon the country. The supplies for both armies were principally foraged from the neighborhood, so that provisions were scarce, and it became absolutely necessary to resort to effective measures, and in force, to replenish our commissary.

A portion of the 14th Iowa regiment was of the party. The colonel commanding was ordered to proceed as far into the country as, in his judgment, he thought best, and yet return to camp by night-fall, with what provisions he might be able to get on the way. It fell to my lot to be of the party, the first of the kind I had ever attended, and I eagerly seized upon the opportunity to acquire the new experience to be derived from this official foray. Our entire line of march, it is true, had been an official devastation, but our especial party was now about to enter upon a licensed raid, with the understanding that we were to secure, in the provision line, all we could and what we could, regardless of the protests and persuasions of those who were compelled to "stand and deliver."

We set out quite early in the morning, and had proceeded several miles, when the column halted for the purpose of arranging details for active operations.

The position in the column, held by the detail from my regiment, when we came to a halt, was immediately at the intersection of the highway and a narrow road leading off to the right. A short distance down this road could be seen a large railway water-tank.

The colonel directed the major to take the detail from the 14th Iowa regiment and make a detour of the country, rejoining the main column by another intersecting road beyond our present position, but to destroy the water-tank on our way. This, in fact, was the chief object of our detour. Our detail consisted of about thirty enlisted men, a major in command, and the chaplain. We never could understand why the chaplain was detailed for this foray; but then, the chaplain was a soldier, and the moral effect of his presence was no doubt great. We plundered the helpless citizens of that stricken country with a prayerful equanimity, and with an ease of conscience born of the presence and example of this Christian soldier that precluded all compunction.

So the chaplain was the head and front of this extra detail. He rode with the major, and both were on the alert for any raiding bands of the enemy.

Hood's army was known to be in the vicinity; we were, therefore, assuming no little risk in thus detaching ourselves from the main column. In fact, the entire party on this foraging expedition was courting danger. It was a hazardous undertaking, so far from the main army, even for so large a party.

Arrived at the water-tank, we set about getting wood for the fire. A convenient fence furnished an ample supply.

In giving the numerical strength of our force, I had overlooked an essential adjunct of a complete and successful foraging party—the plantation mule and cart. A soldier on the lookout had fallen in with one, and by some means had so completely won his muleship's confidence, that he followed, dragging the cart, with the most passive resignation.

The cart was already taxed to about two-thirds of its capacity with the product of its captor's individual exertion, and this consisted chiefly of that luxury of the march, fine spring chickens.

In a few minutes the pile was ready for the torch. The chaplain claimed and secured the honor of applying it, but none too soon, although the fire caught, and the flames spread rapidly, enveloping the doomed structure—for it was scarcely done when we was startled by an excited cry from the alert major, "Fall in! Fall in!"

We knew what it meant, and so, following the lead of the major, we rallied behind the convenient railway enbankment, where we formed a line of battle.

The cause of the alarm was now apparent. Through the heavy timber to the left of us, some distance away, could be seen a body of cavalrymen, far outnumbering our little party, galloping down upon us. The major was startled too, and without giving another command for five minutes, surveyed nervously the approaching enemy. In a battle we certainly should have come off victorious, notwithstanding their greater number, for we were entrenched, as it were, and were better armed.

That the major was unequal to the emergency, we were satisfied from the beginning, but the fact was clearly manifest when he finally issued his next command:

"Let's run, boys, they're coming!"

Away he rode at dangerous speed, the chaplain following over the ties of the railway track. We deemed it expedient to obey the command, and soon we were all in full flight, each one taxing his energy to rival his fellow in alacrity and desire to prove his subordination.

It was more than a hasty retreat, and worse than a confusion; it was a military display bordering on the ludicrous, and not the least ludicrous part of it was the passive mule, abandoned to his fate by his forager, but following, as if conscious also of the danger. Rattling and bounding over the ties, in imminent danger of falling headlong down the steep embankment, came the mule and laden cart, the latter discharging its load of precious freight in scattering consignments with every lurch of the crazy vehicle.

The mule covered our retreat. Steadily and with wonderful accuracy he kept on his way and the cart on the ties, but gradually losing ground. It was a fruitless undertaking on the part of the mule; he would certainly be taken as a straggler, for the distance was rapidly widening between us, and the enemy more rapidly gaining on him.

Going through a deep cut and around a curve in the track we lost sight of both the mule and the enemy. A short distance beyond the cut we came upon an intersecting road leading in the direction of our main column. Filing into this road we were enabled to slightly increase our speed, but for a short distance only. The major and chaplain were far in advance, when we were startled by the loud tramping of horses' feet immediately in our rear. Realizing that our attempt to escape was futile, we halted as one man, and surveyed our enemy with feelings of wretched concern.

On they came, daring and dust-covered, but seemed as little inclined to aggression as we were to resistance; in fact, they looked upon us with cool indifference, and rode by with the utmost nonchalance.

We took up our march now with feelings of utter amazement, and these were intensified when we saw the major and chaplain exchanging congratulations with the cavalry officers. The cavalrymen rode on, and when the major and chaplain permitted us to overtake them we were informed that we had not been chased by the enemy at all, but by a troop of Federal cavalrymen out in a sort of independent lark of their own.

We said but little about this adventure on our return, on the major's account, but utter secrecy was out of the question. Occasional gibes of the malicious and comments of the less discreet, concerning the fighting qualities of the major, could not be restrained. He came to be known as the "fighting major." The epithet was the personification of irony. The major had not been long with us, and it was said that this was his first experience of the realities of war. From this time he seems to have faded gradually from view. I have no recollection of ever seeing him again. It was an utter vanishing.

Soldiers who have seen much of active service in the field, or on the march, have become familiar with adventures of this class, and while they inspire one with a keen sense of the ludicrous, yet the effect is often beneficial. To be chased by a fancied or real enemy has a tendency to prove the metal that is in us, and they suffice often to convert the coward into a valuable soldier. Perhaps no less often the pompous officer and the blustering high private are revealed in their true colors. At all events, a harmless scare or ludicrous incident of this nature will generally tear asunder the mask, no matter how nicely adjusted or rigidly guarded.

A PRETTY TRAITOR.

Louis Goddu.

AMONG those of the First New York (Lincoln) Cavalry who were captured at the disaster of Winchester, for which General Milroy has been both condemned and commended—commended for having averted a worse disaster—were three men who are now well-known citizens of New York: one a prominent and wealthy newspaper proprietor, of foreign birth, but who was then a very poor young man without vocation; another, a managing editor, who was the accredited correspondent of a large New York daily, and later its managing editor; and the third, now an invalid upholsterer, who was once a rich merchant, and at the time of this narrative was a bold and adventurous sort of jack-of-all-trades.

These three men were, after their capture, taken to Andersonville Prison. I will call them by their first names only—Joseph, George, and Charley, respectively. Many readers will, in the course of this narrative, discover their identity.

Twelve days after entering the prison, they made their escape in a manner which compassed many thrilling incidents, and which rivaled Latude's wonderful attempts to escape during the thirty years' captivity he endured for having dared to love the Pompadour.

Joseph, George, and Charley had been placed within that now famous stockade. Charley one day whispered to his companions that he had made an important discovery. No, it was not a loaf of bread, nor yet a chunk of unspoiled bacon. He had discovered something by which, he said, they could regain their liberty. It was nothing less than a tunnel, which led from a well in the south side of the enclosure to its outward limits, as he, at least, supposed. It began six feet below the mouth of the well, and to reach outside the stockade it must have been at least 150 feet long. When told of this, Joseph and George, being skeptical, asked:

"Charley, have you become demented, poor boy? Well, it is no wonder."

No, he had not. He led them to the spot, and, sure enough, there was the tunnel in the well. Some of the 25,000 prisoners, who had become desperate, had conceived the plan of removing a few stones on the side of the well, and, with half canteens (they having split them in two), took turns at burrowing, worm-like, their way through the sand, which they at first let fall, and later carried into the well. That was the only means of escaping detection. It was not necessary to avoid the observances of their fellow-prisoners; only that of the guards, whose orders were of the strictest character, and who promptly shot any prisoner who attempted to escape.

II.

One dark, rainy night—and they were frequent—Joseph and George, preceded by Charley, who had right of preëmption, so to speak, descended into the well, George holding Charley by the hand, and Joseph, true to his instinct of always being on the safe side, holding George. The tunnel was less than three feet in diameter, and while Charley, who was a lightweight, found no great difficulty in crawling on all fours, his larger companions, who had long legs, did not find it so easy. They repeatedly were on the point of giving up, for to return was out of the question, and they would have perhaps died there had not spunky little Charley suggested that he tow George, and George should tow Joseph. Again the latter had the better end of the bargain—the better end of the line. To this "line," figuratively speaking, he has adhered ever since. Whether he derived his inspiration from this ever-to-be-remembered incident, or whether from natural instinct, he only can tell. Jean Valjean's journey through the sewers of Paris, with Marius in his arms, and sewerage up to his belt, was a pleasure excursion compared to the tedious march, if it can be so called, of these three men fleeing from a slow death, perhaps to meet a speedier one. If it is unpleasant as a reminiscence, the reader can perhaps imagine what it was as a reality.

Finally Charley cried out in his ecstasy:

"Daylight, boys, daylight!"

Bang! bang! came from two of the guards who had heard a voice as if coming from underground, but could not trace it.

It is a strange fact that guards often shot at the first sound they heard, as if, like a snake shaking his rattles, to warn their prey, even though they saw no one.

So Charley had to smother his emotion, and incidentally his companions, who were still in the tunnel, and, as they had not heard the shots, had turned propellers, and were pushing Charley out despite his efforts to remain in the tunnel. As he would go no further, and gave no explanation, for he dared not speak, Joseph suggested to George to prod him with his knife, saying he would do likewise to him (George).

Joseph again at the right end.

Finally Charley, having waited till the guards' footsteps had gradually died out in the distance, told his companions to follow him as he emerged from the tunnel. He did not have to send out cards of invitation.

Softly and stealthily they walked into a thicket, expecting to be shot at every moment, thinking that perhaps the guards had sent some of their companions away to the other end, in order that their footsteps might deceive those who were attempting to escape, and were themselves lying in wait for the fugitives. But they reached the near-by woods in safety.

They traveled at night through the woods at the rate of about ten miles per night. During the day they remained concealed in the bushes. They journeyed for three days and three nights in this fashion. For three days and three nights they had nothing to eat. But hunger was not a novel experience to them.

On the fourth night they came to a negro cabin. Its sole occupant was a young colored woman. Charley, having grown half desperate and three-fourths crazy, opened the door with a kick, and, approaching the wench with his open knife in his hand, which he brandished wildly, exclaimed:

"If you don't give me all you have to eat in the house, I'll make rashons outer ye!"

"Fo' de Lawd, massa, I ain't got nuffin to eat. You, massa, must be crazy," she said, with surprising coolness.

And she burst into the convulsive laughter peculiar to Southern negroes of those days especially. This rather staggered Charley, who forthwith instituted a search for "grub." Under an inverted jug in a corner he found a loaf of corn bread; hidden in the fireplace he discovered a jug of molasses. He confiscated them without legal proceedings, which caused the negress, who was young and rather good-looking, to again burst into laughter. Charley approached and scrutinized her. She instantly stopped and stood stock-still, as though Charley were a Medusa, upon whom she had looked and had suddenly turned to stone. Charley, astonished, turned to go at the behest of the pangs of hunger. He had no sooner crossed the threshold than she had another spasm of laughter, exclaiming:

"Go way, white man! Go way fro' me, now!"

Charley did not know, until told of it by his companions, that that was intended as an invitation to come near her, and he acted upon her injunction literally. Together the three famished men sat under a tree and ate the best meal of their life. The corn bread was a dish a Brillat Savarin had prepared for some royal guest; the molasses, Ambrosian nectar. They reckoned not upon their laxative properties—for the time being. They were famished, and hunger knows but one argument.

The repast finished, Charley returned the jug to the wench and gave her two dollars in greenbacks, telling her she could buy molasses and cornmeal with it, as she did not know that greenbacks were money and had purchasing power. (For a time it looked to many as if such would eventually be the case.)

Charley, contrary to his companions' advice, tarried in the negress's house. It was unfortunate that her mode of saying, "Charley, come to my arms!" had been explained to him. This cost him nine months of imprisonment and nearly his life.

III.

Bloodhounds were set on their trails. The negress had told them this would probably be the case. She offered to shelter all of them, at the risk of being severely punished for it. Charley remained. Joseph and George departed, but they separated. The former reached the Opequan River and later Harper's Ferry, where he rejoined the Federal troops. George's experience was more romantic and eventful. Charley's was very sad.

George heard the bloodhounds and pursuers coming. He knew playing 'possum with bloodhounds was useless. He started on a run, and in a few minutes espied a light. He was now between Scylla and Charybdis. He went to the house wherein he saw the light. He did not knock *at* the door, he knocked the door *in*. There he found a woman of about forty-five and a young lady of twenty or twenty-two. They commented on the fact that he disregarded formalities.

"Ladies," said he, "I have escaped from Andersonville prison. You know what it is, or at least have some faint idea of its horrors. Bloodhounds are pursuing me; if I am recaptured I will be made to suffer worse tortures than ever before. *Do* shelter and conceal me. I have made legitimate warfare upon the South, but I am a man. I have a mother, a sister, such as you. Think of it, if your son or brother were captured by bloodhounds and human enemies, and returned to that terrible place! Ladies, I implore, *do* save me!''

By this time the hounds were at the threshold. The young lady—a pretty brunette, who, I afterward learned, traced her ancestry to the south of France—uttered not a word, but caught George by the arm, and leading him to the back door told him to get into the well, which stood near the door; to lower himself into it in the bucket and hold on to the rope till she rescued him.

As she returned into the house the men and hounds entered it through the front door. The hounds forthwith bounded for the rear door, but were somewhat baffled by the fact that the young lady had returned, thus breaking the trail, and they stood for a moment seemingly confused. The soldiers threatened the women with all sorts of punishment for sheltering a ''Yank.'' But the mother was not the kind of woman to undo the work of her daughter, with whom she lived alone, as her husband and sons were in the Confederate army. The men instituted a thorough search, but to no avail. Finally their leader *ordered* the daughter to get him a drink of fresh water. Her proud spirit rebelled against coercion, but she knew that to hesitate would endanger her *protégé*. So she went to get him a drink of water. Unfortunately there was none in the house. She was in a dilemma. But, prompted by her desire to shield the stranger, and nettled by the *order* of the chief, she took the pail in which drinking water was usually kept, went out through the rear door, which she closed behind her, and, lowering her head down the mouth of the well, whispered to George to cling to the stones on the sides till she had hoisted up the bucket and filled her pail, saying she would lower the bucket immediately thereafter.

George did as bidden, but the stones were slippery, and he presently lost his hold and dropped into the bottom of the well. She heard him fall and uttered a faint cry of terror. Not losing her presence of mind, however, she lowered the bucket forthwith. George swam in the well till the bucket reached him, and again got into it, steadying himself by the ropes.

As water breaks a trail, the hounds, which had vainly attempted to follow the young lady, were now completely at sea, so far as George was concerned. So the pursuers went out and set the hounds on another trail.

George remained at this house till the Federal troops recaptured and retained the place. He was again forced into service and continued to act as correspondent for his paper.

The parting with the two women who had saved him had been very affecting, and he and the young lady had promised to correspond as soon as it was practicable. When he had been gone for a few days the young lady ingenuously but seriously asked:

''Mother, would it be treason to love a 'Yank,' you think?''

''Love a 'Yank,' my child! Why, certainly it would be treason.''

''Well, then, mother, I'm afraid I am becoming a traitor.''

The mother smiled and paid no further attention to her ingenuous but warm-blooded daughter's remark, feeling certain it could never have a sequel. But, as the *denouement* will prove, there was a reversal of the French proverb: ''*L'amour fait beaucoup, mais l'argent fait tout.*'' It was *love* which proved omnipotent.

IV.

George's time expired. He reported to his newspaper in New York. He was sent to New Orleans. He was not now simply war correspondent; he also corresponded with the pretty brunette who had concealed him in a well, to whom he wrote such puns as, ''All is *well* that ends *well*,'' etc. While at New Orleans he was made prisoner. When released he was sent to Texas. He had been unable to correspond regularly with his little Southern friend for some time, being sent from place to place. Three months after Appomattox he was recalled to the office in New York, and told to go back South to take a retrospective view of the situation as it was then. He had been made a major and was proud of his uniform, but preferred not to wear it when sent to write up the South.

George (as will appear later) resolved to eventually make his way to the scene where his fate had for many days been in the hands of a pretty ''rebel,'' and had been decided by her. She had not only saved him many months of imprisonment, but probably preserved his life. All her hatred of ''Yanks'' had gradually melted into, first, forgiveness born of pity, and then real affection. She had been taught to hate ''Yanks,'' but after all they were men, she would say to her mother. Perhaps George was forced into the war, and did not come to kill Southern people of his own accord. And had not her father and brother been making war upon the North, too? There were two sides to the question, her own broad mind permitted her to admit. But was it simply breadth of mind? Was not Cupid shooting darts into her young heart? Indeed, it was besieged by the conquering hero, Love, but she did not fully realize it.

How different this kind of warfare from the one which had just devastated the South and so crippled the North—in which her father and two brothers perished! Warfare between friends! Arbitration should supplant all other kinds.

Jeannette B—— (for that was her name) one day astonished her mother with her charitable reasonings, her forgiving disposition, and her inclination to forgive the "Yank" they had harbored. In fact she thought he was different from what she had been told Yanks were. "Perhaps he was an exception," she would say to her mother.

Mrs. B—— understood her daughter's heart far better than Jeannette did herself. She comprehended the situation. But she was a thoroughbred Confederate, and forthwith determined to put an end to the correspondence between Jeannette and George. She intercepted his letters and destroyed them without reading them. But this not only "aggravated the case," as she would term it, but made her daughter so miserable that she almost resolved to give in. But no, her Southern blood and the memory of the loss of her husband and sons bade her be firm. She finally said to her daughter that she had been told by some one who had seen George in Maryland that he had married a Southern girl there. This Jeannette at first refused to believe, but the mother pursued the conspiracy further and caused the announcement of his marriage to be published in a New York paper, which she said to Jeannette had been sent her.

Then Jeannette was forced to believe. She said nothing. She simply pined away. Her whilom red cheeks paled. Her bright black eyes receded into their sockets and lost much of their lustre. Her gayety gave way to moroseness. From a semi-hoyden she became a misanthrope. Still she uttered not a word of complaint. But she seemed to feel instinctively that her mother was to blame for her disappointment, although she could not explain how.

Ere long her mother began to regret the step she had taken, although she had acted, as she thought, for the welfare of her daughter. She wanted her to marry a pure-blooded Southerner, who had saved much property from the war-

wrought wreck and ruin, as he had interests in the North. Of this, Jeannette would not hear. "Money is potent, but love is omnipotent," was now the way the proverb read.

Her mother's dilemma increased daily, for she could not undo what she had done, and to continue as she had begun meant the wrecking of her daughter's happiness and perhaps the sapping of her very life. What was she to do? She was asking herself that question, almost in despair, when she heard a knock at the door.

Jeannette opened it and George entered.

V.

It is difficult to say whether the daughter or the mother was the more pleased at this sudden and unexpected apparition. If they were both pleased their delight did not spring from the same source.

George found Jeannette much changed in features and manners, but said nothing about it. She was much more reserved than she had been when he remained at their house in seclusion. He could not understand why she should be, after they had improved their acquaintance by a protracted correspondence. He was equally mystified by the affability of Mrs. B——, for she had previously treated him with contemptuous coldness.

After an hour's conversation, in which George related his experience and the object of his new mission, he asked Jeannette to take a stroll in the garden, as he felt that there was much mystery which he would like to elucidate, if possible. Jeannette consented almost mechanically. He offered her his arm, which she declined at first, but afterward accepted. He felt that her reserve was caused by something extraordinary, as it contrasted greatly with her former ingenuous *abandon*—the *abandon* of innocence.

"Miss Jeannette," he began, "there is a mystery here which I would ask you to explain. You are so changed! You are not the same Jeannette who sheltered me from my pursuers, who bade me such an affectionate good-bye. Tell me, Miss Jeannette, what has happened you?"

"Nothing has happened *me*," replied the loving but proud Southern maiden.

"Why have you not answered my last letters?"

"I have answered all the letters I have received from you."

"You did not reply to the last three I wrote you."

"Yes, I did. Did you not receive an answer to your letter of June 13th?"

"Yes, but I wrote you three more after that."

"I did not receive them."

A horrible thought had flashed to her mind. She knew her mother's opposition to George's attentions as expressed in his letters, which she, like the pure, innocent child she was, had shown to her mother. She began to suspect her mother of having intercepted them. But no, she could not suspect her own mother, who had always been so good, so loyal, of such base treachery. Besides, had she not seen the announcement of George's marriage in a New York newspaper which she supposed he had sent?

"I cannot understand that," said George. "In my last I informed you that I was coming South again, and that, although my presence in this house was foreign to my professional mission, I would certainly pay you a visit. I was also telling you what my intentions were in coming here—the real object of my coming to Winchester."

"I never received such a letter," replied Jeannette, whose excitement grew as he spoke.

"But since I did not receive your letter," she continued, after a pause, "will you not tell me what its contents were—what the unprofessional object of your mission to Winchester was? Was it mere curiosity to see how a trusting, deceived girl looked—how she withstood deception? If so, sir, you had better make haste and depart."

"Jeannette, why speak you thus to the man who loves you above all other women on earth? Could you think me so base as to be able to deceive a girl who has befriended me as you have, when you could have cast me into the jaws of the hounds and the hands of my enemies?"

"I was very much surprised, but——"

She did not finish the sentence, for he interrupted her.

"Jeannette, there has been treachery here. Some one has intercepted my letters, and there is a dark plot behind it. I am incapable of deceiving anyone, far less you, dear Jeannette."

And he bent to kiss her hand, which he almost forcibly held in his own. She withdrew it quickly and told him he had no right to do so and she would not permit it. Then she suddenly turned and said:

"I asked you to tell me the real object of your visit to this house. If you care to tell me, do so now, or else let us part once more, and this time forever."

Seeing it was time matters were brought to a crisis, he said:

"I came here, Jeannette, with the intention of marrying a Southern girl, if she would have me."

"What do you mean, sir, by telling me such a thing, you who have already married a South——?"

"I mean, Jeannette," he interrupted again, heedless of what she had begun to say, "that I came here to ask you if you would marry me?"

She shrank from him.

"Oh, I am well aware of the objection your mother would have to your marrying a 'Yank,' but love, Jeannette, knows no Mason and Dixon's line. Besides, the war is over. A treaty of peace has been signed. The North and the South have made up. Why should you remain disloyal to the Union? Why should your mother oppose our union?" he said, half smiling.

"But you *are* married!" she exclaimed.

"I married? That is news, indeed. I think, however, if such an event had taken place I should know something about it."

"But I have seen the announcement of your marriage to a Maryland girl in a New York paper!"

He thought she was joking and taunting him, and he only laughed for reply.

"I have the clipping of such an announcement right here," she said, as she drew it from her bosom.

George began to look serious. He took the clipping and sure enough he read the announcement of his marriage.

"It is the base fabrication of some enemy!" he exclaimed.

"Then you are not married?"

"Certainly not, but I will be as soon as you say the word," he replied.

"Oh, heaven!" she exclaimed, and then swooned.

He carried her tenderly in his arms into the house. Mrs. B—— was frantic on seeing her daughter in such a state and began to upbraid George for being the cause of it.

"Do not blame him, blame yourself, mother," said Jeannette, as she revived. "*You*, mother, are the cause of it. *You* are the one who deceived me! *You* have brought me to the verge of insanity and the grave—*you*, my mother," cried Jeannette, the lamb having become a lioness, almost a tigress. "I *do* love this 'Yank,' as you persist in calling him, and I *will* marry him in spite of all your ill-guided opposition. If that is treason, make the most of it."

"My child, forgive me, as I have for your sake forgiven this man, this 'Yank.' It was all for your own good. But now I see my error and I will consent to your marrying the man of your choice if you will forgive me."

"Only a mother could be forgiven such an act," said Jeannette, after a pause. "And now that I am about to be made happy, I *will* forgive you, mother," she said, as she extended one hand to Mrs. B——— and the other to George.

VI.

They were married two days later. They went to New York, where they have lived ever since in happiness, and they seem to love each other to-day as much as on the day of their marriage. George has held the position of managing editor of three first-class dailies, and is in good circumstances, well known by many, and well liked by all.

Joseph went West. He also became a journalist. He bought a decadent paper in a Western city, made a great success of it, then removed to New York, where he bought another tottering newspaper, which has since made him a millionaire. This being a true story, he is included in this narrative, not because he was a necessary character to a drama, but because of the faithfulness of the narrator.

Charley, as previously stated, followed many callings. In 1868 he established a large wholesale furniture house in the Bowery. He failed, and to-day he ekes out a precarious existence as an upholsterer in a small frame house on West 127th Street.

THE SWORDS OF GRANT AND LEE

T. C. Harbaugh

"Fame hath crowned with laurel
The swords of Grant and Lee."

Methinks to-night I catch a gleam of steel among the pines,
And yonder by the lilied stream repose the foemen's lines;
The ghostly guards who pace the ground a moment stop to see
If all is safe and still around the tents of Grant and Lee.

'Tis but a dream; no armies camp where once their bay'nets shone;
And Hesper's calm and lovely lamp shines on the dead alone;
A cricket chirps on yonder rise beneath a cedar tree
Where glinted 'neath the summer skies the swords of Grant and Lee.

Forever sheathed those famous blades that led the eager van!
They shine no more among the glades that fringe the Rapidan;
To-day their battle work is done, go draw them forth and see
That not a stain appears upon the swords of Grant and Lee.

The gallant men who saw them flash in comradeship to-day
Recall the wild, impetuous dash of val'rous blue and gray;
And 'neath the flag that proudly waves above a Nation free,
They oft recall the missing braves who fought with Grant and Lee.

They sleep among the tender grass, they slumber 'neath the pines,
They're camping in the mountain pass where crouched the serried lines;
They rest where loud the tempests blow, destructive in their glee—
The men who followed long ago the swords of Grant and Lee.

Their graves are lying side by side where once they met as foes,
And where they in the wildwood died springs up a blood-red rose;
O'er them the bee on golden wing doth flit, and in yon tree
A gentle robin seems to sing to them of Grant and Lee.

To-day no strifes of sections rise, to-day no shadows fall
Upon our land, and 'neath the skies one flag waves over all;
The Blue and Gray as comrades stand, as comrades bend the knee,
And ask God's blessings on the land that gave us Grant and Lee.

So long as Southward, wide and clear, Potomac's river runs,
Their deeds will live because they were Columbia's hero sons;
So long as bend the Northern pines, and blooms the orange tree,
The swords will shine that led the lines of valiant Grant and Lee.

———

Methinks I hear a bugle blow, methinks I hear a drum;
And there, with martial step and slow, two ghostly armies come;
They are the men who met as foes, for 'tis the dead I see,
And side by side in peace repose the swords of Grant and Lee.

Above them let OLD GLORY wave, and let each deathless star
Forever shine upon the brave who led the ranks of war;
Their fame resounds from coast to coast, from mountain top to sea;
No other land than ours can boast the swords of Grant and Lee!

THE OLD LOG CABIN ON THE RAPIDAN.

WALKER Y. PAGE.

THERE is no truth more obvious or capable of demonstration than that, if the vexed questions which from time to time arise, involving the rights, the honor, and the dignity of nations, and oftentimes opposite sections of the same nation, culminating eventually in national and sectional strife, and entailing miseries beyond the reach of history to depict, were submitted to the adjudication of those (the soldiers) who brave the dangers and bear the heat and burden of the fray, "grim-visaged war," with his attendant train of national, physical, and moral evils, would forever "smooth his wrinkled front," and peace—perpetual peace—would reign supreme,—the glorious exponent of an advanced and perfected civilization.

It is only those—the *stay-at-homes*—to whose delicate nostrils the smell of powder would be an offence, and the clash of contending arms a vulgar horror, who are willing to stir up strife and send soldiers to the field of battle, while they themselves occupy the soft and safe and lucrative places far out of reach of shot and shell.

It is the poor soldier alone, who spends his days amid scenes of carnage and death, and his nights in tantalizing visions of home and family and fireside, under the cold canopy of heaven, and wakes to bear again the brunt of battle, and either lays down his life upon the bloody field, or is carried back to his home the maimed and worthless remnant of his former self, who can really appreciate what war is, and who feels that if the *casus belli* had been submitted to him and his comrades in arms for settlement, the millions of money (much of which has found its way into the pockets of those same non-combatants) and the ocean of brothers' blood which cries to heaven, and seeks for retribution somewhere and somehow, might have been saved to the honor of our common manhood and brotherhood, and the glory of our common country.

The foregoing remarks were suggested by a conversation held with a friend upon the conduct and outcome of our late civil war, its far-reaching effects, and its influence, wise or otherwise, upon our republican institutions, and their ability to maintain and perpetuate the experiment of free government.

My friend, who is now a minister of the gospel, but who, during the war, was Lieutenant G——, of the Federal army, is one who recognizes the fact that the war ended thirty years ago, and who now finds congenial companionship among those who then stood upon the opposite side of the fence; is literally a man of peace, who not only preaches peace, but exemplifies it in his life, remarking, in a recent conversation upon what he considered *real peace* contrasted with its "counterfeit presentment,"—

"I want to emphasize what I said about the soldiery and their feelings toward the war and toward each other (I mean, of course, the soldiers of both sections), and, by way of illustration, let me narrate one of the many little incidents of the war bearing upon the subject of our conversation, all of which I saw, *et quorum pars fui,* and I mention it to show that as between the soldier of the 'blue' and the soldier of the 'gray' no bitterness existed, even while duty called upon them to cut each other's throats in battle.

"It was in the winter of 1863-64, when the Union and Confederate armies were encamped opposite each other, and not more than a mile apart, upon the banks of the Rapidan, in the State of Virginia,—we, of the Federal army, under the command of General U. S. Grant, and the Confederates under the command of General Robert E. Lee. The particular division to which I belonged was commanded by that rough-hewn, but brave and kind old soldier, General Alexander H——. The immediate situation would probably be better designated as 'Dumpling Mountain.'

"As I have before stated, the picket lines of the two armies were not more than a mile apart; and whether it came of the strict surveillance of their officers, or from that feeling of comradeship so characteristic of soldiers even of opposite and contending armies, true it was that our winter-quarters were seldom disturbed by the interchange of compliments in the shape of powder and ball between the two picket lines.

"One evening, when I was in charge of a portion of the Federal lines, I noticed, just at dusk, fifteen or twenty 'Johnny Rebs,' without muskets, coming down the hill some distance beyond their lines. Of course, I and my command were

507

at once upon the *qui vive* to find out what was up.

"As they were unarmed, I concluded they were upon no hostile mission, and contented myself with watching their movements closely. They were evidently thus far beyond their lines for a purpose, and that purpose I determined then and there to discover.

" Following cautiously in their rear with my men, I soon found out whither their steps were tending. In the distance stood an old deserted and partially dilapidated negro cabin, and to this they were evidently directing their steps.

" By some subtle intuition, hard to be explained, I found myself arriving at conclusions not the result of the reasoning process, but which, nevertheless, were a forecast of the truth.

" I said to myself, these fellows are surely Methodist boys, and they are going to that old cabin, bent on having an old-fashioned Methodist prayer-meeting, secure from the gibes and jeers of their impious comrades. They are foolish enough to think that in leaving their muskets behind them they have not violated any of the rules of warfare, and are therefore safe from molestation even from an enemy.

" I knew full well that all such reasoning was fallacious, but, having in vivid remembrance the prayer-meetings of my early youth, where I was wont to kneel beside my father and mother at the same altar, and from whose sacred precincts I had gone out into the world of conflict, danger, and death, with their ever-to-be-remembered blessings upon my head and in my heart, I resolved to reconnoitre, and if it was as I supposed (being a Methodist myself), I determined not only to protect them in their devotions, but to share in their exercises myself.

" Taking fifteen of my men with me, fully armed, we started slowly toward the log cabin. Coming within twenty rods of it, I stopped to listen, and sure enough the words of that dear old hymn, ' Jesus, lover of my soul,' came clear and sweet upon the crisp night air, sung, as though their hearts responded to every line, by those Confederate boys. I at once ordered my men back to the Federal line, and taking one Christian young man with me, walked boldly up to the cabin.

" Greatly to my astonishment, I found that they had not so much as a single guard on duty. Ordering my man to stand his musket against a tree that stood near the door, and unbuckling my own side-arms and throwing them on the ground beside the musket, we marched *sans ceremonie* into their midst.

" Imagine, if you can, the surprise of those Confederate soldiers when they realized that there were Union soldiers in their very midst. Nevertheless they greeted us kindly, and, after a suggestion by one of them that our arms might be stolen if left outside, he went out and brought them in, after which the exercises of the meeting were resumed, as though nothing had occurred to interrupt them.

" At the close of the meeting, I explained to the boys, after I had told them how much I had enjoyed it, what a dangerous thing they were doing in coming so far beyond their lines, and that the fact of their leaving their arms behind them was no protection to them, and did not in the least alter the case.

" I told them that though we were fighting on opposite sides, God was the God and Father of us all, and would listen to our united petitions in that log cabin just as surely as from any cathedral upon earth ; that I was with them heart and soul in their devotions, which had done me much good, but that I would advise them to discontinue their meetings, unless they had some assurance that they could hold them unmolested, to which end I promised them to see General H—— the next morning, and get his permission for them to hold their meetings in the old log cabin throughout the winter and ensuing spring.

" General H—— was, as I have before said, a rough man, an exceedingly rough man, to those who did not know that the rough phases of his character were all on the surface ; and besides being a hard swearer, yet at heart he was one of the kindest men I ever knew. I was rather doubtful as to the result of my mission in behalf of the log-cabin worshippers, notwithstanding my knowledge and belief in his genuine kindness of heart. I conjectured it might be giving him credit for more than his due to suppose that he cared a grot for religious meetings of any kind. However, I was resolved to try, as at the worst I could only get a cynical reprimand.

" I visited him in his tent the next morning, and no sooner had I begun to speak of the prayer-meetings that were being held by the ' Johnny Rebs' at the old log cabin, than he interrupted me in his rough and quasi-sarcastic manner, by saying, ' And you were there, were you not ? I never knew a prayer-meeting to be around without your making an infernal fool of yourself,' etc., etc. Then he asked, 'Did they pray for me?' 'I think they did, general,' I replied; 'for, while praying for sinners in general, they put up special petitions for the *greatest sinner who wore a uniform.*'

"'All right,' responded General H——. 'You tell those fellows, blast 'em, that they can hold prayer-meetings there every night in the week if they want to.' And he was as good as his word, for he forthwith issued an order to be given to every officer who, in turn, should have charge of that portion of the line, which order was to the effect that they, the 'rebs,' should remain undisturbed while holding religious services in said log cabin, and he who violated it would catch ballyhoo.

"I myself had never again the pleasure of meeting those 'boys in gray' at their regular Thursday evening meetings, but many were the 'boys in blue,' officers and men, of the Federal line, who, from time to time, joined in their devotions, and doubtless participated in those promised blessings which come assuredly to 'them that fear the Lord.'

"It needs no casuist to tell us how it was, that on that bleak and wintry field, between two mighty and hostile armies, the name of Him who is the 'Prince of Peace' should have the power to still the passions of men inured to scenes of blood and carnage, and bring to those poor war-worn soldiers that peace which passeth all understanding, keeping and sustaining their hearts and minds even amid all the horrors of a bloody and fratricidal strife.''

My reverend soldier friend had finished his story of the log cabin; but, after a moment or two of silence, a silence upon which I hesitated to intrude, as he appeared to be in deep thought, suddenly he resumed. "I am disgusted," he said, in rather a nervous and impetuous manner; "I am thoroughly disgusted with the incessant cry of *peace, peace,* when there is no real peace.

"Can there be genuine peace while sectional hate, like a poisoned barb, is rankling in the hearts of each? Those men who so loudly maintain that we have peace mistake the cessation of hostilities for that peace which should have come, *and was intended to come,* at Appomattox. True, we have 'shaken hands across the bloody chasm'; and, with the soldiers, I am proud to assert, their *hearts* were in their *hands;* but there is no disguising the fact that there are those (and I fear their name is legion) who, though the war ended thirty years ago, are still harping upon its issues, either in boast of victory or chagrin of defeat, and 'cut such fantastic tricks before high heaven as make the angels weep.' "

No! I fought through the war, and bear upon my person honorable wounds received in defence of my country, and now I invoke real, abiding, perpetual peace for my reunited country, and not that heartless mockery of peace which is paraded every day before my eyes.

I have thought long and earnestly, and, I may add, prayerfully, upon this subject, and now I will outline to you my plan for an ever-enduring peace, which has grown to a conviction, that it is *the* thing, and the only thing, that can reach alike the Northern and the Southern heart.

It is this:

Let the soldiers of the North erect a monument to General Lee. Let the soldiers of the South erect a monument to General Grant.

Let these monuments lift their pinnacles toward heaven, as pointing to that throne where everlasting peace abides. Let them be erected at the nation's capital, or some midway point between North and South, with an entablature on each representing "Peace personified," with this simple inscription, "*Esto perpetua,*" and upon the plinth of one and the other inscribed, "Erected by the soldiers of the North to General Lee," and "Erected by the soldiers of the South to General Grant."

Then we shall indeed have peace as lasting as those monuments, as we shall have wrought in imperishable marble the grand idea of him who said, "Let us have peace!" for in all time to come no American could ever gaze upon those monuments and dream of civil war.

IN THE RANKS UNDER GENERAL LYON IN MISSOURI—1861.

THE OBSERVATIONS OF A PRIVATE SOLDIER.

EARLY in the month of June, 1861, a detachment of recruits, myself among the number, arrived at Fort Leavenworth, where we expected to find transportation and supplies for crossing the plains to New Mexico. We had been assigned to the 2nd Dragoons and 1st Cavalry, United States Army, which are now known respectively as the 2nd and 4th Regiments of Cavalry. We had not been at Leavenworth more than three days when we were suddenly marched on board a steamboat and sent down the river to Kansas City, then an enterprising place of 5,000 inhabitants. Upon leaving the steamboat we were directed to camp in the centre of a grove of magnificent trees of many varieties. The spot overlooked the muddy Missouri River, and excellent springs were everywhere at hand.

Information was now received that, instead of going to New Mexico, mounted on fine horses, we were destined to spend the summer on foot in an active and possibly bloody campaign in Missouri, whose citizens were greatly agitated upon the subject of secession, while many of them had already been enrolled under the banners of the new Confederacy. This intelligence caused great joy among us, and our commanding officer was censured by the men for not beating up the camps of the enemy at once, for enthusiasm among young soldiers is hard to restrain until they come out of their first engagement. Our company was now merged with Plummer's Battalion of the 1st United States

GENERAL S. D. STURGIS, U. S. A.

Infantry, and had for our commander Lieutenant Henry C. Wood, a native of Maine, who subsequently attained high rank in the Adjutant-General's Department.

Our stay of two weeks in this place was employed in constant drilling and target practice. In this latter exercise, in addition to individual firing, we were required to fire by volley, and were then marched up to the target to observe the effect of our skill. It was customary for the officer in command to point out a conspicuous tree or rock and request each man to guess its distance from the spot we occupied. A careful measurement was then made, and those who had displayed the best judgment received compliments, and some were made sergeants or corporals. Indeed, excellence in any direction was speedily rewarded by these appointments, and almost as speedily revoked; for, in a body of men, few of whom had been more than two months in the service, but who were commanded by veteran officers, promotions and reductions were numerous enough.

About the middle of the month the suburbs of the town were enlivened by the arrival of the 1st and 2nd Regiments of Kansas Infantry, and several companies of regular Cavalry; and four brass cannon were soon added to the force. The battery was placed under the command of John V. Dubois, a young officer who had served in the Mounted Rifles, but who now took a fancy to the noise and smoke of artillery.

510

Captain Washington L. Elliott was acting in-spector-general of this force while here and his authority was felt as if it had been a physical burden. Those who were disposed to act up to the regulations found it an easy matter to get along with him, but he demanded of each sol-dier the full measure of his obligations to the government, and every infraction of discipline was met by instant punishment, which, though not cruel, was sure to be remembered. His favorite method of curing disobedient soldiers was to make them walk round a ring about sixty feet in circumference, each man carrying a knapsack filled with stones. The walk was enforced during an entire day or night, unless interrupted by sudden orders to march. To break up whiskey drinking kept him well em-ployed, but to little purpose. He succeeded in driving away a horde of peddlers who had in-fested the ground, but not before they had car-ried off most of the surplus clothing of the men; and drunkenness being still undiminished, he personally searched the pickets upon their return to camp, until he found that liquor had been constantly carried by them in their musket-barrels. As he did not discover this trick until the morning of our departure for the southwest, no punishment was inflicted. Elliott declared this to be the cleverest performance of the kind he had heard of in the army, and that it had not been excelled at West Point.

The troops collecting at Kansas City were formed into a temporary brigade, and were com-manded by Major Samuel D. Sturgis, of the 1st United States Cavalry, who, by the courtesy of Colonels Mitchell and Dietzler, of the Kansas Regiments, was allowed to rank them, although both were qualified by experience for their com-mands.

We had no means of finding out where this expedition was to strike, but the newspapers gave it out that our ultimate destination was Arkansas, and that for the present we might be called on to support General Lyon, who was at this time operating against the forces of Clai-borne F. Jackson, Governor of the State, who had been driven from his capital and was in flight to the Arkansas border.

Before leaving our present quarters for good we made a night march to Liberty, and another to Independence, where armed bands of seces-sionists were assembled. The enemy fled at our approach on each occasion, and though we accomplished nothing, these movements gave us an idea of the manner in which troops advance

to attack, besides furnishing other impressions of value to soldiers which could not be obtained except through experience. The number of fires in the deserted camp indicated to some extent the strength of the enemy, and from the condi-tion of the burning embers could be estimated how long the camp had been abandoned, and consequently the distance of the fugitives from the locality.

At length on the 24th of June, Sturgis set out. A long line of canvas-covered wagons, each drawn by six fat mules, seasoned to service and

GENERAL NATHANIEL LYON, U. S. A.

conducted by experienced wagon masters and drivers, carried food for thirty days and a sup-ply of ammunition for an extended campaign. In the absence of most of the able-bodied men of the town—who appeared to have cast their fortunes with the opposing side—we were cheered by crowds of boys and girls who lined the streets and roads. We reached Westport in the afternoon, and as this was the first hostile force which had appeared in the place, the side-walks were crowded with people and the win-dows of the dwellings were adorned with many handsome faces. But it was easy to observe by their conduct that they would have been better pleased to see us march in any direction but the south.

We accomplished twenty miles during the first day and camped near running water. The command moved along at this agreeable rate until the 2d of July, when it reached Clinton, the chief town of Henry County. Here we were obliged to remain several days, for the river was flooded to such an extent as to be utterly impassable, and the bridges had been burned by the enemy.

Independence Day was celebrated in the usual military style. The troops were paraded and the battery fired a salute—a shot for each of the States of the Union, the States at war with us being included. Those of the men who could obtain apple-jack kept up the celebration in a private manner. But much of the supply of the this beverage was cut off early in the day. A lieutenant with a squad of cavalry had been detailed to scour the town and close up every place where intoxicating liquors could be had; and so energetic were the efforts of the officer in this matter that, while making his report to the commanding officer, he fell to the ground through exhaustion.

While waiting for the river to subside, a general court-martial was held for the trial of soldiers for marauding. It was known as a drum-head court-martial, and the fate of the men was anticipated throughout the camp before the court assembled. There was no evidence produced to show that goods of value had been stolen; the circumstance that the property of citizens had been found in possession of the men was deemed sufficient to convict. On the afternoon of the 6th the sentences of the court were carried out. Five men, belonging to different organizations, were stripped to their waists and marched to a caisson placed near the centre of the troops on parade. They were then called up, one at a time, their hands tied to one of the wheels, and after receiving fifty lashes, well laid on, were drummed out of the service in a body. The acting assistant adjutant-general of the command, who subsequently became a major-general, superintended this business. His voice could be heard all along the line, calling out to the bugler to lay on the lash harder and harder. The citizens of Clinton showed surprise and horror at this extraordinary scene. They took the unfortunate men in charge, and after supplying their wants, had four of them enlisted in a regiment then forming in the interest of the Union. The fifth man procured a horse, joined the staff of General Lyon, served as a scout, and perished at the battle of Wilson's Creek.

Had these men been convicted of such an offence at a later period of the war, among soldiers who had long been associated together, they would have been released by their friends before the day of punishment arrived. But Sturgis was the severest of commanders; and

although no houses had been entered and no women insulted, he determined to strike a blow that would serve as a menace to plunderers for some time to come. His efforts for protecting the property of citizens would have done credit to the police of any city, and his orders were faithfully carried out. For cooking food only decayed logs or the fallen limbs of trees could be used. To carry a fence rail to a camp-fire was a serious matter. Farmers were at liberty to visit the camp and dispose of their produce, but no soldier was allowed to enter a dwelling or an out-house without permission.

We crossed Grand River on the 7th and camped near the forces of General Lyon, the united commands numbering about 4500 men, with ten pieces of artillery.

On the 12th of June Governor Jackson, of Missouri, issued a proclamation calling for 50,000 volunteers to support the cause of the South. No points were designated for them to assemble, but a large force was known to be gathering under the governor's eye at the capitol of the State. Lyon at once determined to strike Jackson at home; and on the second day after the proclamation he set out for Jefferson City, taking with him Totten's Battery, 150 regular infantry, and the 1st Missouri Infantry—this regiment having for its colonel the famous Francis P. Blair. Lyon then commanded the Department of the West, and bore a brilliant reputation for his defence of the arsenal and the capture of Camp Jackson in St. Louis. Thousands of people cheered his little command and wished him success as the boats left the levee and steamed up the Mississippi River. The expedition reached Jefferson City on the afternoon of the next day. A company of regulars under Sergeant Hare led the advance to the capitol building, where the national flag was hoisted without opposition and without any expressions of disrespect on the part of the inhabitants. It was soon learned that the governor had left many hours before for Boonville, several miles up the river. A regiment of infantry having arrived by rail, it was established in Jefferson City, and Lyon, having frightened for a time the rebellious element and encouraged the hopes of those favorable to the Union, took the boats once more, and at seven o'clock on the morning of the 17th landed his troops eight miles below Boonville. He advanced in order of battle for about a mile, when Governor Jackson's skirmishers were encountered, who made a creditable resistance until forced back upon the main body.

Lyon moved with great caution, for he met with a straggling fire from every hill-top and piece of woods. Jackson's men had no artillery to answer Totten's well-served guns; but they conducted themselves so well that Lyon did not reach the town until the afternoon. The defeated Missourians then moved in a southerly direction, under the command of General Marmaduke, but no pursuit was made. Their ultimate capture was considered a certainty, as Colonel Franz Sigel, with two regiments of infantry, had been despatched to the southwestern part of the State to intercept them.

A gentleman of St. Louis, who had accompanied the Federal command, took a position overlooking the contending forces and counted the shots fired by the battery. Then, supposing that each discharge of artillery resulted in the death of ten Confederates and the wounding of many more, he telegraphed to a newspaper that he had seen three hundred of the enemy's dead on the field, and that the wounded were innumerable. General Lyon, in reporting the affair to his government, gave his own loss as four killed and seven wounded, and that of Jackson unknown.

The conduct of Lyon thus far in the prosecution of the war does not appear to have been appreciated by the President, for, since leaving St. Louis, the State of Missouri had been placed under the command of General McClellan, whose headquarters were in Cincinnati, and on July 3d another change was made and the State given over to General Fremont, whose headquarters for nearly three weeks later were at the Astor House, in New York, when they should have been at St. Louis. If Lyon felt chagrined at this want of confidence he made no sign of it in his letters or in his conversation with his associates. Without asking for instructions he proceeded in the direction of Springfield by rapid marches. In that section were to be found many loyal citizens, and it was there that the advancing forces of McCulloch were to be met. He left Boonville for Clinton on the 3d of July with 2,400 men, having been detained by floods of rain and the want of sufficient wagons, and crossed Grand River one day in advance of Sturgis.

The latter visited Lyon on the morning of the 9th and invited the general to inspect his brigade, but Lyon declined, giving as a reason that the men needed rest, and that he did not wish to burden them with the labor of polishing up and standing in the sun for an unreasonable length of time. He consented, however, to pass through the camp and take a look at things. Three o'clock in the afternoon was the hour named for him to appear, and Dubois was instructed to have his battery in readiness to fire a salute.

The news of Lyon's intended visit was circulated through the camp, and all kinds of amusement were given up to get a view of a commander who had already become famous. It was not generally known in what style he would appear, but we looked for some imposing figure borne on by a wild charger and followed by a glittering staff, all at full speed, jumping fences and ditches, and riding over every one who happened to be in the way. While waiting for this event, Major Sturgis came in view on foot, accompanied by a person who was dressed like a farmer. The major drew a white handkerchief from his pocket as an understood signal to the battery, and eleven cannon-shots were fired—the regulation salute for the arrival of a brigadier-general. The men stood in irregular lines like citizens of a town watching a procession. Lyon stopped at several points and made remarks. Halting in front of the spot we occupied, he said, loud enough to be heard: " Major, your men appear to be in fine condition. They are splendid fellows. Such men as these should not be frightened by bullets." "You are right, General," replied Sturgis. "These men will not turn their backs to the enemy."

Lyon seemed to be about the average height, having an active and wiry frame. His manner, though studiously mild and agreeable, was betrayed by a countenance unmistakably agressive. His dress was characteristic of military men of experience, but was much criticised by the troops. While in St. Louis he was presented, by an admirer, with a white hat of the dress pattern. This, with a change of linen dusters, he wore on all occasions during the campaign until the moment of his death. The general proceeded as far as the line extended, stopping very often, probably to repeat what he had said in our presence.

Lyon and his staff then started for Springfield, where they arrived on the 13th, having accomplished fifty miles in one day, and leaving the army far in rear. But the troops were pushed with diligence until they came within easy call of his headquarters.

On the 14th we reached a fine stream of water fed by many springs, which was highly appreciated by the troops. On the afternoon of this day the command was again obliged to witness punishment, but of a more serious nature than had been suffered by those who had been drummed out at Clinton. Joseph W. Cole, of the 1st Kansas Regiment, in a quarrel over a game of cards the day previous, stabbed to the heart a companion named Michael Stein. For this offence he was condemned to be shot, and as the murder was altogether inexcusable he was allowed but twenty-four hours to prepare for leaving the world. Twelve muskets were loaded with full cartridges and twelve more

GENERAL STERLING PRICE, C. S A.

without bullets. They were then mixed in such a manner that their contents could not be determined with certainty. So carefully had this work been performed that no member of the firing party could be accused of contributing to the death of a man, however unworthy of life, who was powerless to resist. The brigade of Sturgis having been ranged on three sides of a square, a detail of twenty-four men took up the arms, and after receiving the victim from the camp-guard, marched to the side of the square destitute of troops. The prisoner passed very close to our company, and was easily known, as he carried no weapons. He appeared to be about twenty years of age and of dark complexion, though somewhat pale near his cheek bones, but he conducted himself bravely. However just his sentence, it was impossible not to feel a melancholy interest in the fate of one whose last short journey could be measured with a rule, and whose remaining minutes could be counted upon the fingers of one hand. He walked steadily to the place of execution, which was

marked by a bank of fresh earth, a grave, and a long box made of rough boards. The guard was then placed fifty feet distant, the prisoner halfway between. As the doomed man declined any religious ceremony the proceedings were carried out with dispatch. After being made to kneel a white bandage was placed over his eyes and his hands were tied behind him. The officer in charge lingered a moment to pat him on the shoulder and to whisper a cheering word, and then gave a signal. Not a sound at this moment broke in upon the stillness of the scene, and all eyes were turned in one direction. Instantly, in a clear voice, which could be heard far out on the prairie, came the commands— "Ready, aim, fire." The crash of musketry was followed by a loud moan, the body of Cole darted upward and backward, and that was the last of the Kansas volunteer.

The army soon reached an elevated and well-wooded locality in the vicinity of Springfield, where it remained for nearly a fortnight. No body of soldiers during the Civil War had less cause for complaint than those under Lyon and Sturgis. The roads, since leaving the Missouri River, were so level and soft that the infantry could travel without shoes if they wished. The ration was not only ample but of far better quality than was furnished in later years. The transportation was so abundant that a wagon was assigned to each company. In each wagon were stored five Sibley tents, the cooking utensils, the food, and the baggage of the men, as we were not obliged in those days to carry our knapsacks or blankets while on the march. Infantry officers of all grades were allowed to ride if they could find horses, and nearly all availed themselves of the privilege.

Since leaving Clinton we stood in little danger of being drummed out for plundering, for the country was thinly settled, and the land, though rich, was poorly cultivated. It was mostly of the prairie kind, and covered with tall grass. Such was the height of the grass that those employed on picket and guard duty returned from their services saturated from head to foot with dew, and when we began the march in the morning it was easy to tell who had been on guard during the night by the mist arising from their clothes.

The time had now arrived when a battle could not long be delayed. The forces of McCulloch and the hostile Missourians under Price had joined, and were not more than fifty miles away, and were said to be anxious to make our acquaintance. The defeat of McDowell in Virginia had become known to them, and they were loud in their boasts that they would soon show us the way to the Mississippi River or the Missouri, whichever we might select. "We can whip five to one," was the cry that came over the hills from the Arkansas line. Keen-eyed, dashing fellows often rode through the camp and chatted with our troops. They made no secret of being fresh from McCulloch's headquarters, and some of them took courage to say that we were no match for the men of Arkansas and Missouri. Others again assured us that our enemies could not stand more than a single blast of artillery, and that we might occupy the land at our pleasure. The presence of these visitors was not only tolerated but encouraged, for it was the policy of our officers to treat all civilians as friends. If they brought us valuable news, well and good; if they reported our affairs to the enemy, we lost nothing, as McCulloch had knowledge of our strength and our weakness.

Our notions of our own superiority were not less extravagant and not less conscientious. We judged the enemy by their conduct at Camp Jackson and Boonville. We looked upon them with contempt, and we were taught to believe that we could manage any body of men that could be found on the road. The majority of us felt, no doubt, that the bullets would fly only in one direction, and that the destruction of our enemies could be brought about by a simple physical exertion. All we had to do was to shoot them down when they came within range and follow the retreating survivors.

Just at this time a sergeant of dragoons, a man of Southern birth, deserted to the enemy, taking his horse and equipments. He gave an excuse for passing the advance-guard in broad daylight, and was soon at full speed toward Cassville. No more dangerous man could have been lost in this manner, as he was employed in the commissary department, and knew the exact number of men under Lyon.

CHAPTER II.

ON the last day of July we passed through Springfield, the most considerable town within a circuit of a hundred miles, and rested for the night in the fields west of the town. Rumors passed through the camps that McCulloch was rapidly approaching and that his cavalry was raising clouds of dust on all the roads leading from the South. It was evident that our general was in no doubtful mood, for in the morning the entire army advanced with limited transportation and an increased supply of ammunition. Late in the day we camped on Wilson's Creek, a clear but sluggish little stream, which rises near Springfield, and, after wandering through the valleys of Green County to its southern border, contributes to James's Fork of White River. The troops were camped in such a manner that if attacked little time would be consumed in getting the lines in order. Early on the following day, which was Friday, the 2d of August, we started out in a westerly direction. The command moved cautiously and frequently halted for more than half an hour at a time. Our battalion being well in advance, we could see squads of our cavalry scouring the country to the right and left of the road, so as to detect any hostile force that might be concealed or found marching over the fields. We proceeded slowly for most of the day along the dusty Fayetteville road. No water could be found, and the dust covered us to such an extent that a companion could not be recognized except by his familiar voice.

About four o'clock in the afternoon, shots were heard ahead, and the advance-guard was instantly deployed, Plummer's battalion on the right, Steele's on the left, and Totten's battery in the centre, the main column being about a mile in rear. The land was uneven and covered with boulders and scrub-oak; but we forced our way through until a point was reached where a pretty clear view could be had for a mile and a half. There was now every indication that serious work was at hand, for a lively skirmish was going on in Steele's vicinity, and the glitter of arms and the movements of horsemen could be observed in our front, but at a considerable distance.

Having nothing to do for the moment, our eyes were naturally turned toward Steele's men, and while watching the puffs of smoke which emerged from their muskets, Company C, of the 4th United States Cavalry, appeared and pressed at full speed upon the enemy, who were dismounted cavalry. The charge was conducted by Captain David S. Stanley. Some of the regulars flourished sabres, but most of them handled pistols, and they presented a fine sight for the short time they were in view.

It was now our turn to do something, as the horsemen in our front had dismounted and begun to advance. Captain Plummer, who was a heavy-set man and who looked like a well-dressed bear, rode in front of the battalion and said to us: "The moment you men take up the double-quick I want you to yell at your best, for it's half the victory. Remember, the more noise you make, the less fighting you will have to do." We then pushed forward at a rapid pace. Totten having found a piece of level ground for his guns, at once opened fire, when, by spontaneous emotion, we doubled our speed, each man shouting at the top of his voice. As the men in the front rank dashed through the bushes, those in rear were nearly blinded by the rebounding branches. Numerous rabbits started up during our progress through the underbrush, and, becoming crazed with the tumult, ran in all directions, some of them passing through the ranks.

When we came to a halt, the enemy, having mounted their horses, were perceived to be flying in disorder over the open country toward the main road. Totten's shells followed them long after they reached the woods, though their loss was insignificant. They proved to be the advance guard of McCulloch's army, consisting of 700 men under General Rains. This officer had been instructed not to risk his men by attacking our lines, but simply to display his force in such a manner as to make it appear much larger than it really was, and thus compel our commander to show his strength. Rains having satisfied himself, from the rising dust in our rear, that Lyon's entire army was present, drew off his command and sent a faithful report of his observations to McCulloch, who was ten miles further to the west.

It being near sunset, we fell back a mile or so to the only stream of water in the neighborhood, our battalion camping near the headquarters of Lyon. He had selected a log cabin by the side of the road, and we stacked arms within a few feet of him. He sat alone in the doorway, twirling between his fingers a flower which he had plucked from a stem within his reach. His countenance seemed full of anxiety and trouble. His repeated solicitations for men and supplies, and a disappointment for every request, had sapped his health and marked his appearance. He brightened up, however, when the passing volunteers recognized him and cheered him. The regulars passed him without making a demonstration, for they never cheer an officer, however high his rank.

There were some fine springs in the vicinity, and the men of the different organizations crowded about them as if they were so many public houses. Those who belonged to Steele's infantry and Stanley's cavalry were listened to with great attention, for they were the only troops who got to close quarters with the enemy. It came out that the Missourians under Rains were by no means wanting in courage. Steele acknowledged that he could with difficulty drive them; and Stanley's forty-two troopers, who charged through their ranks, were glad to cut their way back, after losing four killed and six wounded.

It was told of one of the Missourians that, having discharged his piece and being unable to reload in time for a trooper who was close upon him, he clubbed his weapon and struck the horse a blow that brought him to the ground. He then dashed out the brains of the rider, who had fallen with his horse, but had no sooner done so than his own skull was split open by a sabre cut. But the conduct of the cavalry must have been creditable, for Captain Stanley, who was always prompt to recognize merit, named three of his sergeants for promotion, and Albert Coates, James Irwin, and Thomas C. Sullivan received commissions in the regular army for services performed on that day.

On the morning after the skirmish at Dug Springs, the army advanced to Curran, which is twenty-four miles from Springfield. We were now within six miles of the enemy, who were encamped on Cane Creek. There was but one house in the town of Curran. This solitary building seemed to have done duty as a post-office, general store, and bar-room. The floor was well worn, and the surroundings bore evidence that cross-road horse races had been decided and celebrated here with enthusiasm. All the furniture had been removed except a bench and a few broken chairs. Nothing was to be seen upon the walls but a piece of writing, which informed all who could read it that no more favors would be granted to customers until old scores had been settled. Headquarters were established here during the day, and no appearance of the enemy being observed, Lyon summoned his chief officers for a consultation. When they were seated, the general (according to the notes of Captain Gordon Granger) addressed them and said:

"Gentlemen, before leaving Springfield I became aware that the enemy was moving upon us in great numbers. Supposing that the most formidable of their columns held the advance, I at once started out to engage it. It may be that we came out a day too soon; but I can now see that their generals are unwilling to risk a battle in this region except with their united commands, and I am well satisfied that their divisions are now within supporting distance of each other. In regard to the number of their men in the field, I have reason to believe that we are opposed by not less than 15,000. The most effective and dangerous of these are the troops of McCulloch's brigade, numbering at least 4,000. Next come the State troops of Arkansas, under General N. B. Pearce, who are as well armed and as well disciplined as most of our volunteers. In addition to these are several thousand Missourians under General Sterling Price. Not more than half of Price's men could be trusted to lead an attack, but the poorest of them, coming inio view at a critical moment, might create a panic in our ranks. The circumstance that a portion of them defeated Sigel about a month ago is evidence that they are not to be despised. They have fifteen pieces of artillery and an abundance of ammunition for them. This overwhelming force is in our front and cannot be more than six or seven miles distant." [Major John M. Schofield, Lyon's chief of staff, now senior major-general U. S. A., then produced the latest returns of the Federal command as follows: Infantry, 5,300 men; artillery (sixteen pieces), 268 men; cavalry (four companies), 250 men.] "The condition of this force for aggressive purposes," Lyon continued, "I am sorry to say, is not encouraging. You are aware that for the past ten days we have been reduced to half rations. No article of food could be obtained in abundance except fresh beef, and in consequence of this being improperly cooked many of the men are sick. The supply of clothing has long since been exhausted, and hundreds of men are badly in want of shoes.

"I felt confident when leaving Springfield that a decisive battle would have been fought before this. Now that we are disappointed, I have called you together that we may exchange views upon the situation and determine what is best to be done. The country in front of us, to the spot where the enemy is established, is hilly and wooded for the entire distance, and there is little water on the way. In my opinion, therefore, it is folly to remain here any longer. There are several regiments of cavalry under McCulloch, and though some of them are poorly equipped, their numbers might induce the slender garrison at Springfield to lay down their arms, and I would not be surprised if at this moment the roads in our rear were crowded with mounted men on their way to our base of supplies.

"Even if we push further and fight a successful battle, we are in no condition to improve the victory; but if we fall back from this and make a stand at Springfield, our enemies will necessarily divide their forces in the attack, and with a united front we can easily beat them in detail."

All the officers present at the conference favored a battle if it could be brought about in a tolerably open country. But as the enemy showed no inclination to come out of his wooded stronghold, it was considered wise to retire, the movement to begin at midnight.

The Missouri militia, under Governor Jackson, having on the 5th of July routed the forces of Sigel at Carthage, immediately went into camp under the command of General Sterling Price for organization and drill. Their improvement was rapid, and on the 29th of the month, 7,000 strong, they took the field and joined McCulloch at Cassville, which is fifty miles distant from Springfield. Price then waited on McCulloch and tendered him the supreme command. The Confederate general informed him that he did not wish the control of the Missourians, giving as a reason that they had devoured all their provisions, and in the event of a retreat for a further supply the blame would rest upon him.* It was represented to

him that the corn in the fields was then in a condition for food, and this, with the meal and flour from the mills at hand, would be sufficient for their support until the capture of the Federal army and its splendid commissary. McCulloch then accepted the command, and immediately put his entire force in motion toward Springfield. He arrived at Cane Creek, thirty miles from his objective point, on the 2d of August, with one division, and sent back orders to hurry up the others, as the Federal army was massed not more than ten miles to the east. The entire Confederate Army of the West concentrated on Cane Creek on August 3d, and remained inactive for two days, though Lyon took no pains to hide himself during the whole of this time.

McCulloch was advised by Price that now was the time to attack Lyon, who, in case of defeat, would be obliged to make his way over rough fields and through troublesome ravines, and would necessarily be cut off by the cavalry sent in his rear.

The Confederate commander, generally prone to delay, yielded to this advice, and at one o'clock, on the morning of the 5th, his army took up the march for Lyon's camp. Hebert's Louisiana infantry took the lead, followed by Woodruff's battery; this constituted the advance-guard, and was instructed to attack the enemy on sight. Two hundred yards in rear followed the main body, making its way in the darkness in the following order: 3d Arkansas, Colonel John R. Gratiot; battalion Arkansas volunteers, Lieutenant-Colonel D. McRae; General R. H. Weightman's division of Missourians, with artillery; General N. B. Pearce's Arkansas brigade, and Reid's battery; the remainder of the Missouri militia, under General Sterling Price, in irregular brigades, commanded by Generals William Y. Slack, John H. McBride, James S. Rains, Monroe M. Parsons, and John B. Clark. The strictest silence was enjoined; no drums were to be beaten, and all orders were to be given in a low tone. All the cavalry was kept in rear, but when the battle opened four regiments of McCulloch's were to move to the right, and an equal number of Price's to the left upon the flanks and rear of Lyon, and make it their business to drive the fish into the net.

The Confederate troops pushed on in good humor to Curran, confident that they would soon enjoy the fine sport they had so long wished for. Hebert reached the deserted Federal camp at daylight and met a farmer's boy

---

*Some claim that McCulloch demanded the supreme command, but McCulloch's statement is accepted. See Rec. Rebellion, Vol. III, p. 745.

moving about, who informed him that Lyon's men had left hours before, and were well on their way to Springfield. Some kind of pursuit was made until the middle of the day, when the annoying heat and dust obliged the Confederates to go into camp. In the afternoon of the next day they rested on Wilson's Creek where it is crossed by the Fayetteville road. They were then put in readiness to march against Springfield during the night, where Lyon was safely quartered, but a threatened storm caused McCulloch to wait for a more favorable time.

The hostile forces of Lyon and McCulloch occupied their respective positions three days longer. It is a matter of surprise to many persons that two armies, after traversing hundreds of miles in search of each other, the troops on both sides confident of superiority and clamoring for battle, should spend so much time in devouring their food when a few hours' march would bring them together. The reasons for this inactivity were not widely known at the time; but they are as numerous as might be supplied by the captain of a ship for not putting to sea, or by a gentleman of fashion in reduced circumstances for not going abroad.

If there is any truth in figures, Lyon was badly off for troops. Of the 5,800 men he now had in hand, many of Sigel's men claimed their discharge before the day of battle, and the term of service of the First Iowa would expire on the 18th, as they were all three months' men. Sigel went among his soldiers and begged them to stand by him at this critical time, when an alarm from the pickets was momentarily expected. Notwithstanding his entreaties, two-thirds of the officers and some of the men declined to serve any longer. The vacancies in the battery were filled by men from the infantry, but they were ignorant of artillery drill, and proved inefficient in action. The First Iowa Infantry, under Colonel William H. Merritt, was composed of better material. A mass meeting of the regiment was held, in which every man might have his say, and it was determined that, although the government could claim them no longer than the 18th of the month, they would remain in the field until it suited Lyon's pleasure to send them home. As to their wages, they informed the general that they had no use for money, and it would make no difference if they were never paid.

Of the 5,300 available men now left to Lyon,*

Vide Major Schofield's official report.

about 1,000 of them were soldiers of the regular army, and the moral effect of this force in the minds of the Confederates was immense. McCulloch was no stranger to military affairs, and he knew the value of men who were accustomed to obey with alacrity and who were improved by vigorous drill. It should be known, however, that regular soldiers, unless controlled by a sufficient number of competent officers, are not likely to be formidable in battle, and it happened that of the fourteen companies of regulars then in Springfield, five of them were commanded by sergeants, and but twelve commissioned officers could be found for the remaining nine. The resignation from the army of nearly all the officers of Southern birth in the early months of 1861, the great number of those of the North who all at once received high promotion in the volunteer service, and the sudden demand by the government for staff officers of experience, created this state of affairs. Four of the companies were made up of recruits who were assigned to regiments in the territories, who were halted on their transit for emergencies, and who had seen little more service than the volunteers ; the non-commissioned officers of these received no more pay than the privates, and stood little chance of promotion for meritorious conduct. Such was the condition of the regular troops under Lyon, and persons familiar with the conduct of men in battle will readily comprehend the disaster that is imminent when the voice of their chief is no longer heard, or heard in the agonies of death. Their efficiency was not further enhanced by the fact that they were distributed irregularly throughout the command, not more than four companies to be found together.

As to our volunteers, McCulloch declared that he could dispose of them with ease. And why not? They had been in the field no longer than his own men, and were obliged to face at least two to one ; and it would require a bold and impudent writer to maintain that McCulloch's officers were not as competent to lead their men in action as any that might be found north of the Ohio River. But neither McCulloch nor the most enthusiastic admirer of volunteers on our own side imagined for a moment that, when the day of trial arrived, the representatives of Kansas, Missouri, and Iowa would stand their ground hour for hour and shed their blood drop for drop with the steadiest regulars in Lyon's command.

McCulloch manœuvred for delay so as to allow Lyon's three months' men to leave for home, though he did not divulge his secrets to Price.

The troops of Sigel he still looked upon as difficult to handle, but once out of the way, the Federal army and its wagon train might be considered an easy prey to the overwhelming force of infantry and cavalry which could be hurled against it.

McCulloch, although deplorably short of ammunition and supplies, was surrounded by more men than he was able to handle. On the 30th of July he wrote to L. P. Walker, the Confederate Secretary of War:

I have the honor to report that I am now at this place (Cassville) with my command on my way to Springfield. Since my communication of the 18th, I have been busily engaged in preparing my force for a forward march, and have also been urging on the commanders of the different forces near me to be ready to coöperate with me.

By furnishing the Missouri force with all the ammunition I could spare, and also what could be spared from General Pearce's command, I have given them sufficient to warrant them in again taking the field. General Price, with his force of between 9,000 and 10,000 men, is encamped around Cassville. His effective force will hardly reach 7,000, and they are nearly all armed with shot-guns and common rifles. General Pearce, of Arkansas, is within ten miles of Cassville with his command of 2,500 men. His command is well armed. My brigade is also near me, amounting to about 3,200, nearly all well armed.

Three days later McCulloch was joined by Greer's Texas Cavalry, which increased his force by nearly 1,000 choice men. There could be no doubt, therefore, that on the morning when Lyon forced a battle he found at least 13,000 well-conditioned troops to dispute his advance.

In addition to this effective force were three or four thousand Missourians who had no regimental organizations. They marched along in companies or squads, and were commanded by men of local prominence in the neighborhoods from which they emerged. They were rated by McCulloch as no better than robbers, but in their own estimation they were as good as the best. These brave fellows had left comfortable homes behind them; had traveled over a vast extent of territory, resting at night without shelter, sustaining themselves with food which a Federal soldier would throw away, and were armed with no better weapons than they carried at home in pursuit of game. The strictest orders were given to keep this mob at least twenty miles in rear of headquarters, but the orders were defied, and McCulloch complained bitterly to Price for allowing them to encroach upon the fighting element of his army.

During our stay of three days in Springfield, the avenues of approach were well guarded by pickets. The bulk of the force was massed in one spot, so as to fall with celerity upon the strongest of the columns moving to the attack. Although a number of skirmishes occurred between advanced parties, there was no general alarm. Every man was kept ready for instant action. The tents and baggage were packed away in wagons, and we were obliged to sleep in gardens and groves. Two days' rations and one hundred rounds of ammunition were kept constantly in hand, and no man was allowed to pass the line of sentinels without written permission.

We had been on half rations for some time, but the food was so abundant that we were not aware of the reduction until informed of it by newspapers ten days old. There being no other cause for complaint, the troops began to grumble, and accused the government of starving them in order to save a little money. I have often thought that soldiers are never happy without some cause for discontent; but the prospect of immediate hostilities soon drove away considerations of personal concern.

CHAPTER III.

IT was now the 8th of August, and Lyon had given up all hope of relief from Fremont. He had written many begging letters, and had sent messengers of high social and military standing to St. Louis to picture the situation and to implore assistance. But none of these appeals met with encouragement. On the afternoon of this day he summoned his chief officers for his last council of war. After representing to them the state of affairs as it existed in his own mind, he desired each of them to give his ideas of what should be done—whether to attack the enemy in the morning or retreat at once in an easterly direction.

The majority of the council voted to remain in Springfield and stand in readiness to be attacked, but for a second choice they favored a retreat, as they considered it madness to strike the enemy on their own ground, whose force was estimated to be fifteen thousand men of all arms and conditions. They claimed that by marching all night the army would be twenty miles away before the enemy could be aware of the move.

GENERAL DAVID S. STANLEY.

According to the diary of Captain Gordon Granger, Lyon, after giving an attentive ear to their views, addressed them as follows:

"Gentlemen, your reasons for retreat or for standing still are plausible enough. But, after all, an attack upon the enemy's camp is not so full of danger as you imagine. Their line now extends a distance of three miles along Wilson's Creek. Their best troops are in the centre, and

GENERAL J. M. SCHOFIELD.

at either end are masses of Missourians and others who are not so well disciplined, and who, if put to flight, would carry consternation and dismay to the ranks of the more reliable men. My plan is to advance to-night and at daybreak attack them with as much vigor as we can display. The enemy are aware of our weakness, and when they find our shells bursting among them at such an early hour it will readily occur to them that we had been suddenly reinforced. You must understand that I do not expect a decisive victory on this occasion. The utmost we can hope for is to drive McCulloch from the field and to cripple him to such an extent that he cannot pursue us in case we are compelled to leave. I am aware that in this pointed progress through their camp we are likely to receive a check, but we must bargain for this, and cultivate a disposition to meet emergencies. The volunteers are crying out, 'What are we doing here?' 'Are we to be surrendered without a battle?' I know the spirit of these men, and depend upon it, if they are not moved at once upon the enemy they will begin to look upon their officers as inferior to themselves. If we remain another day in this place the loss of the entire wagon-train and a fugitive retreat will follow."

GÉNERAL FREDERICK STEELE.

He was then interrupted by a report from the pickets, and, after giving some instructions, resumed:

"You must bear in mind that we are in the midst of a population who are faithful to the government. They look to us for protection as children do to their parents. If we leave them without making a reasonable effort in their defence, a change of sentiment will take place among them, and thousands of able-bodied men may be forced into the service of the South. For a hundred miles north and east of us all available men will be swept into the ranks of the enemy, and their families left in danger of insult and plunder. To retire without a battle will subject us to the ridicule of our friends and our foes, and it will seriously damage the prestige of the Federal arms. To those of you who wish to follow the fortunes of this war and expect to rise above the rank you now hold, I will take the liberty to say that your chances for promotion will not improve by a retreat from this place without a fight."

The council was adjourned without a definite understanding as to future operations, but the officers left the room pretty well convinced that Lyon would not retire except through force of arms.

Everything was in readiness for an advance, but toward sundown a heavy detachment returned from scout duty so exhausted that it could not be depended upon for a night march. It was therefore determined to wait another day.

During the afternoon of August 9th I was hailed by Lieutenant Wood, who directed me to take a note to Captain Plummer, who was then at Lyon's quarters. I soon reached my destination, but was informed that I must wait awhile, as the captain was engaged with the commanding general. While loitering around, I got a close view of many army officers then in Springfield who had been called to headquarters for instructions. They were all faithful and courageous sentinels of the republic, and many of them, before the close of the war, reached fame and high command. Among them were Samuel D. Sturgis, David S. Stanley, Gordon Granger, John M. Schofield, Thomas W. Sweeny, Charles C. Gilbert, Frederick Steele, Joseph B. Plummer, James Totten, Franz Sigel, Eugene A. Carr, George L. Andrews, William M. Wherry, Peter J. Osterhaus, Robert B. Mitchell, George W. Deitzler, Frank J. Herron, and Powell

GENERAL GORDON GRANGER.

Clayton. I was glad to observe that they appeared cheerful. They acted like men who were about to engage in a game the result of which was already determined in their favor.

Schofield, the chief of staff, conspicuous by his long beard, came up to a group of officers, and, being asked for information, "Gentlemen,"

GENERAL FRANZ SIGEL.

he said, "it's all settled; we are to advance within an hour, and if we don't have a fight in the morning McCulloch will be to blame." Then they shook hands all around, and, having a large black bottle convenient, began to celebrate the victory which they had in prospect. Lyon and Plummer soon came out, whispering and dragging after them rusty sabres that would force an inspecting officer to suicide.

It was just previous to this time that Colonel Sigel, during an extended interview with Lyon, got permission to separate his brigade from the army and attack the enemy's right, three miles from the chief point of battle.

The little Army of the West needed but a word to be put in motion, and before dark the streets of Springfield were alive with troops and ambulances on the way to McCulloch's camp. The ranks seemed full. No absentees were reported, and not more than a dozen men were in the hospital. The men looked fresh and vigorous, and were not burdened with baggage. As we passed the public square, Lyon was observed sitting on a gray stallion, in conversation with his staff. He was very near the spot where, twenty-two years later, in the presence of a vast multitude, a monument was unveiled to commemorate his services and his glorious death.

Sigel, with six cannon and about twelve hundred men, took an obscure road leading south, with instructions to attack the right and rear of the enemy. His men sang German songs on the

march and carried on with great liveliness. Lyon and Sturgis, with the main column of forty-one hundred men and ten cannon, marched in a westerly direction on the Little York road, and were to fall on the left or front of the enemy, as convenience might suggest.

It now seemed as if the two armies were about to try their luck in a midnight battle, for the Confederates had received orders to march against Lyon at the same hour and over the same roads. But it happened that it began to rain about dark, and as a large portion of them had nothing better than cotton bags to protect their ammunition, McCulloch once more decided to wait for moonlight hours.

Toward midnight, after many unaccountable delays on the road, seven miles had been traversed, when the command rested in an extensive hay-field. Most of our company made a rush for a fence near by, for protection from the rain, but were instantly brought back by Lieutenant Wood and forced to lie down in rows where our muskets had been stacked. We were allowed fence-rails for pillows, however, which, with the blankets, secured us comfortable beds.

"This is hard on rich men's sons," said one, as he lay in the rain.

"We'll look like this when McCulloch gets through with us," said another.

Just at daylight, after enjoying a rest of nearly four hours, every man was awakened and a line of battle was formed. Plummer's battalion

GENERAL P. J. OSTERHAUS.

was already on the left, and extending to the right were the 1st Kansas and 1st Missouri infantry. Totten's and Dubois' batteries followed close in rear. Half a mile further back came Steele's battalion, the 2d Kansas and the 1st Iowa, intended as the reserve. But three hundred yards in front of everything was the skirmish-line. Captains Yates and Maurice, of the 1st Missouri, with their companies, were thrown out in the centre, Gilbert's company of regulars on the left, and Osterhaus' two companies of the 2d Missouri on the right.

In this order Lyon pushed forward through the wet grass to the promised field of battle. Between five and six o'clock the enemy's pickets were met and driven in. But Cawthon's regiment of Confederate Missourians came to the front and contested our advance for a mile or more. We passed a rude cabin near a cow-path, and in the door stood a group of children dressed in their night-clothes who had been aroused from their beds by the commotion. They looked with surprise at so many hunters all dressed alike, and evidently wondered what particular game we were in search of. The innocents of Oak Hills had not long to wait for sights and sounds which they would remember for many a day.

The weather now became favorable. The mist had ascended above the tops of the trees, and the sun was forcing its way through mountains of silver and gold. As we reached the summit of a wooded hill a clear view could be had for about a mile. At a short distance to the left and front were Gilbert's skirmishers. The outposts of the enemy were flying before them. Their advanced line and its reserve moved with great regularity and gave evidence of fine drill. The skirmishers were now at work along the entire line, and it was not long before masses of the enemy were observed.

Arriving upon a partially cleared piece of ground our battalion was brought to a halt, the troops to the right of us moving along. Lyon and his staff then rode up, our company being thrown into disorder for a moment to clear a way for them. The general made earnest gestures to Schofield, who rode beside him. His eyes looked weary from loss of sleep, but the great event of his life supplied a buoyancy, and he was heard to say, " In less than an hour they'll wish they were a thousand miles away."

On a commanding ridge slightly to the left and about half a mile distant, Woodruff's Arkansas battery was established, guarded by numerous infantry. Directly in front and considerably nearer than Woodruff were large bodies of the enemy partly concealed by the elevated ground and the underbrush. The general, after a hasty glance, turned to his inspector-general and said: "Sweeny, it looks as if they mean business. But we'll send them a blast, and if they break we'll put all the artillery at work and keep them on the run."

Captain Totten was then ordered to unlimber his guns and load for action. Totten was a smooth-faced, pleasant-looking man about forty years of age. A few months before this he was stationed at the capital of Arkansas and was in charge of the arsenal there. He was neglected by his superiors, and being menaced by a formidable mob of Confederates surrendered his com-

GENERAL EUGENE A. CARR.

pany and the property of the government. The unfortunate captain and his men were allowed to proceed north, but before leaving they were required to hold up their right hands and swear that they would not bear arms against the Confederate States during the war then in progress. The victors at Little Rock, now dressed and drilled as soldiers of the Confederacy, were again in view, and Totten and his men were about to give them an idea of the value they placed upon such an oath.

Six hundred yards had been named as the distance, and everything being ready the first cannon-shot was fired. A loud and prolonged shout at once broke out among our troops as if to announce their numbers and their intentions. Mingled with this fire more shots followed, the gunners taking unusually long to aim. Lyon examined the situation for more than a minute, then handing his field-glass to an officer he assumed a fiery and determined look, for he became satisfied that the enemy in his front was not disposed to get out of his way. Turning to our battalion commander, "Captain Plummer," he said, " cross the creek at the nearest point and move down the valley until you meet with opposition. You will have plenty to do when you reach the wagon-train you see burning. Do your best to keep any force in check, for I can give you no assistance." The battalion then moved down the rocky hillside to perform its little part in the operations of the day.

Lyon, after despatching Plummer to the valley, pushed on with the main body as fast as the uneven ground and the stubbornness of Cawthon would allow until he came to a rugged and wooded bank running east and west, and which served as a natural breastwork. It rises about eighty feet above the lowland, and was subsequently named Bloody Hill by the farmers of the neighborhood, as on its crest and slopes fell most of the men who perished during the battle. Here the line rested and the regiments raised their standards.

The camps of McCulloch and Price were full of life at daybreak, as the proposed attack upon Lyon had not been abandoned. The men were still under arms and ready for the march. About five o'clock McCulloch was a visitor at the tent of the great Missourian, and was invited to breakfast. While thus engaged, Price informed McCulloch that he had reliable information of Lyon's intentions, and that the evacuation of Springfield and a hasty retreat had been set down for the next day. He urged a forward movement at once, and threatened, if his views were not respected, to cancel all former agreements and force his way through Springfield with the troops of Missouri alone. McCulloch had been puffed into notoriety by the Southern press as a promising warrior and conqueror, though he had not ranked high in the old Federal army. Price had seen service in Mexico, and was familiar with the organization of militia, and was beyond doubt an abler man to conduct a campaign or a battle than the one who gave him orders. McCulloch, fearing that Price meant what he said, and that his own troops might be forced to serve as auxiliaries to the militia of Missouri, determined to act with vigor at once, and promised to make known his plans by noon.

At this moment a horseman arrived with intelligence that Lyon was surely approaching, and that within a mile the hills were lined with men wearing the blue uniform. Both generals treated the story with doubt. An attack by Lyon with his fifty-three hundred men was considered a piece of temerity altogether incredible. A snow-storm at that hour, they imagined,

would not be more surprising. But the roar of Totten's battery convinced them of their danger, and they dropped their cups and overturned the table in their eagerness to take the field. No sooner had they mounted their horses than the artillery of Sigel announced that the right wing of the camp was also in peril.

GENERAL THOMAS W. SWEENY.

It was at once arranged that Price should face to the north with the Missourians and encounter Lyon, while McCulloch took care of Sigel. Price formed his line with remarkable skill and celerity. Cawthon, fatigued by his fight with the Federal advance, occupied the extreme right, and one after the other toward the left were the brigades of Slack, Clark, Parsons, and McBride. Guibor's battery found a place between McBride and Parsons. With this formation the Missourians marched up the southern slope of Bloody Hill and took refuge in the thick mass of scrub oak which everywhere abounded.

A dangerous gap separated Slack and Cawthon for awhile, but the arrival of Weightman, the most energetic and promising of the Missouri brigadiers, perfected the line. Price now awaited Lyon's further advance.

Crossing Wilson's Creek, where his own fine brigade and Pearce's troops were encamped, McCulloch instructed Colonel James McIntosh to dismount the 2d Arkansas Cavalry, and with Hebert's 3d Louisiana Infantry, proceed up the valley and turn Lyon's left, or use his judgment as matters developed ; and this was the force Plummer was destined to engage. Our battalion at this moment barely numbered three hundred men. Plummer was assisted by Captain Daniel Huston and Lieutenant Henry Clay Wood,* all of the 1st United States Infantry. We crossed the creek without trouble, but were opposed on the eastern bank by a jungle of willows and reeds, and had to push and pull each other through, our shoes being filled with water and sand. The narrow valley we entered was covered with patches of Indian corn of moderate height. In this a momentary halt was made to dress the line, when we again moved forward rapidly, facing due south.

When about three hundred yards from the enemy, the experts of the 2d Arkansas began to try their skill at our ranks, but they aimed too high. Many corn-tops fell at our feet and some bayonets were struck, but no complaints were heard among the men. The whistling bullets increased in number as we advanced, and arriving close to a rail face, which hemmed in the cultivated part of the valley, "Halt and commence firing" was heard, when we knelt down to our work.

Plummer, being mounted until the fighting began, saw that the troops he was approaching were not so numerous as to make him feel uneasy, but they were being quickly reinforced, until he found himself confronted by more than a thousand men. He had intended to strike and intimidate the 2d Arkansas and drive it back upon the 3d Louisiana, but the fence spoiled his calculations. The fence was lined with briars and weeds, while beyond was a level stretch of ground studded with brush, thick and dark with foliage, and there, at a distance of about one hundred and fifty yards, the enemy lay. As we fired blindly, and as the fence caught a portion of the bullets, the execution on either side for a time was trifling. "Aim between the rails on a level two feet above the ground," was passed along. The Confederates also improved in their work, and it was not long before those mournful sounds arose to the right and left, which when heard can never be forgotten.

Both sides were armed with muzzle-loading smooth-bores, which carried three buckshot and a ball. They were formidable weapons at close range when well aimed, but we could see nothing. The men frequently asked, "Where are they?" "What do you see?" We were

guided mainly by the sounds of musketry and the voices of men concealed in the dense thicket in front.

The splendid motions we had been taught at drill and parade in anticipation of this bloody day were not practised here. Each man assumed a position to his liking—most of them on their knees and leaning well forward. To load and fire by the old process, with ramrod, required much room, and the ranks were thrown into great irregularity. But everything worked well, and all hands manfully faced the storm.

The voice of Captain Plummer was ever in our ears. He passed constantly along the line in rear of the battalion. "Keep cool, my boys, you are doing well, you are mowing them down!" he would cry out at times. And he attracted swarms of bullets which rattled in the cornfield like drops of rain driven by violent winds. The main armies to the right of the creek had found each other, and the crash of their batteries gave vigor to our arms and elevation to our thoughts.

While all this was going on, Huston and Wood were shouting, instructing us how to aim, to be of good cheer, and not to mind the affairs of the wounded. The tumult was deafening. The loud moans of those who were struck in the stomach, the sharp cries of pain when bones were broken, and the curses of those who received slight wounds filled the air and increased in volume as the fight went on. In the beginning we felt nervous and confused, like anyone suddenly introduced to danger; but we became warmed up with the excitement, and most of the men acted as if they had found an agreeable employment. It was well known that we faced great odds, but as the officers cheered, the men remained active and confident, and showed no disposition to retire.

Quarrels broke out among the men, for those in front complained that their cheeks were singed by the fire of their companions in the rear rank; and ramrods which had been left on the ground for convenience were taken up by others and not promptly returned,

The contest was of short duration. Events did not turn out as Plummer had wished. His little band, though reliable and steady, was fast thinning out. A reinforcement was not looked for, nor could it be supplied. A retreat would invite humiliation. The approach of the enemy would be the signal for the dissolution of his force. And in a moment of frenzy he determined to cross the fence. A bugler was called

*Henry Clay Wood, Colonel and Assistant Adjutant-General, U. S. A., was given a medal by the President of the United States for distinguished gallantry in the battle of Wilson's Creek, Mo., August 10, 1861, where he was wounded while serving as first lieutenant, commanding a detachment of recruits.

to sound the advance, but the bugler was found to be dead. Plummer then attempted to dash through the ranks, sword in hand, and lead a charge in person. But he had barely undertaken the task when a bullet shattered one of his ribs, which threw him into a violent passion. "What's the matter with you?" he said to one who was making his way to the rear. "I am shot through my right cheek," answered the soldier, and the flowing blood proved the truth of his words. "Go back to your place, you villain!" exclaimed Plummer; "you must not mind flea-bites. Sergeant," addressing a non-commissioned officer, "shoot this man down if he refuses to fight." It was found more perilous to leave the ranks than to remain firm.

The Confederates were repeatedly urged by their officers to charge, but they appeared to have minds of their own to consult. Now and then, indeed, a bold man in gray came on with a yell, but he met with instant death. Plummer became hoarse from giving orders and weak from loss of blood. But his heart and soul were still in the fray, and as long as his subordinates kept the men to the mark he determined to hold the field. Observing that the noise among the recruits had somewhat abated, "Keep up the fire on the left!" he cried. He was answered by moans; for, of the sixty-six young men under Wood, who passed the creek less than an hour before, nine had perished, and twenty-five, including their commander, had been wounded.

Many of the latter kept on fighting, or assisted the more unfortunate by such rude skill in surgery as they could exercise. The calls for water were loud and constant; but no water was at hand; and as the able-bodied men momentarily expected death or mutilation, these appeals were treated as if they had not been heard.

At length, after vigorous effort, the Confederates, with a great shout, emerged from their cover, and as their long line neared the fence, with McIntosh and Hebert at the head, the battalion began to break and finally gave way. We made for the reeds which bordered the creek in good order and all together, and were not pursued. Twenty-eight dead were left on the field, and of the fifty-two wounded about half came along with their weapons. McIntosh owned up to a loss of one hundred and one in this quarter, of whom twenty-three were commissioned and non-commissioned officers; and the record on either side is creditable to any soldiers in action.

Dubois, on the left of Bloody Hill, had all along watched the affair in the cornfield and instantly opened his four cannon upon the victorious enemy and drove them in confusion out of range; the wounded we had left behind coming in for a share of the danger.

———

[The portraits accompanying this article appear through the courtesy of Mr. James E. Taylor, the well-known war artist, from whose superb collections the originals were obtained.—ED.]

TO MY WIFE.

Joseph McArdle, of Company F, 163d New York Volunteers, was for some years First Assistant Chief of the Kansas City Fire Department, and noted for his bravery and zeal in the discharge of duty. He died a little over a year ago from the effects of pneumonia, contracted while fighting a disastrous fire. A self-contained and somewhat diffident old soldier, he was loved by his comrades, especially by veteran Company A, but few suspected that he possessed any talent in a literary way. Among his papers, however, was found the following little poem, written in 1864, dedicated to his wife, and containing sentiment worthy to be perpetuated. F. P. McKEIGHAN.]

AT midnight, on my lonely beat,
  When darkness veils the wood and lea,
A vision seems my view to greet,
  Of one at home who prays for me.

The roses bloom upon her cheek;
  Her form seems to me like a dream;
And on her face, so fair and meek,
  A host of holy beauties gleam.

For softly shines her flaxen hair;
  A smile is ever on her face;
And the mild, lustrous light of prayer
  Around her sheds a moonlike grace.

She prays for me, that's far away—
  The soldier in his lonely fight;
And asks that God in mercy may
  Shield the loved one and bless the right.

Until, though leagues may lie between,
  The silent incense of her heart
Steals o'er my soul with breath serene,
  And we no longer are apart.

So, guarding thus my lonely beat,
  'Mid darkening wood and dreary lea,
That vision seems my view to greet,
  Of her at home who prays for me.

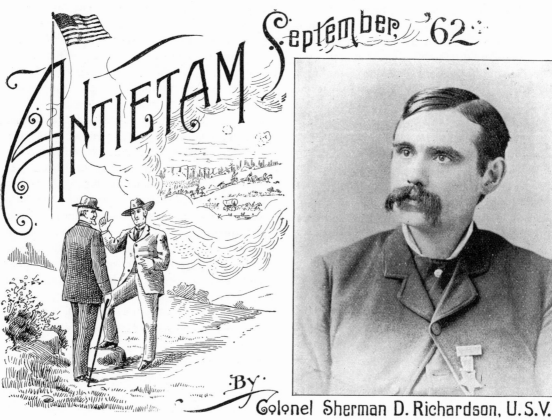

Antietam September, '62

By Colonel Sherman D. Richardson, U.S.V.

I'VE wandered o'er Antietam, John,
  And stood where foe met foe
Upon the fields of Maryland
  So many years ago.
The circling hills rise just the same
  As they did on that day,
When you were fighting blue, old boy,
  And I was fighting gray.

The winding stream runs 'neath the bridge,
  Where Burnside won his fame ;
The locust trees upon the ridge
  Beyond are there the same.
The birds were singing 'mid the trees—
  'Twas bullets on that day,
When you were fighting blue, old boy,
  And I was fighting gray.

I saw again the Dunker Church
  That stood beside the wood,
Where Hooker made the famous charge
  That Hill so well withstood.
'Tis scarred and marred by war and time,
  As we are, John, to-day ;
For you were fighting blue, old boy,
  As I was fighting gray.

I stood beneath the signal tree,
  Where I that day was laid,
And 'twas your arms, old boy, that brought
  Me to this friendly shade.
Tho' leaves are gone and limbs are bare,
  Its heart is true to-day
As yours was then, tho' fighting blue,
  To me, tho' fighting gray.

I marked the spot where Mansfield fell,
  Where Richardson was slain,
With Stark and Douglas, 'mid the corn,
  And Brant amid the grain.
The names are sacred to us, John ;
  They led us in the fray,
When you were fighting Northern blue,
  And I the Southern gray.

I thought of Burnside, Hooker, Meade,
  Of Sedgwick, old and grave ;
Of Stonewall Jackson, tried and true,
  That strove the day to save.
I bared my head—they rest in peace—
  Each one has passed away ;
Death musters those who wore the blue
  With those who wore the gray.

The old Pry mansion rears its walls
  Beside Antietam's stream,
And far away along the south
  I saw the tombstones gleam.
They mark each place where " Little Mac "
  And Robert Lee that day
Made proud the South, tho' wearing blue,
  The North, tho' wearing gray.

Yes, John, it gave me joy to stand
  Where we once fiercely fought.
The nation now is one again—
  The lesson has been taught.
Sweet peace doth fair Antietam crown.
  And we can say to-day
We're friends, tho' one was fighting blue
  And one was fighting gray.

A ROMANTIC INCIDENT OF THE WAR,

ENDING IN THE DEATH OF COL. ULRIC DAHLGREN.

Thad. J. Walker.

SOMETIME, early in the year 1863, as my memory serves me, I think it was in the month of January, while on picket duty near Winchester, in the lower part of the Shenandoah Valley, the first incident connected with this interesting and pathetic story

THADDEUS JAMES WALKER—1894.

occurred. I was standing in a clump of trees and bushes near the bank of the Opequan Creek, beside my horse, carbine in readiness for any alarm, when I heard a faint halloo from another clump of bushes not far distant in my front. I was at once on the *qui vive* for business.

It was a clear, cold morning, the air crisp and fine, and I listened intently, watching closely the bushes in front of me about a hundred yards away, for we knew that the Union pickets were in close proximity to us in our front.

Again came the halloo, and cautiously, from under the shadow of the trees, came three men, seemingly without arms, dressed in what afterwards proved to be a mixed uniform of blue and gray. Seeing them without arms and one of them waving a white handkerchief or rag (there were no handkerchiefs in the army—at least in ours—at that time, but the piece of white material was sufficient evidence to my mind that they wished to come over), I ordered them to do so, one at a time.

After a short talk with them I found them to be deserters from the Union cavalry, who stated that they were tired of the war, "fighting for the niggers," etc., and wished to be sent to Richmond. I was very much taken with the spokesman of the party, who was a good-looking and very intelligent young man about twenty-two or three years of age, with bright eyes and face. I finally concluded to take them into camp headquarters, then about two miles away.

When confronted by our major, Harry Gilmor, of the 2d Maryland Cavalry, he questioned them sharply and closely, and finally concluded to send them up the valley to Staunton and turn them over to Colonel J. Q. C. Naidenbush, who was at that time provost marshal of that place. The men were then placed under guard for the night.

Just at that time I was expecting a short furlough, or "horse detail." I obtained it and

Thaddeus James Walker was born in Chesterfield County, near Petersburg, Virginia, on July 15, 1847, his parents removing shortly afterward to Richmond, Virginia, where his boyhood was spent, until the breaking out of the war. He enlisted March 7, 1862, in the "President's Guard," Captain W. S. Reed; after serving one year in and around Richmond, was transferred to Company D, 2d Maryland cavalry, commanded by Major Harry Gilmor, and served in the Valley of the Shenandoah; was captured near Bethesda Church by the Pennsylvania "Bucktails," on May 26, 1864; taken to Point Lookout, where he remained over eight months; was paroled at Lynchburg, Virginia, after Appomattox. Mr. Walker is now a resident of Philadelphia.

started for home in Hanover County, Virginia, near Old Church,—about sixteen miles from Richmond,—with the three prisoners in my charge. We were soon on our way next morning, after an early and not very elaborate menu of rancid bacon and corn pone, with coffee made from roasted acorns. (Don't smile; this was a good breakfast compared to some we had.)

We were soon off, the stage rattling up the pike containing at least two hearts filled with buoyancy, for my companion (as I had learned to call the spokesman formerly alluded to) was an exceedingly congenial and companionable fellow, who, by his engaging manner and his pleasant conversational powers, soon ingratiated himself into my good opinion, and we felt as if we were old college chums who had met again after a long separation. How little did I think then that my congenial companion was one of the most famous and daring young cavalry officers of the Union army, who was in our lines on one of the most dangerous and hazardous errands a soldier could be engaged in! But to my story.

Arriving at Staunton, I proceeded direct to the headquarters of the provost marshal, Colonel Naidenbush, who paroled them; under oath of allegiance to the Confederacy, I think. Upon this point I will not be positive, yet it seems to me that must have been the only means by which they could be released to go where they chose. After a few hours in Staunton, spent in making ourselves more presentable in the way of clothing, etc., my companion and myself bade good-bye to the other two men, who remained in Staunton, and we were soon on a train bound for Richmond, I intending to remain there over night and go out to my home on the Totopotomoy Creek in Hanover County the next morning.

To shorten my story, my companion accompanied me to my home. I had formed such an attachment for him that I felt loath to part with him, and I extended the invitation, which was at once accepted. We reached home the next morning, and I feel sure that he never forgot the cordial and home-like reception accorded him in that old Virginia farm-house. Lieutenant Murray (his assumed name) soon endeared himself to all of us—mother, father, and three brothers—as he had already to myself, and joined heartily in the sociabilities of the neighborhood, visiting with me wherever I went, and being a brilliant talker, with gentlemanly manners, he always found a welcome. I had noticed that on several occasions when dancing was enjoyed he always declined. How vividly I could recall and remember a short time later *why* he did not and why he would not share my room with me, and on one bracing morning refused to accept my banter for a short race up the lane! I did not know then that the poor fellow had but one foot, the other being a splendid imitation made of ivory.

I must mention that during his stay at my home he paid two visits to Richmond and in some plausible manner obtained a permit from General Winder, who was then provost marshal of Richmond and who it seems had as much confidence in him as I had, to visit the fortifications and other points around the city, and which pass I was told by himself on his return he made good use of. He also, on two or three occasions, went to the Old Church tavern and post-office, ostensibly to get mail.

He was in correspondence with his mother, I believe, and received several letters from Belair, Harford County, Maryland, while with us. He often expressed himself as having "two mothers," as mine had been as kind to him as if he had been one of her own sons. He was attacked with chills and fever, the prevailing disease of that section, and it was the careful nursing of my dear mother that restored him.

A day or two after his recovery he again visited Old Church and *never returned*.

But I must digress a little. During one of our visits in the neighborhood he was introduced to a very estimable and cultured young lady, Miss S. K. H., who, strange to say, doubted him from the first moment she was in his company, and I have yet in my possession a letter from her, advising and warning me against him. How strangely her suspicions were verified will be shown later on in my story.

I began to feel now that his visits to Richmond were for the purpose of learning all he could of the city.

Just after he disappeared General Kilpatrick made a raid through our neighborhood, and again, strange to relate, our farm was not visited or disturbed, and after events assured me that this immunity was due to my companion, "Lieutenant Murray"; also that his visits to Old Church, which was on the main road to the Peninsula and the route General Kilpatrick was supposed to take, were for the purpose of holding communication with him, by signals or otherwise.

Some days afterwards, it may have been a week or more,—I cannot remember the dates now,—a daring raid was made upon Richmond by Kilpatrick and Colonel Ulric Dahlgren, presumably for the purpose of capturing Jefferson Davis and his Cabinet. And on the night of the memorable 3d of March, on the banks of the Mattapony River, Colonel Dahlgren and a small body of his men became separated from the main body of his command, and in the darkness of night ran into a body of Confederate cavalry, commanded by Captain Pollard, of Richmond, who fired a volley, killing Colonel Dahlgren, some of his staff, and several of his men.

Now comes the sad sequel to my story. The body of the brave but unfortunate young colonel was captured and taken to Richmond, and, I believe, embalmed, but I have never learned what became of his body (would be glad if any reader of this article can give me the information). While his body was lying in Richmond one of the first to visit it was Miss S. K. H., of Hanover, who at one glance identified the body as that of poor Murray, my prisoner, my companion, and my friend. My father, uncle, and others who had seen him, also identified the body as that of my friend, Lieutenant Murray. I shall always believe that he was a true friend at heart, though an enemy in disguise, and as I look back into the dim vista of those past dark days of blood and strife, when brother was fighting brother, I shall never forget my feelings of bitter sorrow and regret when I heard the news. I was then with my command and could not see him.

It may be said that he was a "spy," and that he imposed to some extent upon the hospitalities and confidence of his friends, but I have never felt in my heart an unkind memory for him. Was not our noble patriot, Nathan Hale, a spy, and yet a trusted friend of our glorious Washington? Was not the brave, unfortunate Andre a spy, and though an enemy, a brave and chivalric one? And does it not seem to require a brave, courageous spirit to embark in such desperate enterprises, one who will dare and die, if needs be, for the cause he espouses and which he deems right? And I recall just here one of my own comrades, of my own command,—poor Andy Leopold,—who was hung in the Old Capitol Prison at Washington for the same offence. As all seems fair in love and war, he, poor fellow, dared and died for the cause that he too loved.

Was not poor Murray (I shall always remember him by this name) just as brave and chivalrous? Why should not I, his friend, drop a silent tear in his memory and earnestly trust in the hope that a just and merciful Providence will give us a happy reunion in that eternal camping-ground above the stars, where the martyred loved ones who have passed on before us are awaiting the last "bugle call" to welcome us to a home where there are no wars and no tears?

STATISTICS OF THE CIVIL WAR.

IT is manifestly impossible to secure absolutely correct statistics of the Civil War. The Adjutant-General's office gives the following as the number of casualties in the volunteer and regular armies of the United States:

Killed in battle, 67,058; died of wounds, 43,012; died of disease, 199,720; other causes, such as accidents, murder, Confederate prisons, etc., 40,154; total, 349,944; total deserted, 199,105. Number of soldiers in the Confederate service who died of wounds or disease (partial statement), 133,821; deserted (partial statement), 104,428. Number of United States troops captured during the war, 212,608; Confederate troops captured, 476,169. Number of United States troops paroled on the field, 16,431; Confederate troops paroled on the field, 248,599. Number of United States troops who died while prisoners, 30,156; Confederate troops who died while prisoners, 30,152. It is a striking coincidence that the last statement shows a difference of only four men in a total of more than 60,000.

Gettysburg was the greatest battle of the war; Antietam, the bloodiest. The largest army was assembled by the Confederates at the Seven Days' Fight; by the Unionists at the Wilderness.